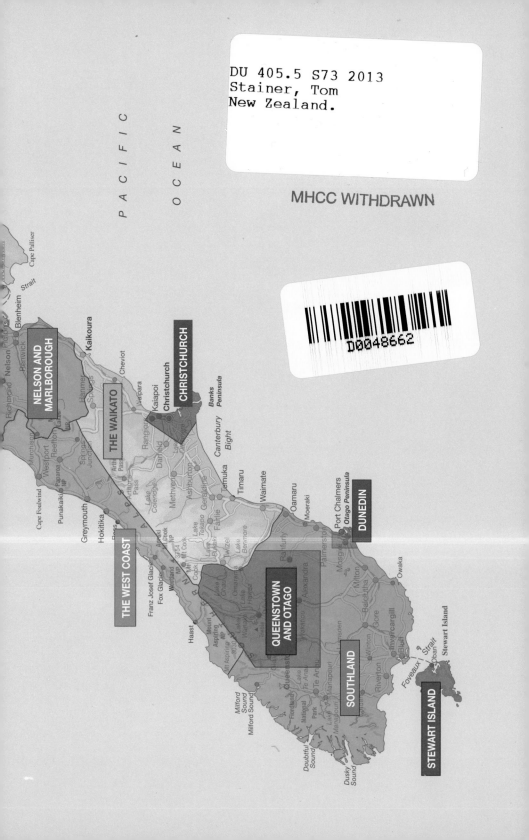

NEW ZEALAND

APA PUBLICATIONS L

Part of the Langenscheidt Publishing Group

The first Insight Guide pioneered the use of creative full-colour photography in travel guides in 1970. Since then, we have expanded our range to cater for our readers' need not only for reliable information about their chosen destination but also for a real understanding of the culture and workings of that destination. To achieve this, they rely heavily on the authority of locally based writers and photographers.

Insight Guide: New Zealand is structured to convey an understanding of the country and its people as well as to guide readers through its wealth of attractions:

The **Best of New Zealand** at the front of the guide gives you our pick of the country's top sights and umissable experiences.

The **Features** section, indicated by a pink bar at the top of each page, covers the natural and cultural history of New Zealand as well as illuminating essays on the Maori heritage, society, culture and daily life, food and wine, architecture, the arts, the environment and outdoor activities.

The main **Places** section, indicated by a blue bar, is a complete guide to all the sights and areas worth visiting across New Zealand. Places of special interest are coordinated by number with the maps.

The **Travel Tips** listings section, with a yellow bar, provides full information on transport, hotels, restaurants, activities from culture to shopping to sports and a detailed list of outdoor activities, and an A–Z section of essential practical information.

The contributors

This fully revised and updated edition was commissioned by **Tom Le Bas** and managed by **Tom Stainer**. The entire book was comprehensively updated by **Donna Blaber**, a travel journalist based in Whangarei in Northland but spending months each year on the highways and back roads across the country.

The tenth incarnation of Insight New Zealand builds on the best-selling earlier editions largely written by **Craig Dowling**, who has lived and worked as a journalist in Auckland, Wellington and Christchurch. Other past contributors include **Denis Welch**, who wrote the chapter on Contemporary Art and Literature. The feature on Performing Arts, Music and Film was written by **Philip Matthews**, while lending her expertise to the info panel on Contemporary Maori Art was

Ngarino Ellis. Cuisine is a subject close to the heart of ex-restaurateur **Lois Daish**, and complementing it is the feature on Wines by **Keith Stewart**, an art and wine critic. The chapter on Outdoor Activities was the work of sports enthusiast **Angie Belcher**. **Michael King** wrote about the Arrival of the Maori and the Modern Maori, **Gordon McLauchlan** described the Voyages of Discovery, Settlement and Colonisation, and **Terence Barrow** wrote about Maori Art.

The Places chapters were originally written by **Peter Calder** (Auckland and Surroundings); **Jack Adlington** (Northland); **Joseph Frahm** (Coromandel); **Colin Taylor** (Rotorua); **Janet Leggett** (The Waikato); **John Harvey** (Taranaki, Wanganui and Manawatu); **Geoff Conly** (Poverty Bay and Hawke's Bay); **David McGill** (Wellington); **William Hobbs** (Nelson and Marlborough); **John Goulter** (Christchurch); **Les Bloxham** (Canterbury, West Coast); **Anne Stark** (Queenstown and Central Otago); **Robin Charteris** (Dunedin); **Clive Lind** (Southland); and **Brian Parkinson** (Stewart Island).

The superb photography comes courtesy of **Andy Belcher** and **Peter James Quinn**. The book was indexed by **Penny Phenix**.

Map Legend

– – – –	Province Boundry
–•– •–	National Park/Reserve
– – – –	Ferry Route
✈ ✈	Airport: International/Regional
🚌	Bus Station
❶	Tourist Information
☗ † ✝	Church/Ruins
∴	Archaeological Site
◰ ⌂	Castle/Ruins
☪	Mosque
✡	Synagogue
∩	Cave
🛈	Statue/Monument
★	Place of Interest
⸙	Beach
▲	Mountain Peak
🗼	Lighthouse
🚠	Cable Car
⛳	Golf
🎿	Skiing

The main places of interest in the Places section are coordinated by number with a full-colour map (eg ❶), and a symbol at the top of every right-hand page tells you where to find the map.

Contents

THE BEST OF NEW ZEALAND: TOP ATTRACTIONS

Discover New Zealand's unique attractions – breathtaking landscapes, exciting adventure activities, absorbing museums, indigenous culture... here, at a glance, are our recommendations.

△ **Glacier Walking, Franz Josef or Fox Glacier**. Explore stunning blue glacier ice and crevasses on a half- or full-day glacier walk, led by knowledgeable and safety-conscious guides. All the gear, including crampons, is provided. See page 271

△ **Rakiura National Park, Stewart Island**. Discover this seldom-explored 170,000-hectare (420,000-acre) paradise of wondrous beauty – a dense wilderness of podocarp rainforest, granite peaks, freshwater wetlands and deserted beaches. See page 313

▷ **Maori culture**. New Zealand's indigenous culture can be experienced by attending a traditional *kapa haka* (song-and-dance show) performed at venues nationwide; at a *hangi* feast; and on guided walking tours of local *marae* (open courtyards) and meeting houses. See page 54

◁ **Adventure sports**. Whether you like your adrenaline via bungee, surfboard, zorb, or with an ice pick, New Zealand has a variety of outdoor adventures sure to get your blood pumping. See page 114

△ **River adventures, Queenstown.** The South Island's adventure-sport capital makes a fabulous base for getting out on the water. Speed along the Shotover River in a jet boat or experience some thrilling whitewater rafting. See page 286

△ **White Island, Bay of Plenty.** See the pure, raw energy of nature at work on the world's most accessible marine volcano. Hike across this unique lunar landscape pockmarked with fumaroles to view its colourful and ever-changing crater lake. See page 176

◁ **Thermal Wonderland, Rotorua.** Visit Rotorua to see New Zealand's most vibrant and colourful thermal parks such as Whakarewarewa, Hell's Gate and Waimangu. Wai-O-Tapu has several highlights, including the Lady Knox Geyser, the bubbly 'Champagne Pool', and brilliantly hued silica terraces. See page 189

◁ **Waitomo Glow-Worm Caves, the Waikato.** Venture underground on a guided tour to see limestone stalactites and stalagmites. The highlight is an awe-inspiring boat ride through enormous caverns, radiantly lit by millions of tiny glow-worms. See page 167

▷ **Waipoua Forest, Northland.** Stroll through the vertiginous canopy of tangled foliage in this mighty Northland kauri forest, where sights such as New Zealand's oldest living kauri tree – the mammoth Tane Mahuta – are, quite simply, unforgettable. See page 159

▽ **New Zealand food and wine, Hawke's Bay and Marlborough.** Tempt your taste buds with cuisine inspired by the freshest of locally gathered produce, perfectly matched to a selection of fine regional wines. See page 204

THE BEST OF NEW ZEALAND: EDITOR'S CHOICE

Our selection of the best outdoor experiences and adventures and the top cultural and historical sights.

View of Mt. Taranaki from Cannington Road, New Plymouth.

MUST-SEE NATURAL SCENERY

Bay of Islands, Northland. A rugged 800km (500-mile) coastline embracing 144 islands and steeped in history, where beauty knows no bounds. Page 151.

Aoraki Mount Cook National Park, Canterbury. Admire New Zealand's highest mountain and the mighty Tasman Glacier, in this vastly contrasting landscape of mountains and plains. Page 264.

Tongariro National Park. There's plenty to do year-round – from hiking the acclaimed Tongariro Crossing, kayaking and mountain-biking during the summer months, to skiing in the winter. Page 191.

Abel Tasman National Park. Paradise on earth for campers, kayakers and hikers. The Coastal Track offers exceptional views. Page 242.

Milford Sound. Marvel at the sight of magnificent Milford Sound, then join a cruise or guided kayaking trip to see its thundering waterfalls and marine life. Page 308.

Fiordland National Park. Take a scenic flight over a pristine environment offering a wealth of truly breathtaking scenery. Page 307.

BEST ARTS AND CULTURAL EXPERIENCES

Te Papa Tongarewa – Museum of New Zealand. A great introduction to New Zealand and home to a fine collection of Maori artefacts and interactive displays. Page 217.

Whakarewarewa Thermal Village. See culture in action at the geothermally powered Maori village and the adjacent Te Puia Maori Arts and Crafts Institute in Rotorua. Page 183.

Waitangi Culture North Show. Visit Waitangi, where New Zealand's founding document was signed. By night the Treaty House comes alive with a cleverly choreographed performance of the Bay of Islands' history, performed by local Maori. Page 153.

Nelson Art Trail and the Suter Gallery. Visit the studios of local artists by following Nelson's Art Trail and don't miss the Suter Gallery, which lies at the heart of the city's thriving art scene. Page 241.

The bronze statue of Wairaka at the mouth of the Whakatane river, Bay of Plenty.

BEST ADVENTURE / OUTDOOR ACTIVITIES

Diving at the Poor Knights Islands. Discover a microcosm of underwater diversity amid dense kelp forests, arches and caverns, including Riko Riko, the world's largest sea cave. Page 161.

Tandem Skydiving. Free-fall attached to a parachute and a skydiving professional who pulls the cord just in time for the perfect touchdown. Page 184.

Bungee Jumping, Queenstown. Take the plunge off where it first began, the Kawarau Bridge, home of the bungee, or have a go at the Nevis Highwire or the Ledge. Page 288.

Jet-Boating, Queenstown. Jump in and hold on tight for jet-boat-powered thrills and spills on the Shotover River. Page 286.

Whitewater Rafting. New Zealand has several fast-flowing rivers including the Shotover, the Tongariro and Rangitikei, and is one of the top whitewater rafting destinations in the world. Page 191.

Whale Watch Kaikoura. Cruise over the edge of the continental shelf to spot sperm whales as they resurface. Page 259.

Glacier Hiking. Hike through ice caves and peer down deep crevasses on a hiking or heli-hiking tour at Fox and Franz Josef Glaciers. Page 271.

Morning surf, Kaikoura.

BEST MAORI EXPERIENCES

Waitangi Culture North Show. Waitangi's *whare runanga* (meeting house) comes to life at night with a dramatic and cleverly choreographed performance of the Bay of Islands' chequered history, performed by Northland Maori. Page 153.

Tamaki Maori Village. Local guides introduce Maori culture, myths and legends, action songs and *poi* dance, stick games, the world famous haka and traditional hangi food, and if you

Tamaki Maori village.

wish to do so you can stay overnight in the *marae.* Page 189.

Te Puia Maori Arts and Crafts Institute. See culture in action and watch the work of master carvers and weavers at Rotorua's Te Puia New Zealand Maori Arts and Crafts Institute. Page 183.

Whakarewarewa – The Living Thermal Village. Spend time with a modern-day tribe who still live among mud pools and hot thermal springs, and who use thermally heated waters for cooking, washing and heating on a daily basis. Page 183.

Terenga Paraoa Tours. Guided walks of Whangarei taking in some of the city's most famous sites, including the sacred Parihaka Pa and the legendary Paranui Valley. Page 161.

BEST HISTORICAL SIGHTS

Oamaru, Otago. New Zealand's largest collection of protected heritage buildings is found here. Crafted from a creamy-textured local limestone, they are a rare sight to behold. Page 300.

Dunedin. Amble around this southern city and enjoy its unique Scottish Victorian, Edwardian and Art Deco architectural heritage. Don't miss the Flemish Renaissance-style railway station, the city's most photographed building. Page 293.

Russell, Bay of Islands. Highlights include the old Duke of Marlborough Hotel, Pompallier and Christ Church. The latter survived the Battle of Kororareka in 1845, and is marked with musket-ball holes. Page 153.

Arrowtown, Otago. Journey back in time along the streets of this picturesque former gold-mining town. Visit its museum and see rusty relics lining the Arrow River. Page 287.

Mission House and Stone Store, Kerikeri. New Zealand's oldest surviving European buildings and adjoining historical site of Kororipa Pa, Hongi Hika's base between 1780 and 1826. Page 156.

Dunedin railway station.

A lush setting on the Milford Track.

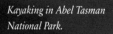

Kayaking in Abel Tasman National Park.

Maori warriors at a traditional haka.

Rotorua's Lady Knox geyser erupts punctually each morning at 10.15.

AOTEAROA

How did New Zealand become home to so many natural marvels? An ancient myth may hold the answer...

Dolphin-watching, Kaikoura.

New Zealand – called Aotearoa, 'land of the long white cloud', by the Maori – is a breathtakingly beautiful land of majestic snowcapped peaks and unexplored rainforests, of pristine lakes swarming with trout and turquoise ocean bays speckled with wooded isles, of glaciers and fiords, geysers and volcanoes. And you don't have to travel far to experience its sensational landscapes – an Alpine peak can be just a short drive from a barren desert, a primeval beach minutes from a busy city. There are kauri forests and kiwi fruit plantations, modern cosmopolitan cities and backcountry sheep stations. This land of plenty produces some of the world's finest food and wine.

All this is ranged across the two similarly sized main islands, North and South, plus Stewart Island off the southern tip and Great Barrier Island in the North, and a scattering of uninhabited islands, some of which are nature reserves. The North Island has the largest population, though there are still large expanses of empty landscapes; the South Island is more spectacular still, filled with mountains, glaciers, and deep fiords. It is a combination of a land that time forgot, completely uninhabited until relatively recent times, and a land that is impossible to forget. But first, it was the land of the Maori.

Lake Wakatipu.

Anthropologists tell of a remarkable migration as the Polynesian ancestors of the Maori moved through the Pacific, arriving here by outrigger canoe from about AD 800. Europeans arrived in the late 18th century, and despite a degree of conflict, New Zealand's past has few of the crimes against indigenous peoples that scar the history of nearby Australia. It is also a nation with a proud tradition of enlightened social policies.

Its natural wonders have made New Zealand a recreational paradise, and New Zealanders love the outdoors – from the rugby fields to the ski fields, from barbecues to bungee jumping. Active yet reflective, New Zealanders take pride in what they have and what they do. Above all, they are eager to share their marvellous country and its bounty with all visitors.

Lake Pukaki and Aoraki Mount Cook.

THE LAND

An archipelago of more than 700 islands, New Zealand perches atop two tectonic plates, the creators of a landscape filled with wild contrasts and awe-inspiring natural phenomena.

Of all the land masses on earth, the islands of New Zealand are the most isolated, surrounded on all sides by great expanses of ocean. But this has not always been the case. For several hundred million years, New Zealand lay on the edge of the supercontinent Gondwana. Finally, some 80 million years ago, during the heyday of the dinosaurs, a huge sliver of land that was to become the North and South islands broke away from Gondwana and headed out into the Pacific. Almost immediately it began to sink and the sea washed further and further inland. Mountains eroded to low hills and waves ate them away. It was only at the 'last minute' – geologically speaking – that compressive plate movements came to the rescue, pushing the land up and out of the sea. As these forces continued, hills grew to become jagged mountains, volcanoes erupted, and these were carved by water and ice to form the landscape of today. Around 60 million years ago it reached its present distance from Australia.

Boiling mud pools, Rotorua.

The lay of the land

New Zealand extends for some 1,500km (900 miles) from the subtropical North Cape in the Far North of the North Island to the sub-Antarctic wilderness of Stewart Island in the stormy southern latitudes. Both the main islands are largely mountainous, although there are also extensive areas of plains and plateaux. One-third of the country is made up of national parkland, forest parks, and reserves, so many of its landscapes remain in a near-pristine state. Travellers who wish to experience a true 'wilderness' will be easily satisfied by a wealth of natural phenomena: sooty volcanoes,

RAIN AND THE RAINFOREST

When air currents are forced to rise over the Southern Alps of New Zealand, moisture drops, causing considerable rainfall – sometimes over 5,000mm (200 inches) a year – on the west coast. On the other side of the mountains, though, there's a corresponding rainfall shadow, so that only a few kilometres from the wettest parts of New Zealand, the annual rainfall can be as low as 300mm (12 inches). Odd as it sounds, the high rainfall can actually be totally incompatible with the survival of the rainforests, as the soil is rapidly leached of the nutrients it needs to sustain them, resulting in stunted vegetation.

ancient glaciers, bubbling mud pools, irides-cent lakes and magnificent stands of temper-ate rainforest. The extreme environment has helped to ensure a relative lack of human impact on the land.

The largely volcanic North Island reaches 2,796 metres (9,173ft) at Mount Ruapehu in the Central Plateau, with range upon range of rolling hills tumbling to the sea. While Rotorua is famous for its gushing geysers and pools of boiling mud, naturally formed hot springs can be found island-wide. Lake Taupo, itself formed by a massive eruption,

Admiring the view across Lake Wakatipu near Queenstown.

forms the liquid heart of the North Island and lush farmlands radiate from its epicen-tre, covering expansive valleys and plains. Although its land area is somewhat smaller than that of the South Island, the North's coastline is longer, thanks to its multitude of deep inlets, mangrove-filled estuaries and sheltered harbours ribboned with sandy beaches. Crashing surf and darker sands pre-dominate in the west, while to the east the coastline is tamer, a seemingly endless string of golden sands punctuated by rocky head-lands and offshore islets.

In the South Island the land rises from the Canterbury Plains in the east to the Southern Alps in the west: the highest peak

in the country is Mount Cook at 3,754 metres (12,316ft), but there are numerous majestic snowcapped peaks rising above 3,000 metres (10,000ft). The west coast is marked by plung-ing cliffs and wild beaches and backed by dense swathes of temperate rainforest. To the east, snow-fed rivers nourish the prosper-ous farmlands of the Canterbury Plains. In Marlborough at the northernmost point of the South Island lie the drowned sea-valleys of the Marlborough Sounds, which form a unique topography of channels, peninsulas and islands. In the southern regions huge ancient glaciers bulldozed rock to form spec-tacular lakes, and with over 360 known gla-ciers in action today, with Franz Josef and Fox glaciers recognised as the largest and most readily accessible, the landscape is constantly changing.

New Zealand's third isle, Stewart Island, located some 30km (19 miles) off the south-ern tip of the South Island, features rugged beaches, swampy valleys, large areas of for-est and peaks including Mount Anglem, the island's highest at 980 metres (3,215ft). For information on the climate of New Zealand see page 375.

> New Zealand's volcanic nature can be destructive, but overall is a blessing in disguise. Volcanic rocks rejuvenate the landscape, weathering to form the country's richest soils, a fact well recognised by the agricultural industry.

Plate tectonics

New Zealand currently sits upon two huge moving 'plates', the Indo-Australian plate and the Pacific plate, the former pushing under the latter, causing the land to rise and creating wrenching forces beneath the surface result-ing in earthquakes and volcanoes. The South Island's Alps were formed by plate movement over the last 2 million years – a mere blink in geological time – and they continue to rise by several centimetres a year.

During the formation of the Alps, world-wide cooling became extreme and the Ice Age ensued. During its colder intervals huge gla-ciers appeared flowing down valleys, and this combination of young mountains and huge glaciers has created landscapes rating among the most spectacular to be found on earth. In Fiordland, the rock walls of ancient glacial valleys drop vertically thousands of feet directly into the sea, while on the other side of the Alps, lakes such as Wanaka and Wakatipu are the result of glacial 'bulldozing'. Further north, the Fox and Franz Josef glaciers plunge towards sea level through the mid-altitude rainforests – a unique sight.

Not all New Zealand's recent history has been one of uplift. In the north of the South Island, the Marlborough Sounds were produced when an extensive river system was drowned. In the North Island the major geological story is of volcanoes, and in a complex situation a whole variety of volcanic types has been produced.

The city of Auckland is built amongst numerous small, perfectly formed, extinct volcanic cones, created by gentle outpourings of lava and ash. As naturally defensive positions, most were terraced and palisaded by Maori to form *pa* (forts). In the Central Plateau a different form of lava produces a very dangerous, explosive type of volcano. About AD 130 – long before any humans arrived on the islands – one of the largest volcanic explosions in historical times formed Lake Taupo. This spread hot ash over a large part of the North Island, flattening huge areas of forest.

Mineral resources

New Zealand's most precious materials are closely tied to the history of the Southern Alps. The Maori's sacred *pounamu* (or greenstone) was formed from exotic rock existing deep below the earth's crust. Altered by heat and pressure during mountain-forming processes, these rocks were pushed to the surface in isolated places on the west coast of the South Island. Its rareness, beauty and material properties in a culture where metal was unknown gave *pounamu* a high value.

Gold also existed in the quartz veins of 'schist' rock, the main component of the Alps. As the mountains grew, they also eroded, and as the lighter and softer minerals of the schist washed away, gold, by virtue of its high density, became concentrated in the nooks and crannies of river beds, exploited during several 19th-century gold rushes across the country.

Dinosaurs and other fauna

The most striking aspect of New Zealand's indigenous fauna is its absence of large four-footed land animals, in particular mammals (other than two species of bat that are found nowhere else), as well as its complete lack of snakes. This was originally attributed to the timing of New Zealand's breakaway from Gondwana, but recent discoveries suggest that carnivorous and herbivorous dinosaurs, as well as flying pterosaurs, were living in New Zealand at that time. The only fossil evidence of land-based, four-footed animals since the dino-

Volcanic landscape, Rotorua.

saurs is a single crocodile jawbone discovered near St Bathans, in Central Otago. Crocodiles, however, do not exist in New Zealand today.

Mammals, too, may once have been part of a 'native' fauna that developed before New Zealand broke away from Australia. The present absence of large land animals – other than birds – is almost certainly a result of extinction over the past 80 million years. With nothing to prey on them, birds proliferated, and some, lacking the need, eventually lost the ability to fly. Of the very distinct New Zealand animals, such as the extinct moa, the kiwi and tuatara (three-eyed centenarian lizards), there is no ancient fossil record. For more on local wildlife and plants see page 101.

DECISIVE DATES

Traders and Explorers

c.AD 800–1000

The first Polynesians arrive in New Zealand.

1642

Abel Tasman is the first European to sight the country.

1769

Captain James Cook is the first European to explore, and set foot in, New Zealand.

1790s

European seal hunters and whalers move into the region.

Whaling was important to the economy in the past.

1809

First European settlers arrive in Russell.

1817

Anglican Mission established at Bay of Islands.

1818

The Maori 'Musket Wars' begin; 12 years of inter-tribal conflict kills 20,000 people.

Colonisation

1830s

Early European settlements grow in size; beginnings of trade with New South Wales.

1840

Maori chiefs sign the Treaty of Waitangi. Auckland becomes the capital. New Zealand Company colonists reach Wellington and establish settlements.

1845

Maori leader Hone Heke cuts down the flagstaff at Kororareka (Russell); 1,000 Maori take arms against the British.

1848–50

Otago and Canterbury are settled.

1852

Taranaki colonisation begins.

1856

New Zealand becomes a self-governing British colony. Gold rush and land struggles.

1860–72

Maori Land Wars (New Zealand Wars); vast tracts of land are confiscated.

Arrowtown is a historic gold mining town in Central Otago.

1861

Otago gold rush begins.

1865

Wellington becomes New Zealand's capital.

1866

Cook Strait submarine telegraph cable is laid.

1867

Maori are given the vote.

1868

Raids by Titokowaru and Te Kooti throw the country into crisis.

1869

Te Kooti is defeated. Otago University is established.

1870

First rugby match is played in New Zealand.

1877

Treaty of Waitangi ruled null by Chief Justice Prendergast. Free compulsory education is introduced.

1882

The first refrigerated agricultural produce cargo is dispatched to England.

1886
Mount Tarawera erupts.

Social Reforms and World Wars

1893
Women are given the vote, 25 years before Britain and the US.

1896
Maori population drops to 42,000 (from 100,000 in 1769).

1898
The world's first old-age pension for men is introduced.

1899–1902
New Zealand troops fight in the Boer War.

1908
Ernest Rutherford awarded Nobel Prize for Chemistry. Population exceeds 1 million.

1915
New Zealand suffers heavy losses in Gallipoli campaign of World War I.

1918–19
Influenza kills 6,700.

1938
Health care and social security are introduced.

1939
World War II breaks out. New Zealand suffers heavy losses.

An Independent Nation

1947
New Zealand becomes fully independent.

1951
ANZUS defence alliance with Australia and the US is signed.

The devastation caused by the Christchurch earthquake.

1953
New Zealander Edmund Hillary becomes the first person to climb Mount Everest.

1962
Maurice Wilkins shares Nobel Prize in physiology and medicine for discovery of DNA.

1965
New Zealand troops are sent to Vietnam.

1975
Parliament passes the Treaty of Waitangi Act, establishing a tribunal to investigate claims.

1981
Anti-apartheid protests during South African rugby team tour create civil unrest.

1985
Greenpeace protest vessel Rainbow Warrior is bombed in Auckland. Government bans visits by ships carrying nuclear weapons.

1987
Maori becomes an official language by law.

1993
Proportional representation election system, Mixed Member Proportional, is introduced.

1995
New Zealand wins the prestigious America's Cup.

1997
The National Party's Jenny Shipley becomes New Zealand's first woman prime minister.

1999
Labour Party leader Helen Clark is elected prime minister.

2005
Civil Union Act is passed.

2008
John Key's National Party is voted into power following Helen Clark's nine-year reign.

2010
Christchurch is hit by a magnitude 7.1 earthquake. New Zealand signs the 'Wellington' Treaty with the US. The Pike River Mine disaster kills 29 miners on the West Coast.

2011
A magnitude 6.3 earthquake devastates Christchurch; 185 lives are lost and the CBD and historic buildings destroyed. New Zealand wins the Rugby World Cup.

2012
The nation works to rebuild Christchurch city. The Tuhoe tribe reaches a historic Treaty agreement with the Crown over governance of Te Urewera National Park.

2013
The first census since 2006 is held (it was postponed in 2011 due to the Christchurch earthquakes).

2014
General election year.

ARRIVAL OF THE MAORI

Polynesian settlers are thought to have arrived in New Zealand from around AD 800–1000. Having established themselves on the islands, they evolved a sophisticated and highly organised culture.

Human habitation in New Zealand dates back only around 1,000 years, making this the world's last sizeable land area – outside of the polar regions – to be settled by man. The origin of its first people, the Maori, is the source of much controversy. Nineteenth-century scholars said Maori were wandering Aryans, others believed they were Hindu, and some thought that they were a lost tribe of Israel. Linguistic and archaeological evidence has led to the current consensus that the Maori are a Polynesian people, and that their ancestors (Austronesian people who originated in Southeast Asia) sailed south from the Asian mainland some 2,000 to 3,000 years ago. Some went southwest, ultimately to Madagascar; others journeyed southeast along the Malaysian, Indonesian and Philippine island chains.

The Pacific Austronesians travelled through the Melanesian islands, reaching Fiji by about 1300 BC and Tonga before 1100 BC. It was here that Polynesian culture as recognised today evolved. And it was from East Polynesia that a migration was launched to New Zealand. There is some controversy over the dates of the southward migration: archaeological evidence dates the Maori's earliest encounters with New Zealand at around AD 800; some anthropologists, however, believe that some migrations took place hundreds of years later – possibly as late as AD 1280. Today, it is generally agreed the migration took place in stages, over several hundred years.

Whatever the date, the land was unlike anything that Polynesians had hitherto encountered. It was far larger and more varied than the Pacific islands they had colonised previously. It was temperate rather than tropical and

Maori children on a morere swing, a tall pole with ropes attached to its top.

sufficiently cold in much of the South Island to prevent the growing of traditional crops. Other than bats, there were no mammals until rats *(kiore)* and dogs *(kuri)* were brought over by the new colonists.

The ancestors of modern Maori showed great fortitude and adaptability. The lack of meat was compensated for by an abundance of seafood and aquatic mammals. Inland waterways contained additional resources – waterfowl, eel, fish and shellfish – and there were nearly 200 species of bird, many of them palatable. The land provided a staple diet of native fern root and nurtured imported cultivated crops such as taro, kumara, yam, gourds and the paper mulberry.

The most coveted food source, however, was the huge flightless bird, the moa, which offered a plentiful food supply. Some early groups of Maori based their entire economy around moas, until over-hunting led to their extinction (see page 102).

Maori culture

Ethnologists recognise two distinguishable but related phases in Maori civilisation. The first is New Zealand East Polynesian, or Archaic Maori, and the second, Classic Maori, the culture encountered and recorded by the earliest

Waitangi Treaty Grounds carving.

European navigators (see page 69). When James Cook observed New Zealand in 1769, New Zealand Polynesians had settled throughout the land. The language they shared was similar, although dialectal differences were pronounced. While some regional variations were apparent, Maori culture was largely homogeneous throughout the country.

Competitive tribalism, for example, was the basis of Maori life. The family and *hapu* (sub-tribe) were the units of society that determined who married whom, where people lived, where and when they fought other people and why. Tribal ancestors were venerated, as were gods representing the natural elements. Life was bound up in a unified vision

in which every aspect of living was related to every other. And the universal acceptance of concepts such as *tapu* (sacredness), *mana* (spiritual authority), *mauri* (life force), *utu* (revenge) and a belief in *makutu* (sorcery) regulated all aspects of life.

Maori society was stratified. A few people were born into *rangatira* or chiefly families; all others were *tutua* (commoners). They became slaves if they were captured in warfare. Immediate authority was exercised by the *kaumatua*, the elders. Whole communities, sharing a common ancestor, were under

> When items of food became scarce in a kainga (village) or pa (fortified settlement), the inhabitants had a rahui, or prohibition, laid on them to conserve precious supplies.

the jurisdiction of the *rangatira* families whose authority was in part hereditary and in part based on past achievement. Occasionally federations of *hapu* and tribes would come together and join forces under an *ariki* (paramount chief) for joint ventures such as waging war against foreign elements, trading or foraging for resources. The most common relationship among even closely related *hapu*, however, was fierce competition.

Communities ranging from a handful of households to those comprised of more than 500 lived in *kainga* (villages). These were usually based on membership of a single *hapu*. The *kainga* would be close to water, food sources and crops. Some settlements, called *pa*, were fortified – many of them elaborately constructed with an interior stronghold, ditches, banks and palisades. More often the *kainga* were adjacent to hilltop *pa*, to which communities could retreat when under attack.

Communal patterns of life in Maori settlements were organised around food gathering, food growing and (in areas where fighting was common) warfare. Cultivation and foraging were carried out by large parties of workers.

Maori warfare

Warfare was an important feature of Maori life in most parts of the country. It was conducted to obtain territory abundant in food or other natural resources; to avenge insults; to obtain satisfaction from *hapu* whose members had transgressed the social code; or to resolve serious disagreements over authority.

Prior to the introduction of the musket with the arrival of the Europeans, most warfare was not totally destructive, with the most common weapons being *taiaha* (long wooden-bladed swords) and short clubs known as *patu* and *mere*. It often involved only individuals or small raiding parties, and ambush or short, sporadic attacks. Even when larger groups fought, the dead rarely amounted to more than a few score. Fighting was rarely carried out far from

settlers distributed Mayor Island obsidian; Nelson and D'Urville Island inhabitants traded argillite. Sometimes food such as mutton birds was also preserved and bartered. People travelled long distances for materials and food delicacies. Although the Maori's ocean-going vessels disappeared by the 18th century, canoes were still widely used for transport on New Zealand's waterways.

Medical examination of pre-European remains reveals that few Maori lived beyond the age of 30. From their late 20s, many suffered from arthritis, and infected gums and loss of teeth due to a

Illustration of a Maori war dance.

home except when a migration was under way. (Migrations were seasonal, undertaken by most tribes, and principally related to the harvesting or gathering of food.)

For individual men, as for tribes, *mana* (spiritual authority) was paramount. An individual's *mana* was intensified by victory and diminished by defeat. Courage and combat skills were also essential ingredients in initiation and acceptance, especially in the case of chiefs.

Other aspects of Maori life

In spite of competition, warfare and tribal demarcations among Maori, trading was extensive. South Islanders exported *pounamu* (greenstone), highly valued for carving. Bay of Plenty

diet of fern roots. The healthy-looking 'elderly' men whose condition Captain James Cook commented favourably on in 1770 may have been, at the most, around 40 years of age.

The population, probably 100,000 to 120,000 when Cook landed, were so long separated from other cultures they had no concept of nationhood. But they were fiercely assertive of their ancestry and *hapu* membership. To that extent they led a tribal existence, but what they shared strongly, no matter which tribe they were born to, was a deep and profound affinity with the land and its bounty. They called the land Aotearoa: 'the land of the long white cloud'. For details of Maori art and more on ancient Maori society, see page 69.

Captain James Cook arrives at Golden Bay in 1769.

VOYAGES OF DISCOVERY

A Dutchman searching for a 'Great Southern Continent' first stumbled upon New Zealand in 1642, but it was another 130 years before any European returned.

The southern Pacific was the last habitable part of the world to be reached by Europeans. It was then only gradually explored at the end of long-haul routes down the coast of South America on one side and Africa on the other. Once inside the rim of the world's largest ocean, seafarers faced vast areas to be crossed, always hundreds, even thousands of miles away from any familiar territory. So it required not only steady courage to venture into this region but a high degree of navigational skill.

The islands of the South Pacific – tucked away near the bottom of the globe – remained the domain of Polynesian peoples for nearly 150 years after the Europeans first burst into the western Pacific. Furthermore, New Zealand was ignored for another 130 years after its initial 1642 sighting by the Dutchman Abel Janszoon Tasman. It was left to the Englishman James Cook to put the South Pacific firmly on the world map in the latter part of the 18th century.

The Dutch traders

European knowledge of the Pacific Ocean had gradually expanded during the 16th and 17th centuries. This was the era in which Spanish and Portuguese seafarers such as Magellan and Quiros, and England's Francis Drake, made their epic expeditions.

Then, towards the end of the 16th century, the Dutch emerged as the great seafaring and trading nation of the central and western Pacific. They set up a major administrative and trading centre at Batavia (now Jakarta) in Java early in the 17th century, an operation dominated by the Dutch East India Company. For the ensuing 200 years

18th-century sketch of Cook's ship Endeavour.

the Dutch were a major power in the region, though for most of that period the voyages of exploration were incidental to the activities of trade.

The Dutch ships eventually found that by staying south after rounding the tip of Africa at the Cape of Good Hope and catching the consistent westerlies almost as far as the western coast of Australia, they could make the journey to Java more quickly than by adopting the traditional route – sailing up the east coast of Africa and then catching seasonal winds for the journey eastwards. As a result, islands off the west coast of Australia and stretches of the coast of the unknown continent itself began to be noted on charts.

Tasman's visit

An ambitious governor of Batavia, Anthony van Diemen, showed a more imaginative interest in discovering new lands for trade than most of his predecessors. In 1642 he chose Abel Tasman to lead an expedition south, to be accompanied by a highly competent navigator, Frans Visscher. The proposed voyage would take them first to Mauritius, then southwest to between 50° and 55°S in search of the great southern continent, Terra Australis Incognita. The expedition, aboard the vessels *Heemskerck* and *Zeehaen*, was then to travel eastwards if no land had been found to impede their progress and to sail across to investigate a shorter route to Chile, a rich trading area and the preserve of the Spanish. As it turned out, the expedition ventured only as far as 49°S before turning eastwards, whereupon it made two great South Pacific discoveries – Tasmania (or Van Diemen's Land, as he named it at the time) and New Zealand (which he called Staten Landt).

On 13 December 1642, Tasman and his men saw what was described as 'land uplifted high' – the Southern Alps of the South Island – and, in

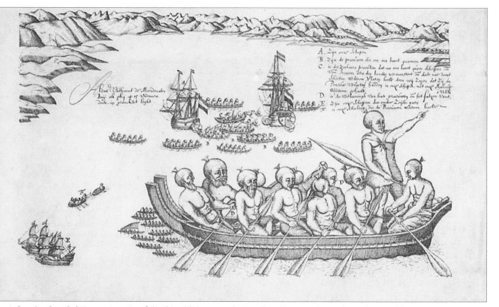

A drawing by Abel Tasman's artist of the skirmish between the Dutch explorers and Maori people at Golden Bay.

TASMAN'S NEAR MISS

Tasman's first and only encounter with the Maori was disastrous. When a canoe rammed a small boat that was travelling between the *Zeehaen* and the *Heemskerck*, fighting broke out and there was loss of life on both sides. Tasman called the place Massacre Bay and continued his journey northwards. He did not land again. What Tasman failed to realise was that he had actually been inside the western entrance to the stretch of water separating North and South islands, now known as Cook Strait. A voyage eastwards of only a few kilometres would have revealed this to him, and perhaps it might be known today as the Tasman Strait.

strong winds and heavy seas, sailed northwards up the coast of Westland, before rounding Cape Farewell and entering what is now known as Golden Bay. Tasman's voyage was not immediately regarded as a major success (see box), but ultimately he was given his due for a gallant and well-recorded exploration.

Cook's exploration

Within a year or two, other navigators had established that New Zealand could not be attached to a huge continent which was thought may extend all the way across to South America. The name was therefore changed from Staten Landt (the Dutch name for South America) to New Zealand, after the Dutch province of Zeeland.

Over a century passed before serious exploration resumed in the region. It was primarily to observe the transit of Venus over the disc of the sun in June 1769 that the English Captain James Cook was dispatched to the South Seas in the 373-ton Whitby-built barque, *Endeavour*. He was instructed to sail to Otaheite (Tahiti) for the transit and then to sail southwards as far as 50°S latitude on another search for the great southern continent, charting the positions of any islands he might incidentally discover.

Cook rounded Cape Horn and entered the Pacific Ocean for the first time on 27 January

with the Maori, and he was taken ashore with Cook the next morning. But the Maori were in a threatening mood and Cook ordered one of them shot to make them retreat. That afternoon, the firing of a musket over a canoe (merely to attract attention) brought an attack on the boat from which the shot had been fired; a few more Maori were shot. Cook had quickly learnt that the native population was powerful, aggressive and brave. (Rather than commemorating the bloodshed, the bay was named Poverty Bay to record the fact that the English failed to find the supplies they wanted there.)

Oil painting showing Captain James Cook arriving at Queen Charlotte Sound.

1769. After observing the transit of Venus and investigating other islands (which he named the Society Islands), he sailed south and then west. On 6 October, a ship's boy, Nicholas Young, sighted the east coast of the North Island where it is today called Young Nick's Head.

Two days after this first sighting of what Cook knew to be the east coast of New Zealand, the land reported by Tasman, the *Endeavour* sailed into a bay where smoke could be seen – a clear sign that there were inhabitants. Their first visit ashore ended with violence when a band of Maori attacked four boys left guarding the ship's boat; one of the attackers was shot dead.

It was discovered that a Tahitian chief on board the *Endeavour*, Tupaea, could converse

COOK'S CREDENTIALS

The son of a Yorkshire labourer, James Cook was born in 1728. He served as an apprentice seaman on a collier, and then volunteered as an able seaman with the Royal Navy during the Seven Years War. He helped survey Canada's St Lawrence River, an essential preliminary to the capture of Québec by General James Wolfe, and enhanced an already growing reputation as a marine surveyor by charting the St Lawrence and part of the Newfoundland and Nova Scotia coasts. In 1766 he observed an eclipse of the sun; both the Royal Society and the Admiralty were impressed with his report, and this led to his appointment to the South Seas voyage.

James Cook made two major cartographical errors: attaching Stewart Island to the South Island as a peninsula, and mapping Banks Peninsula as an island.

First friendly encounter

The *Endeavour* sailed south into Hawke's Bay, and then north again around the top of East Cape. It spent 10 days in Mercury Bay, so called because an observation of the transit of the planet Mercury was made there. In Mercury to study closely the flora and fauna of the area, and while the ship was being cleaned, the smaller boats undertook detailed survey work.

The *Endeavour* left for home at the end of March 1770, sailing up the east coast of Australia, through the Dutch East Indies and then rounding the Cape of Good Hope to complete a circumnavigation of the world. The expedition was an extraordinary feat of seamanship, putting New Zealand firmly on the map and gathering a huge amount of data. Cook seemed to personify the Great Discoverer as defined by his biographer,

Replica of the Endeavour.

Bay, for the first time, the explorers made friends with the local Maori and traded trinkets for supplies of fish, birds and clean water. They were shown over the Maori settlement and inspected a nearby fortified *pa*, which greatly impressed Cook.

The expedition circumnavigated New Zealand and with brilliant accuracy made a chart of the coastline which proved basically reliable for more than 150 years. Cook and his crew spent weeks in Ship Cove, in a long inlet which he called Queen Charlotte Sound, on the northern coast of the South Island, refurbishing the ship and gathering supplies. The stay gave the two botanists aboard, Joseph Banks and Daniel Solander, a wonderful opportunity

Beaglehole: 'In every great discoverer there is a dual passion – the passion to see, the passion to report; and in the greatest this duality is fused into one – a passion to see and to report truly.' Cook's first voyage was one of the most successful and detailed expeditions of exploration in all history.

Return visits

Cook twice again led expeditions into the Pacific – from 1772 to 1775 and from 1776 to 1780. During the second of these, he twice took his ship south of the Antarctic Circle where no vessel was known to have gone before, but he was unlucky in that he did not become the first person ever to see the Antarctic continent.

It was to Dusky Sound in the South Island fiords that Cook repaired for rest and recovery after the extreme hardships faced by his crew in the southern ocean. During the seven weeks his expedition was there, the crew set up a workshop and an observatory, and restored their health with spruce beer (to defeat scurvy) and the plenitude of fish and birds. They made contact with a single family of Maori in an area which was never thickly populated, then or now. They planted seeds on the shore of the sound, and then sailed for their favourite anchorage in Ship Cove at the top of the South Island.

On Cook's way home from New Zealand during his second voyage a few years later, he gave pigs, fowl and vegetable seeds to a Maori community near Hawke's Bay, returning again to Ship Cove on his third voyage. By now he had a friendship with some of the local Maori that had lasted nearly 10 years. In his journals, he referred to the Maori as 'manly and mild' and wrote that 'they have some arts among them which they execute with great judgement and unwearied patience.'

By then he had done such a thorough job of charting the coasts of New Zealand that there was little else for explorers to discover without

> Captain Cook was killed in January 1778 in Kealakekua Bay, Hawaii, after a series of thefts from his expedition led to a skirmish with locals.

going inland. But a number of navigators followed during the remaining years of the 18th century – Frenchmen Dumont d'Urville (who arrived only two months after Cook first set foot in New Zealand) and, later, Marion du Fresne; an Italian, Don Alessandro Malaspina, who commanded a Spanish expedition; and George Vancouver, who had served with Cook.

First European settlement

In 10 years, within the decade of the 1770s, Cook and his contemporaries had opened up the Pacific entirely, and, in 1788, Sydney, in Australia, was established as a British convict settlement. The first Europeans to make an impact on New Zealand, however, were the sealers, with the first gang put ashore on the

southwest coast of the South Island in 1792. There was a brief boom in the early years of the 19th century, but it wasn't long before the seals were in short supply and the ships had to venture further south to the sub-Antarctic islands.

Next, in the last years of the 18th century, came the whalers – some of them driven from the Pacific coast of South America because of the dangers brought about by the war between Spain and Britain. Ships from Britain, Australia and the United States hunted the sperm whale in this region, and visits brought their crew members into frequent contact

An English visitor is greeted by native Maori.

with the Maori of Northland at Kororareka (later renamed Russell).

At first, relations between Europeans and Maori were friendly. But visits were infrequent for a few years after the burning of the brig *Boyd* and the massacre and eating of its crew in Whangaroa Harbour in 1809. This was a reprisal against previous punishment of high-born Maori seamen by Pakeha (European) skippers.

The inland exploration of New Zealand took place mostly during the early to mid-19th century, mainly those parts that were fairly accessible from the coast. Vast areas of the South Island, however, were not successfully explored by Europeans until the 20th century.

SETTLEMENT AND COLONISATION

The colonisation of New Zealand was debated and
fought over by Maori, missionaries, politicians,
settlers and land speculators.

The bleak experiences of Abel Tasman – and
the much more successful endeavours of
James Cook nearly 130 years later – had
no immediate impact on New Zealand. The
Dutch were preoccupied with the Indonesian
archipelago; the British were consolidating and
expanding their trading territories in India.
New Zealand, it seemed, had little to offer a
colonial power.

Across the Tasman Sea, Australia's Botany
Bay was established as a penal settlement in
1788. This was a direct result of America's victory in the War of Independence (previously
convicts were sent to America), but Aotearoa
– the land of the long white cloud – was
mostly ignored.

Sealskins and whale oil

As the 19th century began, with Europe in
the midst of the Napoleonic Wars, demand
increased for commodities such as sealskins
and whale oil. Seals and whales were plentiful in New Zealand waters, and skippers from
Sydney's Port Jackson and Hobart in Van
Diemen's Land (Tasmania) wasted no time
in putting to sea. Numerous skippers found a
convenient watering hole at Kororareka (now
Russell) in the Bay of Islands. The anchorage
there was calm and well protected, and there
was a ready supply of kauri wood for spars
and masts.

Kororareka, with its new European arrivals, rapidly became a lusty, brawling town;
the missionaries who arrived there damned it
as the 'hell-hole of the Pacific'. The newcomers carried dangerous baggage which in time
completely eradicated some of the Maori
tribes, and seriously decimated others: muskets, hard liquor or 'grog', prostitutes, and a

Samuel Marsden introduced Christianity to New Zealand.

THE WAIRAU MASSACRE

Despite the Treaty of Waitangi, land claims soon
became a matter of bitter dispute. In 1843, Arthur
Wakefield (brother of Edward Wakefield) led a
party of armed Nelson settlers into the fertile
Wairau Valley. It was his contention that the land
had been bought by the New Zealand Company
from the widow of a European trader, who had
previously given the Maori a cannon in exchange
for it. The local chief, Te Rauparaha, and his
nephew, Rangihaeata, thought otherwise, and
when the two sides met violence inevitably broke
out. Te Rauparaha's wife was shot and the Maori
killed 22 Pakeha, including Wakefield himself.

host of infectious diseases – many of which proved fatal – to which the Maori had never previously been exposed and therefore had no natural resistance.

Despite all this, contacts between Maori and Europeans were essentially peaceful – although isolated hostilities occurred in the early decade of the 19th century. A barter trade flourished, the Maori trading vegetables and flax for a variety of European trinkets, tools and weapons. The Maori helped cut down giant kauri trees and drag the trunks from bush to beach; they crewed on European sealing and whaling ves-

But the missionary-tradesman-teachers in whom Marsden had placed his faith were in fact an ill-assorted bunch who could hardly be regarded as a civilising, evangelising force by the people they had come to convert. With so many of them involved in gun-running, adultery and drunkenness, it is not surprising that 10 years passed before the first Maori baptism. Not until the 1820s did the Maori begin to find Christianity an attractive proposition.

The missionaries did accomplish some good. Thomas Kendall was instrumental in compiling the first grammar and dictionary

The Emigrants, c.1850, engraved by Elizabeth Walker.

sels; they were physically strong and vigorous, but also proud – a fact often overlooked by most Europeans.

Colonial law but no colony

In 1817, mainly in response to lawlessness in the Bay of Islands, the laws of the Colony of New South Wales in Australia were extended to include New Zealand. Around this time, the Reverend Samuel Marsden arrived from that fledgling colony across the Tasman Sea. A dedicated evangelist, he believed that missionary tradesmen should not only encourage the conversion of Maori to Christianity but also develop their expertise in carpentry, farming and European technology.

of the Maori language, and in 1820 accompanied two famous chiefs, Hongi and Waikato, to Britain.

By 1830, Maori were involved in export trading. In that year 28 ships made 56 voyages to New South Wales, carrying substantial cargoes, including tons of Maori-grown potatoes.

The inclusion of New Zealand within the framework of the laws of New South Wales did not, however, make New Zealand a British colony. And, in any case, the legislation did not prove very effective. The governors had no way of proving charges nor of enforcing their authority while a ship was in New Zealand waters, and they had no authority over foreign vessels and their crews.

Perhaps surprisingly, the early missionaries were generally united in wanting to see New Zealand avoid large-scale colonisation. They hoped to be allowed to spread what they saw as the benefits of Christian civilisation among the Maori, leaving them uncorrupted by the depravity introduced to earlier colonies by European settlers and adventurers. On the other hand, many believed that organised and responsible settlement would be able to avoid the disasters inflicted by Europeans upon indigenous peoples of other countries. The most influential proponent of this view was Edward

Engraving showing Maori chiefs.

Gibbon Wakefield (see page 39).

On a less idealistic level, there was also pressure among Britons for new colonies with land for settlement, and the notion that if Britain did not take sovereignty over New Zealand and populate it with European immigrants, some other colonial power – most probably France – would do so.

Land conflict

The issue of formal colonisation was allowed to drift, yet by the 1830s the scramble for land was in full swing – a scramble that was to produce tragic results within 20 years.

The Maori had no concept of permanent, private ownership of land. Traditionally tribes would inherit land, and if it were sold a chief's authority was generally strong enough to have a sale accepted by most members of the tribe. Sometimes, however, this process was complicated by conflicting claims of ownership among tribes, and such claims could involve large areas. Many land transfers between the white settlers (known to the Maori as Pakeha) and Maori led to conflicts in the 1860s; some of them are still being legally contested today.

There was also the problem of what was being bought. The settlers, and rapacious speculators in Britain, thought they were buying outright freehold land, but in many cases, the Maori believed they were merely leasing their lands for a fee.

The missionaries were not skilled in matters of British law, and certainly not in the area of land conveyancing. The time had finally come for government intervention, however reluctant. In 1833, after the arrival in the Bay of Islands of James Busby as 'British Resident', the move was made. The notion of 'Resident' was vague. A Resident, in most cases, had the full backing of His or Her Majesty's Government as a diplomat representing British interests in a territory that had not yet been annexed by the Crown. He could advise local chieftains, he could cajole – but he had no real power because no treaty or agreement had yet been reached.

Busby did what he could. He attempted to create unity and overall sovereignty among the disparate Maori by formally establishing a confederation of Maori chiefs. Then, in 1835, he proposed that Britain and the United Tribes of New Zealand, as it was termed, should agree to an arrangement under which the confederation would represent the Maori people and gradually expand its influence as a government while the British government, in the meantime, administered the country in trust.

Busby won personal respect from the Maori. Even so, he keenly felt his own impotence and was well aware that he would never be able to achieve law and order here without the backing of some adequate force.

The Wakefield Scheme

In the course of the 1830s it had become obvious that land buying was going to cause serious trouble. Speculators were gambling on Britain taking over and settling the country, while Busby, the British Resident, was powerless to prevent such 'deals' from taking place. Colonisation was inevitable. In 1836, Edward Gibbon Wakefield, a British politician who had been a strong advocate of migration to the new colony of South Australia, told a committee of the House of Commons that Britain was colonising New Zealand already, but 'in a most slovenly and scrambling and disgraceful manner.'

In 1837, at the behest of the government of New South Wales, Captain William Hobson, commanding HMS *Rattlesnake*, sailed from Sydney to the Bay of Islands to report on the situation. Hobson suggested a formal treaty with the Maori chiefs and the placing of all British subjects in New Zealand under British rule. Hobson's report provoked a response, but it was Wakefield's influence that ensured the outcome.

Wakefield disliked the results of colonisation in the United States, Canada, New South

> The missionary William Colenso arrived at Paihia in 1834 and set up a printing press that played a major role in the development of Maori literacy. Among his achievements was a translation of the New Testament into Maori.

Wales and Tasmania. He believed that if land was sold at 'a sufficient price' to 'capitalist' settlers, labourers among the immigrants would stay in the new communities working for landowners – at least for a few years – until they could afford to buy land for themselves at the 'sufficient price.'

Land prices were crucial to Wakefield's system, and New Zealand was his testing ground. Unfortunately he underestimated the aspirations of immigrant labourers and he did not foresee the readiness with which they would move out of the centralised settlements to areas they considered more profitable.

During the late 1830s and early 1840s Wakefield helped establish the New Zealand Company. This became a joint stock company, so that the people involved would bear the costs of establishing the settlements they planned.

The Treaty of Waitangi

Around this time the British government at last responded to the anti-colonial feelings of the missionary groups. Britain decided that the Maori should be consulted on their own future, and that their consent should be obtained before any formal annexation of their country. The result was the Treaty of Waitangi, signed at Waitangi in the Bay of Islands on 6 February 1840 by Hobson (now appointed Lieutenant-Governor) on behalf of the British government. The treaty was later taken to other parts of the country for signing by most of the Maori chiefs. The Tuhoe of Te Urewera, were among those who did not sign.

Ironically, the famous treaty was never actually ratified. Within a decade the Chief Justice,

A portrait of Kotowatowa, a Maori chief.

Sir William Martin, ruled that it had no legal validity because it was not incorporated in New Zealand's statutory law. The date of the original signing of the treaty is now considered to be the 'founding day' of New Zealand as a British colony.

The treaty itself, the opposite of what the missionaries had hoped to achieve, remains a bone of contention. The text of the document was written in English and apparently amended by Hobson after it was first explained to the assembled Maori leaders. A rather loosely translated version in Maori was signed by most of the Maori leaders. The Maori had put much faith in advice from the missionaries, being told that they were signing a solemn pact, under which

New Zealand sovereignty was being vested in the British Crown in return for guarantees of certain Maori rights. Many Europeans (and also Maori) genuinely believed this, and for some years the British government upheld the agreement.

It is almost impossible now to regard the treaty objectively. In the context of its time it was an example of enlightened respect for the rights of an indigenous population. But because it was never ratified, and never truly honoured by the land-hungry white settlers, it is easily construed these days as an expedient fraud and is the focus of some civil dissent.

received its first settlers shortly afterwards, and in 1841 a subsidiary of the Company, based in Plymouth, England, established New Plymouth.

The South Island was not ignored. Captain Arthur Wakefield, one of Edward's many brothers, arrived at Nelson in 1841 and was followed by some 3,000 settlers in 1842.

Signs of trouble

In the Bay of Islands, Hone Heke, a prominent Maori leader and signatory to the Treaty of Waitangi, quickly became disenchanted with the treaty's implications. Although Kororareka

Lyttelton, South Island, in 1880.

The formal British annexation of New Zealand implicit in the 1840 Treaty of Waitangi was quickly followed by the arrival of ships carrying immigrants organised by Wakefield's New Zealand Company. The *Tory*, despatched prior to the signing of the treaty, arrived early in 1840, carrying immigrants who were to settle in the Wellington area. The Wanganui district

> *Pakeha, the Maori term for the white settlers, is a word in common use in contemporary New Zealand; some find it offensive – the original translation is thought to be 'white pig' – but for most it is simply a functional term.*

(Russell) had been the de facto 'capital' of New Zealand before the signing of the treaty, Lieutenant-Governor Hobson decided that Auckland was to be the new capital. Trade from Russell declined and Hone Heke got fractious. He and his warriors demolished the flagpole (the symbol of royal authority) on four occasions, and once sacked the entire town, as British settlers scampered off into the woods or took to boats. George Grey, who arrived as Governor in 1845, called in the army to suppress the rebellion. With the help of Maori dissidents who refused to support Heke, Grey won the day.

Such open conflict did nothing to encourage emigration, and the New Zealand Company went into a terminal decline. It became almost bankrupt in the late 1840s, surrendered its charter, and handed over to the government some 400,000 hectares (about 1 million acres) of land for which about $500,000 were due; in 1858 the Company was dissolved.

Nonetheless, in its last decade of operation the New Zealand Company remained active, lending its organisational support to members of the Scottish Free Church who established Dunedin in 1848, and to the Anglicans who founded Christchurch in 1850. It helped to open up the pasturelands of the Canterbury Plains, and settlers imported sheep, mostly merinos, from Australia, marking the beginnings of large-scale farming.

In 1852 the colony was granted self-government by Britain with the passing of the New Zealand Constitution Act (the first New Zealand parliament convened in 1854).

Wakefield, who did not set foot in New Zealand until 1852, achieved much, but also lived to see that his ideal of cohesive but expanding communities, complete with 'capitalists' and 'labourers', was not viable. The immigrants didn't necessarily make the choice for 'town life', and many left the fledgling settlements to establish agricultural or pastoral properties well beyond the confines of the towns. However, thanks largely to Wakefield's efforts, the settlement and colonisation of New Zealand were achieved in a more orderly manner than had been the case, several decades earlier, in Canada and Australia.

The New Zealand Wars

The new colony, however, was facing problems. There had been a great deal of speculation in land sales, and many Maori were beginning to realise this: land was being sold for as much as 20 times what they had been paid for it.

A direct result of this injustice was the election in 1858 of a Maori 'King' (later called the *Kingitanga* or Maori King Movement) by tribes in the North Island around the Waikato region. There had never been such a title among the Maori, who owed their allegiance to a tribe or sub-tribe, but it was hoped that the *mana* (spiritual authority) of a king, uniting many tribes, would help protect their land against purchase by the Pakeha (white settlers). However, it didn't work out that way.

In Taranaki, another group of tribes rose up against the government in June 1860 following

a blatantly fraudulent land purchase by the colonial administration, the Waitara Land Deal. British regular troops, hastily assembled, were virtually annihilated south of Waitara.

For the next few years, the North Island was ablaze with clashes between Maori and Pakeha. The New Zealand Wars were marked by extraordinary courage on both sides. The conflicts were frequently indecisive, but bloody. On the Pakeha side, the brunt of the early fighting, until 1865, was borne by British regular troops, 14 of whom received Britain's highest battle honour, the Victoria Cross. Between 1865

The NZ Wars were marked by bloody clashes.

and 1872, locally raised militia and constabulary forces played an important role – assisted by some Maori tribes who had decided not to join the Maori King's confederation. The 'official' end of the conflict came in 1872, with the Maori exhausted by a lack of food and heavy losses, although sporadic fighting continued until formal surrender in 1881.

Despite war, the country's prospects continued to improve. The discovery of gold in the South Island led to a fresh influx of migrants in the early 1860s, and the pursuit of pasture was opening up vast tracts of the country. The increasing importance of the southern lands caused the capital to be moved from Auckland to Wellington in 1865.

A NEW NATION

The 20th century saw a series of unprecedented economic, social and political challenges for the people of New Zealand.

Progress towards full independence from Britain began almost as soon as the Maori-Pakeha Land Wars began to settle down. In the 1870s, colonial treasurer Sir Julius Vogel, who borrowed heavily overseas for public works construction, notably railways, sparked an economic boom. A flood of immigrants followed, mainly from Britain but also from Scandinavia and Germany.

But Vogel miscalculated the negative impact of his borrow-to-boom credo. In 1880, New Zealand narrowly averted bankruptcy following steep falls in wool and grain prices. A full-scale depression quickly set in, with unemployment spreading rapidly. In 1888, more than 9,000 settlers left the colony, most of them for Australia, which had remained relatively prosperous.

The years of hardship may have had an impact on the emergence of New Zealand as one of the most socially progressive communities in the world. In 1877 free, compulsory and secular primary school education became law and two years later, every adult man – Maori and Pakeha alike – won the right to vote (see box, page 49).

Richard John Seddon statue in front of the Beehive building, Wellington.

Lamb for the world's tables

There were some other signs of hope, too, with the emergence of a new industry that was set to pave the way in years to come. In 1882, the refrigerated vessel *Dunedin*, loaded with sheep carcasses, made the voyage to England, arriving three months later. The trip was an arduous one, but the meat arrived safely and profits were much higher than in New Zealand. Farmers subsequently began to breed sheep for meat as well as wool, and the frozen meat industry became an economic staple. This, combined with the expansion of dairy exports in the early 20th century, saw the affluence and influence of farmers grow.

New Zealand politely refused an invitation to become part of the new Commonwealth of Australia and was subsequently upgraded by the British Empire from 'colony' to 'dominion' in 1907 (a largely symbolic change of status, but one which would pave the way to full independence within 40 years). The new Reform Party squeezed into power four years later; the new prime minister, William Massey, a dairy farmer, helped consolidate New Zealand's position as an offshore farm for Britain.

World Wars and depression

War brought a new sense of nationalism to New Zealand, and at the same time reinforced the country's ties to Britain. Between 1914 and 1918, 100,000 men joined the Australia-New Zealand Army Corps (Anzac) forces fighting with the Allies in Africa and Europe.

The Great Depression of the 1930s hit hard. Curtailed British demand for meat, wool and dairy products led to severe unemployment and several bloody riots. The new Labour Party swept into power in 1935 and managed to pull the nation out of the doldrums. Under

Back home, a successful economic stabilisation policy and full employment made the 1940s a decade of relative prosperity, and the country emerged from the war with a stronger sense of nationhood and identity. It was an appropriate time, in 1947, for the government to adopt the Statute of Westminster and formally achieve full independence from Britain.

The Labour Party, however, had by then lost its vigour, and its defeat in 1949 ended an era. The victors were the National Party, who ran on a platform extolling private enterprise. The 1950s began with a political tremor as this new

Anzac Day dawn service, Gisborne.

Prime Minister Michael Savage, New Zealand again moved to the forefront of world social change, establishing a full social security system.

Savage also led the country into World War II. This time, nearly 200,000 Kiwis were called to battle, many of them engaged in the Pacific campaign, others in North Africa, Italy and Crete. More than 10,000 died. American writer James A. Michener once claimed that the bravest soldier in each of the World Wars was a New Zealander – Bernard Freyberg in the first and, in the second, Charles Upham, 'a stumpy, square-jawed chap' whose 'behaviour under fire seems incredible'. Upham won the Victoria Cross twice.

WORLD WAR I

By the time World War I ended, almost 17,000 New Zealanders had lost their lives. Indeed, the casualties were out of all proportion to the country's population, then about a million. The futility was underscored by the debacle that took place on Turkey's Gallipoli Peninsula, from 25 April 1915 (a day now marked in memoriam every year as 'Anzac Day') until British naval evacuation some eight months later; the affair cost the lives of 8,587 servicemen from Australia and New Zealand. This heroic tragedy, dramatised some years later in Peter Weir's film *Gallipoli*, gave New Zealand a new identity within the British Empire.

government abolished the Legislative Council, the upper house of the national Parliament. New Zealand became one of the few democratic nations with a unicameral legislature. This gave inordinate power to the executive – a Cabinet made up of members of the ruling party. The power to change the law dramatically, and within hours, enabled the Labour Party to transform the nation's economy, and its entire social structure, between 1984 and 1990 (see page 46).

One of the first actions taken by the unicameral House was the ratification of the ANZUS (Australia–New Zealand–United States) security pact in 1951, sealing the nation's defence requirements.

End of isolation

The first post-war revolution, however, came with the end of isolation. Before mass travel became a possibility, New Zealand's hotels shut at 6pm, restaurants were forbidden to sell liquor and a rigid 40-hour, five-day working week meant shop hours were strictly controlled and most families spent weekends at home. Society remained in that time warp until the 1950s, when passenger ships began their trade again. Thousands of young Kiwis went away for their 'OE' (overseas experience), almost always to London, and for the first time could compare their society with others.

Air travel and advances in telecommunications in the 1960s and '70s led to radical changes in this narrow, closed, highly controlled society. By the 1980s, shops were staying open into the evenings and weekends, most restrictions were lifted from hotels and taverns, New Zealand wines began to rank among the world's best, and restaurants and cafés made eating out part of the national culture. On the back of such sophistication, tourism boomed.

The transition has not always been smooth. In the early 1970s New Zealand began grappling with the problem of diversifying both its production away from bulk commodities and its markets away from Britain. When oil prices soared, debt began to pile up as both Labour and National administrations borrowed and hoped primary production prices would pick up. It was a matter of marketing to other nations, something New Zealanders had never needed to do. They had lived well for so long, simply by farming well and trading

with Britain, that Britain's transition into the European Economic Community (EEC) in 1973 left them in confusion.

Tumultuous times

During the 1970s, New Zealand's sheep population rose past 70 million for the first time as farmers received state payments to boost stock numbers. Primary industry was widely subsidised and manufacturing tightly protected from 1975–84 under Sir Robert Muldoon's National government. Meanwhile, trade barriers imposed on Britain by EEC membership,

Prince William on a visit to Wellington.

combined with rocketing oil prices, sent the cost of industrial goods sky high.

Muldoon's government doubled the tight measures imposed by Labour on immigration, imports and the dollar. A pugnacious man, Muldoon provoked the anger of trade unionists by imposing a wage freeze, but held his line in the face of numerous strikes and demonstrations.

By the end of the 1970s and the beginning of the 1980s, internal inflation was raging so strongly (up to 17 percent) that farm costs skyrocketed and the Muldoon ministry humiliatingly had to bolster subsidies to New Zealand farmers. All the regulation and readjustment caused an agony of doubt about the short-term future of the economy. By 1984, unemployment had reached 130,000 and the national overseas debt stood at NZ$14.3 billion.

When a new Labour government came to power towards the end of 1984, the situation changed rapidly: farm and other production subsidies were withdrawn, import licences abandoned, wage structures dismantled and a broad policy of economic laissez-faire put in place.

On returning to power in 1990, the National Party under Jim Bolger quickly made it clear that they would keep faith with economic

the Christchurch earthquakes in the latter half of 2010 and early 2011, have rattled the bones of New Zealanders. Although these events have brought them together as a people, they have also reminded them of the shaky geological nature of the isles upon which they live.

Foreign affairs

New Zealand began to assert itself on the international stage during the 1960s, as France stepped up its campaign of nuclear testing in its Polynesian-governed islands. There were several mass demonstrations, and strong

Robert Muldoon campaigns for election in 1975.

deregulation. In the mid-1990s the economy began steadily to recover and the government eased up slightly on its expenditure and its tight monetary policy. Immigration was encouraged, and as the population steadily grew, demand for houses rose sharply, and between 2003 and 2008 the price of land, particularly coastal property, soared. The latter has remained high, even with the global downturn. In 2012 Auckland's property market experienced a mini-boom due to a lack of housing in the city.

New Zealand continues to hold its own during the current worldwide recession, its dollar remaining strong against all major overseas currencies, including the British pound. However, a spate of natural disasters, including

NO NUKES

In 1987 Labour passed the Nuclear Free Zone, Disarmament, and Arms Control Act. The US Congress downgraded New Zealand's defence status from ally to 'friend'. Prime Minister David Lange responded by saying that the security alliance was a price worth paying to keep New Zealand nuclear-free. The next year, 52 percent of New Zealanders said they would rather break defence ties than let nuclear-armed ships visit. By 1990, public opinion was so strong that the new National government was forced to maintain the Lange government's anti-nuclear stance. New Zealand remains a nuclear-free zone.

anti-nuclear sentiment reached its peak in New Zealand when the Labour government refused nuclear-armed or nuclear-powered US naval vessels entry to New Zealand ports in 1985. The Americans insisted on their right as allies under the ANZUS Pact and broke off all defence arrangements with New Zealand. Labour, under Prime Minister David Lange, pledged to set up a nuclear-free zone around the shores of New Zealand, and to renegotiate the 33-year-old ANZUS security pact to force the US to keep nuclear armaments out of New Zealand ports. Division within the Labour gov-

New Zealand has also turned its economic attention northwards to the burgeoning Asian economies, and China is currently New Zealand's second-largest trading partner. Chinese demand for New Zealand commodity exports, especially dairy products and wood, has risen rapidly and is a major factor in the recent surge in New Zealand's commodity prices. China is expected to become increasingly important for New Zealand in the coming years. Business is also booming with the United States (New Zealand's third-largest trading partner), Japan and Korea. Trade

China is one of New Zealand's most important trading partners.

ernment on other issues had grown so wide, however, that Lange resigned in 1989.

Early in the post-war period, New Zealand had come to realise that its best economic hope for the future was some sort of pact with Australia. In 1965, the New Zealand Australia Free Trade Agreement was signed. The plan was gradually to dismantle trade barriers between the two countries, but progress was slow. In 1983, the two governments signed the CER (Closer Economic Relations) pact, and by the beginning of the 1990s, free trade was virtually in place across the Tasman Sea. Today, Australia is New Zealand's largest trading partner. New Zealand has some $51 billion invested in Australia, while Australia has $107 billion invested in New Zealand.

with Taiwan, Hong Kong, Malaysia, Indonesia, Singapore, Thailand, India and the Philippines is also growing. Although still important, trade with countries in the European Union is declining.

Maori redress

During the 30 years of social and economic turbulence that began in the 1960s, New Zealand proved to be one of the most stable democracies in the world. But there remained a festering sore beneath the surface, caused by injustices to the Maori over a century before.

The 1984–90 Labour government finally acknowledged the validity of Maori claims for land, fishing grounds and other assets that were illegally taken from them – claims that were based on the 1840 Treaty of Waitangi. The Labour government set up the Waitangi Tribunal to consider these claims, and this process continues today. Many land claims have been conceded, and property, particularly land held by the government, has been given back to Maori ownership. Major fishing concessions have also been awarded. In 2012 the National Party, led by John Key, granted Tuhoe people – a tribe who chose not to sign the Treaty of Waitangi in 1840 – governance, but not outright ownership, of Te Urewera National Park.

Electoral reform

Dissatisfaction with the rapid pace of change and with the performance of government was expressed in a referendum on electoral reform. In 1993, the country voted to scrap traditional first-past-the-post elections in favour of a proportional system called the MMP (Mixed Member Proportional).

In the 1996 elections, the National Party, led by Jim Bolger, won 44 seats in the 120-member house, while the Labour Party won 37. The New Zealand First Party, having won 17 seats, including four Maori seats (areas mainly populated by

Maori rights protestors during Queen Elizabeth's 1989 visit. The banner reads 'Honour the Treaty of Waitangi'.

Although there is a consensus throughout the nation that redress is due, some tension has prevailed over particular Waitangi claims. But in more recent times, rather than the tension spilling over as it has in the past, the parties involved have engaged in discussion over various problems, to find a way forward. Current issues include the question of Maori customary rights to the water held in New Zealand's rivers and lakes. Progress towards settlement of land claims continues and is high on the political agenda, but whatever progress is made, it never pleases everyone. The difficulties, however, continue to be worked through as they arise and are seen by most as the growing pains of a new nation.

Maori who had previously voted for Labour), held the balance of power and emerged as the coalition partner in a new government with the National Party. The situation became volatile after 1996; in 1997 Prime Minister Bolger resigned.

In December 1997, Jenny Shipley became the country's first female prime minister, replacing Bolger as leader of the National Party. But weakened by the break-up of her coalition party and a floundering economy, Shipley lost the 1999 elections to a Labour Party-led coalition, helmed by another woman, Helen Clark. Clark's tough-as-nails approach, aided by a strong domestic economy and lower unemployment rate, clinched her and the Labour Party a second term at the 2002 elections and a third term in 2005, albeit by the narrowest of margins.

In 2008, the National Party, led by John Key, swept into power, and Helen Clark resigned as leader of the Labour Party. The National Party, still led by John Key, also won the 2011 election and formed a minority government. New Zealand's next election will be held in 2014.

A new confidence

New Zealand was once dominated by a self-denigrating 'cultural cringe' which saw it constantly measuring itself unfavourably against other countries. This was compounded by New Zealanders returning home from overseas experiences, and immigrants from wealthy countries, who, missing the infrastructure (if not the population count) of their homeland, made

> On 31 December 1999, New Zealanders made much of the fact that their country was the first in the world to enter the new millennium. This reflected a growing awareness of the nation's uniqueness and individuality.

constant comparisons between New Zealand and the rest of the world.

Although New Zealand has long ceased to be a smaller version of Australia or a pale reflection of England, the process of defining New Zealand's identity was facilitated by several factors, not least among them the introduction of the MMP system in 1993, which established a truly representative government. In the elections

immediately following its adoption, there were more Maori and women MPs, and the first Pacific Island, Asian and Muslim MPs were elected. This in turn made it clear that New Zealand was no longer a bicultural, Maori-Pakeha society, but a multicultural one. For more on New Zealand's multicultural society, see page 53.

Today New Zealand has emerged as a proud, strong, multicultural nation; a nuclear-free, socially forward democracy with a robust currency and strong trade ties. It has a bright future ahead and a distinct South Pacific Island flavour at its heart.

A Maori performs a traditional hongi greeting.

AN ENLIGHTENED LIBERAL NATION

New Zealand has a long history of enlightened social innovation. In 1877, free education became available for all children aged between seven and 14. Two years later, universal male suffrage became law. In the 1890s, under the Liberal Party government, sweeping land reforms were introduced, breaking down the large inland estates and providing money for first mortgages to put people on the land. Industrial legislation provided improved conditions for workers as well as the world's first compulsory system of industrial arbitration. The aged poor were awarded a pension.

The country became the first self-governing nation to grant the right to vote to all adult women in September 1893, when the Governor approved the Electoral Bill passed by Parliament 11 days earlier. This marked the end of an epic struggle by suffragettes, led by Kate Sheppard. A seven-year campaign culminated in the 1893 petition for the enfranchisement of women. It was then the largest petition ever gathered in Australasia.

The principal minds behind these great social reforms were William Pember Reeves, a New Zealand-born socialist, and Richard John Seddon, who became prime minister when Ballance died in 1893. Seddon's legendary toughness and political judgement gave him enormous power within the party and throughout the nation.

Droving sheep over Orari Saddle near Fairlie.

Celebrating Polynesian culture at the annual Pasifika Festival, Auckland.

PEOPLE

In multicultural New Zealand, Maori, Pakeha and Pacific Islanders have been joined by a diverse mix of new arrivals, all helping to shape the distinctive New Zealand character.

New Zealanders, while numerically rare by global standards, are found the world over, with around a million living overseas. The other 4.5 million live at home in what Kiwis dub 'Godzone', one of the most beautiful and least crowded countries on the planet. Yet at the same time New Zealand is also one of the world's most urbanised and suburbanised nations, with three quarters of its residents living in the four main centres, and the rest scattered across the rural spaces in between. The population of Auckland alone exceeds that of the entire South Island, while half the South Island population is to be found in and around Christchurch. You're less likely to run into anyone in Westland, where, perhaps more than anywhere else, one can sense that New Zealand has been home to humans for only a very short time – probably, in fact, less than 1,000 years (see page 27). By any standards, this is a very young country.

An Auckland café.

Despite the overwhelming majority of urbanites, farming remains the backbone of the economy. It is a way of life valued by close-knit rural communities throughout the land. Voluntary activity runs everything, and in the countryside you will also find the warmth, friendly neighbourhood security and community spirit that once set the tone for the nation as a whole. As for the legendary black-singletted, gumboot-clad Fred Dagg-like character (invented by the satirist John Clarke), the doyen of the family farm with a dog at his heel – he's increasingly rare. Chances are, today, the guy working in the cowshed hails from Mumbai or Manila.

However, many an urban office worker may be only one generation away from the farm. Until the 1950s, the rural–urban split was roughly 50/50, but that changed with the post-war drift of jobseekers to the cities, where they purchased the stock-standard quarter-acre (about 1,000 sq metres) of land.

Although New Zealand is still a paradise of sorts, growing crime – the main offenders being drunk and drug-fuelled youths – renders urban areas rather less so today. Meanwhile, in cities, the quarter-acre has shrunk to a mere eighth of an acre. Regardless, the traditional vegetable plot, once an essential in most Kiwi families, has enjoyed a revival, and those without space simply make use of public land to grow their crops. There's been a distinct shift in focus towards sustainable living and today, although pricey, the ideal for many people is a semi-self-sufficient lifestyle, with a plot of land, around

0.5 to 2 hectares (1 to 5 acres), located within an hour's drive of a major city.

Modern Maori

The indigenous people of New Zealand, the Maori or *Tangata Whenua* (people of the land), first settled on the islands at some point between the 9th and 13th centuries AD. More than two centuries after the earliest European settlers arrived, the Maori now make up about 14.6 percent of the population, with most living in the North Island. The Maori language (*Te Reo*) is spoken throughout New Zealand

Maoris make up around 15 percent of the population.

and the vast majority of place names are of Maori origin.

If one single person can be credited for the survival of Maori culture into modern times, it must be the great parliamentarian Sir Apirana Ngata (1874–1950). By the late 1920s, knighted and made Minister of Native Affairs, Ngata had devised legislation to develop Maori land, established a school at Rotorua and initiated a work programme for the building of Maori community facilities. Working with Ngata to implement national policy at a local level was a group of community leaders including Princess Te Puea Herangi of Waikato. Te Puea was the force behind the *Kingitanga*, or Maori King Movement, formed in 1858 to unite and strengthen the Maori community and to halt the loss of Maori land (see page 41).

After her death in 1952, Te Puea's great-niece, Te Arikinui Dame Te Atairangikaahu, led the Kingitanga for the next 40 years, during which it grew in stature. The five-day *tangi* (funeral service) following Te Atairangikaahu's death in August 2006 brought Maori together on an unprecedented scale. Her eldest son, Tuheitia Paki, has succeeded as king.

In the 1930s the living standards of Maori rose considerably under the Labour government's welfare programme, ensuring the physical survival of the race, which had been threatened by diseases introduced by European settlers. (Numbers never dropped perilously low, however: the Maori population, estimated at around 100,000 when the Europeans arrived, had declined to 42,000 by 1900, and after this date numbers began to recover.)

THE HUI, TRADITIONAL MAORI GATHERING

For visitors, the *hui* offers the most revealing glimpse of Maori culture. It will usually be held on a *marae* (the open courtyard in front of the meeting house) under the supervision of the *tangata whenua,* or host tribe. Visitors are called onto the *marae* with a *karanga* – a long, wailing call. The visitors enter led by their own women, dressed in black. Then follows a *tangi* (ritual weeping) for the dead. This is succeeded by the *mihi* (speeches) of welcome and reply, made by male elders. At the end of each speech, the orator's companions stand and perform a *waiata* (song). Once these formalities are over, visitors move forward and *hongi* (press noses) with the locals.

The food served on such occasions is special: meat and vegetables are cooked in a *hangi* (earth oven). There will be seafood, with delicacies such as shellfish, *kina* (sea egg), eel and dried shark. Other treats include fermented *kumara* and *titi* (mutton bird, also known as the sooty shearwater), and *Rewena* (a scone-like loaf) will accompany the meal. Eating together communicates goodwill, and acceptance of hospitality is as important as offering it.

There are many tourist operators in New Zealand, particularly in Rotorua, who can organise *marae* visits, which often include a *powhiri* (formal welcome) and a *wero* (challenge).

Following World War II, however, there was a major shift in Maori society. A decline in rural employment and a rapid expansion of secondary industry in urban areas brought Maori into the cities in increasing numbers, and by the 1980s less than 10 percent remained in rural settlements. For the first time, Maori and Pakeha found themselves living alongside one another.

This new relationship brought difficulties. With no ready access or encouragement to further their education, many new urban Maori became trapped in low-paying jobs. Housing conditions were also poor. That led to stereo-

university, and laws ban discrimination in the workplace. Legal aid and translation facilities are now available in the courts, and Maori ranks alongside English as an official language.

Maori values, too, remain beneath the cloak of Western appearances. Concepts such as *tapu* (sacredness), *noa* (the passing of *tapu* to a person, ie a blessing), *wairua* (things of the spirit) and *mana* (spiritual authority) all persist in modern Maori life. Yet poverty remains a problem in many areas, and Maori still make up a disproportionate number of the prison population. Some commentators have suggested the

Colourful costumes at the Pasifika Festival.

typing that further hindered their prospects. It was a harsh and different world, lacking the support network offered by the extended family in the rural environment. Some born in the new environment reacted in a strongly antisocial manner. The Maori crime rate increased, adding further to a negative Maori stereotype.

The problems, however, have been recognised, and since then much progress has been made. The education system in New Zealand adapted accordingly and *Kohanga Reo* (language nests) were set up to expose pre-school Maori to their language and customs. Increasingly, the current school curriculum reflects the importance of Maori culture, programmes have been established to encourage Maori to study at

social problems are deep-rooted, perhaps going back as far as European colonisation. Regardless of this, the Maori profile has increased dramatically and a more positive image has replaced the old negative stereotype.

Non-Maori increasingly show respect for Maori rituals and for places that are *tapu* (sites of sacred objects, historic events or burials). There are many places throughout New Zealand that are sacred to Maori. Visitors are urged to recognise the cultural significance of these places and treat them with respect.

Britain in the South Seas

Starting in earnest around 1830, hundreds of years after the arrival of the Maori, the pioneering

English, Scottish, Irish and Welsh settlers arrived in New Zealand. The original plan, mooted by the New Zealand Company, was to establish a 'Better Britain' or 'Britain of the South'. Unlike Australia, however, a criminal record did not provide a one-way ticket. Instead, industrious immigrants, respectable, hard-working rural labourers and cultured men of capital were determinedly sought. Prosperity and respectability were promised in exchange for hard work. The idea of owning one's own land, deeply entrenched in the Kiwi psyche, arrived with the settlers for whom it was largely an impossibility back home.

Land issues were a constant source of conflict between the Maori and the Europeans in the early days (see page 38). The Europeans' land-grabbing ways, and later wars between the two groups, did nothing to endear many of the new arrivals to the native population. The greatest conflicts arose over the mutual misunderstanding of what constituted land ownership. Even today, reparation is still being made for land issues surrounding the 1840 Treaty of Waitangi (see page 39).

For the first 50 years of European settlement, almost half the newcomers were English, with significant numbers of Welsh (the original

Women queue to cast their votes, 1899. New Zealand was the first country in the world to introduce universal suffrage.

NOTEWORTHY NEW ZEALANDERS

In 1991 the Reserve Bank of New Zealand announced that new banknotes were required and suggested that the portrait of the Queen on some of the banknotes be replaced by those of notable New Zealanders. This was a significant moment for New Zealand, being seen as a meaningful break with the colonial past. The nation nominated worthy candidates. The illustrious Nobel Prize-winning scientist Sir Ernest Rutherford topped the bill. The first to split the atom, he looks pensively from the NZ$100 note that bills him as Lord Rutherford of Nelson. National hero, the late Sir Edmund Hillary polled a close second. Once voted the country's most trusted citizen in a

nationwide poll, Hillary was respected as much for his conquest of Mount Everest as for his humanitarian and conservation causes. He looks towards the mountains in the distance on the NZ$5 note.

Kate Sheppard graces the NZ$10 note. An intelligent Christian socialist, Sheppard led the women's movement whose efforts made New Zealand the world's first sovereign state to give women the vote. Maori leader Apirana Ngata adorns the NZ$50 note. The first Maori to obtain a degree, Ngata in 1905 entered Parliament as member for Eastern Maori, a seat he held for 38 years. The notes are still the same today, albeit now in plastic rather than paper.

statistics lumped both together). Nowhere in New Zealand does this heritage survive better than in the city of Christchurch, whose founders transplanted a complete cross-section of English Episcopalian society, with an earl and a bishop (both of whom soon fled the privation of the pioneering scene) at the top and the labouring classes at the bottom. The utopian Episcopalian dream might have foundered, but Christchurch has prospered and remains about as close to the mother country as it is possible to get outside of England itself.

The Scots made up the second-largest immi-

in large numbers during the Otago gold rushes of the 1860s.

The pioneers brought with them their Northern Hemisphere traditions, language, festivals, faith and food, some of which have passed unchanged into 21st-century Kiwi culture. With menus intact, a small minority continue to enjoy haggis on Burns Night and Hogmanay, and eggs at Easter, as well as roast, fruit mince pies and steamed fruit pudding at Christmas, eaten in the midst of summer. However, most now ignore traditions in favour of a Kiwi institution – the good old New Zealand barbecue.

Panning for gold in Otago.

grant group, at 24 percent. Their pioneers, a stiff-backed band of Free Kirk (Church) Presbyterians, arrived in 1848, driven by the urge to escape economic depression and the schism that had developed between their Church and the Church of Scotland. This clannish but brave little community possessed the determination and toughness to endure the notoriously bleak winters and the rugged terrain of Otago, where they created a 'Scotland of the South'. Their main city, Dunedin (the old Gaelic name for Edinburgh), became New Zealand's most populous town for a time in the 19th century.

A sizeable number of Irish immigrants, many of whom were diggers who followed the gold trail down from California and Australia, arrived

KIWI INGENUITY

It is said that a New Zealander can fix anything with a length of No. 8 fencing wire. New Zealanders' inventiveness and do-it-yourself mentality arrived with the early European settlers, who found themselves in an untamed land, devoid of the trappings of civilisation. Machinery had to be fixed with whatever was available. Necessity has endowed New Zealand with more inventors per capita than anywhere else. Among them are Sir William Hamilton, who invented the Hamilton jet boat, and Richard 'Mad' Pearse, who designed his own planes and reputedly flew before the Wright brothers.

What Makes a Kiwi

The fact that New Zealand is a small country a very long way from anywhere else has helped to shape the locals' distinctive outlook

New Zealanders are as homogeneous – or as diverse – as the people of any other nation in this age of globalism, the internet and international air travel. That said, the isolation and insularity of this

Fun at the Pasifika Festival.

country have bred some distinct qualities and characteristics.

One that is likely to be noticed early on by visitors is known as the 'cultural cringe', the belief that, because New Zealand is so small and remote, anything from another country is bound to be superior to the local version. This characteristic indicates a desperate need for approval from foreigners. The first question visitors are likely to be asked is: 'How do you like New Zealand?' (The correct answer is: 'It's wonderful, I'm thinking of moving here.')

As a consequence of this dependence on overseas approval, the New Zealanders who have succeeded overseas are the ones who are most respected at home – the likes of Sam Neill, Kiri Te Kanawa and the late Sir Edmund Hillary. However,

increasingly, those who succeed overseas but choose to remain in New Zealand, like Sir Peter Jackson and Bret McKenzie, are held in the highest regard.

Tall poppies

Another corollary of New Zealand's size is that it is quite easy for an individual to shine. Anyone engaged in any form of endeavour is likely to be among the top five in his or her field simply because there won't be many more than five people engaged in it. This is directly connected to the so-called 'tall poppy' syndrome, meaning that anyone who rises above the crowd will be cut down in a frenzy of negative criticism generated by envy. This is often quoted but simply not true, and the syndrome may well be the invention of an over-sensitive elite who cannot abide any suggestion that they fall short of perfection.

The notion of a tall poppy springs from the fact that, despite the wide gap between rich and poor, New Zealand is still at heart an egalitarian society, the legacy of the utopians who colonised it. There is a class system, but it is far less rigid and confining than in most other Western democracies.

New Zealanders are a relatively laconic race, so it's paradoxical that when they do speak, they talk very quickly, packing a greater number of words into a breath than most other native English-speakers. At the same time, their conversation labours under a conspicuous drawl. Those who recoil at the length of time it takes a New Zealander to meander through a vowel should be warned that many linguists theorise that the English-speaking world is undergoing a Great Vowel Shift which will eventually see everyone talking like 'thus'.

A highly active sense of humour is a strong part of the national make-up, though it often goes unnoticed because it is so dry. If a New Zealander says something that sounds absurd, he probably means it to be, but he won't drive it home with series of hearty guffaws and thigh-slapping.

Though New Zealanders are overwhelmingly urbanite in number, their heritage has given them many rural values which persist beyond the farm gate – diligence, support for others, strong community spirit, practicality (with a concomitant distrust of intellectuals) and a can-do attitude. The phrase 'No. 8-wire spirit' holds that a New Zealander can solve any practical problem with a piece of No. 8 fencing wire. New Zealanders are certainly ingenious; they are also diverse, imaginative and entertaining hosts.

The gold rushes also brought a host of fortune seekers from many nations flooding into the country through Dunedin, the nearest port to the Otago goldfields. Among the newcomers were Germans, Scandinavians, Poles, French, Italians and Chinese. Yet, despite the influx of these new immigrants, as the 19th century progressed the unmistakably British character of New Zealand continued strongly, bolstered by the arrival of another 100,000 Europeans – mostly British – in the 1870s.

Old prejudices also persisted, and were bolstered by a few new ones. In many a Protestant

> 'If an English butler and an English nanny sat down to design a country, they would come up with New Zealand.' Anon

like never before. The 1970s saw a severing of traditional ties with Britain after it joined the European Economic Community in 1973, and an end to assisted British immigration. A new wave of immigrants, from Asia and the Pacific, followed. Added to the mix are a growing number of refugees and asylum seekers, attracted by

Rugby Union – a national passion.

mind, there was a distinctive 'us' and 'them' mentality – 'them' being the Catholic Irish. This prejudice persisted well into the 1950s. And, predictably, most of the European arrivals displayed racial prejudice towards the Maori.

The new New Zealanders

Up to the 1960s, there was little to challenge the original plan of a distinctly British New Zealand. Most immigrants were British, and those who were not, for example the 30,000-strong Dutch community who arrived in the 1950s, were expected to adopt the local ways and get on with it. But with the 1960s came television and cheap air travel, which opened New Zealand to the world and the world to New Zealand

New Zealand's progressive humanitarian stance, liberal politics and world-leading social welfare. Today they continue to arrive from various hot spots around the globe – Afghanistan, Iran, Somalia, Burundi and Zimbabwe. Overall, about 23 percent of New Zealand's residents today were born overseas, with more of these living in Auckland than anywhere else in the country.

While certain Kiwi characteristics prevail, the 21st-century New Zealander is becoming increasingly difficult to define. Statistically speaking, if you were to gather together 100 randomly selected New Zealanders, you would be in the company of roughly 68 Europeans, 15 Maori, nine Asians, seven Pacific Islanders and one person from a minority cultural group. The median age would be 36 years for males and 38 years for females, 14 would be over 65 years old and 31 would be from Auckland.

While traditional fish-and-chips remains the favourite for the rest of New Zealand, Asian foods are the takeaway of choice in Auckland, New Zealand's most ethnically diverse region and home to the country's largest Asian population. Today, the Chinese form the largest Asian immigrant group, followed by Indians. Within these groups are families who have been in the country for several generations. The rest of the Asian community come mainly from Korea, the Philippines, Japan, Sri Lanka

The majority of the Pacific Islanders today are New Zealand-born. Their contributions to New Zealand culture are considerable, particularly in the fields of sport and music. All Blacks Sonny Bill Williams and Victor Vito, and former All Blacks Tana Umaga and Jonah Lomu, shot-put champions Valerie Adams and Beatrice

> New Zealand's former prime minister, Robert Muldoon, once remarked that 'New Zealanders who leave for Australia raise the IQ of both countries'.

Contestants prepare for a waka (canoe) race in Rotorua.

and Cambodia. Their reasons for coming vary; some came for education, others to invest or transfer their skills, and many to establish their families in a less crowded, cleaner and healthier environment.

Pacific Islanders

Auckland's distinctly multicultural character contrasts markedly with the rest of the country. South Auckland, in particular, is home to the largest Pacific Island population in the world. The first Pacific Islanders (other than the Maori) were brought by missionaries to New Zealand for biblical training; after World War II, they mostly came to fill labour shortages.

Faumina, Silver Fern netballers Temepara George, Bernice Mene and April Ieremia, hip-hop artist King Kapisi and rapper Scribe – to name but a few – are all Kiwi heroes. The largest group among the Pacific Islanders are the Samoans, whose payments to relatives back home provide half of Samoa's foreign exchange. Cook Islands Maori and Tongans make up the next largest groups, followed by Niueans, Fijians and Tokelauans. Indeed, many more Niueans, Cook Islands Maori and Tokelauans are found in New Zealand than in the islands themselves.

Of the many tongues spoken in New Zealand, the most common after the official languages of English, Maori and New Zealand sign language is Samoan, followed by French, Cantonese and German.

The big OE

New Zealanders have long been ranked among the world's most travelled citizens. A significant proportion of those who emigrate here are likely to spend a large amount of time away from their new home visiting relatives in other countries. And many New Zealanders themselves emigrate: just why 1 million of them live overseas has everything to do with New Zealand's geographical remoteness and the national rite of passage known as the big OE – Overseas Experience.

and settled there permanently. Today an estimated 600,000 New Zealanders have relocated to their large neighbour across the Tasman Sea, attracted by higher wages, warmer northern Australian climates and close proximity to home. Another 50,000 Kiwis are overseas in countries other than Australia and Britain. Most, having satisfied their curiosity, return home to bring up their children or to retire. Settling back in has its challenges, though: the more travelled find it less easy to adjust to the limits of their homeland's insular shores, particularly if they are not fans of rugby, netball or the great outdoors.

Working the land.

Lasting anything from a few years to decades, the OE was originally a sea journey home to Britain and Europe for the early settlers. It then became an essential cultural escape for New Zealand artists and writers of the 1920s and 1930s, stifled by the insular, tight-lipped narrow-mindedness of home. From the 1960s onwards, cheaper air travel brought the rest of the world within the reach of more Kiwis who chose to escape and explore their past and the world at large, and pursue lives around the globe.

The main Meccas of Kiwi pilgrimage remain Britain and Australia. Between 1976 and 1982, 103,000 New Zealanders moved to Australia

The next generation

The first generation live between two cultures, that of the land of their birth, and that of their parents' homeland. While some stay in touch with their parents' culture, others struggle with identity issues. Many first-generation Pacific Island New Zealanders regard the loss of language as the main reason for their generation's lack of confidence and equate fluency in their parents' language as the key to preserving their culture. Yet with each passing generation, cultural anxiety may lessen. The multicultural Kiwi melting pot bubbles on with the healthy addition of increasing mixed parentage and new immigrants.

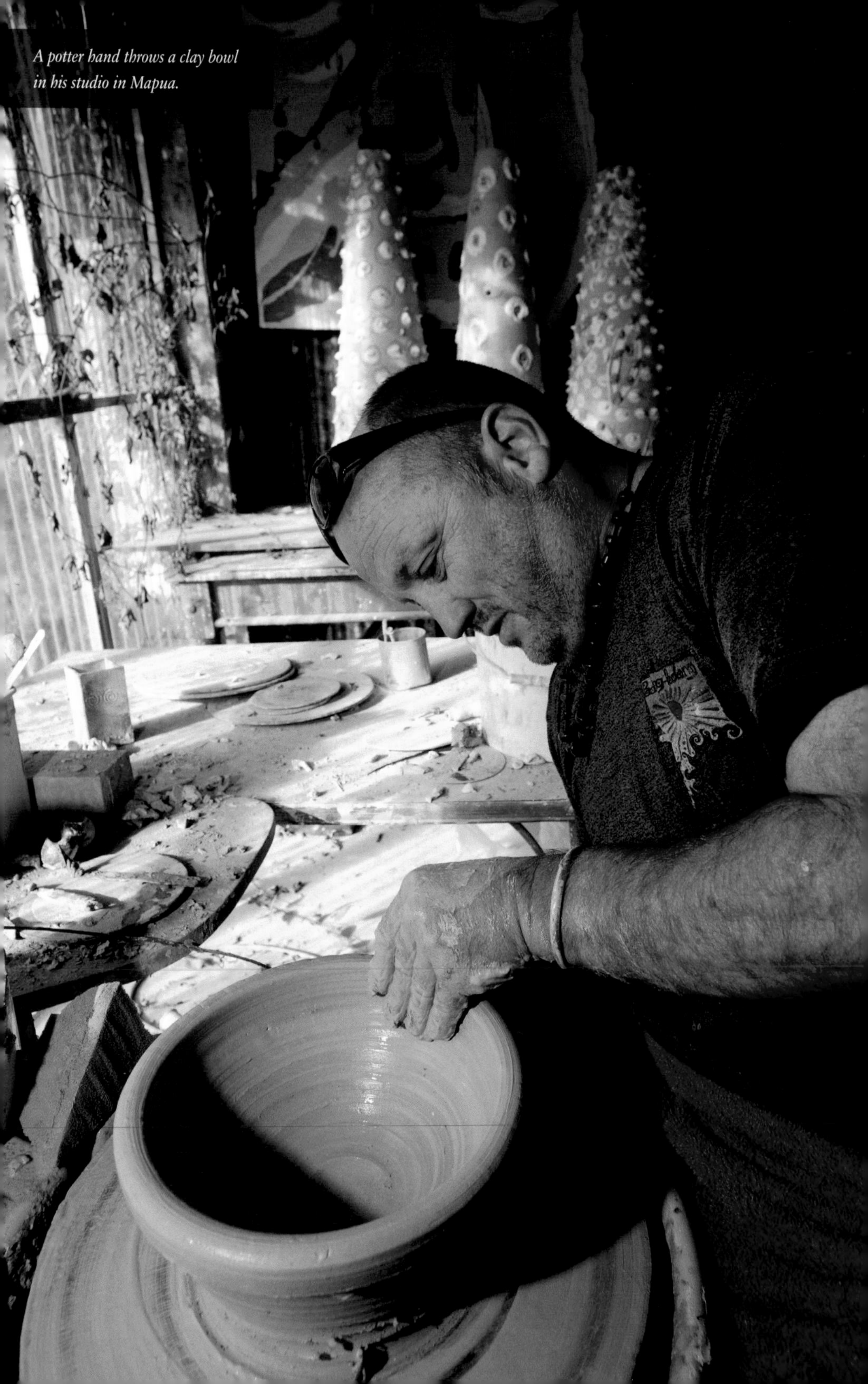

A potter hand throws a clay bowl in his studio in Mapua.

CONTEMPORARY ART AND LITERATURE

Behind much of New Zealand's art and literature lies a degree of tension between the landscape and the people who inhabit it.

Many New Zealanders have always had something of an ambivalent attitude towards the arts. Grants to artists and writers by the state funding agency once regularly aroused derision, as if wastrels and idlers were getting money for nothing. Today philistinism is never far from the surface. But in spite of this – or perhaps precisely because of it – a robust indigenous culture has flourished. The very isolation of artists has forced them to forge their own way, without too much reliance on overseas models or local encouragement.

The practical do-it-yourself tradition of New Zealanders in other fields – notably farming and home renovation – shows through in the work of artists as diverse as the inventive Michael Parekowhai and the masterful Ralph Hotere, whose paintings frequently incorporate materials like corrugated iron and old timber. New Zealand's contribution to the 2003 Venice Biennale, an installation by Michael Stevenson, featured a Trekka (the country's only locally designed vehicle) alongside a Moniac (a water-driven computer that, not surprisingly, never went into production anywhere).

It remains a scandal that there is no national art gallery in New Zealand. The remains of what used to be one have been squeezed into an upstairs space at Te Papa, and although the museum itself is a must, don't expect to find a truly representative display of New Zealand art here. Instead you should trawl the fine range of city and provincial galleries – notably the superb Christchurch Art Gallery (see page 249). The long wavy line of its glass-and-metal exterior hints at the shape of the *koru*, a stylised fern frond that also decorates the tails of Air New Zealand planes and symbolises growth and harmony. Wellington's City Gallery, the

'Solace in the Wind' sculpture by Max Patte overlooking Wellington Harbour.

Auckland Art Gallery, the Dunedin Public Art Gallery, the adventurous Govett-Brewster Art Gallery in New Plymouth and the Eastern Southland Art Gallery in Gore, not to mention Te Puia in Rotorua, are all stimulating.

Fine art

One of the first artists to be exhibited at the new Christchurch Art Gallery when it opened in 2003 was W.A. (Bill) Sutton, the long-lived local painter (1917–2002) whose spare, semi-abstract landscapes seem to symbolise the artist's relationship with the land – often perceived in New Zealand art as empty, brooding, even hostile to humans.

The hugely popular realist landscapes of Grahame Sydney, though softer in style, catch some of this mood. Sydney's work has been likened, with good reason, to that of Andrew Wyeth. The godfather of New Zealand art, as it were, is Colin McCahon, whose work moved beyond simple landscapes with religious connotations to vast, dark, mystical incantations whose brooding power lay as much in the prayers inscribed upon them as in their massive cubist forms.

But contemporary New Zealand art is not all gloom and doom. McCahon's less tor-

particular attention. Terry Stringer's work often playfully exploits the tension between the firmness of bronze, one of his favourite media, and the softness of his subject matter. Something of a traditionalist, though often with a postmodern edge, Stringer is also an accomplished portrait painter.

Experimentation with light is regarded as the province of the painter, but Neil Dawson creates sculptures in which the shadows cast by the work can be equally as important as the shapes he has moulded out of such favoured materials as aluminium and steel.

Civic Square, Wellington.

mented successors have been more inclined towards playfulness and postmodern irony in their work, particularly artists like Joanna Braithwaite, Shane Cotton, Dick Frizzell, Don Driver, Richard Killeen, Peter Robinson and the quirky Bill Hammond, of whose surrealist paintings it has been said: 'Everything about them is odd.'

Sculpture and pottery

Sculpture has always laboured to find its feet in New Zealand. The size of the country and a perception that money spent on art is not money well spent has meant that public commissions are rare and grudging. Sculptors tend to work on a small scale, but there are two who merit

BESTSELLER

The bestselling book in New Zealand history is not a volume of verse, nor an internationally esteemed novel such as Keri Hulme's Booker Prize-winning *The Bone People*. It is the *Edmonds Cookery Book*, initially published in 1908 to promote the use of Edmonds Baking Powder. By 2003, in its 51st edition, it had sold some 4 million copies in a country whose population had only just reached that figure. A centenary edition was published in 2008; like its predecessors it is determinedly old-fashioned, and this has been part of its appeal to many, including overseas visitors who purchase a copy as a souvenir to take home.

His dramatic *Ferns* hover above the Civic Square in Wellington, and his major overseas commissions include the Globe at the Pompidou Centre in Paris, and Canopy for the Queensland Art Gallery in Brisbane.

It's not entirely clear why pottery has long been such a popular creative endeavour in New Zealand. There are two representative currents. The first is the rough-hewn, hands-on, earth-connecting style. One iconic name in this field is Barry Brickell at Coromandel's Driving Creek Railway and Potteries (see page 171). The other strand is a more 'fine art' approach

represented by John Parker, who has worked for years producing pottery solely in white, in which an elegant severity of form and line is a major concern.

Outside the mainstream of New Zealand art – and outside the country for much of his life – is Len Lye (1901–80). Lye worked in numerous media but is mainly remembered as a kinetic sculptor and pioneer of direct film, in which he scratched and otherwise worked directly on film to create entrancing abstract images. These were set to music in a way that has resulted in them being described

Christchurch Art Gallery interior.

LOCAL ARCHITECTURE: STYLE OR KITSCH

With the possible exception of Napier – rebuilt largely in Art Deco style after an earthquake flattened the town in 1931 – no major town or city in New Zealand has achieved any notable architectural unity or harmony. Perhaps the most noteworthy is Dunedin, which retains a certain prewar charm and is distinctive for its use of the local white Oamaru stone.

While Maori themes have sometimes been incorporated into the design of New Zealand's European-style public buildings, they have not influenced architectural thinking to any great degree. Examples of English Gothic may still be seen – in Wellington's splendid Old St Paul's Cathedral for instance – built not with stone

but with timber. John Scott's Futuna chapel in suburban Wellington is a highly regarded modernist work; but perhaps the capital's finest public building is the postmodernist Wellington Central Library, whose designer, Ian Athfield, pillared the front face with metallic versions of the nikau palm tree. The adjacent Athfield-designed Civic Square is equally striking.

For architectural impact, the country's two best-known buildings run the gamut from the sublime to the ridiculous. Work out which is which. One is Auckland's Sky City Tower poking out like a giant ice-lolly stick and the other is Frederick Hundertwasser's public toilet in Kawakawa, Northland.

as proto-music videos. The Govett-Brewster Art Gallery in New Plymouth (see page 207) holds the Len Lye collection and archive, and regularly exhibits his work. His arresting sculpture *Wind Wand* has been installed on the New Plymouth foreshore.

Literature

The first New Zealand writer to attract significant attention outside her own country was Katherine Mansfield, whose delicate short stories have – despite her own gloomy prediction – survived numerous changes of fashion

New Zealand-born British writer Katherine Mansfield.

and can be read with as much pleasure today as when they were written, mostly in the 15 years or so before her death in 1923 at the age of 34. New Zealand in the early 20th century was claustrophobic for the young writer, and in 1908 Mansfield left her country, with some eagerness, in pursuit of a career – first in London and later in Switzerland and the south of France. She never returned.

Not until 1985 was another New Zealander as widely read, when the Booker Prize was awarded to Keri Hulme for *The Bone People*. The book has been translated into some 40 languages and has sold millions of copies worldwide. A difference between the two writers that summarises the development of New

Zealand literature is that Mansfield's work, with its lightness of touch, was only marginally concerned with New Zealand issues, while Hulme's monumental work was almost aggressively focused on issues of national identity and biculturalism alongside more universal themes.

Incredibly, it was only as recently as 1972 that the first book by a Maori writer was published in New Zealand – Witi Ihimaera's short-story collection *Pounamu Pounamu*. Ihimaera went on to become one of the country's leading novelists: his 1987 novel *The Whale Rider* was

> The South Island city of Nelson is renowned for its wealth of talented artisans, and the region possesses more working artists per capita than anywhere else in New Zealand.

a hit film in 2002. Another work that was successfully adapted for the big screen was *Once Were Warriors* by Alan Duff, a sensational book that took the country by storm in the 1990s. According to the *Oxford Companion to New Zealand Literature*, it was 'the first New Zealand novel to deal full on with the actualities of modern urban Maori life'.

Novelists to have made their mark since then include Elizabeth Knox, who broke into the international market with *The Vintner's Luck*, a fantasy about a 19th-century Frenchman's encounters with an angel, and Lloyd Jones, who followed *The Book of Fame* – a remarkable quip on the 1905 All Blacks' rugby tour of Britain – with the completely different *Here at the End of the World We Learn to Dance*. His bestselling novel *Mister Pip* won several awards, including the 2007 Commonwealth Writers' Prize Best Book Award. It was also shortlisted for the Man Booker prize.

The field of history and biography has been dominated for many years by the late Michael King, who moved on from pioneering biographies of Maori woman leaders (Te Puea, Whina Cooper) to the lives of two of the country's greatest writers: Frank Sargeson and the late Janet Frame. Historians such as Deborah Challinor, Miles Fairburn, James Belich, Anne Salmond and Philip Temple have helped to move the writing of history away from the recording of purely political and economic matters to more finely shaded explorations of society, culture and Maori–Pakeha relations.

Children's literature is spearheaded by such international successes as Lynley Dodd, famous for the *Hairy Maclary* series for younger children, and Joy Cowley, whose novel *The Silent One* was memorably filmed and whose reading texts are widely used in the field of education the world over. And then there is the late Margaret Mahy, who through her books and through readings and public appearances achieved national treasure status.

New Zealand does have an unofficial poet laureate, but it is not a position that is widely recognised. Only one poet has achieved the kind of stature that might be called legendary: the passionately nationalistic James K. Baxter, who was famous for wandering through the country barefoot with long hair and a Jesus-like beard in the last years before his death in 1972 at the age of 46. Since Baxter's death the favoured style has been cooler, more distanced and ironic, less given to big-picture stuff – less given, in fact, to ideas. Bill Manhire would be the leading exponent of this school. The old

Detail from The Treaty of Waitingi, The Black and White of It, at the Auckland Museum.

Poetry

Poetry does surprisingly well in New Zealand. Though the average volume of verse sells no more than a few hundred copies, dozens are published every year, while poetry workshops and creative writing courses are booming. When the American poet Billy Collins visited New Zealand, he was mobbed like a rock star. Most major cities have poetry cafés, bars or venues where open readings are regularly held; and a remarkable number of literary festivals have sprung up around the country, some as adjuncts to arts festivals. The Auckland Writers and Readers Festival and the Writers & Readers Week of Wellington's biennial International Arts Festival are the pick of these.

preoccupation with forging a 'New Zealand identity' has long been discarded because New Zealand writers are surer of their place in the world now. Even Allen Curnow, the country's senior poet until his death in 2002, moved a long way from the romantic nationalism of his youth to what one commentator described as a more 'vividly colloquial' style: dry and abbreviated and razor-sharp.

Most Maori poets and novelists write in English, but there is a great deal of crossover between the languages. If you read the self-deprecating poems of Colquhoun, for instance, you'd be hard-pressed to know if he was Pakeha or Maori. It is more than likely you would conclude that he is simply a modern New Zealander.

the aforementioned Edward Cattlin

fully entitled to hold the afore desc

land without any hindrance or let

ness—

Henry Hesketh

Tho Jones

waich

garko

ea.ali.ali

uitie

John Iouwaic

Iukawaira

ANCIENT MAORI ART AND SOCIETY

Maori works of art are not only beautiful to look at, but also reveal a great deal about their society's beliefs, history and social structure.

The classic art of New Zealand Maori is an unsurpassed Pacific tribal art. Many creative styles and much skilled craftsmanship yielded, and continue to yield, objects of great beauty. To appreciate the achievements of Maori arts and crafts, it is invaluable to have an understanding of the materials used, the techniques of crafts, design and symbolism, and the economic, social and religious requirements that inspired the making of artefacts.

Cultural connections

Traditional Maori artefacts fell into three distinctive categories. The first was communally owned objects, such as *waka* (war canoes). The second category consisted of personal items (see panel, page 70), such as garments, *pounamu* (greenstone) ornaments, combs, musical instruments and indelible skin tattoos, while the last category encompassed artefacts of ritual magic kept under the guardianship of *tohunga* (priests) – godsticks, crop gods and anything else used in ceremonial communication with gods and ancestral spirits.

Periods of Maori art merge, yet there are four distinctive eras: Archaic, Classic, Historic and Modern. The Archaic Maori, immediate descendants of the Polynesians who first settled the land, survived by hunting, fishing and foraging. Their art, including carvings and bone and stonework, is characterised by austere forms that, as pure sculpture, can surpass much of the later work.

In time, the cultivation of the sweet potato *(kumara)* and other crops, along with an advanced ability to exploit all natural resources of forest and ocean, allowed a settled way of village life. With this came food surpluses, a tightly organised tribal system and territorial

Carving on a Maori meeting house.

boundaries. These were the Classic Maori, and their altered society supported dedicated craftspeople within each community.

The third period of Maori art, the Historic, underwent rapid changes due to the adoption of metal tools, Christianity, Western fabrics, newly introduced crops, muskets and cannon. The fourth phase, the Modern, was under way before 1900, and remains with us. The great rise in interest in Maori culture *(Maoritanga)* in recent decades is in step with a renaissance of Maori culture.

Displaying hierarchy

Society and the arts have always been associated with fighting chiefs who had a hereditary right to control tribal affairs. They were the best dressed, ornamented and accoutred: tribal prestige *(mana)* depended on these leaders.

People dressed according to rank – chiefs *(rangatira)*, nobles *(ariki)*, commoners *(tutua)*, and slaves *(taurekareka)* – yet when engaged in daily routine work both high and low classes used any old garments. Men and women wore a waist wrap, plus a shoulder cloak when weather or ceremony required. Pre-pubescent children usually went about naked.

The special indication of rank was the facial tattoo. Men's faces were marked in painful, deep-

Elaborate moko tattoo.

grooved cuts made by bird-bone chisels dipped in a sooty pigment, which looked blue under the skin. Northern warriors often had additional tattoos over buttocks and thighs. Women were deeply tattooed on their lips and chin, made blue by the use of comb-type 'needles'.

This remarkable artwork can still be seen on Maori mummified heads, a process involving steaming, smoking and oiling: heads so treated remained intact and retained hair, skin and teeth. Out of respect for Maori beliefs, such heads are rarely exhibited in New Zealand's museums.

Art for the gods

Religious inspiration in Maori art was based on the prevailing beliefs about gods and ancestral spirits. In pre-Christian times supernatural beings were believed to inhabit natural objects. Rituals and chants were thus necessary to ensure the successful pursuit of any task.

In traditional Maori society the sexes were kept apart in all their craft activities. While men worked the hard materials of wood, bone and stone, women used soft materials (see page 72) or prepared flax fibres used in making garments and decorative *taniko* borders. It was believed women were *noa* – non-sacred – and the male, conversely, a *tapu* (sacred or holy) being. This put females in a subservient posi-

> *With no written language, the indigenous Maori relied on sophisticated oral traditions. Considerable mana (prestige) was bestowed on the best orators.*

tion which precluded them from high religious practices and from crafts and activities in which high gods and ancestral spirits were directly involved.

Priests used wooden godsticks *(tiki wananga)*, bound with sacred cords and dressed in red feathers to communicate with gods and ancestral spirits to protect the welfare of the tribe. Stone crop gods *(taumata atua)* were placed in or near gardens to promote fertility in growing crops.

Wooden burial chests were used to contain the bones of the deceased. Maori burial practice, at least for persons of rank, required an initial burial, then a recovery of the bones a year

PRECIOUS POSSESSIONS

The personal possessions of the Maori demonstrate their most exquisite artwork. Combs, feathered garments, treasure boxes, cloak pins, greenstone ornaments (including *hei-tiki* ancestral pendants) and weapons were often given a 'personal touch' to reflect the *mana* (spiritual authority) of their owner. Wooden treasure boxes *(wakahuia)* were made to contain some of the more precious items, such as greenstone ornaments or feathers. These lidded boxes, designed to be hung from house rafters, were ornately carved on all sides, but especially on the underside since they were so frequently looked at from below.

or two later when a final, ceremonial burial would take place. Monuments and cenotaphs of various forms were erected in memory of the dead. Some were posts with carvings of stylised humans called *tiki* (see below), while others took the form of canoes buried in the earth deeply enough to stand vertically.

Symbols and motifs in Maori art

In Maori art the human form, dominant in most compositions, is generally referred to as a *tiki* and represents the first created man of Maori mythology. The *pounamu* (green-

birth figures were often placed between the legs or on the bodies of *tiki* representing descending generations. The out-thrust tongue was an expression of defiance and of protective magic.

Often *tiki* figures have slanted, staring eyes, clawed hands with a spur thumb, a beaked mouth and other bird-like features. These motifs probably stemmed from the belief that the souls of the dead and the gods used birds as spirit vehicles.

The *manaia*, another major symbol, is a beaked figure rendered in profile with a body that has arms and legs.

Carving at the Waitangi Treaty Grounds, Northland.

Carved pounamu (greenstone) pendant.

stone) *hei-tiki* pendant is the best known of ornaments. *Tiki* represent ancestors and gods in the sculptural arts, and may be carved in wood, bone or stone. In ceremonial meeting-house architecture, ancestral *tiki* were carved on panels supporting the rafters or on other parts of the structure. They were highly stylised with large heads to fill in areas of posts or panels. This design also stressed the importance of the head in Maori belief – along with the sexual organs, it was the most sacred part of the body.

Sexual organs were often exaggerated in both male and female carved figures; both penis and vulva were regarded as centres of potent magic in promoting fertility and protection. Small

Whales (*pakake*) and whale-like creatures appeared on the slanting facades of storehouses. Some fish, dogs and other creatures occurred in carvings, but on the whole they are rare; there was no attempt to depict nature in a naturalistic way. *Marakihau*, fascinating mermen monsters of the *taniwha* class (mythical monsters), appeared on panels and as greenstone ornaments. *Marakihau* were probably ancestral spirits that took to the sea and are depicted on 19th-century house panels with sinuous bodies terminating in curled tails. Their heads have horns, large round eyes and tube tongues, and were occasionally depicted sucking in a fish.

The *koru*, a well-known symbol based on an emerging fern frond, is today often used as a symbol of New Zealand, including Air New Zealand's company logo; the symbol signifies new life, adventure, an awakening.

Craft tools and materials

The tools and materials of the Maori craftwork were limited to woods, stone, fibres and shells; metal tools did not exist until after the arrival of the Europeans. Adzes, the principal equipment for woodcarvers, were made of stone blades lashed to wooden helves. *Pounamu*, the nephritic jade also known as greenstone, was the most valued blade material and was sacred.

Carving a Maori mask.

Found only on the western coast of South Island, this rare commodity was widely traded. Chisels, stone-pointed rotary drills and various wooden wedges and mallets completed the Maori tool kit.

The introduction of oil-based paints ousted the old red ochre pigment *(kokowai)*, which can be seen today only in traces on older carvings. The later practice of overpainting old carvings with European red paint was unfortunate as it obliterated much patination and often the older ochres, resulting in the loss of the poly-chrome-painted work of the Historic period.

The iridescent *paua* (abalone) shell was used as inlay in woodcarving, and textile dyes were made from barks. A deep-black dye was obtained by soaking fibres in swamp mud.

Flax plaited into cords provided fine fibre for garments and baskets. As there were no metal nails and the Maori did not use wooden pegs as an alternative, war canoes, houses and food stores were assembled using flax cord. Weavers fashioned intricate ceremonial clothing from feathers, flax and other materials.

The New Zealand forests contained larger trees than Polynesians would previously have seen. This enabled them to build bigger dugout canoes, and also contributed to the woodcarving tradition. Durable totara and kauri trees, the latter found only in the warm, northern parts of the North Island, were favoured by carvers, and bone was used in many ways. Whalebone was especially favoured for weapons, while sperm whale teeth made fine ornaments, and feathers decorated weapons and cloaks.

MAORI MEETING HOUSES

During the Historic era, the meeting house *(whare runanga)* increasingly became the focus of Maori social life and of a Maori art revolution. It played a vital role throughout the 19th century, when meetings were held to discuss issues affecting the tribe.

The walls of meeting houses were decorated with *tukutuku* panels or sections of ornamental latticework used to cover walls between carvings. Each panel consisted of vertical stakes and horizontal rods (traditionally made of bracken-fern or *totara* wood), and flexible materials such as flax were used to form a pattern which told a story that would be 'read' and passed on by *kaumatuas* (seniors) from one generation to the next.

Many ornate meeting houses can still be seen throughout the North Island, including Whare Runanga at Waitangi in the Bay of Islands. They were usually named after an ancestor, and the construction symbolised the actual person; the ridge pole was his spine, the rafters were his ribs, and the facade boards, which at times terminated in fingers, were his arms. At the gable peak was the face mask.

Many communal houses can be visited, and a fine example is Tama-te-Kapua at Ohinemutu, Rotorua, built in 1878. While others are often on private property, visitors are welcome as long as they get permission beforehand.

Modern Maori Art

Maori art is an important cultural phenomenon, and is one that embraces modern media and form as well as respecting the past

There are hundreds of Maori artists working in New Zealand today, and their work spans many media, from the newest technologies to the arts of their Maori forefathers. Contemporary Maori art is as diverse as the Maori people themselves, and wherever you travel to in New Zealand, you will easily find exhibitions and galleries that reward exploration.

During the 20th century Maori art formed into two main streams. The first consisted of arts based in the *whare whakairo* (carved meeting house), such as *whakairo* (carving), *kowhaiwhai* (painting) and *tukutuku* (woven panels). The second stream was that of modern media, such as Western-style painting. Many Maori artists welcomed new artistic movements introduced into New Zealand, such as modernism and postmodernism, and have interacted within these styles in their own particular way, fusing the indigenous with the global.

By the 1960s, Maori were showing their artworks at galleries, both individually and collectively. There have been successive generations of artists, starting with the *kaumatua* (senior citizens) generation of men and women such as Ralph Hotere, Paratene Matchitt, Arnold Manaaki Wilson, Sandy Adsett, Fred Graham and others. Their work showed New Zealand that Maori art deserved to be exhibited in a gallery setting rather than be seen merely as anthropological specimens.

During the 1970s and 1980s a new group emerged, including artists such as Emare Karaka, Robyn Kahukiwa, Kura Te Waru-Rewiri and Shona Rapira-Davies. Much of their art was overtly political, including symbols of protest, bright colours and expressive paint styles. Since then, a further wave of artists has emerged, such as Brett Graham, Michael Parekowhai, Natalie Robertson, Areta Wilkinson and Lisa Reihana, many of whom have been trained in universities. Their work ventures into new territories in terms of media, such as digital/video installation, and in so doing challenges the ideas of what Maori art is in form. Galleries are now opening dedicated solely to Maori art, such as the Kura Gallery (19 Allen Street, Te Aro, Wellington), Maori Art Gallery (Boatshed 2, Frank Kitts Park, Wellington), Kotuku Maori Art Gallery (SH6, Whataroa) and Native Agent (New North Road, Kingsland, Auckland).

The traditional Maori house is still an important centre for contemporary arts. Many contemporary *whare whakairo* maintain aspects of the traditional in terms of the basic architectural structure and choice of design elements (carving, painting and woven panels), yet innovate with the range of materials and imagery used. Master carvers, such as Pakaariki Harrison, are highly sought after, and travel around the globe to talk about their work.

The number of publications about Maori art has

Maori meeting houses (whare runanga), traditional focal point for social, cultural and spiritual life.

increased, and they examine both the tribal arts and the modern. Most notable is the fact that all of these publications are written by Maori, for Maori.

The face of the Maori is also changing, and *moko* (tattooing) is a visible expression of the culture. Traditional sites on the body to ta *moko* (tattoo) are still used, especially the face (full facial for men, lips and chins for women) and thighs and legs of both men and women. *Tohunga ta moko* (tattoo specialists), both men and women, practise around the country. Since the mid-1970s there has been a renaissance of *moko*, and it is not uncommon to see wearers sipping lattes in upmarket cafés. Most use modern gun machines, yet there is a trend towards learning more about traditional tools.

MAORI HANDICRAFTS

The Stone Age culture of the Maori developed extraordinary skills using the simplest of resources, and traditional crafts are flourishing once again.

Traditional Maori handicrafts are undergoing a renaissance in New Zealand, and the vast majority of young Maori entering the arts world begin their journey by learning to carve and weave at Te Puia, the Maori Arts and Crafts Institute in Rotorua. With an ever-increasing demand for authentic souvenirs and traditional Polynesian crafts, many up-and-coming Maori artisans have created a niche through crafting unique one-off items for collectors, which have nothing at all in common with the mass-produced items found in most souvenir shops.

Among the various crafts on offer, intricately carved *pounamu* (greenstone) and bone carvings are particularly sought after, as well as items hand-carved from precious native woods including kauri and totara. Other popular products include masks and handmade *poi*, the latter a dynamic feature of Maori performing arts, used to convey a myriad of poetic meanings. The *poi*, intricately woven balls on a plaited string, are spun in mesmerising circles and fluttered overhead by advanced dancers. Carved *Ti Rakau* (a Maori stick game) is a traditional handicraft often purchased for children. Each player requires one pair of carved wooden sticks to perform a series of movements, steadily progressing to slick tosses and catches.

Carving wood at Te Puia, the Maori Arts and Crafts Institute in Rotorua.

Maori carvings inside a meeting house near the Treaty House in Waitangi.

Carving Workshops

While functional everyday items were important to early Maori, so were personal keepsakes such as *tiki* good-luck charms and *hei-tiki* pendants, usually worn round the neck. Several studios around New Zealand provide day or week-long workshops with experienced instructors for those who would like to learn the basics of this art form and ultimately carve their own.

A greenstone hei-tiki (an ornamental neck pendant). Known as pounamu, greenstone was valued by Maori for its hardiness and beauty, and was used to make tools and jewellery. Of the two types to exist, only one – nephrite – is found in New Zealand.

This Maori war canoe, at Waitangi, is named Ngatokimatawhaorua, and is the largest one in New Zealand.

COMMUNAL WAR CANOES

War canoes, ornately decorated with both sculpture and painting, were objects of great prestige in a Maori community. Most were painted red, with black and white detailing, and festooned with feathers. The magnificent 35-metre (115ft) war canoe at Waitangi was carved from the trunks of two huge kauri trees from the Puketi Forest. It took 27 months to build, and was launched in 1940 to mark the centenary of the Waitangi Treaty.

The streamlined hull is at no point more than 2 metres (7ft) wide, but the canoe was big enough for 160 warriors to sit without treading on one another's feet. Propelled by 80 paddles, the canoe reached an impressive speed in the sheltered waters of the Bay of Islands, and the seafaring skills of the Maori were brought vividly to life for the spectators.

In their quest for a new homeland, the Maori crossed the vast and often turbulent Pacific in hand-built boats; not slender war canoes like this one, but more stable outriggers with greater space for food and personal belongings. In 1985, a 21-metre (69ft) replica of one of these traditional boats sailed from Rarotonga in the Cook Islands to New Zealand. The 5,000km (3,100-mile) journey took just over five weeks, with the crew steering by the stars, moon and tides, just as the Maori had once done.

...ulpture of Tawhiri, the Maori god of wind and storms, in ...aglan.

Maori woven flax bag.

Peter Jackson's epic The Lord of the Rings, filmed in New Zealand.

MUSIC, THEATRE AND FILM

Music, theatre and their sister arts have struggled
to survive in New Zealand as meagre resourcing
stifled creativity, but recently have become more
confident and secure.

Given New Zealanders' reputation as a
laconic, almost self-effacing people, it
may seem remarkable that they can be
persuaded to engage in any of the performing
arts at all. Many New Zealanders have found
it necessary to go overseas to find work that is
commensurate with their talent, notably Kiri Te
Kanawa, Russell Crowe and Sam Neill.

While there is pride in their success, it is
the New Zealanders who have remained and
continued to strive with, work for and speak
to their own people who are most admired.
Peter Jackson's insistence that Hollywood had
to come to him to make his movies inspired a
confidence in the 'local product' that resulted
in a tremendous upsurge of all kinds of creative activity in the first years of the 21st century.

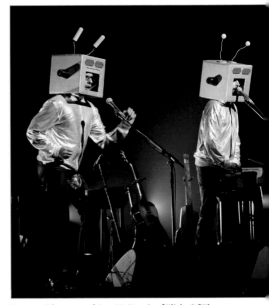

*Jemaine Clement and Bret McKenzie of Flight Of The
Conchords perform in concert.*

Classical music

The New Zealand Symphony Orchestra
(NZSO), based in Wellington, was formed in
1946 amid a post-war optimism in which the
nation's few intellectuals, composers, painters
and actors conspired to invent a national culture (such groups as the Royal New Zealand
Ballet and the New Zealand Players were born
in the same era). Composers including Douglas
Lilburn, Jack Body, Hirini Melbourne, Gareth
Farr and Philip Dadson have created a rich and
diverse repertoire, some of it drawing on Maori
and Polynesian styles.

But New Zealand's most famous practitioner
of classical music remains the soprano Kiri Te
Kanawa. A true diva, she seldom performs at
home. However, New Zealand is a prolific
producer of good singers, including the sopra-
nos Hayley Westenra and Malvina Major, and
the up-and-coming bass baritone Jonathan
Lemalu; a performance by the New Zealand

Opera (usually at The St James in Wellington
or Aotea Centre in Auckland) is a fairly safe bet.
The company is sometimes accused of making
safe choices, but productions are frequently
first-rate. However, anyone hoping to see an
opera written by a New Zealander should
plan to be in Wellington for its biennial New
Zealand Festival, a highlight of the performing
arts calendar.

Ballet and modern dance

The history of dance in New Zealand is one
of struggle and perseverance, writ large. Dance
is costly to develop and tour, and it was something of a miracle that the Royal New Zealand

Ballet celebrated its 50th anniversary in 2003. It has a reputation for hard work and commitment, but the tutu-and-fairy-dust expectations of audiences often keep it from more groundbreaking work.

New Zealand's two leading modern choreographers, Douglas Wright and Michael Parmenter, emerged from the trail blazed by the influential modern dance troupe Limbs, and went on to produce stunning, moving and important work.

Black Grace, an Auckland-based all-male troupe who combine the physicality of rugby players and the grace of ballet dancers, is renowned for its energetic blend of modern dance and Maori and Polynesian forms. Catch them if you happen to be in Auckland.

Theatre

Richard and Edith Campion, the parents of the film director Jane Campion, inaugurated professional theatre in New Zealand when they formed the New Zealand Players in 1953. Before this, theatre-lovers only had sporadic visits by condescending British companies or community repertory groups.

Royal New Zealand Ballet.

THE CONTEMPORARY MUSIC SCENE

New Zealand's first real international export was Split Enz, known as much for its theatrical talents as its music until its disbandment in 1984. These days, this tradition continues in the works of Bret McKenzie and Jemaine Clement, of *Flight of the Conchords* fame, who have enjoyed success on the international stage.

Other names that are perhaps not as well-known but are well worth looking out for include rapper Scribe; hip-hop, R&B and reggae success stories Nesian Mystik, King Kapisi and Che Fu; and talented pop artist and singer-songwriter Bic Runga, who has successfully infused European pop rhythms with Polynesian influences. Her live performances are spine-tingling, as are those of her sister Boh, lead singer of rock band Stellar. Currently rocking everyone's socks off in New Zealand and Australia are the gravelly tones of Gin Wigmore, who released her second album, *Gravel and Wine,* in 2011, and Lady Hawke, best known for her hit singles 'Paris is Burning' and 'Delirium'. Also making waves in the New Zealand scene are Kimbra (who scooped five trophies at the 2012 New Zealand Music Awards), Tiki Tane (once lead singer of disbanded group Trinity Roots), Katcha Fire (New Zealand's premier reggae band) and Fat Freddy's Drop (combo dub, reggae, soul). Even the winner of the 2009 *Australian Idol* was a Kiwi, Tauranga-born Stan Walker.

Summarising the suspicion visited upon all arts in those years, playwright Bruce Mason remembers such repertory groups being 'ignored, sometimes actively abhorred by the average Kiwi.'

The New Zealand Players folded in 1960 but inspired a whole new generation of actors and professional companies. The first was Wellington's Downstage, which survives even though its position as the top theatre in the country's unofficial 'theatre capital' was lost to the rival Circa some years ago. Circa has a reliable company of actors who perform inter-national work and local plays, notably those classics and, when they're feeling adventur-ous, new local works. Beyond Downstage and Circa, these theatres are Palmerston North's Centrepoint, and Dunedin's Fortune. The Auckland Theatre Company (ATC) does not have its own theatre, but usually performs at the Aotea Centre's Herald Theatre or Auckland University's Maidment. ATC's productions have been criticised as being conservative, but more and more local plays are being staged as the company grows, and it has a large pool of capable actors, most of whom are pleased to get a break from less challenging TV work.

Singer Stan Walker performs on stage.

national work and local plays, notably those written by Roger Hall.

No history of New Zealand theatre is pos-sible without mentioning Hall, a British emi-grant with a style of middle-class, middle-aged and middlebrow comedy that both connects with the audience's fears, desires and interests and reminds them of British TV comedies. More challenging playwrights have emerged since, including Duncan Sarkies, Jo Randerson, Hone Kouka and Briar Grace Smith; the latter two have written about New Zealand history from a Maori perspective.

Professional theatre in New Zealand exists on a diet of the latest intelligent British or American blockbuster, revivals of the

MAORI MUSIC AND DANCE

Music has always played a major role in Maori life, and as far back as the Classic (pre-European) era, instruments were fashioned from wood, whalebone and even stone. Traditional chants and songs (*waiata*) are an important feature of ceremonies such as funerals (*tangi*) and weddings. So too is Maori dance, which is both rhythmic and physical, with the beat added by the slapping of chest and thighs with the hand, foot-stamping or sometimes the hitting of sticks. *Kapa Haka* (Concert Parties) now take part in competitions each year to find the best performers, and some groups travel the world to share their impressive, entertaining cultural arts.

New Zealand's avant-garde theatre scene is less visible, but Auckland's Silo and Wellington's Bats can both feel like tiny pockets of anti-establishment resistance. The work can be patchy but is more often daring and inspired. Stylistically, the avant-garde theatre scene is pitched somewhere between lively stand-up comedy and the more traditional dramatic fare on offer at places like Silo and Bats.

In the 1990s, comedy found a permanent venue at Auckland's Classic, and there is a big comedy festival in March every year. The coun-

A scene from The Piano.

try's comedy profile has risen dramatically with the global popularity of Bret McKenzie and Jemaine Clement, together known as the Flight of the Conchords. This Grammy Award-winning duo cleverly combines a unique mix of razor-sharp and witty observation, with characterisation and acoustic guitar music, to win over audiences worldwide. As well as their own TV series, which premièred on HBO, and a series on BBC radio, the pair, along with fellow comedian Rhys Darby (also of Flight of the Conchords), starred in the horror comedy *Diagnosis Death*. Bret and Jemaine have played parts in a number of other films, including The Hobbit, directed by New Zealand film director Peter Jackson.

Festivals provide opportunities for new works to debut and existing works to tour. The biggest is Wellington's biennial (on even years) New Zealand International Arts Festival. Christchurch, New Plymouth, Taupo, Tauranga, Nelson and the Bay of Islands also have their own arts festivals.

See Travel Tips page 351 for contact details of theatre and performing arts venues.

Film

New Zealand directors produced the occasional film prior to the 1970s, the most notable being those by John O'Shea, who specialised in bicultural themes. His films included *Don't Let It Get You* and the interracial melodrama *Broken Barrier*, a kitsch musical masterpiece featuring a young Kiri Te Kanawa. However, it wasn't until Roger Donaldson's 1977 thriller *Sleeping Dogs* that a wave of commercial film-making was launched – which continues to this day.

> Auckland's Civic Theatre is an architectural marvel built in 1929 featuring Buddhas, elephants, panthers and a replica of the Southern Hemisphere sky.

Donaldson moved on to Hollywood to direct *Cocktail*. In 2005 he released *The World's Fastest Indian* – a movie about the life of Kiwi speed motorcycle racer Burt Munro, filmed near Invercargill.

Other New Zealand directors to emerge around this time were Geoff Murphy with *Utu*, who went on to direct a string of US action movies, and arthouse favourite Vincent Ward with *Vigil* and *The Navigator*. Ward went on to write the story for *Alien 3*, and also worked on *The Last Samurai*, which was filmed in New Zealand. His recent works have included *River Queen*, and *Rain of Children*, which documents the life of an elderly Maori woman and her schizophrenic son. The film was nominated for best documentary at the Asia Pacific Screen Awards, and best director at the Australian Directors Guild Awards.

One of New Zealand's most successful exports is Jane Campion, who followed her globally successful *The Piano* (1993) with a number of other works, including *Bright Star*, which was nominated for a Palme d'Or.

But to make it big you do not have to leave New Zealand, as Sir Peter Jackson proved when he did the impossible by making *The Lord of the Rings* trilogy, which won 11 Oscars, as well as pleasing critics, Tolkien fans and audiences who had never even heard of the book. Fans of the series had to wait until 2012 for *The Hobbit: An Unexpected Journey*, the first of a trilogy of films adapted from J.R.R. Tolkien's book The Hobbit. It was filmed in secrecy in New Zealand and fans were again wowed by the special effects and dramatic scenery that has become a highlight of Jackson's works (see

Other notable directors include Niki Caro, who followed her international hit *Whale Rider* with *North Country*, starring Hollywood actress Charlize Theron, and the screen adaptation of best-selling Kiwi novelist Elizabeth Knox's *The Vintner's Luck*. Andrew Adamson has made his mark with worldwide blockbuster films such as *Shrek* and *The Chronicles of Narnia: the Lion, the Witch and the Wardrobe*. He also directed *Prince Caspian*, the second in the Narnia series. One whose works are well worth watching out for is Taika Waititi, a New Zealand Maori of Te-Whanau-a-Apanui descent, best known for

Oscar-winning actress Anna Paquin.

Russell Crowe is honoured with a star on the Hollywood Walk of Fame, Los Angeles.

Exploring Middle-earth, page 82).

Aside from directing, Jackson is part of the renowned Wellington-based Kiwi special-effects company Weta Workshop, and is one of the founders of Weta Digital. The latter won an Oscar in 2010 for its work on *Avatar*, which quickly became the world's bestselling movie.

New Zealand screenwriter and film director Andrew Niccol hit the big time when he co-wrote and produced *The Truman Show*, which garnered an Oscar nomination for best original screenplay and a BAFTA in the same category. His more recent work includes writing and producing the comedy-drama *The Terminal*, starring Tom Hanks, and the political crime thriller *Lord of War*, which starred Nicholas Cage.

his Oscar-nominated and multi-award-winning short film *Two Cars, One Night*, and for *Eagle vs Shark*. More importantly, Waititi directed and starred in the 2009 Kiwi movie *Boy*, the bestselling home-grown film in New Zealand, not to mention award-winner at the prestigious Berlin Film Festival in 2010.

For its size, New Zealand seems to have given the world a disproportionate number of international film stars, notably Sam Neill (who started out in the aforementioned *Sleeping Dogs*), and the Oscar winners Anna Paquin and Russell Crowe. Among the contemporary generation of film actors, Keisha Castle-Hughes, Danielle Cormack and Joel Tobbeck are three standout performers.

EXPLORING MIDDLE-EARTH

New Zealand's sumptuous landscapes provided local director Peter Jackson with the perfect fantasy backdrop for one of the most ambitious projects in cinematic history.

The landscapes of Middle-earth, the fantasy creation of J.R.R. Tolkien, are filled with dramatic mountains, wild forests, verdant pastures and grasslands. When the decision was made to create a definitive film version of the famous book, New Zealand was quickly chosen as the real-life equivalent.

New Zealanders, who have something of a weakness for praise from other parts of the world, are still immensely proud of the success of *The Lord of the Rings* trilogy and perhaps even more so of Jackson's recent release, The Hobbit: An Unexpected Journey – the first in a new trilogy of films adapted from Tolkien's popular masterpiece The Hobbit. The films tell a continuous story set in Middle-earth 60 years before The Lord of the Rings and follow the adventures of Bilbo Baggins, who goes on an epic quest to reclaim the lost Dwarf Kingdom of Erebor from the fearsome dragon Smaug accompanied by 13 dwarves led by the legendary warrior Thorin Oakenshield. The journey takes them through a wealth of wild New Zealand backdrops, swarming with goblins and orcs, deadly wargs and sorcerers. For a detailed guide to the locations used in the film, see www.movie-locations.com.

Peter Jackson directs a battle scene during the filming of part The Two Towers.

The Dead Marshes, where Frodo and Sam were stalked by Gollum (pictured), were filmed at a swamp called Kepler Mire on the Kepler Track.

From almost any point in the South Island you can enjoy views of the Misty Mountains, along which the Fellowship trudged before being broken. Of course, hereabouts (and on a the maps) they are known as the Southern Alps.

Tongariro National Park provided the location for Mordor.

THE TOLKIEN TOURIST BOOM

The Hobbit: An Unexpected Journey and *The Lord of the Rings* trilogy of movies were shot at locations that ranged almost the entire length of New Zealand, and, while some computer enhancements were inevitably employed, many of the sites are natural, unique and almost unbelievably spectacular. The movies continue to spark interest in the country and its pristine landscapes, and *The Hobbit* has also re-ignited a boom in commercial tours, to take fans to the various locations.

While some of the places featured in the movies are relatively inaccessible or on private land, and can only be visited under the aegis of a tour operator, others are easy to reach by individuals. Anyone can get a glimpse, for instance, of large tracts of 'Mordor' or the 'Misty Mountains'. But don't expect to find actual movie sets – due to the environmental considerations so dear to New Zealanders' hearts, all but one of them, Hobbiton in Matamata (www.hobbitontours.com), where the complete set remains, have since been demolished.

e only movie set that has been left in place is Hobbiton, the
ne of Bag End itself, or at least the front door – the interior
s a set in Wellington. It stands on private land at
atamata but can be visited for a fee (see page 166). Much
his verdant, intensely farmed area will suggest the peaceful
re to visitors.

Viggo Mortensen and Liv Tyler on the set of part III, The Return of the King.

Frodo is tormented by the power of the Ring.

Chef Adam Dixon prepares rabbit at the Clevedon Village Show.

CUISINE

Kiwi cooking is distinguished by ingredients that are fresh and flavourful, and a style that fuses a medley of influences, reflecting the country's cultural diversity.

At the heart of New Zealand's exuberant cuisine is the pristine freshness of its fruit and vegetables, meat, seafood and dairy products. Most often, the principal ingredients on your plate will have been grown within a two-hour drive of your table. But what New Zealand cooks do with those ingredients has none of the simplicity of a traditional peasant cuisine. Indeed, there are very few indigenous foods eaten at all. Except for the wealth of seafood, the raw materials are descended from those brought here from many parts of the world, each one finding a suitable environment, whether in the year-round warmth of the north or the less benign climate of the south.

Cosmopolitan cuisine

When it comes to culinary styles, New Zealand cooks have a lot in common with their counterparts in Australia and California. Although all are located on the rim of the Pacific Ocean, they are less influenced by their place on the map than by a common mood of buoyant confidence, a love of vibrant flavours and a willingness to sample whatever food they come across. Mediterranean influences are encouraged by the fact that peppers, aubergines, olives, asparagus and garlic are easily grown. Pesto and hummus are as popular here as anywhere in the world. As are the foods of Asia – curries, stirfries, sushi and miso soup are commonplace.

New Zealanders also bring ideas from their travels abroad and keep up with international trends through books, magazines and television. In addition, each cultural group living in the country – Pacific, Indian, Chinese, Japanese, Greek, Cambodian, Croatian, Dutch, Thai, German and many others – has added its own colour and flavourful ingredients to the

Food van at Otara market.

culinary melting pot, through importing speciality foods, opening restaurants and continuing to cook its traditional food at home.

Colonial roots

The culinary styles of England, Scotland and Ireland, the homelands of the largest number of immigrants since colonial times, remain a powerful element, particularly in home cooking. A typical weekend family get-together meal will consist of roast beef, chicken or lamb, served with crisp golden potatoes, pumpkin, parsnip and kumara (sweet potato) baked in the same pan and served with gravy, mint sauce, peas and silver beet (Swiss chard) or broccoli. In summer, the traditionally high status (and exceptional standard) of local meat is reflected in barbecues with a variety of steaks, lamb chops and sausages, or an array of seafood served with freshly baked bread, corn on the cob and salads.

Despite the influence of other cuisines, many main courses in restaurants still take the traditional form of a fine piece of meat or fish accompanied by vegetables. Many locals are dab hands when it comes to home-baked scones, pikelets and muffins, as well as cakes and biscuits, plus jams, marmalade, chutney and pickles.

Maori cooking

Many of the country's indigenous foods – birds, berries and fern root – were laborious to gather, prepare and preserve. Such traditional Maori delicacies include mutton birds (the distinctly fishy-flavoured young of the sooty petrel), freshwater eels and seafood such as *paua* (abalone), *pipi* and *tuatua* (clam) and *kina* (prickly sea urchin). While the *kumara*, a sweet potato brought from Polynesia, enhanced the range of nourishing foods that could be grown in warmer regions, Maori cuisine benefited enormously from the arrival of

Unloading a catch of albacore tuna at Napier Harbour, Hawkes Bay.

PAVLOVA

If New Zealand has a national dessert, it is the pavlova, traditionally eaten at Christmas barbecues. And if Australia has a national dessert, it is also the pavlova. The two countries maintain a rivalry over where this giant meringue, smothered in whipped cream and fresh fruit, was first concocted. A side issue is the best way of preparing the confection. Two things are incontestable, however: first, that the dessert was originally made in honour of Russian ballerina Anna Pavlova, who visited both countries more than a century ago; and second, that it is an unbeatable way to consume a large amount of sugar in one sitting.

pigs and other farm animals, vegetables, fruit and grains from Europe and America.

Seafood has always been a vital part of the cuisine, and its continuing importance is recognised in the customary rights extended to Maori to allow the gathering of controlled species, such as the rare *toheroa*, a type of clam. The traditional Maori meal most likely to be offered to visitors is the *hangi* (earth oven), a tender and flavourful feast in which meat and vegetables are packed into baskets and steamed over hot rocks in a covered pit. A hearty broth ('boil-up') includes pork or beef, potatoes, onions, carrots and watercress, *rauraki* or *puha* (sow thistle) and sometimes dumplings ('doughboys'). *Paraoa rewana*

('Maori bread') is a large wheaten loaf made with flour and potato.

Fresh fruit

Each season brings with it an amazing range of fresh fruit, none of which is native to New Zealand. However, over the past two centuries each has become a much-loved part of the local cuisine, and several are now important exports. Fruit and vegetable shops and supermarkets stock a good range, although some fruit is barely ripe when sold and needs to be kept for a few days. Delicious tree-ripened fruit can be bought juice. Kiwi fruit, with tart green flesh or the more mellow, golden-fleshed types, marketed under the Zespri label, have been joined by a cherry-sized, smooth-skinned variety.

Autumn also brings apples, including the flavoursome Braeburn, pears, notably the luscious Doyenne du Comice, *nashi* – an apple-shaped type of pear with crisp, juicy white flesh – and glossy orange non-astringent persimmons, which should be eaten while they still feel hard in the hand. Varietal honey and locally grown chestnuts, walnuts, hazelnuts and macadamia nuts are other treats to look out for on your travels.

The kiwi fruit is native to southern China; it was introduced to New Zealand in the early 20th century.

direct from roadside stalls right where it is grown, throughout the country. Weekend farmers' markets nationwide are an increasing phenomenon, and a significant number of supermarkets, stalls and speciality shops offer organic produce.

Autumn is perhaps the most exciting season of all, when subtropical fruit, grown in the warmer parts of the country, is widely available. First in the season is the *tamarillo* or tree tomato, an intensely tart ruby-red fruit with a smooth skin and bright orange interior laced with black seeds. Then comes the *feijoa*, a scented, oval green fruit with a smooth skin and flavour reminiscent of pineapple and strawberries. The wrinkled purple passionfruit holds a spoonful of black seeds in an aromatic golden

A lot of citrus fruit also ripens in the winter – easy-to-peel mandarins, navel oranges, tangelos (super-juicy New Zealand oranges) and the New Zealand grapefruit, an unusual variety with golden peel and sweet-sour golden-hued flesh. Strawberries start to ripen in spring, and by December they will be joined by raspberries, blackberries, loganberries, boysenberries and black and red currants. By Christmas, cherries, the first of the stone fruits, will also be ripe; small boxes of top-quality fruit are a popular gift.

As summer progresses, other stone fruits appear – plums, peaches (locally bred Golden Queens, white-fleshed early in the season and with deep golden flesh later), nectarines, peaches and apricots – and in their primary growing regions of Hawke's Bay and Central Otago can often be bought from roadside stalls.

From the seas

In every season of the year commercial fishing boats bring in a wonderful variety of species, from the delicate hoki, gurnard and flounder, to the local favourites, the flavoursome tarakihi and snapper, flaky blue cod and firm John Dory, as well as the meaty hapuka and bluenose. All year round, excellent farmed Pacific salmon is available. Salmon and other species are often enjoyed skilfully smoked.

Apple harvest, Riwaka.

While winter is the season for highly regarded Bluff oysters, the closely related Nelson variety is a delectable alternative. Farmed Pacific oysters are also often available. Large and succulent Greenshell mussels, which are farmed in the Marlborough Sounds, can be bought live from most supermarkets. Smaller shellfish collected from sandy beaches include *pipi, tuatua* and little neck clams, known locally as cockles. Abalone *(paua)* cling to the rocks along many shores and can be collected in controlled numbers. Another springtime treat is dredged scallops, while eels are particularly delicious when smoked.

Salted mutton birds are also sometimes available from seafood providers. These are the chicks of *titi* (sooty shearwaters), which are collected from a few tiny islands near Stewart Island. Their rich meaty flavour is relished by aficionados. Crayfish, also known as rock lobster, is found along the Kaikoura coast.

Meat and dairy produce

Wide grassy pastures are the year-round home of millions of lambs and sheep, raised for wool as well as meat, cattle for beef and milk, and also smaller numbers of deer. The pastures, known locally as paddocks, are licked by salty sea breezes, which give the meat a delicious and distinctive flavour. All local meats are available throughout the year. A rack of lamb, seared on the outside and still pink inside, is always delicious, or for old-fashioned comfort, look for braised lamb shanks. Lamb's liver, known as lamb's fry, is also good. For steak-lovers, fillet is the most tender, while sirloin, porterhouse, rump or Scotch fillet have a richer flavour. Tender farm-raised venison, often marketed as Cervena, is best when cooked quickly and served medium rare.

Milk, butter and cheese have long been an important part of local cuisine. Thick cream and tangy yoghurt are of excellent quality. More than 60 varieties of cheese are produced in New

> *New Zealand's abundant produce is widely available at the ubiquitous roadside stalls dotted around the country roads. Larger stalls sometimes have a cashier; at others, customers simply leave payment in the honesty box.*

Zealand – look out for Aorangi, kirima, blue supreme and Dutch-style cheeses made by several small producers – although cheddar remains the most popular and is widely available, from creamy mild to richly aged. Sheep and goat cheeses are a relatively new and growing part of the scene.

There are plenty of feral deer, pigs and goats in the bush for hunters (see Travel Tips page 364), although you don't often find wild meat on a restaurant menu. If you do, you can rest assured that it has been processed in a licensed abattoir and will be safe to eat. Trout, abundant in many rivers and streams, are reserved for licensed anglers and not permitted to be sold. To dine on trout you must catch your own. Big-game fishing – and eating the catch – is another attraction.

Picnic supplies

One takeaway meal that has a long local history is the meat pie. These are sold in convenience stores, bakeries and petrol stations, where they are heated to order. The single-serve pies are oval, round or square and most contain ground or diced beef in gravy. A layer of cheese is a popular addition, and some pies are topped with mashed potato instead of pastry.

Also at the bakeries and some cafés you will find sweet goodies that will often be the same distinctively New Zealand specialities that are traditionally baked in the home – Anzac bis-

spot by the sea. The seagulls will help out with the leftovers.

Fine dining

New Zealand has a large number of world-class restaurants, even in more remote locations, where they flourish in the guise of luxury lodges and vineyards. The variety of food is dazzling. It can range from a reinvention of that controversial classic, tripe, to the finest of freshly caught game and seafood. Inspiration is eclectic – drawing from the world's great cuisines – and creativity seemingly boundless as chefs strive to find

Mussels, a New Zealand favourite.

cuits, afghans with chocolate icing and walnut on top, peanut brownies, ginger crunch, bran or cheese muffins, and banana cake. The coffee is almost always espresso and often made with beans roasted by small speciality businesses. A range of teas and herbal teas is always available, as well as local mineral water and fruit juices.

Despite the presence of the usual international franchises, owner-operated fish-and-chip shops still provide the most popular takeaway meal, comprising thick golden chips (French fries) and fish deep-fried in batter or crumbs, as well as seasonal oysters, scallops, sausages and other items. Wait while your meal is cooked to order, wrapped in absorbent paper or piled on a cardboard tray. Then take it to eat at a pretty

a balance between respect for their ingredients and the true artist's desire to improve on nature.

The relatively small size of the market means that competition is intense, which in turn helps keep standards high. But top-end restaurants in Auckland, Wellington and other cities are vulnerable to a domestic tendency to faddishness. It is not unusual for a new restaurant to be booked solid for its first three months, then find itself almost empty as the next shiny new establishment to open catches the locals' attention. However, plenty of fine restaurants have survived changing times and tastes to assure a memorable dining experience.

See Travel Tips page 340 for a list of recommended restaurants across the country.

The Farming Life

Although New Zealand's prosperity was built on its farm produce, changing times have made life tough for farmers.

It's early morning, high summer in the heart of the South Island. Daniel Jamieson, second-generation farmer, father of two and sometime recreational cricket player, has breakfast with his wife, then

heads outdoors to start work on the land where he was born and raised. More than 600 dairy cows await him and his staff in a high-tech milking shed not far from where the woolshed once stood. Daniel remembers the heat, sweat and dust of summer shearing back when he used to be a sheep farmer. In the early 2000s he and his wife were among the first on the plains of North Canterbury to switch from sheep to dairy. Now theirs is one of many grazing cattle herds, in a region where sheep had been raised for nearly a century.

Fields of change

Such changes are sweeping the rural heartland of New Zealand. The rapid spread of dairy farming from traditional North Island regions like Waikato, Taranaki and Manawatu to former sheep-farming strongholds in Canterbury, Otago and Southland has been one of the biggest trends, but is certainly not the only shift to alter the look of the land.

Thousands of hectares of pine trees now cloak hills too steep to support profitable livestock farming, particularly in parts of the North Island. Horticulture, including an abundance of apples, stone fruit and kiwi fruit, remains a mainstay in the Bay of Plenty, Gisborne, Hawke's Bay, Nelson and Otago, but new crops, particularly in the form of large-scale vegetable production, have made inroads into other fertile coastal areas. Profitable new crops such as olives, avocados and lavender have emerged. Grapes now flourish on many hillsides. Deer, ostriches, emus, alpacas and goats are all in commercial production. The expansion of dairy farming and forestry is predicted to continue for some time.

The humble sheep, it seems, is under siege. For decades a cornerstone of New Zealand agriculture, and indeed of the nation's export-driven economy, pastoral sheep production and its supporting industries have arguably borne the brunt of radical political and market changes. The loss of secure markets in the UK when Britain joined the EEC was the first blow, and was followed after 1984 by the systematic dismantling of extensive farm subsidies. New Zealand's rural industries are now among the least subsidised in the world.

New growth

Farmers met these challenges head-on. They've scoured the world for fresh opportunities and continued as guardians of New Zealand's largest industry, responsible for producing more than half of the country's merchandise exports, with dairying currently the biggest single export earner of all: New Zealand has positioned itself well with Asia, and the export of dairy products to this region is a major growth industry.

Traditional commodity sales to Europe may have withered, but sophisticated new products have found buyers elsewhere, most notably throughout Asia and in Australia and the US. The same spirit of innovation that allowed New Zealand to begin refrigerated shipment of frozen sheep carcasses way back in 1882 has led to rapid advances in food-processing technology and farm production systems, not to mention a whole new attitude down on the farm.

The sheer diversity of New Zealand's land-based exports, from powdered deer antler and fresh flowers to chilled gourmet meat cuts and boutique cheeses, reflects only part of the transformation that has taken place. Equally important has been the farmers' willingness to adapt to new market trends. For the thousands who remain committed to the nation's sheep industry, this has meant increasingly specialised production of specific types of meat and wool. For others, it has meant branching out into different types of agriculture or horticulture.

Pressures and possibilities

New Zealand's farmers have been quick to respond to the increasing worldwide consumer concern about chemical residues, animal welfare and food safety. Gifted with a sparse population, clean air and water,

end of the scale there has been a boom in lifestyle block ownership, with plots of land ranging from 0.5 to 2 hectares (1 to 5 acres).

Possession of the land itself remains a source of contention in some areas, such as Taranaki, as many Maori tribes seek redress for the grievances of the past, including the confiscation of land. The process of government compensation for these losses has largely centred on cash settlements, with some return of public land to Maori ownership. While today's farmers face little risk of being themselves dispossessed after 150 years of European settlement, indigenous land claims have nonethe-

and a productive, temperate climate, the country's exports of organic products have shown tremendous growth, and strict animal welfare codes and quality assurance programmes have now been implemented in many of New Zealand's rural industries.

Contrary to the doomsayers of the mid-1980s, who predicted the industry would barely survive without subsidies, farms owned and operated by rural families have remained the backbone of New Zealand agriculture. Admittedly, these properties now tend to be bigger than they used to be and with fewer staff. One or other of the spouses is likely to have a job off-farm to help supplement income; and the tradition of passing land down to the children is by no means as secure as it used to be. In addition, there are a growing number of 'mega-farms' owned by large corporations. At the other

less heightened tensions in some small rural communities.

Protecting the future

Beyond these domestic issues, and beyond its borders, insect pests and animal and plant diseases from other countries continue to pose serious threats to New Zealand. An example is the recent introduction of *Pseudomonas syringae pv actinidiae* bacteria (PSA), which has infected kiwi fruit vines in many places. Border control is among the strictest in the world as the country strives to protect itself from tiny invaders which could scupper multimillion-dollar export markets.

Having survived a multitude of changes and challenges, it's hardly surprising that farmers like Daniel Jamieson have much on their minds these days.

WINES

New Zealand, a latecomer to the world of wine-making, now produces outstanding vintages that are sold worldwide.

New Zealand was the last temperate place on earth inhabited by humans, so it is no surprise that it is also the last (suitable) place on earth to make wine. Still, it has made an impressive run, especially in the realm of small-scale, high-quality production.

It all began in the Bay of Islands in 1819 when Samuel Marsden introduced the grapevine, and James Busby, the official British Resident, planted the first vineyard on his property at Waitangi in 1833. A couple of years later the very first New Zealand wine was produced. It was sampled by French admiral Dumont d'Urville, who pronounced it to be light, sparkling and delicious.

From there on the history of wine-making in New Zealand becomes obscure (prepare to hear a different story depending on who you are talking to). It is undisputed fact, however, that early French settlers planted small vineyards at Akaroa in the South Island and, more importantly, that members of the Marist Catholic brotherhood established a winery at Mission Estate in Hawke's Bay in 1865. This is now a commercial venture and is known as New Zealand's oldest existing vineyard.

By the end of the 19th century, small commercial vineyards were established in other parts of Hawke's Bay and in the Auckland–Northland region. All suffered from the scourge of prohibition politics between 1900 and 1920. For decades the industry languished, until finally in the 1980s vineyards were again established and by the 1990s several distinct wine-growing regions were formed. Today, each has its own wine trails to follow, featuring vineyards of every size and description, many offering a cellar-door experience.

Luscious grapes at a Renwick vineyard.

International standing

If New Zealand has a 'signature wine', it is Sauvignon Blanc, produced here with as much – and often greater – success as anywhere in the world. But hot on its heels are the reds from the nation's superb Pinot Noir grapes. Lawson's Dry Hills Wines (www.lawsonsdryhills.co.nz) in Marlborough (a region best known for its superb Sauvignon Blanc) won Double Gold for the Best Pinot Noir at the 2012 San Francisco International Wine Competition and a Silver Medal at the same show for its stunning 2011 Pinot Gris. White wines such as Pinot Gris and Riesling are becoming increasingly popular; the family-run Seifried Estate (www.seifried.co.nz) won the Best Ice Wine at the same competition for its 2011 Sweet Agnes

Riesling. Needless to say, New Zealand wines are the only complement to the local cuisine that visitors should consider during their stay.

With an eye on the export market, New Zealand wine-makers are enthusiastic participants in international competitions, and many return home every year bearing medals. Enthusiasm has equally been applied to marketing, as a high proportion of the country's wine production is exported – around 113 million litres (25 million gallons), with further growth expected.

Over the past 10 years export markets have diversified significantly. While wine exports to

Wineries in this area have a strong sense of old-time hospitality. Kumeu Valley, northwest of the city, is home to the fabulous Kumeu River Vineyard (www.kumeuriver.co.nz), as sophisticated as anything in Burgundy, and with Chardonnay to match. Down the road, both Matua Valley (www.matua.co.nz) and Westbrook (www.westbrook.co.nz) could be in California, with their visitor centres and tasting platters, while Soljans (www.soljans.com) is more like an upmarket café with a winery attached – but the wine is every bit as good as the food.

Also close to Auckland is exotic Waiheke

Vineyards at Renwick.

all of New Zealand's trading partners remain strong, export statistics from the New Zealand Winegrowers' Association show that sales of New Zealand wine to mainland China more than doubled during 2012.

North Island wineries

Wines produced on Auckland's west coast are among the finest you will find anywhere in the country. It's a region dubbed 'Dally Country' because the wine culture is based on the sterling efforts of immigrants from the Croatian province of Dalmatia. Many of the wineries, including Babich (www.babichwines.co.nz) at the original site in Henderson, are still run by descendants of the Dalmatian founders.

Island, where Te Whau Vineyard (www.tewhau.com) and Mudbrick Vineyard (www.mudbrick.co.nz) provide the ultimate Pacific idyll. The Matakana wine trail, 40 minutes' drive north of Auckland, is also worth exploring.

Hawke's Bay and Wairarapa

Down the lumpy eastern coast of the North Island is Hawke's Bay, where wine-making operates on a large scale. This lifestyle destination had at the last count more than 80 wineries, most of which offer a cellar-door experience. Drive or cycle the region to enjoy the Mediterranean microclimate and the delicious produce offered at roadside stalls along the way. Wine trail highlights include Craggy Range Vineyard (www.

craggyrange.com), set beneath breath-taking Te Mata Peak; Mission Estate (www.missionestate. co.nz), established by Marist Brothers in 1851 and housed inside a former seminary building; Taradale's award-winning Church Road (www. churchroad.co.nz) wines; and the boutique vineyard of Clearview Estate (www.clearviewestate. co.nz), with its range of organic wines. Here you can enjoy lunch among the vines or relax at an informal dining table and chairs built around an 80-year-old olive tree.

Further south is Gisborne, renowned for its long sunshine hours and award-winning chardonnay. Wairarapa, at the bottom of the North Island, is another exciting wine region, and the centre of Pinot Noir excellence. At its heart is Martinborough, where the wineries are so close to each other, you can see a few of them on foot. Don't miss places like Ata Rangi (www.atarangi. co.nz), Martinborough Vineyard (www.martin borough-vineyard.co.nz) and Te Kairanga (www.tk wine.co.nz); the wines are very popular and sell fast, so don't expect everything to be available.

South Island wineries

Marlborough is the only place in New Zealand that actually feels like a totally dedicated wine community – not unlike Burgundy, with winery visitor centres crying out for your attention. Two A-list establishments are Montana (www. brancottestate.com) and Cloudy Bay (www.cloudy bay.co.nz). Also well worth a visit is Villa Maria's impressive modern winery (www.villamaria.co.nz), and Allan Scott (www.allanscott.com), a family owned and operated vineyard with a tremendous vineyard restaurant.

The wine-growing region of Nelson is different altogether, ravishingly bucolic, sun-baked, both maritime and mountain-lined and full of potters and artists. Wineries here include Neudorf (www. neudorf.co.nz), which is one of the country's best producers, and the aforementioned and family-run Seifried Estate (www.seifried.co.nz).

Wineries at Waipara in North Canterbury, such as Pegasus Bay (www.pegasusbay.com) and Mud House Winery and Café (www.mudhouse wineryandcafe.co.nz), produce top Pinot Noir, but for the greatest wine-and-landscape spectacle, go south to central Otago, where mountains soar over clinging vineyards, the lakes are deep blue-green, rivers rush down craggy valleys with chilly enthusiasm, and you can sit outside, sip wine and gaze at the mountains against a crisp sky. Pinot Noir is king here, but there are some scintillating Rieslings, too. Almost every winery that is open to the public is worth a visit, notably Gibbston Valley (www.gvwines.co.nz) and Chard Farm (www.chardfarm.co.nz), which are both good for their food as well as their wine.

For that final memory of New Zealand wine, meander down to Mt Difficulty Wines (www. mtdifficulty.co.nz), near Cromwell, and Black Ridge (www.blackridge.co.nz), in Alexandra, to experience wine craft at its mythical best – challenging, fiercely individual and triumphantly satisfying. See Travel Tips page 373.

New Zealand produces excellent sauvignon blanc.

WINES OF CHARACTER

New Zealand wine has a character, a crystalline purity of fruit flavour, that no one has yet been able to explain. It is certainly not the climate, mostly maritime, and like the landscape tremendously varied – and in the South Island classified in wine-growing terms as distinctly cool. It may be the soil, which is uniquely young by geological standards, or it may be how bright daylight is here, a similar phenomenon to that of Cognac in France, where locals say it contributes to the finesse and concentrated flavour of that region's brandy. The clean air may also contribute. Most likely it is a combination of all these things.

Autumn colours at Wanaka Lake.

Hollyford Valley.

FLORA, FAUNA AND THE ENVIRONMENT

Conservationists wage constant war against introduced pests like possums, stoats and deer in a battle to save unique species of flora and fauna.

New Zealand is one of the most isolated places in the world. The vast expanse of ocean that has separated these islands from any other appreciable land mass for millions of years has meant that local flora and fauna have evolved in complete isolation from the rest of the world. Because of this lonely evolutionary history, around 80 percent of New Zealand's plant species and 25 percent of its birds are found nowhere else on earth, and the same applies to nearly all of the country's insects and marine molluscs.

When people first arrived here around AD 800, the only terrestrial mammals to be found were bats. The islands were, instead, a haven for over 120 species of birds, 70 of which were unique to New Zealand. Many were flightless, and, with a lack of mammals, the top predator in the ecosystem was the giant Haast eagle, preying on the flightless moa (see page 102), up to 20 times heavier than itself. However, it was no match for humans or the four-legged predators they brought with them, and it is now extinct.

With human settlement came increased frequency of fire, resulting in the permanent removal of large areas of forest and the extinction of numerous bird species. Hunting brought the demise of the moa within a few hundred years, while introduced rats and dogs took their toll on other birdlife long before the first Europeans arrived. The arrival of Europeans from the late 18th century onwards sped up what the Maori had begun. Large areas of forest were milled or burnt. The introduction of browsing mammals and farming dramatically altered the landscape. Introduced European species such as weasels, stoats, cats and various rodents wrought havoc on the

The native, flightless kiwi is New Zealand's national symbol.

native birdlife. Possums, rabbits, wild goats and deer browsed native plants so heavily that they killed them.

Conservation measures

While environmental strategies including the management of marine resources, sustainable use of water, the reduction of waste and improvement of energy efficiency have been implemented nationwide, New Zealand's most pervasive environmental issue remains the decline of its unique plants, animals and ecosystems. Over the past 30 years conservation efforts, including extensive pest eradication programmes and reforestation projects, have succeeded in rescuing many species from the brink of extinction. New Zealand's land and marine reserves – some of which have no public access to ensure they remain pristine – have also been extremely successful.

Many species, including the tuatara, which have been around for 250 million years (see page 103), are bred in captivity before being placed in predator-free island sanctuaries.

The kiwi

New Zealand's national icon, the kiwi is highly protected. It is the only bird known to have nostrils at the end of its bill and it

and the Okarito brown kiwi (rowi; restricted to western parts of South Island). The total kiwi population is estimated to be around 70,000.

Introduced predators are the kiwis' biggest threat. Stoats and cats kill 95 percent of kiwi chicks before they are six months old – well short of the 20 percent survival needed for a population to increase. Eggs are also lost when possums disturb nests, and adult kiwis are often killed by ferrets and dogs. New Zealand's Department of Conservation (DOC) works to protect nests in the wild by trapping, shooting and poisoning predators, raising chicks

The kea parrot can be found in the mountains of New Zealand.

also has one of the largest egg-to-body weight ratios of any bird, with the egg averaging about 15 percent of the female's body weight. Kiwis live in pairs and mate for life, sometimes as long as 30 years.

There are five recognised species, all unique to New Zealand: the Great spotted kiwi (roroa; the largest species and fairly numerous in parts of South Island); the Little spotted kiwi (some 1,300 live on Kapiti Island off the southwest coast of North Island (see page 223), with smaller introduced populations on other offshore islands); the Brown kiwi (the most common of the five, still widespread in the central and northern North Island); the tokoeka (fairly common in the southern parts of South Island);

THE MOA

This giant, flightless bird, once a mainstay of the Maori diet, weighed up to 250kg (550lbs) and could be 3 metres (10ft) tall. Its size, and lack of natural predators, made it easy prey for the early human settlers, and all 10 species of the bird were hunted to extinction by the early 16th century. Nevertheless, it became as big in myth as it was in stature, with stories of sightings including that of two gold prospectors in the 1860s, and an alleged sighting on the beach of Martins Bay at the end of the Holyford Track in the early 20th century. Theories of their survival in the southwest of South Island persist, but are considered a near-impossibility by zoologists.

in captivity and releasing them into the wild when they are able to defend themselves, and researching and working with landowners in areas where kiwis live on private land.

The largest project, Operation Nest Egg (www.projectkiwi.org.nz), collects wild kiwi eggs and young chicks in the summer breeding season and looks after them in captive-rearing facilities until they reach about 1.2kg (2.6lbs) in weight and can better fend for themselves, then releases them back into their wild home, where they have a good chance of survival. The project relies on the knowledge, time and commitment of hundreds of different institutions and individuals involved in hatching the eggs and raising the chicks, as well as the ongoing financial support of the New Zealand public.

Operation Nest Egg has been particularly effective for rapidly recovering the populations of the rarest kiwi, the Okarito brown kiwi, or rowi, whose numbers have recovered by some 25 percent over six years, and re-establishing populations that had hitherto declined to just a few individuals. To preserve unique gene pools and adaptations of each population, chicks are always returned to the wild populations they came from and are never mixed up.

Tuatara

These medium-sized reptiles, the only survivors of the order Sphenodontia which comprised many species during the age of the dinosaurs, are of huge international interest to biologists and are under active conservation management.

Tuatara once roamed the mainland, but until recently experts thought this was no longer the case, believing they survived in the wild only on 32 offshore islands free of rodents and other introduced mammals that prey on their eggs. However, in early 2009 scientists were astonished by the discovery of a wild tuatara at the Zealandia Karori Sanctuary Experience in Wellington, the first sighted on the mainland for over 200 years. Rats are considered the most serious threat, and visitors to Kapiti Island have their bags thoroughly searched prior to their arrival on the island, while conservation initiatives focus on keeping existing habitats free of rodents. Captive tuatara play an important part in conservation, education and research, and can be seen at Southland Museum, Wellington Zoo and Auckland Zoo.

Bats

Bats are New Zealand's only native land mammals and in the past have been a challenge to move successfully to safer locations due to their finely honed homing instincts.

However, the DOC team at Pukaha Mount Bruce managed to crack the code when they transferred pregnant bat mothers to their facility where the pups were born, then transferred them to pest-free Kapiti Island, and in doing so were able to pull off the world's first ever successful translocation of bats for conservation purposes.

A tuatara at the National Aquarium of New Zealand.

Yellow-eyed penguin

New Zealand is also home to the world's rarest penguin (one of six species found on the islands; see page 104), the hoiho (noise shouter), or Yellow-eyed penguin, named for its call and distinctive yellow headband. These penguins are found along the southeast coast of the South Island, Stewart Island, the Auckland Islands and Campbell Island, and their total number is estimated to range between 6,000 and 7,000, with around 427 breeding pairs found on the South Island's southeast coast. Chicks are threatened by stoats, rats, cats and dogs. These last also worry adult penguins and they are banned from entering penguin breeding areas. In some readily accessible sites the popularity of ecotourism is also having an effect on nest survival rates. On beaches where there is extensive unsupervised human interaction (adult penguins need ready access to their nests and chicks), chick survival rates can be lower than 1 percent. A DOC species conservation plan was put into place in 1985 and has achieved considerable success since. Another notable success story has been that of the Penguin Place project at Otago Peninsula in the South Island, where private landowners converted their farm to a penguin sanctuary when penguins began to nest there some 23 years ago.

Yellow-eyed penguin.

There are five other penguin species in New Zealand, but three of these (Rockhopper, Snares and Erect-crested) are restricted to the remote sub-Antarctic islands far to the south. The Blue penguin (korora) is the world's smallest penguin and its range extends across all of New Zealand's coasts – one of the best places to see it is on the Banks Peninsula near Christchurch, as well as the Otago coast. The Fiordland penguin (tawaki) is restricted to the fiords of South Island, parts of the southern coast and Stewart Island.

Kakapo

The kakapo is the world's only flightless parrot, which historically inhabited all three islands but is now confined to areas of Fiordland and Stewart Island – two of the most remote spots in the country. Kakapo have also been transferred to predator-free islands. In 1974 it was unclear whether any existed at all, then, incongruously, a population of males was found in Fiordland followed by a population of males and females on Stewart Island. The Department of Conservation has nine people working full-time on kakapo-related projects (www.kakaporecovery.org.nz), but the bird remains at great risk, with only 120 to 130 birds thought to exist.

Where to see wildlife

It is relatively easy to see whales, seals and dolphins, as well as marine birds such as albatrosses and penguins, on boat trips from Kaikoura (see page 238) on the upper east coast of the South Island. Sightings of half a dozen sperm whales and pods of several hundred dolphins

MARINE MAMMALS

New Zealand's marine fauna is diverse, and all marine mammals in New Zealand waters are fully protected by law. Incredibly, sightings of almost half of the world's cetaceans (whales, porpoises and dolphins) have been reported here. Also seen are the endemic Hector's dolphins (found nowhere else), rare beaked whales, New Zealand sea lions (found only in New Zealand's southern waters), and the widely distributed New Zealand fur seals. Other seals that visit New Zealand's shores include the Southern elephant seal and the leopard seal, both of which are found in larger numbers in Antarctic and sub-Antarctic waters. The most common threat to the nation's populations of large whales, including the Southern right whale and the humpback whale, is habitat degradation, global climate change, fishing by-catch, entanglement and accumulation of pollutants in the oceans.

Didymo, a slimy organism otherwise known as rock snot, is found in some South Island rivers, and conservation controls to prevent its spread include disinfecting fishing gear at an approved cleaning station prior to departure on a fly-fishing trip.

New Zealand's Marine Exclusive Economic Zone, covering some 4,053,049 sq km (1,564,882 sq miles) of ocean, is the fourth-largest zone in the world, and is still being definitively mapped.

are common. Back on shore, Kaikoura has a seal colony located not far from the town centre.

A number of offshore islands have been cleared of predators and have become wildlife hotspots, home to a variety of endangered birds, reptiles and insects. Islands such as Tiritiri Matangi and Kapiti off the coast of North Island, Motuara in the Marlborough Sounds and Ulva off Stewart Island are all easy to visit, and here, for example, you can see birds such as the takahe, the saddleback and the stitchbird, and get some idea of what New Zealand must have been like before Europeans arrived.

weed control, propagation and fencing to prevent stock and possums from dining on newly planted trees. Mysterious illnesses are also preying on the mighty kauri, and visitors should heed signs to protect these trees, whose roots are easily damaged, and use the sterile foot baths provided before entering and leaving forested areas.

New Zealand boasts some of the most spectacular stands of forest in the world. There is not much that can beat the magnificent kauri forests of Northland, the splendid broadleaf-podocarp forests of Pureora or Whirinaki in

The waters off Kaikoura are one of New Zealand's prime dolphin-watching areas.

Native flora

The trees and forests of New Zealand are also unique, evolving in isolation for millions of years. Eighty percent of the native flora is found only here, and ranges from magnificent kauri forests, ferns and flaxes, dune plants, Alpine and sub-Alpine herb fields, to stands of rainforest dominated by rimu, beech, matai and rata. The last, along with its northern partner, the pohutukawa, which once completely painted the coastline red in the summer with its tiny crimson petals, has been ravaged by introduced possums, and although these trees can still be seen they are under conservation management by Project Crimson, which is assisting with pest and

the central North Island, or the great, ancient beech forests that you pass through when crossing over the Main Divide in the South Island.

It is also worth taking a bit of time to seek out the Alpine vegetation, which includes some 600 species of plants, the vast majority of which are endemic. Although the best known is the Mount Cook lily, which is actually a type of buttercup, there is a host of other striking and unusual plants, such as the vegetable sheep – a strange, decidedly woolly looking plant which grows together in 'flocks' – and the Spaniards, to mention just a couple. Many of these plants have evolved in a peculiar way in order to cope with the sometimes harsh environment.

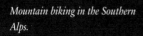
Mountain biking in the Southern Alps.

OUTDOOR ACTIVITIES

With wide open spaces and a healthy lifestyle, New
Zealanders are passionate about sport and adventure
– and are keen to share it with others.

New Zealanders embrace the great outdoors,
and easy access to the oceans and wilderness areas is just one explanation for the
great Kiwi sporting passion. In fact, it would
be difficult to grow up in this country without
spending a significant amount of time hiking in
the mountains, fishing the rivers or riding the
surf. Many of the country's most adored heroes
are those who have achieved great things on the
world's outdoor stages: the late Sir Edmund
Hillary, the late Sir Peter Blake, the All Blacks
rugby team and the Silver Ferns netball team.

From the moment children start school, sport
and physical activity are a big part of the educational curriculum. More than 90 percent of the
country's young people are actively engaged in
sport through clubs or schools. This has helped
make New Zealand a breeding ground for
sportsmen and women, and a playground for
adrenaline-seeking adventurers.

Team sports

Rugby union is the main national sport. More
than 141,000 people play club rugby, and the
national team, the All Blacks, is among the most
successful in the world. February marks the start
of the season with the regionally based Super
15 Competition, and it all ends in late October
with the National Provincial Championships.

A good season for the All Blacks guarantees
A-list celebrity status for players whose names
and personal details will dominate nearly
every tabloid and magazine in the country for
months. The nation's obsession with the sport
can be felt most strongly during international
matches, when tens of thousands of fans decorate themselves in supporting colours. Failure
to win results in collective mourning and a general postmortem of each player's performance.

Inside a zorb.

Cricket is the main summer game, and New
Zealand takes part in the Test Match series and
other international competitions. Cricketing
heroes include the legendary Sir Richard
Hadlee, a Christchurch man who had a record-
breaking career between the early 1970s and
1990 and was knighted for his services to the
game. The excitement of one-day matches has
raised the profile of what a lot of people considered a rather dull and tedious pastime.

The women's winter sport of netball also has
a high profile, partly due to television coverage
of all major international events and the feisty
competitiveness between New Zealand and its
greatest rival, Australia. Volleyball has moved
outdoors onto New Zealand's most beautiful

beaches. Beach volleyball for two- or four-person teams has become a popular spectator sport and is sufficiently casual for teams to be thrown together at the last minute.

Other team sports – hockey, soccer, touch rugby, rugby league and basketball – all have healthy numbers of followers, with the games' codes taught in schools throughout the country. On any winter Saturday, nearly every sports field in the country will be busy with children participating in one or more sporting events. Large numbers of parents gather along the sidelines, cheering, calling and offering unnecessary

wild game species for trophy hunting. The main hunting period is from March to September during the 'rut', when the big males are looking for mates. Hunting here can be challenging and conditions harsh; a high level of fitness is therefore necessary.

Trout fishing became popular after its introduction by British settlers, and the seasons vary between the two main islands. Both start in October, but in the North it finishes at the end of June, while in South Island the season closes at the end of April. Licences can be obtained from any sports shop in any one of the 22 fishing districts.

Fishing amid spectacular scenery.

instructions to their protégés.

Hunting, fishing and skiing

Many sports considered elite in other parts of the world are readily accessible in New Zealand. Very few towns are without a carefully manicured golf course and fast-growing club memberships. No longer the domain of the retired population, golf has a growing popularity among younger people.

There are ample opportunities for hunters to bag deer, chamois, wild pigs, goats and tahr (a Himalayan goat species). In an effort to diversify, farmers in more remote areas actively encourage hunters onto their properties. The Southern Alps hold some of the world's finest

Game fishing is equally popular in New Zealand. Ever since writer Zane Grey alerted the world to the game-fishing opportunities in the Bay of Islands, fishermen have dreamed of reeling in a giant marlin or swordfish. Although many like to take their catch home, others prefer to tag and release the giant specimens caught off the east coast of Northland and the Bay of Plenty. Game fishing is possible throughout the year, but the period from mid-January until the end of May is considered the prime time.

Clear blue skies, lofty mountains and dazzling snow slopes guarantee the popularity of skiing and snowboarding here, with commercial ski fields, Nordic cross-country and heli-ski areas. The North Island has three fields, two on Mount

Ruapehu and another on Mount Taranaki. The South Island fields are spread throughout the Southern Alps, with Queenstown's Remarkables Ski Field and Coronet Peak being the southernmost and among the best. These fields are a favourite training venue for Northern Hemisphere ski teams. Heli-ski and glacier-skiing operators offer an extensive range of off-piste skiing from July to October.

Take a hike

New Zealand has some of the greatest walks in the world. From remote Fiordland forests to the

> On the last Monday of January, the Auckland Anniversary Regatta takes place. With more than 1,000 entries, it is the world's biggest one-day yachting event.

Bookings with DOC are required for some of the most popular and world-renowned tracks, such as the Milford, Heaphy and Routeburn. The number of visitors is closely monitored to ensure preservation of the special nature and wildlife of these pristine areas.

Snowboarding in Queenstown.

vast wilderness areas of Te Urewera National Park, the volcanic plains of Tongariro National Park or heli-hiking on the Franz Josef Glacier, there is no disputing the diversity and beauty of the walks available.

If you are particularly energetic, you can walk the length of the country on marked trails (see Travel Tips page 363). Details of most walks, regardless of duration or recommended fitness level, are available from information centres and Department of Conservation (DOC) offices. New Zealand walks are safe. There is no dangerous wildlife and tracks are well signposted and maintained. However, be aware that the weather is extremely changeable, and walkers of every level must always go well prepared.

On the water

On any fine weekend the waters which embrace Auckland ripple with the wakes of thousands of watercraft. From Westhaven to Buckland's Beach, from the East Coast Bays to Whangaparaoa, they fly in the prevailing westerly breeze, skimming like tiny white butterflies over the water with barely a gap between them. Then, as the shore is left behind, they spread out, revealing themselves as a mix of yachts, launches, fizz boats, windsurfers and jet skiers. The scenario is repeated all around the country's coastline.

Winning the America's Cup, the world's oldest sporting trophy, in 1995 highlighted the sport, which reached a climax in 2000 when

Team New Zealand defended, and won the America's Cup for a second time.

Adrenaline action

Early in the 19th century, 'adventure' meant people pushed to the edge of human endurance. There were things to be discovered, unexplored territories to be conquered, land to chart. Those were the days before double-edged harnesses, poly-prop garments and satellite navigation. Adventure, real adventure, meant facing hardships, discomfort and often death. Today's adventurers need only

55 metres (180ft) high. Speeds of up to 125kmh (77mph) have been recorded.

Parasailing, paragliding and skydiving are other ways to obtain an adrenaline fix while also getting an aerial sightseeing tour. During the summer months, commercial parasailers operate on most of the major lakes. Small airfields near main tourist destinations will generally have gliding or skydiving centres on site or nearby. For many, completing a tandem skydive is high on their list of 'must-do' adventure activities. Taupo, Christchurch, Wanaka and Queenstown are notably popular areas for

Paragliding over a beautiful Queenstown landscape.

the spirit of adventure, some cash and a slight dose of insanity.

New Zealand's capacity for inventing and commercialising adventures is legendary (see page 114). Leaping from aeroplanes, mountains and bridges, pounding down untamed rivers and over terrifying waterfalls, sinking beneath surging seas in search of wrecks or swimming with sharks are all readily available.

Fly by Wire is indicative of Kiwi ingenuity. Invented and patented worldwide by Neil Harrap, the adventure is the world's first flight offering full pilot control of a high-speed, tethered plane. Based at Queenstown, the planes are suspended from an overhead suspension point

A BRIEF HISTORY OF BUNGEE

Life was easy for adolescent males in ancient Vanuatu in the Pacific. To prove their manhood, all they had to do was climb a bamboo tower, tie some fine ropes around their legs and jump. Finding an appropriate rite of passage today is less simple, but bungee-jumping still rates as one of the biggest challenges for people who want to prove their courage. Modern-day bungee-jumping was started in England by the Oxford Dangerous Sports Club, but was commercialised in New Zealand by A.J. Hackett and Henry Van Asch, who brought it into the spotlight in 1987 with a jump from the Eiffel Tower.

skydiving. After leaving the plane, jumpers will spend the first 30 seconds in freefall, plummeting to the ground at 200kmh (124mph) before enjoying the leisurely drift down to earth. Others might prefer a hot-air balloon ride over the Canterbury Plains or aerobatics in a biplane near Southland. For those wanting a more sedate aerial adventure, Wairarapa, Matamata and Omarama are renowned for their superb gliding conditions.

Surfing and diving

For many thrill-seekers, the waters of New Zealand are the biggest, wildest and most exciting playgrounds of them all. Big-wave surfing, windsurfing, kite surfing and scuba diving pit the participant's human-sized strength and courage against one of nature's most powerful and untameable elements.

Kite surfing is one of the country's fastest-growing water sports. Surfers use the power of both the waves and the wind to propel themselves as high as 30 metres (100ft) into the air and can cover some long distances across the water. Riders are strapped by their feet to 'surfboards' and connected to a billowing kite by a harness. Kite surfing has been described as a combination of aerobatics, windsurfing and skysurfing.

New Zealand's coastline and offshore islands have some of the best temperate-water diving in the world. From the rocky headlands of the Far North to the fiords of the deep south, you can explore wrecks, enter dark caves, meander through forests of black coral trees, frolic with fish and confront camera-shy sharks. The coastal waters reflect the diversity of the land, providing a huge range of diving experiences within a very small area.

The Poor Knights Islands, off the coast from Tutukaka, are undoubtedly the jewel of New Zealand diving. Affectionately referred to as 'The Diver's Knights', the labyrinth of caves, archways, air-bubble caves, and drop offs, combined with the prolific fish life which thrives due to the island's Marine Reserve status, ensure the diving is nothing less than spectacular. Experienced divers could never be disappointed with dive sites like Taravana Cave, Kamakazi Drop Off, Northern Arch and Wild Beast Point. For the less experienced and meandering photographers, Maomao Arch, Middle Arch and the Cream Garden offer colour and action at shallow depths. Close by lie two scuttled frigates, the *Tui* and the *Waikato*. Both make great wreck dives, as does the *Rainbow Warrior*, which lies further north at Matauri Bay. Dive operators at Tutukaka offer a variety of trips and cater for divers at all levels. Gear and guides are provided for those who require it.

South Island diving is colder but no less exciting. The Russian cruise liner *Mikhail Lermontov*, lying in 36 metres (120ft) of water near Port Gore in the Marlborough Sounds, excites wreck divers; the cave system of the Riwaka Source in the Takaka Valley challenges cave divers; and Fiordland intrigues budding marine biologists.

Tackling the morning surf at a Kaikoura beach.

The heavy rainfall in Fiordland makes it one of the wettest places on earth and is also responsible for creating unique diving conditions. A permanent layer of tannin-rich fresh water up to 10 metres (32ft) deep sits above the seawater. The result is a great sunblocking filter, which tricks deep-dwelling creatures into the shallow depths. The 14 fiords support the world's biggest population of black coral trees, about 7 million colonies, some up to 200 years old and in depths only accessible to sport divers.

Whitewater thrills

Every year thousands of adrenaline-hungry thrill-seekers climb into kayaks or bouncy orange inflatable rafts and attempt to navigate some of the most scenic, dramatic and dangerous rivers imaginable. Undaunted by nature's obstacles, they plummet over waterfalls and career through sharp-rocked rapids in a frenzy of foam and madness. Then, when the waters are quiet, they let their crafts and their minds drift in aimless contentment. There are more than 80 commercial whitewater rafting operations in New Zealand, carrying a total of 130,000 clients annually on 57 rivers. Between Christmas and the end of February each year about 13,000 people will pour down the Shotover River alone. The rapids encountered range from grades one to five, so you can choose

Boards are purpose-built for comfort, and sledging adventures depart daily from Queenstown.

Deep down and dirty

Cavers Dave Ash and Peter Chandler took the underground experience into the commercial realm when they established The Legendary Black Water Rafting Company at Waitomo in 1987. Cavers float on inner tubes through underground flooded caves lit with glow-worms and decorated with stalactites and stalagmites, before surfacing to warm up with hot soup and crumpets. Be prepared to get wet, cold and

Whitewater rafting on the Kaituna River, Rotorua.

your level of excitement. Participants are provided with wetsuits, life jackets and helmets.

Kayaking is a more sedate pursuit, and trips on fresh or coastal waters are available everywhere. Fiordland is high on the list of most spectacular kayaking sites, with towering mountains rising sheer from the mostly navigable fiords. Abel Tasman National Park is also memorable for day, overnight or longer adventures. The pretty coastline is speckled with safe overnight campsites, and the chance of being accompanied by dolphins or an inquisitive seal is high.

Sledging or river surfing (also known as hydro-speeding) is a fun way to get up close and personal with New Zealand's white water.

scared. The same company can also introduce you to wilder adventures, including abseiling. Another reliable operator, Waitomo Adventures (which measures its adventure danger level at 'Rambo Rating'), will have you abseiling down waterfalls or dropping 100 metres (330ft) down into a gaping hole in the earth known as The Lost World. The South Island's answer to

Inexperienced rafters need to listen to all the instructions handed out before setting off: take note of how to front paddle and back paddle, how to swap sides and how to hold on tight!

Waitomo is found on the west coast, where The Wild West Adventure Company provides a similar range of heart-stopping activities.

Canyoning is the exploration and descent of steep-sided, confined river gorges using specialised ropes, abseiling skills, and sometimes the less specialised arts of jumping and swimming. The Deep Canyoning Company introduced it to New Zealand when it began exploring the spectacular gorges carved out of the schist rock around Wanaka. The thrill comes from abseiling down, in and behind huge cascades and witnessing the grandeur

There are various bungee-jumping sites throughout New Zealand, with one of the most notable being on the Auckland Harbour Bridge. The Bridge Walk to the jump site is equally exciting for spectators. The Mokai Gravity Canyon bungee over the Rangitikei River is one of the North Island's most scenically spectacular. Jumpers who opt for the South Island have a choice of Queenstown jumps. They can leap 43 metres (141ft) off the original bungee site at Kawarau Bridge, drop 47 metres (154ft) off the Ledge bungee in central Queenstown, or brave the Nevis Highwire bun-

Plunging off Bob's Peak with Lake Wakatipu as a backdrop, Queenstown.

of the rock sculptures. Canyoning tours also depart from Auckland.

Off the edge

New Zealanders seem to have an obsession with throwing themselves off things, and the higher the better. None is higher in New Zealand than Auckland's Sky Tower. This is the site of Skyjump, best described as base-jumping without the parachute. Jumpers are escorted to a lift, which takes them to the 53rd floor of the 328-metre (1,076ft) tower. After donning a harness and having equipment checked, they make their way to the edge of a platform where, after summoning together their last reserves of courage, they leap off the building towards the city, 192 metres (630ft) below.

gee, the ultimate high-wire jump of 134 metres (440ft) from a gondola that overlooks the meeting of the Nevis and Kawarau rivers.

A similar thrill is on offer at the Shotover Canyon Swing, where you jump in a harness from 109 metres (358ft) and freefall 60 metres (197ft) into the canyon before a twin rope system pendulums you in a smooth 200-metre (656ft) arc at 150kmh (90mph).

Skywire rides, where you are strapped into a two or four-seat carriage and carried at high speeds of 100kmh (62mph) across wide open valleys by cable, are found at a number of locations, including Queenstown and Nelson.

See also page 360 of Travel Tips and its regional listings for contact details of operators.

THRILLSEEKERS' PARADISE

There's no end to the variety of adventure sports in New Zealand. Just as your heartbeat slows to normal, a new crazy activity comes along.

New Zealanders have become famous for their willingness to jump off bridges, speed down shallow rivers, or roll down hills inside inflatable balls. They're happy to help others do the same, too, and have introduced new heart-pumping sports to the world – but they do it safely. Every week thousands of visitors experience the heady euphoric feeling of an adrenaline rush.

Some New Zealanders are addicted to adrenaline. It's the best legal drug you can get, but like any drug you have to get more of it in different forms. So adventure addicts now consider bungee-jumping 'boring' – abseiling and kite-surfing are currently their ways to get a high. Another favourite thrill is jetboat rides down river gorges, travelling at breakneck speeds perilously close to the rocky banks.

The industry is strongly regulated and the operators highly trained. They've all been to the same charm school and so delight in making any activity seem more dangerous than it really is. They reason that the higher you think the risk is, the higher the adrenaline rush when you 'miraculously' survive the experience.

Should you ask your parachute jump partner how long he's been doing tandem jumps, he'll tell you that today is his first time with a paying customer. Stand on a bridge and ask how many jumps a bungee rope is used for before it's retired, and you'll be told '100, and yours is the 99th'. Such tricks are simple but extremely effective. In fact, the adventure sports industry in New Zealand has a remarkably good safety record.

Nobody has ever satisfactorily explained why New Zealanders are so successful at dreaming up new adventure activities. It must be a combination of the beautiful outdoors and their isolation from the rest of the world. They have to get their kicks at home and they will try anything once. If it works, they will develop it for their visitors' fun and enjoyment.

Glacier walking on what appears to be a living, moving, creaking, mountain of ice is awe inspiring. You may be roped up to your guide in case you slip and fall down a crevasse.

Black-water rafting through underground caves at Waitomo.

A cyclist takes a bend on a track above Nelson at sunset.

ZORBING YOUR WAY DOWN THE HILL

Zorbing is the epitome of New Zealanders' love of the bizarre. An NZ Air Force pilot described zorbing as 'the same sensation as spinning loops and barrel rolls and then crashing to the ground in a jet. Only in a Zorb it doesn't hurt.' Lesser mortals say it's like 'being inside a tumble drier'.

The Zorb is actually two spheres, one suspended inside the inflated outer one. The view from inside is a tumbling blur of blue sky and green grass which eventually seems to blend into one as you bounce and fall and roll down a hillside. Aficionados throw a bucket of water in first (it's called a Zydro Ride) just to remove any chance that they can cling to the sides. To take it to the next level you can try the Zig-Zag track, a cross between a waterfall and roller coaster.

Like many adventure sports, it's almost as much fun to watch as to participate. It starts with mirth as a vacuum cleaner working in reverse is used to pump up the Zorb, and finishes with hilarity as the dizzy participant tries to climb out of the sphere.

Zorbing is probably the safest of all the adventure sports. Like all of them, there is no logical reason to do it. The late Sir Edmund Hillary, New Zealand's most-loved adventure sportsman, probably climbed Everest in 1953 for the same reason as today's adrenaline seekers: because it's there.

Zorbing in Rotorua.

...1p off the tallest ...n-made structure in country, the Sky ...ver in Auckland, ...iched only by a wire.

Tandem skydiving is a 30-second, 200kmh (120mph) freefall with a professional attached to your back. The 4-minute final descent by parachute is the perfect way to calm down.

Dawn breaks over Te Mata peak, Hawke's Bay.

Whangara village on the North Island's east coast.

Mitre Peak in Milford Sound.

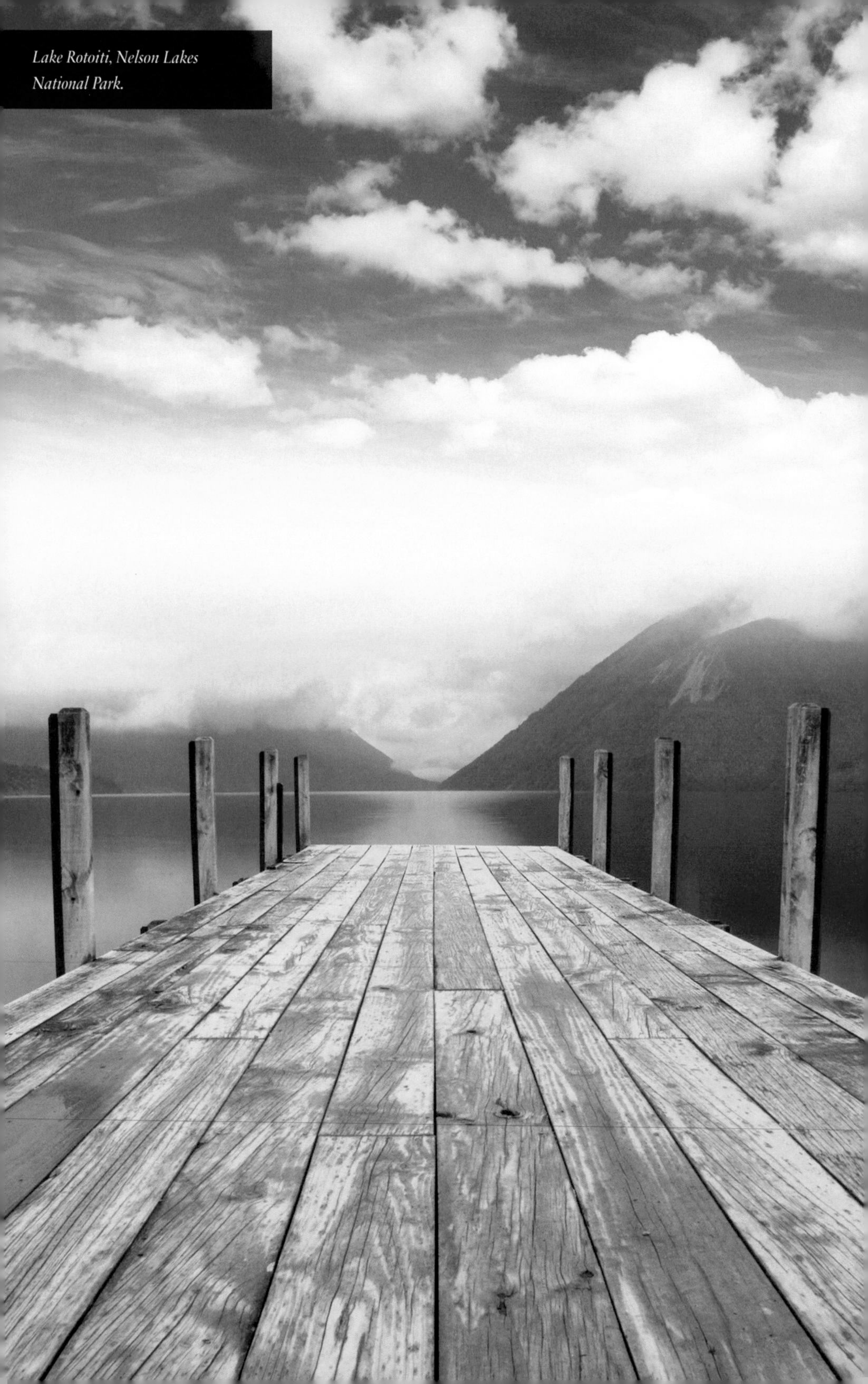

Lake Rotoiti, Nelson Lakes National Park.

INTRODUCTION

A detailed guide to the entire country, with principal
sites clearly cross-referenced by number to the maps.

Champagne Pool, Rotorua.

People aside – albeit friendly, heart-warming people
– it's the places in New Zealand that arouse your
sense of wonder and make you catch your breath.
The pristine beauty of Milford Sound, the silver dazzle
of the Southern Lakes, the bush-wrapped solitude of
Lake Waikaremoana, the boiling surprises of the thermal
regions… these have inspired even the most travelled of
visitors to wax lyrical.

The indigenous Maori's story of creation explains that
land and human beings are all one – flesh and clay from
the same source material. Their emotional attachment to
place is profound and it has influenced Pakeha culture,
contributing to the national belief that 'clean and green' is
a philosophy, not just a tourism marketing tool.

Initially the first European settlers tried to make New Zealand's countryside look British. They cut and burnt the forest and sowed grass, but
when they had spare time to look around, they
soon realised how special their new home was.
The North Island's spas and hot pools earned an
early reputation for their curative powers. As early
as 1901, the government hired an official balne-
ologist and formed a tourist department, the first
government-sponsored tourism promotion organisation in the world.

Oriental Bay, Wellington.

The thermal regions still draw enormous attention from travellers, but nowadays it's mainly the
unsullied, uncluttered landscape, and the sense
of space and timelessness that bring thousands of
visitors to its shores. Some come just to soak in the
scenery, others to learn about Maori culture, while
an ever-increasing number want to walk in the wilderness; for them a
tramp through this scenic wonderland is a sort of purification rite.

New Zealand's remoteness from the rest of the world has served both
to limit the number of visitors and preserve the land from over-exploi-
tation. Those who did come were delighted by what they found packed
into a country whose length can be driven in a couple of days, and whose
width can mostly be crossed in a few hours.

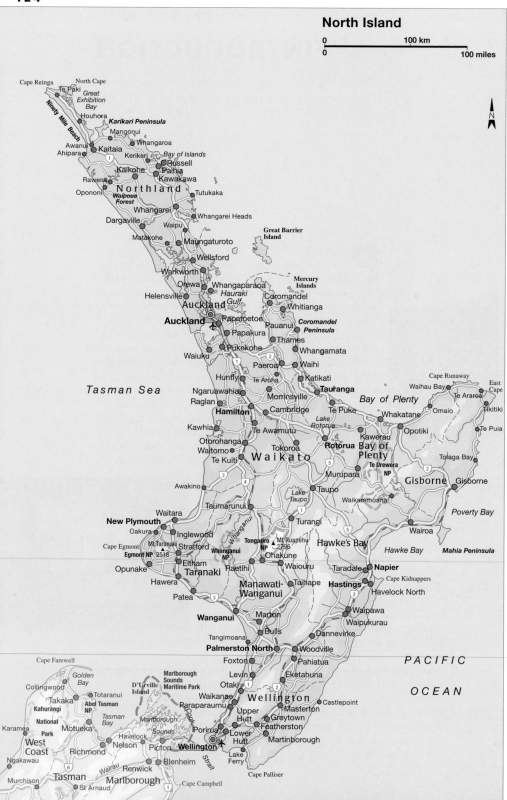

North Island

0   100 km
0   100 miles

Cape Reinga   North Cape
Te Paki
Great Exhibition Bay
Houhora
Ninety Mile Beach   *Karikari Peninsula*
Mangonui
Awanui   Whangaroa
Kaitaia
Ahipara   Kerikeri   *Bay of Islands*
Russell
Kaikohe   Paihia
Rawene   Kawakawa
Opononi   *Waipoua Forest*   Tutukaka
Northland
Whangarei
Dargaville   Whangarei Heads
Waipu
Matakohe   Maungaturoto   *Great Barrier Island*
Wellsford
Warkworth   *Mercury Islands*
Orewa   Whangaparaoa
Helensville   *Hauraki Gulf*   Coromandel
Auckland   Whitianga
Auckland   Papatoetoe   *Coromandel Peninsula*
Papakura   Pauanui
Waiuku   Pukekohe   Thames   Whangamata
Paeroa   Waihi
Huntly   Te Aroha   Katikati
Ngaruawahia   Morrinsville   **Tauranga**   Waihau Bay   Cape Runaway
Raglan   *Tasman Sea*   Cambridge   Te Puke   East Cape
Hamilton   *Bay of Plenty*   Te Araroa
Kawhia   *Lake Rotorua*   Whakatane   Omaio   Tikitiki
Te Awamutu   Kawerau   Te Puia
Otorohanga   **Rotorua**   Opotiki
Waitomo   Tokoroa   **Bay of Plenty**
Te Kuiti   **Waikato**   Tolaga Bay
Awakino   *Te Urewera NP*   **Gisborne**   Gisborne
Murupara
Taupo
Waitara   Taumarunui   Waikaremoana   *Poverty Bay*
New Plymouth   *Lake Taupo*   Wairoa
Oakura   Inglewood   Turangi
Cape Egmont   Stratford   Mt Taranaki   Tongariro NP   Mt Ruapehu   **Hawke's Bay**   *Hawke Bay*   *Mahia Peninsula*
Egmont NP   2518   *Whanganui NP*   2796
Opunake   Eltham   Ohakune   Taradale   **Napier**
Taranaki   Raetihi   Waiouru   Cape Kidnappers
Hawera   Taihape   **Hastings**   Havelock North
Patea   **Manawati-Wanganui**   Waipawa
Marton   Waipukurau
Wanganui   Bulls   Dannevirke
Tangimoana   **Palmerston North**   Woodville
Foxton   Pahiatua   *PACIFIC*
Cape Farewell   Levin   Eketahuna   *OCEAN*
Golden Bay   *Marlborough Sounds Maritime Park*   Otaki
Collingwood   *D'Urville Island*   Waikanae   **Wellington**   Castlepoint
Totaranui   Paraparaumu   Masterton
Takaka   *Abel Tasman NP*   Upper Hutt   Greytown
Kahurangi   *Tasman Bay*   Porirua   Featherston
National   Motueka   *Marlborough Sounds*   Lower Hutt   Martinborough
Karamea   **Park**   Havelock   **Wellington**
West Coast   Richmond   Nelson   Picton   Lake Ferry
Ngakawau   Renwick   Blenheim   *Strait*
Murchison   Wairau   Cape Palliser
Tasman   St Arnaud   **Marlborough**   Cape Campbell

NORTH ISLAND

The North Island is New Zealand's hub, where
frenetic activity is a feature of business, leisure and
even the Earth itself.

Maori dance performance.

The North Island, according to Maori legend, is the fish pulled from the sea by Maui. And what a catch it is, with a superb range of sights to see and things to do. New Zealand's largest and (by far) most worldly cities – Auckland and Wellington – are located here. Auckland, home to more than a quarter of New Zealand's population, is the largest Polynesian city in the world, and its wide range of shops, restaurants and activities make it truly cosmopolitan.

Laid-back Northland, in the subtropical far north beyond Auckland, has a strong Maori heritage and was one of the first areas settled by Europeans. Visit the Bay of Islands townships of Paihia and Russell and it's easy to understand why. Activities here centre on the sea: sailing, big-game fishing, pleasure cruising. There are also numerous sites of historical interest, from the place where the Treaty of Waitangi was signed to the nation's oldest stone building.

Whangarei yacht harbour.

Like most of New Zealand, a change of scenery is never far away. An hour's drive south through fertile dairy country is Waikato – its name borrowed from New Zealand's longest waterway, the Waikato River, which winds its way through the region. On the east coast the Coromandel Peninsula's beautiful beaches and secluded bays urge travellers to slow down, while the East Cape and its remoteness offers a special charm of its own.

Inland things heat up considerably. Hot mineral springs, boiling mud, geysers and volcanoes have led to Rotorua's title: 'thermal wonderland.' Fly-fishing is popular further south at Lake Taupo, New Zealand's largest lake. The fertile grounds of Taranaki and the Manawatu are among the most intensely farmed regions in New Zealand, and their small service towns provide friendly stopover points for travellers. Though situated at the bottom of the North Island, Wellington, the nation's capital, is at the centre of New Zealand both geographically and culturally. Within its harbour-fringed confines are the head offices of many of the country's major companies.

Queen Street.

AUCKLAND

Auckland is one of the world's most sprawling cities, yet you can easily walk across its narrowest point in less than 20 minutes. Volcanoes and the sea define its landscape, but its people are still defining themselves.

Auckland is built on an isthmus located between two stunning harbours and has, from the beginning, been defined by the water that surrounds it. The harbour that laps at the foot of what would become the city's main street was called Waitemata – sparkling water – by the pre-European Maori, and from every vantage point, man-made and natural, the aptness of the name can still be seen today.

Even when the sun is not shining – and Aucklanders like to think of their city as a sun-kissed gem of the South Pacific – the water glistens, silver under overcast skies, and becomes positively diamantine when the clouds part.

So insistent is the sea – nosing up creeks and estuaries and lapping on the shores of a hundred bays – that less than a mile of *terra firma* stops it from cutting Auckland completely adrift. The 19th-century townships that have linked up to make the 21st-century city were sprinkled along an S-shaped isthmus which at its narrowest point is barely 1.3km (¾ mile) wide. Across this corridor of land runs Portage Road, the original crossing point between two harbours. Here, Maori would beach and haul their canoes across the only break in an aquatic highway leading from the sheltered eastern bays of Northland and joining up with the Waikato, the country's longest river, which leads to Lake Taupo, the liquid heart of the North Island.

The City of Sails

Waitemata Harbour is the gateway to the island-studded boating paradise of the Hauraki Gulf. Ownership of recreational boats – from ostentatious gin palaces and deep-sea fishing craft to aluminium 'tinnies', battered rowboats and kayaks – is reputedly the world's highest per capita. Not for nothing has Auckland branded itself 'The City of Sails'.

Main Attractions

New Zealand Maritime Museum
Queen Street
Sky Tower
Civic Theatre
Toi o Tamaki Art Gallery
Albert Park
Auckland War Memorial Museum
Antarctic Encounter and Underwater World

The Sky Tower is 328 metres (1,076ft) tall.

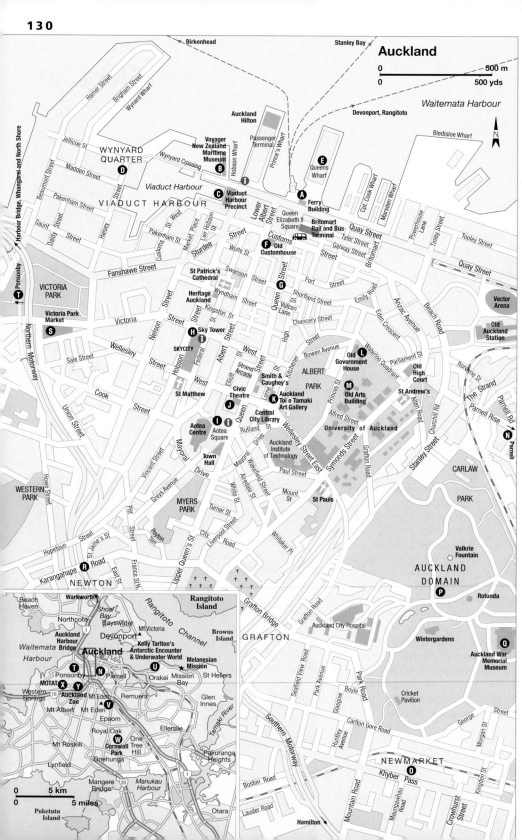

Auckland

Birkenhead
Stanley Bay

500 m
500 yds

Waitemata Harbour

Devonport, Rangitoto

Bledisloe Wharf

Passenger Terminal

Auckland Hilton

Prince's Wharf

Cpt. Cook Wharf

Marsden Wharf

Powerhouse Lane

Tinley Street

Tooley Street

Voyager New Zealand Maritime Museum **B**

Hobson Wharf

Wynyard Crossing

WYNYARD QUARTER **D**

Hamer Street
Brigham Street
Wynyard Wharf

Jellicoe St
Madden Street
Pakenham Street
Beaumont Street

Gaunt Street
Daldy Street

Harbour Bridge, Whangarei and North Shore

Ponsonby **T**

VICTORIA PARK

Victoria Park Market **S**

Victoria Street
Nelson Street
Hobson Street
Federal Street
Albert Street

Fanshawe Street
Sturdee Street
Customs Street
Wolfe St

Pakenham St
Market Place
Cr Hobson
Cr Hobson St

Viaduct Harbour

VIADUCT HARBOUR **C** Viaduct Harbour Precinct

St Patrick's Cathedral

Heritage Auckland

Sky Tower **H**
SKYCITY

St Matthew

Swanson Street
Wyndham Street
Kingston St
West Street

Queen Street
Customs Street
Galway Street
Tyler Street
Britomart
Quay Street

Queen Elizabeth II Square
Britomart Rail and Bus Terminal

Old Customhouse **F**

Ferry Building **A**

Queens Wharf **E**

Lower Albert Street

Emily Road
Anzac Avenue
Beach Road

Vector Arena

Old Auckland Station

Fort Street
Shortland Street
Vulcan Lane
Chancery Street
Bowen Avenue
High Street

G

Eden Crescent
Waterloo Quadrant
Parliament St

Old Government House **L**
Old High Court

St Andrew's

ALBERT PARK

Smith & Caughey's
Civic Theatre **J**
Strand Arcade
Elliott Street
Lorne St
Rutland St

K Auckland Toi o Tamaki Art Gallery

Old Arts Building **M**
Princes Street

Ronayne St
The Strand
Parnell Rise
Parnell
Parnell Rd

St Andrew's

Aotea Centre
Aotea Square **I**
Town Hall

Wellesley Street East
Symonds Street

University of Auckland

Central City Library

Auckland Institute of Technology

Alfred Street
Grafton Road
Stanley Street
Churchill Rd
Alten Road

CARLAW PARK

Mayoral Drive
Vincent Street
Greys Avenue
Pitt Street
City Road
Liverpool Street

White St
Airedale St
Wakefield Street
Paul Street

Mount St
St Pauls

Valkrie Fountain

AUCKLAND DOMAIN

WESTERN PARK

Howe Street
Union Street
Cook Street

MYERS PARK

Turner St
Peyton Tce

Whitaker Pl

P

Rotunda

Hopetoun Street
St Lukes St
France St N
Upper Queen's St

Karangahape Road

NEWTON **R**

Grafton Bridge

Grafton Road

Auckland City Hospital

Wintergardens

Cricket Pavilion

Q Auckland War Memorial Museum

Seafield View Road
Park Avenue
Park Road
Boyle
Glasgow
Huntley Avenue
Carlton Gore Road
George Street
Morgan St

Southern Motorway

Mountain Road
Maungawhau Road
Crowhurst Street

NEWMARKET **O**

Khyber Pass

Boston Road
Lauder Road

Hamilton

Inset map

Beach Haven
Warkworth
Northcote
Shoal Bay
Bayswater
Mt Victoria
Devonport

Rangitoto Island

Rangitoto Channel
Browns Island

Kelly Tarlton's Antarctic Encounter & Underwater World

Auckland Harbour Bridge

Auckland **T** **N**
Ponsonby
Parnell

MOTAT **X** **Y**
Auckland Zoo **V**
Western Springs
Mt Eden

Melanesian Mission

Mission Bay
St Heliers
Orakei **U**

GRAFTON

Waitemata Harbour

Mt Albert
Epsom
Remuera
Glen Innes
Ellerslie
Tamaki River

Royal Oak
W **Cornwall Park**
Onehunga
One Tree Hill
Pakuranga Heights

Mt Roskill
Lynfield

Mangere Bridge
Manukau Harbour
Otara
Puketutu Island

5 km
5 miles

GRAFTON

The city's Anniversary Day, the last Monday in January, is marked by a regatta – first staged in 1840, it's as old as the city itself – which crowds the harbour with as many as 1,000 sailing craft of all sizes in an organised mayhem of spectacle and competition.

A nation of boat owners produced a team of world-beating sailors. Team New Zealand was operating on a budget a fraction of the size of its competitors' when it snatched the coveted yachting trophy the America's Cup in 1995 and successfully defended it in 2000. The pain of losing the cup to the affluent Swiss-based Alinghi syndicate in 2003 was somewhat eased by the knowledge that the victor boat's key crew members were all New Zealanders. America's Cup excitement continues in foreign waters, however many New Zealanders watch the series with keen interest, hoping to lure the event back to NZ.

Turbulent history

A geological newborn, Auckland came to life with a bang. Some 53 volcanoes were created by eruptions which started between 60,000 and 140,000 years ago. The youngest – the bush-clad Rangitoto Island (see panel), whose blue-green hulk dominates the downtown waterfront view – last erupted only six centuries ago, burying a Maori settlement on adjoining Motutapu Island.

The city's human history is no less turbulent than its geological past. The ancestors of the Maori are believed to have arrived from eastern Polynesia around AD 800 (the exact timing continues to be debated heatedly). Traditional lore tells of incessant bloody intertribal warfare which gave Auckland its early Maori name, Tamaki Makaurau, meaning 'battle of a hundred lovers': the poetic description alluded not to a love story but to the conflict, which was as fierce as a suitors' rivalry.

Contact between Maori and the white people they would come to call *Pakeha* occurred haphazardly in this part of New Zealand from the 1770s, as traders and whale-hunters sought shelter along the coast. The British settlement of Auckland officially began with the visit of Samuel Marsden in 1820 (see panel), and the developing

The handsome Ferry Building dates from 1912.

town became the national capital for a time following the signing of the Treaty of Waitangi in 1840.

Auckland's recent growth has been fuelled by a series of immigration booms, beginning with an influx of Asians in the early 1990s which saw many wealthy immigrants settle in the southeastern areas of Howick and on Auckland's North Shore, along with legions of students seeking a Western education. At first the change caused palpable unease among long-established Kiwis who felt the ethnic composition of the city had changed too fast, but they soon realised that it had breathed new life into the place, making Auckland reinvent itself as a vibrant Pacific-Asian metropolis.

An early arrival described Auckland as 'a few tents and huts and a sea of fern stretching as far as the eye could see'. Today, the gaze of the modern visitor ranges over a sea of suburbs. The sprawl of Greater Auckland covers 1,016 sq km (392 sq miles), an area considerably larger than London; in proportion to its population of 1.5 million, it is one of the world's largest metropolitan areas; today, however, land in the inner city that is available for high density housing is running out, so residential construction must go up, not out.

Generally, Aucklanders live, work and shop in the suburban hinterland, which is dotted with busy shopping malls, and venture into the city only on special occasions. From the mid-1980s the inner city area developed rapidly, with unexciting office towers and apartment blocks built from the mid-1990s through to 2005. However, interesting modern architecture can be found around the Viaduct Harbour, the site of the America's Cup village, the Wynyard Quarter and along the waterfront at Queens Wharf.

Early in 2010 Auckland became a 'Super City': the four cities that made up the Auckland region (the CBD, Manukau, Waitakere and North Shore City) were blended into one under a single 'Lord Mayor'. Super city or not, Auckland remains undeniably the country's economic powerhouse. As the largest city in New Zealand, its population has steadily increased, and projections on population growth indicate it will reach 2 million by 2031. Aucklanders produce and consume a large share of the national wealth, and this fact engenders a fair degree of hostility and resentment from those who choose to live in smaller cities and provincial centres.

Auckland Harbour

Urban sprawl and a lack of an Auckland-wide train system can make getting around the Greater Auckland area something of a challenge. Taxis are expensive by world standards, although there is a fairly efficient system of buses and ferries. The city centre's main historic highlights are, however, easily reached on foot.

The sturdy red-brick **Ferry Building** Ⓐ on Quay Street at the foot of Queen Street is a good place to start an exploratory ramble. The 1912 building, which once housed the offices of harbour officials, now contains two of downtown's

A BARGAIN BUY

British Auckland officially began with the visit of the enterprising Reverend Samuel Marsden in 1820. The Sydney-based missionary named the fledgling settlement after the Earl of Auckland, George Eden, the Viceroy of India (the town of Russell, further north, was already established as the main settlement on the North Island – see page 153). Marsden crossed the Auckland isthmus on board the sailing ship *Coromandel* in November, the first European to do so, and his arrival heralded a process of land purchase which remains deeply problematic to this day.

It is more than likely that the Maori – whose traditional relationship with the land rendered the concept of ownership as meaningless – did not believe they were selling their real estate but rather accepting gifts in return for letting the new settlers live on their land.

Certainly the newcomers got a bargain: they purchased the area that now comprises the heart of Auckland for 50 blankets, 20 pairs of trousers, 20 shirts and other assorted sundries plus £50 cash, with another £6 paid the following year. The 1,200 hectares (3,000 acres) that the British settlers purchased covered the area from today's Freemans Bay to Parnell and inland as far as Mount Eden. Today, just 604 sq metres (6,499 sq ft) of downtown land in the city is worth at least NZ$1.6 million.

better restaurants, and behind it you can board the ferries to the North Shore and the islands of the Hauraki Gulf (for details see margin, page 148).

If you stand in the street with your back to the building, the Viaduct Harbour precinct, including the excellent **Voyager New Zealand Maritime Museum** Ⓑ (daily 9am–5pm; tel: 09-373 0800; www.maritimemuseum. co.nz), is barely three minutes' walk to your right. Its collection covers maritime history all the way back to the earliest Polynesian explorers. Vessels on display include the *Rapaki* floating steam crane and *KZI*, the yacht that launched New Zealand's America's Cup obsession when it sailed and lost in San Diego in 1988. Check in at the SailNZ kiosk (tel: 09-359 5987; www. explorenz.co.nz; daily) a few paces to the east of the museum for a chance to explore Auckland Harbour aboard a former America's Cup boat.

New Zealand's defence of the America's Cup prompted the redevelopment of the **Viaduct Harbour** Ⓒ. Site of the Southern Hemisphere's largest super-yacht marina, the Viaduct is a fashionable restaurant and bar precinct offering that conjunction of fine food and water views which so many find irresistible. When the ostentatious super-luxury yachts are in port, particularly at the height of summer, they are a major attraction in themselves. Beyond the Viaduct Harbour, and reached via a footbridge, lies the new **Wynyard Quarter** Ⓓ, a revitalised section of the waterfront – an extension of the Viaduct Harbour – dominated by open spaces, a playground, basketball courts, restaurants and the rippled architecture of the new Viaduct Events Centre. A novel way to get around the precinct is aboard the heritage tram, which completes a loop every 15 minutes. Returning back through Viaduct Harbour, walk the length of Prince's Wharf to see the **Auckland Hilton**, on the water's edge, cleverly designed to suggest a cruise liner and one of Auckland's better examples of postmodern architecture.

Back on Quay Street, immediately behind the Ferry Building is **Queens Wharf** Ⓔ, a unique vantage point to view the Waitemata Harbour. As you enter the wharf the vertical steel and

For a bird's-eye view of the city, try a half-hour guided climb over the Auckland Harbour Bridge. A maze of catwalks and surprising twists and turns add to the thrill of this outdoor adventure. Contact Auckland Bridge Climb, Curran Street, Westhaven Reserve, tel: 09-360 7748; www. bungy.co.nz.

To bound off the 328-metre (1,076ft) Sky Tower, contact Skyjump, tel: 09-368 1835, or visit www. skyjump.co.nz.

Queen Street, in the heart of downtown Auckland.

timber art forms recall the industrial and architectural structures of its former life as a working wharf (completed in 1913). Now transformed into a public waterfront space, it's home to a new building, The Cloud, and a renovated old one, Shed 10, part of Auckland's makeover for the Rugby World Cup 2011. The caterpillar-looking 'Cloud', designed by Jasmax, is an events venue, 180 metres (590ft) long, which can accommodate up to 5,000 people. Shed 10, a historic cargo shed built in 1910, is the only original building left on the wharf, and its upgrade continues along with Auckland's plans to revitalise the waterfront area. Projects include a 10km (6-mile) long promenade and recreational trail along the waterfront, a new cruise terminal next to Shed 10 and a classic-boat marina with berths for Auckland's heritage vessels, such as the *Kestrel* ferry. Also planned is a series of parks and a light rail system linking the waterfront to the city.

Back at the Ferry Building, and just across **Quay Street** is **Queen Elizabeth Square**, dominated by the city's main transport hub, **Britomart**. This is housed in the former Chief Post Office, a neoclassical building dating back to 1910. As you leave the square to cross **Customs Street**, look again to your right (west). A block away, on the corner of **Albert Street**, is the **Old Customhouse** ⑤ which was the financial heart of Auckland for more than 80 years. Designed in French Renaissance style, the building was completed in 1889 and is one of the last remaining examples of monumental Victorian architecture to be found in a central business district where the wrecker's ball has been far too busy.

Queen Street central

Downtown Auckland keeps long hours, and shops seeking the tourist dollar stay open until late in the evening on weekdays and through the weekends. **Queen Street** ⑥ – the city's main drag, is one of the few places in New Zealand which is busy 24/7. Cheap noodle houses, ethnic restaurants and internet cafés cater to the city's huge number of foreign

students, bars attract the young, and convenience stores serve inner-city apartment dwellers, although there is also a sprinkling of upmarket boutiques and fashion brand stores. Much of corporate New Zealand headquarters itself in the Queen Street valley.

Some excellent restaurants do good business in the streets that radiate out from Queen Street, but it's the inner suburbs – particularly Parnell to the east and Ponsonby to the southwest – where some of the city's best eateries are to be found. If you're so inclined, check out the touristy souvenir stores in the lower part of Queen Street: the prices, while not cheap, will not be extortionate, though often half of the merchandise will be made in China – check the label.

As you walk south up the main street, pause at the intersection of Queen and Fort streets. Waves lapped the shore at this spot less than 150 years ago when Shortland Street, a block further up, was the main street; back then Queen Street was a bush-covered gully along which ran a canal serving as an open sewer.

You will have hardly failed to notice, some 500 metres (550 yards) to the southwest, the cloud-piercing **Sky Tower** ⓗ (tel: 09-363 6000; www.sky city.co.nz; daily 8.30am–10.30pm, Fri and Sat until 11.30pm) on Hobson Street, the western ridge of the valley. At 328 metres (1,076ft), it was the butt of many jokes when it was built in the mid-1990s: critics saw its giant syringe shape as an apt symbol of the gambling addiction being generated by the casino at its foot. But it is now a familiar and dramatic feature of the city skyline – best seen from the harbour or from Devonport's North Head. Visitors are whisked in high-speed lifts to the top for a view, which, on a clear day, can stretch more than 80km (50 miles). Those less prone to vertigo might like to consider the 192-metre (630ft) high 'Skyjump' off the tower (contact Skyjump; tel: 09-368 1835; www.skyjump.co.nz) – New Zealand's adventure-sport fixation is not restricted to the countryside.

Civic pride

Back down to earth on Queen Street, and some 400 metres (1,300ft) to the south is **Aotea Square** ⓘ, dominated by the monolithic **Auckland City Council** administration building, and, on the western side of the square, the city's main cultural complex, the **Aotea Centre**. The latter was built over the howls of derision from those who could not understand why the city's pre-eminent public building was not being sited on the waterfront. The Aotea Centre's 2,300-seat multi-purpose theatre is acoustically problematic, to say the least – most classical music performances take place in the beautifully restored and acoustically warm **Town Hall** on the square's southeastern boundary – but it is popular as a convention centre. The Aotea Centre, The Civic, Auckland Town Hall and Aotea Square all come under the collective administrative umbrella **The Edge** (tel: 09-357 3355). For programme details, check www.the-edge.co.nz.

Just down the road to the north at the corner with Wellesley Street is the opulent **Civic Theatre** ⓙ. Built

Auckland Toi o Tamaki Art Gallery.

TIP

Auckland's pre-eminent private art gallery is the Gow Langsford Gallery at 26 Lorne Street, opposite the Auckland Art Gallery. Many of New Zealand's leading contemporary artists and a selection of international artists are represented here (tel: 09-303 4290; www. gowlangsfordgallery.com; Mon–Fri 10am–6pm, Sat 10am–4pm.

Albert Park.

in 1929, this was one of the world's finest atmospheric picture palaces, though now is mostly used for touring musicals and shows. Its ornate construction was a sign of the times – it employed many hundreds of tradesmen during the Great Depression – and the labyrinthine stairways are watched over by hundreds of glittering elephants. From 1997 to 1999 it underwent a multimillion-dollar refurbishment for the millennium, its mock sky, complete with twinkling stars, making its interior one of the city's finest sights.

Aotea Square and the Civic Theatre are separated by the city's major cinema centre. A block to the east in **Lorne Street** is the **Central City Library** (tel: 09-377 0209; www. aucklandcitylibraries.com; Mon–Fri 9am–8pm, Sat–Sun 10am–4pm). Even in the internet age, its reading room remains popular with homesick travellers and immigrants devouring the foreign press.

A further block east on the corner of Wellesley Street East and Lorne Street is the **Auckland Toi o**

Tamaki Art Gallery 🅚 (tel: 09-379 1349; www.aucklandartgallery.govt.nz; daily 10am–5pm; free daily tour of collections at 11.30am and 1.30pm; free, except for special exhibitions), which holds historical collections and fine exhibitions of contemporary art from New Zealand and overseas. Visitors are likely to be intrigued by the idealised 19th-century portraits of Maori by Gottfried Lindauer and Charles Goldie.

North of the gallery off Kitchener Street, an access path leads into **Albert Park**, set on a ridge of thick ash formed by early volcanic eruptions. However, the main CBD pedestrian access to the park is at the floral clock at 33–43 Princes Street, constructed in 1953 to commemorate Queen Elizabeth II's first visit to New Zealand. Once the site of a Maori village and then a defence post, it became a park administered by Auckland City Council from 1879 onwards. Paths, gardens and trees were established, and an elaborate Victorian fountain was built as a centrepiece. Albert Park House, formerly the gardener's cottage (now housing an aggregation of clocks and ceramics), was added, along with a statue of Queen Victoria, unveiled in 1899 to mark her 60th jubilee.

From the park you can enter the leafy grounds of the **University of Auckland**. At the corner of Princes Street and Waterloo Quadrant, in part of the university grounds is the **Old Government House 🅛**, built in 1856 as the home of the Governor. The building appears to be made of stone, though in fact its exterior cladding is all kauri, the wood of the magnificent species of tree which once dominated the New Zealand bush and was the building material of choice until well into the 19th century.

The university's central attraction, however, a few metres south on Princes Street, is the **Old Arts Building 🅜**, with its intricate clock tower. It was completed in 1926 in

Gothic style and immediately dubbed The Wedding Cake by locals because of its decorative pinnacled white-stone construction.

Note the refurbished **High Court**, some 250 metres (270 yards) to the northeast, where a series of grinning griffins and gargoyles adorn the exterior walls. It stands near the corner of Anzac Avenue and Parliament Street, whose name is another vestige of Auckland's former status as New Zealand's capital. It was only pressure from the gold-rich South Island and new settlements further south in the North Island that resulted in the movement of the capital from Auckland to Wellington in 1865.

East of the city centre

Continue east through the park known as **Constitution Hill**, named after the fact that businessmen took a 'constitutional' walk up its steep slope from their Parnell homes to their city offices. Follow Parnell Rise, turning into Parnell Road for 2km (1¼ miles) and walk up through **Parnell** . It's an oddity of the city's history

– some say it's because the upper classes didn't like the sun in their eyes on the way to and from work in the city – that the suburbs east of Queen Street have always been the city's more affluent. So it's no accident that Parnell oozes a refined style. It's also the gateway to **Newmarket** Ⓞ, a busy shopping strip which is home to some of fashion's big-name outlets, and **Remuera**, where the serious, old money lives. Parnell largely overcame the unfortunate faux-heritage refurbishment of the 1970s, which hideously attempted to re-imagine it as a pioneer village in low-maintenance materials.

At the end of Parnell Road, past the Anglican Cathedral, enter the **Auckland Domain** Ⓟ by turning right on Maunsell Road. This 75-hectare (185-acre) park is the city's oldest, with duck ponds, playing fields, traditional statuary and the Wintergardens – two large glasshouses displaying temperate and tropical plants.

This route provides easy access to the **Auckland War Memorial Museum** Ⓠ (tel: 09-309 0443; www.

Albert Park combines Edwardian design features with some mildly incongruous contemporary sculpture.

The Auckland War Memorial Museum.

WHERE

The impressive Manaia Maori cultural performance takes place at the Auckland War Memorial Museum (daily; performance and tour, 11am, 1.30pm; performance only, 12pm, 2.30pm). Admission to the show is by ticket only (performance and tour NZ$35, child $17.50; performance only NZ$25, child NZ$12.50). Tel: 09-309 0443.

An evening view of the city skyline.

aucklandmuseum.com; daily 10am–5pm; children free), which presides over the rambling grounds of the Domain. Despite the name, the museum is not devoted to war artefacts but deals with subjects as diverse as natural history, ethnology and archaeology. The building was erected in 1929 as a memorial to soldiers who died in World War I. It houses one of the world's finest displays of Maori and Polynesian culture, with some artefacts dating as far back as AD 1200. A highlight is the 35-metre (115ft) war canoe *Te-Toki-A-Tapiri* (The Axe of Tapiri), carved in 1836 from a single giant totara tree and designed to seat up to 100 warriors.

Southwest of the centre

Auckland is the world's biggest Polynesian city. Almost 266,000 New Zealanders – about 7 percent – are of Pacific Island ethnicity, with more than 67 percent of them residing in the Auckland region. In some cases, Auckland's Polynesian population outnumbers those back at home (for instance, nine out of 10 Niueans live here) and in most cases, more than half are New Zealand-born. Most of the Pacific peoples settled in the central part of the city in the mid-20th century, particularly in Ponsonby and adjoining Grey Lynn, until soaring property prices and the accompanying gentrification of those suburbs saw the islanders migrate again, to the Manukau region in South Auckland (see page 145).

Heading southwest from the Domain for some 1.25km (¾ mile) brings you to **Karangahape Road** Ⓡ – known to locals as K Road – which runs west from Grafton Bridge, and is an iconic city-centre strip which attracts a bustling crowd for its alternative nightclubs, cafés and ethnic dining options. Traces of the city's Pacific connections linger in shops displaying brilliantly coloured floral cloth, and where the occasional taro, yam, papaya and other tropical foods can be found. These days the vibe in this part of town is distinctly Indian, and for most visitors this is the raffish but undeniably charming side of the city (even if the western end is home to some of the city's sex industry

– the rest of which lurks downtown in Fort Street).

About 1km (0.5 mile) north of K Road is the **Victoria Park Market** **S** (tel: 09-309 6911; www.victoria-park-market.co.nz; daily 9am–5pm; free), built on the site (and under the tall brick chimney) of what was the city's rubbish destructor until the 1970s. The market has just had a $20 million refurbishment and is a seven-day lure for café hoppers and shoppers. The quality of most merchandise is high and while retail fruit and vegetable stalls also operate here, it is not a farmers' market.

Further west still – a 10-minute walk up Franklin Road or a short bus ride up the hill – is **Ponsonby** **T**. This ribbon of road, festooned with the best selection of restaurants in town, is the sister of Parnell, about the same distance from Queen Street. Once home to hirsute students and whole streets of Pacific Island immigrant families, Ponsonby today is filled with refurbished turn-of-the-19th-century villas on pocket-handkerchief sections which fetch ludicrous prices at auctions, and the streets are full of the elegant and the self-regarding. It's not exactly Rodeo Drive – many of the city's more creative types live on its narrow streets – but it's definitely Auckland's Golden Mile.

Along Tamaki Drive

A return to the Ferry Building is as good a place as any to start Auckland's waterfront drive – the ribbon of tarmac that runs east from the port around the harbourside makes for a scenic tour of the city's waterfront. Quay Street becomes **Tamaki Drive**, which winds some 8km (5 miles) along the seafront. The safe beaches are good for swimming at high tide and excellent for picnics. Rangitoto Island looms ahead, seemingly close enough to touch. The footpath is busy with cyclists and walkers on sunny weekends, and bicycle-, boat- and windsurfer-hire businesses ply a roaring trade.

En route, **Kelly Tarlton's Antarctic Encounter and Underwater World** **U** (tel: 09-531 5065, 0800-805 050; www.kellytarltons.co.nz; daily 9.30am–5pm) can be considered a virtually compulsory stop. This facility is constructed in what used to be a sewage pumping station. Today dozens of varieties of fish, including sharks, can be viewed from a moving walkway passing through a huge transparent tunnel. A 41-year-old 250kg (550lb) stingray with a metre-wide wingspan, named Phoebe, is the star attraction at Stingray Bay. The Seahorse Kingdom features seahorses from around the globe, including the world's only spiny sea dragon on public display. The Antarctic section features a Snow Cat ride to view the colony of King and Gentoo penguins, while the partially submerged Shark Cage provides the chance to see School, Wobbegong and Broadnose Sevengill sharks in a whole new way.

Mount Eden and Cornwall Park

Towering just 3km (2 miles) south of the city centre is the 196-metre (643ft)

Kelly Tarlton's Antarctic Encounter and Underwater World.

The 19th-century town hall at Ponsonby, one of the city's most exclusive neighbourhoods.

On Anniversary Day, Auckland's yachts race in New Zealand's largest regatta. The city has the highest boat ownership per capita in the world, and it's easy to see why, with the myriad islands of the Hauraki Gulf lying beyond the beaches and bays of Waitemata Harbour.

volcanic cone of **Mount Eden** , Auckland's highest point. Long extinct in volcanic terms, it offers a 360-degree panorama of the region almost as good as the view from the Sky Tower. In an old lava pit on the eastern side, at 24 Omana Avenue, is **Eden Garden** (tel: 09-638 8395; www.edengarden.co.nz; daily 9am–4.30pm), which provides a heady floral display, including the largest collection of camellias in the Southern Hemisphere. It was created in 1964 on the site of an abandoned quarry and is run by volunteers. A café operates on site from 9am–4pm daily.

Another 3km (2 miles) southeast, in **Cornwall Park** (tel: 09-630 8485; www.cornwallpark.co.nz; daily 7am until dusk; free), is the landmark cone of **One Tree Hill** and the obelisk which crowns the tomb of the 'Father of Auckland', Sir John Logan Campbell, the entrepreneur who set up Auckland's first commercial store at the bottom of Shortland Street on 21 December 1840. Campbell was the city's most prominent businessman until his death in 1912 at the age of 95. The 135-hectare (334-acre) estate encompassing One Tree Hill, which he donated to the people of Auckland after becoming the city mayor, was given its name in 1901 when Campbell hosted Britain's Duke and Duchess of Cornwall. He also built **Acacia Cottage** in 1841. Now Auckland's oldest building, the restored cottage is preserved in Cornwall Park at the base of One Tree Hill.

The Maori name for One Tree Hill is Te Totara-i-ahua, in deference to the sacred totara tree that stood here until 1852, when the early settlers replaced it with a pine. Today, the 'One Tree' sobriquet is something of a misnomer: the lone pine tree that used to stand on the summit was cut down in 2002, after failing to recover from a chainsaw attack by a Maori activist who was seeking to draw attention to political grievances.

Transport Museum and Zoo

At Western Springs, just off the northwestern motorway, the **Museum of Transport and Technology** (MOTAT; tel: 09-815 5800; www.motat.org.nz; daily 10am–5pm) has over 300,000 items in its collection, including working vintage vehicles, aircraft and machinery and excellent hands-on applied science displays. The museum also has an aircraft built by New Zealander Richard Pearse, who, some devotees claim, flew it in March 1903, several months before the Wright Brothers. Volunteer enthusiasts operate many exhibits at the weekends.

A brief ride from MOTAT in an old tram (or, alternatively, a pleasant walk eastwards around the lake at Western Springs Park) leads to **Auckland Zoo** (tel: 09-360 3805; www.aucklandzoo.co.nz; daily 9.30am–5.30pm, last admission 4.15pm), home to New Zealand's largest aggregation of native and exotic animals. Here you can see the kiwi, New Zealand's unique flightless bird, and the tuatara, a 'living fossil' which has not changed since the age of the dinosaurs. (for more on these and other local wildlife see page 102).

Trendsetting Kiwi Fashion

Something of a late starter in the global sartorial stakes, New Zealand's fashion industry has now taken off

New Zealand fashion may not have fully come of age just yet, but somewhere around the turn of the new millennium it developed the ability to walk. At that time, New Zealand designers began developing a distinctive style of their own.

In 1997, four home-grown labels – Moontide, World, Wallace Rose and Zambesi – took part in Australian Fashion Week for the first time. Two years later, Kiwi designers took part in London Fashion Week. 'There seems to be a remarkable difference between Australia and New Zealand. New Zealanders have a darker outlook. Less show-offy. More intellectual,' observed French Vogue. Since then Kiwi fashion has been regularly showcased during Paris Fashion Week, launching New Zealand fashion further into new global markets. NOM*D has featured in the designers' room at Liberty's of London. Kate Sylvester has more than 50 stores worldwide and New Zealand designer Rebecca Taylor, who has worked in New York for many years, has a range of celebrity followers, including Ashley Judd, Cameron Diaz and Minnie Driver.

Overseas fashion writers and opinion shapers are no longer the novelty at major New Zealand fashion events such as the World of Wearable Arts Awards, which is hosted in Wellington and attracts entrants from around the globe, and New Zealand Fashion Week, held in Auckland. Whatever the truth of *Vogue*'s pronouncement, the New Zealand style is less individualistic than it is a brilliant assimilation of a variety of influences. As in so many other areas, the country's isolation has forced the locals to come up with their own solutions – in fashion no less than in agriculture. While still heavily influenced by Northern Hemisphere designs, many designers draw on Polynesian and Asian styles, while others amass a globally eclectic mix and turn it into a coherent whole. (Much contemporary young Polynesian fashion, in turn, is strongly influenced by US hip-hop culture.)

Often those who do best in the fashion industry are those who market themselves as their brand – Karen Walker, Trelise Cooper and Sharon Ng are notable examples. Many of the prominent designers (and labels) who are matching local popularity with some overseas success – Walker, Cooper, Kate Sylvester, Scotties, Zambesi and WORLD – are based in Auckland. But New Zealand's biggest city doesn't have the field entirely to itself.

While Wellington has stores representing the better-known local labels, other names to look out for include Andrea Moore, Madcat and Voon. Leading labels NOM*D, Carlson, Mild Red and Dot Com all call Dunedin home, and the student influence gives the city's fashion a slightly funkier air than the fashion favoured in other centres. Well supported, Dunedin is a hub for up-and-coming designers.

Other invigorating fashion is occurring on the fringes, produced by names that may well be big one day, or, fashion being fashion, disappear altogether. Away from Auckland's High Street, Lorne Street and Chancery you'll find the odd gem on Karangahape Road, but to find what bubbles beneath Auckland's polished veneer, head to the small studios of Ponsonby Road. Here you will often come face to face with the designers in their role as cashier, fabric cutter and seamstress all rolled into one. Elsewhere, cutting-edge design is likely to be found in various small studios dotted around Dunedin.

As for men's fashion, for a Kiwi male to care about his appearance is still, except in certain circumstances, regarded as anomalous.

Modelling a Karen Walker design.

Sunset at Piha beach.

AUCKLAND'S SURROUNDINGS

Auckland's hinterland exhibits different flavours depending on whether you travel west, north, south – or east, to the 47 islands of the Hauraki Gulf.

Auckland is a sprawling city, the urban area extending for miles along the shores of the Hauraki Gulf, far to the south around Manukau Harbour and west to the fringes of the Waitakere vineyards. Beyond the suburbs, the countryside quickly becomes attractive, particularly to the north and west, where the kauri forests of the Waitakere Ranges are a major attraction. To the east, the blue waters of the Hauraki Gulf are dotted with islands, making this one of the world's most rewarding sailing destinations. Many of the islands are stunningly beautiful, notably Great Barrier Island, which can be reached from downtown Auckland in a couple of hours by ferry. The coasts on both sides of the northern peninsula extending towards Northland are blessed with wonderful sandy beaches, and are rather more windswept on the western shore.

Aucklanders are passionately, obsessively, blindly devoted to the motorcar, as the rush-hour snarl on the motorways quickly reveals. Decades of political prevarication have prevented the development of an effective, useful rail system, and the buses all too often become gridlocked in traffic at busy times of day. Any visitor who wishes to avoid an eye-watering taxi bill will want to rent a car to make the most of a short stay by exploring beyond the city limits. Alternatively, there is no

shortage of organised tours which take in the most important sights in the city's environs.

To the west

Travelling from downtown Auckland, the visitor's first taste of Auckland's western suburbs is at **Henderson ❶**, west of SH16 at the Lincoln Road turn-off. The valley here was settled early by Dalmatian and Croatian wine growers. Today, their dynasties are commemorated in many of the street names, and the

Main Attractions
Kauri forests, Waitakere Ranges
Muriwai Beach
Devonport
Rangitoto Island
Waiheke Island

A Kumeu winery.

roads of modern West Auckland are studded with vineyards, some world-class, others old family operations whose rough reds are still sold in half-gallon flagons.

Beyond the city limits, stay on SH16 and you'll come to **Kumeu ❷**, 20km (12 miles) past the Henderson turn-off, where weekend farmers run horses on their farms. Here are to be found some of the more substantial vineyards, like **Kumeu River** (www.kumeuriver.co.nz), **Westbrook** (www.westbrook.co.nz) and **Matua Valley** (www.matua.co.nz).

In common with most of the developed world, the suburban areas of west Auckland are lined with shopping malls and bland commercial and light industrial developments. However, just beyond this, a mere 20km (12 miles) from downtown Auckland, lie the thickly forested **Waitakere Ranges**. Here tall kauri trees, giant ferns and nikau palms create a beautiful environment for bushwalkers – known locally as trampers – and for film-makers. The popular TV series *Xena* and *Hercules* were filmed here in the **Waitakere Ranges Regional Park**. The ranges are easily explored by following the aptly named **Scenic Drive** (SH24), which runs for 28km (17 miles) along their spine from Titirangi to Swanson. Some 5km (3 miles) from the **Titirangi ❸** end of the drive, the **Arataki Visitor Centre** (tel: 09-817 0077; http://regionalparks.auckland council.govt.nz/aratakivisitorcentre; daily Nov–Mar 9am–5pm, Apr–Oct 10am–4pm) is the place to plan detailed explorations, with a series of walks of varying degrees of difficulty and suggestions for camping out overnight. The centre also has an excellent range of authentic New Zealand-made souvenirs and books.

West coast beaches

Beyond the ranges, the west gets truly wild: the edge of the land is stitched by a line of black-sand surf beaches, windswept and pounded by the waves of the Tasman Sea. The northernmost beach, 32km (20-mile) long **Muriwai ❹**, is actually designated a public road (4WD only), leading north to the Kaipara Heads at the

Red-and-yellow flags mark safe places for swimming.

WAITAKERE CITY

Auckland's frontier is out west. The Waitakere region, 15km (9 miles) west of downtown Auckland on State Highway (SH) 16, burst into life in the mid-1950s when a causeway road was laid across part of the upper harbour, bringing the west much closer to the city, but on the coast it still maintains a distinctive wildness. Residents are nick-named Westies, but any generalisation masks this region's variety. Artists, craftspeople, back-to-nature bush-lovers, business owners, and substantial Maori and Polynesian populations are all part of Waitakere's mix. Well known as the eco-area of Auckland, Henderson has several eco-friendly structures, including the council building, which has won many awards for its tussock-covered roof, its clean lines and sustainable design.

entrance of Kaipara Harbour. Close to the township (also called Muriwai) is the Takapu Gannet Colony which, seen up close from viewing platforms, is one of the region's great sights. The breeding season, from September to May, is the best time to visit. Muriwai was one of the most important visual inspirations for the late Colin McCahon (see page 64), New Zealand's pre-eminent artist.

At the southernmost limit of **Waitakere City** and the Waitakere Ranges is Whatipu, where the sea seems to boil as it pours into the tidal Manukau Harbour. In between, the line of beaches raked by the sea includes **Piha**, the surfers' paradise and a favourite of holidaymakers, and **Karekare ❺**, where the spectacular opening sequence of Jane Campion's *The Piano* was filmed.

Be aware that these west coast beaches are very dangerous for swimming and their death tolls include many unwary tourists. Beaches are patrolled during the summer months, and for your own safety it is wise to swim between the flags. Also be wary of rogue waves that have been known to overwhelm people sitting on the rocks.

South Auckland

The words 'South Auckland' are loaded for Aucklanders. The suburbs strung out on each side of the southern motorway beyond Otahuhu unquestionably include some of the region's most economically depressed neighbourhoods – although there are parts of **Manukau City**, the region's southern city, that are extremely affluent. Here is to be found the social and physical landscape depicted in the 1994 movie *Once Were Warriors*, which showed the cost of drinking, domestic violence and gang warfare on Maori families.

Otahuhu ❻, 14km (9 miles) south of Auckland on SH1, gives a good glimpse of Manukau's cultural diversity: wander down the main street, where Asian and Pacific traders jostle cheek-by-jowl.

Some 3km (2 miles) further south is the colourful and noisy **Otara Market** (Sat 6am–noon) on Newbury Street in

Otara market.

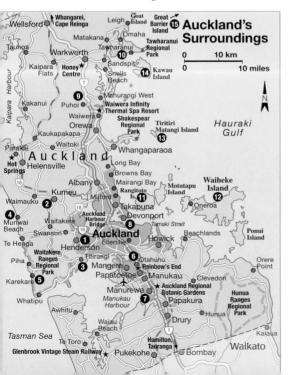

FACT

The landmark Kiwi film *Once Were Warriors*, based on a novel by Alan Duff and directed by Lee Tamahori, was released in 1994 to rave reviews. Set in south Auckland, it takes a painful look at the problems that plague working-class Maori families.

the Otara Shopping Centre (take the East Tamaki Road/Otara turn-off on SH1). With more than 250 stalls vying for attention, this is New Zealand's largest street market, and everything from a wide selection of clothes, art and jewellery to fresh fruit and vegetables is on display. Standing in the midst of this multicultural community is **Mangere Mount**, which rises to 100 metres (330ft) and overlooks Manukau Harbour.

Travel another 5km (3 miles) south to **Rainbow's End** (tel: 09-262 2030; www.rainbowsend.co.nz; daily 10am–5pm), the country's premier theme park, with crazy rides you won't find anywhere else in New Zealand. If you like that kind of thing, the park's 'Power Surge' ride is comparable to a spin and tumble in a washing machine.

Elsewhere in Manukau, about 5km (3 miles) south of Rainbow's End, are the **Auckland Regional Botanic Gardens** (tel: 09-267 1457; www.aucklandbotanicgardens.co.nz; daily 8am–8pm; free) near **Manurewa** ❼, with a dazzling variety of species.

Manukau Harbour, which marks the city's western border, lacks the scenic charm of the east coast's Waitemata Harbour. At low tide its mudflats stretch for miles, and are home to numerous species of wader and other birds. It's uncrowded, too: many Aucklanders ignore it, partly because it used to be polluted with industrial and domestic run-off. The clean-up has been a triumph of conservation planning.

North Auckland

The opening of the **Auckland Harbour Bridge** in 1959 transformed the region immediately north of Auckland from countryside into city almost overnight. At a stroke, what had been a string of sleepy seaside settlements backed by rolling pastureland became part of the city.

Today the bridge, a 1km (0.5-mile) long 'coathanger' stretching from the north end of the city centre at Fanshawe Street to Northcote Point across the harbour, carries an average of 141,000 vehicles a day. City and harbour views can be enjoyed with the help of

Devonport basks in the sunshine.

DIVINE DEVONPORT

A 10-minute ferry ride (30 times daily) across the harbour from downtown Auckland, Devonport is a waterside haven full of charm. Its streets are lined with preserved colonial villas and bungalows, many of them accommodating cafés and small boutiques selling local crafts, antiques and collectables. There are sandy beaches to relax on, and an enormous public playground for children is right on the waterfront. Looming overhead are the volcanic cones of Mount Victoria and North Head, affording fine views of downtown Auckland and the eastern bays. At North Head there are old gun emplacements and connecting tunnels to explore, or linger in town following the Old Devonport Walk, a mapped route linking historical sites and museums of note such as the Devonport Historical Museum.

an enterprising operator, **Auckland Bridge Climb** (tel: 0800-286 4958; www. aucklandbridgeclimb.co.nz) which offers a 1.5-hour guided climb. This being New Zealand, there's a chance to take a bungee jump off the bridge at the end of the tour. Two things the public can't do on the bridge motorway, however, is walk or ride a bicycle, although city planners often discuss opening a bridge walkway for the public.

The region to the north of the bridge is known as the North Shore, a sprawling area of suburbia and industrial development fringed by the beautiful white-sand beaches. The fastest way to reach nearby **Devonport** ❽ is to hop aboard one of the regular ferries departing from the Quay Street Ferry Building (see margin, page 148) in downtown Auckland. This is a decidedly affluent area with many grand Victorian houses, arts and craft galleries and a plethora of bars and cafés (see panel).

To the north of Devonport the coastline becomes an attractive procession of sheltered coves and white-sand beaches; Takapuna Beach, Milford Beach, Mairangi Bay, Browns Bay and Long Bay, all of which offer tremendous views of the Hauraki Gulf.

Two of these, Takapuna and Browns Bay, have good shopping areas, cafés and restaurants, and overlook Rangitoto Island. Long Bay, a large regional park offering several good hikes, also has a large playground and a café right on the beach.

Rodney District

But it's still further north, beyond North Shore City, that the day-tripper really begins to reap rewards. The **Northern Motorway Tollway**, completed in 2009, has opened up access to the region as never before.

The motorway bypasses the suburbs of Orewa and Whangaparaoa (the name means 'bay of whales'), a region that was semi-rural pastureland and beach cottages barely a generation ago, but is now Auckland's northernmost dormitory suburb, and

as a result has lost much of its former charm. There are some pleasant spots, though: the suburban neighbourhoods run down to safe swimming beaches and the well-manicured **Shakespeare Regional Park** at the tip of Whangaparaoa Peninsula is still a nice picnic spot.

Some 6km (4 miles) north of Orewa is **Waiwera Infinity Thermal Resort** (tel: 09-427 8800; www.waiwera. co.nz; daily Sun–Thu 9am–9pm, Fri– Sat 9am–10pm). Tucked under the brow of the hill, the pools (whose Maori name means 'hot water') are one of only two thermal areas in the Auckland region (the other is at **Parakai**, near Helensville, 55km/34 miles northwest of the city on SH16).

If you continue to the end of the Northern Motorway Tollway, just after passing through the Johnson Hill Tunnels, watch out on the left for the sign to **Puhoi** ❾, the country's earliest Catholic Bohemian settlement. If you're passing by, be sure to stop for a drink at the **Puhoi Tavern**, full of old-world charm and pictures of the early Bohemian migrants and

WHERE

The Riverhead Ferry's riverway and inner harbour chartered cruises provide a unique view of Auckland's sights and suburbs. They depart from Westhaven Marina, 10 minutes' walk west of Auckland CBD (tel: 09-376 0819; www.riverheadferry.co.nz).

One of the spectacular islands of the Hauraki Gulf.

farming paraphernalia on display, watch cheese-makers at work at Puhoi Valley Cheese (tel: 0800-423 133; www. puhoivalley.co.nz) or drop by the **Puhoi Bohemian Museum** (tel: 09-427 8987; www.puhoihistoricalsociety.org.nz; summer daily 1–4pm; rest of year Sat–Sun 1–4pm) on Puhoi Road.

Beyond the Puhoi Junction, the countryside begins to open up. Interesting places to stop and stretch your legs include the **Honey Centre** (tel: 09-425 8003; www.honeycentre. co.nz; daily 8.30am–5pm; free), 4km (2½ miles) south of Warkworth, where you can buy varieties of New Zealand's excellent honey and watch the bees making it behind the glass walls of working hives. Its café serves a wide range of honey-inspired ice-cream flavours. **Warkworth** itself is a pretty riverside country town and the access point for some of the region's real gems. Turn east on the Matakana–Leigh Road for a drive through the wine-growing area of **Matakana** and take in **Tawharanui** ❿, 25km (16 miles) from Warkworth, the northernmost of the regional

Connells Bay sculpture park, Waiheke Island.

parks, where – on a weekday at least – you stand a pretty good chance of having an endless white-sand beach entirely to yourself.

To the north is Omaha, a popular surf destination, and **Leigh**, home to Goat Island, the site of the Cape Rodney-Okakari Point Marine Reserve, where, in the shallows, the friendliest fish in the nation eagerly snap around your feet. Great snorkelling and diving are on offer through Goat Island Dive (tel: 0800-348 369; www.goatislanddive.co.nz). For those who prefer not to get wet feet, the **Glass Bottom Boat** (tel: 09-422 6334; www. glassbottomboat.co.nz), usually found on the water's edge, offers good viewing.

Hauraki Gulf islands

No visitor should leave without venturing onto the waters of the beautiful island-dotted **Hauraki Gulf**, or at least the inner harbour. All the islands described here, with the exception of Kawau Island, are easily accessible by fast ferry from Auckland's Ferry Building along Quay Street (see page 132).

In many ways the most striking island to visit is **Rangitoto Island** ⓫ – just 8km (5 miles) northeast of Auckland – the 600-year-old dormant volcano which dominates the city's skyline. The summit is a bracing, though not hugely demanding, walk, and there is a tractor-trailer trip (tel: 09-367 9111; www.fullers.co.nz) for those who don't fancy the exertion. Take stout shoes; the volcanic lava pathway butchers fancy leather. From the 260-metre (850ft) summit there are unforgettable 360-degree views of the city, the northern bays and the Hauraki Gulf. A causeway joins Rangitoto with **Motutapu Island**, which, by way of contrast, is mostly covered in farmland.

Barely 19km (12 miles) from downtown Auckland is **Waiheke Island** ⓬, the most populated of the Gulf islands. A generation ago it was a retreat for the impecunious and the artistic who had to brave the bouncy, hour-long ferry ride into town. These days a high-speed catamaran makes the commute shorter, and as a result the island's population and profile have changed beyond recognition. Much of the work of local craftspeople is now world-class rather than hippie-cottage. The steep slopes overlooking the many beautiful bays are now sprinkled with architect-designed houses where once only simple cottages stood. A highlight is **Connells Bay Sculpture Park** (guided tours, tel: 09-372 8957; www.connellsbay.co.nz), with an array of mesmerising sculptures in magnificent surroundings.

Chic cafés line the streets of the main settlement, **Oneroa**. The island's bus service is infrequent – it's tied to the ferry timetable – but taxis and rental cars are cheap and the walking is pleasant.

Waiheke has a burgeoning wine industry, too. And while it can be comfortably sampled in a day trip, if you decide to stay a while, you'll find accommodation to suit even the most extravagant of tastes.

Tiritiri Matangi Island ⓭, which must rank as one of New Zealand's greatest conservation success stories, makes for a lovely day trip from Auckland with **360 Discovery Cruises** (tel: 0800-360 3472; www.360discovery.co.nz; daily, departs 9am); guided tours are an option. Reclaimed from weeds and feral predators resulting from several centuries of settlement, it has been restored to a superb open wildlife sanctuary populated by many species of endangered New Zealand birdlife, including the Little spotted kiwi, *takahe* and Red-crowned parakeet *(kakariki)*.

Further to the north again, **Kawau Island** ⓮, 46km (29 miles) from Auckland, is a sleepy retreat ranged around a sheltered harbour popular with yachties. For those without a boat of their own, Kawau Water Taxis (tel: 0800-111 616; www.kawauwatertaxis.co.nz), located one hour's drive north of Auckland, provide transport. The stately **Mansion House** (tel: 09-422

8882; daily 11am–4pm), in the bay of the same name, was the country home of one of the early governors, Sir George Grey. It was he who introduced the wallaby, more commonly associated with Australia.

Those with more time to spend might set aside a couple of days to explore **Great Barrier Island** ⓯, the gulf's most remote outpost, 90km (56 miles) northeast of Auckland. This is truly another country, where the small permanent population lives without mains power; electricity is supplied by private generators or alternative sources. The 700 or so islanders, who refer to their home as 'the Barrier', are renowned as among the country's most reclusive; most live in Port Fitzroy on the southwest coast, the port of arrival for ferries from Auckland. There are some superb walks and beautiful beaches along the island's 30km (20-mile) length, and it is also popular for diving, fishing, surfing and camping. In addition to the regular ferries there are also sightseeing cruises and flights, although to drop in for an hour is rather to miss the point.

TIP

For more information on what to do on Great Barrier Island, phone the Great Barrier Information Line (tel: 09-429 0767; daily 8am–6pm) or visit www.greatbarrierisland.co.nz.

Great Barrier Island is known for its beautiful beaches.

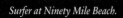
Surfer at Ninety Mile Beach.

NORTHLAND

Northland's picturesque charm makes it a dream for 'lifestylers', who grow their own food and yearn for semi-self-sufficiency; it's also an ideal holiday and retirement spot. But its dramatic beachscapes and vast open landscapes conceal a sometimes troublesome past.

Auckland
Wellington
Christchurch

Main Attractions
The Bay of Islands
Waitangi National Trust Treaty Grounds
Russell
Cape Reinga
Ninety Mile Beach
Waipoua Forest
Poor Knights Islands

Tribal warfare, bloody clashes between Maori and Pakeha, debauchery, insurrection, missionary zeal, a treaty of peace and promises – all are part of Northland's turbulent historical make-up. But today this subtropical side of New Zealand has much more to offer than its past. It is a friendly, welcoming place where you can relax and enjoy the sun, food, sights and distinctive, almost 'island', way of life. The irregular peninsula juts upwards some 450km (280 miles) from the farmlands north of Auckland to the rocky headlands of Cape Reinga, and is famed for its scenery, fine game fishing, unspoilt white-sand beaches and magnificent kauri forests.

The region is often labelled the winterless north because of its mild, damp winters and warm, humid summers. A distinctive feature is its pohutukawa trees, which in early summer rim the coast and decorate the hinterland with their bright red blossoms.

Bay of Islands

For those wanting to explore the region freely, **Paihia ❶**, a Bay of Islands township on the far northeast coast, is a good base to work from. It's a smooth and scenic 3½-hour (240km/150-mile) drive up SH1 from Auckland via the Northern Motorway and Northern Motorway Tollway.

Further on, the route becomes a single-lane road, travelling north through the small farming towns of Warkworth and Wellsford to **Waipu**, an excellent lunch stop. Take time to visit the **Waipu Museum** (tel: 09-432 0746; www.waipumuseum.com; daily 10am–4.30pm), one of New Zealand's best small museums, which highlights the extraordinary journey of the town's original Scottish settlers. Its gift shop is a treasure trove of New Zealand products. Those with a torch can explore the limestone formations

Kawakawa's famous toilets.

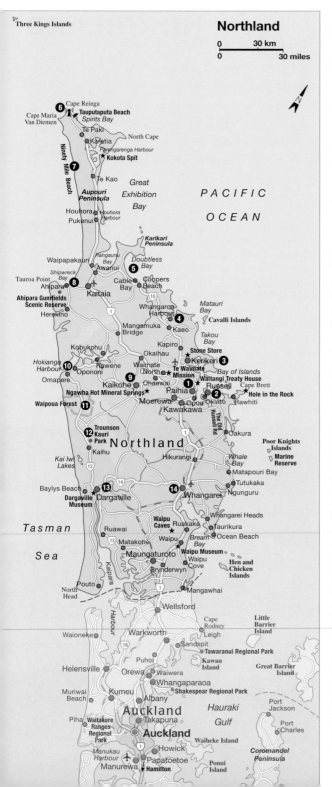

and glow-worms of Waipu Caves or spy upon endangered fairy terns at the Waipu Cove Wildlife Refuge on Johnson Point Road, en route to the beach itself – a popular place to picnic, swim and surf. From Waipu it's a further 40km (25 miles) up to Northland's largest city, Whangarei (see page 160).

Leave the main highway at **Kawakawa** – home to New Zealand's most interesting public toilets, a bizarre baroque confection designed by Austrian artist emigrant Frederick Hundertwasser – and snake around the harbour to the seaside resort of Paihia.

Paihia lies at the heart of the **Bay of Islands**, the cradle of New Zealand. The Bay's irregular 800km (500-mile) coastline, embracing 144 islands, is steeped in historical association as the site of the country's earliest European settlement.

Polynesian explorer Kupe is said to have visited the bay in the 10th century, followed by another canoe voyager, Toi, some 200 years later. Captain James Cook discovered the harbour for Europeans in 1769. Impressed, he gave the sheltered waters of the bay their current name. In the scattered group are eight larger islands and numerous islets; the largest measures 22 hectares (54 acres). Many are uninhabited; some are privately owned; others are reserves. The region's small permanent population is multiplied during the traditional New Zealand summer holiday period, from Christmas to late January, when thousands of Kiwis head north to camp, boat, swim, fish and relax. A visit during this period requires accommodation reservations well in advance.

Since the 1950s, Paihia has been revamped to meet the challenge of tourism. Modern hotels surround a neat, expanded shopping centre, with a good variety of eating places and modest nightlife. The wharf, its focal point, caters for island cruises and fishing trips around the bay. Places of historical note are marked with bronze plaques along the sandy seafront. It is also a town of many firsts: New Zealand's oldest Norfolk pine stands here; a mission station was created on the town site in 1823, and missionaries built and launched the country's first ship, the *Herald*, here in 1826; and from the first printing press, brought from England in 1834, was published the first Bible in Maori. Paihia's colonial history is very obviously etched in the town's graveyard.

Waitangi Treaty House

The most significant act in New Zealand's early history took place on the lawn of the **Waitangi Treaty House**, set in the Waitangi Reserve about 2km (1¼ miles) north of Paihia across a one-way bridge that also leads to the Waitangi golf course. The house is now part of the **Waitangi National Trust Treaty Grounds** (tel: 09-402 7437; www.waitangi.net.nz; daily 9am–5pm, until 7pm Dec–Mar; cultural performances at 11am, 1pm, 3pm). The nightly cultural show (www.culturenorth.co.nz), which is held at dusk, explores the history of the Bay of Islands and is well worth seeing.

On 6 February 1840, with Governor William Hobson signing on behalf of Queen Victoria, Maori chiefs and English gentlemen agreed to end Maori–Pakeha conflict, guarantee the Maori land rights, give them and the colonists Crown protection and admit New Zealand to the British Empire. At the time of the signing, the house was the home of James Busby, British Resident in New Zealand from 1832 to 1840.

The gracious colonial dwelling, with its commanding views of the bay, later fell into disrepair. It has since been restored, and today the Treaty House is a national museum. Also worth visiting is the adjacent Maori meeting house, or *whare runanga*, where one of the world's largest war canoes, the impressive 35-metre (115ft) *Ngatokimatawhaorua*, is proudly displayed.

Russell – former Sin City

Runaway sailors, escaped convicts, lusty whalers, promiscuous women,

TIP

Russell is something of an epicurean hotspot and a haven for chefs of renown, who create culinary masterpieces with the pick of the Bay of Islands' legendary produce.

The Waitangi Treaty House.

brawlers and drunks: **Russell ❷**, 15km (9 miles) northeast of Paihia, formerly known as Kororareka and dubbed 'hell-hole of the Pacific', has seen them all. Russell is easy to get to as it's linked by a regular foot-passenger ferry service from Paihia. A vehicular ferry also travels between the port of **Opua**, 9km (6 miles) south of Paihia, and **Okiato** near Russell.

Colonists first arrived in 1809, making Russell New Zealand's first white settlement. Today it's small, quiet and peaceful, though things liven up at Christmas and New Year with the influx of boaties and other visitors.

The town was briefly New Zealand's capital, and in the early 1830s lust and lawlessness prevailed, with up to 30 grog shops operating on the tiny waterfront. Shocked early settlers responded by building **Christ Church**, at the corner of Robertson and Beresford streets, two blocks east of the harbour, in 1835. It is New Zealand's oldest surviving church; its bullet-holed walls are grim reminders of the siege that took place in 1845.

FISHING IN THE BAY OF ISLANDS

Deep-sea fishing for some of the world's biggest game fish is a major lure in the Bay of Islands. The main fishing season is from December to June, when the huge marlin are running. Many world records for marlin, shark and tuna have been set here. Yellowtail kingfish, running on until September, provide good sport on light rods. Snapper, one of New Zealand's favourite table fish, is also plentiful.

Fighting fish up to 400kg (880lbs) are caught in the bay, the majority are tagged and released, but those that are weighed-in attract appreciative crowds. At the end of the day listen out for the low tolling of a bell; this signals that a large fish has been caught and is being weighed on the wharf. Competitions for line-fishing and surf-casting are frequently held, and, despite the 'seasons', fishing is a year-round sport here. Charter boats are available at Paihia or Russell for half- or full-day hire, and on a share basis. But a more laid-back fishing experience is also possible. The towns' numerous small wharves are seldom without at least one small-scale angler hopefully dangling a line in the water.

The bay is also popular as a sea-kayaking destination, with its numerous sandy coves within short reach of each other. In the summer months the waters become crowded with Northland yachties; other yachts are sailed by their owners up from Auckland for a holiday on the water.

Maori chief Hone Heke, who signed the Treaty of Waitangi in 1840, later became discontented over government land dealings when the promised financial rewards did not materialise. In 1845, he defiantly chopped down the British flagstaff, symbol of the new regime, on Maiki Hill at the northern end of the beach. Meanwhile, Chief Kawiti, an ally of Heke, burnt and sacked Church property. A showdown duly took place in 1846 near Kawakawa, at Kawiti's *pa*, Ruapekapeka. A strong Redcoat force captured this formidable fortress, somewhat unfairly on a Sunday when the converted Maori were busy worshipping their new Christian God. Heke was eventually pardoned and his men freed.

Pompallier (tel: 09-403 9015; www.pompallier.co.nz; daily Nov–Apr 10am–5pm, May–Oct 10am–4pm) is housed in the sole surviving building of the French Catholic missionaries, who erected it in 1842 to serve as their printing press. Today, extensively restored as a working museum, its original printing press, bookbindery and tanning pits reproduce the Roman Catholic books in the Maori language, which were printed here in the 1840s. **Russell Museum** (tel: 09-403 7701; www.russellmuseum.org.nz; daily Feb–Dec 10am–4pm, Jan until 5pm), one block east on York Street, provides an excellent account of the Battle of Kororareka, whaling, game fishing, and early Maori and European history. The **Duke of Marlborough Hotel** (tel: 09-403 7829; www.theduke.co.nz), one of the country's oldest, is a pub of great character dishing up steaming plates of seafood chowder, local Orongo Bay oysters, and freshly caught fish and chips.

The Old Russell Road

There is an alternative route to Russell, turning off to the coast 17km (11 miles) north of Whangarei. Known as the Old Russell Road, along the way there is a lot to linger over, including **Mimiwhangata**, an 800-hectare (2,000-acre) Coastal Farm Park under marine conservation offering excellent snorkelling and diving. Birdwatchers will be enthralled by the local populations of NZ dotterel, Pied stilt and oystercatcher, and 30 or so kiwis also make their home here.

Oakura was once the site of 10 Maori *pa*, and the pretty horseshoe of Bland Bay is anything but insipid, with deep-blue waters, Department of Conservation parklands, numerous hikes, and a myriad of scattered islands. **Rawhiti** is the starting point for the **Cape Brett Walkway**, a hilly, seven-hour one-way hike, with a DOC hut at the end where hikers can camp overnight, or the option to catch a water taxi to Paihia. A slightly less strenuous option is the three-hour return hike to the ruins of an old whaling station in the **Whangamumu Scenic Reserve**.

The Old Russell Road continues through scenic Parekura Bay, past rows of oysters at Orongo Bay to Russell.

Trips on the bay

The true beauty of the islands in the bay can best be appreciated on one of the daily 'Cream Trips' operated by **Fullers** (www.fboi.co.nz) from both Paihia (Marsden Road; tel: 09-402 7422) and Russell (Cass Street; tel: 09-403 7866). These seven-hour boat trips retrace the voyages of bygone days when cream was regularly collected from island farms. Mail and provisions are still handled this way today. The Fullers cruise covers about 96km (60 miles), and passengers can see the island where Captain Cook first anchored on his 1769 voyage; the cove where French explorer Marion du Fresne, along with his 25 crew members, was slain by Maori in 1772; and the bays where the earliest missionaries landed.

Fullers also offers a shorter four-hour cruise to the Cape Brett lighthouse and Piercy Island, and, weather permitting, the boat passes right through the famous **Hole in the Rock** at the end of Cape Brett. For a bit more of a thrill, try the Mac Attack (tel: 09 402 8280; www.macattack.co.nz),

Russell wharf.

a 90-minute blast to the Hole in the Rock and Cathedral Cave and back in a powerful catamaran with a top speed of 100kmh (62mph).

With its remarkably clear waters, the Bay of Islands is also a diving paradise. By world standards, top-quality diving is cheap and accessible, with numerous reliable commercial operators (see Travel Tips, page 365).

Kerikeri and surroundings

The next major stop in Northland is **Kerikeri ❸**. Located 23km (14 miles) north of Paihia, beside a pretty inlet, it is a township of unusual interest and character, which has a rich backdrop of early Maori and European colonial history. Here, missionary Samuel Marsden planted the country's first vineyard in 1819. Today, much of New Zealand's finest citrus and subtropical fruits, including avocados, are grown on Kerikeri's fertile volcanic soils.

The township and its immediate environs, with a population of 5,000, form a thriving centre for handicrafts and cottage industries. The climate and relaxed lifestyle have attracted many creative residents, along with wealthy retirees from other New Zealand centres. Two vineyards and a plethora of quality restaurants do nothing to discourage new residents. The oldest surviving European building in the country, **Mission House**, formerly **Kemp House** (tel: 09-407 9236; www.historic.org.nz; daily May–Oct 10am–4pm, Nov–Apr until 5pm; tours on the hour), is on Kerikeri Road, 1km (½ mile) to the east of the township. It was built in 1822 of pit-sawn kauri and totara. The **Stone Store** (tel: 09-407 9236; daily May–Oct 10am–4pm, Nov–Apr until 5pm; free) next door, completed in 1836 to house New Zealand mission supplies, is the country's oldest standing European stone building. It still serves as a shop and has a museum upstairs (charge).

Just to the northeast, the site of **Kororipa Pa** should not be overlooked. This was celebrated warrior chief Hongi Hika's forward army base between 1780 and 1826. Maori warriors were assembled here before launching raids on tribes throughout North Island. It can be reached via a short walkway. For a longer hike, take the path upriver (beginning beside Kemp House) to the impressive cascade of Rainbow Falls.

Across the river from the Stone Store on Mission Road is The Parrot Place (tel: 09-407 6454; www.theparrotplace.co.nz; daily 10am–5pm), subtropical gardens filled with a huge variety of native and exotic parrots from around the world, including the New Zealand kakariki and the endangered Antipodes Parrot.

Around 15km (9 miles) southwest of Kerikeri is **Waimate North**, New Zealand's first inland settlement for white people. Built in 1831–2, the **Te Waimate Mission House** (tel: 09-405 9734; www.historicplaces.org.nz; Nov–Apr daily 10am–5pm, May–Oct Mon–Sat 10am–4pm) in Waimate North was the home of Bishop George Augustus Selwyn, New Zealand's first Anglican bishop.

Cape Brett.

North to Cape Reinga

In Maori mythology, Cape Reinga is where the spirits of the dead depart on their homeward journey to the ancestral land of Hawaiki. Coach tours now make their way up this legendary flight path, along the Aupouri Peninsula to its northernmost point, and return via Ninety Mile Beach. As tourist hire cars frequently get trapped on the sands of Ninety Mile Beach (mainly due to the drivers' lack of experience at driving on sand), coaches and four-wheel drive vehicles, which leave from Paihia, Kerikeri, Kaitaia and other Far North towns daily, are the best option if you wish to travel one-way via the beach. The east-coast (SH1) route traverses the worked-out gum fields of the Far North, a relic of the huge kauri forests that once covered this region. The dead trees left pockets of gum in the soil, which early settlers found to be a valuable export, used to make fine varnish. So valuable, in fact, that it triggered a 'gum rush' – by the 1880s, more than 2,000 men were digging up a fortune.

In **Whangaroa Harbour** ❹, a deep-sea fishing base 25km (16 miles) north of Kerikeri, lies the wreck of the *Boyd*. The ship called in for kauri spars in 1809 and sent a party of 11 ashore. However, the group was murdered by the local Maori inhabitants, who donned the victims' clothes, rowed back to the vessel and massacred the rest of the crew, then set fire to the ship. Reliably serene now, Whangaroa is another popular destination for yacht cruises (tel: 09 405 1663; www.snowcloud.co.nz) to the Cavalli Islands and sea kayaking.

About 24km (15 miles) further is **Doubtless Bay** ❺, named by Cook, with its string of gently sloping sandy beaches, including **Coopers Beach**, lined with pohutukawa trees, and **Cable Bay**, with its peach-coloured sands and an array of pretty shells. Accommodation and places to eat are available at both beaches, and at the nearby and picturesque fishing village of Mangonui.

At **Awanui**, the Aupouri Peninsula begins and the road passes through **Pukenui**, **Houhora** and **Te Kao**, to

Hokianga Harbour.

TIP

Ancient kauri is the oldest timber on earth, retrieved from swamps and dating back 30,000–50,000 years. At the Ancient Kauri Kingdom (tel: 09-406 7172; www. ancientkauri.co.nz) on State Highway 1 at Awanui, 8km (5 miles) north of Kaitaia, it is turned into beautiful craft pieces.

Cape Reinga with its lighthouse. The whole district is rich in Maori folklore. At **Cape Reinga ❻** itself, 130km (80 miles) north of Doubtless Bay at the tip of the **Aupouri Peninsula**, a gnarled pohutukawa, at least 800 years old, grows out of the rocks at the foot of the cape. Spirits are said to slide down its roots into the sea to begin their journey to the underworld. Views from the cape, where the lone lighthouse stands guard, are impressive.

You can see the turbulent merging line of the Pacific Ocean and Tasman Sea, the **Three Kings Islands**, 57km (35 miles) offshore, neighbouring capes, including Cape Maria Van Diemen, and numerous secluded beaches. Steep trails lead down to several of these, including Te Werahi and Twilight Beach. Alternatively, take the road to Tauputaputa Beach, perfect for picnicking. The Te Paki sand dunes provide the perfect setting for sand surfing, and boards can be hired from Ahikaa Adventures (www.ahikaa-adventures.co.nz), which operates from a truck parked on site. For the complete sea-and-sand experience, join a kayaking tour at Karatia and paddle across the **Parengarenga Harbour** to the striking headland and sun-bleached dunes of **Kokota Spit** at the harbour mouth. This is the last landfall for migratory godwits flying across the planet to the Arctic.

Ninety Mile Beach

Ninety Mile Beach ❼, south of Cape Reinga and running along the western side of the Aupouri Peninsula, is actually 60 miles (96km) long (there are numerous explanations for this quirk, the most plausible being an early mapping error). It is lined with tall dunes and hillocks of shell and flanked by the Aupouri Forest, populated by bands of wild horses of thoroughbred stature. The route back to Paihia is via the service hub of **Kaitaia**, New Zealand's northernmost town, the gateway to the seaside settlement of **Ahipara ❽**. Located at the southernmost end of Ninety Mile Beach, surfers come from all over the world to ply the waves here and at adjacent **Shipwreck Bay**.

Behind Shipwreck Bay is the **Ahipara Gumfields Scenic Reserve**, a ghostly and fascinating wilderness area where prospectors once excavated kauri gum from the sand. Hike or join a Tuatua Tours quad-bike adventure (tel: 0800-494 288; www.tuatuatours.co.nz) to explore the reserve and **Tauroa Point**, where there is an intriguing cluster of shanties with no running water and no power, used by transient seaweed-gatherers.

The west coast

From Ahipara, a more interesting west-coast route leads back to Auckland either via **Herekino** and **Kohukohu**, crossing the Hokianga Harbour by vehicular ferry, or via **Kaikohe ❾**, 150km (93 miles) south of Cape Reinga, where a hilltop monument to Chief Hone Heke offers tremendous views of both coasts. Nearby are **Ngawha Hot Mineral Springs** (tel:

Sand-surfing on Ninety Mile Beach.

09-405 2245; daily 9am–9pm), with tempting mineral-rich waters for a refreshing soak. From here it is a 40km (25-mile) drive west to **Hokianga Harbour** , a long sheltered harbour with a score of ragged inlets that keep the place quiet, serene and rural. At Horeke, a tiny hamlet where houses and the pub overhang the water line, is the Wairere Boulders Nature Park (RD1, Okaihau; tel: 09-401 9935; www. wairereboulders.co.nz), an amazing collection of fluted basalt boulders that seem to flow down the valley like a stream. Felix and Rita Schaad rediscovered the boulders in the mid-1980s – they'd been lost to the bush for 100 years or more. After extensive research they located photographs of the boulders taken in 1873 by photographer, D.L. Mundy. The couple were keen for others to enjoy the boulders and so, after much hard work, opened an extensive network of tracks. Volcanic in origin, the boulders are truly remarkable and it's a great place to stop and stretch your legs.

If you're following the west-coast route south via **Herekino** and **Kohukohu**, you **will find the latter township is** stamped with the architecture of the early 1900s, when it was a thriving timber town. Take time to wander its streets, visit the wharf, the country's oldest stone bridge and the Village Arts Gallery (tel: 09-405 5827; www.villagearts.co.nz; daily 10am–4pm), and peer through abandoned cannon from the *Boyd*, before catching the vehicular ferry to **Rawene**, the gateway to northern Hokianga.

Rawene perches at the tip of the peninsula with many of its buildings hanging over the waterline, their foundation posts buried firmly in the sand. The village is home to some noteworthy buildings: the old courthouse and gaol, the Masonic Hotel, Clendon House, The Ferry House and several old churches. The police station is also of note, for it was here in 1898 that the Mahurehure *hapu* of the Ngapuhi refused to pay the small fee required

for licensing the ownership of a dog, marking New Zealand's last armed conflict. Refreshments are best taken at the Boatshed, a picturesque café overhanging the harbour.

Further towards the harbour mouth, the tiny seaside resort of **Opononi** briefly became world-famous in the summer of 1955–6, when a young dolphin began frolicking with swimmers at the beach. When 'Opo' the dolphin died in somewhat mysterious circumstances, the nation mourned. She is remembered in a song and a monument.

The road then heads south through the **Waipoua Forest** , with its 2,500 hectares (6,200 acres) of mature kauri trees, the largest stand of kauri left in the country. New Zealand's largest living kauri tree, Tane Mahuta (Lord of the Forest), is around 2,000 years old and is located a five-minute walk away from the car park. Its mighty girth spans 13.8 metres (45ft), yet this colossal kauri has fragile and easily bruised roots, and a well-formed wheelchair-friendly boardwalk has been constructed to protect them.

Waipoua Forest, home to the most extensive stands of kauri trees in the country.

Waipoua Forest offers several other excellent walks. The road to the DOC Visitor Centre follows a pretty stream with picturesque picnic spots and gas BBQs on its banks.

Further south at **Trounson Kauri Park** ⓬ near-perfect growing conditions for large kauri are found, and a 40-minute loop track meanders among thick native bush dominated by the magnificent trees, as well as kauri grass, taraire, kiekie, neinei and ferns.

Dargaville ⓭, 90km (56 miles) south of Hokianga Harbour, was founded on the timber and kauri gum trade. In Harding Park, **Dargaville Museum** (tel: 09-439 7555; www.dargavillemuseum. co.nz; daily 9am–5pm) is built of clay bricks brought in from China as ship's ballast and is full of memorabilia from this stretch of coast, including shipwreck artefacts and Maori carvings. There is also a display of the environmental vessel *Rainbow Warrior*, which was bombed by French agents in Auckland Harbour in 1985. It was scuttled near Kerikeri in 1987 and is now an artificial reef, teeming with marine life and popular with divers.

Clapham's National Clock Museum, the national chronometer display at Whangarei.

Whangarei and the Poor Knights Islands

From Dargaville, State Highway 14 leads east to **Whangarei** ⓮, a deep-sea port with a picturesque harbour and an industrial presence – the town is home to a glassworks, cement plant and an oil refinery. The Town Basin area on the waterfront, where international yachties moor their vessels, draws visitors from far and wide to dine at its wharf-side cafés and peruse its boutique stores. Also a hub for talented Northland artisans, its galleries and studios offer something for every taste. Watch as molten glass is transformed into delicately blown vases at Burning Issues Gallery, and take a step back in time at **Clapham's National Clock Museum** (tel: 09-438 3993; www. claphamsclocks.co.nz; daily 9am–5pm). Here you can see the largest collection of clocks and music boxes in the Southern Hemisphere, featuring clocks dating back to the 17th century. The historic Reyburn House Art Gallery is at the Town Basin inside Whangarei's oldest existing early settler's home, while the Whangarei Art Museum,

located within the Hub at the i-site information centre, has an extensive collection of early NZ colonial art as well as contemporary Maori art.

For panoramic views of the city and harbour visit Mount Parihaka or take the scenic drive to **Whangarei Heads** and hike up Mount Manaia for excellent views of **Bream Bay** and the **Hen and Chicken Islands**. Terenga Paraoa Tours (tel: 09-430 3083; daily 9.30am) depart from the i-site visitor centre at the Town Basin and take in some of the city's famous sites, including the sacred Parihaka Pa and the legendary Paranui Valley. Visit the Whangarei Falls, plunging 25 metres (82ft) into a deep, bush-fringed pool, hike through the AH Reed Kauri Park filled with 500-year-old kauri trees and a cascading waterfall, or take kids to befriend Sparky the one-legged kiwi at the **Native Bird Recovery Centre** (SH14, Maunu; tel: 09-438 1457; www.nbr.org.nz; daily 9am–5pm; donation). There are plenty of hotels and restaurants in the city, as well as safe swimming beaches.

The road out to the **Tutukaka** coast offers some real gems, including the orchards of Huanui, and the quaint village of Ngunguru, once a busy port and now devoted to recreational water sports, with great fishing, a boat ramp, ski lane, and picnic tables for enjoying takeaways alfresco overlooking the water.

The bustling nautical township of Tutukaka is the gateway to the **Poor Knights Islands** and some of the best diving, snorkelling and game fishing in the world. The islands stand alongside a spectacular marine reserve, and are also home to the world's largest sea cave, **Riko Riko**, a mammoth watery cavern covered from top to toe with lichen and moss. It's worth taking a speedboat tour across the water to experience its amazing acoustics and colourful parades of fish.

Further up the coast a horseshoe of holiday homes encircle **Matapouri Bay**, while Woolley's Bay and Sandy Bay are popular for swimming and surfing. A 20-minute hike through groves of ancient puriri trees and kowhai brings you to the isolated cove of **Whale Bay**, where pohutukawa trees overhang the sands.

Whangarei Falls.

Abseiling into the magical 'Lost World' cave at Waitomo.

THE WAIKATO

Dairy production and agriculture flourish in these rich, fertile lands south of Auckland, lands which also have a wealth of historical artefacts and cultural traditions.

The central and western region of the North Island is one of New Zealand's great agricultural areas. Grass grows quickly here, and the free-grazing dairy herds that crop these fertile plains daily have brought prosperity to generations. The grass is fed by a mild, wet climate. On the flats – the area has more flat arable land than anywhere else in the North Island – farm diversification has expanded the production of fruit and vegetables. The Waikato is also thoroughbred horse-breeding country, and dairy cattle studs abound.

Much of the now-green pastures were the spoils of land wars between Maori and Pakeha in the 1860s. The Waikato was once relatively well populated by Maori tribes and its land communally owned, according to ancestry. This was a landscape of dense bush on the hills, with peat swamp and *kahikatea* (white pine) forests covering the extensive areas of flat land and the low hills of the Waikato and Waipa river systems.

The New Zealand Wars changed everything; it took nearly 20 years for the British and colonial forces to subdue Maori tribes who were intent on keeping what was left of their land. What land was not confiscated by the government was effectively taken through the 1862 legislation which forced the traditional Maori group ownership to be individualised. Single

owners were easy prey for land agents, and the way was opened for the gradual taming, during the early 20th century, of the natural wilderness into the intensively farmed land it is today.

Capital of the Waikato

Hamilton ❶, New Zealand's fourth-largest city, lies 136km (85 miles) south of Auckland on the banks of the **Waikato River**, New Zealand's longest waterway. Known to the Maori as Kirikiriroa, the city was renamed by Europeans after Captain Fane Charles

The Waikato is one of New Zealand's most productive agricultural areas.

TIP

To experience the real pulse of Hamilton, walk beside the river following the city's new 11km (7-mile) walkway and cycle path. It meanders along both banks of the river and runs right through the centre of Hamilton.

Hamilton Gardens.

Hamilton of the HMS *Esk*, who was killed at the Battle of Gate Pa, near Tauranga, in 1864.

It was the Waikato River, long a vital Maori transport and trading link to the coast, that first brought the Europeans to the area and led to the establishment of Hamilton in the 1860s. The first businesses grew on the riverbank, and today the commercial hub of the city runs parallel to it on the west bank.

The city centre's most notable riverbank attraction is the **Waikato Museum** (tel: 07-838 6606; www.waikato museum.org.nz; daily 10am–4.30pm; free), at the southern end of the main thoroughfare, on the corner of Victoria and Grantham streets. Of particular note in its collection of fine arts, ethnography and Waikato history are 15,000 Tainui (Waikato's Maori tribe) artefacts, including wood and stone carvings, woven flax garments and tribal items. National and international touring exhibitions are a regular feature, but permanent displays worth noting are a magnificent war canoe and a contemporary Tainui carving and weaving commissioned for the museum's opening in 1987. Located within the complex is the **Exscite Centre** (tel: 07-838 6606; www. exscite.org.nz), an interactive science and technology centre which boasts among its delights an earthquake simulator.

Just south of the city centre on SH1 are the 58-hectare (143-acre) **Hamilton Gardens** (tel: 07-838 6782; www. hamiltongardens.co.nz; daily 7.30am– 5.30pm, until 8pm Nov–Mar; free). Organised by various themes, including a tranquil Japanese garden and an Indian Char garden, these grounds are the city's most popular attraction.

The Waikato River is now a recreational asset for the region but it is also of primary importance for the power stations, which harness the waters to provide one-third of the nation's hydroelectric power. Behind each dam there are artificial lakes, popular spots for fishing, boating and rowing.

Maori stronghold

On the Waikato River north of Hamilton is **Ngaruawahia** ➋, the hub of the Maori King Movement (see page 41) and an important Maori cultural centre. On the east riverbank

is the **Turangawaewae Marae**, its name meaning 'a place to put one's feet'. It contains a traditionally carved meeting house and a modern concert hall, and is open to the public on special occasions. The **Waingaro Hot Springs** (tel: 07-825 4761; www.waingarohotsprings.co.nz; daily 9am–9.30pm) are 24km (15 miles) west of Ngaruawahia en route to **Raglan**.

Mount Taupiri, 6km (4 miles) downstream from Ngaruawahia, is the sacred burial ground of the Waikato tribes, with graves sprawling over the hill alongside the motorway. Nearby, the Waikato's waters are used to cool a massive coal-and-gas-fired power station at **Huntly**. Its two 150-metre (500ft) chimneys tower over the town.

Cambridge

The bucolic town of **Cambridge ❸** also sits on the Waikato River, 24km (15 miles) southeast of Hamilton. The charming **St Andrew's Anglican Church**, tree-lined streets and village green give it a very English atmosphere. Cambridge is the renowned heart of the local equine industry. This is celebrated in mosaic tiles in the town centre, where local legends such as Zabeel, Sir Tristram and Empire Rose are commemorated, along with famous locally raised Olympians, including cyclist Sarah Ulmer and rowers Georgina and Caroline Evers-Swindell. Cambridge is well known for its boutique shopping; authentic New Zealand souvenirs can be purchased from Cambridge Country Store (www.cambridgecountrystore.co.nz) at 92 Victoria Street. It is also the location of **New Zealand Horse Magic** (tel: 07-827 8118; www.cambridgelodge.co.nz; Mon–Fri 10am–2pm, bookings essential), 6km (4 miles) south of Cambridge on SH1. Tours of this horse stud showcase a huge variety of horse breeds, including the New Zealand wild horse and the Kaimaniwa, as well as famous New Zealand racehorses such as Rough Habit and Christopher Vance. Visitors can ride a horse at the conclusion of a tour.

Provincial towns

To the east of the river are the Waikato towns of Morrinsville, Te Aroha and

Maori carvings at Turangawaewae Marae. The complex is open to the public on special occasions.

Kayaking on the Waikato River.

Mangapu Cave in the amazing Waitomo subterranean complex.

Sunrise over a Waikato paddock. The area around Cambridge is a prime horse-breeding area.

Matamata. **Matamata** ❹ is well known for its thoroughbred race-horse stables. A three-storey block-house built by an early landowner, Josiah Clifton Firth, in 1881, stands as a reminder of the settlers' insecurity after the Land Wars with the Maori. It's now part of the **Firth Tower Historical Museum** (tel: 07-888 8369; www.firthtower.co.nz; Thu–Mon 10am–4pm; free entry to grounds only), an entertaining interactive experience for families, sited on the Firth family homestead built in 1902.

Nearby, several walking tracks lead into and over the **Kaimai-Mamaku Forest Park**, including one to the pictur-esque **Wairere Falls**. Fans of *The Lord of the Rings* will enjoy a visit to **Hobbiton** (tel: 07-888 9913; www.hobbitontours.com; daily tours at 9.50am, 11.05am, 12.20pm, 1.35pm, 2.50pm, 4.05pm, 5.20pm) at 501 Buckland Road, Hinuera, about 15 minutes out of town, where part of Peter Jackson's latest movie, *The Hobbit,* was filmed and many of the set pieces are now permanent features on the land-scape. For more on *The Lord of the Rings* film locations, see page 82.

Morrinsville is a centre for the surrounding dairy land, with its own large processing factory, while **Te Aroha** ❺, on the Waihou River, was once a gold town and fashionable Victorian spa sitting at the foot of 952-metre (3,123ft) bush-clad **Mount Te Aroha**. The world's only known hot soda-water fountain, the **Mokena Geyser**, is here in the **Hot Springs Domain**, the 18-hectare (44-acre) thermal reserve that is the heart of the town's spa fame. The geyser erupts at 30–40-minute intervals, gushing at its highest to a modest 4 metres (13ft), while an elaborate piece of plumbing allows visitors to sample its allegedly health-giving waters down in the town itself. The **Te Aroha Mineral Spa** (tel: 07-884 8717; www.tearohamineralspas. co.nz; daily 10.30am–9pm, until 10pm Fri–Sun) features public and private pools – some in original 19th-century bathhouses – whose mineral waters are reputed to be good for aches and pains.

Southwest of Hamilton, heading towards Waitomo, is **Te Awamutu** ❻, which has been dubbed 'the rose town' for its gardens and rose shows.

One of the country's oldest and finest churches, **St John's Anglican Church**, built in 1854, stands in the main street. Another, St Paul's, built in 1856, lies to the east in Hairini.

The **Te Awamutu Museum** (tel: 07-872 0085; www.tamuseum.org.nz; Mon–Fri 10am–4pm, Sat 10am–1pm, Sun 1–4pm; donation) houses, alongside numerous important Maori treasures, a permanent exhibition entitled 'True Colours', dedicated to the history of local-boys-made-good the Finn brothers, of the rock band Split Enz.

Waitomo Caves

In the northern part of King Country, so named for its connections with the Maori King Movement, is **Waitomo**. It is famous for its caves and glow-worm grottoes, such as the sublime **Waitomo Glow-Worm Caves** ❼ (tel: 07-878 8228; www.waitomo.com; daily Apr–Nov 9am–5pm, Dec–Mar 9am–6.30pm, tours depart every half-hour).

Waitomo is also a hotbed for blackwater rafting, which is underground and in the dark. One of the most reliable operators is **Waitomo Adventures** (tel: 07-878 7788; www.waitomo.co.nz), which offers a two-hour black-water journey as well as various permutations of abseiling down underground holes and waterfalls, and a seven-hour Lost World adventure where participants abseil in and walk, swim and climb out. The same company also leads tours through the spectacular St Benedicts Caverns, discovered only in 1962 and long inaccessible to all but speleological specialists.

Before a visit to the caves, stop by the **Waitomo Caves Discovery Centre** (tel: 07-878 7640; www.waitomodiscovery.co.nz; daily 8.45am–5.30pm, Jan–Mar 8.15am–7pm), beside Waitomo Village's visitor centre. It has informative displays on the geography and history of the caves.

At **Te Kuiti**, 19km (12 miles) to the south, charismatic Maori leader Te Kooti Rikirangi took refuge from the British in 1864 and built a carved meeting house, later given to the local Maniapoto people as a gesture of thanks for their protection. Some 32km (20 miles) to the west of Waitomo are the thundering **Marokopa Falls**, a 10-minute walk from the main Te Anga Road.

Waitomo glow-worm.

WAITOMO WONDERS

The glow-worms of Waitomo Glow-Worm Caves are a truly stellar sight. Stairs lead down to the 14-metre (46ft) high Cathedral, adorned with stalactites and stalagmites on every conceivable surface, formed by the action of water on limestone over hundreds of thousands of years. It's incredible, but the highlight comes at the end: an awe-inspiring boat ride through enormous caverns, by the radiant light of millions of tiny glow-worms. These caves were long known to Maori; the first Pakeha to visit them was surveyor Fred Mace in 1887. Today three caves are open to the public – the Glow-Worm Cave, Ruakuri and Aranui – plus the self-guided Piripiri Cave located a 30-minute drive away, and best explored with a torch and solid footwear, as the ground is both slippery and steep.

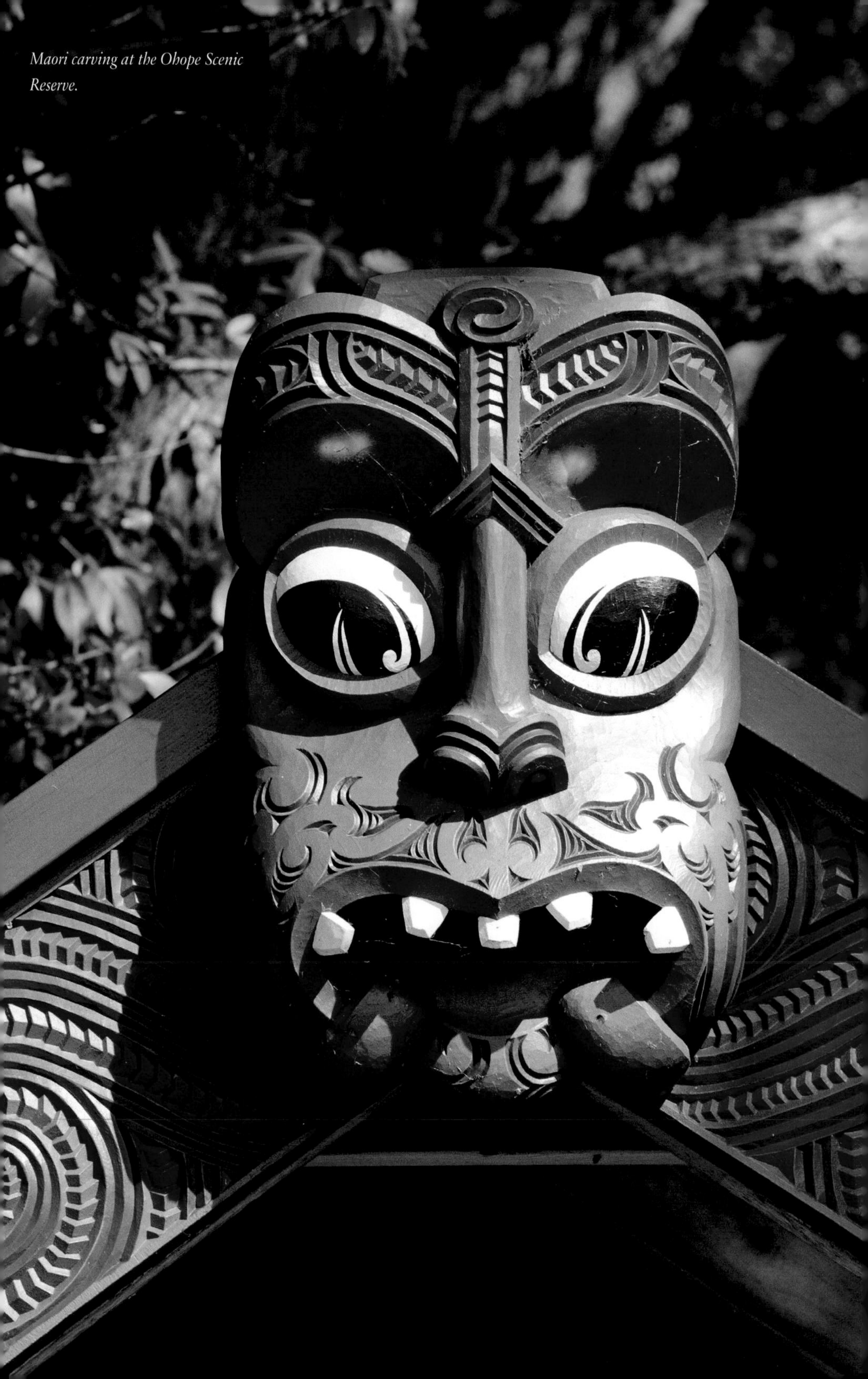

Maori carving at the Ohope Scenic Reserve.

COROMANDEL AND THE BAY OF PLENTY

This northeastern area is a place where the great outdoors comes to life in the form of camping, tramping and boating. The less energetic can laze at any number of glorious beaches.

The popular phrase 'Coromandel: Mine Today, Gone Tomorrow!' reflects the strong feelings of its inhabitants that the region's greatest asset is not its abundant mineral wealth but its natural attractions. The region once yielded abundant treasures, and early European settlers who flocked here were gold-seekers and bushmen. Reminders of these earlier bonanzas abound, with colonial buildings, old gold-mine shafts and the like. Today, people flock to the area for a less material and much more accessible treasure: activities in the great outdoors, including diving, fishing, boating, swimming, camping, tramping and fossicking for gemstones.

Thames and environs

At the base of the **Coromandel Peninsula, Thames ❽** was officially declared a goldfield in August 1867. The ensuing gold rush swelled the town's population to 18,000 at its peak, and there were more than 100 hotels. Today there are just four, the oldest-standing being the **Brian Boru Hotel** (1868) on the corner of Pollen and Richmond streets, at the southern end of town.

To appreciate Thames's past, one should head further north to the **Mineralogical Museum** and adjacent **School of Mines** (tel: 07-868 6227; Wed–Sun 11am–3pm, daily during Jan) on Cochrane Street. This was one of 30 schools of mines around the country that used to provide practical instruction to a burgeoning population of miners. Around 500 metres (1,640ft) to the northeast on Tararu Road is **Goldmine Experience** (tel: 07-868 8514; www.goldmine-experience. co.nz; Dec–Feb daily 10am–4pm, Mar–Nov Sat–Sun 10am–1pm), an old gold mine now turned into a tourist attraction, where members of the Hauraki Prospectors' Association demonstrate the technology used to retrieve gold.

Main Attractions

Driving Creek Railway
Hahei and Cathedral Cove
Hot Water Beach
Waihi Arts Centre and Museum
Mount Maunganui
White Island

Cyclists race at Mount Maunganui.

In Waihi, a bronze statue of a Maori warrior stands beside a Cornish pumphouse, a relic of Martha Hill Mine, which was once the richest gold mine in New Zealand. The pumphouse was based on a design used in tin mines in Cornwall, England.

Kauaeranga Valley is the site of the **Department of Conservation Visitors Centre** (tel: 07-867 9080), 10km (6 miles) northeast of Thames. The first kauri spars were logged here in 1795, mainly for the use of the Royal Navy. By 1830, kauri trees were being cut in greater numbers, and the decimation of the forests was to continue for a century. Late in the 1800s, huge kauri timber dams were built across creeks on the peninsula to bank up water and then float the logs to sea. About 300 such dams were constructed, more than 60 of them in the Kauaeranga Valley. Many are still there, slowly disintegrating. Today the valley is a favourite spot for camping and tramping, and visitors have plenty of access to the wilderness along more than 50km (30 miles) of tracks.

Coromandel and surroundings

From Thames, follow the winding route north along the **Firth of Thames** up the west coast of the Coromandel Peninsula. The views across the water to Auckland in the far distance are spectacular. **Tapu**, 19km (12 miles)

north of Thames, is the junction for the **Tapu–Coroglen Road**, a scenic route climbing to 448 metres (1,470ft) above sea level. The **Rapaura Watergardens** (tel: 07-868 4821; www.rapaurawatergardens.co.nz; daily 9am–5pm), 7km (4 miles) along this road, feature gentle walks, abundant native flora, lily ponds, bridges, streams, a waterfall and sculptures of *punga* (a native fern), as well as the delightful café, **Koru at Rapaura** (tel: 07-868 4821; daily 9am–3pm). The road continues over the peninsula to the east coast but it is rough and, in winter, somewhat dangerous. Most travellers to the east coast prefer to make the journey across at **Kopu**, just south of Thames, or take SH25 or the 309 Road, further north at Coromandel township.

Coromandel ❾ township, 55km (35 miles) north of Thames, near the northern end of the peninsula, offers a quiet, alternative life for creative types. The town and peninsula were named after the Royal Navy ship HMS *Coromandel*, which called into the harbour in 1820 seeking kauri spars. The township was less peaceful when it became the site of New Zealand's first gold find, by Charles

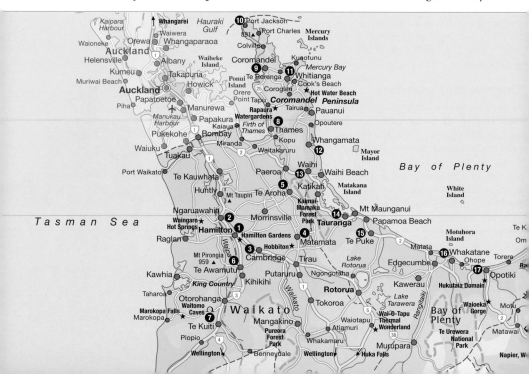

Ring in 1852. More than 2,000 people dashed across the gulf from Auckland at the news, but on arrival they found that the gold was deeply embedded in quartz rock and expensive to extract. It wasn't until 15 years later that a gold-bearing reef rich enough to warrant expensive extraction machinery was discovered. You can see the machine extraction process in action at the **Coromandel Battery Stamper** (tel: 07-866 7933; www. coromandelstamperbattery.weebly.com; daily 10am–3pm), 3km (2 miles) north of the township at 410 Buffalo Road. Over 100 years old and fully operational, this huge machine, used for processing gold from rock, is powered by New Zealand's largest working waterwheel. Tours are led by a trained geologist.

Coromandel has an air of the past about it and even at the peak of the summer holiday season the pace is slow and the lifestyle relaxed. Its sleepy history is recorded in the **Coromandel Historical Museum** (tel: 07-866 7251; Mon–Fri 10am–1pm, Sat–Sun 1.30–4pm) at 841 Rings Road, which offers a glimpse of life in the gold-rush days. There is even a jailhouse at the back.

One of New Zealand's most idiosyncratic attractions is located some 3km (2 miles) north of town on Driving Creek Road. The **Driving Creek Railway and Potteries** (tel: 07-866 8703; www.drivingcreekrailway. co.nz; daily 10am–5pm), the creation of potter, conservationist and engineer Barry Brickell, is noted as much for its quirky train service as for the quality of its crafts. Brickell himself designed the train, built originally for carting clay from the hills for his pottery work. The miniature train takes passengers on a one-hour return trip into the hills, and up to the mountain-top terminus, 'Eyefull Tower,' for great views.

Beyond Coromandel, 28km (17 miles) north, is **Colville**, with the last store before Cape Colville and the northernmost tip of the peninsula. Enthusiasts insist that visitors cannot experience the full spirit of the peninsula unless they travel to the end of this road.

En route, the road skirts the **Moehau Range**, whose 891-metre (2,923ft) peak is the highest point in the area. Keep an eye open for a rare native frog (*Leiopeima archeyi*),

FACT

Driving Creek's narrow-gauge mountain railway runs on tracks only 388mm (15 inches) wide. Trains depart at 10.15am and 2pm daily, with more frequent departures Dec–Mar (bookings recommended).

White sands and striking rock formations make Cathedral Cove one of the most attractive beaches on the east coast.

Central North Island

0   50 km

0   50 miles

N

PACIFIC

OCEAN

which lives only on the Coromandel Peninsula.

The unspoilt beauty and isolation of **Port Jackson** and Fletcher Bay are worth sampling. **Fletcher Bay**, at the end of the road, is also the starting point for the **Coromandel Walkway**, a three-hour walk to **Stony Bay**. If you prefer less energetic pursuits, visit Stony Bay by taking the road just north of Colville, crossing the peninsula to Port Charles and returning via Kennedy Bay on the east coast to Coromandel township.

Whitianga and nearby beaches

Two roads lead from Coromandel Town to Whitianga, situated on the opposite coast of the peninsula. The first, the SH25, runs via the holiday resort of Matarangi and Kuaotunu Beach. The second route, some 15km (9 miles) shorter, is the 309 Road, which climbs to 300 metres (1,000ft) before descending to approach the town from the south along the Whitianga Harbour edge. En route, at number 471, is the Water Works (tel: 07 866 7191; www.

L&P in concrete form, Paeroa.

thewaterworks.co.nz), a quirky waterpark and a fun place to visit with kids.

Whitianga is said to have been occupied for more than 1,000 years by the descendants of the Polynesian explorer Kupe. Kauri gum was shipped from Whitianga from 1844, peaking in 1899 with the shipment of 1,100 tonnes. Today's visitors enjoy fishing, swimming and rock-hunting, with the last drawing those in search of the area's gemstones: jasper, amethyst, quartz, chalcedony, agate and carnelian.

Whitianga township is on the shores of **Mercury Bay**, with the mouth of **Whitianga Harbour** at its southern end. If you follow the road south skirting the harbour to **Coroglen** (formerly Gumtown) and travel for a further 8km (5 miles), you will reach a junction that provides access to two of Coromandel's most important highlights. The first of these is **Cook's Beach**, where Captain Cook first hoisted the British flag in New Zealand in November 1769 to claim the territory in the name of King George III. While here, he also observed the transit of Mercury; a cairn and plaque at the

LEMON AND PAEROA

The pride and joy of the small country township of Paeroa is a large concrete representation of a soft-drink bottle. The mineral waters of Paeroa were used to make Lemon and Paeroa, an indigenous soft drink and national icon. L&P, as it is now known, has long been mass-produced commercially, and the bottle, which used to stand beside the main road, was moved back several metres in 2002 because photographers angling for a good view were creating a traffic hazard. Bottles of L&P can be purchased at most supermarkets or at a dairy, the Kiwi lingo used to describe a convenience store. Today L&P comes packaged in either a can or a bottle which bears a distinctive yellow-and-brown label; the drink itself is said to taste somewhat like fizzy home-made lemonade.

summit of the dramatic Shakespeare Cliffs mark the occasion.

Nearby is **Hahei**, a wonderfully beguiling stretch of white sand, and a popular location for any number of water activities thanks to its crystal clear waters. A track at the northern end of Hahei leads to **Cathedral Cove**, which is notable for its majestic rock formations. Also accessible by sea, it is a popular kayaking location.

The second essential site on the peninsula is **Hot Water Beach**, 9km (6 miles) south of Hahei, where thermal activity causes steam to rise from the sand and visitors can dig a thermal hot pool on the beach, using 'sandcastle' walls to keep the sea out or let it in to regulate the temperature. It is a great way to relax travel-weary bodies from the bumps and bends of the roads.

The next centre southwards is **Tairua**, on the harbour of the same name. The area is dominated by 178-metre (584ft) **Mount Paku**; a walkway leads to the summit for views of nearby Shoe and Slipper islands. Across the harbour is the affluent resort town of **Pauanui**, billed as a 'Park by the Sea'

but described by some as almost too tidy to be true. **Whangamata** ⓬, 40km (25 miles) further south, is a popular family holiday spot and one of the prime surfing beaches of the peninsula.

Inland from Whangamata

From Whangamata the road winds inland; 30km (19 miles) south is **Waihi** ⓭, where a rich gold- and silver-bearing lode was discovered in 1878. **Martha Hill Mine** was the greatest source of these minerals. Shafts were sunk to a depth of more than 500 metres (1,640ft) and in a period of over 60 years, more than NZ$50 million worth of gold and silver was retrieved. Fascinating mining relics are on display at **Waihi Arts Centre and Museum** (tel: 07-863 8386; www.waihimuseum.co.nz; daily 10am–3pm) at 54 Kenny Street. Today, gold is still being mined from a venture which has laid bare the original mine shafts on Martha Hill.

The bullion trail led through the Karangahake Gorge to **Paeroa**, 20km (12 miles) from Waihi, from where the ore was shipped to Auckland. The

Ohope beach on the Bay of Plenty.

Karangahake Gorge Walkway offers river views and old mining relics along the way.

A road running through the Athenree Gorge south of Waihi leads to SH2 and on to **Katikati**, where hundreds of outdoor murals depicting the locals' lifestyle adorn numerous buildings, along with sculpture and other installations.

Tauranga and the Bay of Plenty

Some 30km (19 miles) to the southeast of Katikati is the coastal city of **Tauranga** ⓴, which is both a tourist focal point and an important commercial centre served by the country's busiest export port. Located at the western end of the **Bay of Plenty**, Tauranga (meaning 'safe anchorage') has a relaxed feel despite the obviously high level of commercial activity connected with the port. Its chief attractions are a benevolent climate and access to numerous white-sand beaches not far from the centre of town.

Tauranga has an interesting history. Flax trading became established here after the missionaries had arrived in 1838. In 1864, during the New Zealand Wars, Tauranga was the site of fierce fighting during the Battle of Gate Pa. That battlefield was the scene of heroic compassion when Maori warrior Hene Te Kirikamu heard fatally wounded British officers calling for water, and risked death in taking it to them.

The site of the original military camp, the **Monmouth Redoubt** and the mission cemetery, holds not only the remains of the British troops killed at Gate Pa but also the body of the defender of the fort, Rawhiri Puhirake, killed during the subsequent Battle of Te Ranga. **The Elms Mission House** (tel: 07-577 9772; www.theelms.org.nz; Wed, Sat, Sun 2–4pm), in Mission Street, was built in 1847 by Reverend A.N. Brown (who treated the wounded from both sides at the Battle of Gate Pa) and occupied by members of the Brown family until 1991. Its library, finished in 1839, is the oldest in the country.

Across the harbour from Tauranga is the township of **Mount Maunganui**.

View from the summit of Mount Maunganui over the Bay of Plenty.

Built around the 231-metre (758ft) dormant volcano, it affords views of Tauranga and the surrounding area. Near its foot are several fine beaches and the Mount Maunganui Hot Pools and Bay Wave (tel: 07-575 0868; www.tcal.co.nz; Mon–Sat 6am–10pm, Sun 8am–10pm) on Adams Avenue, which provides a place to soak or swim, year-round.

For more down-to-earth thrills, travel south to Papamoa Beach and visit Blokart Heaven (tel: 07-572 4256; www.blokartheaven.co.nz; daily 10am–5.30pm) at 176 Parton Road, where wind-powered blokarts, a cross between a go-kart and a land-sailer, can be hired and raced around a purpose-built speedway track.

The Bay of Plenty was named by Cook, and his description proved prophetic. Perhaps the greatest evidence of plenitude was the phenomenal growth of the furry kiwi fruit, which has made the township of **Te Puke** ⓯, 28km (17 miles) southeast of Tauranga, the 'Kiwi Fruit Capital of the World.' Just beyond Te Puke is **Kiwi 360** (tel: 07-573 6340; www.kiwi360.com; daily 9am–4pm, tours hourly), an orchard park, information centre and restaurant, with 'kiwi karts' to take visitors for trips around the park. Extreme jet-boat rides are on offer nearby at Spring Loaded Adventures (tel: 07-533 1515; www.longridge.co.nz; daily 9am–4pm, hourly departures) at 316 State Highway 33, up the Kaituna River.

Along the coastal road to Whakatane

About 100km (60 miles) southeast of Tauranga and 85km (53 miles) east of Rotorua is **Whakatane** ⓰, at the mouth of the Whakatane River and the edge of the fertile Rangitaiki Plains. Until it was drained 70 years ago, the area was a 40,000-hectare (100,000-acre) tract of swampland.

Whakatane takes its name from the arrival of the Mataatua canoe from Hawaiki at the local river mouth. Legend records that the men went ashore, leaving the women in the canoe, which began to drift away. Though it was *tapu* (forbidden) for women to touch paddles, the captain's

Maori carving at Kohi Point, Whakatane.

FURRY FRUITS

Te Puke's horticulture has brought much prosperity to the region. The kiwi fruit, originally known as the Chinese gooseberry, was introduced to New Zealand from China in 1906, and thrived best in the Bay of Plenty. In the 1970s and early 1980s, fuelled by strong demand and high prices, many of Te Puke's farmers became rich from a harvest of only a few hectares. Over the years, cultivation expanded swiftly throughout other New Zealand regions, as well as to other countries including Chile, New Zealand's main kiwi fruit competitor. As iconic as it may be, these days the humble green kiwi fruit is just another orchard crop, and one that has been ravaged by PSA, a fruit disease which growers in the region have been battling to control, so far to no avail.

TIP

Be sure to stop at Te Kaha Beach Resort (tel: 07-325 2830; www.te kahabeachresort.co.nz) along the town's main road on a cliff. It's a great place to meet the locals, especially if there is a rugby game on to kick-start the conversation.

daughter, Wairaka, seized one and shouted: *Kia whakatane au i ahau!* ('I will act as a man!'). Others followed suit and the canoe was saved. And thus the settlement was named Whakatane – to be manly. A bronze statue of Wairaka now stands on a rock at the river mouth. Above the area known as The Heads is Kapu-te Rangi ('Ridge of the Heavens'), claimed to be the oldest Maori *pa* (fortified village) site in New Zealand, established by the Polynesian explorer Toi.

Whakatane is known as an eco-tourism centre, and one of its major attractions is **White Island**, in the midst of the Bay of Plenty 50km (30 miles) from the shore. Clearly visible from the town, the island is an active volcano. Daily boat trips with **White Island Tours** (tel: 07-308 9588; www.whiteisland.co.nz; tour departs daily at 8.15am and 9.15am), located on The Strand East, include guided tours of its sulphuric moonscape, where jagged red ridges rise around yellow and copper fumaroles. Despite the formidable terrain, the island has an incredible allure, since this is the only place

The bronze statue of Wairaka.

in the world where you can easily see an active marine volcano at such close proximity. Scenic flights pass over its steaming cone, which was mined for sulphur ore between 1885 and the mid-1930s. In 1914, 12 men lost their lives here during a violent eruption. The island is also known for its thriving colonies of sea birds. Whakatane is also a good base for excursions that take you to swim with the dolphins that thrive in the bay.

Just over the hill, 7km (4 miles) from Whakatane, is the popular **Ohope Beach**, described with some justification by former New Zealand Governor-General Lord Cobbam as 'the most beautiful beach in New Zealand.'

The last centre of note between Whakatane and the eastern boundary of the Bay of Plenty at Cape Runaway is the rural centre of **Opotiki** ⑰. Here in 1865 missionary Reverend Carl Volkner was murdered by a Maori rebel leader, Kereopa of the Hau Hau sect, in a gruesome episode which saw Volkner's head cut off and placed on the church pulpit, with the communion chalice used to catch his blood.

Some 8km (5 miles) to the south-west of Opotiki is the **Hukutaia Domain**, with some beautiful walks through the lush landscape. Many of the plants here are rare, and one of them is in a class of its own – a puriri burial tree, Taketakerau, estimated to be more than 2,000 years old. It was discovered in 1913 when a storm broke off one of its branches to reveal numerous human bones that had been interred by Maori. The bones were later re-interred and the *tapu* (sacred or taboo) status lifted from the tree.

Towards East Cape

From Opotiki there are two routes to the east coast: across or around. The route across is the more straightforward and follows SH2, which runs through the spectacular Waioeka Gorge. The gorge narrows and becomes steeper before crossing into

the deep rolling hills that line the descent into Gisborne. The alternative route, which follows SH35 around East Cape, provides some of the most beautiful coastal driving the country can offer. The road winds along the coast for 115km (71 miles) to Cape Runaway. En route it crosses the Motu River and passes through the small settlement of **Te Kaha** ⓲, with its pretty crescent-shaped beach. As you drive around the coast from Te Kaha you will notice the distinctive **Raukokore Church**, an Anglican place of worship built in 1894, jutting out from the road almost into the sea. Nearby is **Waihau Bay** ⓳, a popular camping area and spot for divers to hire a boat and explore the rich sea bed just metres from the shore. Several more beautiful bays are passed on the way to **Whangaparaoa**.

Rounding the cape, the next stop is **Hicks Bay** ⓴, which offers glowworm caves for the adventurous nighttime hill climber, and horse rides by day. **Te Araroa** is 10km (6 miles) further along. In the school yard by the road is a 600-year-old pohutukawa tree, Te Waha o Rerekohu, believed to be New Zealand's largest, with a total of 22 trunks, a girth of 19.9 metres (65ft) and an overall spread of 37.2 metres (122ft). The manuka tree also holds a special place in this community: harvested from much of the East Cape region, the leaves are brought to Te Araroa's manuka oil plant, Tairawhiti Pharmaceuticals, for extraction.

There's a turn-off here that leads 21km (13 miles) to **East Cape** ㉑ and its lighthouse. It is New Zealand's most easterly point and one of the first places in the world to see the new day.

Heading south from Te Araroa, SH35 runs inland through largely barren scenery. It passes through **Tikitiki** ㉒ with its **St Mary's Church**, built in 1924 to honour Maori servicemen killed in World War I. The building's Maori design is one of the most ornate in the country.

Just off the highway is **Ruatoria**, centre of the Ngati Porou tribe. Don't be surprised to see locals riding into town on horseback, or horses tied up outside the store. The hotel at **Te Puia**, 25km (16 miles) further south, has hot springs on site, and a short drive further on is **Tokomaru Bay**, where it is a delight to see the coast again. This entire stretch of coast, down to **Gisborne** (see page 197), is popular with surfers and holidaymakers for its unhurried pace and wide expanses of beach. The small roads leading off the main highway are rewarding to explore. Notable is **Anaura Bay**, where there is a campsite, and **Tolaga Bay**, the site of New Zealand's longest wharf.

Closer to Gisborne is **Whangara** ㉓, another beautiful white-sand beach and the location for the New Zealand film *Whale Rider*. As you approach Gisborne from Whangara, stop at **Wainui Beach**, where there is a range of accommodation. It is close to the town and provides a convenient beach location while you visit the city.

One half of the husband-and-wife team that run the Cheddar Valley Pottery, located near Ohope.

Carved posts (pouwhenua) at Waiotahi Beach, near Opotiki.

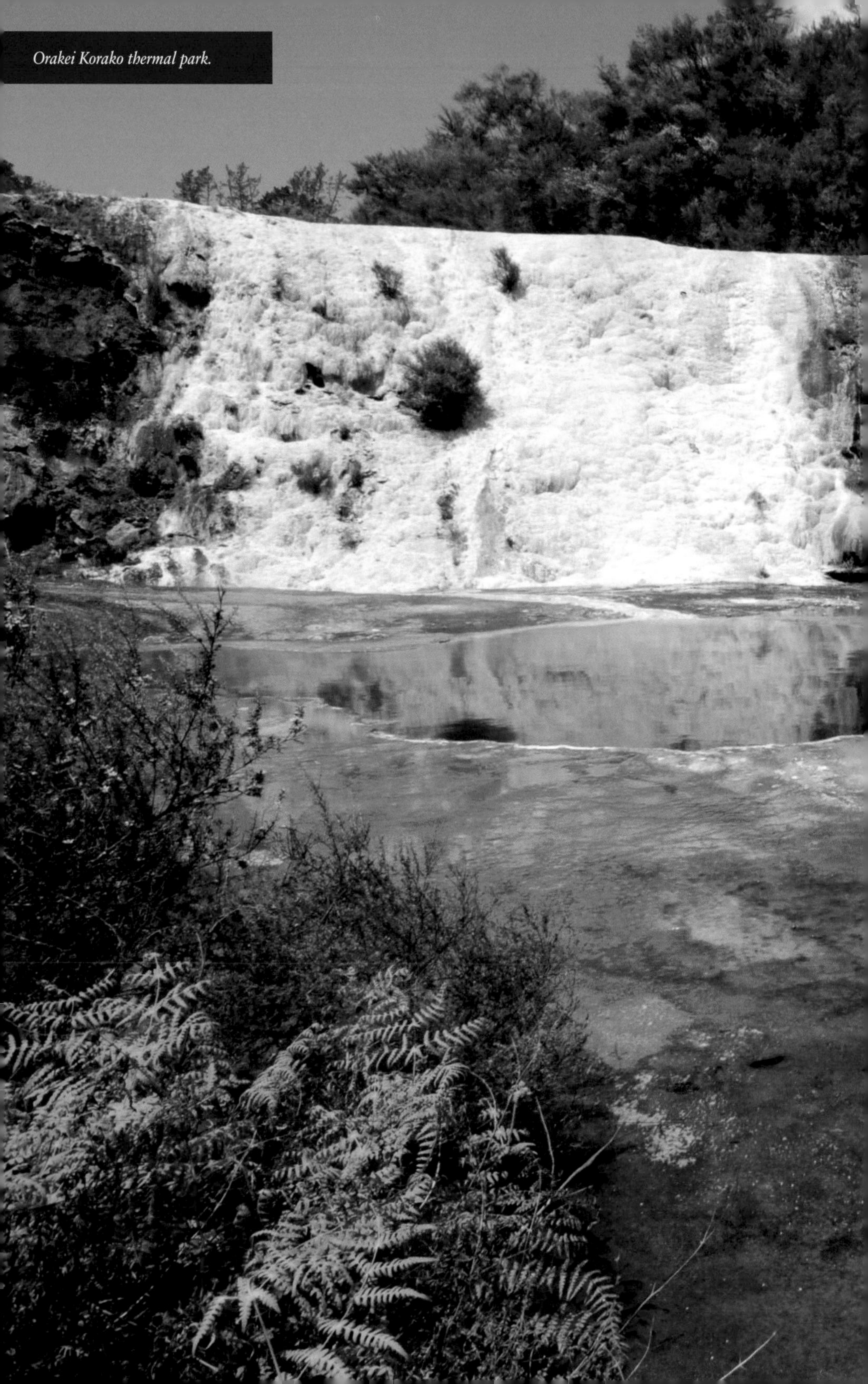

Orakei Korako thermal park.

ROTORUA AND THE VOLCANIC PLATEAU

Auckland

Wellington

Christchurch

On the surface it's quiet and even genteel, but Rotorua's tranquillity is punctuated by the hot and steamy thermal activity that has attracted tourists and health-seekers since Victorian times.

Of his visit to Rotorua in 1934, playwright George Bernard Shaw declared: 'I was pleased to get so close to Hades and be able to return.' Shaw was not the first to draw an analogy between Rotorua and the fire and brimstone of the underworld. To pious Anglican pioneers the region must have had all the hallmarks of Dante's Inferno – a barren wasteland of stunted vegetation, cratered with scalding cauldrons, bubbling mud pools and roaring geysers hurling super-heated water into a sulphur-laden atmosphere.

Today, this part of central North Island represents pleasure and not torment – a place of thermal wonders, lush forests, green pastures and crystal-clear lakes teeming with trout. Anglers, campers, swimmers, water-skiers, yachtsmen, pleasure boaters, trampers and hunters are all drawn to the region. This is one of the major holiday areas in New Zealand, and the principal focus for adventure-sport activities on the North Island.

Rotorua is on a volcanic rift which stretches in a 200km (120-mile) line from White Island off the coast of the Bay of Plenty to Lake Taupo and the volcanoes of the Tongariro National Park in the Central Plateau of the North Island.

Cultural hotspot

Rotorua was settled by descendants of voyagers from the legendary Maori homeland of Hawaiki. Among the arrivals in the Te Arawa canoe around AD 1350 was the discoverer of Lake Rotorua, named in Maori tradition as Ihenga, who travelled inland from the settlement of Maketu and came across a lake he called Rotoiti, 'little lake.' He journeyed on to see a much larger lake, which he appropriately called Rotorua, the 'second lake.'

About 68,000 people, around 35 percent of whom are Maori, reside in the Rotorua urban area and nearby smaller towns. This is the greatest concentration

The home of the Rotorua Museum is known as "Tudor Towers".

of Maori residents of any New Zealand centre, and makes the town a national focus of Maori culture. Visitors will not fail to notice the strong smell of sulphur, all part of the geothermal activity, which pervades the entire area. Most people, fortunately, become accustomed to it in a matter of minutes.

City-centre attractions

Rotorua ❶ is 234km (145 miles) south of Auckland, following State Highway (SH) 1 through Hamilton to Tirau and turning southeast on SH5. Set beside the clear trout-filled waters of Lake Rotorua, the town is fairly compact. The downtown area is centred between two main thoroughfares, Fenton Street and Randolf Street.

At least some of a visitor's time here will be spent soaking in hot mineral water, an activity which can be enjoyed in an apparently infinite variety of ways. In 1874, former New Zealand premier Sir William Fox urged the government to 'secure the whole of the Lake Country as a sanatorium owing to the ascertained healing properties of the water.' This immediately sparked off the development of Rotorua into a spa town. The building of its first sanatorium began in 1880 and, although the sulphurous waters of the baths are still regarded by some as useful in the treatment of arthritis and rheumatism, most people enjoy them simply as a pleasant form of relaxation.

East of the northern end of Fenton Street in the lovely grounds of the **Government Gardens** is the magnificent Tudor-style bathhouse, built in 1908 as a spa centre. Housing the **Rotorua Museum** ❹ (tel: 07-350 1814; www.rotoruamuseum.co.nz; daily 9am–8pm), it contains, alongside art exhibitions, fascinating displays of slightly sinister-looking apparatus used for various forms of hydrotherapy more than a century ago. Permanent exhibitions tell the story of the local Te Arawa people and the devastating eruption of Mount Tarawera (see page 189) in 1886.

A one-minute walk from the museum are the historic **Blue Baths** (tel: 07-350 2119; www.bluebaths.co.nz; daily 10am–6pm), which occupy a Spanish mission building, first opened in 1933. These heated non-thermal freshwater pools were beautifully restored in 1999; bathing is reasonably priced.

A short stroll south of the museum is the **Polynesian Spa** ❸ (tel: 07-348 1328; www.polynesianspa.co.nz; daily 8am–11pm). Choose from the 26 thermal pools, each having its own special mineral content and varying temperatures. The Priest Pool was named after a Father Mahoney, who pitched his tent alongside a hot spring on the site in 1878 and bathed in the warm water until he reportedly obtained complete relief for his arthritis. Four years later the spa was established. Some pools are off-limits to children, and private pools and spa treatments are also available.

Behind Government Gardens and its various attractions is the pleasant Lakefront Walk – a route which

Visit a local marae for a taste of Maori culture.

WHERE

Rotorua's i-site Visitor
Centre (tel: 07-348
5179; www.rotoruanz.com)
in Fenton Street will
provide assistance with
hire cars, coach
excursions and
sightseeing. The majority
of Rotorua's
accommodation is on
Fenton Street, running
north–south across the
city. It is only a short
drive to the popular
tourist attractions of the
surrounding region, but
having your own
transport is ideal.

follows the lake past the boat ramps of Motutara Point, before winding through wetlands and the thermal areas of the Sulphur Point Wildlife Sanctuary, where a variety of wetland birds carefully pick their way through the steam.

Legends of the pools

To the east of Government Gardens is the wharf. Sightseeing cruises on the *Lakeland Queen* (tel: 07-348 0265; www.lakelandqueen.com; daily 8am, 1pm, dinner cruise Sat only, 7pm), a 32-metre (105ft) paddle steamer, depart from the lakeside jetty. On its early morning cruise you can view the sunrise over **Lake Rotorua** while enjoying a hearty breakfast. If you're not an early riser, opt for a lunch or dinner cruise.

If you wish to explore **Mokoia Island ⓒ**, in the middle of Lake Rotorua, home to the rare saddleback, stitchbird and North Island robin, contact Mokoia Waiora Island Experiences (tel: 07-349 0976; www.mokoiaisland.com; daily). Scenic flights aboard float planes are also available

from the wharf area with Volcanic Air (tel: 07-348 9984; www.volcanicair.co.nz).

Further along the lakefront is the historic Maori village of **Ohinemutu ⓓ**, once the main settlement on the lake. Its Tudor-style Maori **St Faith's Church**, built in 1910, is notable for its rich carvings, a window depicting a Maori Christ figure who looks as though he is walking on the waters of Lake Rotorua, and a bust of Queen Victoria. The church was presented to the Maori people of Rotorua in appreciation of their loyalty to the Crown and is a noteworthy expression of how some of the Maori adopted Christianity into their traditional culture.

The adjacent 19th-century **Tamatekapua Meeting House** took 12 years to carve and is named after the captain of the Arawa canoe, Tama Te Kapua. It is said that Hine-te-Kakara, the daughter of Ihenga, Rotorua's discoverer, was murdered and her body thrown into a boiling mud pool. Ihenga subsequently set up a memorial stone, calling it Ohinemutu, or 'the place where the young woman was killed.'

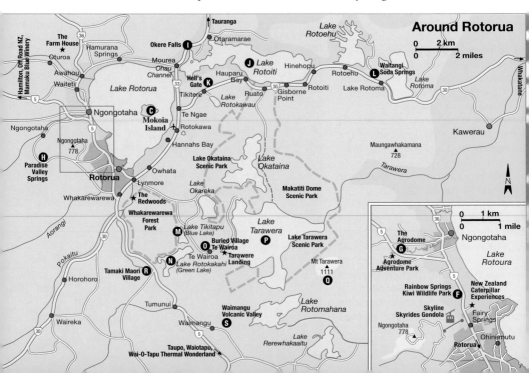

Around Rotorua

Mud and geysers

At the southern end of Fenton Street in a thermal area known as **Whakarewarewa** Ⓔ is **Te Puia**, home to two major attractions. The first is the impressive **Te Puia New Zealand Maori Arts and Crafts Institute** (tel: 07-348 9047; www.tepuia.com; daily 8am–6pm), where skilled Maori carvers and flax weavers can be observed at work. The intricately carved archway to the area depicts Hinemoa and Tutanekai embracing (see panel). The second is the famous **Pohutu Geyser** ('Big Splash'), thundering to a height of more than 30 metres (100ft) up to 20 times a day. Guided tours leave on the hour and include the arts institute and the mud pools, hot springs and geysers of the thermal park. Also on site is Rotowhio, a replica of a traditional Maori village, where cultural shows are held daily at 10.15am, 12.15pm and 3.15pm. In the evening concert performances and a *hangi* (traditional Maori earth-oven meal) are held here.

To the west of Te Puia is **Whakarewarewa – The Living Thermal Village** (tel: 07-349 3463; www.whakarewarewa.com; daily 8.30am–5pm), whose residents, the Tuhourangi/Ngati Wahiao people, inhabit an otherworldly terrain of bubbling mud pools and hot thermal springs. Tribal people have, for generations, used thermal waters for cooking, washing and heating. The charge includes a guided tour, which departs hourly, and cultural performances held daily at 11.15am and 2pm. For a small charge, a real treat is to sample a traditionally cooked meal, steamed to perfection in a purpose-built box held in place over a geothermal pool; this is held daily between noon and 2pm.

Behind the village lies the Whakarewarewa Forest, a popular place to hike or mountain bike. Mountain bikes can be hired at the entrance to the forest from Planet Bike (www.planetbike.co.nz), who also take guided tours.

Rainbow country

About 4km (2½ miles) northwest of Rotorua off SH5 on Fairy Springs Road is the delightful **Rainbow Springs** Ⓕ (tel: 07-350 0440; www.

Croquet in Government Gardens, in front of the Blue Baths.

The waters at the Polynesian Spa in Rotorua emanate from two deep thermal springs.

Wai-O-Tapu.

the only one of its kind open to the public in the world. On your 45-minute guided tour, you can view kiwis, native geckos and skinks, plus adult and juvenile tuatara, New Zealand's living 'dinosaurs', in a nocturnal house. There are also New Zealand native and exotic birds, and 'Captain Cooker's' wild pigs, introduced by the famous explorer himself. The park's latest attraction, The Big Splash (daily 9am–5pm) is a unique waterslide attraction which takes nine minutes to complete. En route the ecological evolution of New Zealand is brought to life, from the time of the dinosaurs, through to the arrival of humans.

Opposite Rainbow Springs is the New Zealand **Caterpillar Experience** (tel: 07-347 3206; www.caterpillar experience.co.nz; daily 8.30am–5pm), a museum displaying vintage earthmoving machinery.

Also close to the springs is the terminus for **Skyline Skyrides** (tel: 07-347 0027; www.skylineskyrides.co.nz/rotorua; daily 9am–late), one of Rotorua's main adventure attractions, but with plenty

rainbowsprings.co.nz; daily 8am–11pm, until 10pm Apr–Oct). Its natural pools, set amid 12 hectares (30 acres) of lush landscaped gardens, teem with thousands of Brown and Rainbow trout. These fish, which swim here from Lake Rotorua to spawn, can be hand-fed and viewed through an underwater window. The Kiwi Encounter at Rainbow Springs (daily 10am–4pm) is a unique incubation facility, hatchery and nursery,

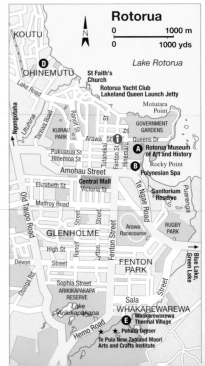

on offer for the less cavalier as well. Ride a gondola midway up **Mount Ngongotaha** for a breathtaking view of the city, lake and surrounding countryside. The more adventurous can plunge downhill again in a high-speed luge cart. The speed of the carts can be controlled, and there are three tracks totalling 5km (3 miles), including a relatively leisurely 'scenic' option with bays where riders can stop to take photographs. The Sky Swing takes the children's playground favourite a few notches higher, reaching a height of 50 metres (165ft) and speeds of 120kmh (75mph).

About 10km (6 miles) northwest of Rotorua, on Western Road near **Ngongotaha**, is the spacious **Agrodome** Ⓖ (tel: 07-357 1050; www. agrodome.co.nz; daily 8.30am–5pm), located on 160 hectares (395 acres) of pasture. Three times a day (9.30am, 11am and 2.30pm) 19 trained rams (showcasing New Zealand's 19 major breeds) are put through their paces by extremely well-trained sheepdogs. It's an educational and entertaining performance, and visitors receive

handfuls of freshly shorn wool. Children love the chance to bottle-feed a lamb, though they're often less enthusiastic about the genuinely rural accompanying odours. There are a huge number of other activities, including an organic farm tour which departs at 10.40am, 12.10pm, 1.30pm and 3.40pm daily and provides the chance to feed sheep, deer, alpaca and emu by hand.

At the adjacent **Agroventures Adventure Activities** (tel: 07-357 1050; www.agrodome.co.nz; daily 8.30am–5pm), many thrilling rides are on offer, including Freefall Xtreme, which recreates the sensation of skydiving with a column of wind that holds the adventurer 5 metres (16ft) in the air. Also available are bungee jumping, jet-boat racing, zorbing (see page 115), the Shweeb Velodrome, the world's first human-powered monorail racetrack, and the Swoop, which is an exhilarating combination of bungee jumping and flying that sees visitors being whisked 100 metres (330ft) through the air at 130kmh (80mph).

Bathing in a thermal pool.

MAORI LOVE STORY

Rich with Maori folklore and legend, one of Lake Rotorua's greatest Maori love stories is set on the island of Mokoia: the romance of Hinemoa and Tutanekai. Hinemoa lived on the mainland and, against her family's wishes, fell in love with Tutanekai, a young island chieftain. Their marriage was forbidden, so the couple secretly planned for Hinemoa to paddle across the lake following the sound of Tutanekai's flute at night. When Hinemoa's family beached the canoes she was forced instead to swim across the lake, warming herself in the hot pool that bears her name, before reuniting with Tutanekai. Today visitors can join a boat cruise and bathe in Hinemoa's Pool, while spotting rare birds including the saddleback, stitchbird and North Island robin.

There are more trout at **Paradise Valley Springs**  (tel: 07-348 9667; www.paradisev.co.nz; daily 8am–5pm), 11km (7 miles) northwest of Rotorua on Paradise Valley Road, which reside in a series of sparkling blue spring-fed pools. You'll also find a pride of lions (often with cubs to pat), and a wealth of native New Zealand and exotic wildlife. Lion-feeding takes place daily at 2.30pm; the kea and possums are fed at 3pm. The newest addition to the park is an elevated tree-top walk through native bush passing the roosts and nests of native birds.

To protect sports fisheries, it has been made illegal to buy or sell trout in New Zealand, but many visitors can still enjoy a fresh trout dinner, as the fish is an easy catch, with guides claiming a 97 percent daily 'strike' rate. In fact, no trip to Rotorua or Taupo is complete without a fishing expedition on the lakes. Guides supply all tackle and will meet clients outside hotels, with trailer boats ready for action, or at the boat harbour. **Clearwater Cruises** (tel: 07-362 8590; www.clearwater.co.nz) and **Mana Adventures** (tel: 07-348 4186; www.manaadventures.co.nz) both provide a variety of trout-fishing excursions.

Rainbow trout on most lakes around Rotorua and on Lake Taupo average 1.4kg (3lbs) and on Lake Tarawera (see page 188), where they are tougher to catch, fish of 3.5–5.5kg (8–12lbs) are not uncommon. The icing on the cake after a day of fishing is having a hotel or restaurant chef prepare the catch – a service speciality which most are well used to providing.

Some 8km (5 miles) north of the Agrodome on SH5 is **Off Road NZ** (tel: 07-332 5748; www.offroadnz.co.nz; daily 9am–5pm). This is for those who like to go very fast and make a lot of noise, especially in self-drive four-wheel-drive vehicles or Off Road's monster truck, over rough and challenging terrain. Nearby is the **Mamaku Blue Winery** (tel: 07-332 5840; www.mamakublue.co.nz; daily 9am–5pm), New Zealand's largest blueberry winery, where orchard and winery tours, farm and bush tours, museum tours, and home-made blueberry ice creams are available.

Along Central Road, past Ngongotaha township at Sunnex Road (off Central Road), the **Farm House** (tel: 07-332 3771; www.thefarmhouse.co.nz; daily treks at 10am, 11.30am, 1pm, 2.30pm) hires out ponies and horses for riding over 245 hectares (605 acres) of bush-edged farmland and leads treks throughout the day. Carrying on clockwise around Lake Rotorua, the scenic road continues past Hamurana Springs, where there is a large reserve with swings and a picnic area, to **Okere Falls** ❶ where, after a short walk through native forest and down a cliff side, the **Kaituna River** can be viewed thundering through a narrow chasm into the swirling pool below. This is the place to tackle the highest commercially rafted waterfall in the world with **Raftabout** (tel: 07-343 9500; www.raftabout.co.nz; daily 9am, 12.30pm, 3.30pm). Pick-up in

One of Rotorua's serene lakes.

Rotorua is available free of charge, one hour prior to your trip.

Knocking on Hell's Gate

Crossing the Ohau Channel outlet, which leads from northeastern Lake Rotorua into **Lake Rotoiti ❿**, an eastbound turn onto SH30 towards Whakatane takes you to the very door of **Hell's Gate ❿** (tel: 07-345 3151; www.hellsgate.co.nz; daily 8.30am–8.30pm), reputedly the most active thermal reserve in Rotorua. The Maori name, Tikitere, recalls the legend of Hurutini, who threw herself into a boiling pool because her husband treated her with contempt. Tikitere is a contraction of *Taku tiki i tere nei* ('My daughter has floated away'), bestowed by George Bernard Shaw. The volcanic activity here covers 4 hectares (10 acres), highlighted by the hot-water **Kakahi Falls**, the largest of their kind in the Southern Hemisphere. Hell's Gate is home to the **Wai Ora Spa**, where you can experience the cosmetic benefits of a mud bath. Follow this with a soak in sulphur-infused waters for silky smooth skin.

Further down SH30 you can reach the southern shores of Lake Rotoiti, followed by **Lake Rotoehu** and **Lake Rotoma**. A side road between the lakes heads off to **Waitangi Soda Springs ❿**, located in front of the campground. Here hot water percolates in the Waitangi Stream, where you can take a dip. Heading south of Lake Rotoiti is unspoilt **Lake Okataina**, the starting point of a walking track to Lake Tarawera (see page 188).

The eruption of Tarawera

Southeast of Rotorua, past the airport and suburb of Lynmore, is the turn-off to the forest-clad **Lake Tikitapu ❿** (Blue Lake) and **Lake Rotokakahi ❿** (Green Lake), a favourite stomping ground for joggers and a retreat for those who enjoy walking or riding along the well-marked and graded trails. Horses, ponies and kayaks are available for hire. The trails lead through pine forest and native bush. On a fine day, follow the signs to the lookout points between the lakes to observe that, although they

Geyser at Wai-O-Tapu.

Jetty at Lake Tarawera, with Mount Tarawera in the background.

Waimangu Cauldron.

are side by side, one is blue and the other green.

The road continues to Lake Tarawera via the **Buried Village** ⓞ (tel: 07-362 8287; www.buriedvillage.co.nz; daily Nov–Mar 9am–5pm, Apr–Oct until 4.30pm), destroyed on 10 June 1886 when a devastating eruption of Mount Tarawera blasted rock, lava and ash into the air over a 15,500-sq-km (6,000-sq-mile) area and buried the villages of Te Wairoa, Te Ariki and Moura, killing 147 Maori and six Europeans. The Buried Village contains items excavated from Te Wairoa, including the *whare* (hut) of a *tohunga* (priest) who foretold the disaster (see panel) and was unearthed alive four days after the eruption. There is an inescapably eerie feeling here as you walk past the remnants of Maori and European buildings frozen in time at the moment a community was extinguished.

From the Buried Village, it's a short drive further east to **Lake Tarawera** ⓟ, with **Mount Tarawera** ⓠ ('burnt spear') looming in the distance. From Te Wairoa, before the eruption, many Victorian tourists were rowed across Lake Tarawera to the fabulous Pink and White Terraces, two huge silica formations which rose 250 metres (820ft) from the shores of **Lake Rotomahana** and were billed as one of 'the eight wonders of the world' (see panel). Today, you can retrace the route to the former site from **The Landing** at Lake Tarawera (tel: 07-362 8502; www.thelanding laketarawera.co.nz), with **Clearwater Cruises** (tel: 07-362 8590; www.clear watercruises.co.nz). Alternatively, pedal boats and kayaks can be hired from The Landing to explore the thermal activity at **Hot Water Beach** and Lake Tarawera's sheltered inlets and bays. **The Landing Café** (tel: 07-362 8502), located within the cruise centre, is rightly famous for its gourmet pizzas and lakeside dining.

If you fancy a bird's-eye view, flights over Mount Tarawera's crater and thermal lakes depart from Te Puia, Agrodome Park and Skyline Skyrides. The flights are operated by **Helipro**

(tel: 07-357 2512; www.helipro.co.nz), which has exclusive landing concessions on both Mount Tarawera and Mokoia Island. A thrilling landing on the mountain's slopes allows close inspection of the 6km (4-mile) long, 250-metre (820ft) deep chasm caused by the volcanic explosion.

Waimangu Valley

On SH5, some 14km (9 miles) south of Rotorua, is the **Tamaki Maori Village** ® (tel: 07-349 2999; www.maoriculture. co.nz; daily 6.30pm). The brainchild of two enterprising brothers, Doug and Mike Tamaki, the site features a recreated pre-European Maori village, where local guides introduce Maori culture, myths and legends, action songs and *poi* dance, stick games and the world-famous haka (Maori War Dance). Sharing of food is an important Maori custom and tickets include a traditional *hangi* (earth oven) buffet feast. If you wish, you can prolong the experience, with an overnight stay in the *marae*.

Around 20km (12 miles) south of Rotorua, still on SH5 going towards Taupo, is the turn-off to **Waimangu Volcanic Valley** ❺ (tel: 07-366 6137; www.waimangu.com; daily 8.30am–5pm). This unspoilt thermal area contains the **Waimangu Cauldron**, the world's largest boiling lake. An easy walk downhill from a tearoom leads past bubbling crater lakes, hot creeks and algae-covered silica terraces to the shores of Lake Rotomahana, where a launch can be taken to the intensively active **Steaming Cliffs** and the former site of the lost Pink and White Terraces.

Waimangu is one of the more colourful thermal attractions, presenting a vivid palette of hues that only adds to the otherworldly impression it creates. The **Waimangu Geyser** was once the biggest in the world, reaching dizzy heights of 500 metres (1,640ft). Today it has less force and is dwarfed by Pohutu (see page 183), New Zealand's biggest geyser.

About 10km (6 miles) further along SH5, a loop road leads to another thermal area, **Wai-O-Tapu Thermal Wonderland** ❷ (tel: 07-366 6333; www.waiotapu.co.nz; daily 8.30am–5pm). *Wai-O-Tapu*, Maori for 'Sacred Waters', is the home of **Lady Knox Geyser**, which erupts daily at 10.15am in a spectacular spurt of super-heated water and steam. Other attractions include the bubbly **Champagne Pool**, tinted silica terraces and **Bridal Veil Falls**. Good coffee and meals are available at the on-site café.

About 70km (43 miles) south of Rotorua and 37km (23 miles) north of Taupo is the 'Hidden Valley' of **Orakei Korako** ❸ (tel: 07-378 3131; www.orakei korako.co.nz; daily 8am–4.30pm), which is a cave and thermal park comprising geysers, hot springs, mud volcanoes, underground caves and some of the largest silica terraces in the world. The geothermal area is accessible only by a short boat cruise across **Lake Ohakuri**, which is included in the charge. Maori chiefs painted themselves in the mirror pools here, hence the name, Orakei Korako – 'adorning place'.

TARAWERA'S GHOSTLY SIGHTINGS

Adding to the area's mysterious aura is the tale of a ghostly war canoe full of mourning, flax-robed Maori seen by two separate boatloads of visitors on Lake Tarawera on the misty morning of 31 May 1886. Earlier that morning, the visitors had ventured out by boat from Te Wairoa, the launch point for trips on Lake Tarawera, to view the famous Pink and White Terraces rising from the shores of nearby Lake Rotomahana.

When this sighting was reported back at Te Wairoa it filled the local Maori villagers with terror, for the ceremonial war canoe that had been described to them had ceased to exist in the region for over 50 years. Tuhuto, the tohunga (priest) of Te Wairoa, prophesied that the apparition was 'an omen that all this region will be overwhelmed'. Some Maori even left the area, but many stayed.

On a chilly moonlit night 11 days later, Mount Tarawera fulfilled his prophecy to the letter, blasting the Pink and White Terraces off the tourist map forever, though not from Rotorua's memory. The eruption lasted some five hours, and an area measuring some 15,540 sq km (6,000 sq miles) – including the village of Te Wairoa – was covered with ash, lava and mud. Rotorua never seems to have come to terms with the loss of the terraces, and you may be surprised how often you are reminded of them during your stay.

The route to Taupo

If you've somehow emerged from Rotorua without being exposed to its geothermal wonders, you can rectify the omission on the way to Taupo. Some 7km (4 miles) before Taupo, just below the junction of SH1 and SH5, visitors will encounter the **Wairakei** ❹ geothermal area. At **Wairakei Terraces** (tel: 07-378 0913; www.wairakeiterraces.co.nz; daily 9am–5pm), natural silica terraces wiped out for the construction of a power station in the area have been recreated artificially and there's a series of hot thermal mineral pools in which to bathe. **Wairakei** also hosts a **Maori cultural experience** every evening at 6pm, which includes singing and dancing, followed by a *hangi* meal (bookings essential). Tours of the power station are also available. Super-heated water is drawn from the ground through a series of bores, enabling dry steam to be piped to electricity turbines in a nearby powerhouse.

Before reaching Taupo at the **Wairakei Tourist Park** on the Waikato River, you will encounter a world

first, the geothermally heated **Huka Prawn Farm** (tel: 07-374 8474; www.hukaprawnpark.co.nz; daily 9am–4pm). Visitors can observe, hand-feed, catch and eat prawns here; tours of the farm depart hourly between 10am and 2pm. Another stop is the **Volcanic Activity Centre** (tel: 07-374 8375; www.volcanoes.co.nz; Mon–Fri 9am–5pm, Sat–Sun 10am–4pm), which explains all you need to know about geothermal and volcanic activity in the region – one of the most active areas on earth.

A further 200 metres (650ft) down the road is the **Huka Honey Hive** (tel: 07-374 8553; www.hukahoneyhive.co.nz; daily 9am–5pm; free), where you can learn all about bees and purchase a bottle of New Zealand's famous manuka honey to take home.

A nearby loop road leads to the spectacular **Huka Falls**, where the full force of the Waikato River hurtles from a narrow gorge over an 11-metre (36ft) ledge. Enough water goes over the falls every second to fill two Olympic-sized pools. When lit by sunshine, the water takes on a brilliant ice-blue colour before crashing into a foaming basin below. A footbridge passes over the river, offering spectacular views, and on the other side there are a number of pleasant hikes, including the walk downstream to **Aratiatia Rapids**, where the Rapids Jet (tel: 07-374 8066; www.rapidsjet.co.nz; daily 9am–5pm) offers sensationally wicked jet-boat rides. Alternatively, book a white-knuckle ride with **Hukafalls Jet** (tel: 07-374 8572; www.hukafallsjet.com; daily 10am–5pm), whose jet boats depart every 30 minutes and skim across the water near the base of the falls. A short distance along the loop road on the banks of the Waikato River is the renowned **Huka Lodge** (tel: 07-378 5791; www.hukalodge.co.nz), an exclusive retreat for the well-heeled.

Also located between Wairakei and Taupo, on Karapiti Road, is **Craters of the Moon** (tel: 06-385 4114; www.

The 1,111-metre (3,645ft) summit of Mount Tarawera.

cratersofthemoon.co.nz; daily 8.30am–6pm), a 45-minute walk through a wild thermal area where you can gaze into a frightening abyss of furiously boiling mud and see steam rising from natural fumaroles in the hillside.

From here, the resort town of Taupo is only about 5km (3 miles) away.

Lake Taupo

Taupo is an abbreviation of Taupo-nui-Tia ('the great shoulder cloak of Tia'), which takes its name from the Arawa canoe explorer who discovered **Lake Taupo** ➎, New Zealand's largest lake. The lake covers some 619 sq km (240 sq miles) and was formed by volcanic explosions over thousands of years. It is now the most famous trout-fishing lake in the world, yielding in excess of 500 tonnes of rainbow trout annually. The rivers flowing into the lake are equally well stocked, so that fishermen frequently stand shoulder-to-shoulder at the mouth of the Waitahanui River, forming what has come to be known as the picket fence.

Apart from its trout-fishing fame, Taupo offers a full range of activities, from sedate boat and kayak trips on its lake to skydiving, bungee jumping and other adrenaline-pumping sports. A major New Zealand events destination, both accommodation and restaurants are easy to find at this family-oriented township. For more information, drop by the **Taupo i-site Visitor Centre** at 30 Tongariro Street (tel: 07-376 0027; www.laketauponz.com; daily 8.30am–5pm).

Mount Ruapehu

At the southern head of Lake Taupo is the breathtaking 7,600-sq-km (2,930-sq-mile) **Tongariro National Park** ➏, containing the three active volcanic peaks of **Mount Tongariro** (1,968 metres/6,457ft), **Mount Ruapehu** (2,796 metres/9,173ft) and **Mount Ngauruhoe** (2,290 metres/ 7,513ft), which starred as Mount Doom in the film trilogy *The Lord of the Rings* (see page 82).

The most scenic route from Taupo leaves SH1 at **Turangi** heading for **Tokaanu**, not far from the Tongariro Power Station, and winds up steeply up through native bush and around

TIP

There are several useful websites on skiing in New Zealand, but skiers heading to Mount Ruapehu should check out www.mtruapehu.com. It has information on skiing at both Whakapapa and Turoa.

White-knuckle jet-boat ride on the Waikato River.

the shore of Lake Rotoaira. The alternative route is to turn off the main highway at Rangipo on to SH47.

According to Maori legend, when the priest and explorer Ngatoro-i-rangi was in danger of freezing to death on the mountains his fervent prayers for assistance were answered by the fire demons of Hawaiki, who sent fire via White Island and Rotorua to burst out through the mountain tops. To appease the gods, Ngatoro cast his female slave into the Ngauruhoe volcano – called Auruhoe, by the local Maori. Mount Ngauruhoe, with its typical volcanic cone, is the youngest and most active of the three volcanoes and still bubbles and spits lava and ash occasionally. A major eruption in 1954 continued intermittently for nine months. More recently, Mt Tongariro made its presence known, spewing tons of ash sky-high during 2012.

Mount Ruapehu is a perpetually snowcapped volcano with a flattened summit stretching 3km (2 miles) and incorporating an acidic, bubbling crater lake and six small glaciers. Ruapehu has blown out clouds of steam and ash a number of times in the past 100 years, raining dust over a 90km (56-mile) radius in 1945, and closing the nearby Whakapapa and Turoa ski fields in 1996. On 24 December 1953, 151 people died in a tragic train disaster when a *lahar*, or violent discharge of water and mud, roared down the Whangaehu River from the Crater Lake. Fortunately, when the lake burst its banks again in March 2007, an alarm system provided warning before a torrent of mud and debris again poured through the river gorge.

Top-class skiing

Mount Ruapehu is the major ski area of the North Island, with the action taking place at two locations, comprising 1,800 hectares (4,450 acres) of slopes. **Whakapapa** on the mountain's northwestern face has excellent beginner slopes as well as more challenging areas. **Turoa** is on the southwestern slopes, with magnificent views of Mount Taranaki. Accommodation abounds in the area, with Turoa skiers tending to base themselves at **Ohakune**, while those skiing at Whakapapa stay at **Whakapapa Village**, where the historic **Chateau Tongariro Hotel** (tel: 07-892 3809; www.chateau.co.nz), built in 1929, is found, or at **National Park**, a village located about 15km (9 miles) away. Tour operators also offer whitewater rafting down the Tongariro and Rangitikei rivers.

Outside of the July–October ski season, Tongariro National Park has fine walks, such as the 16km (10-mile) **Tongariro Crossing**, which covers spectacular scenery in a matter of seven or eight hours. Rangers at the **Whakapapa Visitor Centre** (tel: 07-892 3729) have details on walking tracks and huts. The walk can be achieved in a day, but two days allows time for diversions, such as the summits of Mount Ngauruhoe and Mount Tongariro. The hike begins and ends at different locations but inexpensive transportation can be booked through your accommodation.

Hiking a crater rim at Tongariro National Park.

Spas

Kiwis make good use of their country's natural resources – rejuvenating in the therapeutic waters of a toasty sulphur pool has become a national pastime.

Since the 1800s, New Zealanders have been soaking in the country's natural mineral waters, and the Maori have been doing so for a good deal longer. Although long embedded in the nation's psyche, Kiwi spa culture has made a huge comeback from its humble beginnings, when visitors were invited to 'come and take the waters'. These days there are a number of major commercial spa resorts scattered around the country where, after the obligatory slide into a soothing thermal pool for a long, hot soak, you can treat yourself to any number of optional beauty treatments.

The major thermal resort towns of Rotorua (North Island) and Hanmer Springs (South Island) offer a range of mineral-water options, from public family pools to private adults-only mineral spas. Smaller thermal springs are located in towns such as Te Aroha, New Plymouth, Maruia and Kaikohe.

Commercial spa pools are treated in order to make them completely safe to bathe in, but it is a real treat to visit one of the all-natural, non-chlorinated sites. These are often set beside – or form part of – a stream and surrounded by towering native forest in National Parks and reserve land.

Other hotspots are found in idyllic settings amid the sands fringing lakes and sea. Here visitors are welcome to soak in delicious warmth, without parting with a single cent. However, you will need to remember to keep your head above water to avoid ingesting any harmful amoebas.

Amoebas aside, thermal pools have long been revered for their healing qualities, and they vary greatly in mineral composition and supposed health benefits; common minerals include silica, sodium, calcium, potassium and lithium.

The vast majority of New Zealand's spa experiences are in the northern half of the North Island. Auckland offers three spa complexes within a 45-minute drive of the CBD: **Parakai Hot Springs** to the west, **Waiwera Infinity Thermal Spa** to the north and **Miranda Hot Springs,** a short drive beyond the city limits to the south.

However, it is Rotorua's active volcanic wonderland of spouting geysers, bubbling mud pools and natural thermal springs and spas, set amidst jewel-like crater lakes, that is New Zealand's epicentre of bathing delight (see Thermal Wonders of Rotorua, page 194). Unbeatable experiences include **Wai Ora Spa** at Hell's Gate in Tikitere, where heavenly mud spas provide the chance to detoxify for a modest fee, then relax in a toasty, non-chlorinated sulphur pool, and the **Polynesian Spa**, overlooking Lake Rotorua in the CBD. It caters for everyone, with family pools, adult-only pools and private pools, as well as the peaceful Lake Spa retreat, where you can relax while watching the sun set.

Stunning natural locations in the region include **Parengarenga Pools** at Lake Rotoiti and **Te Wairoa** at Lake Tarawera, both of which are accessible only by boat. Easier to reach is **Kerosene Creek** on SH5, just south of Rotorua near Wai-O-Tapu. Here, a hot burbling stream offers a variety of pools, and you can seek out your own warm soaking spot in among the rocks.

Hot springs and mineral pools at Hanmer Springs, a town in the Canterbury region.

THERMAL WONDERS OF ROTORUA

This strange, steamy landscape of bubbling springs and mud pools, saturated in Maori lore and history, has been attracting tourists for more than a century.

Rotorua has been a top tourist resort for decades. A century ago genteel folk came to the spa from all over the world to promenade and take the waters. So it's a little surprising to learn that New Zealanders call the town 'Stinkville' and 'Rotten Egg Town'. All becomes clear when you take your first breath of the sulphur-laden mist, but you'll soon forget the odour as you explore the surreal steamy surroundings. Every geyser, every spring, it seems, has a curious name with a story attached. The Lobster Pool in Kuirau Park is so named because of the shade its acidic waters tinted fair European skins, and a concentrically ringed mud pool is charmingly named 'Gramophone Record Pool'.

Lunar Rebirth

One of these stories relates to the moon. Rotorua's healing waters have been described as 'Wai-ora-a-Tane' (Living Water of Tane), where according to Maori legend the dying moon bathes each month in the great mythical lake of Aewa. Here, she receives the gift of life to sustain her on her journey through the heavens.

It's important to obey the signposts and keep to the paths in this region, where the earth is a bit less stable than most of us are used to. The thermal pools may look tempting, but some of them are boiling hot or highly acidic. If your vision gets blocked by steam, stand still until it clears – don't stagger on blindly.

Hot sand in Rotorua.

Whakarewarewa. This famous thermal area's full name is Whakarewarewatanga-o-te-a Wahiao, which means, 'the uprising of a war party of Wahiao'. New Zealand's highest geyser, Pohutu, bursts forth several times a day for up to 40 minutes at a time, reaching heights of 20–30 metres (65–100ft). The nearl Prince of Wales Feathers geys generally goes off just before Pohutu.

A hangi, a traditional Maori way of cooking food using rocks buried in the ground to heat a pit oven. Volcanic stones are preferred as they can withstand high temperatures.

nner parties and concerts are sometimes held in the misty,
ereal atmosphere of the Champagne Pool at Wai-O-
u Thermal Wonderland, just south of Rotorua. The
ol is actually quite green and steamy, and
esn't really look like Champagne at all, but
izzes enthusiastically near the shoreline.

Tudor Towers.

CROQUET AT THE BATHHOUSE

How very English! Splendid buildings like Tudor Towers, the town's most frequently photographed edifice and a superb backdrop to a croquet match, give Rotorua its genteel charm. The elegant building that graces Government Gardens was originally constructed as a bathhouse in 1908, complete with ancient sculptures in the foyer. To the left and right of the entrance foyer, double doors led to men's and women's bathhouses, where treatment could be obtained for rheumatism. The baths had facilities for Aix massage, steam baths and mud baths.

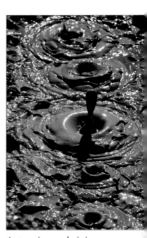

A steaming mud pit in a geothermal area on North Island.

The building is no longer a bathhouse – if you want a dip in a thermal pool, the nearby Polynesian Pools, built in 1886 and the site of Rotorua's first building and bathhouse, is open daily.

Today, Tudor Towers houses the Rotorua Museum (see page 181), with a number of collections tracing the development of painting and printmaking in New Zealand, as well as contemporary paintings. There is also a kauri gum collection and a wildlife display, plus exhibitions about the local Te Arawa people who first settled the area. A video on the 1886 Mount Tarawera eruption shows how the magnificent Pink and White Terraces, formed of silica deposits, were annihilated.

POVERTY BAY AND HAWKE'S BAY

Hawke's Bay and its neighbour, inappropriately named Poverty Bay, are home to a wealth of bountiful vineyards, colourful history, interesting architecture, and New Zealand's most easterly city.

Main Attractions

Gisborne
Lake Waikaremoana
Mahia Peninsula
Art Deco Architecture, Napier
Hawke's Bay Wineries

The Mahia Peninsula is a great place to spot whales as they pass by in spring.

There are several reasons why Gisborne and the area around it are special to New Zealanders. Situated on 178 degrees longitude, Gisborne is noted for being the first city in the world to greet the rising sun each day, a fortunate accident of geography made much of at midnight on 31 December 1999, when it led worldwide television coverage of the turn of the new millennium.

It is also a historic coast: Young Nick's Head, a promontory across the bay from the city of Gisborne, was the first piece of land that British explorer Captain James Cook and the crew of his ship *Endeavour* sighted in 1769. Cook's landing site is at the foot of Kaiti Hill, a great viewing platform for Gisborne and the surrounding areas.

Over the Turanganui River stands an impressive statue of Captain Cook, and further around the beachfront is a statue of Nicholas Young, the cabin boy on the *Endeavour* who was credited with being the first on board to sight land.

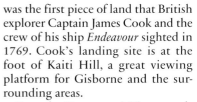

WHALE STRANDINGS

The Mahia Peninsula has a long whaling history. Extensive commercial operations began in the 1830s, and it soon became the principal whaling point on the mid-eastern section of the North Island, with 11 stations located from Waikokopua to Mahanga. Whaling has long since ceased, and Sperm and Beaked whales are often spotted cruising past the peninsula. Unfortunately strandings (around 30 per year) are common, as the whales get confused by the unusual topography of the peninsula, and after following the land's curvature, find themselves wallowing in shallow waters. The largest recorded stranding was in April 1943, when 300 False killer whales came ashore; these days locals are better equipped to give those stranded a helping hand.

Gisborne

Cook, who got most things right, erred badly, however, in calling the region **Poverty Bay** because 'it did not afford a single article we wanted, except a little firewood'. Poverty Bay retains the name grudgingly. It is now sheep and cattle country, rich in citrus, apple and kiwi fruit orchards, vineyards, vegetable gardens and a variety of food crops which all support a large processing industry. With around 15 wineries in the area, it's no surprise that its wines – particularly Chardonnay and Gewürztraminer – are among the best in the country and should be sampled at one of the many vineyards open to the public.

Poverty Bay offers spellbinding coastal vistas of white sands and sparkling blue waters, accompanied by the scarlet blossom of the *pohutukawa*, often known as the New Zealand Christmas tree because it is at its best and brightest in late December. Some of this vibrancy rubs off on **Gisborne** ❼, a city of sun and water, parks, bridges and beaches. Water sports are a recreational way of life and the city is a magnet for surfers, with reliable conditions at the nearby beaches of Wainui, Okitu and Makorori.

The 'City of Bridges', Gisborne is situated on the banks of the Taruheru and Waimata rivers and Waikanae Creek, all joining to form the Turanganui River. On Stout Street, adjacent to the city centre, **Tairawhiti Museum** (tel: 06-867 3832; www.tairawhitimuseum.org. nz; Mon–Sat 10am–4pm, Sun 1.30pm–4pm; free) recounts the region's ancient and recent history. A section of the main building is a maritime museum, made up from parts of the steamship *Star of Canada*, which was wrecked on Kaiti Beach in 1912.

Gisborne lingers over its association with Cook, but the area's historic wealth pre-dates his visit. Maori landholdings – some of them leased to Europeans – are extensive. Meeting houses are numerous and can be seen at many Maori settlements along the coast. Most feature carved lintels, panels and beams in traditional style, embellished with the unorthodox painting of patterned foliage, birds and mythical human figures. One of the

Eastwoodhill Arboretum.

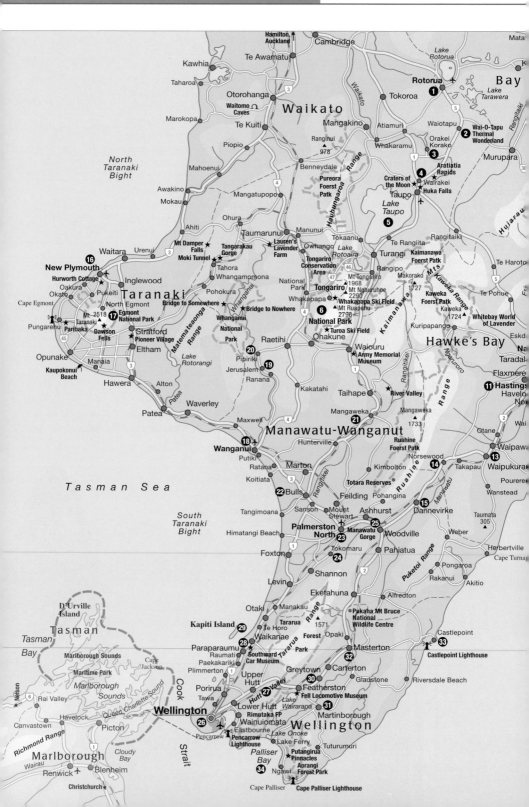

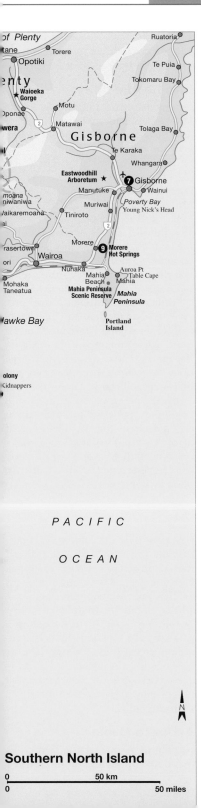

largest meeting houses in the country is **Te Poho-o-Rawiri** (visits by arrangement only; **Gisborne-Eastland Visitor Centre**, tel: 06-868 6139), at the base of **Kaiti Hill** on Queens Drive. Built in 1925, it did not use the traditional ridgepole structure because of its size. However, it still contains some impressive *tukutuku* (woven reed) panels and magnificent carvings. Almost every Maori settlement on the coast has its treasured meeting house.

As a major forestry centre, it's quite appropriate that Gisborne is the location of New Zealand's largest tree collection, at **Eastwoodhill Arboretum** (tel: 06-863 9003; www.eastwoodhill.org.nz; daily 9am–5pm). Located just 30 minutes west of town via Patutahi, it was founded by Gallipoli veteran soldier W. Douglas Cook. His lifetime's work sprawls over some 70 hectares (173 acres).

Legendary Te Kooti

While Poverty Bay is tranquil today, it has been the site of many tribal battles in the past. One of the most interesting stories concerns the Maori prophet Te Kooti, who in the 19th century led a rebellion against settlers. He was exiled to the distant Chatham Islands, hundreds of kilometres off the east coast of the North Island, along with dozens of other Maori arrested in the 1860s – but that wasn't to be the end of him. He masterminded a daring

Children's artwork at the Tairawhiti Museum in Gisborne.

escape back to the mainland and, believing God had appeared to him and promised he would save the Maori as he had saved the Jews, founded a religious movement which still exists, called *Ringatu* ('The Upraised Hand'). The government sent an army in pursuit, but Te Kooti proved a formidable enemy in the wild bush of the **Urewera Range**, striking back with guerrilla attacks that kept him free and the government harassed. He was eventually pardoned in old age and allowed to live with his followers in the King Country (see page 167).

Many of Te Kooti's old haunts have been preserved in **Te Urewera National Park ❽**, 212,000 hectares (524,000 acres) of rugged mountains, forests and lakes, much of it still inaccessible to all but the toughest trampers. Located some 164km (102 miles) northwest of Gisborne via Wairoa, the park's highlight is **Lake Waikaremoana** ('Lake of the Rippling Waters'), rich in trout and with bush thick to the water's edge on all but the eastern side, where it is hemmed in by steep cliffs. Chalet, motel and motor-camp accommodation is available at Waikaremoana (tel: 06-837 3826; www.lake.co.nz), and there are tramping huts throughout the park.

Into Hawke's Bay

Poverty Bay runs southwards to the Mahia Peninsula, where it merges into the **Hawke's Bay** region. Sitting near the neck of the peninsula separating the two bays is **Morere**, 60km (37 miles) south of Gisborne, worth visiting if only to soak in a pool at the **Morere Hot Springs ❾** (tel: 06-837 8856; www.morerehotsprings.co.nz; daily 10am until late). The Nikau Pool is the best; reached via a short track, it is set among a beautiful forest of ferns, and there are several rewarding hikes through the surrounding native forest.

Further on in **Nuhaka**, a road provides access to the dramatic, high white cliffs of the **Mahia Peninsula**. On the south side of the peninsula is **Mahia Beach**, a popular place with a large camping ground, friendly store and links-style golf course. Follow the road across the peninsula to Maungawhio Lagoon, a paradise for birdwatchers, and on to the small settlement of **Mahia** itself, located on a rocky coastline with a series of small sandy beaches punctuated by rocky outcrops boasting numerous rock pools.

Auroa Point provides great views of dramatic Table Cape, and whales are often seen passing through here.

Back on SH2 some 40km (25 miles) past the town of **Wairoa**, a turn-off leads northwest to Te Urewera National Park (see page 200). Continue west on SH2 to Lake Tutira, a bird sanctuary, where you can stop to stretch your legs on one of two tracks. The walk around adjacent Lake Waikopiro takes 20 minutes, while the Tutira Walkway consists of two loops which take 2–5 hours.

From here it's a further 125km (78 miles), approximately 1½-hours drive, south to Napier.

Art Deco Napier

Napier ❿ is one of the two cities that make up the region of Hawke's

RISING FROM THE ASHES

Hawke's Bay was where New Zealand's worst earthquake tragedy took place on 3 February 1931. Buildings crumpled under the impact of a 7.9 Richter Scale earthquake. What the shock did not destroy in Napier and Hastings, fire finished off. The resulting death toll of 258 included a number of people killed by falling parapets. The city of Napier was closest to the epicentre, and heroic deeds were performed by rescuers and by naval personnel from the HMS Veronica, which happened to be in harbour (along Napier's seafront today there is a colonnade named after the naval sloop).

As elsewhere in the world, the early 1930s was a time of economic depression, but a passionate government and a sympathetic world came to Hawke's Bay's post-quake aid with funds for a massive relief and rebuilding campaign. The opportunity was taken to widen streets, install new underground telephone lines, and a strict earthquake-proof building code was enforced, giving rise to a brand new city with architecture inspired by the Art Deco movement of the time.

It could be said that Napier today is a kind of memorial to the earthquake. Much of its suburban area, stretching out to the once-independent borough of Taradale in the southwest, is built on the 4,000 hectares (10,000 acres) of former marshland the earthquake pushed up.

Bay – the other is Hastings. Napier and Hastings may be twin cities but both are strongly independent and even competitive. Napier is a seafront city with a population of 55,000, while Hastings is an agricultural marketing centre of some 67,000. To their west plains sweep away to the Kaweka and Ruahine ranges, rugged areas for hunters and trampers. Both are thriving cities today, and there is little indication of the massive destruction they suffered in the tragic earthquake that rocked Hawke's Bay in 1931 (see panel).

The large-scale destruction wrought by the 1931 earthquake gave Napier a chance to reinvent itself, and a new city arose from the ashes with a distinctive Art Deco facade. Napier's collection of Art Deco buildings in the inner city, with their bold lines, elaborate motifs and pretty pastel colours, is recognised internationally. Widespread appreciation, however, has come only in the past decade. Napier's people are fiercely proud of the city's heritage. Building owners are encouraged to restore and preserve the facades, and civic leaders have done their bit too, developing the main street in a sympathetic fashion.

While New Zealand is well known for the effort it puts into preserving its many natural assets, it does not have a good record for preserving its architectural heritage. To this end, Napier's **Art Deco Trust** (www.artdeconapier. com) was formed in 1985 by a visionary group. Without their efforts, it is entirely possible the construction-crazy 1980s would have seen 'progress' do as much damage to the buildings of the 1930s as the earthquake did to their predecessors. The trust organises a number of activities, including informative daily walks for visitors at 10am and 2pm, as well as spearheading the annual Art Deco Weekend held in February, when the whole town seems to step back in time to the 1930s. The Trust also runs the **Art Deco Shop** at the Deco Centre, 163 Tennyson Street (tel: 06-835 0022), which stocks a wide range of gifts and souvenirs relating to Napier's Art Deco heritage.

TIP

Napier's Art Deco Trust organises a range of daily guided walks; booking is not essential. The 1-hour morning walk (NZ$16) departs at 10am from Napier Visitor Centre on Marine Parade. The 2-hour afternoon tour ($21) departs at 2pm from the Art Deco Shop at 7 Tennyson Street. From Dec–Feb, an evening walk ($19) also departs at 5pm from the Napier Visitor Centre. For further information contact the Art Deco Trust (tel: 06-835 0022; www.art deconapier.com).

The style of Napier's County Hotel contrasts with the city's Art Deco buildings.

Marine Parade at Napier. The city's Art Deco buildings are among the finest in the world.

Kiwi fruit, grown around Hastings, used to be known as Chinese gooseberries.

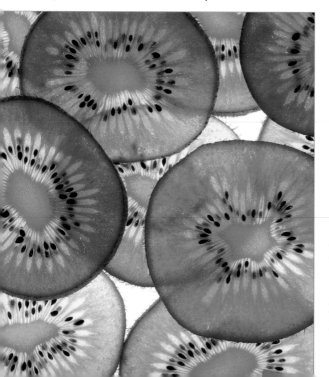

One exception to Art Deco's stranglehold on Napier's claims to architectural merit is the magnificent **County Hotel** (tel: 06-835 7800; www.countyhotel.co.nz) on Browning Street. Previously the County Council Chambers, it is a resplendent example of the Victorian-Edwardian Classical Revival style. And it is not just the design that harks back to those times. Quaintly, if not rashly, a complimentary decanter of port is always available in its library.

Another highlight of Napier is the city's 2km (1¼-mile) long **Marine Parade**. A large recreational collection of gardens, sculptures, fountains, earthquake memorials and varied visitor attractions, the seaside promenade is dominated by towering rows of Norfolk pines. Look out for the **Statue of Pania**, a maiden of local Maori legend who fell in love with a young chief but later lost her life and that of their child to the sea.

At No. 65 is **Hawke's Bay Museum** (tel: 06-835 7781; www.hbmag.co.nz), which houses displays on the earthquake, and Maori art and culture.

Also on Marine Parade is the **National Aquarium of New Zealand** (tel: 06-834 1404; www.nationalaquarium.co.nz; daily 9am–5pm), which opened in 2002. Housed in a distinctive stingray-shaped building are more species than in any similar establishment in New Zealand. A moving footpath carries viewers under the 'oceanarium', while sharks, stingrays and many other varieties of fish glide by. Land-based species are also featured: kiwis, tuatara and glow-worms among them. It's a hands-on, interactive experience in the manner that is now de rigueur for museums around the world.

Residential **Napier Hill** overlooks the city centre. This was one of the earliest parts of the city to be developed by Europeans, as is evident in some of the fine Victorian and Edwardian homes and the maze of twisting, narrow streets, designed before motorcars were anticipated. On the north side of the hill, next to the busy port, is another historic locale, **Ahuriri**, the cradle of Napier and the site of the first European settlement in the area; today it is home to a number of excellent seafood restaurants. A scenic road winds up **Bluff Hill** to a lookout, for views over the city, harbour and bay.

Fruitful Hastings

Some 21km (13 miles) south from Napier, architectural treasures from the post-earthquake period are also a feature of **Hastings ⑪**, with a good number of them in the Art Deco and Spanish mission style. Despite this and despite their physical proximity, though, Hastings is rather a different city from Napier – laid out in a flat and formal fashion, and surrounded by rich alluvial plains which host a huge range of horticultural crops. Hastings's main role is, as it is proudly called by locals, 'The Fruit Bowl of New Zealand'. A Mediterranean-type climate, pure water from an underground aquifer, and innovative growers have made this one of the most important apple-growing regions in the world. Apricots, grapes, peaches, nectarines, plums, kiwi fruit, pears, berries and cherries also grow profusely and are on offer from roadside stalls during the harvesting season, along with tomatoes, sweetcorn, asparagus and peas.

Despite the horticultural bounty, the twin cities rely heavily on farming, which has generated the region's historic wealth. Only pine forest farms are challenging the supremacy of sheep and cattle in the rolling hinterland. The pastoral farms are the legacy of Victorian settlers who laid claim to huge tracts of Hawke's Bay, and made their fortunes from wool and, later, sheep-meat, beef and hides.

All this may be lost on younger visitors more likely to be awed by Hasting's **Splash Planet** (tel: 06-873 8033; www.splashplanet.co.nz; Nov–Feb daily 10am–6pm, Mar–Oct Sat–Sun only, 10am–5.30pm), a family-friendly water theme park with more than 15 attractions and motorised rides, and a hit with toddlers, teens and the young at heart.

Around 3km (2 miles) across the plain from Hastings is 'The Village', as the pretty, genteel town of **Havelock North** is known locally. It sits in the shadow of **Te Mata Peak**, a limestone mountain with a summit accessible by car. From the top you can enjoy the sweeping views or, if you are daring enough, you may go hang-gliding or paragliding from the steep cliff on one side. Havelock North is also the home of major honey producer **Arataki Honey**, which has more than 17,000 hives. Its **Visitor Centre** (tel: 06-877

Sheep-shearing demonstration at Wool World, Clifton Station, in Hawke's Bay.

The east coast resorts offer superb beaches and the most reliable weather in the country.

The country's oldest wine maker, Mission Estate Winery, in Hawke's Bay.

Gannet Beach Adventures (tel: 06-875 0898; www.gannets.co.nz; daily) to what is thought to be the largest mainland gannet colony in the world. During the breeding season from June to October the cape is closed to visitors for scientific study. The Cape's name harks back to an incident in which local Maori attempted to abduct a Tahitian youth from the serving staff of Captain Cook's *Endeavour* while it lay at anchor nearby because they thought he was a kidnapped Maori.

Hawke's Bay is the oldest of the country's wine-growing regions and sees itself as the finest. There are over 80 wineries established around Napier and Hastings. Certainly it enjoys ever-increasing recognition for the quality of its Chardonnay, Sauvignon Blanc and Cabernet Sauvignon. Wine enthusiasts often wax lyrical over wineries like **Trinity Hill** (www.trinityhill.co.nz), **Te Mata Estate** (www.temata.co.nz) and **Church Road** (www.churchroad.co.nz). Church Road is one of New Zealand's leading producers and one of its oldest, having been founded in 1897. This

7300; www.aratakihoneyhb.co.nz; daily 9am–5pm) has a live 'Bee Wall' where you can see an entire colony at work, from the queen to the drones.

Gannets and wineries

Hastings and Napier may enjoy distinctive identities but they share some significant attractions – the Cape Kidnappers gannet colony, for example, and the local wine industry.

Cape Kidnappers ⑫ is 18km (11 miles) from Hastings and a 20- to 30-minute drive from either city, followed by a ride along the beach aboard a tractor-towed trailer with

was where pioneer wine maker Tom McDonald earned the title of father of quality red-wine-making in New Zealand. Church Road has the country's only **wine museum**, which can be viewed on a winery tour departing from the cellar door at 11am and 2pm daily. The museum has antiquities from the Mediterranean dating back to 1000 BC, including amphorae and other vessels. A wine tasting is held at the end of the tour.

There are numerous wineries in the region, all open to visitors. Many offer free wine tastings and have a restaurant on site. If you cannot find a willing designated driver, book a winery tour with one of the many operators in Napier or Hastings.

South of Hastings

Around 50km (31 miles) south of Hastings, pastoral farming is the reason for the existence of another set of Hawke's Bay twin towns, Waipukurau and Waipawa. Near **Waipukurau** ⑬ is a hill with one of the longest names of any place in the world: Taumata-whakatangihangakoauauotamatea-pokaiwhenuakitanatahu. The 57 letters translate into 'The hill where the great husband of heaven, Tamatea, caused plaintive music from his nose flute to ascend to his beloved'.

Further south again, another culture has left its mark. In the 19th century, hardy Norwegian and Danish settlers cleared the rainforest in southern Hawke's Bay, which was so dense it had discouraged all others. They established such towns as Norsewood, 85km (53 miles) south of Hastings, and Dannevirke ('Dane's Work'), another 20km (12 miles) further south. The Scandinavian flavour is still evident at **Norsewood** ⑭. Although a tiny town, it has a well-known woollen mill producing a range of knitted goods bearing the settlement's name. **Dannevirke** ⑮ actively promotes its historic links with Scandinavia, though it once, probably wisely, rejected a plan to erect a giant statue of a Viking. Dannevirke is a farm service town and a convenient staging post on the busy highway between Manawatu to the south and Hawke's Bay to the north.

Ascending Te Mata peak the hard way.

Cricket practice with Mount Taranaki in the background.

TARANAKI, WANGANUI AND MANAWATU

These predominantly rural regions encompass scenic splendour peppered with quiet, pleasant townships and crowned by Mount Taranaki's majestic peak.

The 169km (105-mile) Te Kuiti–New Plymouth road leads southwards through a varied landscape. There is rugged farmed hill country, the Awakino River Gorge, and a beautiful stretch of coast with cliffs and placid sandy bays offering glimpses of **Mount Taranaki**, in full view on a clear day. The road passes by a striking memorial to the famous Polynesian anthropologist Sir Peter Buck just north of Urenui, his birthplace. Approaching New Plymouth, Taranaki's main centre, the land flattens to fertile dairy plains which encircle the dormant volcano of Mount Taranaki, a near-perfect, permanently snowcapped cone soaring to a height of 2,518 metres (8,261ft).

New Plymouth

With Mount Taranaki as its backdrop, the town of **New Plymouth ⑯**, home to 48,000 people, spreads along the coast. Its location, fertile soil and climate were immediately attractive to European arrivals in the 1840s. Early missionaries and settlers found a Maori population depleted by intertribal wars, yet land disputes between the Maori and newcomers still beset the settlement. War broke out in 1860 and eventually placed New Plymouth under virtual siege.

Visitors should start at **Puke Ariki** (tel: 06-759 6060; www.pukeariki.com;

Mon–Fri 9am–6pm, Sat–Sun 9am–5pm; free), a museum, public library and visitor centre rolled into one. Located on Ariki Street in the town centre, its exhibits and interactive displays will help you get acquainted with the history and culture of the Taranaki region. The museum also includes the historic **Richmond Cottage**, home of three of the first settler families.

To the east at 42 Queen Street is the **Govett-Brewster Art Gallery** (tel: 06-759 6715; www.govettbrewster.

New Plymouth.

*Blooms at Pukeiti
Rhododendron Trust.*

com; daily 10am–5pm; free), home to a notable collection of contemporary art, including works by Len Lye, a New Zealand artist and filmmaker (see page 65). **Taranaki Cathedral Church of St Mary** (tel: 06-758 3111; www.taranakicathedral.org.nz) on Vivian Street, completed in 1846, is the oldest stone church in New Zealand, and the newest to be consecrated as a cathedral, early in 2010.

New Plymouth is best known for its beautiful parks. At **Pukekura Park** (daily 7.30am–7pm, Dec–Mar until 8pm), a few blocks southeast of Govett-Brewster Art Gallery, lakes, gardens, a fernery, fountains and a waterfall are all lit in rainbow colours by night. The park is also home to the **Brooklands Zoo** (tel: 06-759 6060; daily 9am–5pm; free).

A pleasant **Coastal Walkway** runs the length of New Plymouth – fully 7km (4 miles) from the Waiwakaiho River Mouth to Point Taranaki. At roughly the mid-point, opposite Puke Ariki, is Len Lye's soaring 45-metre (148ft) kinetic sculpture *Wind Wand*, a popular New Plymouth landmark.

Around the town

Heading south 8km (5 miles) from New Plymouth, via Carrington Road, is **Hurworth Cottage** (tel: 06-756 8606; Sat–Sun 11am–3pm). One of the region's earliest homesteads, it was built in 1855 by Harry Atkinson, a young immigrant from England, who later became premier of New Zealand.

Some 12km (7 miles) out of town on Pukeiti Road is the **Pukeiti Rhododendron Trust** (tel: 06-752 4141; www.pukeiti.org.nz; daily 9am–5pm), a 320-hectare (791-acre) park established in 1951, which showcases one of the world's best displays of rhododendrons and azaleas in a native bush setting.

Winter skiers and summer hikers will enjoy **Egmont National Park** ⑰, encircling the peak and slopes of **Mount Taranaki**, with its more than 300km (180 miles) of bush walks. Climbing the summit is not supremely difficult, but weather conditions change extremely quickly here, so it's important to have all the right gear, or for safety take a guided hike (see margin note). The easiest access to the park is via **Egmont Village**, 20km (12 miles) southeast of New Plymouth. The **North Egmont Visitor Centre** (tel: 06-756 0990; daily 8am–4.30pm) here can help with more information on what to do in the area.

Surf Highway

The Surf Highway, SH45, which horseshoes around the bulbous Taranaki coastline from New Plymouth to Hawera, connects with SH3 up to New Plymouth for a complete circumnavigation of Mount Taranaki. There are plenty of reasons to tarry along the way on this beautiful coastal road.

Oakura, 15km (9 miles) southwest of New Plymouth, is a trendy beach

TALES OF TARANAKI

Maori legend tells of how Mount Taranaki split from the mountains of the Central Plateau and came to reside in the Taranaki region. Pihanga, a small mountain and the beauty of the Central Plateau, set her heart on Mount Tongariro, spurning the advances of gentle, Zen-like Mount Taranaki, breaking his heart. While Mount Ruapehu and Mount Ngauruhoe looked on in wonder, mighty Mount Taranaki fled west, his sheer bulk carving the Whanganui River and his tears filling it into a raging torrent. Mount Taranaki found his way to the coast and stopped, in a region which has since been known as Taranaki.

It's not hard to imagine the rhythmic pounding of the ocean soothing his shattered ego, the strong westerly wind clearing his mind, and clouds providing a thick cover when he's feeling morose.

outpost with a number of excellent cafés lining the main thoroughfare. Lucy's Gully nudges the edge of the Egmont National Park, while at **Okato** the Stony River Walk provides crystal-clear waterholes for a refreshing dip.

At **Pungarehu**, turn right at the school to Cape Egmont lighthouse (built in 1881), for beautiful views on a clear day. Back on SH45, turn right to Parihaka to see the gravesite of the great Maori chief Te Whiti-O-Rongomai, who died here in 1907, aged 90.

In the 1870s, when Europeans settled on land confiscated from the Maori by the British following the Taranaki Wars, Te Whiti encouraged peaceful protest among his people. His campaign of passive resistance and civil disobedience ended at Parihaka in November 1881, when he was arrested. Earlier that day hundreds of British soldiers and militia marched to the *pa* (Maori fort) ready for battle, but to their surprise they were met by rows of children singing and dancing. As Te Whiti was led away he remained strong, telling his assembled followers, some 2,000 Maori, 'Be you steadfast in all that is peaceful.' Nevertheless, his words had no impact on the British troops and, in one of New Zealand's darkest moments, non-resistant Maori were raped and assaulted, crops destroyed and homes ransacked.

From Pungarehu the road continues on to **Opunake**, 65km (40 miles) from New Plymouth, where colourful murals decorate the town from top to toe. Opunake's landmark building, the eye-catching **Everybody's Theatre**, with Marilyn Monroe and Charlie Chaplin still gracing its billboards, is charming inside, with traditional movie chairs and posters. A tiny Art Deco building houses the boutique Egmont **Soap Factory** (Mon–Fri 9am–5pm, Sat until 1pm), where everything is made from scratch, and across the road the eclectic **Sugar Juice Café** dishes out homemade fare.

In **Manaia**, an air of prosperity radiates from the freshly painted band rotunda and granite war memorial obelisks, surrounded by historic buildings. Wide streets lead inland to **Dawson Falls**, where numerous hikes into Egmont National Park await the adventurous, and out to the coast to windswept **Kaupokonui Beach, a popular camping area**.

In spring **Hawera** is blooming, and good views of the countryside can be enjoyed from its historic **Water Tower** on High Street. The town has some off-beat attractions, including Kevin Wasley's **Elvis Presley Museum** (tel: 06-278 7624, 027-498 2942; www.digit alus.co.nz/elvis; by appointment only), a shrine literally packed from floor to ceiling with memorabilia, and the **Tawhiti Museum** (tel: 06-278 6837; www.tawhitimuseum.co.nz; Sept–May Fri–Mon 10am–4pm, Jun–Aug Sun 10am–4pm), an intricately detailed labour of love by artist Nigel Ogle, in which the history of the immediate area is recreated in handcrafted life-size displays and scale models. From Hawera, SH3 leads southeast to

TIP

The best time to explore Egmont National Park is during the flower season from Dec–Mar, or to ski its snows in July–Aug. In the summer, call into the Egmont Visitor Centre for detailed maps to hike independently; or for guided walks, contact Top Guides, tel: 021-838 513, 0800-448 433; www.topguides.co.nz.

Taranaki waterfall.

Wanganui, or north to New Plymouth to complete a loop of Mount Taranaki, passing through **Eltham**, **Stratford** and **Inglewood**.

Stop in Eltham to explore its wealth of Edwardian and Victorian buildings on a self-guided walking tour, and Stratford to experience its **Clock Tower** glockenspiel playing Romeo and Juliet at 10am, 1pm and 3pm. The **Taranaki Pioneer Village** (tel: 06-765 5399; www.pioneervillage.co.nz; daily 10am–4pm) is also well worth a visit. Novelty train rides depart from here daily at 11am, 1pm and 3pm. Inglewood is home to the **Fun Ho! National Toy Museum** (tel: 06-756 7030; www.funhotoys.co.nz; daily 10am–4pm), and from here it's a short drive back to New Plymouth via Lake Mangamahoe, where the mirror image of Mount Taranaki reflects perfectly on a clear day.

Wanganui

Heading southeast along the coast from Hawera, SH3 passes through lush farming countryside to **Patea**, and on to **Wanganui** ⑱, a city most famous for its river – the Whanganui (note the extra 'h'), which is New Zealand's longest navigable waterway and much loved by canoeists and jet-boaters.

The main attraction in town is the superb **Whanganui Regional Museum** (tel: 06-349 1110; www.wanganui-museum.org.nz; daily 10am–4.30pm) on Watt Street, a treasure trove of Maori artefacts, including the Te Mata-O-Hoturoa war canoe, and also featuring a remarkable collection of paintings by well-known New Zealand artist Gottfried Lindauer. Built in the form of a Greek cross, the elegant **Sarjeant Gallery** (tel: 06-349 0506; www.sarjeant.org.nz; daily 10.30am–4.30pm; free) graces the hill above the museum.

Before exploring Wanganui further, take a trip up to the **Memorial Tower** on **Durie Hill**. An elevator (daily 8am–6pm), built in 1918, climbs 66 metres (216ft) inside the hill, although the 176 tower steps are worth the trouble on a fine day. You'll be rewarded with a magnificent view of the city and river.

Settler's cottage in Taranaki.

About 2km (1¼ miles) south along Putiki Drive is **Putiki Church** (St Paul's Memorial Church). The exterior is plain white, but its interior is adorned with magnificent Maori carvings and *tukutuku* (weaving) wall panels.

Bason Botanical Reserve and **Bushy Park** scenic reserve, on the western outskirts of the city, are both within easy reach on SH3. With duck ponds and a range of short walks the parks are popular with families.

Heading upriver

The sooty departure of the lovingly restored coal-fired PS *Waimarie* from the **Whanganui Riverboat Centre** (tel: 06-347 1863; www.riverboats.co.nz; 2-hour cruise Mon, Fri 11am, 1-hour cruise Sat 10.30am, 12pm, 3-hour cruise Sun 11am) provides a satisfying window into the days when paddle steamers plied the river. There is also an excellent museum on site. Alternatively, follow the river up the 79km (49-mile) **Whanganui River Road** to Pipiriki, a journey of about two hours, 30km (19 miles) of which is unsealed.

As you approach the village of **Jerusalem** ⑲, you will understand why French Catholic missionaries established themselves along this bend in the river in 1854, and why New Zealand poet James K. Baxter chose the serenity of this site for a commune in the late 1960s. The mission remains today, but the commune disintegrated after Baxter's death in 1972. Prior to the establishment of the mission, Jerusalem was a larger Maori village known as Patiarero. In 1883 Mother Mary Aubert arrived and opened a school for Maori children. Her keen interest in native herbs led to the preparation of healing remedies and the subsequent establishment of a home for incurables.

Pipiriki ⑳ is the gateway to **Whanganui National Park**. From Pipiriki you can get to the **Bridge to Nowhere**, more accurately a bridge in the middle of nowhere, built to service a new settlement for soldiers after World War I, but subsequently abandoned when they were forced out by the 1930s depression and farming difficulties. It can be accessed by a 40-minute walk from the Mangapurua landing, a two-day tramp from the Whakahoro Hut via the Kaiwhakauka and Mangapurua valleys, or by canoe or jet boat (contact Bridge to Nowhere Lodge, tel: 0800-480 308; www.bridgetonowhere-lodge.co.nz).

Another route leads into the interior north of Wanganui; SH4 travels through the scenic Parapara Ranges and on to Tongariro National Park.

White-water thrills

To the east of Wanganui and north of Palmerston North (see page 212) on SH1, **Taihape** and **Mangaweka** ㉑ provide access to the swift-flowing, canyon-carving **Rangitikei River**, famed for its excellent white water. At **River Valley** (tel: 06-388 1444; www.rivervalley.co.nz; daily) near Taihape, gorges of violent white water, Grade 5 rapids and deep pools make for one

Power-boating on the Whanganui.

of the top whitewater-rafting destinations in the world. Or you can take a hair-raising 80-metre (260ft) bungee jump into the river at **Mokai Gravity Canyon** (tel: 06-388 9109; www.gravity-canyon.co.nz; daily 9am–5pm) on New Zealand's highest bridge bungee, and catch a water-powered chair-lift ride back to the top, where a 172-metre (560ft) high flying fox and a 50-metre (164ft) freefall swing awaits. Onlookers can take in all the action from the viewing deck.

In Mangaweka itself, the **Mangaweka Adventure Company** (tel: 06-382 5744; www.mangaweka.co.nz; daily 8.30am–5.30pm) offers great family fun with a one-hour splash-about on stable sit-top kayaks, a scenic introduction to the river's gentler side, plus rafting and kayaking tours ranging from one hour to four days.

South of Wanganui

The SH3 proceeds southeast from Wanganui to Palmerston North, 74km (46 miles) away. The largest township en route is **Bulls** ㉒, where there are 100 or so intriguing signs ranging from the medical centre 'Cure-a-bull' through to the police station 'Constabull', all niftily tucked in amid colourful murals and a pervasive aura of civic pride. Here you can add to your agricultural education with a visit to **Flock House**, an agricultural training institute. Built in 1895, it was purchased in 1923 by the New Zealand Sheepgrowers, who ran a scheme to train the sons of British seamen's widows as farmers.

Palmerston North

On the approach to Palmerston North is **Mount Stewart**, with fine views of the rich pastures of Manawatu, the region surrounding the city of Palmerston North. A memorial near the road commemorates early settlers. It's a short hop from here to the historic homestead and gardens at **Mount Lees Reserve. Palmerston North** ㉓ itself is the flourishing centre of agricultural Manawatu, with **The Square** as the city's focal point. Named in Maori as Te Marae-O-Hine or 'Courtyard of the Daughter of Peace', it commemorates a female chieftain named Te Rongorito who sought an end to intertribal warfare during the early days of European settlement.

West of The Square, at 396 Main Street, is **Te Manawa** (tel: 06-355 5000; www.temanawa.co.nz; daily 10am–5pm), an institution combining history, art and science in its museum, art gallery and interactive science centre. To the northwest, at 87 Cuba Street, is the **New Zealand Rugby Museum** (tel: 06-358 6947; www.rugbymuseum.co.nz; daily 10am–5pm). This shrine to the national sport displays items from blazers to whistles, with a section devoted to the country's famous All Blacks team.

Roads radiate outwards from the centre of 'Palmy'. **Fitzherbert Avenue** leads to the city's other major focal point, the **Manawatu River**. The river is crossed by only one bridge, used by thousands of cars and bicycles each day en route

The fertile plains east of Mount Taranaki are ideal for dairy farming.

to **Massey University** and a number of science research stations. Also over the bridge is the **International Pacific College**, and New Zealand's largest army base, at Linton. Given the number of educational institutions in Palmerston North, it's not surprising it calls itself the Knowledge Centre of New Zealand.

On the city side of the Manawatu River is the city's much-loved **Victoria Esplanade** (daily; free), an enchanting reserve featuring botanical gardens, a miniature train (tel: 06-354 8868; www.esplanaderail.org.nz; Sat–Sun 1–4pm, Dec–Jan 10am–5pm), a children's playground, an aviary and an education centre and conservatory. Don't miss the **Dugald Mackenzie Rose Garden** at the Esplanade, which has an international record for developing new varieties of the flower.

A stone's throw away, also on Park Road, is **Lido Aquatic Centre** (tel: 06-357 2684; www.lidoaquaticcentre.co.nz; Mon–Thu 6am–8pm, Fri 6am–9pm, Sat–Sun 8am–8pm), a water park replete with slides and chutes. Native bush reserves are close by.

Exploring Manawatu

A short drive south of Palmerston North on SH57 is **Tokomaru** ㉔, and its creative **Tokomaru Steam Engine Museum** (tel: 06-329 8867; www.tokomarusteam.com; Mon–Sat 9am–3.30pm, Sun 10.30am–3.30pm). A railway track circles the grounds, and there are various contraptions on display, from steamrollers to sewing machines.

SH56 heads west to beaches at Tangimoana, Himatangi and Foxton, well patronised by locals and linked by bracing coastal walks. **Feilding**, 20 minutes north of Palmerston North on SH54, is a large town which boasts two squares, a motor-racing track and racecourse, and a stock sale on Friday mornings. Take a NZ$10 insider tour of the yards and auctions on a **Feilding Stock Saleyard Tour** (tel: 06-323 3318; www.feilding.

co.nz/saleyardtours.htm; Fri 11am). The Feilding Stock Saleyard has the capacity to hold 35,000 sheep, and with a total turnover of around 1.2 to 1.3 million animals per week, these yards do more business than any other in the Southern Hemisphere. Bookings are essential.

Perhaps the most dramatic route in or out of Palmerston North and the Manawatu region is via the rugged **Manawatu Gorge** ㉕, to the east. SH3 first passes through the country town of Ashhurst. From here you'll get a good view of the **Tararua Wind Farm** (www.windenergy.org.nz), an impressive array of 40-metre (130ft) high 660kw turbines.

The route travels past **Pohangina** and **Totara** reserves, an area of virgin native bush favoured for picnics, then narrows, clinging to the southern side of the Manawatu Gorge and linking the region to Hawke's Bay. On the opposite bank of the river is the Hastings and Napier railway line, opened in 1891. Drive with care: this winding, and at times narrow, road demands your constant attention.

Manawatu River at dusk.

The Beehive.

WELLINGTON

Vibrant Wellington, the seat of government as well as the unofficial cultural centre of the country, has a cosmopolitan buzz that is readily discernible.

Tawhiri-ma-tea, the Maori god of wind and storm, fought many fierce battles with his earthbound brother gods in Wellington and the Wairarapa. No wonder, then, that the Cook Strait, the stretch of water separating this end of the North Island from the South Island, has long been known as one of the most treacherous short stretches of open water in the world. The early Maori saw the North Island as a great fish, rich with food for their families. Today the mouth of the fish is as pretty a capital city as any in the world. Wellington's great blue bowl of harbour is only mildly scarred by its port reclamations and the high-rise offices set below green hills dotted with white wooden houses.

San Francisco's twin

Named after Arthur Wellesley, the first Duke of Wellington and victor of the Battle of Waterloo, **Wellington** ❻ has long been compared to San Francisco, and accurately so. In addition to a susceptibility to earthquakes and a punishingly hilly topography, both cities have a superb coastal location with ocean vistas, an abundance of cool, sunny weather, and a shared penchant for old wooden houses done up in rainbow colours: the city's dwellers have made their homes some of the most architecturally attractive in New Zealand.

A desirable seaside suburb.

Like San Francisco, Wellington has a cable car, zooming out of its city belly on Lambton Quay to a fine view of the harbour, beside the ivy-clad, red-brick Victoria University. That it is also the seat of government has not seen it go short when it comes to funding public buildings.

Wellington is, however, rendered less than perfect not just by its earthquake risk but also with the near-constant presence of a nagging, often chilly wind. A cartoon image of residents bent double as they struggle to

Main Attractions

Te Papa Tongarewa – Museum of New Zealand
Civic Square
Museum of Wellington City and Sea
Wellington Cable Car
Zealandia Karori Sanctuary Experience
Kapiti Island
Martinborough Vineyards
Putangirua Pinnacles

Wellington

0 —————————— 500 m
0 —————————— 500 yds

Porirua

Katherine Mansfield's Birthplace

Hutt Valley, Silver Stream Railway, Petone Settlers' Museum

New St Paul's Cathedral

National Library

Old St Paul's Cathedral

Hill Street

Backbencher Pub

Aitken St

Thistle Inn

Archives New Zealand

New Zealand Portrait Gallery

Parliament Buildings

Beehive

Cenotaph

Old Government Buildings

Railway Station

Thorndon Container Terminal

PIPITEA

Lewisville Road

Tinakori Road

ANDERSON PARK

EARLY SETTLERS MEMORIAL PARK

Lady Norwood Rose Garden

Botanic Gardens Cafe

WELLINGTON

Zealandia Karori Sanctuary Experience

BOTANIC

Education and Environment Centre

Carter National Observatory

GARDENS

Wellington Cable Car Museum

KELBURN

KELBURN PARK

Centennial Fountain

Victoria University

Cable Car

Plimmer Steps

BNZ Building

Wellington City Library

City Gallery

Old Town Hall

Michael Fowler Centre

Film Centre

Circa Theatre

Te Papa Tongarewa Museum of New Zealand

State Opera House

LAMBTON

Terrace

Events Centre

Museum of Wellington City and Sea

FRANK KITTS PARK

WELLINGTON CENTRAL

Queen's Wharf

Wellington Harbour (Port Nicholson)

Lambton Harbour

Clyde Quay Wharf

Clyde Quay Marina

Freyberg Pool

Royal Port Nicholson Yacht Club

Oriental Parade

ORIENTAL BAY

Mt Victoria

TE ARO

GLOVER PARK

Garrett Street

St James Theatre

Cuba Mall

Courtenay Place

Bats Theatre

Downstage Theatre

Embassy Theatre

Wakefield Street

Cambridge Terrace

Kent Terrace

MT VICTORIA

CHARLES PLIMMER PARK

Colonial Cottage Museum

Arthur Street

Webb Street

Buckle Street

National War Memorial & Carillon

BASIN RESERVE

BASIN RESERVE

CENTRAL PARK

Massey University

Rugby St

St Marks

NAIRN STREET PARK

Tennis Centre

Wellington Polytechnic

ALEXANDRA PARK

Mt Victoria Tunnel

Wellington College

Hataitai (bus) Tunnel

MT COOK

Wellington Zoo

make their way against a chilly southerly bringing icy blasts borne down from the Southern Alps is not too far from the truth.

In the second half of the 1970s the city was shaken by a man-made storm, as a downtown area of quaint Victorian wedding-cake two- and three-storey premises was demolished on the grounds of it being an earthquake risk.

However, the skyscrapers of steel and glass that replaced them should serve to keep city-goers safe in the event of any major seismic movements. The city is again undergoing a flurry of future proofing, in the wake of the recent Christchurch earthquakes.

After the decade of demolition in the 1970s, Wellington tarted up the few old buildings left, such as Victoria University, downtown relics like the baroque St James Theatre on Courtenay Place and the government buildings centred around The Terrace, which are built of native woods in the masonry style of European architecture.

Despite moving its port operations a mile or so north to a new container complex around this time, Wellington remained one of the country's busiest ports and still is today. This is mainly due to the all-weather sailing of the Cook Strait rail ferries and foreign fishing vessels that call here for registration and provisioning.

The buildings left behind when port operations moved north are a major part of Wellington's reinvention of itself after the public port service, a major employer, was decimated in the 1980s.

Physically confined by the sea on one side and the Rimutaka Ranges on the other, the capital went about the job with gusto. Today it is a hub of creativity; writers and artists are well supported here, and the city offers some of the finest shopping in New Zealand.

The heart of the city

Any exploration of the city should start on Cable Street at **Te Papa Tongarewa – Museum of New Zealand A** (tel: 04-381 7000; www. tepapa.govt.nz; daily 10am–6pm, until 9pm Thu; free), which is regarded as one of the finest in the country and houses some of the most important *taonga* (treasures) of New Zealand. There is no better introduction to the country to be found under one roof, and its aggressively postmodernist approach guarantees mental stimulation of a kind not always found in New Zealand museums.

Within its well-designed interior are a wide range of exhibits and experiences. Examples include Te Marae, a contemporary Maori gathering place, and Awesome Forces, where you get to experience the powerful geological forces that shape New Zealand's landscape. Don't miss the earthquake house. There are also discovery and state-of-the-art time travel and virtual reality centres, cafés, a souvenir shop, children's shop and a bar. Visitors

Inside Te Papa Tongarewa, one of New Zealand's finest museums.

Coastal scenery around Wellington.

should set aside one full day to make the most of this landmark museum.

Leaving the museum and turning right out on the old wharf area, you will see a building with a wedding-cake facade at 1 Taranaki Street, which was rescued from the demolished Westport Chambers to make a home for one of the city's liveliest and most innovative professional theatres, **Circa Theatre ❸** (tel: 04-801 7992; www. circa.co.nz). The building is a perfect example of the born-again look that has transformed the original port area.

If you turn left after leaving the museum you'll find the city's two other major theatres. **Bats Theatre** (tel: 04-802 4175; www.bats.co.nz), found by turning right from Cable Street onto Kent Terrace, is an intimate venue, home of the fringe, that presents diverse and challenging theatre. Turn right again on Marjoribanks Street to encounter the skewwhiff concrete, iron and wood pyramid of **Downstage Theatre** (tel: 04-801 6946; www.downstage.co.nz) at 12 Cambridge Terrace, which offers great shows, a licensed bar and accommodation. The

country's first professional theatre, established in 1964, Downstage marks the southern tip of **Courtenay Place**, one of the city's hip bar and restaurant centres.

To discover the commercial, retail and historic centre of Wellington, follow the wharf north from Circa Theatre to a place where a lagoon has been carved out beside two traditional city rowing clubs. Here, intricately carved arches lead across the main road to **Civic Square ❸**. In between the remnants of Wellington's Victoriana, colourful and architecturally impressive buildings and malls, and a slew of cafés, brighten the scene. Nowhere is this more apparent than in the generous pink-and-beige piazza of Civic Square.

On one side of the square is the **Michael Fowler Centre** – the unmistakable steel colander housing the city's municipal chambers – and the rectangular **Old Town Hall**, saved after testimonials from visiting conductors, such as the late Leonard Bernstein, rated it one of the best symphonic halls in the world, a fitting venue for the home-base of the New Zealand Symphony Orchestra. The Michael Fowler Centre and Old Town Hall are the focus of the annual New Zealand Fringe Festival, reinforcing Wellington's status as the capital of the performing arts in New Zealand.

On the other side of Civic Square is the **Wellington City Library** (tel: 04-801 4040; www.wcl.govt.nz; Mon–Thu 9.30am–8.30pm, until 9pm Fri and 5pm Sat, 1–4pm Sun). The library's interior is like an industrial plant of exposed metal and awash with natural light; outside, its gorgeous plaster curve is decorated with metal palms. All was designed by the city's leading architect, Ian Athfield.

In between is the **City Gallery** (tel: 04-801 3021; www.citygallery.org.nz; daily 10am–5pm; free), which hosts a collection of contemporary local and international artworks in its 1930s Art Deco-style building.

WELLINGTON'S FOUNDING FATHER

The citizens of Wellington have shown scant respect for their Pakeha founding father, the English politician and advocate of emigration Edward Gibbon Wakefield. There is no memorial to Wakefield in the city other than his gravesite, perhaps partly due to lingering disapproval over a prison term he served for allegedly abducting an heiress; she was willing, but her father was not, and he brought a successful court case against the young Wakefield. It was in London's Newgate Prison that the unfortunate Wakefield witnessed at first hand the miserable lot of England's poor, and was moved to devise a scheme that offered a chance to those with nothing by encouraging them to emigrate to Australia and New Zealand.

In practice, though, his ideas of orderly settlement proved to be something of a mess (see page 38). Idealists were thin on the ground in the new lands, and speculators as thick as shovels in a gold rush. Wakefield's brother, William, was in charge of acquiring land for the new emigrants, but he had only four months to do so. His quick deals with the Maori included buying Wellington for 100 muskets, 100 blankets, 60 red nightcaps, a dozen umbrellas and such goods as nails and axes. Wakefield claimed to have bought for £9,000 the 'head of the fish and much of its body', a total of about 8 million hectares (20 million acres).

Wellington's wharves

The streets between Wellington's central city skyscrapers are narrow and windswept with few parks or open spaces, but the city's office workers are never more than a stone's throw from the wharves, with views of wide open skies and invigorating sea breezes. Turn right from the Civic Square towards the water and follow the **wharves** north again. These are open to the public; lunchtime joggers zip past the Russian and Korean fishing crews, and restaurants in converted stores offer haute cuisine. If you're not hungry, you can still see what the sea has to offer at the **Museum of Wellington City and Sea ⓓ** (tel: 04-472 8904; www.museumofwellington.co.nz; daily 10am–5pm; free) at Queens Wharf. The museum houses a captivating collection of maritime memorabilia.

Part of the museum is **Plimmer's Ark Gallery**, which contains the excavated remains of the 150-year-old sailing ship *Inconstant*, later known as Plimmer's Ark. Edward Gibbon Wakefield's (see page 39) controversial role in the struggles of the early settlers may explain why the title 'Father of Wellington' was conferred on John Plimmer instead. A merchant settler who displayed less idealism, Plimmer complained that a place represented to him as 'a veritable Eden' had proved 'a wild and stern reality.' In fact, he had little cause for complaint – he had converted the wreck of the *Inconstant*, the fallout from a bad day, into a flourishing trading enterprise on the beach. Like many of his fellow entrepreneurs, Plimmer added his own wharf, eventually becoming one of the solid citizens of the emerging town, and his wreck ended up as the boardroom chair in the country's Bank of New Zealand.

Lambton Quay and the Parliamentary District

Follow Grey Street, heading inland from the City and Sea Museum, until you reach Lambton Quay, turn right and you'll find **Wellington Cable Car ⓔ** (tel: 04-472 2199; Mon–Fri 7am–10pm, Sat 8.30am–10pm, Sun 9am–9pm). Given the city's

Civic Square.

FACT

The heritage building housing the Museum of Wellington City and Sea was first constructed in 1892 as the Bond Store (customs house), a warehouse where everything from coffee to corsets was stored until duty was paid. In fact, it is safe to say that from 1892 until after World War I, much of what Wellington ate, drank and wore had spent time here.

precipitous downtown topography, the cable car, which runs every 10 minutes and terminates at the Botanic Gardens (see page 221), is a popular route between the shopping precinct and the numerous offices uphill. At the top is the Cable Car Museum (tel: 04-475 3578; www.wellingtoncablecar.co.nz; daily 9.30am–5pm; free), a small museum popular with transport enthusiasts. A free shuttle to Zealandia (see page 221) departs on the hour from here.

Now a major shopping strip, **Lambton Quay** was once the beachfront where Plimmer and his fellow traders set up shop, its narrowness prompting reclamations ever since. The result today is that Lambton Quay is now several blocks from the harbour.

If you make a return trip on the cable car, you can continue north on Lambton Quay for 600 metres (660yds) to the **Old Government Buildings ❻**, the second-largest wooden building in the world. Constructed in 1876, it comprises 9,300 sq metres (100,000 sq ft) of timber. The tides lapped at

City views on the Wellington Cable Car.

this site before land was reclaimed in 1840. Directly opposite, politicians, top public officials and business folk buzz around the capital's unique circular Cabinet offices, known as **The Beehive ❼**. A large amount of the administrative and financial clout of the country is centred here.

Built in the late 1970s, the copper-domed Beehive is a soft contrast with the square marble angles of the adjacent **Parliament Buildings ❽** (tel: 04-817 9503; www.parliament.nz; Mon–Fri 10am–4pm, Sat 10am–3pm, Sun 11am–3pm; free), completed in 1922, and the Gothic turrets of the **General Assembly Library**, dating back to 1897. Free tours depart on the hour, but it is recommended to arrive 15 minutes in advance, to allow for security screening. To one side of the Beehive is the historic, red-brick **Turnbull House**, tucked below the skyscraper 'Number One The Terrace,' office for the Treasury, with the Reserve Bank across the road. North of the Beehive and Parliament are the **New St Paul's Cathedral**, larger than its predecessor (see below) and

with a pink concrete facade, as well as the **National Library ❶** (tel: 04-474 3000; www.natlib.govt.nz; Mon–Sat 10am–5pm; free). Within this is the **Alexander Turnbull Library**, housing a remarkable collection of New Zealand and Pacific history.

Leave the National Library via Aitken Street, turn left on Mulgrave Street and, surrounded by pohutukawa trees, you'll see **Old St Paul's ❽** (tel: 04-473 6722; daily 9.30am–5pm; free), a small but impressive Gothic Revival-style cathedral made entirely of native timbers, even down to the nails. Consecrated in 1866, this is the most noteworthy of the city's 30 churches; many of these were built in the wooden adaptation of the soaring stone Gothic style that was a unique colonial feature.

About 10 minutes' walk further north is the district of **Thorndon**, location of **Katherine Mansfield's Birthplace** (tel: 04-473 7268; www.katherinemansfield.com; Tue–Sun 10am–4pm) at 25 Tinakori Road. The two-storey family home where the writer was born in 1888 has been beautifully restored and features an authentic Victorian town garden.

Wellington's suburbs

On the fringes of the city centre lie some of Wellington's premier attractions. Just over 1km (½ mile) southwest of Old St Paul's are the luxuriant grounds of the **Botanic Gardens ❿** (tel: 04-499 4444; www.wellington.govt.nz/services/gardens; daily sunrise–sunset; free), notable for the formal glory of the **Lady Norwood Rose Garden**. The gardens are perfect for a stroll, and in the summer months the colourful blooms are truly spectacular. There is also a good children's adventure playground here.

The **Carter National Observatory** in the Botanic Gardens (tel: 04-910 3140; www.carterobservatory.org; Mon, Wed, Thu, Fri 9am–5pm, Tue, Sat 10am–9.30pm, Sun 10am–5.30pm) gives enlightening talks and demonstrations

about the southern night sky. There are also planetarium shows.

Another 1km (½ mile) southwest of the Botanic Gardens is the remarkable **Zealandia Karori Sanctuary Experience ❶** (tel: 04-920 9200; www.sanctuary.org.nz; daily 10am–5pm, last entry 4pm) on Waiapu Road. This oasis has 35km (22 miles) of tracks covering 252 hectares (623 acres) of regenerating forest. This is a chance to see – or at least hear – birds such as kiwi, *weka* and morepork in their natural environment. Night guided tours are also available (booking is essential; tel: 04-920 9200). The sanctuary hit the headlines in 2009 when a tuatara was discovered here, the first sighting on the mainland for over 200 years.

Wellingtonians are seasoned campaigners when it comes to environmental battles. From the late 1960s, citizens of the gentrified Thorndon neighbourhood cut their conservation teeth when opposing the construction of an urban motorway; the campaign managed partly to achieve its aims. A more successful protest took place on

Tulips soaking up the sun at the Botanic Gardens.

An antique telescope at the Carter National Observatory.

the other side of the city in the raffish community of the Aro Valley below the Victoria University, when students and residents repelled council plans to demolish their wooden cottages in favour of concrete.

A high-profile example of the latter campaign can be seen in the presence of the **Colonial Cottage Museum**  (tel: 04-384 9122; www. colonialcottagemuseum.co.nz; Sat–Sun noon–4pm, Dec–Mar daily noon–4pm), at 68 Nairn Street, close to the corner of Willis Street (which runs south from the city centre). The museum is located in Central Wellington's oldest building, a four-bedroom house dating from 1858. The house was to be demolished in the 1970s, but the tenacity of its occupant, a granddaughter of the original builders, inspired local support and it was saved.

From Te Aro, head southeast to the **Basin Reserve** cricket ground, which was a lake before an earthquake drained it. To the southeast of the basin is the suburb of **Newtown**, its narrow streets teeming with new migrants from the Pacific, Asia and Europe. At the local school, you can hear 20 different languages spoken, while shops that look like the clapboard facades of a Hollywood Wild West set sell exotic foods from a dozen lands. Newtown is also the site of **Wellington Zoo** Ⓝ (tel: 04-381 6755; www.wellingtonzoo.com; daily 9.30am–5pm). This is New Zealand's oldest zoo, built in 1906 and now run on the natural habitat conservation model favoured by zoos worldwide.

The Hutt Valley

To enjoy the rest of what Wellington has to offer, head north again, leaving the city via the Hutt Road (NH2) and heading for the topographically blander environment of the **Hutt Valley** ㉗, the cities of **Lower Hutt** and **Upper Hutt** and their satellite suburbs. The first settlers had little to thank Edward Gibbon Wakefield for when they were dumped on a beach at the swampy bottom of the Lower Hutt Valley. After their tents flooded, the settlement moved to the narrow, but dry, site of the present city. The abandoned Lower Hutt area, today's **Petone**, meaning the End of the Sand, evolved into a working-class industrial town. Times have changed, and the flat shoreline is now a recreational area and the workers' cottages have been gentrified. The **Petone Settlers' Museum** (tel: 04-568 8373; www.newdowse.org.nz/psm; Wed–Sun 10am–4pm) commemorates the early struggles. The museum is notable for its close involvement with the local community and is as much about the present as the past.

Further up the valley at Silver Stream, home to the exclusive red-brick Catholic St Patrick's College, is a chance to ride on a hillside steam train at the **Silver Stream Railway Museum** (tel: 04-543 7348; www.silver streamrailway.org.nz; Sun only 11am–4pm). It is operated by a group of volunteers and has one of the largest

Wellington Zoo resident.

collections of working vintage steam trains in New Zealand.

Head back south towards Wellington and take the eastern turn-off to explore some of the small communities tucked into the steep eastern bays. **Wainuiomata**, famous for its rugby league club, is the gateway to the **Rimutaka Forest Park**, which provides a natural barrier between Wellington and the Wairarapa. The park features several good wilderness hikes, including the Whakanui Track, the McKerrow Track and the Mount Matthews track, leading to the summit of Mount Matthews.

Another hilly route leads to **Eastbourne**, across the bay from Wellington. It can also be reached by ferry or a drive around the bays from the city centre, and is worth a visit for its craft shops and simply as a quiet contrast to the city. It is an easy 8km (5-mile) hike around this coast to view the **Pencarrow Lighthouse**, the country's first permanent lighthouse. This 1859 cast-iron structure was 'manned' at the time by one Mary Jane Bennett, New Zealand's only woman lighthouse keeper.

Wellington's environs: the Kapiti Coast

At weekends many Wellingtonians head northwest to the **Kapiti Coast**. One of the many good beaches in the area is at **Paraparaumu** ㉘, 57km (35 miles) from the capital, where there are water slides and water-sports facilities, and a range of accommodation options. It can be reached by commuter train in 45 minutes, or one hour by car (due to traffic).

It is possible to join tours from Paraparaumu to the unspoilt native bird sanctuary of **Kapiti Island** ㉙, the capital of the warrior chief Te Rauparaha, who ruled the Wellington region when the Pakeha arrived. Cats, goats and dogs blighted the native fauna of the island until the Department of Conservation embarked on an eradication programme, and Kapiti is now a valuable sanctuary for several species of native birds such as the *kakariki*, *takahe*, *kea* and kiwi. As well as hiking and birdwatching, the island has two marine parks which hug its northern shores and provide

TIP

If time does not permit a day trip to Kapiti Island, visit Nga Manu (tel: 04-293 4131; www.ngamanu.co.nz), a 15-hectare (38-acre) park in Waikanae dedicated to the preservation of New Zealand flora and fauna. Breed-and-release recovery programmes for kiwi, brown teal, blue duck and tuatara operate here, and its wetland areas teem with native waterfowl, including scaup (New Zealand diving ducks).

Wellington's environs, with Kapiti Island in the distance.

The Toast Martinborough festival takes place each November.

A kaka (native parrot) at Pukaha Mount Bruce National Wildlife Centre.

excellent snorkelling and scuba-diving opportunities. Marine life is colourful and diverse, with orange and yellow sponges (some of which are extremely rare), *kina*, *paua*, starfish, corals, anemones, octopus and a variety of reef fish including butterfish, blue cod and red mullet. Regular tourists include blue moki and kingfish, and rarer passersby include spotted black grouper, drumfish and magpie perch. All along Kapiti Island's coast white-fronted terns, variable oystercatchers, reef herons, gannets, fluttering shearwaters, and black and spotted shags make their home. **Kapiti Tours Ltd** (tel: 06-237 7965; www.kapititours.co.nz), which is based at Paraparaumu, can take you there; one-hour guided walking tours are also available.

A few kilometres further along the Gold Coast, as it is known, you can enjoy locally made gourmet cheeses and watch sheep-shearing and the milking of cows at the **Lindale Centre** (tel: 04-297 0916; daily 9am–5pm; free), and don't miss out on a tasting of locally made Kapiti ice cream.

Wairarapa region

Beyond the Hutt Valley are the farming lands of the **Wairarapa**. Wellington developed as a port partly for the shipping of the products from these fertile plains.

It takes an hour to drive northeast over the 300-metre (1,000ft) Rimutaka Ranges on SH2; cars sometimes need chains to negotiate the road during winter. In the old days, a Fell locomotive hauled people and goods up the mountain's almost vertical incline to the other side: a land of wide open spaces fringed by a handsome coastline, where it's warmer, sunnier and less windy than the capital. These same broad plains attracted some of New Zealand's earliest European settlers – the ones responsible for its legacy of dollhouse-cute villas and homesteads.

Rolling down the hill into **Featherston**, the **Fell Locomotive Museum** (tel: 06-308 9379; www.fell museum.org.nz; Mon–Fri 9am–2pm, Sat–Sun 10am–4pm) houses the only Fell locomotive left in the world. Fells, of which only six were made, were

designed to cope with steep gradients, such as on the Rimutaka Ranges, where the track passed over a gradient of 1 in 13. Nearby, the small local **Heritage and World War Museum** outlines the grim role the town played as a POW camp for Japanese.

Greytown ③⓪ was New Zealand's first inland town and is arguably the prettiest and most Victorian of them all. City folk flock here to indulge in wine trails, antiques, arts, crafts, speciality shops and local produce. **Cobblestones Museum** (tel: 06-304 9687; www.cobblestonesmuseum.org.nz; daily 10am–4pm) at 169 Main Street, evokes the echoes of clattering stagecoaches and the heavy breathing of tired horses, pulling in with cargoes of new pioneers. Next door at number 177, **Schoc Chocolates** (tel: 06-304 8960; www.chocolatetherapy.com; daily 10am–5pm) crafts divine organic and preservative-free chocolates and truffles on site.

Martinborough ③①, 18km (11 miles) southeast of Featherston, burst onto the world stage in the 1990s as a wine producer, particularly for its Pinot Noir. Take a two-hour vineyard tour departing from Martinborough with The Horse and Carriage (tel: 027-426 2286; www.horseandcarriage. co.nz), or for a more comprehensive tour by vehicle take a day trip with Martinborough Wine Tours (tel: 06-306 8032; www.martinboroughwine-tours.co.nz; daily 10am–4.30pm).

Alternatively, if you're short on time, visit the Martinborough Wine Centre at 6 Kitchener Street (tel: 06-306 9040; www.martinboroughwinecentre. co.nz; daily 10am–5pm), a fine place to learn all about the wineries in the region. Bloom restaurant at Murdoch James (tel: 06 306 9165; www.murdoch james.co.nz or www.bloomrestaurant.co.nz) makes a good lunch stop.

Further north on SH2, the eye-catching daffodil capital of **Carterton** has more historical buildings to explore, plus attractions including **Paua World** (tel: 06-379 4247; www. pauaworld.com; Mon–Fri 8am–5pm, Sat–Sun 9am–5pm, factory tours Mon–Thu 8am–5pm; free) at 54 Kent Street, with displays and information relating to the shellfish and its uses.

Classic car at Martinborough.

WAIRARAPA WINE

The Wairarapa region produces about 3,000 cases of wine per year and its success with Pinot Noir is well known. The potential to grow vines in the region was first recognised by William Beetham over a century ago when he planted vines in Masterton in 1883 and successfully managed to produce a quality vintage. A decade later, Beetham added another vineyard at Lansdowne (also in Masterton), which he planted with vinifera varietals including Pinot Noir. In 1905, prohibition brought an end to the Lansdowne vineyards, but in more recent years, riding the wave of Martinborough's success and wider global awareness of New Zealand wines, a flurry of boutique vineyards owned and run by passionate, quality-driven wine makers have opened.

This is the best place in New Zealand to buy *paua* shell souvenirs of every description. Also in town on Chester Road is **Awaiti Gardens** (tel: 06-379 8478; www.awaitigardens.co.nz; Sept–May Thu–Sun 10am–4pm), 2.4 hectares (6 acres) of rhododendrons, roses and hydrangeas, a gallery and a cottage serving Devonshire teas.

To the west, in the **Tararua Forest Park**, is the beautiful Waiohine Gorge, whose waters flow from the flanks of Arete Peak and Tarn Ridge. There are a number of good hikes here, beginning with a rather precarious-looking swing bridge suspended high above the river, just minutes from the car park. To the east, on the sunny plains beyond Carterton, are the vineyards of Gladstone.

North of Carterton, the town of **Masterton** ❷ hosts the annual **Golden Shears** sheep-shearing competition (tel: 06-378 8008; www.goldenshears. co.nz). Although New Zealand has long shed its image as one giant farm, the Golden Shears is still one of the few regular agricultural events in which the whole country takes an interest.

Masterton's hills and rivers are popular with those who wish to get away from it all, and in the duck-shooting season its population rises dramatically.

For locals, life centres around **Queen Elizabeth Park**, with its historic cemetery, super-sized duck pond, 'Kids' Own' playground, steam train, mini golf and bowls. Across the road at 12 Dixon Street is The Wool Shed, **the National Museum of Sheep and Shearing** (tel: 06-378 8008; www.sheardiscovery.co.nz; daily 10am–4pm), with its Golden Shears Hall of Champions, sheep-shearing display, and information about all facets of wool production.

Other points of interest include peaceful **Henley Lake** and **The Pointon Collection** (tel: 06-378 6710; www.pointoncollection.co.nz; daily 10am–4pm) at 68 McKinstry Avenue, with its vast aggregation of vintage cars and motorcycles, plus a collection of clothes spanning 100 years from the 1860s through to the 1960s.

Worthy excursions from Masterton include the drive north to **Pukaha Mount Bruce National Wildlife**

The rural town of Eketahuna.

Centre (tel: 06-375 8004; www.mtbruce.
org.nz; daily 9am–4.30pm), where threatened species such as the North Island
kiwi, the kokako, and North Island kaka
can be viewed in natural bush aviaries.
Highlights here include Manukura, a
rare white kiwi, and the daily feeding
sessions: tuatara at 11.30am, eels at
1.30pm and kaka at 3pm. Kiwi chicks
are also often seen during the breeding
season from September through to May.

The southeast coast and Palliser Bay

Castlepoint ❸ is one of the few settlements on the ruggedly beautiful southeastern coast, accessed via a long road
from Masterton. The Castlepoint lighthouse is perched among embedded
fossils on a craggy wind-blown bluff,
buffeted by the giant rollers of the
Pacific Ocean and reached via a rickety
causeway – an adventure in itself.

Another lighthouse and scenic drive
of note is the route 60km (37 miles)
southwest of Martinborough to the
rough windswept coast of **Palliser
Bay** ❸. From Lake Ferry take the
Cape Palliser Road southeastwards

to the strange **Putangirua Pinnacles**.
Here a 30-minute walk leads to giant
rock spires, some reaching up to 50
metres (165ft) in height, formed by
the weathering away of silt deposits
over the past 120,000 years.

In **Ngawi**, a picturesque fishing village nestled snugly into the base of the
towering Aorangi Range, rows of rusty
bulldozers, used for pulling fishing
boats ashore, line the beach.

Seals are commonly sighted along
this stretch of coast at the southern
tip of North Island, and at the end of
the road 258 steep steps lead to Cape
Palliser Lighthouse, constructed in 1896
from materials brought by boat, as the
road to the cape was not built until
1941. The windswept shores of Palliser
Bay were once the principal points of
access for early European settlers to the
region. The settlers arrived in the mid-
to late 1800s to set up sheep stations,
build homes and farm the fertile plains.

From the lighthouse you can gain
spectacular views across Palliser Bay
to the South Island, and see Kaikoura's
snowcapped mountains rising sharply
from the sea.

Castlepoint.

*A tui feeds on nectar
at Zealandia Karori
Sanctuary.*

Surfers at Kaikoura.

View from Milford Sound towards Mitre Peak.

South Island

0   100 km

0   100 miles

SOUTH ISLAND

An island of unparalleled scenic beauty and variety, with magnificent snowcapped mountains, fabulous empty beaches and dramatic fiords backed by primeval rainforests.

Detail from Larnach Castle.

Variety is the essence of the South Island, a visual feast of towering snowcapped peaks, broad sun-parched plains, impenetrable rainforests, rich farmlands, spectacular waterfalls, giant glaciers, serene lakes and deep fiords. The boat from which Maui fished the North Island out of the sea, according to the ancient Polynesian legend, seems to have captured much of nature's bounty.

The South Island is remarkably uncrowded. Christchurch, the very English 'garden city' devastated in the 2011 earthquake yet being rebuilt in an architectural revival, remains one of the two main points of entry, together with Picton in the picturesque Marlborough Sounds. Here at the top of the island, a region of sunken valleys and secluded bays, sun-drenched plains record New Zealand's highest sunshine hours, much to the pleasure of grape growers.

Hit the West Coast and things start to get wild; beaches pounded by the turbulent Tasman Sea meet with the immensity of the Southern Alps. Through the winding mountain passes the landscape opens up to one of wide braided rivers and high-country sheep farms. Hot mineral springs seep from the ground where the giant moa once roamed.

swimming with dolphins.

In the southern lakes region, Queenstown and Wanaka offer a magnificent setting with lakes, forests and mountains combining to create a scene of extraordinary beauty, with a range of adventure activities guaranteed to get the adrenaline pumping. To the east and on the coast is Dunedin, a university city where the influence of the early Scottish settlers is plain to see.

The rich farmland of Southland forms the base of the island. And then there is Fiordland, comprising 10 percent of New Zealand's land area but less than one-thousandth of its population. Found here are the renowned Milford Track, Milford Sound, Mitre Peak and Doubtful Sound.

Maui's anchor comes in the form of Stewart Island. Little-known to many New Zealanders themselves, those in the know say its friendly inhabitants and untouched landscapes make it the most phenomenal place of all.

Araroa Bay, Abel Tasman National Park.

NELSON AND MARLBOROUGH

The South Island's northern tip is a haven for wildlife and offers rest, relaxation and a slow pace, which many travellers will welcome after a bumpy journey across the Cook Strait.

Auckland
Wellington
Christchurch

Across Cook Strait from Wellington, the provinces of Nelson and Marlborough are the gateway to the South Island for those arriving on the ferry (the three-hour trip from the capital terminates at Picton in the Marlborough Sounds). This is a picturesque region with marked differences in scenery – the dry scrubland of the east contrasting with the dripping rainforest further west. Collectively, the provinces enjoy the highest number of sunshine hours in the country (2,000–2,400 a year).

New Zealanders holiday here in droves. Nelson's population of 52,000 is said to double at Christmas and New Year. Its Tahunanui Motor Camp, empty much of the year, becomes a small city in its own right. At beach resorts like Kaiteriteri, numbers jump from several hundred to several thousand. Visitors pour into hotels, motels and motor camps in cars full of children, towing caravans or boats, with tents strapped to roof racks.

Across Cook Strait to Picton

Cook Strait is a natural funnel for the strong westerly wind known as the Roaring Forties. On a bad day, this can be one of the most unpleasant short stretches of water on earth. But squeezing through the narrows to enter Tory Channel in the **Marlborough Sounds**

❶ is like entering another world, its sheltered coves and bays beckoning with blissful hues of greens and blues. This complex configuration of sunken valleys has more than 1,000km (620 miles) of shoreline. Nonetheless, the journey down **Tory Channel** and **Queen Charlotte Sound** aboard the ferries gives only a glimpse of the glorious scenery. The shores invite exploration and are dotted with isolated houses, many offering holiday accommodation. Even today, few Sounds residents enjoy the luxury of road access

Main Attractions

Marlborough Sounds
Blenheim Wineries
Abel Tasman National Park
Farewell Spit Eco Tours

Sea kayaking in Torrent Bay.

Northern South Island

0   50 km

0   50 miles

N

Tasman Sea

Karamea Bight

Mangara
Paturau
River
Coll

Heaphy Track

Kahura
Waikorc
▲ 1646
Mt D

*Tasma
Mounta*
Nat

Oparara
Basin

Karamea
Mt Kenda
1762
▲

Karameal **36**

*Wanga
Trac*

Ka

Owen
River

Mokihinui
Hector
Ngakawau Seddonville

Westport Denniston
Cape Foulwind **35**
**Buller
Gorge**

**Ariki
Falls I**

Buller

Murchiso

Inangahua

Ro

Charleston

Punakaiki **Paparoa
NP**

Reefton
37 **Victoria
Forest
Park**

Na

Park

Pancake Rocks **34**

Paparoa Range

Barrytown Ikamatua

Blackball *Grey*

Maruia
Springs

Runanga

Ahaura

Springs
Junction

Greymouth **33** Stillwater

Moana

Lewis
Pass
865

Kumara
Junction **Shantytown**

*Lake
Brunner*

**Lake
Summer
Forest
Park**

*Lake
Sumner*

Hokitika **32** Kumara

Inchbonnie

*Lake
Kaniere*

Otira
912

Mt Longfellow
1898

Hu

Ross

Kowhitirangi

**Hokitika
Gorge**

**Arthur's
Pass
National
Park**

*Puketeraki
Range*

Mt Rolleston
2271

*Lake
Ianthe*

Arthur's
Pass **16**

Abut Head Harihari

31 Okarito
Lagoon

Okarito

*Lake
Wahapo*

Whataroa

West
Coast

2400
Mt Murchison

2644
Mt Whitecombe

Craigieburn
Forest
Park

73

**Broken
River**

ALPS

*Lake
Coleridge*

Porter's
Pass

17

945

Am

Oxford Rangio

Cust

Lake Mapourika

Franz Josef Glacier

Gillespie's Beach

SOUTHERN

*Lake
Matheson*

30

**Aoraki
Mt Cook
National
Park**

2795
Mt Arrowsmith

Springfield
Sheffield

72

Darfield

Kaiap

Christchurc

Hornby

29 Fox Glacier **28**

3498
▲ Mt Tasman
3754

25

Two Thumb Range

Mount Hutt
18

Canterbury

Methven

Burnham
Dunsandel

Lincoln

*Lake
Ellesme
Te Wai*

Karangarua
**Bridge Scenic
Reserve**

**Westland
National
Park**

Aoraki Mt Cook
**Tasman
Glacier**

☀ Aoraki Mt Cook Village

Mount
Somers

Rangitata

Mayfield

*Canterbury
Plains*

Rakaia

Chertsey

77

1

Monro Beach

Knights Point

*Lake
Paringa*

Paringa

24

1951
Ben McLeod

**Peel
Forest
Park**

Tinwald
Ashburton

Haast Beach

*Lake
Moeraki*

Haast

Haast

22
*Lake
Tekapo*

Geraldine **19**

C a n t e r b u r y

Jackson Bay **27**

**Mount
Aspiring

National**

Mt Huxley
2499

Ben Ohau Range

Glentanner
Park

**Mt John
Observatory**

**Church of
Good Shepherd**

21 Fairlie

79

Orari

Waitohi

Temuka

B i g h t

26 Haast Pass
563

*Lake
Pukaki*

Burke's
Pass

Albury

Pleasant
Point

20

Makaroa

23
Twizel

*Lake
Ohau*

*Kirkliston
Range*

*Hunters
Hills*

**Raincliff
Reserve Maori
Rock Art**

Timaru

Pareora

**SOUTHERN
ALPS**

▲ 3030
Mt Aspiring

*Lake
Wanaka*

*Lake
Benmore*

Omarama

*Lake
Hawea*

Otago

Treble Cone
2088 ▲

Queenstown

Wanaka

Lindis Pass
971

Dunedin

Aoraki
Mt Cook

3498

Mt Tasman

2400

SOUTHERN

*West
Coast*

Arriving at Picton by ferry from the North Island. There are frequent daily crossings in both directions between Wellington and Picton: journey time is about three hours, depending on sea conditions. The crossing is frequently rough, so take travel-sickness pills.

to their homes, with launches still the main mode of transport; even mail and the doctor come by boat. The area is encompassed by the Marlborough Sounds Maritime Park.

Derelict buildings from the last whaling station in the country can be seen just inside the entrance to Tory Channel. It closed in 1964, ending more than 50 years of pursuit of the migratory humpback whale by the Perano family.

The most famous of all Pacific explorers, Captain James Cook, spent more than 100 days in and around Ship Cove during his travels. It was on the highest point of Moutara Island in Queen Charlotte Sound that Cook claimed New Zealand for King George III, and the Sound for his queen, an act commemorated by a monument erected near the entrance to Queen Charlotte Sound.

The commercial centre for almost all activity in the Sounds is the attractive town of **Picton ❷**, near the head of Queen Charlotte Sound. As well as being the terminal for the Cook Strait ferries to Wellington, Picton marks the start of the South Island section of both State Highway (SH) 1 and the main trunk railway. It is also the main base for the assorted launches, water taxis and charter boats on which locals and visitors rely for transport.

An old trading vessel, the *Echo*, which is usually drawn up on the beach on one side of Picton's bay, was one of the last of New Zealand's old trading scows to remain in service, and is now a café-bar (tel: 03-573 7498; Wed–Sun 10am–late). Its exploits during World War II, when the US Navy commandeered it, inspired the book and later the film *The Wackiest Ship in the Navy*. A shipping relic of far greater antiquity, the teak hull of the *Edwin Fox*, lies in the purpose-built **Edwin Fox Maritime Centre** (tel: 03-573 6868; www.edwinfoxsociety.com; daily Apr–Nov 9am–3pm, Dec–Mar 9am–5pm) at Dunbar Wharf. Built in India in 1853, the *Edwin Fox*, in her long and colourful history, carried cargo world-wide, troops in the Crimean War, convicts to Australia and immigrants to New Zealand.

Picton has several museums, mostly devoted to its maritime heritage. Much of the activity here centres around the foreshore promenade, where there's a children's playground, mini-golf course, and kids can sail small yachts on a pond for 20c a pop. Further afield, half-day and full-day scenic cruises, kayak trips and dolphin-watching expeditions leave regularly to explore the labyrinthine waterways in the area. Departing from the Town Wharf, **Dolphin Watch Ecotour** (Town Wharf; tel: 03-573 8040; www.naturetours.co.nz) provides a range of trips including a popular wildlife-spotting cruise to Motuara Island Bird Sanctuary at the entrance to Queen Charlotte Sound, where once-endangered saddleback and South Island robins can be viewed at close range, along with a host of other rare and protected bird species. Water taxis also depart from the wharf, and within half an hour you can be dining at a

A Renwick vineyard.

resort, or hiking a short section of the Queen Charlotte Track.

To complete the whole 71km (44 miles) of the track from historic Ship Cove to Anakiwa takes four to five days. A range of accommodation is available, from tent sites and basic rooms through to upmarket rooms in private lodges and resorts.

Blenheim and the wineries

Some 30km (19 miles) south of Picton, **Blenheim ❸** is the administrative centre of sparsely populated Marlborough province. Sitting on the Wairau plain, this pleasant rural service town has blossomed since the establishment in 1973 of the original Montana vineyards, now owned by **Pernod Ricard New Zealand** (www.pernod-ricard-nz.com). Pernod Ricard is New Zealand's largest wine maker, producing a bewildering array of wines. One of its wineries, **Montana Brancott Winery** (tel: 03-520 6975; www.brancottestate.com; daily 10am–4.30pm), is located just south of Blenheim. A guided tour of the vineyard, which departs from the

Heritage Centre at 11am, and 2pm daily, is very informative and takes in some of the winery's special features, including rare, giant *cuves* made of French oak, New Zealand's first traditional Coquard champagne press, and 55-tonne tipping tanks.

Marlborough is one of the country's most important wine-producing regions, with wineries at every turn, including the renowned **Cloudy Bay** (www.cloudybay.co.nz), an abundance of fine restaurants and cafés, and a great variety of places to stay. The annual **Marlborough Wine and Food Festival** (www.wine-marlborough-festival.co.nz) in February celebrates the vital relationship between good food and wine and is an important regional event. Other regional staples – grapes, apples, cherries, salmon, mussels and sheep – all take advantage of Marlborough's warmth to grow fat and juicy. The region's pleasant, sunny climate is down to the rain shadow (and *föhn*) effect produced by the mountains to the west and southwest.

Blenheim has several noteworthy attractions, including the **Millennium Art Gallery** (05-579 2001; www.marlboroughart.org.nz; Mon–Fri 10.30am–4.30pm, Sat–Sun 1–4pm; donations), and the **Marlborough Museum** (tel: 03-578 1712; www.marlborough museum.co.nz; daily 10am–4pm) in the **Brayshaw Museum Park** complex, where the history of the town's early settlers is displayed.

In nearby **Renwick ❹**, 10km (6 miles) from Blenheim, are the vineyards of the Wairau Valley. Here, **Wine Tours By Bike** (tel: 03-577 6954; www.winetoursbybike.co.nz) supply everything for exploring the wine tour, from bikes to wine panniers. Detailed maps provide personalised itineraries, including vineyards, arts and crafts, scenic sights and the pick of seasonal fruits.

Out on the coast, the small settlement of **Rarangi** provides good views of the broad sweep of Cloudy Bay. To get there from Blenheim, drive north on SH1 for 9km (5½ miles), then make a right turn onto Rarangi Road. At the northern end of the beach a hike or drive along the cliffs leads to Whites Bay, a DOC camping ground, and historic Robin Hood Bay, where there's an old stud and mud cottage, built by a whaler in 1854.

South of Blenheim, nothing utilises the long, hot, dry days of summer more than the salt works at Lake Grassmere, 30km (19 miles) southeast of Blenheim, where sea water is ponded in shallow lagoons and then allowed to evaporate until nothing is left but blinding-white salt crystals.

Mussels and gold

SH6, running northwest from Blenheim to Nelson, takes you 39km (24 miles) down the attractive Kaituna Valley to **Havelock ❺**. This fishing and holiday settlement at the head of Pelorus Sound, the furthest point that the Marlborough Sounds penetrate inland, is like a smaller version of Picton, without the bustle of the inter-island ferries but with the same feeling that all the important businesses are waterborne. Pelorus

Casks at Wither Hills winery on New Renwick Road, Blenheim. Their environmentally sustainable vineyards are used to grow grape varieties that include Sauvignon Blanc, Riesling, Pinot Noir, Chardonnay and Gewürztraminer.

The Marlborough region produces almost 80 percent of the country's wine.

The Mussel Pot restaurant in Havelock, whose speciality, unsurprisingly, is green-lip mussels harvested from local waters.

The World of Wearable Art and Classic Cars Museum in Nelson.

and Kenepuru sounds are key to New Zealand's aquaculture industry, their uncrowded and sheltered waters being used for growing salmon in sea cages and green-lipped mussels on buoyed rope lines. Scallops and Pacific oysters are harvested here. To learn more about this industry, join a **Greenshell Mussel Cruise** (tel: 03-577 9997; www.marlboroughtravel. co.nz), departing from the marina. It cruises through the sounds, visiting mussel farms en route; tastings, matched with local Marlborough wines, are provided.

Just beyond Havelock is **Canvastown**, named after the tent village which popped up when gold was discovered on the **Wakamarina River** in the 1860s. It was a short-lived rush, with most of the diggers going south to Otago. Canvastown remembers its brief heyday with a memorial of old mining tools and equipment set in concrete. Visitors can hire pans and still get a 'show' of gold on the Wakamarina.

Rai Valley, further north, provides a rest stop for buses travelling the 115km (71 miles) between Blenheim and Nelson. A smaller road heads off northwards to **French Pass** ❻ at the outermost western edge of the sounds. A narrow, reef-strewn waterway separates the mainland and **D'Urville Island**, resembling a raging river as it tries to equalise the waters of Admiralty and Tasman Bays. New Zealand's fifth-largest island, it was named after 19th-century French explorer Dumont d'Urville, who sailed through the pass in 1827, narrowly avoiding the wrecking of his corvette, the *Astrolabe*, when it was dragged over the reef.

Nelson and environs

Marlborough and **Nelson** ❼ were once a single province but the conservative sheep farmers of Marlborough ceded Nelson in 1859, colonised as it was by progressive artisans and crafts people perceived as troublemakers. It set the tone for a city unlike any other in New Zealand, a hotbed of creative flair.

In part, the city owes its arty identity to Andrew Suter, Bishop of Nelson from 1867 to 1891. Suter

equeathed what is considered to be the country's finest collection of early colonial watercolours to the people of Nelson. They are housed in the **Suter Gallery** (tel: 03-548 4699; www. thesuter.org.nz; daily 10.30am–4.30pm) at 208 Bridge Street, one of the centres of cultural life in the city, along with the **School of Music** (tel: 03-548 9477; www.nsom.co.nz) two blocks south on Nile Street and the **Theatre Royal** (tel: 03-548 3840; www.theatre royalnelson.co.nz) to the west at 78 Rutherford Street, the country's oldest theatre building. One block to the east is Trafalgar Street, with **Christ Church Cathedral** set imperiously at the head of a flight of steps at its southern end.

A few hundred metres north on Trafalgar Street, at Montgomery Square, is **Nelson Markets** (tel: 03-546 5454; Sat–Sun 8am–1pm), a good opportunity to see and buy some of the region's best produce as well as a cross section of local crafts.

On Atawhai Drive at Nelson's northern end is **Founder's Historic Park** (tel: 03-548 2649; www.founders park.co.nz; daily 10am–4.30pm), a collection of historical buildings, including a windmill, a 3D maze, an organic brewery and nautical exhibits in a garden setting. Further north are the **Miyazu Gardens** (daily 8am–sunset; free), a traditional Japanese garden, and a better bet for garden-lovers than **Botanical Hill** on Milton Street at the town's eastern border, although the zigzag track to the 'Centre of New Zealand', at the top of the hill, is popular with hikers.

Art that you can wear

Until 2004, Nelson hosted the world-famous **World of Wearable Art Awards** (WOW), an annual theatrical extravaganza that attracted local and overseas competitors. Designers competed to create the most outlandish garment that encompassed it all – fashion, sculpture and art.

In 2005 the WOW awards show moved to the Queens Wharf Events Centre in Wellington, but the creations from previous competitions have a permanent home in Nelson at the **World of Wearable Art and Classic Cars Museum** (tel: 03-547 4573; www. wowcars.co.nz; daily 10am–5pm) at 95 Quarantine Road. Allow at least an hour to take in the wearable art and classic car galleries, audiovisual theatre and illumination room.

Some of the prettiest churches in the area are found in **Richmond**, 12km (7 miles) southwest of Nelson, and **Wakefield**, 15km (9 miles) southwest of Richmond, where the parish church of **St John's** was built in 1846, making it New Zealand's second-oldest church and the oldest in the South Island. Halfway between Nelson and Richmond, at **Stoke**, is the pioneer homestead **Broadgreen Historic House** (tel: 03-547 0403; www.nelson citycouncil.co.nz/broadgreen-historic-house; daily 10.30am–4.30pm) at 276 Nayland Road. Built circa 1855, this 11-room stately cob house provides a glimpse of an earlier and more genteel era.

The Interislander ferry makes its way through Queen Charlotte Sound, part of the Marlborough Sounds.

The Cool Store Gallery on Mapua Wharf is housed in a converted cool store shed for apples. Ideal for souvenirs, this place only stocks arts and crafts by New Zealand artists, sculptors and jewellers.

FACT

In the past, the availability of relatively cheap smallholdings and seasonal work made Nelson province something of a magnet for people seeking alternative lifestyles. These days, land prices have soared, but house trucks still abound, and the valleys of the Motueka River and Golden Bay continue to attract many people with ideas about holistic living.

Abel Tasman National Park is fringed with superb beaches.

Motueka and Abel Tasman National Park

Nelson contributes a large part of the nation's production of nashi pears, kiwi fruit, berryfruit and apples. It also produces the entire national crop of hops. Flavouring the country's beer, these are grown near **Motueka** ❽, 35km (22 miles) northwest of Richmond on SH60, where large fields of tobacco once filled every paddock. Vineyards in Nelson are increasing in number, particularly in Waimea and the Moutere Hills. Forestry, fishing and ship servicing are other big local industries.

The handicraft revival of the 1960s saw the Nelson region develop as an important pottery centre, largely due to the good local clay, and nowhere more so than in Motueka – a thriving artistic community (with excellent trout fishing on the Motueka River). Potteries still abound, but weaving, silver working, glass blowing and other crafts are also well represented.

Some 20km (12 miles) north of Motueka is the **Abel Tasman National Park** ❾, with its emerald

bays and granite-fringed coastline. This is best savoured by walking the **Coastal Track** (see page 244) connecting **Marahau** at its southern end to **Totaranui** in the north. The full walk takes three or four days, but the less energetic can take coastal launch or yacht services from Kaiteriteri or Marahau to a selection of bays along the way. Kayak trips around the bays, both guided and unguided, have grown in popularity in recent years. A memorial to Abel Tasman, the 17th-century Dutch navigator who first sighted New Zealand, stands at **Tarakohe** on the road to the park that bears his name.

Golden Bay

Ascending to an altitude of 791 metres (2,595ft), **Takaka Hill Road**, a section of SH60 which runs west of the park to **Golden Bay**, is not the country's highest mountain pass, but its 25km (16 miles), featuring a total of 365 bends, makes it the longest single hill drivers in New Zealand will tackle. Rainwater has etched this marble mountain into a bizarre landscape of

rifts, rills, runnels and flutings. A walk of 400 metres from the end of a road up the Riwaka Valley, on the Nelson side of Takaka Hill, will take you to the first visible part of the Riwaka River, where it emerges in full flow from its invisible source inside the hill.

Down a side road to Canaan, **Harwoods Hole** plunges an awesome 183 metres (600ft), giving highly experienced abseilers the ultimate test of plunging into the void. The first descent, taking place in 1957, was marked by tragedy when one member of the party was killed by a falling rock while being winched back up. After the summit is the hill's hairpin bend lookout, with wonderful views down to Golden Bay.

Just 5km (3 miles) west of **Takaka** ⑩, the town which serves as the gateway to Golden Bay, Waikoropupu Springs (also known as Pupu Springs) made world news in 1993 when scientists recorded that New Zealand's largest freshwater springs discharge the world's clearest water – giving near perfect underwater visibility for a stunning 62 metres (203ft). The effect is spectacular. Aquatic plants grow profusely, providing the glorious freshwater equivalent of a coral reef. Further up, at the head of the mist-clad valley, a car park marks the start of the **Pupu Walkway**. This 2km (1¼-mile) section of curving, cliff-hugging water channels and aqueducts remains a tribute to the eight men who built it with picks and shovels in 1901 in order to provide water for the gold sluicers below.

The **Wholemeal Café** (tel: 03-525 9426; www.wholemealcafe.co.nz), established 1977 in Takaka as the Wholemeal Trading Company, was once the only eatery around. Now it competes with nearly a dozen cafés and restaurants around the bay. The **Mussel Inn** (tel: 03-525 9241; www.musselinn.co.nz), about midway on the 30km (19-mile) road north from Takaka to **Collingwood** (the last town near the end of the highway), is something of an institution. The owners believe small is beautiful when it comes to brewing beer, and this microbrewery is one of the smallest in the country.

Golden Bay takes its name from the precious metal that inspired the Aorere gold rush in 1857. Today it is synonymous with the long, lazy curve of sandy beaches that arch northwest up to **Farewell Spit** ⑪. Covered in huge sandhills and scrub, this unique 35km (22-mile) long sandspit, declared a nature reserve in 1938, is the longest in the world and curves out across Golden Bay like a scimitar, with turbulent waves on one side and vast tidal flats on the other. Built from schist sands washed north along the west coast, the spit is slowly growing, spreading, lengthening and widening as the action of the strong winds and currents bring their forces to bear on the constantly shifting sands of this dynamic environment. The Department of Conservation manages the spit, with strict limits on access. Walking is permitted from **Puponga**, 26km (16 miles) from Collingwood, and **Farewell Spit Eco Tours** (tel:

DRINK

Rather than mimic classic styles, the Mussel Inn microbrewery near Takaka invented a whole lot of new ones. Start off with a 'goose' and finish with a 'strong ox'. In between, sink a 'black sheep', 'dark horse' and 'pale whale', to mention a few.

Pupu Springs' pristine waters.

South Island Tracks

The very best way to experience the superior landscapes of the South Island is to take an extended hike along the numerous tracks.

Seeking the great New Zealand outdoor experience can be as simple as a walk in the park. The **Department of Conservation** (DOC) administers walking tracks, including its nine best Great Walks, through national parks scattered throughout the length of the country. These include five in the South Island: the Milford Track, Routeburn Track, Kepler Track, Abel Tasman Coastal Track and the Heaphy Track. See page 363 and visit www.doc. govt.nz for more information, including trail maps and route planning.

Perhaps the most famous is the Milford Track in Fiordland, extending through glorious South Island landscapes for some 53km (33 miles). It leads from Lake Te Anau through a deep river valley and over an Alpine pass to finish four days later at a fiord. The track follows the Clinton River from the head of the

Taking in the views from Takaka Hill, an extension to the Abel Tasman Coastal Track.

lake up to the Mintaro Hut, then crosses the MacKinnon Pass and descends to the Quintin Hut. Packs can be left here while walkers make a detour to Sutherland Falls, the country's highest waterfall. From the Quintin Hut the track heads through rainforest to Milford Sound. Due to its immense popularity, you must book well in advance (ie months before you leave home) if you want to walk the Milford Track. It can be completed either as part of a guided walk or independently as a 'freedom walker'. It attracts people of all ages, but a reasonable standard of fitness is required and all-weather clothing is essential.

Only slightly less well known, but equally spectacular, is the three-day **Routeburn Track** that links the Fiordland National Park with the Mount Aspiring National Park. This track was part of an early Maori route to find greenstone (jade). It leads from the main divide on the Te Anau–Milford Road over Key Summit to Lake Howden before dropping into the Mackenzie Basin. From there it crosses the Harris Saddle into the Routeburn Valley. The highlight is the view from Key Summit. Hut passes for both the Routeburn Track and the Kepler Track (also accessed from Te Anau) are available from the Te Anau DOC office.

A very different experience is offered by the **Coastal Track** at Abel Tasman National Park. This three- to four-day track idles through bush and dips down into golden-sand beaches. Its waterside route has made the Coastal Track immensely popular in recent years and it can be difficult getting hut accommodation, so bring a tent or consider staying at Awaroa Lodge (www.awaroalodge.co.nz). If the tide is in, you occasionally have to divert around the inlets: check tide times in the local paper before you leave or at huts along the way.

The Heaphy Track, from Collingwood to Karamea, takes between four and six days. Most of the track lies within the boundary of Kahurangi National Park. From Brown Hut the track rises through beech forest to Perry Saddle. One highlight is the view from the summit of Mount Perry (a two-hour return walk from Perry Saddle Hut). The track then winds through the open spaces of the Gouland Downs and on to the Mackay Hut. Nikau palms are a feature of the section from Heaphy Hut along the spectacular coastal stretch, where the route drops down along the beach. This is the most beautiful part of the walk, but, as for all the above hikes, bring plenty of insect repellent to ward off sandflies.

Detailed information on these and other tracks can be obtained from offices of the Department of Conservation. There is no charge for using the tracks, and reasonable rates apply to accommodation.

03-524 8257, 0800-808 257; www.fare wellspit.com), a four-wheel-drive trip, departs regularly from Collingwood for the lighthouse and the gannet colony near the spit's end.

Farewell Spit also makes Golden Bay the world's deadliest whale trap. Pilot whales migrating past in summer become stranded in shallows, often hundreds at a time, when armies of residents and holidaymakers can be relied upon to refloat them.

Kahurangi and wild west

Facing the raging Tasman Sea, Nelson's wild western flank can be an inhospitable, even dangerous, coastline, but is always inspiring. From Puponga, the 30-minute walk to **Wharariki Beach** is second to none, with bold cliff lines, arches, caves, rock pools galore and row upon row of massive dunes. The road over Pakawau Saddle gets you to Westhaven Inlet, a marine reserve and a popular place to spot a wide variety of wading and shore birds.

The narrow, dusty road around the inlet affords excellent views. The best reflections are at high tide if it's not windy. Echo Point is worth a stop and a good scream for an eightfold reverberation sound effect. Remnants of the once-thriving town of **Mangarakau** give little hint of an industrious past based on coal, timber, flax and gold. Spare a thought as you drive on past the old school house, another closure. Just off to the right is the overgrown entrance to the town's coal mine, where an explosion of built-up gas killed four miners on 17 January 1958, their first day back after summer vacation. The town's fifth miner, who rushed in to help the others, was seriously gassed.

Nelson Lakes

South of Golden Bay, even four-wheel-drive vehicles are of no use. This is the area set aside for **Kahurangi National Park ⓬**, at 452,000 hectares (1 million acres), the country's second-largest national park and home to more than half of New Zealand's 2,400 plant species, including 67 found nowhere else. Many people come here to hike over 550km (342 miles) of trails, the most popular being the 85km (53-mile) **Heaphy Track** (see page 244), which starts 30km (19 miles) south of Collingwood and ends in Karamea. Overnight accommodation along the way is available, for a small charge, in DOC huts.

There are other oases, too, for people of softer feet and softer muscles. A restored 1920s fishing lodge on the shores of **Lake Rotoroa**, 90km (56 miles) southwest of Nelson in the scenic **Nelson Lakes National Park ⓭** area, boasts 'blue-chip' fishing waters within a short walk of the front door, and 26 top-class fishing rivers teeming with trout are within an hour's drive. **St Arnaud** village on the shores of nearby **Lake Rotoiti** also offers comfortable accommodation and (for winter visitors) two ski fields nearby.

If you don't want to head on to Christchurch or the west coast, another route from St Arnaud follows the Wairau Valley back to Blenheim.

At the crest of Takaka Hill, near the Takaka Hill Road, is Ngarua Cave, which contains the skeletal remains of the now extinct flightless moa bird.

Farewell Spit, the northern tip of South Island, at high tide.

Hagley Park is home to the Botanic Gardens.

CHRISTCHURCH

Devastated by the earthquake of 2011, the South Island's largest city has undergone a major transformation over the past couple of years with its CBD cleared of ruins to make way for new parks and modern quake-proof architecture. Away from the construction zones much remains open, including the city's elegant public gardens and parklands.

C hristchurch, the main city of Canterbury province, has long been New Zealand's Garden City, renowned for its wealth of established gardens and parks, traditional pleasures such as punting on the Avon River, and a plethora of heritage buildings. Since the major earthquake of 22 February 2011, this reputation has been built upon, with new parks filling the spaces where lives were tragically lost and heritage buildings were destroyed or badly damaged.

Although much work has been completed, the rebuilding of Christchurch is expected to continue throughout 2013 and 2014. While it's under way, various construction sites within the inner CBD will be off-limits as contemporary buildings in sympathetic designs replace the 1,000 or so buildings that were demolished.

With many areas within the CBD closed off at various times depending on construction requirements, the inner-city suburbs of Riccarton and Merivale, along Papanui Road, and outlying areas such as Harewood, Burnside and Bishopdale have boomed. The latter, a large region which branches out towards the airport, was totally unaffected by the earthquakes and offers a number of excellent attractions and a range of low-rise places to stay. It's also an ideal base from which to explore attractions

in the wider Canterbury region: riding a hot-air balloon over the city and plains at dawn or following a scenic self-drive route to sample the French charms of Akaroa, out on Banks Peninsula.

Orientation in the Garden City

At the heart of the city in the cordoned 'Red Zone' is the pedestrian-only Cathedral Square, named after Christchurch's pride and joy, the lofty neo-gothic Church of England

Main Attractions

Christchurch Art Gallery
Hagley Park
Botanic Gardens
Punting on the Avon River
Orana Wildlife Park
Akaroa (Banks Peninsula)
Quake Tours

Earthquake devastation.

Cathedral. Its construction began in 1864 but wasn't completed until 1904 due to a lack of funds. Its spire once made it the city's tallest building; however, the 63-metre (208ft) tower was severely damaged in the 2011 earthquake, and much of the Cathedral has since been demolished. To enter the Red Zone you can join an earthquake bus tour which allows access into parts of Christchurch, including Cathedral Square, that are usually closed to the public. The trips provide up-to-date information on the fate of Christchurch's iconic central city buildings, and the opportunity to learn more about how the city is changing. Red Bus (tel: 03 379 4260; www.redbus.co.nz) is the only tour currently permitted to journey into the Red Zone. Also worth trying is Hassle-free Tours (tel: 03-385 5775; www.hasslefreetours.co.nz; daily, departs 10am and 2pm), which offers city tours on open-top double-decker buses. As parts of the city in the Red Zone are slowly reopened, any buildings that remain unsafe will be fenced off.

Re:START **A**, a shopping precinct in Cashell Street, made from shipping containers painted in a bright and colourful palette, have been fitted out as high-end shops and cafés, creating a thriving hub in the CBD.

Although the cathedral remains closed, from its base, a grid of streets spreads across the plains. The central streets assume the names of English bishoprics – minor ones, because by the time the city was planned in the early 1850s, the best names had already been taken for other communities in the province.

At the limits of the city centre run four broad avenues. They enclose a square mile that mirrors the City of London. Within their bounds are extensive parklands and tidy, tree-lined squares with names such as Cranmer, Latimer and Victoria. Winding through the parklands and the city is the Avon River. On one 1849 Canterbury map, the Avon River appears as the 'Shakespeare', and Christchurch as 'Stratford'. Indeed, many locals mistakenly believe that the Avon is named after the river in Shakespeare's Stratford but, in fact,

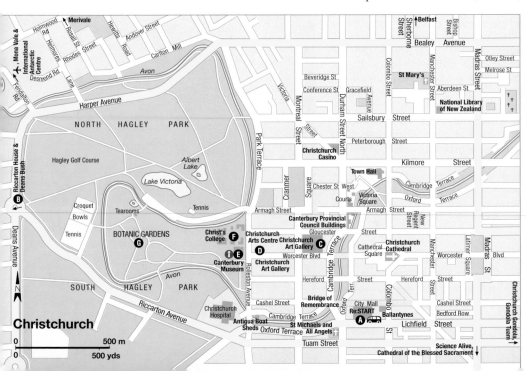

Christchurch

the name is taken from that of another watercourse, a little larger than the Avon, which burbled past the home of the city's pioneering Deans family. The Avon borders the **Riccarton House & Deans Bush** ❸ (tel: 03-341 1018; www.riccartonhouse.co.nz), the Deans' beautiful home at 16 Kahu Road. While the house was damaged in the earthquake and is still undergoing repairs, during daylight hours visitors are welcome to wander through its 1-hectare (3-acre) grounds, which include the sole remnant of native kahikatea forest on the Canterbury Plains. Located in the grounds is Deans Cottage, a colonial cottage built by pioneering Scottish brothers, William and John Deans, in 1843 and the oldest building on the Canterbury Plains, which is also open for viewing.

Christchurch still holds its gardens – acres and acres of them – both public and private, close to its heart. The 'Garden City' label became official in 1997, when Christchurch was named Garden City of the World. Visit in late summer and you will see this aspect of the city at its finest.

Beyond the CBD

Although parts of the CBD will remain closed for some time, the city still offers a number of attractions. Foremost among these sights is the **Christchurch Art Gallery** ❸ (Montreal Street; tel: 03-941 7300; www.christchurchartgallery.org.nz; daily 10am–5pm, Wed until 9pm; free), **a glass-and-steel building housing** an impressive collection of New Zealand art. This contemporary structure withstood the initial violent forces of nature and operated as the headquarters for Civil Defence national and local teams, as well as a base for rescue teams in February and March 2011.

From the gallery heading west along Worcester Boulevard lies the site of the former **Christchurch Arts Centre** ❸. This was originally the home of the University of Canterbury, a mass of dreaming spires, turrets and cloisters. When the university moved to more spacious grounds in the suburbs, the site was dedicated to arts and crafts studios, theatres, restaurants and apartments, all nestled within the granite Gothic shells. A victim of

TIP

Following the 2011 earthquake, the Christchurch i-site Visitor Centre has moved to the Botanic Gardens on Rolleston Avenue, opposite Hagley Park (tel: 03-379 9629; www.christchurchnz.net; daily 8.30am–5pm).

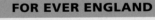

Punting along the Avon River.

FOR EVER ENGLAND

A city does not become more English than England without putting its mind to it. Named after an Oxford college, Christchurch was a planned Anglican settlement, masterminded by one John Robert Godley. Repelled by the egalitarianism and industrialisation of the 19th century, Godley aspired to a medieval notion of a harmoniously blended Church and state, presided over by a benevolent gentry. He founded the Canterbury Association, with no fewer than two archbishops, seven bishops, 14 peers, four baronets and 16 Members of Parliament as backers. The idea was to raise money and find settlers – and only the best sort of migrant needed apply. To qualify for an assisted passage, a migrant had to furnish a certificate from his vicar vouching that 'the applicant is sober, industrious and honest', and that 'he and all his family are amongst the most respectable in the parish'. From such ideals came the first Canterbury pilgrims in 1850. By 1855, 3,549 migrants had made the journey.

Inevitably, things went wrong. Dreams of an ecclesiastical utopia crumbled under the harsh realities of colonial life. It was as difficult to revitalise Anglicanism in New Zealand as it was anywhere else. Yet dreams endure. To be of First Four Ships stock still brings some cachet, even today. The names of those first official migrants are engraved on plaques in Cathedral Square.

the earthquake, it is now one of several vacant plots throughout the city which has been used by 'Gap Filler', a creative urban regeneration initiative to bring live music, outdoor film, art and creative spaces into the CBD. This is the heart of old Christchurch.

Directly across Rolleston Avenue is another Gothic structure, designed by the country's most distinguished Victorian architect, Benjamin W. Mountfort (1825–98). Opened in 1878, this significant landmark was designed to house the **Canterbury Museum** Ⓔ (tel: 03-366 5000; www.canterbury museum.com; daily Oct–Mar 9am–5.30pm, Apr–Sep until 5pm; donation). Besides displays exploring Canterbury's pre-European and pioneer history and a fine collection of decorative art and costume, the museum also devotes space to the discovery and exploration of Antarctica, and to **Discovery** (charge), the museum's natural history centre for children.

Right next door is **Christ's College** Ⓕ, a very Anglican, English public school for boys. The buildings, old and new, are marvellous.

The glass-and-steel frontage of Christchurch Art Gallery.

Beyond, moving further into **Hagley Park**, the 30-hectare (74-acre) **Botanic Gardens** Ⓖ (tel: 03-941 8999; www.ccc.govt.nz/cityleisure/parks walkways/christchurchbotanicgardens; daily 7am–sunset; free) are a truly splendid celebration of the city's gardening heritage, from English herbaceous borders and native sections to glasshouses of subtropical and desert specimens. Considered one of the top botanic gardens in the world, the area is enclosed within a loop of the Avon River as it winds through the 160-hectare (500-acre) Hagley Park. The park also includes a golf course, playing fields, tennis courts and a duck pond.

Thirty-minute guided tours on traditional punts along the meandering **Avon River** (tel: 03-366 0337; www. punting.co.nz; daily 9am–6pm) are Christchurch's premier attraction and depart regularly from the Antigua Boat Sheds at 2 Cambridge Terrace, located at the southernmost end of Rolleston Avenue or the Gloucester Street Bridge.

Port Hills

Further out in the suburbs you can tour countless streets of fine homes. Christchurch's real estate is fiercely class-conscious, along lines that are somewhat inexplicable. **Fendalton** and **Merivale**, northwest of the city, are easily recognised, with their fine trees and secluded gardens, as havens of the wealthy. Yet cross the street and values plummet.

To the south, the **Port Hills** enjoy a clear geographical advantage over the rest of the city. Their elevation lifts them above the winter smog, which can be severe by New Zealand standards. The **Summit Road** Ⓘ, along the tops of the hills, gives tremendous views across the city, the plains and the Southern Alps and, on the other side, the port of Lyttelton and the hills of Banks Peninsula. There are extensive walking tracks over the Port Hills and peninsula beyond. They range from one- or two-hour strolls to ambitious hikes, with shelters to rest in. Ask at an information centre for details.

There are many gardens in the hills. One of the most notable is **Gethsemane Gardens** (tel: 03-326 5848; www.geth semanegardens.co.nz; daily 9am–5pm) on Revelation Drive, a private garden that nurtures many unusual plant species. Its little avenues and tiny trellised chapel are worth a visit, but the highlight, the Noah's Ark – a chapel set inside a large wooden boat – is a must-see.

It's also worth taking a drive or bus to **Lyttelton ②**, 12km (7 miles) to the southeast, the sleepy-looking port over the hill from Christchurch. Close to the epicentre of the February 2011 earthquake, its charming cottages clinging to the slopes sustained immense damage. You can return through the Lyttelton road tunnel or drive over the hill to the beachside suburbs of Ferrymead, Redcliffs and **Sumner ③**. The latter also sustained much damage, but it still retains its air of an artists' retreat. It's slightly bohemian and gets extra busy at weekends, when families come to enjoy its beaches.

Back towards the city, **Ferrymead Heritage Park ④** (50 Ferrymead Park Drive; tel: 03-384 1970; www.fer rymead.org.nz; daily 10am–4.30pm) is a working re-creation of an Edwardian pioneer village complete with cottages, shops, a church and a railway station. Members of 18 volunteer societies keep the village alive, and electric tram rides are available every Saturday and Sunday. A steam train runs the first Sunday of every month from November to February, and the first Sunday of every month March to October. At the weekend lively markets are held here.

Harewood, Christchurch's new hub

Northwest of the city, beyond the inner suburbs of Fendalton and Merivale, is the Christchurch International Airport and the suburbs of Harewood, Burnside and Bishopdale. This area was spared damage by the region's quakes and offers a number of excellent attractions, eateries and places to stay.

At 38 Orchard Road, a short distance from the airport, is the fascinating

TIP

Hire a canoe or paddle boat from Antigua Boat Sheds (2 Cambridge Terrace at the end of Rolleston Avenue; tel: 03-366 6768; www. boatsheds.co.nz), beside the Avon, and explore the river as it winds through the Botanic Gardens and Hagley Park.

Street buskers, part of the city's lively performing arts scene. The World Buskers Festival takes place every year in late January.

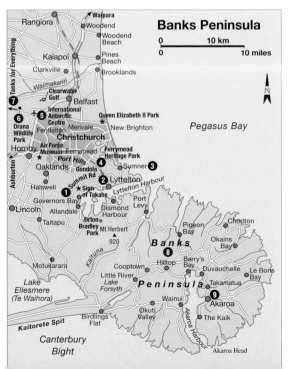

View of Christchurch from Port Hills.

International Antarctic Centre  (tel: 03-357 0519; www.iceberg.co.nz; daily 9am–5.30pm, until 7pm Nov–Mar), which celebrates Christchurch's history as the embarkation point for ice-bound expeditions (see page 314). As part of the 'Snow and Ice Experience' visitors are exposed to Antarctic temperatures, as well as getting the chance to explore a snow cave and ride snowmobiles; Hägglund all-terrain vehicle rides depart every 15 minutes. Generally considered the next best thing to being in Antarctica (if not slightly better because it omits the privations that accompany the real thing), it's well worth a visit. An additional attraction is the New Zealand Little Blue Penguin Encounter, featuring the world's smallest penguins; try to time your visit to coincide with feeding sessions, held daily at 10.30am and 3.30pm.

Harewood is also home to **Clearwater Golf Course** (Clearwater Avenue, Harewood; tel: 03-360 2146; www.clearwaternz.com), a par-72 course where visitors are welcomed. With five tee positions to choose from, players of all levels and abilities will find the course challenging yet enjoyable – and very beautiful, with its series of spring-fed lakes and trout-filled streams set picturesquely against the backdrop of the Southern Alps.

Nearby, at 423 McLeans Island Road in Harewood, is **Orana Wildlife Park** ⑥ (tel: 03-359 7109; www.oranawildlife park.co.nz; daily 10am–5pm), New Zealand's only open-range, safari-style zoo. Visitors can enjoy a hands-on experience with domestic animals in a farm enclosure, but the most attention is given to the rhinoceroses, cheetahs, giraffes, zebras and other exotic species. Feeding sessions are staggered throughout the day; highlights include lion feeding held daily at 2.30pm, and giraffe feeding at noon. You can explore the park at your own pace, or join a guided tour daily at 11.20am and 2.30pm. The park also has excellent displays of New Zealand wildlife, including the rare tuatara (feeding at 1.50pm), and endangered birds such as the kiwi (feeding at 1.30pm), kereru and kaka.

Also on McLeans Island Road is **Tanks for Everything** ⑦ (tel: 03-359

1007; www.tanksforeverything.co.nz; daily), a rather unusual off-road attraction where a fleet of ex-army tanks and other vehicles are available for hire.

Further afield to the south of the city, refined pleasures can be had at a handful of wineries that have dotted the rural outskirts of Christchurch since Canterbury became one of New Zealand's boutique wine-growing regions in the late 1980s. Alternatively, take a day trip north to Waipara, one of New Zealand's most rapidly growing wine regions, where Pinot Noir, Riesling, Chardonnay and Sauvignon Blanc grapes thrive in a warm microclimate.

The Banks Peninsula

If you have time before you head south to the mountains and lakes, you might want a change from the city lights. **Banks Peninsula** ❽, over the Port Hills to the east, is the best destination for a short trip. It is the scene of one of two blunders made by Captain James Cook when he circumnavigated New Zealand in the 18th century. He mapped the peninsula as an island – which would have been correct if he had come several millennia earlier, as the extinct volcanoes which formed the peninsula were once separated from the mainland. (Cook's other gaffe was Stewart Island, at the southern tip of the South Island, which he linked to the mainland.)

The once bush-covered hills of Banks Peninsula were long ago logged for timber, but there are still some small remnants of bush and plenty of delightful valleys and bays. Sheltered microclimates support many horticultural products and plants that cannot be cultivated anywhere else this far south, including kiwi fruit. There are also some exotic nuts and herbs grown in the area.

French-influenced Akaroa

To experience the real charm of the region, seek out **Diamond Harbour**, Okains Bay, Okuti Valley and **Port Levy**. These places are fertile, inviting and unspoilt – in many other parts of the world they would be bristling with condominiums. But the real gem of the peninsula is **Akaroa** ❾, about 80km (50 miles) from Christchurch. This little settlement

EAT

If driving to Akaroa from Christchurch, stop off at the Hilltop Café and Bar (tel: 03-325 1005; www. thehilltop.co.nz), just past Little River. Situated on the volcanic rim of the crater that forms Akaroa Harbour, it offers spectacular views, and good coffee and cuisine.

Scenery on the Banks Peninsula.

Shaky Ground

While Christchurch rebuilds its shattered CBD, low magnitude aftershocks continue to rumble beneath residents' feet.

As the citizens of Christchurch lay sleeping on the morning of 4 September 2010, an earthquake of magnitude 7.1 hit the city. The epicentre was beneath the township of Darfield, 40km (25 miles) to the west. Remarkably, due to the timing of the event and the relative depth of the quake, there was no loss of life. Nonetheless, a state of emergency was declared and much of the city's infrastructure was damaged, with several heritage buildings rendered structurally unsound and further harm caused by the hundreds of high magnitude/shallow-depth aftershocks which occurred in the following weeks.

Less than six months later, on 22 February 2011, a second major earthquake shook the city. With a magnitude of 6.3 it was significantly less powerful than the September quake, but this time the epicentre was just 3.5km (2 miles) below the surface,

Rebuilding Christchurch.

and just 9km (5.5 miles) southeast of the city centre. And this time it struck right in the middle of the day, when the city centre was crowded with shoppers and office workers. It had a devastating effect, literally shaking Christchurch's early 19th-century architecture to the ground, claiming 185 lives as it did so.

New Zealand was placed under a National State of Emergency for several weeks following the event, as all resources the nation had available were directed into Christchurch. Search and rescue teams were dispatched from around the globe to aid local search and recovery efforts.

Today, only a handful of Christchurch's former heritage buildings remain. Work continues to demolish the 1,000 buildings within the CBD that were condemned as structurally unsound and irreparable, and to replace them with structures incorporating contemporary earthquake standards and sympathetic designs. The rebuild is expected to continue for the foreseeable future, and while it's underway, a key part of the inner CBD, dubbed the 'Red Zone', has been cordoned off for safety. Modern architecture in the CBD, built to New Zealand's stringent earthquake building code, for the most part stood firm.

Beyond the Red Zone, tens of thousands of people in the suburbs have been displaced from their homes. The process of rebuilding the city will be a long journey for its residents; some buildings will be reconstructed, others continue to be assessed and reassessed, and repaired or demolished as required.

Some details listed in this book will change as the city is slowly rebuilt; for the latest on the city's reconstruction and other matters relating to the earthquake, see www.ccc.govt.nz, and for the latest news on tourist attractions as they open visit www.christchurchnz.com.

Christchurch Cathedral in the aftermath of the quake.

began its European life in 1838 when a French whaler, Captain Jean-François Langlois, landed on its shores and bought – or so he thought – the entire peninsula from the Maori. Sixty-three settlers set out from France on the *Comte de Paris* to create a South Seas outpost. But they arrived in 1840 to find the Union flag flying. Pipped at the colonial post, the French settlers nevertheless stayed. They planted poplars from Normandy, named streets after places in their home country and grew grapes. By 1843, however, they were outnumbered by the English.

Nonetheless this French outpost lingers on, and has been spruced up for visitors. Little streets, with names such as Rue Lavaud and Rue Jolie, wind up the hill from the harbour front. A charming colonial style predominates, and has been protected by town planning rules. Of most note is the **Langlois-Eteveneaux House**, now fitted out as a display and part of the **Akaroa Museum** (tel: 03-304 7614; www.akaroamuseum.org.nz; daily 10.30am–4.30pm) at the corner of Rue Lavaud and Rue Balguerie.

Churches are also among Akaroa's notable sights. The Roman Catholic **St Patrick's Church** on Rue Lavaud is the oldest in anything like original form. It was built in 1864 and was in fact the third in town to serve Akaroa's French and Irish (hence the name) Catholics. It is a charming and cluttered little building with a noteworthy Bavarian window on the east wall.

The nearby Anglican **St Peter's Church** at Rue Balguerie was built in 1863, and generously enlarged about 15 years later. Compared to St Patrick's, this is a more austere building in the Protestant style. Most distinctive of all is the tiny **Kaik**, a Maori church some 6km (4 miles) south of the township along the foreshore. It is a remnant of a once strong Maori presence around Akaroa Harbour, in a haunting and evocative setting.

In the town of Akaroa, a climb through the domain, called the **Garden of Tane**, is worthwhile on its own count, and will take you to the spectacularly sited graveyard. Its graves must have the best views in the country, and they make up a rich record of the region's history. The **Old French Cemetery**, however, on the other side of town, is a disappointment. It was the resting place of Akaroa's earliest Europeans; the long slog up the hill affords a good view of the harbour, but a benevolent government tidied the place up in 1925, in the process destroying most of the headstones for a mediocre memorial.

Akaroa Harbour, on the south coast of Banks Peninsula, is on the doorstep of the habitat of the rare Hector's dolphin. **Black Cat Cruises** (tel: 03-304 7641; www.blackcat.co.nz; daily 6am, 8.30am, 11.30am, 1.30pm, 3.30pm) depart regularly to catch glimpses of the magnificent creatures.

Many Christchurch people own holiday houses in Akaroa or nearby, and the town can become crowded in January and February. There are many bars, restaurants and cafés – but due to the isolation, restaurants tend to be pricey.

Sheep on the road to Akaroa.

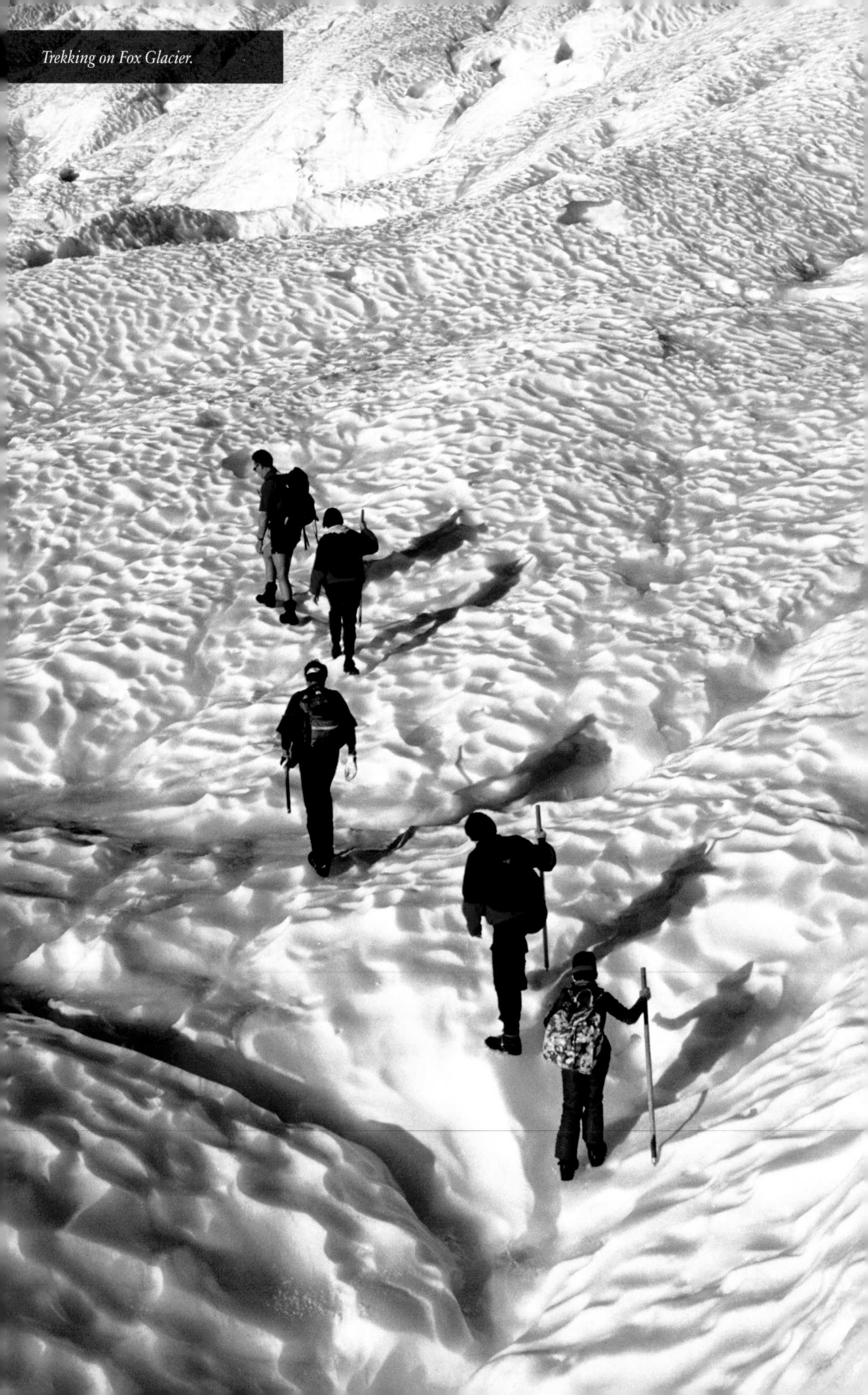

Trekking on Fox Glacier.

CANTERBURY

Canterbury's flat coastal and inland plains are bordered by mountain ranges of breathtaking beauty. There can be no finer place to be – when the wind's in the right direction.

Canterbury is a marriage of mountain and sea, linked by snow-fed rivers that cut braided courses across the plain. The Southern Alps, Pacific Ocean and two rivers (the Conway in the north and Waitaki in the south) form the boundaries of the province, which surrounds Christchurch on the eastern side of South Island.

The popular view of Canterbury as a patchwork plain where lambs frolic under a nor'west sky really does exist. The plain, 180km (112 miles) long and an average of 40km (25 miles) wide, is New Zealand's largest area of flat land. Canterbury lamb, bred for meat and wool, is regarded as the country's best. And the Canterbury nor'wester is a notorious wind, a true *föhn* that creates warm, dry and blustery conditions as it descends from the high peaks to the west. It whips up dust from the river beds and furrowed farmlands, and is blamed for the moodiness of the locals when it blows.

Further west, Canterbury province also encompasses New Zealand's highest mountains and its widest rivers, alongside pastoral and forested hills, some superb beaches, extinct volcanoes and the sheltered bays of Banks Peninsula (see page 253). Settlement is diverse, from cities to high-country sheep stations where genteel English traditions are vigorously upheld.

Newborn lamb on the Canterbury plains.

North Canterbury

Heading north from Christchurch, the main State Highway (SH) 1 crosses the Canterbury Plain to reach **Waipara**, one of New Zealand's most rapidly expanding wine regions. Stop for a tasting at a cellar door, or sample the fare at one of its award-winning wineries, including **Pegasus Bay** (www.pegasusbay.com), Mud House Winery (www.mudhousewineryandcafe.co.nz) and **Waipara Hills** (www.waiparahills.co.nz).

At the town of Waipara, SH7 peals off inland, climbing up the Waiau

Main Attractions

Waipara Wine
Arthur's Pass National Park
Geraldine
Timaru
Lake Tekapo
Lake Pukaki
Aoraki Mount Cook
  National Park

TIP

Choose your poison –
rafting, jet boating,
quad-biking or bungee
jumping – at
Thrillseeker's Adventures
(tel: 03-315 7046; www.
thrillseekers.co.nz), a short
drive from Hanmer.

Swim with a pod of dolphins at Kaikoura.

Valley and the rolling hills of north Canterbury to reach **Lewis Pass**, from where it winds its way down to the west coast. It's an all-weather route which opened in 1939, offering a comparatively gentle, picturesque crossing to the west coast.

North of Waipara the road passes through small rural settlements including **Hurunui**, where a famous limestone tavern (www.hurunihotel.co.nz) was built in 1868 to accommodate weary drovers, and the limestone landscape of **Waikari**, with its ancient Maori rock art and naturally sculpted animal forms.

Further on, in the mountains, is a favourite retreat of Cantabrians. **Hanmer Springs** ⓮, a little Alpine village an easy 136km (85-mile) drive north of Christchurch, is nestled in a sheltered, forested valley. The **Hanmer Springs Thermal Pools and Spa** (tel: 03-315 0000; www.hanmersprings.co.nz; daily 10am–9pm), on Amuri Avenue, has hot mineral pools set in a garden of giant conifers. Few experiences are more pleasurable than relaxing in these open-air pools on a winter's

night, watching the snowflakes dissolve silently in the steam.

A European settler stumbled upon the springs in 1859 and they were harnessed by the government in 1883. Since then their recuperative powers have been used at various times to help rehabilitate wounded soldiers, the mentally ill and alcoholics. The landscaped rock gardens include numerous thermal pools and a separate family area where children can enjoy waterfalls and slides.

Several easy paths meander through **Hanmer Forest Park**, the first exotic forest established by the government in the South Island. More demanding walks to the summits of **Conical Hill** and **Mount Isobel** provide magnificent panoramas. The **Mount Isobel Track**, which passes 200 different kinds of sub-Alpine flowering plants and ferns, is a naturalist's delight.

Hanmer's 18-hole golf course is one of the highest in New Zealand, while fishing, hunting, jet boating, river rafting, bungee jumping, skiing and horse-trekking are also available. Although there is accommodation in the form of small hotels and guesthouses, the main street has retained the low-key atmosphere of a typical rural township.

To the west of Hanmer, SH7 reaches an altitude of 865 metres (2,838ft) at **Lewis Pass**, passing through beautiful beech-covered mountains. The highway descends to **Maruia Springs**, where the **Maruia Springs Thermal Resort** (tel: 03-523 8840; www.maruia springs.co.nz; daily 8am–7.30pm) offers a chemical-free thermal soak in perfectly formed rock pools beside the burbling Maruia River. The route then continues on to the Rahu Saddle, Reefton and Greymouth on the west coast (see page 275).

Inland in the far north of the province, the isolated **Clarence Valley** is worth exploring by four-wheel drive for its rugged beauty, especially upstream. Note, however, that the road that runs along it is not

accessible from Hanmer – there are locked gates at the Acheron River Bridge (downstream from Jack's Pass) and at the Rainbow Station over the Main Divide. The road, originally built to install and maintain the high-voltage transmission lines from the hydro schemes of Otago to Blenheim, Nelson and beyond, is an unsealed, often steep track, suitable only in good weather.

The Kaikoura Coast

Out on the coast, the northern Canterbury shoreline is exposed and rocky, especially around **Kaikoura** ⓯ (population 3,500), some 182km (113 miles) north of Christchurch, situated at the base of a small peninsula which provides shelter for the fishing boats that work out of here. The crayfish or rock lobster that they pursue on this rocky coast is sold freshly cooked from roadside stalls.

More important these days to Kaikoura's economy are the visitors who come to see the sperm whales which congregate a few kilometres offshore. The sonar 'clicks' from the submerged animals, chasing giant squid at depths of a 1km (3,280ft) or more, are tracked by a sensitive hydrophone so the boat can be positioned roughly where the whale will resurface to loll about for around 10 minutes. The highlight of the spectacle takes place when the leviathan throws up its big flukes and disappears. The 2½-hour-long tours, available throughout the year, are operated by **Whale Watch Kaikoura** (tel: 03-319 6767; www.whalewatch.co.nz).

It's ironic that this quaint seaside town, founded on the killing of whales over a century ago, should find new prosperity showing them off. Whale-watching trips can also be taken in a light plane (Wings Over Whales; tel: 03-319 6580; www.whales.co.nz) or helicopter (Kaikoura Helicopters; tel: 03-319 6609; www.worldofwhales.co.nz). The Maori-run whale-watching business has provided a big boost for the town, and it's now a worthy stopover activity on any journey in the area.

Another of Kaikoura's attractions is also found offshore. Dolphin-watching

Whale-watching trip at Kaikoura.

WINTER WONDERLAND

Winter transforms the vast windswept plains and pleated foothills of the Mackenzie Country into a sports wonderland. While local ski fields like Mount Dobson (www.dobson.co.nz), Fox Peak (www.foxpeak.co.nz) and Lake Ohau (www.ohau.co.nz) rely on naturally forming snow, Round Hill Ski Field (www.roundhill.co.nz) in the Two Thumb Range is always open during the winter thanks to its snow-making machines. The ski field offers magnificent views across Lake Tekapo, and its wide gentle slopes are ideal for beginners and those making the transition from skiing to snowboarding who need to put in concentrated effort on predictable terrain. Qualified instructors provide tuition for beginners, intermediate and advanced, and you can hire all the equipment you need.

TIP

One of New Zealand's most spectacular train journeys is the TranzAlpine from Christchurch to Greymouth. It passes through farmland, mountains and valleys on a 233km (145-mile) journey which takes 4.5 hours one-way. Contact Tranz Scenic at tel: 04-495 0775; www. tranzscenic.co.nz.

tours by **Dolphin Encounter** (tel: 03-319 6777; www.dolphin.co.nz; daily 5.30am, 8.30am, 12.30pm) allow swimmers to frolic in the waters with these friendly creatures. The tours are hugely popular, so make sure you book in advance during summer.

Inland from Kaikoura, two parallel mountain ranges thrust skywards, with the highest peak, **Mount Tapuaenuku**, soaring to 2,885 metres (9,465ft). Beyond that is the **Awatere Valley** and **Molesworth Station**, New Zealand's largest sheep and cattle mountain ranch, which stretches over 182,000 hectares (450,000 acres).

South Canterbury: a touch of Switzerland

Canterbury's finest scenery is inland, along the foothills and valleys of the **Southern Alps**. Three main roads provide easy access to passes to the mountains, beyond which lies Westland. Northernmost is the aforementioned Lewis Pass, central is spectacular Arthur's Pass and the surrounding national park of the same name; southernmost is Burke's Pass,

which leads to the Mackenzie Country and the magnificent panorama of glacial lakes and Alps of the Aoraki Mount Cook region.

The quickest route between Christchurch and Westland is the West Coast Road (SH73) through Arthur's Pass, which boasts New Zealand's version of a Swiss village. Although **Arthur's Pass ⑯** township, in the heart of the Southern Alps 154km (96 miles) west of Christchurch, lacks green pastures and tinkling cowbells, it does have chalet-style accommodation and a railway station. The **TranzAlpine** train stops here twice daily on its journey between Christchurch and Greymouth (see page 319). For information on walks and climbs in the area, and on weather conditions, call the DOC information centre (tel: 03-318 9211; www.doc.govt.nz).

Arthur's Pass marks the eastern portal of the **Otira Tunnel**, the only rail link through the mountains. The 8km (5-mile) tunnel, completed in 1923 after 15 years of construction, remains a vital rail link between the west coast and Canterbury.

The Canterbury Plains.

Arthur's Pass is also the headquarters of **Arthur's Pass National Park**. Its proximity to Christchurch and access to numerous tracks of varying difficulty through inspiring scenery, mountain climbing and skiing make the 114,500-hectare (282,930-acre) park one of the most popular in the country. You can also enjoy night skiing on the floodlit slopes of Temple Basin (tel: 03-377 7788; www.temple basin.co.nz) on the main divide of the Southern Alps. Within its borders are 16 peaks over 2,000 metres (6,500ft), the highest being **Mount Murchison** at 2,400 metres (7,870ft), while the most accessible is **Mount Rolleston** at 2,271 metres (7,451ft).

Meanwhile, the 924-metre (3,032ft) Arthur's Pass, named after Arthur Dudley Dobson who rediscovered the former Maori route in 1864, marks the boundary between Canterbury and Westland. Storms are often as intense as they are sudden, dropping as much as 250mm (10 inches) of rain in 24 hours. Bad weather in winter often forces the closure of the highway, which in the Otira Gorge is very steep, with a series of tight bends requiring special care in wet weather and in winter.

The road is not suitable for vehicles towing caravans, and in bad weather it is advisable for camper vans to take the longer, but easier and safer, Lewis Pass route to Westland.

Porter's Pass and Mount Hutt

Arthur's Pass is not the highest point on the West Coast Road. That distinction belongs to **Porter's Pass ⑰**, just 88km (55 miles) west of Christchurch, which traverses the foothills at 945 metres (3,100ft). It's a popular winter destination for day-trippers from Christchurch who enjoy tobogganing and ice-skating at Lake Lyndon and skiing on the many ski fields in the vicinity, such as the commercial field at **Porter Heights** (tel: 03-318 4002; www.skiporters.co.nz) and the club fields at **Craigieburn** (tel: 03-318 8711; www.craigieburn.co.nz), **Broken River** (tel: 03-383 8888; www.brokenriver.co.nz) and **Mount Cheeseman** (tel: 03-344 3247; www.mtcheeseman.co.nz).

TIP

One way to get really stunning views of Canterbury is to drift over it sipping champagne in a hot-air balloon, gazing at the Southern Alps. Aoraki Balloon Safaris operate from Methven (tel: 03-302 8172; www.nzballooning.com).

Geraldine's country-style cinema.

JAMMY GERALDINE

Set on the banks of the Waihi River, Geraldine is a friendly settlement, jam-packed with craftspeople who have moved here for the creative synergy and the relaxed lifestyle. A hive of edible creativity, there are gourmet treats on every corner of this town. Tempt your taste buds at Talbot Forest Cheese, inhale the aromatic world of speciality jams at Barker Fruit Processors, and indulge yourself in the chocolatey confines of Coco, where a legendary Kiwi favourite, the chocolate fish (a marshmallow sweet covered in rich creamy chocolate) can be sampled.

At Michael and Gillian Linton's Giant Jersey, gorgeously soft Perendale, mohair and merino wools are crafted into stylish made-to-measure garments, and at the Belanger-Taylor Glass Studio visitors can witness the fascinating birth of intriguing works of art. Vintage-car enthusiasts will be in their element at the Vintage Car and Machinery Museum, while an evening at the Geraldine classic country-style cinema will never be forgotten. It's customary to be met at the door and personally ushered to your seat – a cosy couch downstairs, or a regular seat up top. Arthouse and mainstream films are screened on an old Ernemann 2 projector and, unless the movie is subtitled, an intermission is standard.

The kea is a native parrot, a fairly common sight in the mountains.

Mount Hutt.

Canterbury's most popular and best-developed ski field is **Mount Hutt** , 100km (60 miles) west of Christchurch and serviced by the small town of **Methven**, 11km (7 miles) away, which provides accommodation to suit all budgets. Ski aficionados regard Mount Hutt as one of the best ski fields in New Zealand. It has a vertical rise of 672 metres (2,205ft) – the longest run stretches for about 2km (1¼ miles) – and is well suited to both skiing and snowboarding.

Nearby is the **Rakaia Gorge**, world-famous for its salmon and its landmark bridges. Experienced local guides lead backcountry fishing excursions, or you can ride the rapids aboard the **Discovery Jet** (tel: 03-318 6943; www.discoveryjet.co.nz; daily).

To Aoraki Mount Cook via Burke's Pass

Although New Zealand's highest peak, Aoraki Mount Cook, is almost directly due west from Christchurch,

the journey by road is a circuitous 330km (205 miles), heading first south, then west, then north again. Getting there, however, is half the fun.

The main route from Christchurch follows SH1 south for 121km (75 miles), marching easily across plain and braided river alike, casually belying the mighty challenges this journey once posed for Maori and pioneer. The wide rivers proved major obstacles to travel and settlement in the 1850s, and difficult river crossings caused many drownings in Canterbury. Throughout New Zealand 1,115 people lost their lives in river accidents between 1840 and 1870, and it was even suggested in Parliament that drowning be classified a natural death. Nowadays motorists speed over the Rakaia, Ashburton and Rangitata rivers without a thought for the hazards that once confronted travellers.

Immediately past the Rangitata River, the road to the Mackenzie Country (SH79) veers off westwards from the main highway. It leads to the foothills and the tiny inland country town of **Geraldine** , 138km (86 miles) southwest of Christchurch. The town nestles into the hills, a base for detours to a historic pioneer homestead in the Orari Gorge and excellent picnic and fishing spots in the nearby Waihi and Te Moana gorges and Peel Forest Park.

Some 31km (19 miles) further south is **Timaru** , the urban heart of the Central South Island, a vibrant town that has preserved much of its Edwardian heritage and buildings. Timaru's first colonists started building a breakwater in 1859, and its harbour was finally completed in 1906. The addition of many stately Edwardian buildings and a striking piazza overlooking Caroline Bay (site of the town's annual summer carnival) has created a respectable town centre with an air of quiet dignity.

The renowned artist Colin McCahon was born here, and many of his works can be seen at the

Aigantighe Art Gallery (tel: 03-688 4424; www.timaru.govt.nz/artgallery; daily; free). The city has an excellent network of walkways. You can visit **the South Canterbury Museum** (tel: 03-687 7212; www.timaru.govt.nz/museum; daily; free) or inhale the heady scents of the 529 named old rose varieties planted in the **Trevor Griffiths Rose Garden** (daily; free).

Head inland to **Pleasant Point**, where the surrounding countryside offers wine tasting at the café at **Opihi Vineyard** (tel: 03-614 8308; www.opihi. co.nz; Wed–Sun 11am–4pm), **Maori Rock Art** at Raincliff Reserve (free) and, in **Upper Waitohi,** the memorial of unsung aviation pioneer Richard Pearse. At **Pleasant Point Museum and Railway** (tel 03-614 8323; www. pleasantpointtrail.org.nz; daily) you can ride the world's only Ford Model T Railcar (departs 11am, 12pm, 1pm, 2pm and 3pm), admire the restored railway relics, or wait in the Old Time Movie Theatre, with a bunch of cinema classics.

The small country town of **Fairlie**, reached by travelling through Geraldine or Pleasant Point, has a tiny historical museum (donation). From here onwards the gentle countryside is left behind as the road, now SH8, rises with deceptive ease to **Burke's Pass** ㉑. At this gap through the foothills a different world stretches beyond – the great tussocked basin known as the **Mackenzie Country**, named after a Scottish shepherd who in 1855 tried to hide stolen sheep in this isolated high-country area.

Long, straight stretches of road take you for about 100km (62 miles) southwest, eventually to **Twizel**(www. twizelnz.com), a town built to provide accommodation for workers on the region's major dam projects, and thought likely to become a ghost town when the projects were completed. Twizel, however, has defied pundits, and today provides a quiet and budget-friendly base for exploring the area.

Winding across the stark, bronzed landscape, 58km (36 miles) from Twizel, the road reaches **Lake Tekapo** ㉒, a lovely turquoise glacial lake reflecting the surrounding mountains. At 710 metres (2,329ft) above sea level, the lake's gorgeous turquoise colour is caused by 'rock flour', finely ground rock particles suspended in glacial meltwater. By the water's edge is the simple stone **Church of the Good Shepherd**. Nearby, the high-country sheepdog which has played an essential role in building New Zealand's prosperity is commemorated in a bronze statue erected by runholders from Mackenzie Country.

For stunning views and stargazing tours take the road to **Mount John Observatory** (tel: 03-680 6960; www. earthandsky.co.nz; daily), where telescopes probe deep space searching for dark matter, black holes and distant planets. Below is Tekapo Springs (tel: 0800-235 382; www.tekaposprings.co.nz; daily 10am–9pm), at 6 Lakeside Drive, a hot pool and day spa complex with an adjoining snow park and ice-skating

The sheepdog monument at Lake Tekapo.

The Church of the Good Shepherd at Tekapo.

The view across Lake Pukaki.

Late autumn colour contrasts make for a fantasy landscape in Aoraki Mount Cook National Park.

rink; during the summer the ice rink converts to roller-skating. Alternatively, you can try your hand at fishing, hiking, mountain biking or horse riding. During the winter **Round Hill Ski Field** (tel: 03-680 6977; www.roundhill.co.nz) offers a pleasant drive to gentle, open slopes and cosy clubrooms.

Beyond Tekapo there is a choice of two routes, either the main SH8 or the **Canal Road**, a scenic route which follows the course of the man-made canal that drains Tekapo's waters to the first of the Waitaki hydroelectric scheme's powerhouses on the southern shore of **Lake Pukaki ㉓**.

Pukaki today is twice the size it was in 1979, when its waters were allowed to flow unimpeded to Lake Benmore. Concrete dams now hold Pukaki in check, forcing it to rise to a new level for use in hydroelectric power generation. About 2km (1¼ miles) north of the turn-off to **Aoraki Mount Cook** is a lookout with spectacular views of the area, including, on a clear day, the towering hulk of the mountain itself.

Aoraki Mount Cook National Park

Travellers on SH80 that skirts the southern slopes of the Pukaki Valley and concludes at **Aoraki Mount Cook Village ㉔**, 99km (62 miles) west of Tekapo, might catch glimpses of the old road undulating above and disappearing into the surface of the lake far below. The newer sealed highway, with an easy gradient, has halved the driving time to the lodge with the million-dollar views, **The Hermitage** (tel: 03-435 1809; www.hermitage.co.nz), with rooms nearly as pricey but worth every cent.

The village is the gateway to the monarch of New Zealand's parks, the **Aoraki Mount Cook National Park ㉕**, where the highest peaks in the land soar above the crest of the Southern Alps. Supreme is Aoraki Mount Cook itself, which until 1991 was 3,764 metres (12,349ft) high. However, the famous mountain lost about 10 metres (33ft) from its summit in that year in a massive avalanche. The re-surveyed official height today is 3,754 metres (12,316ft), which allows it still to retain its standing as New Zealand's highest mountain.

The Aoraki Mount Cook Alpine region was the training ground for the late Sir Edmund Hillary, the first person to scale Mount Everest. The park extends only 80km (50 miles) along the Alpine spine, yet it contains 140 peaks over 2,100 metres (7,000ft), as well as 72 glaciers, including five of New Zealand's largest – the Godley, Murchison, Tasman, Hooker and Mueller. Of these, the **Tasman Glacier** is the largest and longest in the Southern Hemisphere, extending 27km (17 miles) – it has retreated a couple of kilometres in recent times – and in places some 3km (2 miles) wide. The ice in this glacier can reach over 600 metres (2,000ft) in depth. Beneath the glacier the ice-melt forms a large (and ever-growing lake). Glacier Explorers (tel: 03-435 1641; www.glacierexplorers.co.nz) offers an informative cruise of the glacier and terminal lake.

Due to its sacrosanct status within a national park, accommodation in the village has been limited. Nevertheless, in addition to The Hermitage hotel, there are also self-contained A-frame chalets, a camping ground, a well-equipped youth hostel and a great backpackers lodge. Well-defined tracks lead from the village up to the surrounding valleys. These eventually become 'climbs' that are definitely not for novices and should only be tackled with the right equipment, and then only after consultation with the park rangers. Easier mountain ascents are provided by ski-equipped scenic aircraft, which land on the high snowfields.

Skiing is available from July to September, the most exciting run being the descent of the Tasman Glacier. As the spectacular upper reaches of the glacier slopes can only be accessed via fixed-wing skiplane, skiing the Tasman can be an expensive affair. The Aoraki Mount Cook-based **Alpine Guides** (tel: 03-435 1834; www.alpineguides. co.nz) operate ski trips to the Tasman during the season. The same company also organises guided climbs of Aoraki

Mount Cook and mountaineering instruction courses in the summer.

On SH80 near Aoraki Mount Cook Village is a tiny airport from where **Aoraki Mount Cook Skiplanes** (tel: 03-430 8034; www.skiplanes.co.nz) offer magnificent scenic flights to view the glaciers up close and, on some routes, land on them. The Grand Circle Option lasts nearly an hour and flies first to the west side of the Alpine Divide to land on either Franz Josef or Fox Glacier (see page 271) before returning via Tasman Glacier. Flights incorporating a landing on the névé of Tasman Glacier are highly recommended.

The spectacular views of Aoraki Mount Cook, especially when the last rays of the midsummer sun strike its peak in late twilight, form the highlight of many a traveller's exploration of Canterbury. The mountain, named Aoraki (Cloud Piercer) by the Maori, is frequently shrouded in cloud, depriving sightseers of its face. But come rain or shine, this Alpine region is ever masterful, ever dramatic, and a corner of Canterbury where people are dwarfed into comparative insignificance.

FACT

The Aoraki Mount Cook National Park covers approximately 700 sq km (270 sq miles), and was formally gazetted as a National Park in 1953. Together with the Westland National Park, it forms a World Heritage Park.

Sublime scenery at Lake Tekapo.

The west coast.

Fur seal at Cape Foulwind near Westport.

THE WEST COAST

Wild and rugged, this area's inhospitable terrain makes many of its scenic spots difficult to reach: those who persevere will be rewarded with untamed nature at its best.

Main Attractions

Fox and Franz Josef Glaciers
Lake Matheson
Okarito Lagoon
Shantytown, Greymouth
Pancake Rocks, Punakaiki

Most New Zealanders refer to their South Island's western flank as simply 'the Coast', a rugged and primeval region that plummets westwards from the South Island's Main Divide, through luxuriant rainforest hemmed in by a breathtaking coastline. Weeks can be spent exploring this region, which Rudyard Kipling referred to as 'last, loneliest, loveliest, exquisite apart'. No other area in the country is so stamped with identity or character.

In the gold-rush days of the 1860s men lit their cigars with £5 notes and dozens of towns sprang up in the middle of the bush around the promise of buried riches. Yet the hard-drinking, hard-fighting and hard-working men and women of those bygone days have left behind little more than a legend. After decades of decline, the population along the 500km (300-mile) coast is now almost back to what it was in 1867, when it peaked at 40,000 and comprised 13 percent of New Zealand's total population. Today, West Coasters number around 38,000 – a mere fraction of the country's 4.5 million people. Old buildings ramble into misty landscapes and rainforest relentlessly reclaims sites where towns such as Charleston (once home to 12,000 souls and 80 grog shops) boomed.

Living here is still for the hardy. There are more 'settlements' than towns, and no cities. Along with the mist and mountains, a pioneering spirit still hangs in the air. The Coasters who remain have developed a strong identity, with a reputation for being down-to-earth, rugged, independent and hospitable. For years, they made a habit of flouting liquor licensing laws, in particular that which forbade the sale of alcohol after 6 o'clock, which was regarded as some kind of joke originating from the city. Although

Polished paua (abalone) shells.

The Bushman's Centre near Lake Ianthe recreates the lives of the pioneering bushmen – mainly fur trappers – who lived in the west coast region in the 19th century.

The TranzAlpine train en route to Greymouth.

most West Coasters are environmentally evolved, a few still harbour a deep suspicion of 'Greenies', conservationists who want to preserve intact the area's native forests and birdlife. Some locals, struggling to scratch a living from coal-mining and timber-milling, angrily oppose the environmentalist concerns of these outsiders.

Early explorers

The west coast has never seduced its inhabitants with an easy life. It was settled late by the Maori, from about 1400, the main attraction being the much-coveted *pounamu* greenstone at Arahura, the hard and translucent jade traded up and down the country to make fine-quality tools and weapons. Because of the stormy sea conditions along this stretch of coast, the stone had to be arduously carried out on men's backs, first through a route north to Nelson and later across Alpine passes in the Main Divide to Canterbury.

Neither of the two great European discoverers, Abel Tasman and James Cook, was enamoured of what he saw when sailing past the west coast, in 1642 and 1769 respectively. 'An inhospitable shore' was Cook's description. 'One long solitude with a forbidding sky and impenetrable forest' was the view, about 50 years later, of an officer in a French expedition.

Travelling up the coast

The west coast is accessed from elsewhere in South Island via one of three spectacular mountain passes, or through the scenic Buller Gorge that winds back to Nelson in the north. The southernmost route, snaking up from the Southern Lakes and the dry, tussocked scenery of Central Otago, is State Highway (SH) 6. Crossing the 563-metre (1,867ft) high **Haast Pass** ㉖, this was the last major arterial route to be pushed through in New Zealand, completed in 1965. Having descended to the coast, SH6 then follows the seaboard northwards from the town of Haast all the way up to Westport, enabling travellers to follow almost the entire length of the coast as part of a South Island round trip.

The **Haast Visitor Centre** DOC (tel: 03-750 0809; www.haastnz.com; daily Nov–Mar 9am–6pm, Apr–Oct 9am–4.30pm), near the Haast junction, has useful information on attractions in the area. Turn south at Haast township and you enter an especially lonely corner of the country, traversed by a road which extends 36km (22 miles) to the fishing village of **Jackson Bay** ㉗. This small community swells in size during the spring, when whitebaiters descend en masse to the nearby river mouth, an annual occurrence which is repeated beside swift-flowing rivers all along the coast.

Fishing is a major preoccupation in this southern part of Westland. Haast is known for its river fishing, while 45km (28 miles) north at the quiet holiday spot of **Lake Paringa**, anglers are enticed by the prospect of brown trout and quinnat salmon. Meanwhile, eco-tourism is breathing new life into rural communities once entirely reliant on fishing or other local resources. Some 30km (19 miles) north of Haast, at **Wilderness Lodge Lake Moeraki** (tel: 03-750 0881; www.wildernesslodge.co.nz) in South Westland, guests are immersed in the nature experience while cosseted in luxury. For many, gazing up at the Southern Cross and hearing the screech of a kiwi are among the highlights of their stay. In the light of day, there is the Fiordland penguin colony near **Knights Point** to visit, or dolphins to be seen cavorting in the surf off **Ship Creek**.

Fox and Franz Josef glaciers

Many of the country's finest mountains lie in the geographical region of the west coast, comprising that chain of spectacular cloud-piercing peaks called the **Southern Alps**. Aoraki Mount Cook (see page 264) is the highest and a serious challenge to the Alpine climber. Dozens of other peaks over 3,000 metres (9,850ft) are named after early navigators, including Tasman, Magellan, La Perouse, Dampier and Malaspina.

About 120km (75 miles) north of Haast, an astonishing total of 15 metres (49ft) of snow is dumped annually at high altitudes, giving rise

Gold was discovered in the region in the 1860s.

GLEAM OF GOLD

Back in the early days the west coast was so forbidding that European exploration inland did not begin in earnest until 1846. The opinion of one of the early first explorers, Thomas Brunner, who described it as 'the very worst country I have seen in New Zealand', only served to discourage others. His distaste resulted from the great hardships suffered during his nightmarish 550-day journey, when he got so hungry he had to eat his dog. There must be something about this place and desperate eating; the last act of cannibalism reputedly took place here in the late 1800s.

It was only in 1860, after favourable reports of huge low-level glaciers in the south and possible routes through the Alps to Canterbury, that the central government purchased the west coast from the Maori for 300 gold sovereigns. Discovery of gold in 1864 at Greenstone Creek, a tributary of the Taramakau River, would change everything here. Hordes of gold-hungry miners converged on the area from all over the world. New strikes followed up and down the Coast, in the river gorges and gravels, the precious metal even being found in the black sand of the beaches. These 'diggers' brought a cheerful camaraderie that gave a distinctive character to the new province. The boom did not last long, but the surviving town sites, workings and rusty relics provide glimpses of that golden past.

to some 140 glaciers. Uniquely, two of these – **Fox Glacier** and, further up the road, **Franz Josef Glacier** – penetrate the lower forest. Few sights equal the spectacle of these giant tongues of ice grinding down through the temperate rainforest to just 300 metres (1,000ft) above sea level. Explorer and geologist Julius von Haast made the first recorded visit to the glaciers in 1865. His unbridled enthusiasm soon made them known as far away as Europe. Within two decades, guided glacier trips had become fashionable. One old photo of the period shows a party of 90 picnickers high in the jumbled ice. Venturing onto the ice alone has never been recommended, and successions of mountain guides have made their living sharing their glacial passion.

Glaciers constantly advance and retreat, depending upon the accumulation of snow gained in the upper glacier and ice melting in the lower part. An increase in snowfall at the névé results in the glacier advancing. Years of heavy snowfall high in the mountains caused both glaciers to begin a spectacular advance in 1985

which continued until 2009. Such was the progress of Franz Josef Glacier that its sparkling white ice could be seen again for the first time in 40 years from the altar window of St James Anglican Church, which sits against a backdrop of native bush in Franz Josef township. Both the Franz Josef Glacier and the Fox Glacier are currently in a phase of retreating.

Both glaciers are located, about 25km (16 miles) apart, in the **Westland National Park** ㉘, with its 88,000 hectares (217,000 acres) of Alpine peaks, snowfields, forests, lakes and rivers. The main highway, which traverses the park's western edge, passes close to both. As well as guided walks on the ice (see panel), narrow bush-clad roads provide easy access to good vantage points for postcard views from reasonably close vantage points. But take note that the glacier terminals are very fragile, and towering blocks of ice have been crashing down with increasing frequency, resulting in some fatal accidents: it is important to stay within the boundary ropes. Helicopter and skiplane flights

Trekking on Franz Josef Glacier.

over the glaciers provide remarkable views of the greenish-blue tints and the apparently infinite crevasses.

Two small but lively townships, **Fox Glacier** ㉙ and **Franz Josef** ㉚, each with a decent range of accommodation and restaurants on offer, cater to the needs of visitors. **Department of Conservation** offices in Fox Glacier (tel: 03-751 0807; Mon–Fri 9am–4.30pm) and Franz Josef (tel: 03-752 0796; daily Dec–Feb 8.30am–6pm, until 5pm Mar–Nov) provide information about the activities available in the area.

There are some 110km (68 miles) of walking tracks accessible from these townships, passing through the varied native forest and dominated by the lofty peaks of Cook, Tasman and La Perouse. This trio of mountains is stunningly mirrored in **Lake Matheson**, one of the park's three calm lakes formed by the glacial dramas of 10,000 years ago. Just 10 minutes north of Franz Josef Village on SH6 is **Lake Mapourika**, the largest and arguably the most stunning of South Westland's glacial lakes.

Coastal highlights

A short detour 19km (12 miles) west of Fox Glacier township is **Gillespie's Beach**, noted for its miners' cemetery and seal colony. Some 60km (37 miles) further north on the main road, another side road leads to **Okarito Lagoon** ㉛, New Zealand's largest natural wetland, which covers 3,240 hectares (8,000 acres). It is famous as the only breeding ground of the rare white heron. A survey taken just 12 years after the birds' discovery there in 1865 showed only six breeding pairs had escaped the plume hunters.

The town of **Okarito** once boasted 31 hotels, but now only a few holiday cottages and permanent dwellings remain. For the more adventurous, guided kayak trips organised by **Okarito Nature Tours** (tel: 03-753 4014; www.okarito.co.nz) are an excellent

means of exploring the lagoon and the white heron colony.

Further north on SH6 at **Whataroa**, a sedate 20-minute jet-boat ride also takes nature-lovers to a riverside hideaway within the sanctuary to view the colony, now numbering 250. The Maori called them *kotuku*, the 'bird of a single flight', to be seen perhaps once in a lifetime.

Continuing northwards, the main highway passes the idyllic, forest-enclosed and trout-filled **Lake Ianthe** before arriving in the town of **Ross**, at the heart of a once-flourishing goldfield which produced the largest nugget (2,970g/99oz) – the 'Honourable Roddy' – ever recorded in New Zealand. Relics of its once proud history and a replica of the aforementioned nugget can be seen at the **Ross Goldfields Information and Heritage Centre** at 4 Aylmer Street (tel: 03-755 4077; www.ross.org.nz; daily 9am–4pm). Gold panning is a popular activity here; pans can be hired from the heritage centre.

About 30km (19 miles) north of Ross is **Hokitika** ㉜, formerly

Reflections at Lake Matheson.

the 'Wonder City of the Southern Hemisphere' with 'streets of gold' and a thriving seaport. It is much quieter these days, but has regained something of its prosperous feel. It is served by the west coast's main airfield, and its many tourist attractions include a historical museum, greenstone factories, a gold mine, gold panning and a glow-worm dell. A good kiwi-viewing facility is here at the **National Kiwi Centre** (tel: 03-755 5251; www.thenationalkiwicentre.co.nz; daily 9am–5pm) at 64 Tancred Street. You can view kiwis in a recreated habitat, giant eels (best at feeding times 10am, noon and 3pm), tuatara and various aquatic species.

A celebration of the coast's bush tucker is held annually in mid-March at the **Hokitika Wild Foods Festival** (www.wildfoods.co.nz). The one-day gala event gives visitors the chance to sample wild boar, venison, huge roasted larvae called huhu grubs and gourmet 'westcargot' snails, not to mention whitebait patties. At the other end of the culinary scale, the town's **Café de Paris** (tel: 03-755 8933) on Tancred

An ice cave on Fox Glacier.

Street serves authentic European cuisine and has won various awards for its fine fare.

Both **Lake Kaniere** and the **Hokitika Gorge**, 18km (11 miles) and 35km (22 miles) from Hokitika respectively, make worthwhile side trips. Otherwise continue 23km (14 miles) north of the town, to Kumara Junction and the turn-off to the dramatic **Arthur's Pass Highway** (see page 260), the second of the three mountain passes linking the east and west coasts of South Island. A few kilometres along this road is the old gold-mining town of **Kumara**, from where a scenic detour to **Lake Brunner**, the largest lake on the west coast, winds its way through dense native forest.

From Shantytown to Greymouth

Towards Greymouth, about 10km (6 miles) north of Kumara Junction, is **Shantytown** (tel: 03-762 6634, 0800-742 689; www.shantytown.co.nz; daily 8.30am–5pm), a replica of a late 19th-century goldfield town offering

WALKING ON ICE

Guided glacier walks range from a half- to full day, while a more expensive option is a heli-hike, which takes you on a scenic helicopter flight and lands you on the glacier for a guided walk. Adventurous types can try ice climbing. You will be kitted out with a helmet, harness, ice crampons, an axe and a rope. A high degree of fitness is necessary.

Less fit mortals are better off on the half-day glacier walk, which itself is a strenuous affair if you've never walked on ice before. Dress warmly in layers, although you will be provided with boots, socks and gloves, crampons, a Gore-Tex raincoat and a trekking pole.

For walks on Fox Glacier, contact Fox Glacier Guiding (tel: 03-751 0825; www.foxguides.co.nz; daily) who offer a wide range of options with regular departures throughout the day. For Franz Josef, contact Franz Josef Glacier Guides (tel: 03-752 0763; www.franzjosefglacier.com; daily). As the Franz Josef Glacier has recently become unstable, to get onto the glacier ice here now requires a helicopter flight, so it is significantly more expensive than hiking on Fox Glacier, however it comes with free entry to Franz Josef's stunning new Glacier Hot Pools (tel: 0800-044 044; www.glacierhotpools.co.nz), an ideal way to relax afterwards.

Otherwise hop onto a helicopter or light plane for a scenic flight instead. The more expensive trips feature a brief snow landing on either of the glaciers.

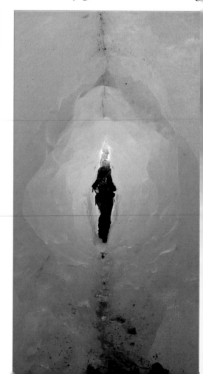

gold panning and a bush steam loco-motive ride to the gold-panning and saw milling areas. Thirty historic buildings include a local saloon, gift shop, bank, jail, church, hospital and school. You are welcome to try your hand at panning for gold, but if that does not appeal, down a locally crafted Monteith's beer instead at the Golden Nugget Hotel.

At nearby **Wood's Creek**, take the 1km (0.5-mile) loop walking track around the New River diggings dating back to 1865. Diggers smeared their bodies with rotten mutton fat to ward off sandflies, risking their lives working in the river and its tributaries, where water levels could rise in a matter of minutes after heavy rain (a frequent occurrence on this coast). Take a torch so you can investigate the tunnels, but leave immediately should the water begin to rise.

Greymouth ㉝, 41km (25 miles) north of Hokitika on SH6, is the terminus of the TranzAlpine train route from Christchurch (see page 260). The largest town on the west coast (population 13,900), it owes its commanding position to its seaport and its proximity to timber mills and coal mines. In 2010, Greymouth hit international news when 29 coal miners at the nearby Pike River Mine lost their lives in a violent underground explosion.

Nowadays the township is reinventing itself as the coast's adventure capital. The pioneering spirit still drives tourist ventures that cajole visitors to try their hand at gold mining, four-wheel-drive quad-bike safaris, dolphin-watching and cave rafting. Greymouth is a good base with enough diversions for a short stay. Enquire at the **i-site Visitor Centre** at 112 Mackay Street (tel: 0800-473 966; www.greydistrict.co.nz).

The **Jade Boulder Gallery** (tel: 03-768 0700; daily Dec–Feb 8am–6pm, Mar–Nov 9am–5pm; free) in Guinness Street showcases greenstone with innovative displays, while **History House** (tel: 03-768 4028; daily 10am–4pm, closed Mar–Nov weekends) features a collection of photographs and memorabilia of the district dating back to the 1850s.

TIP

The entrance fee to Shantytown includes a ride on one of its three vintage steam trains: the 1877 L-Class, 1896 improved F-Class Kaitangata, or 1913 Climax. The ride will take you through rainforest along a line which follows the original 1800s sawmill tram track.

The deer farming industry is highly lucrative in New Zealand.

Carving pounamu greenstone.

The steam locomotive at Shantytown.

Another of Greymouth's varied attractions is tours of **Monteith's Brewery Company** (tel: 03-768 4149; www.monteiths.co.nz; daily 10.30am, 3pm, 4.30pm, 6pm, booking essential) at the corner of Turumaha and Herbert streets. You can see the beer being brewed in open fermenters by coal-fired boilers, learn about each beer's origin and taste profile, and, of course, down a couple at the end of the tour.

A 20-minute drive inland from Greymouth is **Blackball**, a former coal-mining town now enjoying something of a nostalgic renaissance. A room at the Formerly **Blackball Hilton Hotel** (tel: 03-732 4705; www.blackballhilton.co.nz) comes with a hot water bottle if you want one. Spend the day wandering around the old coal workings or explore the start of the **Croesus Track** to Barrytown. Evenings are best huddled around a fire, sipping Monteith's beer.

Pancakes at Punakaiki

Beyond Greymouth, the spectacular Coast Road to Westport hugs the coastline, which, 43km (27 miles) north at **Punakaiki**, takes on the extraordinary appearance of a pile of petrified pancakes. The **Pancake Rocks ㉞** and their blowholes comprise layers of stratified limestone. Reached by a short, scenic walk from the main road, the rocks are best visited when there is an incoming tide, when the brisk westerly wind causes the tempestuous sea to surge explosively and dramatically into the chasms, spouting spray through skylight-type holes.

Take a stroll along the nearby coastal tracks and look out for native wood pigeons (kereru) and tui feeding on the abundant kowhai trees, or hike along the shoreline to see the nests of Westland petrels. Punakaiki is on the edge of the **Paparoa National Park**, where the peculiarities of the

limestone landscape continue inland. Here, rainwater has created deep gorges, fluted rocks and cave networks, many still unexplored.

Some 32km (20 miles) north is **Charleston**, the once-booming centre of the Buller district, with old gold workings nearby. At a junction 21km (13 miles) further to the north, the coastal road becomes SH67, leading to nearby **Westport** ③⑤, a useful launching pad for side trips to attractions in the area.

At **Cape Foulwind**, west of the township, a walkway follows the coast for 4km (2 miles). The highlight is a view of a breeding colony of New Zealand fur seals. About 14km (9 miles) north of Westport, along the Karamea Highway, is the deserted coal-mining town of **Denniston**, once the largest producer of coal in New Zealand. The **Denniston Walkway** climbs the high plateau to the old coal town and provides views of the once breathtakingly steep tramway called the **Denniston Incline**.

The west coast's northernmost town, 97km (60 miles) north of Westport, is **Karamea** ③⑥, gateway to the vast 4,520 sq km (1,745 sq mile) **Kahurangi National Park** (see page 245) with its famous Heaphy Track.

A visit to Karamea is not complete without a trip to the **Oparara Basin**, an area of majestic limestone arches and caves northeast of the town. Westport shop owner Phil Wood and three caving mates discovered the entrance to **Honeycomb Cave**, just 1km (0.5 mile) further up from the **Oparara Arch**, in 1980. So far, the bones of 27 extinct species of birds – giant moa and eagles, even a goose that no one knew existed – have been found in its 17km (11 miles) of passages. Honeycomb Cave, with its delicate straw stalactites, pedestal 'elephant feet' and cascades of rougher flowstone, can be viewed with **Oparara Guided Tours** tel: 03-782 6652; www.oparara.co.nz; daily 8.30am, 9am, 10am, 1.30pm).

Buller Gorge and Reefton

Around 5km (3 miles) south of Westport, SH6 turns inland (becoming the Buller Gorge Highway) to follow one of the South Island's most beautiful rivers, the Buller, through its lower and upper gorges for 84km (52 miles) to Murchison. At this point the west coast is left behind and the road continues to Nelson and Blenheim at the northern end of the island. Prior to Murchison, two branches extend southwards: SH69 and SH65, both of which connect with the Lewis Pass Highway at Springs Junction, the last major route across the South Island.

SH69, which turns off at the Inangahua Junction, traverses one of the most mineralised districts of New Zealand. About 34km (21 miles) south, it enters **Reefton** ③⑦, named after its famous quartz reefs. This region was once abundant with gold and coal. The other route (SH65) winds its way up to the Lewis Pass from the outskirts of Murchison, joining up with the main Lewis Pass Highway at Springs Junction, 72km (45 miles) to the south.

FACT

Heavy rainfall on the west coast – some 5 metres (200 inches) pours annually – accounts for its lush greenery and vibrant colours. In fact, some Kiwis refer to it as the 'wet coast'. When the rain is exhausted and the cloud rolls back from the mountain tops, the air fills with birdsong and – the sole flaw in this Eden – sandflies, with their craving for human blood. Be sure to slather yourself with plenty of insect repellent.

The Pancake Rocks at Punakaiki.

EXPLORING THE NATIONAL PARKS

Among New Zealand's greatest attractions are its publicly owned National Parks, Forest Parks, Scenic Reserves and Regional Parks.

New Zealand's National Parks preserve the country's natural heritage and are highly protected by the Department of Conservation (DOC). Nine of the DOC's most significant 'Great Walks', are located within the park system. For detailed topographical maps and further information on the geology, flora, fauna, historic sites, hiking, conservation initiatives and accommodation of each of the 14 National Parks, visit www.doc.govt.nz.

Tongariro National Park: Tongariro's vast open landscapes frame the volcanoes of Tongariro, Ngauruhoe and Ruapehu. Hikes include the 'Great Walks' Tongariro Northern Circuit and the Tongariro Crossing.

Te Urewera National Park: The misty bluffs and tumbling waterfalls of Te Urewera provide a backdrop for the 'Great Walks' Lake Waikaremoana Track.

Egmont National Park: Mount Taranaki's symmetrical cone lies at the heart of Egmont National Park. Highlights include the Goblin Forest and beautiful Dawsons Falls.

Whanganui National Park: This park offers 230km (140 miles) of peaceful paddling plus the Whanganui 'Great Walks' Journey.

Abel Tasman National Park: With golden beaches, tranquil lagoons and impossibly clear waters, Abel Tasman's most memorable hike is the three-day 'Great Walks' Coastal Track.

Nelson Lakes National Park: Craggy peaks and trout-laden waters dominate the Nelson Lakes National

Lake Matheson in Westland National Park, with Mount Tasman and Mount Cook beyond. The park also contains th Fox and Franz Josef glaciers, and has some great walks.

Milford Sound is pa of the Fiordland National Park. Cru companies allow visitors to travel alo the fiord to open oce and back, a fantasti way to appreciate th stunning scenery.

A young kauri tree at Waipoua Kauri Forest, Northland, a protected forest park. Most of New Zealand's kauri forests were decimated in the 18th and 19th centuries.

kayaking in Abel Tasman National Park.

ount Cook is the crowning glory of the magnificent uthern Alps range. The training ground for Everest nqueror, the late Sir Edmund Hillary, it's a terrain that is to be taken lightly.

Tongariro National Park has vast volcanic landscapes.

Park. Cruise on the lakes, hire a kayak or fish to your heart's content.

Kahurangi National Park: This vast wilderness is renowned for its nikau palms, limestone/marble outcrops and caves, and the Heaphy Track, a 'Great Walks' route of four to six days.

Paparoa National Park: Paparoa's highlights include the Pancake Rocks at Punakaiki, and the Pororari River Track.

Arthur's Pass National Park: Experienced mountaineers flock to Arthur's Pass National Park to tackle its highest mountains. Shorter hikes include the Devil's Punchbowl Waterfall and the Dobson Nature Walk.

Aoraki Mount Cook National Park: This park contains 140 peaks over 2,134 metres (7,011ft) high, including 3,754-metre (12,316ft) high Aoraki Mount Cook, plus 72 glaciers.

Westland Tai Poutini National Park: High peaks, huge glaciers and placid coastal wetlands provide 110km (68 miles) of walking tracks.

Mount Aspiring National Park: Home to the Routeburn Track 'Great Walks' route, as well as the multi-day Greenstone Track and the Dart/Rees River circuit.

Fiordland National Park: New Zealand's most remote wilderness area features 14 fiords and two 'Great Walks' – the Milford and Kepler Tracks.

Rakiura National Park: Hikes here range from 15 minutes to multi-day hikes. On the 'Great Walks' Rakiura Track, Stewart Island kiwi are often spotted.

Lake Wanaka.

QUEENSTOWN AND OTAGO

Located in an area of spectacular natural beauty, it's easy to understand why Queenstown is unashamedly a tourist town, with its huge range of leisure activities and great shopping.

The hub of Central Otago is the jewel in New Zealand's tourism crown. It has become such a popular destination for overseas visitors that some New Zealanders complain that they can't get a look in. In less than 30 years, Queenstown has grown from a sleepy lakeside town into a sophisticated all-year tourist resort, a sort of Antipodean Saint Moritz. This is a place that has been nurtured on tourism, and while other rural towns have struggled to survive, it has flourished. Within a radius of just a few kilometres, the ingenuity and mechanical wizardry of New Zealanders have combined with the stunning landscape to provide an unrivalled range of adventure activities.

Central Otago possesses a personality quite distinct from other parts of the country. Some of the Southern Alps' most impressive peaks dominate its western flank, towering over deep glacier-gouged lakes. Yet the enduring impact is more subtle, encapsulated in the strange landscape chiselled and shaved from Central Otago's plateau of mica schist rock. In the dry continental climate of the inland plateau, the pure atmosphere aids the play of light, evoking nuances few other landscapes permit. The overwhelming impression is of a stark, simple landscape burnished in

glowing browns tinged with white, gold, ochre and sienna. The effect has attracted generations of landscape painters to the area.

Yet scenery alone is not enough to lure people into staking out a patch of earth in what in the past has been an arid and often inhospitable region. Over nine centuries of sketchy human habitation, Central Otago's lure has been successively based on moa, jade, grazing land, gold, hydroelectric power and now tourism.

Pounamu greenstone, the Maori's precious stone.

Thrills on the Shotover River.

Riding the luge down the twisting track on Bob's Peak is heaps of fun. But try the beginners' 'scenic' route before progressing to the more winding advanced route.

Gold in them hills

The first humans to set foot in the region were Maori moa-hunters who pushed inland around the 15th century. However, through over-hunting and the effects of fire, the moa and other birds disappeared for ever. Some of New Zealand's best moa remains have been found in the banks of the Clutha River as it winds through the plateau on its 320km (200-mile) journey to the Pacific.

Europeans first arrived in Central Otago in 1847 when a surveyor blazed a trail for pioneers searching for land to establish large sheep runs. By 1861 the new settlers were squatting on most of the potential grazing land, battling against the harsh environment of winter snows, spring floods, summer droughts and bush fires, as well as wild dogs and other vermin.

These pioneers, predominantly of Scottish origin, were just settling in when, in 1861, the first major gold strike was made in a gully along the Tuapeka River. Central Otago's gold boom had begun. In just four months, 3,000 men were swarming over the 5km (3-mile) valley, probing and sifting each centimetre for glowing alluvial gold. A year on, the population of the Tuapeka goldfield was 11,500, double that of the fast-emptying provisional capital, Dunedin. Otago's income trebled in 12 months, while the number of ship arrivals quadrupled, many of the 200 vessels bringing miners from Australia's goldfields.

As prospectors moved inland to the then inhospitable hinterland of Central Otago, new fields were discovered in quick succession in other valleys – the Clutha at the foot of the Dunstan Range, the Cardrona, Shotover, Arrow and Kawarau. In 1862 the Shotover, then yielding as much as 155g (5oz) of gold by the shovelful, was known as the richest river in the world. In one afternoon two Maori men going to the rescue of their near-drowned dog recovered no less than 11kg (388oz) of gold.

Queenstown

One of the best introductions to **Queenstown** ❶ is to admire the magnificent views of the town and

surroundings from **Bob's Peak** Ⓐ by taking an exciting **Skyline Gondola** Ⓑ (tel: 03-441 0377; www.skyline. co.nz; daily 9am until late) ride from Brecon Street. After the 790-metre (2,592ft) climb, take the chair-lift higher up the peak and ride the thrilling luge downhill, back to the gondola's viewing deck and restaurant complex. From here you can access a range of scenic hikes and mountain bike trails or, by night, join a Skyline stargazing tour to observe and learn more about the night sky (tours usually start around 90 minutes after sunset). During the day, **Ziptrek Ecotours** (tel: 03-441 2102; www.zip trek.com) runs tours riding a series of flying foxes (harnesses swinging from zip-line wires) between tree-top platforms. A flying fox providing an alternative route to Brecon Street has also been installed. The gondola also provides access to the **Queenstown Bike Park**, which features more than 30km (19 miles) of purpose-built tracks catering for all levels of riders. The lift, which allows bikes to be hooked onto the gondola and carried

up to the Park, has been a huge hit since it opened.

Also on Brecon Street is the **Kiwi and Birdlife Park** (tel: 03-442 8059; www.kiwibird.co.nz; daily 9am–6pm). Easy walks through native bush lead to aviaries where you can see tui, bellbird, fantail and kiwi, as well as endangered species such as the black stilt and banded rail. A conservation show runs at 11am and 3pm, and kiwi-feeding is held at 10am, noon, 1.30pm and 4.30pm.

As you would expect from a major tourist hub, Queenstown has a wide variety of accommodation, restaurants, entertainment and shops displaying handcrafted New Zealand products such as suede and leather goods, sheepskin and woollen products, and attractive greenstone jewellery. But for most people, these are mere distractions from the lure of the great outdoors all around. The **i-SITE Visitor Centre** Ⓒ at the corner of Shotover and Camp streets (tel: 03-442 4100; www.queenstown-vacation. com; daily May–Nov 8am–6pm, Dec– Apr 8am–7pm) has all the details you

The Skyline Gondola, with views over Lake Wakatipu.

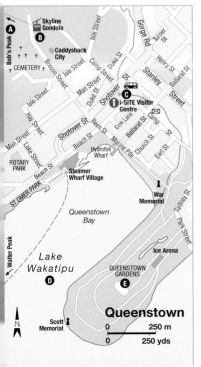

TSS Earnslaw steams across Lake Wakatipu every two hours in summer.

Gondola; here, too, you'll find the **Ledge Sky Swing** (tel: 0800-286 4958; www.bungy.co.nz).

Some of the world's finest scenic flights, on both helicopter and light plane, operate from Queenstown, providing access to spectacular lake, Alp and fiord scenery and locations which cannot easily be reached in any other way. For those with enough daring to dispense with machines, there is also paragliding, hang-gliding and skydiving, strapped to your guide, of course (the Visitor Centre has all the details).

Milder pastimes

Rather more sedate activities are available around the town, too – trout fishing in rivers and streams or an excursion on the steamship TSS *Earnslaw* (tel: 03-249 7416; www.realjourneys.co.nz; daily 10am–8pm, Dec–Mar departures every two hours), a grand old coal-fuelled vessel which has graced the waters of **Lake Wakatipu D** since 1912, when it was first used to carry goods to remote settlements. What's inside is almost as fascinating as the views beyond,

need on how to spend your time in Queenstown.

Commercial water adventures on Queenstown's lakes and rivers include canoeing, yachting, windsurfing, parasailing, water-skiing, canyoning, rafting and hobie-cat sailing. Queenstown is also synonymous with bungee jumping, and you don't even have to leave town to get your first bungee under your belt. A short but spectacular jump called **The Ledge** bungee is found at the top of the Skyline

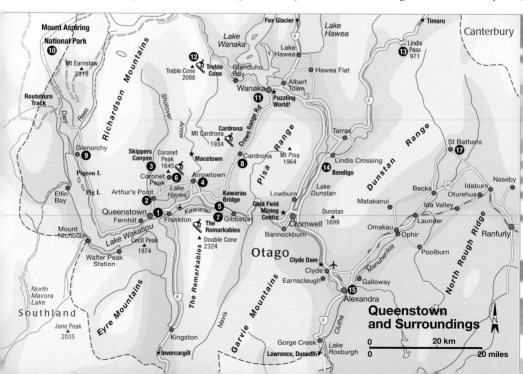

and passengers are encouraged to view the engine room and historic displays. An optional extra is a visit to a working farm in a magnificent location, the **Walter Peak High Country Farm**, where you can have lunch or tea and the chance to see New Zealand's all-important agriculture at first hand. In summer you can also opt to cycle independently on the Walter Peak back-country trail or join a guided cycling trip, or take a guided horse trek.

Queenstown's newest attraction is the 110km (68-mile) Queenstown Trail, which connects the Wakatipu Basin, Gibbston Valley, Arrowtown, Lake Hayes and Queenstown Bay. Cyclists can choose to complete the full multi-day ride or spend a day or even an hour exploring the trail.

Lake Wakatipu is Central Otago's most haunting body of water and has long captured people's imagination with its strange serpentine shape and rhythmic 'heartbeat' (see below), as well as its constant coldness (swimming is enjoyed during summer in other lakes in the South Island – but

here, even during the height of summer, it is nothing short of a teeth-chattering experience). According to Maori legend, the lake is the 'Hollow of the Giant' *(Whakatipua)*, formed when an evil sleeping giant was set on fire by a brave youth, thus melting the snow and ice of the surrounding mountains to fill the 80km (50-mile) double-dog-legged hollow. In fact, the major lakes of Wakatipu, Wanaka and Hawea were all gouged by glaciers, and the peculiar rise and fall of Wakatipu every five minutes is not the effect of a giant's heartbeat, as legend dictates, but of a natural oscillation caused by variations in atmospheric pressure.

Directly opposite the lake from the steamer wharf are the **Queenstown Gardens Ⓔ**, a tranquil, fir-surrounded expanse of broad lawns and rose gardens that also afford excellent views of Walter Peak, Ben Lomond and The Remarkables. If you prefer a more structured horticultural experience, **Queenstown Garden Tours** (tel: 03-441 3990; www.queenstowngarden tours.co.nz) picks you up from your accommodation and takes in three

QUOTE

Lake Wakatipu is indisputably handsome. 'I do not know that lake scenery can be finer than this,' enthused English novelist Anthony Trollope in 1872.

Paragliding over Bob's Peak.

SKIPPERS CANYON

Skippers Canyon is an adventurous scenic drive snaking along a treacherously narrow trail along a schist bluff with sheer vertical drops to the vivid ice-blue of the Shotover River below. Hell's Gate, Castle Rock and Devil's Elbow flash past, before you're deposited in a vast tussock-draped landscape framed by the Richardson and Harris mountains. Steeped in history, the route is littered with old gold-mining settlements and ruins, with informative displays and numerous picnic spots.

Follow in the footsteps of miners at Skippers Bridge, or explore the ruins of the Long Gully Pub, Mount Aurum Recreation Reserve, and the pipeline that once brought water to the goldfield. To get safely there and back (rental vehicles are prohibited) team up with Nomad Safaris (www.nomadsafaris.co.nz).

FACT

Whitewater rafting grades are weather-dependent. If a lot of rain falls the river will be higher and therefore fewer rocks are exposed, making it a lower-grade river, ie Grades 1, 2 or 3. When little rain has fallen there is less water and therefore more rocks and more challenge, hence a Grade 5 river. Rain can come at any time of the year, so the rivers fluctuate, but it does tend to rain a lot less in summer, so there is far more chance of a Grade 5 experience.

Shotover Jet boat.

splendid local residential gardens in the spring, summer and autumn months. Devonshire tea is served.

Outside Queenstown

To enjoy most of the activities for which the area is renowned, you will have to venture a little further from Queenstown itself.

Following the **Gorge Road** north out of town will bring you to **Climbing Queenstown** (tel: 03-450 2119; www.climbingqueenstown.com; daily 9am, 1.30pm), a series of iron rungs, ladders and wires attached to a mountain side, which enables the inexperienced to replicate the experience of rock climbing. Abseiling and rock-climbing options cater for both first-timers and experts.

The region's swift-flowing rivers set the scene for whitewater rafting and jet-boating adventures. The latter is New Zealand's home-grown style of running rivers, upstream as well as down. Propellerless powerboats speed over rapid shallows barely ankle-deep. These nifty craft are thrust along by their jet stream as water, drawn in through an intake in the bottom of the hull, is pumped out at high pressure through a nozzle at the rear. The typical jet boat can skim over shallows no more than 10cm (4 inches) deep, and can execute sudden 180-degree turns within a single boat length. The best-known of the dozen or so commercial options, **Shotover Jet** (tel: 03-442 8570; www.shotoverjet.com; daily 8am–5pm, Jan–Feb until 6pm), takes passengers from **Arthur's Point ❷**, 5km (3 miles) north of Queenstown, on a thrilling ride, up and down the **Shotover River,** skirting jagged cliffs. It is without a doubt one of the more accessible adventure experiences in Queenstown. A free shuttle service from Queenstown is available.

Whitewater rafting on the 14km (9-mile) stretch of the Shotover River, with its Grade 3–5 rapids (see margin), is more challenging than the **Kawarau River** to the east, which has a 7km (4-mile) run more suitable for inexperienced rafters. Several companies – such as **Queenstown Rafting** (tel: 03-442 9792; www.rafting.co.nz) – offer trips with bus transfers to the launch point, wetsuits and a brief lesson before you take off. River sledging, with just a slim board between you and the river torrent, is also popular on the Kawarau River. Trips departing at 9am and 2pm are offered by **River Surfing** (tel: 03-442 5262; www.river surfing.co.nz).

North of Arthur's Point is **Skippers Canyon ❸**, the epicentre of the region's gold-mining activity from the 1860s until recently. Also known as Skippers Grand Canyon, this 8-hectare (20-acre) area encompasses a number of attractions. The dramatic **Skippers Road**, hand-hewn from solid rock, is an adventure in itself. Self-driving is not recommended; a sign advises that car insurance is invalid here. **Nomad Safaris** (tel: 03-442 6699; www.nomad safaris.co.nz) offers daily four-wheel-drive tours into the canyon to the old settlement with a restored schoolhouse, cemetery and the **Skippers**

Canyon Suspension Bridge, which spans the swift waters of Shotover River 102 metres (335 feet) below.

Gold towns

Just past Arthur's Point is the steep road leading to Coronet Peak, but if you continue on straight ahead you will wind up in the tiny village of **Arrowtown ❹**. This is the most picturesque and best-preserved gold-mining settlement in Central Otago and arguably the prettiest small town in New Zealand, never more so than in autumn, when the foliage colours are truly spectacular.

Arrowtown is home to what may well be New Zealand's quirkiest movie house – **Dorothy Brown's Cinema, Bar and Bookshop** (tel: 03-442 1964; www.dorothybrowns.com; 10am–10.30pm) on Buckingham Street, which shows arthouse films in an opulent setting (red possum fur cushions, chandeliers, unusually comfortable seating), with an open fire and a bar.

At the end of Buckingham Street, heading towards the river, lie the evocative remains of the **Chinese Settlement**. At the peak of the gold rush in the 1880s, this sad collection of tiny stone buildings was home to some 60 Chinese miners. Their story is told in the **Lakes District Museum** (tel: 03-442 1824; www.museumqueens town.com; daily 8.30am–5pm) further along at 49 Buckingham Street. There are gold and other mineral specimens, miners' tools, miners' personal effects (typically old photos and old domestic appliances), plus colonial-era memorabilia, a collection of horse-drawn vehicles, a recreated streetscape and a Victorian schoolroom.

Ghost towns are scattered throughout the region, shadows of the calico, sod and corrugated-iron settlements that seemed ugly to visiting English novelist Anthony Trollope in 1872. One such place, **Macetown**, haunts the hills 15km (9 miles) northwest of Arrowtown and is a worthwhile detour. To get there a 4WD vehicle is essential, so it is best visited with a reputable tour company such as **Nomad Safaris** (see page 286). The town now consists of a handful of buildings in

Arrowtown.

TIP

The highlight of the ski season in Queenstown is the week-long Queenstown Winter Festival in July. One of the best websites for skiing in this region is www.nzski.com. Also worth checking out is www.cardrona.com and www.treblecone.co.nz.

various states of ruin, yet has an almost park-like quality, in part thanks to remnants of old gardens which have gone their own way. Macetown began life in the 19th century as a collection of tents for miners who hunted first for gold and, later, quartz. When the resources were exhausted, the town declined. The last mine closed in 1914.

Leaving Arrowtown, take the Arrowtown/Lake Hayes Road back to Queenstown. For most of this section of the trip you will be driving alongside the much-photographed mirror-like **Lake Hayes** and bypassing the luxury **Millbrook Resort**, with its Bob Charles-designed golf course. New Zealand's own distinctive architectural styles are visible in the thoughtfully designed farm dwellings where craftspeople, artists and retired folk enjoy a gentle way of life.

At the junction of State Highway (SH) 6 turn left and you will soon be at the world's first commercial bungee site, the historic **Kawarau Bridge ❺**, 6km (4 miles) south of Arrowtown, opened in 1988 by A.J. Hackett. For those who don't fancy

the real deal, there is the behind-the-scenes **Secrets of Bungy Tour** (tel: 0800-286 4958; www.bungy.co.nz) at the adjacent **Kawarau Bungy Centre**. This includes a look at bungee-cord making and exclusive access to viewing decks. After taking the plunge or just watching the expressions of those who do, you may feel in need of a little something at the centre's **café and wine bar.**

Leaving here, you can return to Queenstown via SH6 or continue on through the Gibbston Valley, calling in to sample wines at vineyards including Chard Farm (www.chardfarm.co.nz) and **Gibbston Valley Wines** (www.gibbstonvalley.co.nz), where tastings are complemented by cheese produced on site.

A.J. Hackett Bungy also runs one of the highest bungee jumps in the world, the mind-blowing 134-metre (440ft) Nevis Highwire Bungy, on the Nevis River (a tributary of the Kawarau), 32km (20 miles) from Queenstown. The site can only be accessed by four-wheel drive and transport is included in the jump fee.

Steamer Wharf at Lake Wakatipu.

Skiing and tramping

The largest ski fields in the region are Coronet Peak, The Remarkables, Treble Cone and Cardrona. **Coronet Peak ❻** is Queenstown's backyard ski field, located just 18km (11 miles) to the north and reached by sealed road. The ski season here extends from July to September (sometimes into October) and is noted for the variety of its terrain and innovations such as night skiing under floodlights. In the summer, sightseers can take chair-lifts to the summit (1,645 metres/5,397ft) for a wonderful view, while thrill-seekers can enjoy a rapid descent in a Cresta Run toboggan.

The second major ski field is **The Remarkables ❼**, 20km (12 miles) east, the rugged range that forms the famous backdrop to Queenstown. Its ski runs are popular with beginner and intermediate skiers, although there are also more challenging runs for the more experienced. The third ski area is **Cardrona ❽**, 57km (35 miles) from Queenstown, on the way to Wanaka via the Crown Range Road. The highest road in New Zealand, it offers a series of stunning views.

Some 42km (26 miles) northwest of Queenstown at the head of Lake Wakatipu is **Glenorchy ❾**, an area of exceptional beauty in a region where exceptional beauty seems to be the norm. For much of the distance from Queenstown, the road follows the shores of Wakatipu's western arm. Some 25km (16 miles) from town you will reach the top of a hill that provides a spectacular view across the lake, with its three islands – Tree Island, Pig Island and Pigeon Island.

Glenorchy is a hotbed of activity. Kayaking, jet boating, horse riding, fishing, canoeing and canyoning are all popular pursuits here. **Dart River Safaris** (tel: 03-442 9992, 0800-327 853; www.dartriver.co.nz) leads groups on many of these activities, including a jet-boat excursion to Sandy Bluff at the edge of **Mount Aspiring National Park ❿**; a wilderness safari incorporating jet boating and a nature trail; and full-day Funyak (inflatable canoe) trips. All explore the **Dart River**, which passes through a landscape of mountains and glaciers, and scenery from Tolkien's 'Middle-earth' (see page 82). The mountains of the Mount Aspiring National Park, a World Heritage Site, loom ahead, dominated by **Mount Aspiring** (3,030 metres/9,941ft). The park and the lonely valleys extending into Lake Wanaka (see below) present unrivalled opportunities for hiking, tramping and fishing in unspoilt wilderness.

Of all the numerous hiking trails in the Wakatipu Basin, the most rewarding is the **Routeburn Track**, which commences at Glenorchy. Winding its way through splendidly isolated country at the head of Lake Wakatipu to the Upper Hollyford Valley, this four-day trek is certainly one of New Zealand's best, but requires a greater degree of experience and fitness than the famed Milford Track in neighbouring Fiordland. High points of the walk include a variety of flora – and some

Wanaka's pristine lake.

fauna – waterfalls and rapidly changing landscapes.

Wanaka and its environs

Wanaka ⓫, 34km (21 miles) north of Cardrona, is a sort of mini-Queenstown (though it dislikes being described so). It may be relatively devoid of the bigger centre's in-your-face commercialism and crowds, but with its own lake, ski fields and everything else that's required of a southern playground, it's still a popular resort – with a good range of accommodation and restaurants. Wanaka's **i-site Visitor Centre** (tel: 03-443 1233; www.lakewanaka.co.nz; daily 8.30–5.30pm) has all the details you need to plan a stay here.

One of the more unusual attractions is Stuart Landsborough's **Puzzling World** (tel: 03-443 7489; www.puzzlingworld.co.nz; daily 8.30am–6pm, until 5.30pm Apr–Nov), about 2km (1¼ miles) south from Wanaka, and a must for families. Its main features are the tilted buildings that make up the complex and challenging 1.5km (1-mile) maze. Inside are numerous fascinating 'how-does-that-work?' optical illusions and holograms, as well as the unique Hall of Following Faces, in which faces of famous people seem to float and follow you everywhere.

Treble Cone ⓬ (tel: 03-443 1406; www.treblecone.co.nz) is a ski resort 19km (12 miles) northwest of Wanaka. Proud of its powder and the number of international awards it has won, it styles itself as the ski field where the locals go, and boasts the longest vertical rise in the district. In the summer it's worth a visit to marvel at the stupendous views.

Follow SH6 east of Wanaka and head north on SH8 to the **Lindis Pass** ⓭, linking northern Central Otago with Mount Cook and the Mackenzie Country. The road winds through some of the most beautiful hill country anywhere in New Zealand.

Former gold-rush towns

Bendigo ⓮, near the Clutha River 40km (25 miles) southeast of Wanaka (off SH8), is a near-perfect ghost town, especially when the wind whistles through the tumbledown stone cottages at the bleak crossroads. The southern extension of SH8 is the main artery to the heart of Central Otago, running parallel with the Clutha River, past the former gold towns of Roxburgh, Alexandra, Clyde and Cromwell. These towns are prosperous today thanks to their connection with Otago's lifeblood: that same mighty Clutha. The river that once surrendered gold has since, through irrigation, transformed parched land into fertile country famous for its stone fruit. Now it is also a major generator of electricity.

The road south of Bendigo runs for 15km (9 miles) to **Cromwell**. This is wine- and fruit-growing country, although Cromwell's greatest asset is **Lake Dunstan**, the body of water on which the town sits. The lake is used extensively for water sports and has an abundance of birdlife. In 1993 a dam was built close to where the Clutha River leaves the Cromwell Gorge near

The road north from Wanaka to Haast Pass and the west coast.

Clyde, 20km (12 miles) southeast of Cromwell. The water behind expanded through the gorge, drowning the old town of Cromwell and much of the lower Clutha Valley. The historic buildings of the Old Cromwell Town Historic Shopping Precinct (www.old-cromwell.co.nz), which were relocated to a new position on the lake, are a major drawcard and house a range of craftspeople and cafés.

Alexandra 🅖, 31km (19 miles) southeast of Clyde, distinguishes itself early by its colourful, blossom-parade tribute to spring. In winter, ice-skating and curling take place on natural ice in the Manorburn Dam. Heading south there are tiny gold-rush towns that have refused to die. The original gold-rush settlement – which was then known as Tuapeka, now **Lawrence** – still survives with a strongly Victorian flavour. Pockets of old gold towns are stitched into the ranges, gullies, gorges and valleys elsewhere in Central Otago.

SH85 leads northeast of Alexandra before looping back southeastwards to the Otago coast. En route it passes through the Manuherikia Valley, offering a worthwhile side trip to historic **St Bathans** 🅖, one of the best-preserved sites in the Otago goldfields. Among its 19th-century wood, stone and mud-brick buildings is the celebrated **Vulcan Hotel**, built in 1882, and famous for its resident ghost. The town stands on the edge of disused goldfields, and contained therein is the **Blue Lake**, whose intense colour is caused by the presence of mica, which reflects the light to memorable effect on a sunny day. Ice-skating and curling are popular sports here in winter. Another worthwhile destination via SH85 is **Naseby**, a quaint hillside hamlet with period buildings, craft shops, a village green, a skating and curling rink, bike trails, a motoring museum, accommodation, and cafés.

Central Otago is an intense experience, whatever the time of year. The area enjoys greater variety between seasons than most other parts of New Zealand. In autumn, poplars planted by the settlers glow gold. In winter, nature transforms power lines into glistening lace-like threads of white across a frosty fairyland.

DRINK

If visiting wineries is more your scene, book a tour with Queenstown Wine Trail, which takes you to premier wineries in central Otago – like Gibbston Valley, Peregrine, Waitiri Creek and Chard Farm. Tel: 03-441 3990; www.queenstownwinetrail.co.nz.

View from The Remarkables.

Moeraki Boulders.

DUNEDIN

Behind the solid, sombre facade of a city built by Scots and leavened in gold-rush wealth lies a lively university town, splendidly placed to take advantage of surroundings rich in natural treasures.

Dunedin reclines, all-embracing, at the head of a bay, a green-belted city of slate and tin-roofed houses, of spires, chimneys and churches, of glorious Victorian and Edwardian buildings, of culture, of learning. In the opinion of its 125,000 friendly citizens, more than 25,000 of whom are students, this is as it should be, for here in the deep south is a way of life, a peace and a tranquillity that few cities can match.

The 20km (12-mile) long Otago Harbour, where container ships and coastal traders now ply in place of Maori war canoes, whaling ships and three-masters, is fringed by roads and green hills, including the 314-metre (984ft) extinct volcano of Harbour Cone on the steep and skinny Otago Peninsula, and the perpetually cloud-carpeted cap of the 680-metre (2,230ft) Mount Cargill.

A proud history

While Dunedin is still a very proud city, it was once also the richest and most populous in all New Zealand. In the 1860s, with the discovery of gold in the Otago hinterland and a rush that rivalled California's, Dunedin rapidly became the financial centre of the country. Immigrants flocked from around the world, head offices of national companies sprang up, industry and civic enterprise flourished.

Dunedin is New Zealand's Scottish city.

Here was the country's first university, medical school, finest educational institutions, its first daily newspaper, first electric trams, and the first cable-car system in the world outside the United States.

Before the gold strikes, it was religious fervour on the other side of the world that led to Dunedin's European colonisation. Disruption in the Presbyterian Church of Scotland gave birth to the idea of a new settlement in the colony of New Zealand where 'piety, rectitude and industry' could

Main Attractions
Dunedin Public Art Gallery
Dunedin Railway Station
Otago Museum
Taiaroa Head
Penguin Place
Larnach Castle
Architecture of Oamaru
Oamaru Blue Penguin Colony

flourish. Free Kirk advocates Captain William Cargill, a veteran of the Peninsula War, and the Rev. Thomas Burns, nephew of poet Robbie, were the leaders. The ships *John Wickliffe* and *Philip Laing* landed 300 Scots in March and April 1848 to a site already chosen by the London-based New Zealand Company and purchased – for £2,400 – from the local Maori. Its first name was New Edinburgh; soon it became Dunedin (Edin on the Hill).

Once gold was discovered inland, there was no holding Dunedin back. In two years, the population of Otago rocketed from 12,000 to 60,000 – 35,000 of them immigrant gold-seekers. Dunedin was the arrival point for the miners, the service centre for the goldfields and the bank for the gold. With all this new prosperity came saloons, gambling dens, brothels and dubious dance halls. Pubs there were aplenty, breweries too. Dunedin to this day has retained a high reputation for its well-patronised licensed premises.

For a quarter of a century, Dunedin boomed. And where Dunedin went, the rest of New Zealand followed, until the gold ran out. Gradually, commercial attractions and a kinder climate in the north led to the decline of the southern cities and provinces. For the past few decades, Dunedin has fought the inevitable drift north. The most significant means of stemming the flow is through its educational prowess: the greatly expanded university – now with more than 21,000 students – together with the College of Education for training schoolteachers and the Otago Polytechnic, pour over 25,000 youngsters into the Dunedin community, consolidating its status as a leading city of learning.

Around the Octagon

To explore Dunedin, start in the **Octagon Ⓐ**, which links Princes and George streets in the heart of the city. Tall, leafy trees bordered by historic buildings make this a popular lunch spot. Immediately west is the **Dunedin Public Art Gallery** (tel: 03-474 3240; www.dunedin.art.museum; daily 10am–5pm; free), the oldest in New Zealand. It houses one of the country's finest collections, with

The Clutha River, inland from Dunedin.

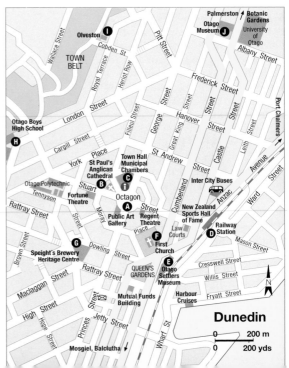

works by Van der Velden, Frances Hodgkins, Constable, Gainsborough, Monet, Pissarro and Reynolds.

Just north of the gallery is **St Paul's Anglican Cathedral B** (daily 9am–5pm), its Gothic Revival pillars rising 40 metres (130ft) to support the only stone-vaulted nave roof in New Zealand. Built between 1915 and 1919, it is constructed entirely of stone quarried from nearby Oamaru (see page 300).

Next door are the century-old **Municipal Chambers C**, which were designed by the noted colonial architect Robert Lawson, and behind it the 2,280-seat **Town Hall**, which was once the largest in the country. The Chambers, also built from Oamaru stone, have been replaced by the adjacent **Civic Centre** as local government offices, although the modern, stepped design of the latter has drawn criticism for the contrast with its Victorian-era antecedents. The city's **i-site Visitor Centre** (tel: 03-474 3300; www.dunedinnz.com; Mon–Fri 8.30am–5.30pm, Sat–Sun 8.45am–5.30pm), as well as conference facilities, are

housed in the Municipal Chambers, whose imposing clock tower and spire were re-erected in 1989 amid an overall spring-cleaning of the city centre.

Moving east down Lower Stuart Street, look out for classic old buildings such as the Allied Press newspaper offices, the law courts and the police station, which are excellent examples of art in stone.

Near the junction of Castle Street and Anzac Avenue is the **Dunedin Railway Station D**, perhaps the finest stone structure to be found anywhere in the country. It earned designer George Troup a knighthood and the nickname 'Gingerbread George'. Built between 1904 and 1906 in the Flemish Renaissance style, it has a 37-metre (121ft) high square tower, three huge clock faces and a covered carriageway projecting from the arched colonnade.

In the main foyer is a mosaic-tiled floor with nine central panels showing a small English 'Puffing Billy'. The original floor was comprised of a total of 725,760 half-inch Royal Doulton porcelain squares. Other

University of Otago and its clock tower.

ornamentation in the station is in original Doulton china and stained glass. From here, trains depart daily for the spectacular Taieri River Gorge (see page 300) and beyond.

On the first floor of the station is the **New Zealand Sports Hall of Fame** (tel: 03-477 7775; www.nzhall offame.co.nz; daily 10am–4pm), the national sports museum that pays tribute to that great New Zealand obsession with a dizzying array of memorabilia and exhibits – such as the arm guard that All Blacks rugby player Colin Meads wore when he played a test match with a broken arm.

Maybe it's not surprising that Dunedin has such a remarkable railway station, as the city has a fascination with trains. *Josephine*, one of the country's first steam engines (a double-boiler, double-facing Fairlie) is protected in a glass case on display beside the **Otago Settlers Museum E** (tel: 03-477 4000; www. otago.settlers.museum; daily 10am– 5pm) at 31 Queens Gardens, just south of Dunedin Railway Station. Established in 1898, and recently renovated throughout, it is one of New Zealand's finest social history museums, showcasing the ancestral journeys of the people who live here today, including southern Maori tribes, Scottish pioneers and Chinese gold miners. Also among its displays is *JA1274*, the last Dunedin-made steam locomotive to haul the main trunk-line trains.

Other city highlights

The country's first skyscraper, the **Mutual Funds Building** (1910), stands near the station, close to the original centre of Dunedin, the Stock Exchange area. Land reclamation has forced many of the fine old office buildings that used to line the harbour into a new role as storage areas (others have been demolished). A gargoyled 'bride's-cake' monument in here pays homage to founder Captain Cargill. It sat atop men's underground toilets until public opprobrium led to the conveniences being closed.

First Church F, in Moray Place, is another Robert Lawson design and

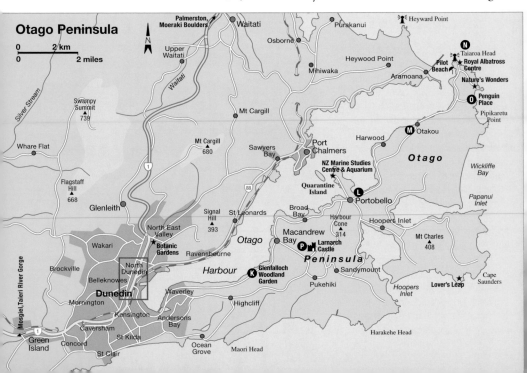

arguably his best work. Actually the third church to be built on this site, it has a magnificent spire rising 54 metres (180ft) heavenwards. Inside, the wooden gabled ceiling and rose window above the pulpit are worthy of inspection.

Two blocks west at 200 Rattray Street lies **Speight's Brewery Heritage Centre** Ⓖ (tel: 03-477 7697; www. speights.co.nz; tours daily 10am, noon, 2pm, 4pm, 6pm, 7pm). You can tour the brewery where the beer in which southerners take so much pride is brewed, and there is, of course, a tasting session at the tour's conclusion.

Many of the banks and other churches in the central city area are of architectural merit, as is the Lawson-designed **Otago Boys High School** Ⓗ tower block, dominant above the city. It is situated just below the **Town Belt**, a 200-hectare (490-acre) and 8km (5-mile) long green swathe that separates the city from its suburbs. A walk here offers some of the best views of the city and its harbour. Listen out for the call of the tui and the bellbird; this expansive green space is an area of wooded reserves and sports fields, golf courses, cotula-turfed bowling greens, huge heated swimming pools and fine swimming and surfing beaches.

Within the Town Belt area also lies 'the jewel in Dunedin's crown', **Olveston** Ⓘ (tel: 03-477 3320; www. olveston.co.nz; booking essential; guided tours only). Built between 1904 and 1906 to the design of celebrated English architect Sir Ernest George for a local businessman, David Theomin, it was bequeathed to the city in 1966. The 35-room house of double brick and oak is rated the best example of a grand Edwardian-style manor found in New Zealand.

North of the Octagon

In the north of the city are the (almost) combined campuses of the University of Otago, Otago Polytechnic and Dunedin College of Education. Dominating the Gothic walls of the university, beside the grass-banked water of the Leith, is the main clock tower. Just west is the fascinating **Otago Museum** Ⓙ (tel: 03-474 7474;

The architecturally impressive Railway Station.

www.otagomuseum.govt.nz; daily 10am–5pm; free) at 419 Great King Street, with Pacific Island and Maori artefacts, maritime relics and colonial-era collections. If you have time for only one museum visit in Dunedin, this has to be it. **Discovery World** (charge) on Level 1 will appeal to children.

Also in the north, on the slopes of Signal Hill, are the **Botanic Gardens** (daily, daylight hours; free). New Zealand's oldest, it covers 65 hectares (160 acres) and is world-renowned for its rhododendron dell and its great variety of gardens.

Otago Peninsula drive

To appreciate fully the **Otago Peninsula** and its views of the city, take the 'low road' and return via the 'high'. The following 64km (40-mile) round trip can take anything from 90 minutes to a full day. The narrow, winding road calls for careful driving as part of it was built by convict labour for horse and buggy traffic. (The prisoners were housed in an old hulk that was dragged slowly along the seafront.)

Aerial view of Dunedin.

The first sight you will see along the curving western coastline is **Glenfalloch Woodland Garden** Ⓚ (tel: 03-476 1006; www.glenfalloch.co.nz; daylight hours), 12 hectares (30 acres) of lovely rambling gardens encircling a 1871 homestead. Visitors are welcome to bring a picnic.

The winding Portobello Road runs along the peninsula coast to **Portobello** Ⓛ, 8km (5 miles) from Glenfalloch. In Portobello village you can visit the **Otago Peninsula Museum** (tel: 03-478 0255; Sun 1.30–4.30pm, or by appointment) and on Hatchery Road the **New Zealand Marine Studies Centre and Portobello Aquarium** (tel: 03-479 5826; www.marine.ac.nz; daily 10.30am–4.30pm). Operated by the University of Otago as a marine laboratory, the centre has a life-size model of a colossal squid, and its aquariums are filled with everything marine from seahorses to octopuses. The touch pool allows a tactile experience with smaller sea creatures.

At **Otakou** Ⓜ, about 4km (2.5 miles) further north, is a Maori church and meeting house which appear to be carved, but are actually cast in concrete. In the cemetery behind are buried three great Maori chiefs of the 19th century – the warlike Taiaroa, Ngatata (a northern chief said to have welcomed the Pakeha to Cook Strait) and Karetai, induced by missionaries to abandon cannibalism and take up the Bible. The *marae* here is sacred to local Maori and is still the most historic Maori site in Otago. (The name 'Otago', in fact, is a European corruption of 'Otakou'.)

Just north lie remains of the whaling industry founded in Otago Harbour in 1831, 17 years before European settlement took root. The old factory is clearly visible and marked by a plaque. Another plaque across the road commemorates the first Christian service held in Otago Harbour, by Bishop Pompalier, in 1840.

Wildlife and a castle

As you crest the hill past Otakou and look towards lofty **Taiaroa Head** , at the tip of the peninsula, glance up. Those huge seabirds resting lazily on the wind are the world's largest birds of flight, rare Royal albatrosses. Incredibly graceful, they swoop, turn and soar with barely a flick of their 3-metre (10ft) wings. They mate for life, and up to 30 pairs from this tiny colony circle the globe before returning here to mate and produce a chick every two years.

The **Royal Albatross Centre** (tel: 03-478 0499; www.albatross.org.nz; daily Apr–Oct 11am–3pm, Nov–Mar 11am–6pm) has viewing galleries and display areas. Escorted groups depart on tours to observe the breeding cycle and the pre-flight peregrinations of the fledglings. A new penguin-watching activity also operates from the centre, Pukekura Blue Penguins (tel: 03-478 0499; www.bluepenguins.co.nz; daily at dusk, time changes daily so check website). While here, take in (for free) the antics of a southern fur seal colony at nearby **Pilot Beach**, and visit

also **Fort Taiaroa**, where the unusual **Armstrong Disappearing Gun**, transported here in 1886 on the perceived threat of an attack by Tsarist Russia, is found. The 15cm (6-inch) cannon is hidden in the bowels of the earth, rising to fire, then sinking again for reloading.

Around 2km (1.25 miles) to the east, along a farm road, is **Penguin Place**  (tel: 03-478 0286; www.penguinplace.co.nz; daily tours at 10.15am, 11.45am, 1.15pm, 2.15pm, then every hour at quarter past until 7.15pm). Here, rare Chaplinesque Yellow-eyed penguins (see page 103) strut in the surf and can be observed at close proximity through a unique system of hides and tunnels. This is a very popular and worthwhile attraction, so bookings are essential.

The MV *Monarch* provides a regular service from Dunedin down Otago Harbour to Taiaroa Head, but for a very different view of the peninsula and its wildlife, contact **Wild Earth Adventures** (tel: 03-489 1951; www.wildearth.co.nz), which leads sea-kayaking tours, visiting the Royal

Larnach Castle grounds.

NOMADIC COMMUNITIES

For much of the period prior to the arrival of Europeans, the coast of Otago was more densely settled than any part of the North Island. The moa-hunters lived here, thriving on fish, waterfowl and the giant, flightless moa bird. But when Captain Cook sailed past in 1770, he missed the harbour entrance and the moa-hunters, noting only long white beaches now called St Kilda and St Clair. 'A land green and woody but without any sign of inhabitants,' he logged. Thirty years later, sealers and whalers gathered in the Otago region, but were not always popular with the locals. In 1813, four sailors were killed and eaten by Maori; then, in 1817, at Murdering Beach, just north of the harbour entrance, three sealers offended natives and were killed.

Larnach Castle features a remarkable range of craftsmanship – a spectacular example being the detail in its Venetian stained-glass windows.

The view across to Dunedin from the Otago Peninsula.

albatross and fur seal colonies by sea and taking in a great variety of other wildlife on the way.

The return route follows the Taiaroa Head access road to Portobello in order to reach the 'high road' leading back to the city. Along the way, visit **Larnach Castle** (tel: 03-476 1616; www.larnachcastle.co.nz; daily 9am–5pm, gardens 9am–7pm), a century-old baronial manor that is New Zealand's only castle. It took 14 years to build (from 1871) as the home of the Hon. William J.M. Larnach, financier and later Minister of the Crown. An English workman, along with two Italian craftsmen, spent 12 years carving the ceilings. The castle fell into disrepair but has now been fully restored, and most of its 43 rooms, including accommodation, are open to the public. The 'high road' that leads back to suburbia has commanding views of the harbour.

Taieri Gorge and railway

Dunedin visitors should not restrict themselves to the city. Within easy reach both north and south there are areas of immense natural beauty, sparsely populated and as yet undiscovered by the tourist hordes.

Special excursion trains run north and sometimes south on the main trunk line from the Dunedin Railway Station (see page 295). On the **Taieri Gorge Railway** (tel: 03-477 4449; www.taieri.co.nz; departs daily Oct–Apr 9.30am, 2.30pm, May–Sept reduced timetable), both vintage 1920s wooden carriages renovated by the Otago Excursion Train Trust and modern air-conditioned steel carriages enter Otago's hinterland through the rugged and spectacularly bridged **Taieri River Gorge** ❶, northwest of Dunedin. You can make a return journey back to Dunedin by the same train, or continue another 19km (12 miles) to the railway's terminus at **Middlemarch** in Central Otago, where coach connections can take tourists onward to Queenstown (see page 282).

North to Oamaru

The Otago coast north from Dunedin is of interest, too. At **Kaitiki Beach** Common dolphins are often spotted, while further north are the bizarre **Moeraki Boulders** ❷, huge round stones that lie 'like devil's marbles' on the seashore. The food baskets of a wrecked canoe according to legend, they were actually formed by the gradual erosion of the mudstone cliffs just behind the beach. Over a period of 60 million years, salts accumulated around the eroded pieces, forming the boulders. Some measure 4 metres (13ft) in circumference.

Oamaru ❸, 117km (72 miles) north of Dunedin, is the site of the largest collection of protected heritage buildings to be found in New Zealand. Crafted from a creamy textured local limestone known as Oamaru stone, these gorgeous Victorian buildings with their huge columns and extensive ornamentation are a rare sight to behold. Pick up a walking map from the information centre (tel: 03-434 1656; www.visitoamaru.co.nz; daily 8.30am–5pm)

at 1 Thames Street, for insights into the features and history behind their exquisitely restored facades.

Also in town are **St Luke's Anglican Church** (1866), the **North Otago Museum** (1882) and the old **Courthouse** (1882–3), its well-proportioned classical design reflecting a Palladian architectural influence. The old **Bank of New South Wales**, with its Corinthian columns, is now home to the **Forrester Gallery** (tel: 03-433 0853; www.forrestergallery.com; daily 10.30am–4.30pm; donation) at 9 Thames Street.

Pop inside the impressive **St Patrick's Basilica** on Reed Street, built in 1893, to see its coffered Renaissance-style ceiling and great dome over the sanctuary. Nearby, at 56 Eden Street, is the house where New Zealand author **Janet Frame** lived for 14 years. A number of extracts from her earlier manuscripts can be seen in Oamaru. Follow Chelmer Street, Toby's route described in *The Edge of the Alphabet*: 'Now up the damp road… the high bank on the right with the houses and gardens in the shadow of it not yet rid of the night dew; on the other side the Town Gardens…' Established in 1876, the latter boast some magnificent trees, shrubs and flowerbeds, and a burbling Italian marble fountain.

Just beyond the information centre is the **Harbour and Tyne Historical Precinct**, the old quarter of town. Here craftsmen sculpt wedges of Oamaru stone, and a local bookbinder practises his age-old craft. The district is full of arty types whose works are on display in the **Grainstore Gallery** (tel: 03-434 8117; daily 8.30am–5pm). Stop for a drink in the olde-worlde bar of the **Criterion Hotel** (tel: 03-434 6247; www.criterionhotel.co.nz) and learn of its resident ghost.

As evening falls, make your way along the waterfront to **Oamaru Blue Penguin Colony** (tel: 03-433 1195; www.penguins.co.nz; daily Nov–Apr 9.30am–11pm, May–Oct 9.30am–8pm) at Oamaru Harbour and take a seat in the open-air grandstand. As it gets dark, the Little Blue penguins come ashore and waddle past to the colony's nesting area. During the day the facility offers a 30-minute behind-the-scenes experience. Yellow-eyed penguins can be seen at the **Bushy Beach Penguin Colony** (free) at Bushy Point from Department of Conservation (DOC) hides.

Waimate's wallabies

Some 49km (31 miles) north of Oamaru is **Waimate** ❹, wallaby country where you can kiss, kill or eat a wallaby, all in a single day! To hunt, team up with the **Ngahere Game Ranch** (tel: 03-689 7809; www.tournz.com), but if a cuddle is more your scene, visit **EnkleDooVery Korna** (tel: 03-689 7197; Sept–June daily 10am–5pm) to befriend hand-reared orphaned joeys.

Waimate's other claim to fame is its strawberries, and the annual 'Strawberry Fare' in December. Head to Waimate's main street for an architectural flashback to the Edwardian era, but don't leave without tasting the **Savoy Tearooms'** famous wallaby pies, a mix of steak, onion, salt and pepper and plum sauce.

TIP

If you want to see the albatrosses at Taiaroa Head, the best time to visit is December to February. No viewing is possible mid-Sept to late Nov. The birds' life cycle is: Sept: adults arrive; Oct: courting and mating; Nov: eggs are laid; Jan to Feb: chicks hatch; Sept: chicks fly the nest.

Mural in Dunedin's Octagon.

SOUTHLAND

Auckland
Wellington
Christchurch

Stepping into Southland's staggeringly beautiful landscape, you could be excused for feeling that you were at the ends of the earth.

I t's the expansiveness of the place that first takes you – wide open spaces with a distinctive quality of bold light which so impressed the early European landscape painters. Signs of Maori settlement go back as far as the 12th century around the southern coast; the first European inhabitants were a determined breed of Scottish settlers who began to arrive in 1848 and within 13 years were demanding provincial government. The 1860s were a time of heady development – in towns, country, rail and roads – to such extent that the state coffers were emptied. As a result, the province was legally and administratively fixed to neighbouring Otago in 1870.

The 100,000 people who proudly call themselves Southlanders today have scant regard for the historical purist's arguments about their legitimacy. They live in New Zealand's southernmost land district – Murihiku, the tail end of the land, as the Maori called it. This 'province' takes in about 28,000 sq km (some 11,000 sq miles), its boundary starting just above the breathtaking hills and valleys of Milford Sound on the west coast, skirting the southern shores of Lake Wakatipu bordering Central Otago, and meandering its way through some of the lushest, most productive farmland in New Zealand to join the southeast coast near an unspoilt area called the Catlins. The grittiness in the local character manifests itself in an agrarian excellence – the region is responsible for a quarter of New Zealand's export receipts.

Contrasts abound in the land itself. On the spectacular west coast, deep fiords lap against towering mountains and snowcapped peaks reach skywards in an area that is called, not surprisingly, Fiordland. In the lee of the mountains are the two extensive plains on which the province's prosperity has

Doubtful Sound.

grown to depend. These lowlands surround the city of Invercargill, extending across the South Island to reach the southeastern coastlands.

Scottish Invercargill

The 50,000 people who live in **Invercargill ⑤** – located some 217km (135 miles) southwest of Dunedin, or 283km (176 miles) south of Queenstown – reside close to an estuary once plied by steamers and sailing ships. The Scottish heritage of New Zealand's southernmost city is well reflected in its street names, many elegant buildings, neat gardens and tree-lined parks. The original town planners were generous in the amount of space devoted to main thoroughfares and public spaces. Today, **Queens Park**, the green heart of the city, provides a wide range of recreational pursuits, from sunken rose gardens and statuary created by Sir Charles Wheeler, to a golf course and swimming pool.

Invercargill's biggest attraction is the **Southland Museum and Art Gallery** (tel: 03-219 9069; www.south landmuseum.com; Mon–Fri 9am–5pm, Sat–Sun 10am–5pm; free) at the Gala Street entrance of Queens Park. There are galleries devoted to the Maori, history and art, but the displays on the sub-Antarctic region – the cluster of islands between New Zealand and the Antarctic – alone make a visit worthwhile. The audiovisual film *Beyond the Roaring Forties* will add immeasurably to your understanding of this windswept and isolated region. Another highlight of the pyramid-shaped museum is a 'tuatarium' where visitors can observe tuatara lizards, last survivors of the dinosaur era, roaming at leisure in a large, natural sanctuary.

At the ground level of the museum is Invercargill's **i-site Visitor Centre** (tel: 03-211 0895; www.invercargill.org. nz), where you can get more information on the rest of the attractions in the city.

Just 10km (6 miles) south of the city centre is **Oreti Beach**, a long stretch of sand popular among the hardy locals for swimming, yachting and water-skiing. The beach is also famous for the succulent *toheroa*, a rare and strictly protected shellfish that grows up to 15cm (6 inches) in length.

Bluff's highlights

About 27km (17 miles) south of Invercargill is the land's-end port of **Bluff ⑥**. The next stop after here is Stewart Island (see page 310) and the cold, stormy sub-Antarctic waters.

Aside from its busy port area (see panel), Bluff is famous, above all, for the plump oysters from the Foveaux Strait, the 35km (22-mile) stretch of water that separates Stewart Island from the mainland. In the early 1980s, the oyster beds were stricken with *Bonamia*, a protozoan disease, but careful management has ensured their recovery and a quota system prevents over-harvesting. Unique to New Zealand, this shellfish is not exported as the local market takes the full quota. The oyster season runs from March to August, with the highlight being the hugely popular annual **Bluff Oyster**

The Routeburn Track.

Southern South Island

0   50 km
0   50 miles

N

Tasman Sea

Greymouth

Westla
Aora
NP
A
Mt O
Vi

Lake Moeraki
Knights Point
Haast Beach
Lake Moeraki
Lake Paringa

West Coast

Jackson Head
Jackson Bay
Haast
Haast

Mt Huxley
2499

Mount Aspiring National Park

SOUTHERN ALPS

Awarua Point

3030
Mt Aspiring
Haast Pass
563

Makaroa

Lake Ohau

Lake Wanaka
Lake Hawea

Omarama

Lake McKerrow
Hollyford Track

Milford Sound
Milford Sound
Hollyford Valley

Matukituki

Treble Cone
2088

971
Lindis Pass
O

21
23 1692 Mitre Peak
Sutherland Falls
22
Homer Tunnel
Routeburn Track

Richardson Mountains

Lake Hawea

Tarras

St Batha

George Sound

Milford Track
Cascade Creek

Hollyford

Glenorchy

Wanaka

Fiordland

Lake Gunn

Avenue of the Disappearing Mountain

Arrowtown

Becks

Murchison Mts
1879
Mt Irene

Mirror Lakes

Lake Te Anau

Queenstown

Cromwell

Dunstan Range

Omakau
8

Secretary Island

Te Anau
Glow Worm Caves

Te Anau Downs

Lake Wakatipu

Remarkables

Clyde

Alexandra

Otago

85

Ra

Doubtful Sound **18**

20

Kingston

National

17

Kepler Track

19
Te Anau Wildlife Centre

Eyre Mountains

Garvie Mountains

see Queenstown and Surr

Deep Cove

West Arm Underground Power Station

16
Lake Manapouri
Manapouri

Athol

Roxburgh

Clutha

Middle

Breaksea Sound

Waiau

Redcliff Wetland Reserve

Five Rivers

8

Resolution Island

Park

Southland

Monowai

Blackmount

Mossburn

Lumsden

Waikaia

Raes Junction

Gabriels Gully

Dusky Sound

15
Lake Monowai

Southland

99

Otahu Flat

Dipton

94

Riversdale

Waikaka

Lawrence

Tuapeka Mouth

Cape Providence
Chalky Inlet

Cameron Mountains

Clifden

13

14
Lake Hauroko

Wreys Bush

Mandeville

Tapanui

Clydevale

Lake Poteriteri

Hump Ridge Track

12

Tuatapere

Orepuki

11 Colac Bay
Te Waewae Bay

Otautau

Aparima

Oreti

Winton

Mataura

Hokonui Hills

Gore

1

Clinton

Balclutha

Kaitangata

Pahia Point

10
Riverton

The Rocks

Oreti Beach

Edendale

Catlins
Mt Pye
720

Forest

Owaka

Molyr
Bay
Nugge

5
Invercargill

Tokanui

Park Papatowai

Chaselands

9 Jack's Blov
Purakaunui Falls

Black Rock Point

6
Bluff
Tiwai Point

Fortrose

Waikawa

8
Cathedral Caves

Foveaux Strait

Waipapa Point

92

7 Curio Bay
Fossil Forest

Codfish Island
28

Mt Anglem
980

25 Acker's Cottage

Ruapuke Island

Mason Bay

27

Paterson Inlet
Oban

26 Ulva Island

Doughboy Bay

Rakiura National Park

Mt Allen
750

24 **Stewart Island**

Muttonbird Islands

Big South Cape Island

Snares Group

Southwest Cape

Downtown Invercargill on a stormy day.

and **Southland Seafood Festival** (www.bluffoysterfest.co.nz) in April/May.

If you're interested in local maritime history, the small **Bluff Maritime Museum** (tel: 03-212 7534; Mon–Fri 10am–4.30pm, Sat–Sun 1–5pm), at 241 Foreshore Road, is worth a visit. Here you can climb aboard and explore the workings of the oyster boat *Monica II*.

East to the Catlins coast

Head southeast of Invercargill for 80km (50 miles) towards the small fishing port of **Waikawa**, reached by a well-surfaced road that passes through rolling countryside which not long ago was covered in bush. This is part of the **Southern Scenic Route**, stretching from Balclutha in south Otago, along the southern coast, past Waikawa, and eventually terminating at Te Anau (see page 308). Heading northeast from Waikawa the scenic route (SH92) takes in much of the **Catlins**, an area whose diverse natural beauty is supplemented by the many opportunities it affords to see such wildlife as fur seals, sea lions, the occasional, awe-inspiring elephant seal and rare Yellow-eyed penguins.

Turn off to Waikawa (the town lies just off the scenic route) and travel a further 6km (3¾ miles) to the remains of a petrified forest buried millions of years ago at a place called **Curio Bay** ❼. This freeze-frame of time has caught every grain of timber in the fossilised stumps; boulders which have been broken open by some unknown force show patterns of leaves and twigs. It's best viewed at low tide. Adjacent is a new bush walkway called the Curio Bay Walkway (free), which demonstrates what the petrified forest would have looked like 180 million years ago. The loop track takes 20 minutes to walk and has interpretation panels to read along the way. Nearby is **Porpoise Bay**, a pleasant swimming beach named after the rare, small Hector's dolphins, with their distinctive black-and-white markings, which frequent the bay. A variety of accommodation is available in this area and it is a good base from which to explore the Southern Catlins.

Further east, 34km (21 miles) from Porpoise Bay, is the vast **Waipati Beach**, where a walkway leads to the spectacular 30-metre (98ft) **Cathedral Caves** ❽. The caves can only be entered two hours either side of low tide. A torch is essential lest you tread on a sleeping seal or sea lion. Travel another 10km (6 miles) north to **Papatowai**, which is home to a few essential stores and the starting point for numerous magnificent beach and forest walks.

Follow the Southern Scenic Route another 24km (15 miles) to **Owaka**, a thriving – albeit remote – township, stopping off at the stunning **Purakaunui Falls** along the way. Follow the road signs to reach this three-tiered waterfall, then hike for 10 minutes on a trail through the forest to the actual cascade. At Owaka, there is café and a limited range of accommodation; it makes a good base from which to explore bush walks and waterfalls, or indulge in some birdwatching. The **Catlins Visitor Centre** here (tel: 03-415 8483; www.catlins-nz.com) can supply you with all the details you need. Some 6km (4 miles) southeast of Owaka is **Jack's Blowhole** ❾, a 55-metre (180ft) deep hole of surging seas located some 200 metres (220yds) from the beach.

From here you can continue 30km (19 miles) north to **Balclutha**, and then either turn northeast to Dunedin or take the faster inland route back to Invercargill and head into isolated Fiordland.

West to the mountains

Invercargill may be flat, but its residents cannot help but raise their eyes westward to the distant mountains that border Fiordland. For those in a hurry, this vast natural area can be reached in less than two hours, travelling northwest across the central Southland plains via Winton and Lumsden: this is prime farmland, carrying several million head of stock. At Lumsden, turn westwards on SH94 towards Te Anau and the highlands: the scenery soon changes, with the rolling tussock country indicating that you are in land of an altogether tougher nature.

Petrified forest at Curio Bay.

INDUSTRIOUS BLUFF

There is no mistaking Bluff's importance as a port. Snake-like conveyor machines, their tails buried in a large building and their heads in ships' holds, load hundreds of thousands of frozen carcasses of lamb and mutton for export to markets across the globe.

Across the harbour, a series of imposing structures is dominated by the Tiwai Point aluminium smelter, which produces 334,000 tonnes of aluminium a year. Tucked away on the lonely Tiwai Peninsula, where non-stop winds disperse smoke-laden effluent, the smelter is the major industrial employer in the south. However, it is an industry that has experienced tough times in 2012/13, mostly due to mounting costs to run the plant, in particular the escalating cost of electricity. Free tours have been put on hold. Call 03-218 5999 for information.

For those with more time, the coastal road to the mountains – the western section of the Southern Scenic Route – makes for a more interesting drive. Some 38km (24 miles) due west of Invercargill is the historic coastal township of **Riverton** ❿. Sealers and whalers made this their home in 1836, and Southland's first European settlement still bears signs of those times. Preservation is a way of life here. In 2002 the New Zealand Historic Places Trust offered a whaler's cottage for sale for the sum of just NZ$1, so long as the owner promised to preserve it according to the trust's specifications.

A further 10km (6 miles) west is **Colac Bay**. Once a Maori settlement, it grew into a town with a population of 6,000 during the gold-rush days of the 1890s, and now is a popular holiday spot for Southlanders. Further west is **Orepuki** ⓫ township, where history merges with the present: an old courthouse is now a sheep-shearing shed. Along the shore, look out for macrocarpa trees turned inwards by salt-laden southerly winds and hunt for semiprecious gemstones on the beach.

Travellers have a fine view of thundering surf between Orepuki and **Tuatapere** ⓬, 20km (12 miles) away. Across **Te Waewae Bay**, where Hector's dolphins and Southern right whales can sometimes be spied, bush-clad mountains loom, the first signs of what is to come. The **Tuatapere Hump Ridge Track** (www.humpridgetrack.co.nz), a 53km (33-mile), three-day circuit, starts and finishes at the western end of the bay.

From the timber town of Tuatapere, where fishing and deer-hunting stories are as common as logs from the town's mills, the road heads inland 12km (8 miles) to **Clifden** ⓭, notable for the nearby **Clifden Suspension Bridge** (built in 1899) and the spooky **Clifden Caves**. The caves can be explored without a guide, but make sure you have a good torch and follow the signposted instructions. From Clifden, a 30km (19-mile) unsealed road leads to New Zealand's deepest lake, **Lake Hauroko** ⓮, set among dense bush and steep slopes. Its name means 'sounding wind' after the exposure it has to winds from both north and south. From here, the **Hump Ridge Jet** (tel: 03-225 8174; www.wildernessjet.co.nz) provides jet-boat excursions down the 27km long Wairaurahiri River through pristine forest to the South Coast.

Continuing north from Clifden, the road passes through Blackmount and then to the **Redcliff Wetland Reserve**, where birdwatchers might catch sight of a Bush falcon in action. The settlement of Monowai is 6km (4 miles) northwest of Blackmount, a base for the recreational Mecca of **Lake Monowai** ⓯, with its excellent fishing and hunting.

Fiordland National Park

Beyond the wetlands is **Lake Manapouri** ⓰, 28km (17 miles) north of Monowai. It has been described as a soft, feminine lake, with a scattering of wooded islands, banks dense with bush and a horizon bounded by the **Kepler Mountains**. It is indeed in a magnificent setting, with the high mountains of Fiordland rising majestically ahead.

The Catlins coast.

With an area of 1.2 million hectares (3 million acres), **Fiordland National Park**  is New Zealand's largest, and forms part of the South West New Zealand World Heritage Area. That first glimpse across Lake Manapouri, to sheer mountains and remote deep valleys on the other side of the lake, gives the observer some understanding of why ancient Maori legends never lose their romantic hold in this wild region.

To experience the scenery first-hand, you can take a launch across Lake Manapouri to its **West Arm**. There was a scheme to raise this lake by 27 metres (89ft) for hydroelectric purposes, but thankfully conservation interests prevailed, although the massive **Manapouri Underground Power Station** was built at West Arm to supply power to the Tiwai Point aluminium smelter (see page 306). Guided tours to the vast machine hall located 200 metres (660ft) underground are operated by **Real Journeys** (tel: 03-249 7416, 0800-656 501; www.realjourneys.co.nz) as part of their Doubtful Sound day excursion.

Riverton was Southland's first European settlement.

The construction of the power station involved the building of a road from West Arm, at the westernmost point of Lake Manapouri, across the wild Wilmot Pass, to the head of **Doubtful Sound** , the deepest of Fiordland's sounds, in an area known as **Deep Cove**. Bottlenose and Dusky dolphins frolic in the deep-blue waters of the fiord, and divers can view black coral, which grows at an unusually shallow depth due to the darker, fresh water, infused with tannins from decaying forest leaves. **Adventure Kayak & Cruise** (tel: 03-249 6626; www.fiordlandadventure.co.nz) runs guided kayaking tours on the Sound. The hub of this magnificent wilderness is the town of **Te Anau** , 22km (14 miles) north of Manapouri, with its many hotels, motels and lodges. According to Maori legend, Lake Te Anau was created when local Maori chief Te Horo found a sacred spring. He asked his wife not to reveal its existence, but after he'd departed on a journey, she nonetheless showed it to her lover. As soon as his face reflected in its waters, a torrent drowned the village and formed the lake.

A highlight of this area is the **Te Anau Glow-Worm Caves** on the western shores of **Lake Te Anau** at the base of the Murchison Mountains. The caves, believed to have been known to early Maori explorers, were only rediscovered in 1948. A trip to the caves takes 2½ hours and can be booked at **Real Journeys** (see page 308) in Te Anau. A walkway and a short punt ride take people to the heart of the cave system, which also features whirlpools, magical waterfalls and a glow-worm grotto. The Department of Conservation runs the **Te Anau Wildlife Centre** (daily 24 hours; free), just outside the town on the road to Manapouri. It is one of the very few places where you can see the rare *takahe*, among other bird species.

Mighty Milford Sound

A spectacular route to the sea through Fiordland is the 120km (75-mile) long

road to **Milford Sound** ㉑ from Te Anau, world-renowned and described by Rudyard Kipling as 'the eighth wonder of the world'. Authors and artists have struggled to put into words the beauty that unfolds as the road, following Lake Te Anau for the first 30km (19 miles), enters dense forests, then passes serenely beautiful places such as the **Mirror Lakes**, 58km (36 miles) from Te Anau, and the **Avenue of the Disappearing Mountain**, where the eyes are not to be believed as the mountain appears to shrink while driving towards it. Forests, river flats and small lakes pass by, until the road drops towards the forested upper **Hollyford Valley** at Marian Camp.

The road then splits in two. One arm ventures into the no-exit **Hollyford Valley**, with its **Gunns Rest**, a basic campground run by one of Fiordland's most interesting characters. At the end of this road is the start of the **Hollyford Track**. The other fork proceeds west, heading steeply up the mountain towards the eastern portal of the **Homer Tunnel** ㉒. Work on this 1,240-metre (4,118ft) unlined tunnel, hewn from solid rock, began in 1935 as an employment project for five men who lived in tents and used only picks, shovels and wheelbarrows. It was completed in 1954, but not before avalanches had claimed the lives of three men. Homer can be Fiordland at its roughest.

From the Milford side, the road drops 690 metres (2,264ft) in 10km (6 miles) between sheer mountain faces, to emerge in the **Cleddau Valley**, with its awe-inspiring **Chasm Walk**, where you can stroll to a series of steep falls formed by the plunging Cleddau River. Back on the road, it's another 10km (6 miles) to the head of Milford Sound, where a small clutch of boats await. These carry visitors from the southernmost end of Milford Sound out to the open sea. The trips are extremely popular, and it is wise to book well in advance. **Southern Discoveries** (tel: 03-441

1137, 0800-264 536; www.southerndiscoveries.co.nz) operate short boat trips that take in most highlights, while **Real Journeys** (see page 308) offer short scenic cruises as well as overnight trips on the *Milford Wanderer* and *Milford Mariner*. These companies also organise trips to the **Milford Deep Underwater Observatory** and Southern Discoveries' **Milford Discovery Centre**, which highlights the region's natural history and geology; it is located on the only floating structure on Milford Sound.

The Sound is dominated by the unforgettable **Mitre Peak** ㉓ – a 1,692-metre (5,551ft) pinnacle of rock – and several landmarks, notably the 162-metre (532ft) **Lady Bowen Falls**. Milford tends to buzz with day-trippers, but remains remarkably empty at either end of the day. It also buzzes with sandflies, so insect repellent should be liberally applied. From Milford Sound, it is possible to travel north towards Queenstown via Te Anau, **Mossburn** and **Kingston**. Alternatively, motorists can proceed northeast towards Dunedin via the Mataura Valley.

TIP

The road trip from Queenstown to Milford Sound is a tiring 4–5 hours each way, so consider booking a coach and boat trip with Real Journeys (tel: 03-249 7416 or 0800-656 501; www.real journeys.co.nz) instead. Better still at the end of the day, take the flight option back to Queenstown.

Bottlenose dolphins, one of the largest species in New Zealand waters.

STEWART ISLAND

Little-known, even to New Zealanders, the country's 'third island' is a wildlife paradise and ecotourist's dream come true.

The Maori called it Te-Punga-o-te-Waka-a-Maui – 'Anchorstone of Maui's Canoe' – the weight that held the other islands of New Zealand together. The most commonly used and known Maori name is, however, Rakiura, meaning 'glowing skies'. One William Stewart, first officer on a sealing expedition in 1809, began charting the island's coasts and lent it the name by which it is now known. Today, **Stewart Island ㉔** metaphorically serves as one of the great foundation stones of the New Zealand environment, acting as a safe haven for many kinds of wildlife which otherwise would struggle to survive. It helps that it has just 28km (17 miles) of sealed roads and a grand total of 350 inhabitants.

Stewart Island can be reached by plane from Invercargill Airport which takes just over 20 minutes, or by express catamaran ferry from Bluff to Oban, across Foveaux Strait, which takes an hour. If you take the ferry particularly in the winter months, be prepared for a fairly rough trip, as the Strait has a well-earned reputation as one of the roughest stretches of water in New Zealand (the winds aren't called the 'roaring forties' for nothing). On the bright side, the larger seabirds such as albatrosses and mollymawks need strong winds to remain aloft, so the rougher the weather, the more you are likely to see.

From the air, Stewart Island looks deceptively small. It is roughly triangular in shape, with the west coast stretching almost 60km (37 miles) from Black Rock Point in the north to the **Southwest Cape**. There are two large bays, Doughboy and Mason with all-weather anchorage provided by Paterson Inlet on the east coast. On the western side, rollers constantly thunder onto the shore from the Tasman Sea. The southeast coast is also fairly exposed.

The South Sea Hotel is Oban's only pub.

Oban and Ulva Island

Centred around Half Moon Bay and Horseshoe Bay, with its charming cottages almost hidden among the trees, **Oban** ㉕ is one of the most delightful settlements in New Zealand. Some of the houses date back to the days when the Norwegians had a whaling base at nearby **Paterson Inlet**, with others built by the descendants of whalers and sealers. There is a wide range of accommodation, from hostels for backpackers to some expensive homestays. (Prices on Stewart Island tend to be a bit steeper than those on the mainland, as just about everything, except fish, needs to be imported.) There is also accommodation available at the local watering hole, the **South Sea Hotel** (tel: 03-219 1059; www.stewart-island. co.nz) at the shore end of Main Road, where many locals congregate at the end of a hard day's work aboard fishing boats, or at Paterson Inlet's mussel and salmon farms.

Rakiura Museum (tel: 03-219 1221; Mon–Sat 10am–1.30pm, Sun noon–2pm), at 9 Ayr Street, holds many items relating to the island's maritime history and pre-European days, and is a good place to learn about the local wildlife.

Not far east of town on the way to Acker's Point is **Acker's Cottage**, New Zealand's oldest surviving whaler's dwelling. Built of stone and clay-mortar, it was constructed by an American whaler, Lewis Acker, and his wife, Mary Pui, in 1835. Acker set up a coastal trading and boatbuilding business, which he operated until the late 1850s. Since then the cottage has been used as a smithy, storeroom, brewery and workshop. More recently it has been restored by the NZ Historic Places Trust and the Department of Conservation and is open for visits.

Kayaking and diving are popular pursuits on the island but if you don't want to get your feet wet, Marine Nature Cruises (tel: 03-219 0034; www.stewartislandexperience.co.nz) provides tours of the bay aboard a semi-submersible.

Around Oban are many delightful shore walks for a wide range of fitness levels. There are some fine stands of trees, and the native fuchsia is particularly prolific. Birdlife is abundant, and, as they are seldom harassed, they will allow you to approach quite near. Kakariki, kaka, bellbirds, fantails, tui and tomtits are among the species commonly encountered, and also the native pigeon, the kereru. The raucous cries of one of the native parrots, the kaka, flying overhead, can often be heard around Oban.

Well worth a visit is **Ulva Island** ㉖, about 3km (2 miles) offshore in Paterson Inlet. It is accessed by water taxi, or, for the more adventurous, a kayak. The island is covered in primeval forest. Mature rimu, totara, miro and kamahi are all present in good numbers, as are smaller plants such as ferns and orchids. Ulva has been cleared of predators in recent years, and a number of endemic

The Rakiura Track.

bird species have been introduced. The most conspicuous of these is the South Island saddleback, but there are also Stewart Island robins, riflemen and yellowheads. Also on Ulva is a flourishing population of Stewart Island weka, a brown flightless bird about the size of a chicken. Signs discourage you from feeding them, but weka are optimists, and certainly not above helping themselves to an unattended lunch. There is also a large population of *tokoeka* kiwis; because they sometimes forage during twilight due to the short nights of midsummer, there is a better chance of seeing them here than in any other part of New Zealand.

Mason Bay ㉗, on the west coast, is another kiwi stronghold. The birds here are often to be seen in the late afternoon foraging among the flax and tussock grasses and even searching for sandhoppers along the beach.

Stewart Island's huge albatrosses are a sight to behold.

A haven for birdwatchers

Another good place for viewing birds is at the relatively exposed **Acker's Point**, 3km (2 miles) to the east of Oban. Larger seabirds such as albatrosses and mollymawks tend to stay out of the sheltered bays, as the winds there are generally not strong enough to keep them aloft. If you walk out to Acker's Point in the evening, you'll hear Blue penguins calling to each other as they float in rafts (or groups) just offshore, waiting until it is dark enough to venture safely ashore to their burrows. During the summer breeding season, you'll also hear the calls of the home-coming sooty shearwater, or *titi*, which nests in burrows under and around the beacon.

Sooty shearwaters generally go by the rather unflattering name of muttonbirds – derived from the taste of their meat: either like fish-flavoured mutton or mutton-flavoured fish. In any event, most people find it a rather unhappy gastronomic combination (although some Maori see it as a delicacy). For the curious, the South Sea Hotel in Oban sometimes features them on its menu.

The waters around Stewart Island offer some of the best opportunities

GIANT SEABIRDS

One of the best places to spot seabirds lies to the south of Stewart Island towards the Snares Group. Although landing is not permitted, sailing or motoring just offshore is, and in the evenings the cacophony of home-coming shearwaters and penguins is impossible to miss.

For dedicated birdwatchers wanting to add magnificent albatrosses, sooty shearwaters and mollymawks to their list, there is no other way of seeing them, and you had better see them while you can. With the relaxed attitude some say is taken by the New Zealand government on enforcing the regulations on long-line fishing in the southern waters, the numbers of these birds are fast plummeting. Several thousand are drowned each year when they get hooked on the fishing lines of boats.

in the world for viewing seabirds. Over half the world's known albatrosses and mollymawks frequent the coastal waters here, along with a plethora of other seabirds, including petrels, shearwaters, skuas, prions, Blue penguins and Fiordland penguins. Also commonly encountered are Cape pigeons, known somewhat irreverently by the locals as 'Jesus Christ birds', because of their habit of pattering across the water. There is also a plethora of seabirds found near the **Snares Group**, 125km (78 miles) from the southernmost tip of Stewart Island (see panel).

Rakiura National Park

However, if you choose to keep your feet on dry land, there is plenty to keep you occupied on Stewart Island itself, as there are about 245km (152 miles) of walking tracks. A particularly good tramp is the 29km (18-mile) long **Rakiura Track**, which starts and ends at Oban and takes three days to complete. There are huts along the way for overnight stays. The tracks in the north take you through stands of totara, rimu and rata, while those in the south run up from beautiful forested bays out into shrublands and sub-Alpine vegetation. These southern areas, around the Tin Range, were until fairly recently home to New Zealand's rarest bird, the kakapo. In the 1970s they were moved to the safety of off-shore islands like **Codfish Island ㉘**, which lies not far off Stewart Island's west coast.

With 85 percent of the island encompassed by the **Rakiura National Park**, there is a multitude of areas to visit and things to do. And even if you are not the tramping sort, there are few other places where it is as pleasant just to sit and take in nature at its finest.

The fern groves, particularly those around **Dynamite Point**, are luxuriant, especially now that the introduced white-tailed deer are being kept under control, and there is a particularly good collection of plants in the gardens at the **Motarau Moana Reserve**, on the road to Horseshoe Bay.

A stream flowing into Mason Bay.

The Last Wilderness

New Zealand has long had a stake in the planet's most extreme environment, one that represents the final frontier for tourism.

Adventurous travellers, like the brave explorers who blazed their trail, are succumbing to the lure of Antarctica, a continent with an exceptional and utterly unique beauty. The coldest, windiest and most hostile place on earth, the frozen continent has teased our curiosity for centuries, and heroes populate its short human history. Those who have been there report awesome encounters with the raw forces of nature, but also times of ineffable, luminous peace and beauty.

The city of Christchurch has long been a base for Antarctic expeditions – Robert Falcon Scott spent three weeks there in 1901 preparing for his journey. Today, a couple of commercial operators (see page 373) sail from Christchurch to Antarctica and the sub-Antarctic islands of New Zealand – far-flung islands teeming with wildlife which have been described as the Galapagos of the South.

Antarctica is the last great wilderness, with close to 90 percent of the world's ice sprawling over an area larger than the United States. If all this ice were to melt, the continent would shrink to about three-quarters of its present size and rising sea levels would inundate most of the world's lowlands.

Antarctica's exploration has close associations with New Zealand. When Abel Tasman arrived off the west coast of New Zealand in 1642 he believed it might be the western edge of a continent that stretched across to South America. Accordingly, he called it Staten Landt, then the name for South America. A year later, when it was decided there was no huge landmass across the South Pacific, the name was changed to Zeelandia Nova.

The next European visitor to New Zealand, Captain James Cook, also showed an interest in a possible southern landmass, the terra australis. In one of the most daring voyages ever made, Cook sailed along 60 degrees latitude and then penetrated as far as 71 degrees south without sighting the legendary continent. He stayed south so long, his crew verged on mutiny. Fifty years later, the Russian navigator Fabian Gottlieb von Bellinghausen circumnavigated the world between 60 and 65 degrees south, dipping to 69 degrees on

Edmund Hillary at Scott Base, 1957.

two occasions, and became the first man to see land inside the Antarctic Circle.

New Zealander Alexander von Tunzelmann, the 17-year-old nephew of a pioneer settler of central Otago, is believed to have been the first person to step ashore on Antarctica, at Cape Adare in January 1895. Exploration on the land began soon afterwards, and New Zealanders took part in the explorations by Englishman Robert Falcon Scott and the Anglo-Irish Ernest Shackleton between 1900 and 1917, and Australia's Sir Douglas Mawson during the years before World War I. As every school kid knows, Scott and his party reached the South Pole in January 1912, only to learn that the Norwegians under Roald Amundsen had beaten them to it. Scott and his team died on their return journey.

In 1923, the territory south of 60 degrees and between 160 degrees east and 150 degrees west was claimed by the British, and placed under the administration of the Governor-General of New Zealand. In 1933 the New Zealand Antarctic Society was formed, although it was another 15 years before the first New Zealand onshore base was established on the continent.

In 1957, Everest conqueror Sir Edmund Hillary led a group of five fellow countrymen on an overland dash to the South Pole. He was supposed to have acted solely as a support for Britain's transpolar expedition, laying down supply bases on the New Zealand side of Antarctica. But Hillary and his small group made such progress that they decided to push for the Pole themselves, becoming the first to make it overland since Scott 45 years before.

Since 1958, parties from New Zealand have explored and mapped huge areas of the frozen continent, and intensively researched the geology of the region. In 1964, New Zealand erected a new base of its own, named Scott Base after Captain Scott, at McMurdo Sound.

Care of resources

Five years earlier, the Antarctic Treaty designed to 'ensure the use of Antarctica for peaceful purposes only and the continuance of international harmony' was signed by 12 nations, including New Zealand. This culminated in a Convention on the Regulation of Antarctic Mineral Resource Activities (CRAMRA) in Wellington in 1988. In 1991, the CRAMRA signatories signed a protocol that prohibits mining on the continent until 2041. It is probable that mineral-bearing rocks of the sort prevalent in Australia and South Africa are common on the Antarctic mainland. There are also known to be huge deposits of sub-bituminous coal and large deposits of low-grade iron ore.

Tourism interest in Antarctica remains strong, but access is still extremely difficult, and likely to stay that way for many years. The majority of tourists travel by ship from southern South America, although a few intrepid travellers make the trip from Christchurch (see page 373). If it becomes easier, protection of this special environment may have to include stringent controls on tourism. For now, visitors who can't get to Antarctica can get a taste of the continent at Christchurch's International Antarctic Centre and Auckland's Kelly Tarlton's Antarctic Encounter and Underwater World (see page 139).

Scott base, population 19.

Mitre Peak at sunrise.

INSIGHT GUIDES TRAVEL TIPS
NEW ZEALAND

TRANSPORT

ACCOMMODATION

EATING OUT

ACTIVITIES

A – Z

TRANSPORT

GETTING THERE AND GETTING AROUND

GETTING THERE

By Air

More than 99 percent of the 2 million tourists who visit New Zealand each year arrive by air.

International Airports

The main gateway is the **Auckland International Airport** (www.auckland-airport.co.nz) at Mangere, 24km (15 miles) southwest of downtown **Auckland**. Bus, shuttle and taxi transfers into the city are available.

There is also an international airport in **Hamilton** (www.hamiltonairport.co.nz), 15km (9 miles) south of the city, although this tends to service only New Zealand and Australian flights.

The airport at **Wellington** (www.wellington-airport.co.nz), the capital city, has restricted access for most wide-bodied aircraft types because of the runway length.

The main gateway into the South Island is via the Christchurch International Airport (www.christchurch-airport.co.nz), close to the city of **Christchurch**. Many international airlines run scheduled flights there.

Direct flights to and from Australia land at and take off from the airport at **Queenstown** (www.queenstownairport.co.nz), 8km (5 miles) east of Frankton.

New Zealand has direct air links with the Pacific Islands, all the major Australian cities, several major Asian destinations, and cities in North America and Europe. Passengers arriving on long-haul flights should allow themselves a couple of rest days on arrival.

By Sea

A few cruise ships visit New Zealand, but there are no regular passenger-ship services to the country. Most cruises in the South Pacific originate in Sydney, Australia, so cruise operators generally fly their passengers to and from New Zealand. However, some cruise lines, including P&O Line (www.pocruises.co.nz), regularly travel to New Zealand, mostly between November and April. Some cargo vessels also take small groups.

GETTING AROUND

By Air

Air New Zealand and Jetstar are the main domestic carriers.

Helicopters are readily available in main cities and in the main tourist resort areas.

Although domestic flights can be expensive, there are plenty of deals around for flying in off-peak times, for example Air New Zealand's Grabaseat website (www.grabaseat.co.nz), and other internet deals rewarding those who book well in advance. Flights can be booked online or with travel agents and accredited agents.

Air New Zealand, Sales and Reservations, tel: 0800-737 000 (reservations) or 0800-737 767 (travel centres); www.airnewzealand.co.nz

Jetstar, P O Box 14 081, Christchurch 8030, tel: 0800-800 995; www.jetstar.com

DVT Caution

To prevent deep-vein thrombosis (DVT) on long-haul flights, take note of the following guidelines:
Be comfortable in your seat.
Bend and straighten your legs, feet and toes every half-hour or so while seated during the flight.
Press the balls of your feet down hard against the floor or footrest to help increase the blood flow.
Do some upper-body and breathing exercises to improve circulation.
Take occasional short walks up and down the aisles.
If the plane stops for refuelling, get off the plane and walk around, if this is permitted.
Drink plenty of water.
Don't drink too much alcohol.
Avoid taking sleeping pills, which also cause immobility.

By Sea

Modern ferries operated by two competing companies, Interislander and Bluebridge, link the North and South Islands. The ferries sail between Wellington and Picton and carry passengers, vehicles and freight. There are frequent daily crossings in both directions, though it is important to book vehicle space in advance during summer. The journey takes about 3 hours, depending on sea conditions.

There is a wide range of facilities and entertainment on board the *Interislander*, including a bar, lounges and a café.

Ferry tickets can be purchased online, and at NZ Post outlets, travel agents and visitor information centres.

The *Interislander*, tel: 04-498 3302 or 0800-802 802; www.inter islander.co.nz

Bluebridge, tel: 0800-844 844; www.bluebridge.co.nz.

A passenger ferry operated by Real Journeys (tel: 0800-656 501; www.realjourneys.co.nz) from Bluff in Southland connects Stewart Island with the South Island.

Passenger ferries (departing from the terminal behind the Ferry Building on Quay Street, Auckland), service Great Barrier Island and Waiheke Island, as well as vehicular ferries. For further information on transporting your vehicle across to either island, contact **SeaLink**, car, passenger and freight ferry services, tel: 0800-732 546; www.sealink.co.nz.

By Rail

By international standards the New Zealand rail network is extremely limited. The infrastructure is there, but rail is mainly used for freight. To travel the country completely by rail is not an option.

The New Zealand government has set aside money to improve the rail network, but progress to date has been slow. Within a decade there should be some improvement. In the meantime, visitors may be interested in the three routes offered by **Kiwi Rail Scenic Journeys**, one in the North Island and two in the South Island. These travel through some of the most spectacular scenery in the world aboard trains comfortably outfitted with a dining car serving light meals and beverages. The routes are:

TranzAlpine: This scenic train journey is also offered as a return one-day trip, and travels between Christchurch in the east of the South Island and Greymouth in the west.

Coastal Pacific: This train travels along the coast and connects Christchurch with the inter-island ferries at Picton. From here you can

Have Pass Will Travel

If you're planning to rely on public transport, consider buying a travel pass that allows a combination of bus, train, ferry and plane travel nationwide at a substantial discount. These include the 12-month **New Zealand Travelpass** from InterCity Group (NZ) Ltd (tel: 0800-339 966; www. travelpass.co.nz) and the Kiwi Adventure Bus Pass from Naked Bus (www.nakedbus.co.nz).

Overnight Campervan Parking

Tourists hiring non-self-contained campervans (no toilet, shower or grey-water storage) and then 'freedom camping' (overnighting at non-designated campsites) is a growing environmental problem in New Zealand, and firm action is taken with offenders. Those hiring or travelling in privately owned non-self-contained vehicles are advised to camp in designated camping areas at Holiday Parks, DOC campsites and other areas. To enforce this, a number of councils nationwide issue instant fines to offenders. Visitors travelling by campervan must also make use of dump stations located throughout New Zealand to empty their grey-water waste; do not dump your waste at the side of the road. Rental vehicle companies provide brochures and details of these during vehicle handover, but if you're unsure of locations while en route, visit the local i-site information centre. For up-to-date information and advice on how to camp in an environmentally friendly manner in New Zealand, visit www. newzealand.com.

catch a ferry across the Cook Strait to Wellington in the North Island.

Northern Explorer: This service runs between Wellington and Auckland.

For ticket information tel: 04-495 0775, 0800-872 467; www. kiwirailscenic.co.nz. Tickets can be purchased online, from any Kiwi Rail accredited agency, travel agents and visitor information centres. Kiwi Rail offers a Scenic Rail Pass (www. kiwirailscenic.co.nz/scenic-rail-pass) which covers the North and South Islands; however, the touring routes are limited compared to travelling by coach.

By Bus and Coach

City transport: Major cities all have extensive local bus services for getting you out and about economically. Check with visitor information centres in each town for details of how they operate. Have coins ready, as you usually pay on boarding. Bus passes are available from visitor centres and local convenience stores.

Inter-city coaches: There is an excellent inter-city coach network throughout the country, using modern and comfortable coaches (some with toilets). It is wise to reserve seats in advance, especially during summer months.

The major bus operators are **InterCity Coachlines** and the **Naked Bus Company**.
InterCity Coachlines
www.intercitycoach.co.nz
Auckland, tel: 09-623 1503
Wellington, tel: 04-385 0520
Christchurch, tel: 03-365 1113
Dunedin, tel: 03-471 7143
Travel and information centres throughout New Zealand can book bus tickets and multi-day passes for visitors aboard InterCity Coachlines.
Naked Bus
www.nakedbus.co.nz

Auckland's free City Circuit bus operates in the city centre.

This low-cost and reliable coach company sells all its tickets online, enabling it to offer cut-price fares on its fleet of comfortable coaches, which travel throughout New Zealand. Free Wi-fi is offered on board and fares starting at NZ$1 can often be found if you are prepared to book well in advance. Should you wish to call, tel: 0900-62533, but note that calls are charged at premium rates of NZ$1.99 per minute.

In addition, several smaller bus and shuttle companies operate regional and inter-city coach services. Check with local visitor information centres for contacts.

Taxis

All cities and most large towns have 24-hour taxicab services. Chauffeur-driven cars are also readily available in major cities.

By Car and Campervan

Driving offers one of the best ways to see New Zealand's extremely diverse landscape, and on any single journey you can expect to enjoy a wealth of spectacular scenery. It is worth noting, however, that some journeys involve winding roads through hill country, and therefore the time to travel from one place to another can take a lot longer than you may expect. To make the most of your time in New Zealand, allow adequate time to journey from one place to another.

Approximate Driving Times
North Island
Auckland–Whangarei = 3 hours
Whangarei–Paihia = 1 hour
Paihia–Cape Reinga = 4.5 hours
Auckland–Hamilton = 2 hours
Hamilton–Rotorua = 1.5 hours
Hamilton–Whakatane = 3 hours
Hamilton–New Plymouth = 4.5 hours
Hamilton–Taupo = 2 hours
Taupo–Napier = 2.5 hours
Whakatane–Napier = 5 hours
Taupo–Palmerston North = 3.5 hours
Palmerston North–Wellington = 2 hours

South Island
Picton–Christchurch = 5 hours
Christchurch–Greymouth = 4 hours
Christchurch–Kaikoura = 3 hours
Christchurch–Mount Cook = 5 hours
Christchurch–Dunedin = 5 hours
Mount Cook–Queenstown = 4 hours
Queenstown–Invercargill = 3 hours
Invercargill–Dunedin = 4.5 hours
Queenstown–Fox Glacier = 7 hours
Fox Glacier–Greymouth = 3.5 hours

Greymouth–Westport = 2 hours
Greymouth–Nelson = 4.5 hours

Road Conditions
Multi-lane highways are few – they generally only provide immediate access to and through major cities – and single-lane roads are the norm. While traffic is generally light by European standards, the winding and narrow nature of some stretches of roads means you can only go as fast as the slowest truck, so do not under-estimate driving times. Main road surfaces are good and conditions are usually comfortable; the main problem you might encounter is wet road surfaces after heavy rains. Signposting is generally good.

Petrol
Unleaded 91- and 96-octane petrol is sold, along with diesel, at all service stations. Compressed natural gas and liquid petroleum gas are also offered. Prices vary from place to place.

Motoring Associations
A comprehensive range of services for motorists is available from the Automobile Association, and reciprocal membership arrangements may be available for those holding membership of foreign motoring organisations.

Automobile Association, Head Office, 99 Albert Street, Auckland City, tel: 0800-500 543; www.aa.co.nz

Documentation: You can legally drive in New Zealand for up to 12 months if you have a current driver's licence from your home country or an International Driving Permit (IDP).

Vehicle Hire
To hire a vehicle, you must be 21 years of age or over and hold a current New Zealand or international driver's licence. Third-party insurance is compulsory, although most hire companies will insist on full insurance cover before hiring out their vehicles. Private accident/medical insurance is highly recommended (see page 378), as although all visitors are entitled to initial, free acute (emergency) care following an accident, this does not apply to subsequent treatment. What's more, under New Zealand law victims do not have the right to sue a third party in the event of an accident.

It is also wise to book rental vehicles in advance. Major international hire firms such as Avis, Hertz and Budget offer good deals for pre-booking. If you have not pre-booked, tourist information desks at most airports can direct you to other operators to fit your budget.

The approximate cost per day for rental of a mid-sized car is NZ$70–80, with competitive rates negotiable for longer periods.

Campervans/motorhomes are very popular in New Zealand and are both an economical and flexible means of exploring the country. The average daily charge during the high season is NZ$250 for a two-berth and NZ$330 for a six-berth.

Vehicle Hire Companies
Ace Rental Cars
Nationwide, tel: 0800-502 277
www.acerentalcars.co.nz
Apex Car Rentals
Nationwide, tel: 0800-939 597
www.apexrentals.co.nz
Avis
Auckland, tel: 09-275 7239
Wellington, tel: 04-801 8108
Christchurch, tel: 03- 358 9661
Queenstown, tel: 03-442 3808
Dunedin, tel: 03-486 2780
www.avis.com
Budget
Nationwide, tel: 0800-283 438
www.budget.co.nz
Hertz
Auckland, tel: 09-367 6350
Wellington, tel: 04-384 3809
Christchurch, tel: 03-366 0549
Queenstown, tel: 03-442 4106
Dunedin, tel: 03-477 7385
www.hertz.com
KEA Campers
Nationwide, tel: 0800-520 052
www.keacampers.co.nz
Wilderness Motorhomes

Rules of the Road

In New Zealand, you drive on the left side of the road and overtake on the right.

Give way to traffic on the right at roundabouts.

If you are turning left, right-turning oncoming traffic should give way to you.

The wearing of seat belts – by the driver and all passengers – is compulsory.

The legal speed limits are 100kmh (60mph) on open roads and 50kmh (30mph) in built-up areas, but watch for signposts superseding these limits.

New Zealand's road signs follow the internationally recognised symbols.

For drink-driving regulations, see page 376.

Nationwide, tel: 09-255 5300
www.wilderness.co.nz

Cycling

If you are fit, cycling is another good way to get around New Zealand. It is becoming increasingly popular, especially in the South Island. However, as the countryside is extremely hilly and mountainous and can be quite hard-going, you may wish to sit some sectors out, and travel aboard an inter-city coach. If doing so, advise the coach company when you book to ensure there will be adequate space for your bicycle. Bikes are also hired out in every destination, and are a fantastic way to get around New Zealand's smaller towns.

TRANSPORT BY REGION

North Island

Auckland

The main gateway to New Zealand is the **Auckland International Airport** at Mangere, 24km (15 miles) southwest of the city's downtown area. Bus, shuttle and taxi transfers are available into the city. You'll find them lined up outside the main terminal. Shared shuttle rides cost from NZ$28 and the Air Bus (www. airbus.co.nz) costs NZ$16 and takes about an hour to reach the city. Shuttles to the North Shore or West Auckland cost slightly more. A taxi takes around half the time, but will cost NZ$60–80.

As New Zealand's largest city, Auckland is well connected by a network of domestic flights and inter-city coaches, as well as rail services.

Change to Road Rules

New Zealand's 'left-turn versus right-turn' road rule changed in 2012, aligning the nation with international standards. All traffic turning right must now give way to a vehicle coming from the opposite direction and turning left. If in doubt visit the New Zealand Transport Authority website for further information (www.nzta. govt.nz). However, the greatest hazard to tourists comes from New Zealanders themselves, as they come to terms with the new rule.

There is a great inner-city bus service (including the free City Circuit service around the immediate city centre every 10 minutes 8am–6pm) and plenty of taxi services to choose from. You'll find taxi stands throughout the central city. Contact **Auckland Co-operative Taxis**, tel: 09-300 3000; www.cooptaxi.co.nz. Flagfall is NZ$3 and trips are charged at NZ$2.60 per kilometre; waiting time is charged at NZ90 cents per minute.

An NZ$16 **Auckland Discovery Day Pass** (tel: 09-366 6400; www. maxx.co.nz) gives you unlimited rides on most buses, trains and ferries for a day. This is also available as a monthly pass for NZ$250 per calendar month. You can buy the pass on any bus, or at the ferry terminal. The Link bus is a convenient way to travel around the inner city. It travels from the Wynyard Quarter to K' Road and returns via the same route following Queen Street. A rides costs only NZ50 cents. The Inner Link travels both clockwise and anti-clockwise in a loop, going through Ponsonby, K' Road and the inner-city suburbs. A ride costs only NZ$1.90.

Auckland also has a commuter train system, **Connex**, linking the Britomart terminal in the city to the outer western and southern suburbs.

For all public transport enquiries, call MAXX, tel: 09-366 6400; www. maxx.co.nz.

Northland

The Bay of Islands is around 250km (155 miles) north of Auckland. **Air New Zealand** operates daily flights from Auckland to **Kerikeri** Airport, Northland's main airport. The flight time is approximately 45 minutes. ABC Shuttle (tel: 022-025 0800; www. abcshuttle.co.nz) provides a regular shuttle service from the airport.

InterCity operates a daily luxury express coach service from Auckland to the Bay of Islands and to Kaitaia in the Far North. Prices are NZ$28–56 one way; or up to $106 if you book a fully flexible ticket. Contact: **Northliner Travel Centre**, Sky City Terminal, Auckland (tel: 09-307 5873; www.intercitycoach.co.nz). Alternatively, seats are available aboard the daily **Naked Bus** (www.nakedbus.co.nz).

The Bay of Islands is 3½ hours' drive from Auckland via the East Coast Highway, or 5–6 hours if you travel past the mighty Waipoua Forest (the largest kauri forest in New Zealand).

Northland is well served by inter-city buses in and out of the region, as

well as bus and taxi services in most large towns.

The Waikato

Hamizlton

Hamilton is located about 2 hours south of Auckland, with bus links to most cities and towns. **Hamilton International Airport** is 15km (9 miles) south of the city, with daily links with major New Zealand cities. Virgin Australia (www.virginaustralia.com) flies direct to Brisbane in Australia and from here connects Hamilton passengers to Asia, Europe and the USA.

Hamilton is also on the main trunk line, with rail services on Kiwi Rail's Northern Explorer **route** between Auckland and Wellington. The Auckland–Hamilton journey takes just over 2 hours.

Hamilton has excellent inner-city bus and taxi services. There are also plenty of car-hire agencies in the city. **Hamilton Go Buses**, tel: 07-846 1975, 0800-4287 5463; www.busit. co.nz

Hamilton Taxis, tel: 07-847 7477; www.hamiltontaxis.co.nz

Coromandel and the Bay of Plenty

About 90 minutes from Auckland and Rotorua, the Coromandel is on the Pacific Coast Highway. There are twice daily flights to **Whitianga** from Auckland with Sunair (tel: 0800-786 247; www.sunair.co.nz). The airline also offers flights to Tauranga, Hamilton and Rotorua. There are also door-to-door minivan shuttle services between Whitianga, Tairua, Thames and Auckland, which cost from NZ$26 through to NZ$94, depending on how far you travel. Contact: **Go Kiwi Shuttles and Adventures**, tel: 07-866 0336; www. go-kiwi.co.nz. Or drive the 2½-hour scenic, winding route following the Pacific Coast Highway from Auckland.

Tauranga/Mount Maunganui

From the Coromandel, you can take the Pacific Coast Highway to the Bay of Plenty. The trip into Tauranga takes 1–2 hours. Alternatively, catch an **InterCity** bus or Naked Bus to Tauranga from most North Island destinations.

Rotorua and the Volcanic Plateau

Rotorua

Air New Zealand and Sunair have flights in and out of Rotorua. The airport is about 15 minutes from the centre of Rotorua. You can also catch one of a number of inter-city coaches, such as the **Naked Bus** and **InterCity**, in and out of all major New Zealand destinations.

Most thermal activities in Rotorua offer shuttle services that will take you from the city centre to their attraction, for a small charge or free of charge. There is a good public bus service with **Bay Bus** (tel: 0800-422 928; www.baybus.co.nz); or with **Rotorua Super Shuttle**, (tel: 07-345 7790; www.supershuttle.co.nz). For taxis, contact **Rotorua Taxis** (tel: 07-348 1111; www.rotoruataxis. co.nz).

Taupo
Taupo is about midway between Auckland (4 hours to the north) and Wellington (4 hours south), on the classic touring route, the Thermal Explorer Highway, which runs through Taupo en route from Auckland to Rotorua and Hawke's Bay. There are direct **Air New Zealand** flights daily from Auckland and Wellington to Taupo Airport with connections to the South Island.

Whakapapa Village/National Park
To get to the Whakapapa Village – National Park area and Ohakune – from where the North Island's ski slopes are easily accessible – take the Northern Explorer train from Auckland, or the **InterCity** or **Naked Bus** service that connects with Ohakune from Auckland and Wellington.

Poverty Bay and Hawke's Bay
Gisborne
Gisborne is an 8½-hour car ride south on the Pacific Coast Highway from Auckland. Regular flights connect major North and South Island centres to Gisborne Airport. Coaches also operate regular schedules from around the country.

Hastings
Hastings is 3½ hours' drive from Gisborne. Regular flights connect major centres to Hawke's Bay airports. Coaches also operate regular schedules from around the country.

Napier
Napier is 3 hours' drive from Gisborne. Regular flights connect major North and South Island centres to Hawke's Bay airports. Coaches also operate regular schedules from around the country.

Taranaki, Wanganui and Manawatu
New Plymouth
Off the beaten track, this region has its own airport, which is serviced by

Air New Zealand. Inter-city coaches also run services. **New Plymouth** can be reached on a 6½-hour drive from Auckland by following SH1 and SH3.

Palmerston North
Palmerston North, the heart of the Manawatu, is about 1 hour's drive south of Wanganui. It is serviced by **Air New Zealand**. Inter-city coaches also run to the region. The town is also on the main Auckland to Wellington trunk line, with rail services on the Northern Explorer.

Wanganui
Wanganui has its own airport, serviced daily by **Air New Zealand**. Inter-city coaches run services to the region. It is a 3-hour drive from Wellington or Taupo, 2½ hours from New Plymouth, and 4 hours from Napier. You can also reach Wanganui from Auckland – an 8-hour drive – via New Plymouth or via Taumarunui on SH4.

Wellington and Surroundings
Wellington
Wellington International Airport has services from Australia and some South Pacific islands, as well as having good regional and national links. It's about half an hour's drive from the city centre – taxis and shuttles cost about NZ$35–40 and the Airport Flyer bus to the CBD costs NZ$6–15, depending on how far you travel. Buses depart every 15 minutes and free Wi-fi is available on board.

Wellington is also well served by inter-city coaches and can be reached from Auckland by train aboard Kiwi Rails' **Northern Explorer**.

Ferry services link Wellington with Picton on the South Island. See 'By Sea', page 318.

Wellington's cable car.

The Wellington public transport system, **Metlink** (tel: 0800-801 700; www.metlink.org.nz), runs regular bus, commuter train and ferry services throughout the city and outer regions, including the Bus-About Pass (NZ$9.50 day pass and NZ$135 for a 30-day pass). There are plenty of taxi stands around the inner city. However, Wellington is so compact that it's easy to walk from one end of Lambton Quay to Courtenay Place.

You can visit historic Somes Island, Petone, Days Bay or Seatoun on the **Dominion Post Ferry** (tel: 04-499 1282; www.eastbywest. co.nz) departing from Queens Wharf, or catch the unique **Cable Car** (tel: 04-472 2199) from Cable Car Lane off Lambton Quay, to the suburb of Kelburn and the top of the Botanic Gardens. Wellington also has a commuter train system, the **Tranzmetro** (contact Metlink on tel: 0800-801 700), linking the city to the outer suburbs as far as Upper Hutt.

South Island

Nelson and Marlborough
Blenheim
Air New Zealand flies to Blenheim, which is on SH1, 36km (22 miles) south of Picton. InterCity and Naked Bus link the township with main centres.

Kaikoura
Kaikoura, the world's whale-watching capital, is midway between Blenheim and Christchurch. It can be reached by road, coach or rail. The journey down the east coast to Kaikoura is picturesque and magnificent.

Nelson
Nelson Regional Airport has regular

air links with Auckland, Wellington and Christchurch, as well as a range of provincial centres.

Coach services link Nelson with Motueka and the southern entrance of the Abel Tasman Park. Contact: **Abel Tasman Coachlines**, tel: 03-548 0285; www.abeltasmantravel. co.nz. You can also hire a car or motorhome and drive to most surrounding towns in less than 2 hours. Contact the nearest visitor centre for more details.

Picton and the Sounds
Ferry services between Wellington and Picton are frequent. The Interislander and Bluebridge ferries take 3 hours to get you across Cook Strait.

Christchurch and Surroundings
Christchurch
Christchurch is served by a busy international airport (which escaped damage in the 2011 earthquake), and has comprehensive road and rail links and a deep-water port. The public bus service from the airport to the city (numbers 3 and 29) costs NZ$3.20–7.50, depending on where you are going, and takes 30–40 minutes; the shuttle takes 20–30 minutes at a cost of NZ$19–25. The more expensive option of a taxi costs NZ$45–65, but it will get you there much faster – about 12–20 minutes, depending on the destination.

If travelling from Greymouth, on the west coast, you should try to take Kiwi Rail's scenic **TranzAlpine** train (tel: 0800-872 467; www.tranzscenic.co.nz), which cuts through some spectacular scenery. Christchurch is also well served by inner-city buses (for information phone Metro Info on 03-366 8855; www.metroinfo.co.nz), and taxi services, as well as inter-city coaches from other New Zealand destinations. The historic tram service was put out of action by the 2011 earthquake but was due to restart in mid-2013.

A dedicated shuttle service to Hanmer Springs leaves from outside the Canterbury Museum on Rolleston Avenue at 9am daily and arrives in Hanmer Springs 2 hours later. It departs Hanmer at 4.30pm daily. Contact: **Hanmer Connection** (tel: 0800-242 663; www.hanmerconnection.co.nz).

Reliable taxi companies operating in the Christchurch region include **Blue Star Taxis** (tel: 03-3799 799; www.bluestartaxis.org.nz) and **Gold Band Taxis** (tel: 03-379 5795; www. goldbandtaxis.co.nz).

The West Coast
If you drive, access is either through the Buller Gorge from Nelson, through the Lewis Pass via historic Reefton, over the high Alpine Arthur's Pass from Christchurch or via Haast Pass from Queenstown. Driving time is 3–5 hours, depending on the point of departure.

There are airports at Hokitika and Westport, with regular scheduled services. A scenic alternative is to take Kiwi Rail's **TranzAlpine** train through the Southern Alps from Christchurch to Greymouth, or vice versa (see page 323 for details). The west coast is also well served by **InterCity Coachlines** and the **Naked Bus Company**.

Queenstown and Otago
Queenstown
Air New Zealand has regular flights to Queenstown, and you can reach it direct from main centres such as Wellington, Christchurch and Auckland. Daily flights operate to and from several cities in Australia. There are daily coach and shuttle services to and from Christchurch, Mount Cook, Dunedin, Te Anau, Wanaka, Franz Josef and Milford Sound.

In Queenstown, you can reach most places by walking or taking a short taxi ride. You'll need to hire a car to get out and really see the countryside, and there are plenty of car-hire companies in Queenstown. Getting to and from Arrowtown is also easy, with a regular coach service.

Wanaka
Wanaka is about an hour's drive north of Queenstown. Alternatively, you can take a shuttle service or inter-city bus. There are also scenic flights – the one from Queenstown to Wanaka takes approximately 20 minutes.

Dunedin and Surroundings
Dunedin
Dunedin has an international airport with direct flights with Air New Zealand (www.airnewzealand.co.nz) from Australia's Gold Coast, Sydney, Melbourne and Brisbane, as well as Auckland, Wellington, Christchurch and Rotorua. Public buses to and from the airport are not available. However, airport shuttles to the city cost from NZ$30 per person and taxis at NZ$90 are also available. The airport is about half an hour south of the city. You can also take a bus to Dunedin from many places on the South Island. Driving from Dunedin to Christchurch takes about 5 hours, while the journey from Queenstown is about 4½ hours.

Dunedin, like Queenstown, is easily covered on foot or by taxi (**Dunedin Taxis**, tel: 03-477 7777; www. dunedintaxis.co.nz). There are also regular city bus services with **Citibus** (tel: 03-477 5577; www.citibus.co.nz). For all Taieri Gorge rail enquiries, go to the **Dunedin Railway Station** in Lower Stuart Street (tel: 03-477 4449; www.taieri.co.nz).

Southland
Invercargill
Invercargill Airport is a 5-minute drive west of the city centre and is serviced by **Air New Zealand** flights. Coach services also connect Invercargill with other points in New Zealand.

Te Anau
Te Anau is about a 3-hour drive south of Queenstown, with shuttle services and inter-city buses between the two towns. **Top Line Tours** in Te Anau (tel: 03-249 8059; www.toplinetours. co.nz) travels from Manapouri to Te Anau every day, or you can charter a 45-minute flight from Queenstown.

Stewart Island
Real Journeys' **Stewart Island Ferry service** (tel: 0800-000 511; www. realjourneys.co.nz) operates daily between Bluff (departs from Bluff Visitor Terminal, Foreshore Road) and Stewart Island (departs from Stewart Island Visitor Terminal, Main Wharf).

The ferry company also runs a connection service to the ferry from Invercargill (pick-up and drop-off at the airport and **i-site** Visitor Centre), Queenstown and Te Anau (pick-up and drop-off at Real Journeys Visitor Centres in both cities). **Stewart Island Flights** also fly directly from Invercargill Airport to Stewart Island (tel: 03-218 9129; www.stewartislandflights.com).

Real Journeys' **Stewart Island Experience** (Stewart Island Visitor Terminal, Main Wharf, Halfmoon Bay, Oban; tel: 0800-000 511; www.realjourneys.co.nz) has cars, scooters and mountain bikes for hire. It also operates various tours and cruises, as do **Aurora Charters** (tel: 03-219 1126; www. auroracharters.co.nz) and a number of other small local operators. Tours range from fishing and sightseeing to birdwatching and nature walks. **Sails Ashore** (tel: 0800-783 9278; www.sailsashore.co.nz) offers a two-hour Island Life **Road Tour** that explores virtually every road on the island, all 28km (17 miles), with an interesting commentary on the island's history.

ACCOMMODATION

HOTELS, YOUTH HOSTELS, BED AND BREAKFAST

Hotels and Motels

International-standard hotels are found in all large cities, in many provincial cities, and in all resort areas frequented by tourists. In smaller cities and towns, more modest hotels are the norm.

Motels are generally clean and comfortable, with facilities ideal for families. Many offer full kitchens and dining tables, and some provide breakfast.

The New Zealand tourism industry uses Qualmark as a classification and grading system to help you find the best accommodation, shopping and activities to suit your needs. There are five levels of grading from one star (minimum) to five stars (best available). Participation in the Qualmark system is voluntary, so if a motel or hotel does not have a grading, its location and tariffs will usually give a reliable indication of what to expect. Expect to pay surcharges for additional occupants and peak season.

Concessions for children are available. Generally children under two years of age are free; two to 12 years attracts half tariff; 13 years and over, full tariff. If you are travelling as a family, look for motels/ self-catering cottages that offer two bedrooms, as these provide good value. By law, Goods and Services Tax (GST) of 15 percent will be included in the price you are quoted.

Farmstays, Homestays, Bed and Breakfasts (B&B)

More New Zealanders are opening their homes to visitors. There are a large number of B&B properties in cities, towns and rural locations,

ranging from historic and heritage buildings to boutique inns.

Farmstays are an excellent way for visitors to see the real New Zealand, which has been dependent on farming since the colonial days. You may share the homestead with the farmer and his family, or, in many cases, have the use of a cottage on the farm. Depending on the farm, you may get the chance to share home-cooked meals with your hosts and join in activities like sheep shearing and fruit harvesting.

If you are on a limited budget, you can try working farmstays. Over 180 farms offer free accommodation, meals and friendly hospitality in exchange for 4 hours of light work a day, doing tasks such as gardening and feeding animals. It is also possible to work flexible hours so that you have time to explore the area. For further information, contact visitor information centres, or check the websites listed below.

Auckland city view.

Rural Holidays New Zealand, PO Box 2155, Christchurch 8140; tel: 03-355 6218; www.ruralholidays.co.nz.

Rural Tours NZ, PO Box 228, Cambridge, North Island; tel: 07-827 8055; www.ruraltourism.co.nz.

Hostels

The **Youth Hostel Association of New Zealand** offers an extensive chain of hostels to members throughout the country. Details of membership and hostel locations can be obtained from its National Office at Level 1, 166 Moorhouse Avenue, PO Box 436, Christchurch, New Zealand; tel: 03-379 9970, 0800-278 299; www.yha.co.nz.

Motor Camps

Most motor camps (caravan parks with tent sites and campervan sites as well) offer communal washing, cooking and toilet facilities. Campers are required to supply their own campervan, caravan or tent, but the majority of camps also have cabins available, ranging from tiny huts to Alpine-style cabins. Some also offer fully self-contained motel units.

Motor camps are licensed under the Camping Ground Regulation (1936) and are all graded by the New Zealand Automobile Association. It is a good idea to check with the AA on current standards with the camps.

In summer, do book ahead, as New Zealanders are inveterate campers. For details, contact:

Automobile Association, Head Office, 99 Albert Street, Auckland; tel: 0800-500 222; www.aa.co.nz.

Top 10 Holiday Parks, 13 Tyne Street, Christchurch; tel: 03-343 8800; www.topparks.co.nz.

NORTH ISLAND

Auckland

Best Western President Hotel
27–35 Victoria Street West
Tel: 09-303 1333
www.presidenthotel.co.nz
Comfortable air-conditioned rooms and standard studios, suites and apartments. Ideally situated between Sky City and Queen Street. **$$$**

Hotel De Brett
2 High Street
Tel: 09-925 9000
www.hoteldebrett.com
A boutique hotel in an iconic and historic Auckland building. Each of its 25 rooms has been individually styled. Private courtyard for guests' use. The on-site Kitchen Restaurant was a recent finalist in the Cuisine NZ Restaurant of the Year Awards. **$$$$$**

Empire Backpackers
21 Whitaker Place
Tel: 09-950 9000
www.aucklandbackpackers.co.nz
Classy, apartment-style inner-city accommodation with good rates for private rooms. A café, bistro and bar are located on site and internet facilities are available. **$**

The Great Ponsonby Art Hotel
30 Ponsonby Terrace, Ponsonby
Tel: 09-376 5989
www.greatpons.co.nz
Located close to all the major attractions, this small hotel in a restored 1898 weatherboard villa offers a range of tastefully decorated rooms and studios, surrounded by New Zealand artworks. **$$$$**

Heritage Auckland
35 Hobson Street
Tel: 09-379 8553
www.heritagehotels.co.nz
A large hotel located downtown near the America's Cup Village and transformed from a landmark building which used to house Auckland's most significant department store. Two distinctive wings offer full services. The Tower Wing has an indoor lap pool, sauna, spa and gym, while the Hobson Street Wing (the old department store) has a rooftop pool, spa and gym. Other facilities include an all-weather tennis court, two restaurants and a bar. **$$$**

Hilton Auckland
147 Quay Street
Princes Wharf
Tel: 09-978 2000
www.hilton.com
This is one of Auckland's premier five-star properties, a contemporary hotel occupying a prime position on Princes Wharf, with uninterrupted views of the Waitemata Harbour from its rooms and suites. Blissful views are also offered from its restaurant and bar. **$$$$$**

Langham Hotel Auckland
83 Symonds Street
Tel: 09-379 5132
www.langhamhotels.com
In the heart of the city, the Langham offers five-star luxury in its 410 rooms. Featuring 24-hour service, butler service, an outdoor heated pool, rejuvenating spa, gym and business centre with high-speed broadband. **$$$$**

Mollies Luxury Boutique Hotel
6 Tweed Street, St Marys Bay
Tel: 09-376 3489
www.mollies.co.nz
An upmarket boutique hotel just minutes away from the shops, cafés and bars of Ponsonby and Herne Bay. Classy rooms, and a gourmet à la carte breakfast delivered to your suite daily. **$$$$$**

Ranfurly Evergreen Motel
285 Manukau Road, Epsom
Tel: 09-638 9059
www.ranfurlymotel.co.nz
On the airport bus route, 500 metres from restaurants and 1km (0.5 mile) from the racecourse and showgrounds, with 12 spacious, self-contained units, sleeping up to five. **$$**

Rendezvous Grand Hotel Auckland
Corner Vincent Street and Mayoral Drive
Tel: 09-366 3000
www.rendezvoushotels.com/auckland
Near the waterfront and within walking distance of the main commercial and entertainment area. The Rendezvous has 452 rooms with 24-hour room service, shops, currency exchange and some executive rooms. **$$$**

Sky City Grand Hotel
90 Federal Street
Tel: 09-363 7000, 0800-804 111
www.skycityauckland.co.nz
Located in the heart of the city adjacent to Sky City Hotel, this is one of Auckland's best hotels, offering 316 immaculate rooms, a spa, gym, indoor lap pool, club lounge and business centre. It also has two restaurants, most notably the highly acclaimed Dine by Peter Gordon (tel: 0800-759 2489), which serves superlative food with imagination and flair. **$$$$**

YHA Auckland International
5 Turner Street
Tel: 09-302 8200
www.yha.co.nz
This five-star hostel offers safe, clean and comfortable accommodation in multi-share rooms, as well as twin, double and en-suite rooms. **$**

Auckland's Surroundings

Devonport

Esplanade Hotel
1 Victoria Road
Tel: 09-445 1291
www.esplanadehotel.co.nz
Built in 1903, this lovingly restored luxury boutique hotel has it all – charm, ambience and friendly service. It's a 10-minute ferry ride from downtown Auckland. **$$$$**

Peace and Plenty Inn
6 Flagstaff Terrace
Tel: 09-445 2925
www.peaceandplenty.co.nz
Enjoy tranquillity and grandeur at this lovingly restored waterfront Victorian villa. Minutes by ferry from the CBD, its guest suites are spacious and ooze colonial charm, yet offer all modern conveniences, including en-suite bathrooms and wireless broadband. Highly recommended. **$$$$**

Great Barrier Island

Earthsong Lodge
Tryphena
Tel: 09-429 0030
www.earthsonglodge.co.nz
Offering panoramic views over olive groves, pasture and native bushlands to the sea, Earthsong Lodge offers three well-appointed and private rooms set in Tuscan villa-style surrounds featuring sheltered cobbled courtyards, fragrant rockeries, box hedges and the scent of lavender lingering in the air. **$$$$$**

Medlands Beach Backpackers and Villas
9 Mason Road
Tel: 09-429 0320
www.medlandsbeach.com
Comfortable family accommodation with great views. Backpackers accommodation **$** Villas **$$**

Tipi & Bob's Waterfront Lodge
38 Puriri Bay, Tryphena
Tel: 09-429 0550

PRICE CATEGORIES

Price categories are for two people in a double room, including GST:
$ = below NZ$100
$$ = NZ$100–150
$$$ = NZ$150–200
$$$$ = NZ$200–300
$$$$$ = over NZ$300

TRANSPORT
ACCOMMODATION
EATING OUT
ACTIVITIES
A – Z

www.waterfrontlodge.co.nz
Right on the waterfront, with
spectacular sea views. Licensed
restaurant and bar. **$$$$**

Kawau Island
The Beach House Resort
Vivienne Bay
Tel: 09-422 8850
www.kawauresort.co.nz
Comfortable accommodation
located on a pristine beach ideal for
swimming, kayaking, snorkelling and
fishing. Spa pool. **$$$$$**
Kawau Lodge
Tel: 09-422 8831
www.kawaulodge.co.nz
An island homestay set amid native
bush, accessible only by water. Queen
rooms with en suites, kayaks for
guests' use, plus sailing and fishing
options. **$$$$**

Orewa/Whangaparaoa
Edgewater Motel
387 Main Road, Orewa Beach
Tel: 09-426 5260
www.edgewaterorewa.co.nz
An older motel complex but it's
one of the very few located right on
the beachfront, with one- and two-
bedroom units to accommodate
families. **$$**
Gulf Harbour Lodge
164 Gulf Harbour Village Drive, Gulf
Harbour, Whangaparaoa
Tel: 09-428 1118
www.gulfharbourlodge.co.nz
Comfortable rooms overlooking the
canals of Gulf Harbour Marina, with
an international-standard golf course
within easy walking distance. Fishing,
diving and boating trips in the Hauraki
Gulf depart daily from the marina.
$$$
Waves
Corner Hibiscus Coast Highway and Kohu
Street
Tel: 09-427 0888
www.waves.co.nz
Modern studio and one- and two-
bedroom units just 50 metres from
Orewa Beach. In-room spa baths and
barbecue facilities. Shops nearby.
$$$$

South Auckland
Bella Vista
14 Airpark Drive, Airport Oaks
Tel: 0800-235 528
www.staybellavista.co.nz
An immaculately kept airport hotel
offering comfortable rooms with
ample free parking. Complimentary
airport shuttle and continental
breakfast daily. Quiet location. **$$**
Jet Inn Airport Hotel
63 Westney Road, Mangere

Tel: 09-275 4100, 0800-538 466
www.jetinn.co.nz
An excellent hotel just five minutes'
drive from the airport and 15km (9
miles) from downtown. Immaculately
clean, with numerous room types
to accommodate different needs.
Swimming pool and restaurant on
site. Courtesy shuttle to airport. **$$$**

Waiheke Island
Beachside Lodge
48 Kiwi Street, Oneroa
Tel: 09-372 9884
www.beachsidelodge.co.nz
Self-contained apartments or bed
and breakfast, near the beach with
views of Blackpool Bay. **$$**
The Boatshed
Corner Tawa and Huia streets, Little
Oneroa
Tel: 09-372 3242
www.boatshed.co.nz
A small, hip, luxury hotel experience.
Amazing rooms with a nautical theme and
incredible attention to detail. The host is a
talented chef and a stay here is
guaranteed to be unforgettable. **$$$$$**

*Waitakere City and West Coast
Beaches*
Auckland Waitakere Estate
573 Scenic Drive, Waiatarua
Tel: 09-814 9622
www.waitakereestate.co.nz
A private paradise surrounded by
rainforest, perched at 244 metres
(800ft) above sea level, yet within
easy reach of the city centre. Quiet
location, restaurant on site. **$$$$**
Bethells Beach Cottages
267 Bethells Road, Bethells Beach
Tel: 09-810 9581
www.bethellsbeach.com
Three special handcrafted cottages
overlooking Bethells Beach, with
plenty of room for families. Peaceful
location just a short walk from the
beach. **$$$$**
Hobson Motor Inn
327 Hobsonville Road, Upper Harbour
Tel: 09-416 9068
www.hobson.co.nz
This inn has fully self-contained units,
plus a swimming pool, spa, sauna
and mini-golf course. Good rates for
long stays. **$$**
Karekare Beach Lodge
7 Karekare Road, Karekare Beach
Tel: 09-817 9987
www.karekarebeachlodge.co.nz
A secluded getaway opposite one of
the coast's most beautiful beaches –
the location for the movie *The Piano*,
it makes an ideal base for local walks.
$$$
Piha Lodge
117 Piha Road, Piha

Tel: 09-812 8595
www.pihalodge.co.nz
This small, award-winning facility
has magnificent views of the sea and
bush, plus a pool and spa. **$$**
Vineyard Cottages
1011 Old North Road, Waimaukau
Tel: 09-411 8248
www.vineyardcottages.co.nz
Set against a vineyard backdrop,
the cottages are comfortable and
well presented, and within easy
driving distance of Muriwai Beach,
the gannet colony, and Muriwai Golf
Course. Other popular activities
include horse riding and the local
wine trail. **$$$$**

Warkworth Area
Bridgehouse Lodge
16 Elizabeth Street, Warkworth
Tel: 09-425 8351
www.bridgehouse.co.nz
Simple yet comfortable rooms in the
heart of Warkworth, overlooking the
Mahurangi River. Bar and restaurant
on site. Riverside walks and excellent
access to local shops and cafés. **$$**
Saltings Estate
1210 Sandspit Road, Sandspit
Warkworth
Tel: 09-425 960
www.saltings.co.nz
Luxurious apartments set on a
vineyard overlooking the water. **$$$$**

Northland

Ahipara
**Ahipara Beachfront Luxury
Accommodation**
14 Kotare Crescent, Ahipara
Tel: 09-409 4007
www.beachfront.net.nz
Just seconds from the sand there are
two self-contained apartments with
sun decks or a garden studio room
with an outdoor patio and adjoining
double bedroom. **$$$**

Bream Bay
Black Sheep Farm
1034 Cove Road, Waipu Cove
Tel: 09-432 0435
www.blacksheepfarm.co.nz
Brand new boutique accommodation
in an elevated character homestead,
between two beautiful white
beaches. Spacious rooms, all with
an en suite and balcony. Ten acres
featuring native bush, organic veggie
gardens, orchards and rare-breed
sheep. Tariff includes gourmet
breakfast. Super Kiwi hosts. **$$$$**
Camp Waipu Cove
869 Cove Road, Waipu Cove
Tel: 09-432 0410
www.campwaipucove.com

Self-contained cabins, camping pitches and places to safely overnight in your motorhome right on the beach. The cabins offer excellent value. Shops and restaurant nearby. $

Doubtless Bay
By the Bay
16 Braemar Avenue
Coopers Beach, Mangonui
Tel: 09-406 1268
www.beachfrontapartments.co.nz
Self-contained beachfront apartments with sea views, just steps from the pohutukawa-fringed sands of Coopers Beach. It's a short walk or drive to nearby shops. Peaceful location. $$$$
Taipa Bay Resort
22 Taipa Point Road
Tel: 09-406 0656
www.taipabay.co.nz
A top-rated complex with its own beachfront café, pool and tennis court. $$$$

Houhora
Deepwater Lodge
SH1, Pukenui
Tel: 09-409 8573
Lovely comfortable lodge with friendly hosts set right on the edge of Houhora Harbour. It's a short walk to local restaurant and shops. $$
Houhora Lodge Bed & Breakfast
3994 Far North Road, Houhora
09-409 7884
www.topstay.co.nz
Comfortable lodge in a three-acre garden. The hosts are knowledgeable Northlanders who will happily cook wholesome meals for guests. $$$
Pukenui Lodge Motel
Corner SH1 and Wharf Road, Pukenui
Tel: 09-409 8837
www.pukenuilodge.co.nz
This comfortable motel is built on the site of a historic homestead. Shared, backpacker-style accommodation is also available. $$

Kerikeri
Kerikeri Homestead Motel
17 Homestead Road
Tel: 09-407 7063
www.kerikerihomesteadmotel.co.nz
In a tranquil area, with views of Kerikeri golf course, each boutique unit has cooking facilities and four have spa baths. Huge pool and outdoor spa. Close to a restaurant and bar. 12 units. $$$
Ora Ora Resort
28 Landing Road
Tel: 09-407 3598
www.oraoraresort.co.nz
This upmarket resort promises a range of pampering options, and its

Gourmet Organic Kitchen serves fine food, wines and beer. $$$$$

Omapere/Opononi
Copthorne Omapere
SH12, Omapere
Tel: 09-405 8737
www.omapere.co.nz
Restaurant, bar and wonderful rooms right on the harbour's edge. A relaxing place to stay close to the Waipoua Forest, Opononi and all the delights of the peaceful Hokianga Harbour. $$$
Opononi Lighthouse Hotel
SH12, Opononi
Tel: 09-405 8824
www.lighthousemotel.co.nz
Self contained one- and two-bedroom units overlooking Hokianga Harbour. Spa pool and barbecue area. $$

Paihia
Blue Pacific Quality Apartments
166 Marsden Road
Tel: 09-402 0011
www.bluepacific.co.nz
Just minutes from Paihia township, these high-quality one- to three-bedroom apartments have breathtaking views of the Bay of Islands. Each has a full kitchen plus a private balcony or courtyard. 11 units and 1 studio. $$$$$
Crows Nest Holiday Villas
20 Sir George Back Street, Opua, Paihia
Tel: 09-402 7783
www.crowsnest.co.nz
Fully self-contained villas overlooking the Opua wharf, Waikare Inlet and Onewhero Bay. Nautical themes, plunge pool, private decks. $$$$$
Edgewater Apartments
8–10 Marsden Road
Tel: 09-402 0090
www.edgewaterapartments.co.nz
Pleasant beachfront location with saltwater lap pool. A range of apartments to choose from, all with a sea view. It's a short, flat walk to the shops, wharf and water activities. $$$$$

Russell
Commodore's Lodge Motel
The Waterfront
Tel: 09-403 7899
www.commodoreslodgemotel.co.nz
These spacious and luxurious self-contained studio apartments open onto a subtropical garden on the waterfront. There's a solar-heated pool, a children's pool, spa and barbecue. 11 units. $$$$
The Duke of Marlborough Hotel
Waterfront
Tel: 09-403 7829
www.theduke.co.nz

'The Duke' holds New Zealand's oldest liquor licence and has been a haven of hospitality for over 150 years. An elegant refurbished hotel, it offers superb dining and well-equipped en-suite rooms of various types, including a self-contained bungalow. It is right on the waterfront, next to the ferry terminal. 25 rooms. $$$$
Motel Russell
16 Matauwhi Road
Tel: 09-403 7854
www.motelrussell.co.nz
Quiet motel only five minutes' walk from Russell. Swimming pool and barbecue area set within a lush subtropical garden. 15 studio, and one- and two-bedroom units. $$$

Tutukaka
Oceans Resort Hotel
The Marina
Tutukaka
Tel: 09-470 2290
www.oceansresorthotel.co.nz
This resort overlooks Tutukaka Harbour and has a heated saltwater swimming pool and comfortable rooms. Its restaurant is world-class and focuses heavily on preparing seafood well. $$$

Waipoua Forest
Waipoua Lodge
SH12
Tel: 09-439 0422
www.waipoualodge.co.nz
Perched on a ridge overlooking the Waipoua Forest, this villa was built as a private home over a century ago. Now restored, it includes three pioneer-style cottages with super-king and queen bedrooms, en-suite bathrooms, lounge and kitchenette. There is a restaurant and bar on site. $$$$$

Whangarei
The Chalets Huanui
264 Ngunguru Road
Huanui, Glenbervie
Tel: 09-437 3001
www.chaletshuanui.co.nz
Set in the countryside on 10 acres of gardens, only 10 minutes' drive from the CBD, and 10 minutes from coast. Cedar chalets with kitchenette and

PRICE CATEGORIES

Price categories are for two people in a double room, including GST:
$ = below NZ$100
$$ = NZ$100–150
$$$ = NZ$150–200
$$$$ = NZ$200–300
$$$$$ = over NZ$300

TRANSPORT

ACCOMMODATION

EATING OUT

ACTIVITIES

A – Z

en suite. A continental breakfast is included in the tariff. **$$$**
Settlers Hotel
61–69 Hatea Drive
Tel: 09-438 2699
www.settlershotel.co.nz
In the city centre, overlooking the river, this quaint hotel has en-suite rooms, a restaurant, spa pool and swimming pool. 53 rooms. **$$**

The Waikato

Hamilton
Barclay Motel
280 Ulster Street
Tel: 07-838 2475, 0800-808 090
www.barclay.co.nz
Luxury spa suites and family units and studios, 21 in all, set around a spacious courtyard dotted with colourful geraniums and potted palms. Solar-heated swimming pool, spa pool and children's playground. **$$$**
Colonial City Motel
23 Thackery Street, Hamilton
Tel: 07-838 2479
www.colonialcitymotel.com
A historic motel built around an original 1920s homestead in a park-like setting just five minutes' walk from Hamilton CBD. **$$**
Kingsgate Hotel Hamilton
100 Garnett Avenue
Tel: 07-849 0860
www.millenniumhotels.co.nz/kingsgatehamilton
Good-value city-centre hotel with 24-hour room service. 147 rooms. **$$**
Ventura Inn and Suites Hamilton
23 Clarence Street
Tel: 07-838 0110, 0800-283 688
www.venturainns.co.nz

Some rooms have king-size beds and spa baths. Central location. Complimentary continental buffet breakfast. **$$**

Matamata
Broadway Motel
128 Broadway, Matamata
Tel: 07-888 8482
www.broadwaymatamata.co.nz
Modern and spacious units set in park-like grounds. Easy walk to shops and restaurants. **$$**
Miro Court Villas
5 Miro Street, Matamata
Tel: 07-888 8482
Matamata's newest motel is in the heart of town and offers five contemporary units with broadband, private courtyards, heat pumps and air conditioning. **$$$**

Ngaruawahia
Arrow Lodge Motel
Market Street, Ngaruawahia
Tel: 07-824 8360
www.arrowlodge.co.nz
Older-style motel with solid walls and 10 quiet, self-contained ground-floor units bordering on reserve land which runs down to the Waikato River. **$**

Te Aroha
Aroha Mountain Lodge
5 Boundary Street
Tel: 07-884 8134
www.arohamountainlodge.co.nz
Cosy lodgings in a picturesque villa close to the Te Aroha Hot Mineral Pools. **$$**
Te Aroha Motel
108 Whitaker Street
Tel: 07-884 9417

www.tearohamotel.co.nz
Twelve spacious and super-clean units in older style located right next door to the Te Aroha Domain and Hot Mineral Pools. It's a short walk to restaurants and shops. **$$**

Tirau
Rose Lodge B&B
4 Rose Street
Tel: 07-883 1162
Email: jennysayers@xtra.co.nz
Provincial setting with friendly hosts. Once a Masonic Lodge, this historic building in the heartland of rural Waikato offers two modern rooms, each with its own entranceway and shady, private veranda. A true gem. **$$**

Waitomo
Waitomo Caves Hotel
Lemon Point Road
Tel: 07-878 8204
www.waitomocaveshotel.co.nz
Victorian-style historic hotel, 19km (12 miles) from Te Kuiti and near the limestone caves. 37 rooms. **$$$**
Waitomo Lodge
SH3, Te Kuiti
Tel: 07-878 0003
www.waitomo-lodge.co.nz
Modern motel complex with easy access to Waitomo Caves' attractions. Comfortable rooms with king-size beds in every unit, country views and some rooms with spa baths. **$$**
Woodlyn Park Waitomo Motel
1177 Waitomo Valley Road
Tel: 07-878 6666
www.waitomomotel.co.nz
Unique modern accommodation set within a ship, an aeroplane, a train and even in hobbit holes! **$$$**

Whangarei yacht harbour.

Coromandel and the Bay of Plenty

Hahei
Cathedral Cove Lodge Villas
Harsant Avenue, Hahei Beach
Tel: 07-866 3889
www.cathedralcove.co.nz
The only true beachfront accommodation at Hahei, just a short walk from Cathedral Cove. Rooms have sea or garden views. 16 units. **$$$$**

The Church
87 Hahei Beach Road
Tel: 07-866 3533
www.thechurchhahei.co.nz
An established property with 11 cosy cottages set in beautiful gardens. Popular restaurant on site. **$$$**

Hicks Bay
Hicks Bay Motel
5198 Te Araroa Road
Tel: 06-864 4880
www.hicksbaymotel.co.nz
This motel has a range of accommodation to suit all budgets, from seasonal campsites and shared bunk rooms to classic Kiwi one- and two-bedroom motel rooms. Friendly hosts, excellent sea views, a pool, playground, country café/restaurant and guest lounge. **$$**

Opotiki
Cape View Cottage
Tablelands Road
Tel: 07-315 7877
www.capeview.co.nz
A quiet, modern country cottage with two separate bedrooms and everything you need for an overnight or a longer stay. This is a great place to take a break, catch up with your laundry and relax in the outdoor spa pool by night. Wide ocean and cape views. **$$**

Pauanui
Pauanui Pines Motor Lodge
174 Vista Paku, Pauanui Beach
Tel: 07-864 8086
www.pauanuipines.co.nz
Set among established gardens, there are 18 self-contained one- and two-bedroom units with full kitchens, large bathrooms, lounge and dining areas. Cooked or continental breakfasts are delivered to your door on request. Heated swimming pool and tennis court, and a golf course nearby. **$$$**

Tairua
Pacific Harbour Lodge
223 Main Road, Tairua Beach
Tel: 07-864 8581
www.pacificharbour.co.nz
Thirty-one island-style lodges, set amid tropical vegetation with shell-covered pathways to the chalets, beach and award-winning restaurant. Spacious units. **$$$$**

Paku Lodge
10 The Esplanade
Tel: 07-864 8557
www.pakulodge.co.nz
Ten modern units right on the waterfront, all with balconies. Kayaks for guests' use. **$$**

Tauranga/Mount Maunganui
Accommodation at Te Puna
Corner Minden Road and SH2, RD6, Tauranga
Tel: 07-552 5621
www.tepunalodge.co.nz
A comfortable motel, good for large groups, with family-size units, some with spa baths. Shared accommodation and cabins also available. **$$**

Bay Palm Motel
84 Girven Road, Mount Maunganui
Tel: 07-574 5971
www.baypalmmotel.co.nz
Modern and very comfortable units with spa baths, a short walk from the beach and shops. Heated swimming pool. 16 units. **$$$**

Oceanside Twin Towers Resort
1 Maunganui Road, Mount Maunganui
Tel: 07-575 5371
www.oceanside.co.nz
A premier resort with studio and multi-room apartment accommodation. The studio rooms are spacious and feature en-suite bathrooms and kitchenettes. The complex also has hot pools, a gym and sauna and is close to shops, restaurants and the beach. The apartments, with en-suite bathrooms and full kitchens, have impressive views. Studio rooms offer the best value. **$$$**

The Terraces
346 Ocean Beach Road, Mount Maunganui
Tel: 07-575 6494
www.terraces-oceanbeach.co.nz
Spacious three-level apartments with full kitchen, laundry and balcony. **$$$**

Thames
Rapaura Watergardens
586 Tapu–Coroglen Road
Tel: 07-868 4821
www.rapaurawatergardens.co.nz
The accommodation here (two separate cottages) is located at a sightseeing attraction – water gardens with gentle walks, abundant native flora, lily ponds, bridges, streams, a waterfall and sculptures of *punga* (native tree fern). **$$$–$$$$**

Tuscany on Thames
SH25, Jellicoe Crescent
Tel: 07-868 5099
www.tuscanyonthames.co.nz
Italian-style motel nestled between the beautiful coast and bush-covered hills. It has modern facilities, including large en-suite bathrooms. 14 units. **$$**

Whangamata
Breakers Motel
324 Hetherington Road
Tel: 07-865 8464
www.breakersmotel.co.nz
Tucked away in a reserve bordering the estuary, this attractive motel building resembles a wave. The units all overlook a swimming-pool complex with a waterfall and large barbecue area, and include a private deck with spa pool. 21 suites. **$$$**

Whitianga
Beachfront Resort
111–113 Buffalo Beach Road
Tel: 07-866 5637
www.beachfrontresort.co.nz
Absolute beachfront with uninterrupted views of Mercury Bay. A range of suites with one to three bedrooms, plus a full range of facilities including a heated spa pool, kayaks, beach games and a barbecue site for guests' use. **$$$$**

Kuaotunu Bay Lodge
SH25, Kuaotunu
Tel: 07-866 4396
www.kuaotunubay.co.nz
An elegant beach house, 18km (11 miles) north of Whitianga, with beach access and a private deck with panoramic views of the peninsula. It's a great winter getaway, with open-fire, underfloor heating and en-suite bathrooms. Three rooms. **$$$$**

Rotorua and the Volcanic Plateau

National Park
Adventure Lodge and Motel
Carroll Street, National Park Village
Tel: 0800-321 061
www.adventurenationalpark.co.nz
Accommodation to suit every budget is found here, from studio motel units and standard lodge rooms through to budget bunk beds. Transport to the ski slopes and hiking tracks is easily arranged. **$–$$**

PRICE CATEGORIES
Price categories are for two people in a double room, including GST:
$ = below NZ$100
$$ = NZ$100–150
$$$ = NZ$150–200
$$$$ = NZ$200–300
$$$$$ = over NZ$300

Ski Haus
Carroll Street, National Park Village
Tel: 07-892 2854
www.skihaus.co.nz
Cheap and cheerful: clean but basic
double, bunk and family rooms, and
campervan sites. Bar and spa pool. **$**

Ohakune
**Hobbit Motor Lodge and
Restaurant**
Corner Goldfinch and Wye streets
Tel: 06-385 8248
www.the-hobbit.co.nz
Beds are normal size, despite the
lodge's name, and accommodation
includes family units and studio
apartments. Also has outdoor spa
pools and a guest laundry. **$$**

Powderhorn Château
Bottom of Mountain Road
Tel: 06-385 8888
www.powderhorn.co.nz
The Powderhorn Château, 20
minutes' drive from Turoa ski
area, combines the ambience of a
traditional European ski chalet with
the luxury of a hotel. There's the
choice of hotel rooms or an eight-
person chalet. Dine at one of two
restaurants, the Powderkeg or the
Matterhorn, soak in the hot pool, or
enjoy a drink around the log fire in
the main bar, the Powderkeg. The
Powderhorn ski and board shop is
next door. 30 rooms. **$$$$**

**Tussock Grove Boutique Hotel and
Cottage**
3 Karo Street
Tel: 06-385 8771
www.tussockgrove.co.nz
Boutique accommodation in a park-
like setting with a restaurant and a
bar. There's a lounge with a log
fire, sauna, spa, drying room and
adjacent tennis court. **$$**

Rotorua
Birchwood Spa Motel
6 Sala Street
Tel: 07-347 1800, 0800-881 800
www.birchwoodspamotel.co.nz
Close to the thermal reserve and golf
course, these luxury units all have a
spa bath or spa pool. 17 units. **$$$$**

Cactus Jacks
1210 Haupapa Street
Tel: 07-348 3121
www.cactusjackbackpackers.co.nz
Budget accommodation for singles
and couples with dorm beds and
single, twin and double rooms. A fun
place to be if you are travelling solo.
Spa pool. **$**

Cottages at Paradise
801 Paradise Valley Road, Rotorua
Tel: 07-357 5006
www.cottagesatparadise.co.nz

Two-bedroom fully self-contained
cottages in the country, set on the
banks of a river. A gourmet breakfast
hamper is provided daily. Peaceful
and highly recommended. **$$$$**

Millennium Rotorua
Corner Eruera and Hinemaru streets
Tel: 07-347 1234, 0800-645 685
www.millenniumrotorua.co.nz
Ask for a room overlooking Lake
Rotorua. You will get a great view from
the balcony. The staff are friendly, and
facilities include a gym and thermal
pools. **$$$$**

The Princes Gate Hotel
1057 Arawa Street
Tel: 07-348 1179, 0800-500 705
www.princesgate.co.nz
Built in 1897 and refurbished to
modern standards, this is Rotorua's
best heritage hotel and its boutique
accommodation comes complete with
spas, a sauna, heated pool, gym and
tennis court. 50 rooms, each with its
own unique decor. **$$$**

Redwood Holiday Park
5 Tarawera Road
Tel: 07-345 9380
www.redwoodparkrotorua.co.nz
A range of accommodation options,
from motel units and tourist flats
through to basic cabins, campervan
sites and tent sites. **$$**

**Silver Fern Accommodation and
Spa**
326 Fenton Street
Tel: 07-346 3849, 0800-118 808
www.silverfernrotorua.co.nz
Twenty contemporary studios, one-
and two-bedroom suites. A day spa is
located on site. **$$–$$$**

Solitaire Lodge
Lake Tarawera, RD5
Tel: 07-362 8208, 0800-765 482
www.solitairelodge.com
Luxury accommodation in a stunning
lake-edge location with superb views.
Suites have timber cathedral ceilings,
large beds, a private deck and
spacious bathroom. There's an open
fire in the main lounge. 10 suites.
$$$$$

Sudima Hotel
1000 Eruera Street, Rotorua
Tel: 07-348 1174
www.sudimahotels.com
Excellent and quiet location next to
the Polynesian Spa and the wide
open spaces of Government Gardens.
Restaurant, bar and private thermal
pools on site. **$$**

Treetops Lodge & Estate
351 Kearoa Road, Horohoro, Rotorua
Tel: 07-333 2066
www.treetops.co.nz
This private eco-wilderness lodge
hidden amongst virgin forest beneath
the imposing Horohoro Bluffs is

surrounded by water and native
bush and is the place to come to
achieve inner calm. The suites are
modern and beautifully presented;
the lodge cuisine is superb. Explore
the property's waterfalls by horse or
on foot, or just relax listening to the
ever-present sound of water and feel
the weight of the world lifting off your
shoulders. **$$$$$**

Wylie Court Motor Lodge
345 Fenton Street
Tel: 07-347 7879, 0800-100 879
www.wyliecourt.co.nz
Resort-style complex, with private
heated pools, in park-like grounds.
Modern facilities include a large
heated swimming pool and
Campbell's Restaurant, popular for its
pasta dishes. 36 rooms. **$$$**

Taupo
Bayview Wairakei Resort
SH1
Tel: 07-374 8021, 0800-737 678
www.wairakei.co.nz
In the heart of the Wairakei Thermal
Valley, this resort is just 9km (6 miles)
north of central Taupo. There is a
sauna, gym, six large spa pools and
two swimming pools. More than 180
rooms and villas. **$$$–$$$$**

Baywater Motor Inn
126 Lake Terrace
Tel: 07-378 9933, 0800-926 822
www.baywater.co.nz
Magnificent lake and mountain views
from this motel, 1km (½ mile) from
the town centre. Self-contained units
have a large in-room spa bath and a
balcony or patio. 12 units. Good deals
are available if you stay two to three
nights. **$$$**

Boulevard Waters Motor Lodge
215 Lake Terrace
Tel: 07-377 3395
www.boulevardwaters.co.nz
Lake-edge motel with luxury features,
such as in-room spas, king-size beds,
underfloor heating and thermal pool.
10 suites. **$$$**

Suncourt Hotel
14 Northcroft Street
Tel: 07-378 8265
www.suncourt.co.nz
Studio and one-, two- and three-
bedroom suites, many with lake
views. Outdoor swimming pool and
heated spa. Children's play area and
two guest laundries. **$$$**

Whakapapa Village
Bayview Château Tongariro
Whakapapa Village, Tongariro National Park
Tel: 07-892 3809
www.chateau.co.nz
Completed in 1929, this is one of
New Zealand's few hotels located

in the middle of a World Heritage park. Known as 'the grand old lady of the mountain', it is renowned for its grandeur, and offers a range of rooms. **$$$$–$$$$$**

Skotel Alpine Resort
Whakapapa Village, Tongariro National Park
Tel: 07-892 3719
www.skotel.co.nz
At the edge of the village, this resort has accommodation ranging from deluxe rooms to straightforward cabins and chalets. Terraces Restaurant and Bar on site. **$$$**

Tongariro Holiday Park
SH47, Tongariro
Tel: 07-386 8062
www.thp.co.nz
Comfortable budget accommodation with cabins, self-contained units, and tent and campervan sites. Café and spa pools on site. **$**

Poverty Bay and Hawke's Bay

Gisborne
Champers Motor Lodge
811 Gladstone Road
Tel: 06-863 1515
www.champers.co.nz
Modern complex, close to the city centre and airport, with luxurious ground-floor units, some with double spa baths. Heated pool in landscaped grounds. Adjacent to a large park. **$$$**

Ocean Beach Motor Lodge
Wainui Beach
Tel: 06-868 6186, 0800-250 800
www.oceanbeach.co.nz
Mediterranean-style luxury motor lodge, at Wainui Beach. Studio, and one- and two-bedroom apartments with spacious private courtyards and designer kitchens. Popular Mexican restaurant on site. **$$$**

The Quarters
Te Au Farm, Nuhaka, Mahia
Tel: 06-837 5751
www.quarters.co.nz
Modern and stylish holiday cottage with expansive ocean views. Complimentary home-made bread and cooked crayfish on arrival. Self-catering, although home-cooked meals are served on request. The surroundings are great for scenic walks, bush tramping, swimming, hunting and surfing. **$$$$**

Hastings
Black Barn
Black Barn Road, RD2
Tel: 06-877 7985
www.blackbarn.co.nz
Beautiful rural vistas from cottages located on a vineyard. Range of

accommodation available. **$$$$$**
Millar Road
Millar Road, Havelock North, Hastings
Tel: 06-875 1977
www.millarroad.co.nz
Brand-new, stylish, top-end vineyard accommodation with expansive rural and sea views. Lots of New Zealand art is on display and all furniture is handcrafted in New Zealand. It is self-catering, but breakfast provisions are provided. **$$$$$**

Omahu Motor Lodge
357 Omahu Road
Tel: 06-870 7061, 0800-166 248
www.omahumotorlodge.co.nz
These quality air-conditioned units, some with spa baths, are opposite Hawke's Bay Hospital. **$$$**

Napier
The County Hotel
12 Browning Street
Tel: 06-835 7800
www.countyhotel.co.nz
Luxurious Edwardian Art Deco building in a central location. Its restaurant serves award-winning international cuisine. **$$$$$**

The Crown
Ahuriri
Tel: 06-833 8300
www.thecrownnapier.co.nz
A great place to stay opposite the Ahuriri waterfront, close to the beach and park. A range of comfortable rooms, from studios to three-bedroom suites. Some rooms have water views. **$$$**

Lawn Cottages
527 Lawn Road, Clyde
Tel: 06-870 0302
www.lawncottages.co.nz
Stylish cottages set in lush gardens in rural Clyde, halfway between Napier and Hastings. Friendly hosts, magical setting. **$$$$**

McHardy Lodge
11 Bracken Street
Tel: 06-835 0605
www.mchardylodge.com
With a fabulous breakfast menu, this is possibly the only former maternity home providing visitor accommodation in the country. **$$$$$**

Te Urewera
National Park
As well as the motor camp beside Lake Waikaremoana (www.lake.co.nz), there are numerous Department of Conservation (DOC) huts dotted around the park. For bookings, contact the Aniwaniwa Visitor Centre.

Taranaki, Wanganui and Manawatu

Hawera
Tairoa Lodge
3 Puawai Street
Tel: 06-385 4882
www.tairoalodge.co.nz
Set on 4 hectares (10 acres) of established gardens with mature rhododendron, magnolia, copper beech and kauri trees, Tairoa Lodge is one of Hawera's oldest residences. Built in 1875 from Northland kauri, it has been restored to its former elegance. A relaxing place to stay. **$$$**

New Plymouth
93 By the Sea
93 Buller Street
Tel: 06-758 6555
www.93bythesea.co.nz
A cosy bed and breakfast on the coastal walkway, near ocean and rivers. Suburban with sea views. **$$$**

Brougham Heights Motel
54 Brougham Street
Tel: 06-757 9954, 0800-107 008
www.broughamheights.co.nz
Well-presented executive and spa-bath units, plus a business lounge and conference facilities. Off-street parking. **$$$**

Copthorne Hotel Grand Central New Plymouth
42 Powderham Street
Tel: 06-758 7495
www.copthornenewplymouth.co.nz
Central hotel, with premier to executive rooms, most with a spa bath, and a first-class café. 60 rooms and suites. **$$$**

New Plymouth Top 10 Holiday Park
29 Princes Street, New Plymouth
Tel: 06-758 2566
www.nptop10.co.nz
Well-presented accommodation including one- to three-bedroom motel-style units set in park-like grounds. Popular with families, with an outdoor swimming pool, spa pools and sauna facilities. **$$–$$$**

Nice Hotel and Restaurant
71 Brougham Street
Tel: 06-758 6423
www.nicehotel.co.nz

PRICE CATEGORIES

Price categories are for two people in a double room, including GST:
$ = below NZ$100
$$ = NZ$100–150
$$$ = NZ$150–200
$$$$ = NZ$200–300
$$$$$ = over NZ$300

Boutique hotel with individually styled bedrooms with contemporary art. The designer bathrooms have double spa baths. Multi-award-winning restaurant. **$$$$**

Palmerston North
Chancellor Motor Lodge
131 Fitzherbert Avenue
Tel: 06-354 5903
www.chancellormotel.co.nz
Close to the city centre, this motel has comfortable units, with fully equipped kitchens, private balconies, and spa baths. **$$$**
Hiwinui Country Estate
Ashhurst Road, Ashhurst
Palmerston North
Tel: 06-329 2838
www.hiwinui.co.nz
Exclusive accommodation on a 485-hectare (1,200-acre) stud farm. Luxurious rooms in a magnificent home with hospitable hosts and an on-site day spa. Farm tours are provided for guests. **$$$$$**
Rose City Motel
120–122 Fitzherbert Avenue
Tel: 06-356 5388
www.rosecitymotel.co.nz
One- and two-bedroom suites, studio and mezzanine units. Sauna, spa pool and squash court. Convenient location, only two minutes' walk from town. **$$**

Wanganui
Anndion Lodge
143 Anzac Parade, Wanganui
Tel: 06-343 3593
www.anndionlodge.co.nz
On the banks of the Whanganui River, with a range of rooms. Saltwater

swimming pool, outdoor spa, sauna and BBQ area. A superior place to stay for little outlay. **$$**
The Flying Fox
River Road, Wanganui
Tel: 06-342 8160
www.theflyingfox.co.nz
Peaceful accommodation in rustic hand-built cottages located beside the Whanganui River. Just getting here is an adventure in itself – the accommodation is reached by cable car. Organic meals are provided on request by the friendly hosts. A truly amazing place to stay. **$$**
Kings Court Motel
60 Plymouth Street,
Wanganui
Tel: 0800-221 222
www.kingscourtmotel.co.nz
Clean, tidy accommodation in a convenient central location. **$$**
Kingsgate Hotel The Avenue
379 Victoria Avenue
Tel: 06-349 0044
www.theavenuewanganui.com
Offers an extensive range of accommodation, just 10 minutes' walk from the city. Restaurant and swimming pool on site **$$**

Wellington and Surroundings

Wellington
Apollo Lodge Motel
49 Majoribanks Street
Tel: 04-385 1849
www.apollo-lodge.co.nz
Clean and comfortable motel units, executive suites and apartments for up to five people, close to the shopping centre and five minutes from Oriental Bay. **$$–$$$**

Copthorne Hotel Oriental Bay
100 Oriental Parade
Tel: 04-385 0279
www.millenniumhotels.co.nz
Fine modern hotel in an excellent location overlooking the harbour and close to the city centre. Exceptional views are offered from the hotel's One80 Restaurant. Heated indoor swimming pool. It's a 10-minute walk to Te Papa Museum and the theatres, restaurants and bars of Courtney Place. **$$$**
Gourmet Stay
25 Frederick Street, Te Aro
Tel: 04-801 6800
www.gourmetstay.co.nz
A brand new and cool little boutique hotel near Wellington's thriving Cuba Street Quarter. The hosts are foodies who, by day, run a superb deli on the ground floor. Needless to say, they can point you in the right direction to dine. **$$**
InterContinental Wellington
2 Grey Street
Tel: 04-472 2722
www.intercontinental.com/wellington
In an excellent waterfront location, this hotel is good for both business and leisure guests. It has a restaurant, bars and room service, and a fitness centre with a heated pool. **$$$$$**
Novotel Capital Wellington
133–137 The Terrace
Tel: 04-918 1900
www.novotel.co.nz
Modern hotel in the centre of the CBD, near Lambton Quay and Parliament buildings, with a swimming pool, gymnasium, restaurant, bar, and city and harbour views. **$$$$**

Mount Taranaki.

Victoria Court Motor Lodge
201 Victoria Street
Tel: 04-385 7102
www.victoriacourt.co.nz
Located near the city centre, the pleasant units and off-street parking make this a good option. From here it is only a short stroll to the eateries of Cuba Street and the shopping facilities of Manners Mall. **$$$**
Wellesley Boutique Hotel
2-8 Maginnity Street, Wellington
Tel: 04-474 1308
www.wellesleyboutiquewellington.com

A charming heritage building transformed into a popular boutique hotel. On-site restaurant. **$$$$**

Outside Wellington
Longwood
78 Longwood Road East, Featherston
Tel: 06-308 8289
www.longwood.co.nz
Named after Napoleon's house of exile on St Helena, Longwood is reputedly New Zealand's largest private home. Gracious, hosted accommodation is provided within

the house, or in a series of equally comfortable but more budget-friendly cottages. The acres of beautifully kept gardens are well worth exploring. **$$$–$$$$$**
The Martinborough Hotel
The Square, Martinborough
Tel: 06-306 9350
www.martinboroughhotel.co.nz
Stylish guest rooms, all with different decor, within a refurbished colonial hotel established in 1882. Located in the heart of Martinborough wine country. **$$$**

SOUTH ISLAND

Nelson and Marlborough

Blenheim
Lugano Motor Lodge
91 High Street, Blenheim
Tel: 0800-584 266
www.lugano.co.nz
Opposite the floral gardens of Seymour Square in the heart of Blenheim, just a short stroll from the shops, restaurants and pubs, Lugano offers studio, one-bedroom and two-bedroom units. **$$$**
Quality Hotel Marlborough
20 Nelson Street
Tel: 03-577 7333
www.marlboroughhotel.co.nz
Contemporary hotel with a good restaurant and large outdoor swimming pool. **$$$**
Uno Piu
75 Murphys Road
Tel: 03-578 2235
www.unopiu.co.nz
Boutique accommodation set in 1.6 hectares (4 acres) of established gardens. Two modern guest suites with en-suite bathrooms and a self-contained cottage. Ten-metre (33ft) pool, cobbled patio and charming hosts. **$$$$$**

Nelson
Beachside Villas Hotel
71 Golf Road
Tel: 03-548 5041
www.beachsidevillas.co.nz
A Mediterranean-style boutique motel in a beautiful garden setting, offering luxurious self-contained apartments. Seven units. **$$$**
Bella Vista Motel
178 Tahunanui Drive
Tel: 03-548 6948
www.staybellavista.co.nz
A bit of a walk from the city centre (30 minutes), but close to beautiful Tahunanui Beach and the harbour entrance. Good cafés and shops

nearby. One unit has a spa bath, while two rooms are wheelchair-accessible. **$$**
DeLorenzo's Studio Apartments
43–55 Trafalgar Street
Tel: 0508-335 673
www.delorenzos.co.nz
These luxury apartments, close to business and shopping areas, are furnished in a modern style and have super-king beds, en-suite bathrooms, spa baths and Sky TV. **$$$**
Kimi Ora Spa Resort
99 Martin Farm Road, Kaiteriteri
Tel: 0508-546 4672
www.kimiora.com
Swiss-style chalet apartments with sea views. The resort has a health complex with an extensive range of spa treatments, heated indoor and outdoor pools, a sauna, steam room, spa pool, tennis courts and fully licensed vegetarian restaurant with panoramic ocean views. **$$$**
Tuscany Gardens Motor Lodge
80 Tahunanui Drive
Tel: 03-548 5522
www.tuscanygardens.co.nz
Studio, one- and two-bedroom family units have full kitchens, but it's only a five-minute walk to local eateries (and the beach). Guest laundry and garden. **$$$**
Wairepo House
22 Weka Road, Mariri
Tel: 03-526 6865
www.wairepohouse.co.nz
A three-storey colonial homestead with rich native timbers, chapel ceilings and sunny decks, set in an apple-and-pear orchard. **$$$$$**

Picton and the Sounds
Bay of Many Coves Resort
Queen Charlotte Sound
Tel: 03-579 9771, 0800-579 9771
www.bayofmanycovesresort.co.nz
In the heart of the Marlborough Sounds, this is a quiet, attractive and

very isolated holiday retreat with a swimming pool, hot tub and massage spa therapy. Kayaks and dinghies are available free of charge, as are wilderness tours within the bay to see shag colonies, seals and dolphins. **$$$$$**
Furneaux Lodge
Endeavour Inlet
Tel: 03-579 8259
www.furneaux.co.nz
This exclusive bush retreat and eco-resort in the heart of the Marlborough Sounds offers a range of luxury suites, self-catering cabins and backpacker hostels. Facilities include a restaurant-bar. All scuba-diving requirements are supplied. Good fishing off the wharf. From here you can embark on the Queen Charlotte hike. Budget hikers' accommodation is also available. **$$$$**
Harbour View Motel
30 Waikawa Road
Tel: 03-573 6259
www.harbourviewpicton.co.nz
Twelve tastefully furnished and self-contained studios with great harbour views. **$$$**
Punga Cove Resort
Endeavour Inlet
Tel: 03-579 8561
www.pungacove.co.nz
Chalets are nestled in the bush, with superb views of the surrounding bay. Each has an en-suite bathroom, modern facilities, a sun deck and barbecue (on request). The Punga Lodge sleeps 10 people, while the

PRICE CATEGORIES

Price categories are for two people in a double room, including GST:
$ = below NZ$100
$$ = NZ$100–150
$$$ = NZ$150–200
$$$$ = NZ$200–300
$$$$$ = over NZ$300

Hagley Park, Christchurch.

studio chalets can accommodate two or three. It has a private beach, with good swimming and excellent fishing. Camping is also available here. **$$$$**

Sennen House
Oxford Street
Tel: 03-573 5216
www.sennenhouse.co.nz
On a quiet street away from the wharf area but within easy walking distance, this historic B&B and self-catering apartments is housed inside a colonial villa built in 1886. Each apartment within the home is beautifully restored and offers a private lounge and full kitchen facilities. **$$$$**

Takaka and Golden Bay
Collingwood Homestead
Elizabeth Street, Collingwood
Tel: 03-524 9079
www.collingwoodhomestead.co.nz
Gorgeous boutique B&B in a colonial homestead, with wonderful hosts. It's a short walk to shops and cafés. **$$$$**

Sans Souci Inn
11 Richmond Avenue, Pohara
Tel: 03-525 8663
www.sanssouciinn.co.nz
Mud-brick eco-lodge set in lush gardens with spotless, sweet-scented composting loos. Also renowned for its delicious slow-cooked dinners. A great place to stay. **$$**

Christchurch and Surroundings

Akaroa
Akaroa Criterion Motel
75 Rue Jolie
Tel: 03-304 7775, 0800-252 762

www.holidayakaroa.co.nz
Twelve luxury studio units and a penthouse apartment, all with harbour views. Fully renovated in 2012. **$$$**

Akaroa Waterfront Motels
56–64 Rue Jolie
Tel: 03-304 7484
www.akaroawaterfront.co.nz
Family-size accommodation on the seafront; within walking distance of shops and restaurants. Stunning beachfront lawn and picnic area, shaded by palms. **$$$**

Christchurch
Airport Gateway Motor Lodge
45 Roydvale Avenue, Burnside
Tel: 0800-242 8392
www.airportgateway.co.nz
Offers a range of clean and spacious studio, one-, two- and three-bedroom units in a country garden setting. Restaurant and bar facilities. **$$$**

Ashleigh Court Motel
47 Matai Street West, Lower Riccarton
Tel: 03-348 1888
www.ashleighcourtmotel.co.nz
A short walk from the museum, shopping centre and gardens, units have kitchen facilities and en-suite bathrooms. Clean, comfortable and quiet accommodation. **$$$**

Belmont Motor Inn
172 Bealey Avenue
Tel: 03-379 4037
www.belmontmotorinn.co.nz
This conveniently located motor inn is only 10 minutes from the city centre and has one- and two-bedroom fully self-contained units. **$$$**

The Charlotte Jane
110 Papanui Road
Tel: 03-355 8882

www.charlotte-jane.co.nz
Near Merivale village, this luxurious boutique hotel is just a 20-minute walk from the city. Converted from an old Victorian school and named after one of the ships that brought Christchurch's founding fathers ashore, its 12 spacious en-suite rooms are tastefully furnished and come with a gourmet breakfast each morning and a glass of sherry or wine in the evenings. **$$$$$**

Chateau on the Park
189 Deans Avenue, Riccarton
Tel: 03-348 8999
www.chateau-park.co.nz
Situated beside Hagley Park, this hotel offers a range of comfortable rooms, as well as a restaurant, pool, day spa and plentiful complimentary off-street parking. **$$$$**

Christchurch YMCA
12 Hereford Street
Tel: 03-365 0502
www.ymcachch.org.nz
Quality accommodation for all budgets, located near the Botanic Gardens and museum. Bunk rooms are also available. **$**

Country Glen Lodge
107 Bealey Avenue
Tel: 03-365 9980
www.glenlodge.com
Luxurious apartments close to the city centre. Extensive facilities, including luxury spa bath units. Children's play area and barbecue area for guests. **$$$**

The George Hotel
50 Park Terrace
Tel: 03-379 4560
www.thegeorge.com
A low-rise luxury hotel on a great site across the road from the Avon

TRANSPORT

ACCOMMODATION

EATING OUT

ACTIVITIES

A – Z

River and Hagley Park. Contemporary rooms with balconies. Ten-minute walk to the city centre. Top-rated fine-dining restaurant. **$$$$$**

Gothic Heights Motel
430 Hagley Avenue
Tel: 03-366 0838
www.gothicheightsmotel.co.nz
Opposite Hagley Park, within walking distance of the museum, city restaurants and Botanic Gardens. Self-contained studio and family units in a quiet location. **$$$**

Heartland Hotel Cotswold
88–96 Papanui Road
Tel: 03-357 1919
www.heartlandhotels.co.nz
Modern comforts are combined with old-world charm and authentic period furnishings at this New Zealand owned and operated hotel, just five minutes from the city. Restaurant and bar on site. **$$$$**

Merivale Manor Motel and Apartments
122 Papanui Road, Merivale
Tel: 03-355 7731
www.merivalemanor.co.nz
Originally built in the 1880s, the manor has been transformed into 10 elegant studios, one- and two-bedroom apartments. Continental breakfast is included in the tariff. Lots of restaurants nearby. **$$$**

Parkview on Hagley
1 Riccarton Road, Riccarton
Tel: 0800-888 020
www.hotelparkview.co.nz
This swish hotel offers spacious soundproofed and self-contained rooms, double-glazing and en suites with a separate shower and spa bath. Most rooms overlook Hagley Park and some feature private balconies. **$$$$**

Sudima Hotel
Corner Memorial Avenue and Orchard Road, Christchurch Airport
Tel: 0800-783 462
www.sudimachristchurch.co.nz
Adjacent to the Antarctic Centre near Christchurch Airport, this solid low-rise hotel has an outdoor swimming pool, and a bar and restaurant. **$$$**

Canterbury

Aoraki Mount Cook National Park

Aoraki Mount Cook Alpine Lodge
Aoraki Mount Cook Village
Tel: 03-435 1860
www.aorakialpinelodge.co.nz
In the heart of Aoraki Mount Cook National Park. Quality self-catering accommodation with superb panoramic views of Mount Cook and the Southern Alps. Guest kitchen, lounge and laundry. **$$$**

The Hermitage Hotel
Terrace Road, Mount Cook
Tel: 03-435 1809
www.hermitage.co.nz
Luxurious accommodation as well as self-contained family-size motel rooms and chalets. All feature amazing scenery at the foot of New Zealand's tallest mountain in the Aoraki Mount Cook National Park. Sauna, clothing outlet, coffee shop, two restaurants and a bar. Sir Edmund Hillary Museum and Planetarium on site. It's well worth splashing out for a Premium room. **$$$$**

Mount Cook Backpacker Lodge
Bowen Drive
Tel: 03-435 1653
www.mtcookbackpackers.co.nz
Modern self-contained units, en-suite dorm and double/twin rooms. Popular bar and grill, laundry, grocery store and tour desk. **$–$$**

Mount Cook Youth Hostel
1 Bowen Drive, Mount Cook
Tel: 03-435 1820
www.yha.co.nz
A modern complex with a wide range of facilities. Single-sex and mixed dormitories, double and twin rooms. Shop, TV room, showers, free sauna and a coin-operated laundry. **$–$$**

Geraldine

Kavanagh House
SH1, Winchester
Tel: 03-615 6150
www.kavanaghhouse.co.nz
Stylishly decorated rooms with en-suite bathrooms. A gourmet fruit and chocolate platter and a cooked breakfast are included in the tariff. Ten minutes' drive to Geraldine or a one-minute walk to Winchester's shops. **$$$$**

Scenic Route Motor Lodge
28 Waihi Terrace, Geraldine
Tel: 0800-723 643
www.motelscenicroute.co.nz
Geraldine's newest luxury motel complex. Quiet double-glazed units, some with spa baths. **$$**

Hanmer Springs

Albergo Lodge
88 Rippingdale Road
Tel: 0800-342 313
www.albergohanmer.com
The priority at Albergo is relaxation, restoration and recreation, with an emphasis on wellbeing. No matter how travel-weary you arrive, you are guaranteed to leave refreshed. The buildings and grounds have been designed along the harmonious principles of feng shui, with whimsical details that create a delightful ambience. All your creature comforts

are here, a highlight of which is the gourmet breakfast. **$$$$**

Alpine Lodge Motel
Corner Amuri Drive and Harrogate Street
Tel: 03-315 7311, 0800-993 377
www.alpinelodgemotel.co.nz
The accommodation, close to shops and a pool complex, ranges from traditional chalets to luxurious tower suites. Facilities vary in each suite. **$$$**

Greenacres Chalets and Apartments
84 Conical Hill Road
Tel: 03-315 7125, 0800-822 262
www.greenacresmotel.co.nz
Separate units in a park-like setting overlooking the Hanmer Basin. Chalets and deluxe townhouse apartments have decks, balconies and full kitchen facilities. Close to Hanmer township and thermal pools. **$$$**

Hanmer Resort Motel
7 Cheltenham Street
Tel: 03-315 7362, 0800-777 666
www.hanmerresortmotel.co.nz
Clean and tidy studios, villas and apartments, which can accommodate up to six people. Two-minute walk to the adjacent Hanmer Springs hot mineral pools. **$$$**

Hanmer Springs Larchwood Motel
18 Bath Street
Tel: 03-315 7281, 0800-755 756
www.larchwoodmotel.co.nz
Spacious rooms, which can sleep up to six, in a garden setting. Handy for squash courts, the hot pools and forest walks. **$–$$**

Kaikoura

Donegal House
School House Road
Tel: 03-319 5083, 0800-346 873
www.donegalhouse.co.nz
Located 3km (2 miles) north of Kaikoura, this award-winning Irish pub has 28 bed-and-breakfast en-suite rooms furnished with an Irish theme. Outdoor spas, three huge open fires, tranquil gardens and a lake. There's also an excellent restaurant and an Irish bar serving more than 100 Irish and Scottish whiskies. **$$$**

Dylan's Country Cottages
268 Postman's Road
Tel: 03-319 5473

PRICE CATEGORIES

Price categories are for two people in a double room, including GST:
$ = below NZ$100
$$ = NZ$100–150
$$$ = NZ$150–200
$$$$ = NZ$200–300
$$$$$ = over NZ$300

www.lavenderfarm.co.nz
Private self-contained country
cottages located on a fragrant
lavender farm. Breakfast is included
in the tariff. **$$$**
Hapuku Lodge & Treehouses
Station Road, RD1, Kaikoura
Tel: 03-319 6559
www.hapukulodge.com
A contemporary country hotel with
lodge and luxurious treehouse
accommodation. Restaurant on site.
Two minutes' walk through fields to
the beach. **$$$$$**
Panorama Motel
266 The Esplanade
Tel: 03-319 5053, 0800-288 299
www.panoramamotel.co.nz
Beachfront location, with
uninterrupted sea and mountain
views from all units. Plenty of off-
street parking for boats and cars. **$$**

Lake Tekapo
Lake Tekapo Scenic Resort
Main Highway
Tel: 03-680 6808, 0800-118 666
www.laketekapo.com
Centrally located accommodation
with good lake and mountain views.
$$$
Lake View Tekapo
6 Lochinver Avenue
Tel: 03-680 6265
www.lakeviewtekapo.co.nz
Luxury accommodation with
uninterrupted lake and mountain
views from every room. Super-king
beds, en-suite bathrooms and all
modern conveniences. **$$$$**

Methven
Canterbury Hotel (Brown Pub)
Mount Hutt Village
Tel: 03-302 8045
www.thebrownpub.co.nz
A historic hotel that has been a haven
for travellers for more than 120 years.
Basic but comfortable facilities. Good
family restaurant. **$**
Powderhouse Country Lodge B&B
3 Cameron Street, Mount Hutt
Tel: 03-302 9105
www.powderhouse.co.nz
A beautifully restored Edwardian villa.
Luxurious bedrooms have private en
suites. Eight-person spa available,
plus breakfast. Three rooms. **$$$**

Timaru
Avenue Motor Lodge
31 Craigie Avenue
Tel: 03-684 8383
www.avenuemotorlodge.com
Timaru's newest motel, with spacious
king studios and one- and two-
bedroom apartments with double spa
baths. **$$$**

The West Coast

Arthur's Pass
Trans Alpine Lodge
Main Road, Arthur's Pass
Tel: 03-318 9236
www.arthurspass.co.nz
Alpine Lodge with great scenery,
cosy open fires and chalet-style
accommodation in the heart of
the Southern Alps. Restaurant
specialises in traditional Kiwi fare:
lamb, pork roast and West Coast
rump steak. **$$**

Fox Glacier
Rainforest Motel
15 Cook Flat Road, Fox Glacier
Tel: 03-751 0140
www.rainforestmotel.co.nz
Clean, spacious motel complex with
views of Alps and rainforest. **$$$**

Franz Josef Glacier
58 On Cron Motel
58 Cron Street
Tel: 03-752 0627, 0800-662 766
www.58oncron.co.nz
Contemporary apartment-style motel
in excellent location directly opposite
the Glacier Hot Pools. Spacious
rooms and two-bedroom units for
families. **$$$$**
Rainforest Holiday Park
46 Cron Street
Tel: 03-752 0220
www.rainforestholidaypark.co.nz
New motel and park complex set
amongst the rainforest. A wide
range of accommodation is offered
here; some is perfect for families
and for those looking for a safe
and convenient place to park their
campervan overnight. **$$$**
Te Waonui Forest Retreat
3 Wallace Street, Franz Josef
Tel: 03-752 0555
www.tewaonui.co.nz
A warm and quiet haven in an
environmentally friendly building amid
lush rainforest. The spacious rooms
feature pillow menus and special
touches at every turn. Local cuisine
is served on site at the Canopy
restaurant. **$$$$$**

Greymouth
Aachen Place Motel
50 High Street
Tel: 03-768 6901
www.aachenmotel.co.nz
Popular studio apartments and units
with friendly hosts and great sea and
mountain views. **$**
Gables Motor Lodge
84 High Street
Tel: 03-768 9991
www.gablesmotorlodge.com

Large units with fully equipped
kitchens. Some have spa baths, while
others have showers. Handy for the
shops, cafés and restaurants. **$$**

Haast
Wilderness Lodge
Lake Moeraki, SH6
Tel: 03-750 0881
www.wildernesslodge.co.nz
The Wilderness Lodge has a stunning
and tranquil setting, with fantastic
bush and coastal walks teeming with
wildlife. Guest-only tours include
hikes to secluded penguin sites.
Breakfast and dinner are included in
the tariff. **$$$$$**

Hokitika
Fitzherbert Court Motel
191 Fitzherbert Street
Tel: 03-755 5342
www.fitzherbertcourt.co.nz
Modern units with self-contained
kitchens, some with spa baths. Near
the town, airport and beach. **$$**
**Shining Star Chalets and
Accommodation**
11 Richards Drive
Tel: 03-755 8921
www.shiningstar.co.nz
Centrally located, these fully self-
contained timber chalets have
their own decks and direct beach
access. Also campsites, cabins and
apartment-style units available.
Facilities include a sauna, spa pool
and playground. Near glow-worm
grotto. **$$$**

Karamea
Karamea River Motels
Bridge Street, RD3, Karamea, Westport
Tel: 03-782 6955, 0800-527 263
www.karameamotels.co.nz
One- and two-bedroom suites on a
private farm, with views across the
wilderness of Kahurangi National
Park. Suites have large private
lounges. Close to the centre of
Karamea. **$$**

Punakaiki
Punakaiki Beachfront Motels
Mabel Street, Punakaiki
Tel: 03-731 1008
www.punakaikicottagemotels.co.nz
Motel units right on the beachfront,
500 metres north of the Pancake
Rocks. **$$$**

Queenstown and Otago

Alexandra
Asure Avenue Motel
117 Centennial Avenue
Tel: 03-448 6919
www.avenue-motel.co.nz

Spacious accommodation close to the aquatic centre and park. Spa baths are available in some units. **$$**

Hillview Park
110 Hillview Road
Tel: 03-448 9582
www.hillviewpark.co.nz
Two-bedroom, self-contained cottage in beautiful gardens in a rural setting on the outskirts of Alexandra. Spa pool. **$$**

Arrowtown
Millbrook Resort
Malaghans Road
Tel: 03-441 7000
www.millbrook.co.nz
Luxury resort in a mountain setting with a range of accommodation. There's a superb golf course, restaurant and spa. **$$$$**

Shades of Arrowtown
9 Merioneth Street
Tel: 03-442 1613
www.shadesofarrowtown.co.nz
These tastefully furnished studios and apartments, in a garden setting, have recently been refurbished. **$$**

Cromwell
Carrick Lodge Motel
10–12 Barry Avenue
Tel: 03-445 4519
www.carricklodge.co.nz
Contemporary motel with 16 suites. Close to shops and restaurants but with rural views of countryside and mountains. **$$**

Pisa Range Lake Resort
1–12 Perrairn Place
Tel: 03-445 3417
www.pisarangelakeresort.co.nz
Five-star resort on the shores of Lake Dunstan, offering a range of accommodation, from studios to three-bedroom villas. **$$–$$$**

Lake Hawea
Lake Hawea Motor Inn
1 Capell Avenue
Tel: 03-443 1224
www.lakehawea.co.nz
On the shores of Lake Hawea and offering a range of accommodation, including comfortable units with balconies. Nine-hole golf course, restaurant and barbecue area. **$$**

Stoneridge Estate
756 State Highway 6
Tel: 03-442 1021
www.stoneridge.co.nz
Stunning views from a magnificent property overlooking Lake Hayes. The lodge is built from giant hardwood beams, stone and slate, and completed with stylish decor. Fresh flowers, fruit basket, Egyptian-

cotton linen. Lap pool and hot tub for guests' use. Late checkout (11am). **$$$$$**

Queenstown
Azur
23 McKinnon Terrace
Tel: 03-409 0588
www.azur.co.nz
This luxury lodge is in the Sunshine Bay area, five minutes from town. Each villa boasts sensational panoramic views, a lounge area with a fireplace and an outside deck. Rates include breakfast, afternoon tea and pre-dinner drinks, plus all transfers. **$$$$$**

Central Ridge Boutique Hotel
4 Sydney Street
Tel: 03-442 8832
www.centralridge.co.nz
Sumptuous well-priced rooms, each with a bath in the en suite. Day spa and restaurant on site. **$$$$**

The Dairy
Corner Brecon and Isle streets
Tel: 03-442 5164
This private, luxury hotel offers stylishly appointed rooms, each with an en suite. Breakfast is served in the renovated old corner store ('the dairy' in Kiwi jargon), and there is a quirky 'honesty box' bar. Outdoor spa pool, large lounge with open fire, and bikes for guests' use. Breakfast and afternoon tea is included in the tariff. One-minute walk into town. **$$$$$**

The Heritage Queenstown
91 Fernhill Road
Tel: 03-450 1500
www.heritagehotels.co.nz
A European-style lodge, with forest-view and lake-view suites, crafted from centuries-old schist and cedar. Facilities include a well-equipped day spa, sauna, gym and swimming pool. **$$$$–$$$$$**

Manata Lodge
111A Tucker Beach Road
Tel: 03-441 3144
www.manatalodge.co.nz
Classy fully serviced and self-contained apartment accommodation available by the night or per week. **$$$$$**

Nugget Point Boutique Hotel
Arthur's Point
Tel: 03-441 0288
www.nuggetpoint.co.nz
Award-winning boutique hotel with a fine restaurant, only 10 minutes' drive from Queenstown. The suites are impeccably furnished, and the more expensive ones have stunning views of the Shotover River and Coronet Peak. Competent staff provide first-class service. **$$$$**

Pinewood
48 Hamilton Road
Tel: 03-746 396
www.pinewood.co.nz
Conveniently located, just five minutes' walk to town and offering well-priced self-contained motel-style units, as well as budget shared dormitory accommodation. **$$**

YHA Queenstown Lakefront
88 Lake Esplanade
Tel: 03-442 8413
www.yha.co.nz
Nestled right on the lakefront among luxury hotels, it would be hard to find another accommodation in New Zealand which offered such good value for money. Choice of private or shared rooms. **$**

Wanaka
Edgewater Resort
Sargood Drive, Lake Wanaka
Tel: 03-443 0011, 0800-108 311
www.edgewater.co.nz
Modern luxury apartments and rooms with large bathrooms – some can be configured to provide family suites. On the edge of Lake Wanaka, with great views. The popular Sargoods Restaurant and Wineglass wine bar is on site. **$$$$**

Oak Ridge Pool and Spa Resort
Corner Studholme and Cardrona roads
Tel: 03-443 7707
www.oakridge.co.nz
Comfortable accommodation a short drive from the town centre. Hot-pool complex on site. **$$$–$$$$**

Dunedin and Surroundings

Dunedin
Fletcher Lodge
276 High Street
Tel: 03-477 5552
www.fletcherlodge.co.nz
Six luxurious rooms a few minutes' walk from the centre of the city. **$$$$$**

Hulmes Court Bed and Breakfast
52 Tennyson Street
Tel: 03-477 5319, 0800-448 563
www.hulmes.co.nz
A beautiful 1860s Victorian mansion in the heart of Dunedin. A large marble fireplace is cosy during winter and there's a relaxing drawing room

PRICE CATEGORIES

Price categories are for two people in a double room, including GST:
$ = below NZ$100
$$ = NZ$100–150
$$$ = NZ$150–200
$$$$ = NZ$200–300
$$$$$ = over NZ$300

TRANSPORT

ACCOMMODATION

EATING OUT

ACTIVITIES

A – Z

with authentic furnishings. Each room features a different decor. **$$**

Larnach Lodge
145 Camp Road, Otago Peninsula
Tel: 03-476 1616
www.larnachcastle.co.nz
Bedrooms with private bathrooms are individually decorated in period style, and each has an amazing view of the ocean 305 metres (1,000ft) below. Lodge guests may dine in the historic Larnach Castle dining room. **$$$$$** There is also a cheaper option with shared bathrooms. **$$$$**

Scenic Hotel
118 High Street
Tel: 03-357 1919, 0800-696 963
www.scenic-circle.co.nz
In a central location, with a spacious and welcoming lobby, this historic landmark hotel has plenty of superior and premium rooms from which to choose; ask for a room away from the road as it can be a bit noisy. There's a great café attached to the hotel, and service is good. **$$–$$$**

Oamaru
Avenue Motel
473 Thames Highway
Tel: 03-437 0091
www.avenuemotel.net.nz
This solidly built motel offers budget-friendly, spacious and comfortably furnished rooms overlooking Milner Park. Short drive to town centre. **$**

Heritage Court Motor Lodge
346 Thames Highway, Oamaru
Tel: 03-437 2200
www.heritagecourtlodge.co.nz
The top pick of motels in Oamaru. Some units have private balconies, courtyards and spa baths. Off-street parking and children's play area. Room service, and restaurant on site. **$$**

Southland

Catlins Coast
Catlins Farmstay B&B
174 Progress Valley Road, Catlins
Tel: 03-246 8843
www.catlinsfarmstay.co.nz
Roomy accommodation on a working farm, midway between Cathedral Caves and Curio Bay. Breakfast is available, and you'll get an exceptionally warm Kiwi welcome here. **$$$**

Colac Bay
Oraka Seaviews
16 Bungalow Hill Road
Tel: 03-234 9005
www.orakaseaviews.co.nz
Fully furnished cottages with sea

views. Set on an enormous beef farm, this is a great place to unwind. **$$**

Invercargill
Beersheba Boutique Accommodation
58 Milton Park Road
Tel: 03-216 3677
www.beersheba.co.nz
Michael and Anne Broad offer warm and thoughtful Southern hospitality in their sprawling home. The 4.4 hectares (11 acres) of landscaped woodland gardens, featuring an enormous pond, provide a restful setting. There's a hideaway cottage offering private, self-contained accommodation, or guests can stay in the Tamarisk or Magnolia rooms within the main homestead. Highly recommended. **$$$$**

Birchwood Manor
189 Tay Street
Tel: 03-218 8881
www.birchwoodmanor.co.nz
Award-winning motel with good family and business accommodation in spacious and affordable units and rooms. Close to supermarket, opposite city centre. **$$**

Riverton
The Globe Backpackers
24 Taramea Bay Road
Tel: 03-234 8527
Shared-room accommodation. It's a short walk to a playground and shops. **$$**

Riverton Rock Guesthouse
136 Palmerston Street
Tel: 03-234 8886
www.rivertonrock.co.nz
A very cool place to stay on Riverton's main street overlooking the estuary. This heritage building has been refurbished throughout, and every room has different decor. **$$**

Te Anau
Aden Motel
57–59 Quintin Drive
Tel: 03-249 7748
www.adenmotel.co.nz
Basic self-contained units with kitchen, close to lake and shops. **$–$$**

Dunluce B&B
Apirama Drive
Tel: 03-249 7715
www.dunluce-fiordland.co.nz
A great base from which to explore Te Anau and Milford. Friendly hosts, beautifully presented rooms and mountain views. **$$$$**

Lakeside Motel
36 Lakefront Drive
Tel: 03-249 7435
www.lakesideteanau.co.nz

Central motel in a garden, near restaurants and with unobstructed views of lake and mountains. Nineteen units with full kitchens and en-suite bathrooms. **$$$**

Luxmore Hotel
Main Street
Tel: 03-249 7526, 0800-589 6673
www.distinctionluxmore.co.nz
Located close to Te Anau's services and attractions, and a short walk through the town (100 metres) to the lake front. The rooms are comfortable and well heated. Popular with tour groups, with 106 rooms. **$$$$**

Tuatapere
Waiau Hotel
47 Main Street, Tuatapere
Tel: 03-226 6409
www.waiauhotel.co.nz
Old-fashioned southern country-pub hospitality at its finest. Clean, comfortable rooms, some en suite. Tariff includes a full cooked breakfast. **$$**

Stewart Island

Greenvale Bed & Breakfast
Kaka Ridge Road, Halfmoon Bay
Tel: 03-219 1357
www.greenvalestewartisland.co.nz
Close to the centre of Oban and the sea, with magnificent views of Foveaux Strait. Exclusive, with just two rooms, individually designed and with king-size beds and en-suite bathrooms. **$$$$$**

Sails Ashore Boutique Lodge
Halfmoon Bay
Tel: 03-219 1151
www.sailsashore.co.nz
Luxury boutique bed and breakfast overlooking Halfmoon Bay and the islands of Foveaux Strait, a short stroll from the village. Two-night stay minimum in summer. Informative island tours are run for guests. **$$$$$**

South Sea Hotel
Elgin Terrace, Halfmoon Bay
Tel: 03-219 1059
www.stewart-island.co.nz
A friendly country-style hotel, a 25-minute walk from town. The restaurant serves local seafood. Also has studio units adjacent to the hotel. Great views and location. **$$**

Stewart Island Lodge
14 Nichol Road, Halfmoon Bay
Tel: 03-219 0085
www.stewartislandlodge.co.nz
Secluded setting with fantastic views of the bay; each suite has a super king-size bed, central heating and en-suite bathroom. Gourmet meals feature fresh local seafood. **$$$**

EATING OUT

RECOMMENDED RESTAURANTS, CAFÉS AND BARS

General

An abundance and variety of quality fresh meat, fish and garden produce fill the New Zealand larder with riches on which a world-class cuisine has been built.

The variety of produce offered by New Zealand's market gardens is perhaps rivalled only by those of California. Vegetables such as asparagus, globe artichokes and silver beet (Swiss chard) – luxuries in some countries – are abundant here, as are pumpkins and kumara, the waxiest and most succulent of the world's sweet potatoes. Kiwi fruit, apples, tamarillos, strawberries, passion fruit, pears, blueberries and boysenberries are shipped all over the globe, but while you are here, it's also well worth trying less famous fruits, such as feijoa, babacos and prince melons.

The waters surrounding New Zealand contain an abundant harvest and are the source of at least 50 commercially viable types of fish and shellfish – including crayfish, mussels, oysters, *paua* (abalone) and the tiny whitebait.

New Zealand lamb is superb and deserves its worldwide acclaim. Dishes that are particularly worthy of note are crown roast lamb and lamb spare ribs. The beef is excellent, too, and game – including venison – is plentiful.

If you want to savour a national dish, you won't go far wrong with a helping of pavlova – a delectable concoction of meringue, topped with fresh fruit and whipped cream.

Where to Eat

Good restaurants abound in the country's major cities and in major resort towns. Many of them specialise in international cuisines, most notably Japanese, Vietnamese, Indonesian, Chinese, Korean, Indian, Italian and Thai.

There are formal restaurants, of course, but New Zealanders tend to be more casual, and outdoor dining is popular in the summer months. If you are invited to a BBQ it is customary to ask what you can bring along to contribute. The answer may range from 'just yourself' through to 'bring a salad'. If you are unsure, take a bottle of wine for your hosts. If the answer, however, is to 'bring a plate', this actually means to fill a dish with food to share with everyone, similar to 'pot luck'.

What to Drink

Wine: New Zealand wines win awards all over the world and are well worth trying. The country's cool maritime climate and its summer rains produce light, elegant, fruity white wines – and, in recent years, some very fine red wines, in particular Pinot Noir. See *Cuisine* and *Wine* chapters for more details.

Wine purchased with your meal at a licensed restaurant will be more expensive: add roughly NZ$10–15 per bottle. Look out for the restaurant's 'house' wines as these can be extremely good, often local, and offer significantly better value.
Beer: New Zealanders, with Australians, are among the biggest beer-drinkers in the world: many of New Zealand's beers – Steinlager, Speights, Macs, Tui, Monteiths – rank with the great beers of Denmark and Germany.

BYO means 'Bring Your Own' bottle, and indicates that a restaurant is licensed for the consumption of alcohol, but not for selling it. At BYO restaurants you are likely to be charged a small 'corkage' fee for supplying glasses and for opening your bottle.

Most nightspots, restaurants and cafés serve liquor, and you can buy alcohol from liquor outlets, wine shops and supermarkets (beer and wine only) – if you're 18 or over.
Water: Drinking tap water in New Zealand is perfectly safe, and in most restaurants this will automatically be supplied to your table in a vessel such as a glass bottle or jug.

Bottled water, either still or sparkling, can also be ordered. Well-known European brands are often available, but you are far better off to order a New Zealand brand such as New Zealand Natural, Waiwera Water, and Stewart Island Rain.

Enjoying a beer.

NORTH ISLAND

Auckland

Angus Steak House
8 Fort Lane
Auckland CBD
Tel: 09-379 7815
www.angussteakhouse.co.nz
A meat eater's paradise that is always busy. A good honest steakhouse serving hearty portions, cooked to your exact order, with optional side dishes including oysters, wedges, fried mushrooms and fries. **$$**

Antoine's
333 Parnell Road
Parnell
Tel: 09-379 8756
www.antoinesrestaurant.co.nz
Elegant, highly innovative gourmet restaurant, on a busy shopping street with many other good eateries located in the same area. The menu offers New Zealand cuisine with French undertones. **$$$**

Cibo
91 St Georges Bay Road, Parnell
Tel: 09-303 9660
www.cibo.co.nz
Housed in an atmospheric former chocolate factory. Asian-influenced New Zealand cuisine and superb service have kept Cibo at the top of its game for more than a decade. The menu features an enormous selection of cheeses sourced from all over New Zealand. **$$$**

De Post Belgian Beer Café
466 Mount Eden Road, Mount Eden
Tel: 09-630 9330
www.depost.co.nz
This very popular bar has a great range of Belgian beers and some of the best mussel dishes anywhere. **$**

Euro Restaurant and Bar
22 Princes Wharf
Tel: 09-309 9866
www.eurobar.co.nz
Fashionable restaurant that is always in the awards limelight. High-quality food and service, with a focus on fresh New Zealand produce. **$$$**

The French Café
210 Symonds Street
Tel: 09-377 1911
www.thefrenchcafe.co.nz
Winner of many prestigious awards, The French Café serves contemporary European cuisine in a friendly and intimate environment. There's a relaxed bar for pre- and post-dinner drinks and a conservatory room that overlooks the courtyard, where you can enjoy dining alfresco. **$$$**

Harbourside Seafood Bar and Grill
1st Floor, Ferry Building, 99 Quay Street
Tel: 09-307 0486
www.harboursiderestaurant.co.nz
Like CinCin on the ground floor, this restaurant offers imaginative seafood cooking. Great views. Bookings recommended. **$$$**

Kermadec
Viaduct Quay (opposite the Maritime Museum)
Tel: 09-304 0454
www.kermadec.co.nz
Very good fish dishes and excellent views from the upstairs balcony. **$$$**

Mai Thai
Corner Victoria and Albert streets
Tel: 09-366 6258
www.maithai.co.nz
Delicious and authentic Thai cuisine. **$**

Monsoon Poon
Corner Customs and Lower Hobson streets
Tel: 09-379 9311
www.monsoonpoon.co.nz
Southeast Asian restaurant and bar offering food from around the region. Open kitchen, so you can watch the chefs at work. **$$**

MooChowChow
23 Ponsonby Road, Ponsonby
Tel: 09-360 6262
Eating at this super-cool place has been likened to dining at food stalls in Bangkok. Delicious, zingy Thai food and fresh fruit cocktails. **$$**

The Observatory Restaurant
Level 52, Sky Tower
Tel: 09-363 6000
www.skycityauckland.co.nz
Venture nearly 200 metres (660ft) up Auckland's tallest structure to the highest restaurant in the tower for buffet-style New Zealand seafood specialities. **$$$**

Prego
226 Ponsonby Road, Ponsonby
Tel: 09-376 3095
www.prego.co.nz
Great food, Italian classics and more cooked with panache. A top restaurant – try to get a table in the front courtyard. **$$$**

Soul Bar and Bistro
Viaduct Harbour
Tel: 09-356 7249
www.soulbar.co.nz
One of the best choices at Viaduct Harbour, with fabulous fish dishes and a great selection for vegetarians. Enjoy some of New Zealand's most popular soul food while appreciating the harbour views. Very popular with locals. **$$**

SPQR
150 Ponsonby Road, Ponsonby
Tel: 09-360 1710
www.spqrnz.co.nz
One of Auckland's most famous and best-loved restaurants, with great cuisine, notably the linguine and clams. It becomes a popular nightspot once the plates are cleared away. Dark interior; pavement tables. **$$$**

Tony's Original Steak House
27 Wellesley Street West
Tel: 09-373 4196
www.tonys.co.nz
Cosy and inviting atmosphere reminiscent of a British pub. Diverse menu of Kiwi favourites and international classics, as well as steak and seafood. **$$**

Vivace
Level 1, 50 High Street
Tel: 09-302 2303
www.vivacerestaurant.co.nz
Italian-style food served tapas fashion makes for a tasty quick meal or a pleasant evening out if you feel like lingering to savour a few of the delights on one of Auckland's better wine lists. **$$$**

Wildfire Churrascaria
Shed 22, Princes Wharf
Tel: 09-353 7595
www.wildfirerestaurant.co.nz
Meat and seafood abound at this Churrascaria, with long skewers of New Zealand beef, chicken, pork, lamb and fish, served continuously by Churrasco waiters, directly onto your plate until you can eat no more. **$$**

Auckland's Surroundings

Devonport
Monsoon Thai Café Restaurant
71 Victoria Road
Tel: 09-445 4263
www.monsoonthai.co.nz
Specialises in contemporary Thai and Malay food, to eat in or take out. **$**

Portofino
26 Victoria Street
Tel: 09-445 3777
www.portofinodevonport.co.nz
An outstanding Italian restaurant where fresh ingredients are used to create a variety of chicken, beef and vegetarian dishes, cooked fresh to order. **$$$**

Great Barrier Island
Claris Texas Café
Hector Sanderson Road
Tel: 09-429 0811
Standard café fare for breakfast and lunch. Daily from 8am. **$**

Currach Irish Pub
Pah Beach, Stonewall, Tryphena
Tel: 09-429 0211

The Ferry Building facade.

www.currachirishpub.co.nz
Authentic Irish atmosphere, great pub food and Guinness and Kilkenny on tap. Travelling musicians are warmly welcomed. **$$**

Kawau Island
Mansion House Café
Mansion House
Tel: 09-422 8903
Open for light snacks and coffee from 10am–4pm. **$**

Orewa
Sahara Café and Restaurant
336 Hibiscus Coast Highway
Tel: 09-246 8828
Mediterranean-style cuisine. **$$**
Walnut Cottage Café
498 Hibiscus Coast Highway
Tel: 09-427 5570
Home-made fare served in a historic 1850s home and garden setting. **$**

South Auckland
Broncos Steak House
712 Great South Road,
Manukau
Tel: 09-262 2850
www.broncossteakhouse.co.nz
As reliable as restaurants with 'steakhouse' as part of the name the world over. A great range of New Zealand steak, cooked to order. **$$**
Volare Italian Restaurant & Pizzeria
91 Charles Prevost Drive, Manurewa
Tel: 09-267 6688
www.volare.co.nz
Famous for its convivial atmosphere, Volare's delicious Italian food has made it one of the most popular restaurants in South Auckland. **$$$**

Waiheke Island
Ajadz
2 Korora Road, Oneroa

Tel: 09-372 2588
www.ajadz.co.nz
The only place to go on Waiheke for a range of stunning Indian dishes. **$$**
The Beachfront Bar Café
1 Fourth Avenue, Onetangi
Tel: 09-372 2565
www.thebeachfront.co.nz
Located right on the beach, this café is a destination in itself. **$$**
Nourish Café
3 Belgium Street, Oneroa
Tel: 09-372 3557
www.nourish.co.nz
Renowned for its breakfasts served until 3pm daily, as well as zesty salads and other seasonal gourmet café fare. Takeaways available. **$**

Waitakere City and West Coast Beaches
Beesonline Honey Centre and Café
791 SH16, Waimauku
Tel: 09-411 7953
www.beesonline.co.nz
It's not just for apiarists – this stylish licensed café serves first-class food with an emphasis on fresh organic produce, local ingredients and honey. Well worth the drive, if only to dine here. **$$**
The Elevation
473 Scenic Drive,
Waiatarua
Tel: 09-814 1919
www.elevationcafe.co.nz
Good food, wine and music in a prime location high on top of the Waitakere Ranges, with fantastic panoramic views of Auckland city. This is a great stopover on a day trip to Piha. Brunch is served at weekends. Dinner reservations are recommended. **$$$**
Macnuts Farm Café and Shop
914 South Head Road
Tel: 09-420 2501
www.macnut.co.nz

Book to tour the macadamia orchard and enjoy lunch from a somewhat macadamia-dominated menu at the farm café. **$–$$**

Warkworth/Matakana
Dragonfly Cafe
615 Matakana Road, Matakana
Tel: 09-422 7348
In gorgeous grounds overlooking a waterfall, this café offers a superb selection of freshly prepared fare. **$**
Leigh Sawmill Café
142 Pakiri Road, Leigh
Tel: 09-422 6019
www.sawmillcafe.co.nz
One of the area's most esoteric cafés, specialising in fresh local fish (straight from the commercial fishery next door) and pizzas. **$$$**

Northland

Doubtless Bay
Mangonui Fish Shop
Beach Road
Tel: 09-406 0478
This place wins prizes for its traditional fish and chips, and its seafront location is unbeatable. When available, be sure to sample succulent blue nose. **$**
Waterfront Café and Bar
Waterfront Road
Tel: 09-406 0850
Reliable fare for breakfast, lunch and dinner, right on the waterfront. **$$**

Kerikeri
Café Blue
582 Kerikeri Road
Tel: 09-407 5150
Great family-friendly indoor and outdoor dining, with a children's playground. Set in an orchard that provides oranges, figs, macadamias and culinary herbs. **$$**
Fishbone Café
88 Kerikeri Road
Tel: 09-407 6065
Good, straightforward café fare and friendly atmosphere. **$**

Paihia
Alfrescos Restaurant & Bar
6 Marsden Road
Tel: 09-402 6797
www.alfrescosrestaurantpaihia.com
Family-run business located right on the bay. Excellent value. Open for

PRICE CATEGORIES

Price categories are per person for dinner, including service and tax:
$ = NZ$15–25
$$ = NZ$25–40
$$$ = NZ$40 and over

breakfast, lunch and dinner. **$$**
Waikokopu Café
Treaty Grounds, Waitangi
Tel: 09-402 6275
www.waikokopucafe.co.nz
This award-winning café is in a shady tropical garden at the entrance to Waitangi Treaty Grounds. The food ranges from breakfast and light snacks to main meals of lamb, beef and seafood. **$**

Russell
The Duke of Marlborough Hotel
Waterfront
Tel: 09-403 7829
www.theduke.co.nz
The Duke of Marlborough has a fine restaurant, where you can't go wrong with the locally caught seafood – mussels and Orongo Bay oysters are brought straight from the sea to the table. **$$**
The Wharf
The Strand
Tel: 09-403 7771
www.thewharfrussell.co.nz
The best waterfront location, with outdoor tables set right beside the beach, beneath giant native pohutukawa trees. Superb fine dining and an excellent wine list. **$$$**
York Street Café
1 York Street
Tel: 09-403 7360
Fresh local food at reasonable prices. The chowder is widely praised. Several vegetarian options as well. Daily 8am–3pm. **$$**

Whangarei
Caffeine Espresso Café
4 Water Street
Tel: 09-438 6925
www.caffeinecafe.co.nz
Serves some of the best coffee in the country and provides mouth-watering meals in a cosy atmosphere. Open for breakfast and lunch. **$**
La Familia Artisan Café & Deli
84 Cameron Street
Tel: 09-438 8404
www.lafamilia.co.nz
European breads, panini, excellent coffee and sweet treats are a speciality. A great place to stop for a quick pick-me-up. **$**
The Pizza Barn
2 Cove Road, Waipu
Tel: 09-432 1011
Legendary pizzas such as the Musterer (smoky lamb, caramelised kumara, red onion, capsicum and mint sauce) and the Gumdigger (an enticing mix of smoked salmon, asparagus, blue vein cheese, basil and pesto) are served in the town's old Post Office building. Diners

regularly drive all the way from Auckland just to eat here. **$$**
Reva's on the Waterfront
31 Quay Side,
Town Basin Marina
Tel: 09-438 8969
www.revas.co.nz
Right on the harbour overlooking moored boats, Reva's has an extensive menu of traditional and contemporary cuisine, pizzas and seafood, and is a regular port of call for cruising yachties. **$$**
Tonic
239 Kamo Road,
Tel: 09-435 1910
www.tonicrestaurant.co.nz
A delicious à la carte menu features old favourites like French onion soup and toffee crème brûlée. The set menu on Sunday evening is popular with locals. Bookings are advised. **$$$**

The Waikato

Hamilton
Domaine Eatery
575 Victoria Street
Tel: 07-839 2100
www.domaine.co.nz
Teeming with locals, this eatery serves tasty Mediterranean-style and Asian-inspired dishes. **$$$**
Gothenburg Restaurant
15 Hood Street
Tel: 07-834 3562
www.gothenburg.co.nz
Tapas, wood-fired pizzas and European fare are served here, in the heart of the popular Hood Street restaurant precinct. **$$**
Iguana Street Bar and Restaurant
203 Victoria Street South
Tel: 07-834 2280
www.iguana.co.nz
Hearty steaks, pasta, pizza, salads and light meals. Set menus and à la carte. **$$**
Lone Star
185 Victoria Street
Tel: 07-839 3005
www.lonestar.co.nz
Ribs, steak, pizza and prawns, served in gigantic proportions – nobody goes home hungry from the Lone Star Café. **$–$$**
The Narrows Landing
431 Airport Road
Tel: 07-858 4001
www.thenarrowslanding.co.nz
Gourmet cuisine with New Zealand and European influences. Huge wooden doors, lots of iron, a metal mesh staircase and candlelight enhance its medieval style. **$$$**
Thai Village Café
The Market Place, Hood Street

Tel: 07-834 9960
www.thaivillage.co.nz
Excellent Thai cuisine with a wide range of curry, rice and noodle dishes. Generous servings and reasonable prices. **$$**

Te Aroha
Domain Cottage Café
Te Aroha Domain
Tel: 07-884 9222
Lovely setting inside a historic building. Café fare daily, 9am–3pm. **$**
Mokena Restaurant
6 Church Street
Tel: 07-884 8038
www.mokena.co.nz
Licensed restaurant serving buffet-style food. **$$**

Other Locations
Bosco Café
57 Te Kumi Road, Te Kuiti
Tel: 07-878 3633
In the heart of King Country, a great stopover for some good hearty food, decent coffee and excellent home-made cake and muffins. **$**
Out in the Styx Café
2117 Arapuni Road, Te Awamutu
Tel: 0800-461 559
www.styx.co.nz
Seasonal food cooked from scratch. The menu changes daily according to the chef's whims, and is served buffet-style. Bookings essential. **$$**
Roselands
579 Fullerton Road, Waitomo Caves
Tel: 07-878 7611
www.roselands-restaurant.co.nz
An award-winning restaurant amid native bush in a rural landscape. The mouth-watering menu is prepared using fresh Kiwi produce. Try the barbecue-style lunch. Open for lunch only. **$$**

Coromandel and the Bay of Plenty

Coromandel Township
Pepper Tree and Bar
31 Kapanga Road, Coromandel
Tel: 07-866 8211
www.peppertreerestaurant.co.nz
Fresh New Zealand cuisine; local green-lipped mussels are a speciality here. The lunch menu offers good value. **$$**

Hahei
Café Luna
1 French Road
Tel: 07-866 3016
Good food and great coffee served by friendly staff. **$**
The Church Restaurant
87 Hahei Beach Road

Tel: 07-866 3797
www.thechurchrestauranthahei.co.nz
Contemporary New Zealand dining
in a renovated church building.
Very popular with locals and Kiwi
holidaymakers. **$$$**

Tairua
Manaia Café and Bar
Corner Main and Manaia roads
Tel: 07-864 9050
Menus change regularly with the
seasons and focus on fresh flavours.
Dine alfresco in the spacious
courtyard or indoors. Happy hour
Fri–Sat 4–6pm; great music and
atmosphere. Open 10am until late for
brunch, lunch and dinner. **$–$$**

Tauranga/Mount Maunganui
Bravo Café and Restaurant
Red Square
Tel: 07-578 4700
www.cafebravo.co.nz
All-day dining, good service and sunny
tables. The spicy mussels, gourmet
pizzas and wood-fired bread are all
excellent. **$$$**
Harbourside Brasserie and Bar
The Old Yacht Club, The Strand, Tauranga
Tel: 07-571 0520, 0800-721 714
www.harboursidetauranga.co.nz
Waterfront dining at its best – watch
the boats come in as you dine on
imaginative cuisine. A wide range of
dishes, from lamb shanks Provençal
to apple-roasted pork rack. Or
try some of New Zealand's finest
seafood here. **$$$**
Blue Restaurant
4 Marine Parade, Mount Maunganui
Tel: 07-574 7554
Popular with beachgoers, this casual
eatery serves breakfast all day,
blackboard lunches and à la carte
dinner. Lunch **$** Dinner **$$**

Whangamata
Nero's
Port Road
Tel: 07-865 6300
www.neros.co.nz
Bistro and gourmet-style pizzas with
exotic toppings and pasta. Takeaway
available. The new outside courtyard
with an open fire is a fabulous dining
area in the summer. **$–$$**

Whitianga
Eggsentric Café and Restaurant
1049 Purangi Road, Flaxmill Bay, Cooks
Beach
Tel: 07-866 0307
www.eggsentriccafe.co.nz
Small selection of fresh, well-
prepared food. Live music often plays
here – check the website for up-to-
date details of performances. **$**

Rotorua, Taupo and the Volcanic Plateau

Central Plateau
Alpine Restaurant and Bar
Corner Clyde and Miro streets, Ohakune
Tel: 06-385 9183
This long-running restaurant is still as
popular as the day it opened. It serves
European-style meals in a warm and
welcoming fine-dining environment. **$$**
Licorice Café
57 SH1, Motuoapa, Turangi
Tel: 07-386 5551
www.licoricecafe.co.nz
Home-cooked Kiwi fare with a good
range of gluten-free and vegetarian
options. **$**
Powderkeg Restaurant and Bar
Mountain Road
Tel: 06-385 8888
www.powderhorn.co.nz
Good-value meals are served beside
a roaring fire on huge, slab tables and
benches. Open 7am until late. **$$**
Utopia Café
47 Clyde Street
Tel: 06-385 9120
Enjoy superb coffee, all-day breakfasts
and delicious café meals. **$**

Rotorua
Abracadabra Café/Bar
1263 Amohia Street
Tel: 07-348 3883
www.abracadabracafe.com
A Moroccan-themed café/restaurant
open for breakfast, lunch and dinner.
Tapas and meze are served from
5pm until closing and are excellent
value. Rates highly for its cuisine,
cleanliness and service. **$–$$**
Bistro 1284
1284 Eruera Street
Tel: 07-346 1284
www.bistro1284.co.nz
An award-winning restaurant in a
historic 1930s building. **$$$**
Brew
1103 Tutanekai Street
Tel: 07-346 0976
www.brewpub.co.nz
Contemporary New Zealand brewpub
fare served with casual café-style
service. Open daily. **$$**
Capers Epicurean
1181 Eruera Street
Tel: 07-348 8818
www.capers.co.nz
Casual deli-style café serving freshly
prepared fare including salads, hot
dishes, cakes, slices, sandwiches and
wraps, for breakfast, lunch and dinner
and everything in between. Highly
recommended. **$**
Fat Dog Café
1161 Arawa Street
Tel: 07-347 7586

www.fatdogcafe.co.nz
This popular café filled with locals is
open 9am–3pm for burgers, paninis
and light snacks, and for dinner until
late. **$$**
Indian Star
1118 Tutanekai Street
Tel: 07-343 6222
www.indianstar.co.nz
If you've been holding out for a good
curry, this is the place to go. **$$**
Katsubi Restaurant and Sushi Bar
1123 Eruera Street
Tel: 07-349 3494
Authentic Japanese and Korean
cuisine is served at this restaurant
specialising in sushi, teriyaki,
tonkatsu and bento. **$**
Lakeside Café Memorial Drive
Tel: 07-349 2626
Serves light lunches and morning and
afternoon teas right on the lake, with
seating indoors and out. **$**
The Landing Café
Lake Tarawera
Tel: 07-362 8502
www.thelandinglaketarawera.co.nz
Nestled on the shores of Lake
Tarawera, this café features a
mouth-watering menu served in an
unsurpassed lakeside setting. **$$**
Lewishams Café and Restaurant
1099 Tutanekai Street
Tel: 07-348 1786
www.lewishamsrestaurant.co.nz
Established nearly 30 years ago with
a strong local following, Lewishams
serves European cuisine with Pacific
Rim accents. Daily 9am until late. **$$**
Sabroso
1184 Haupapa Street
Tel: 07-349 0591
www.sabroso.co.nz
A great little Mexican and Latin American
restaurant with good food and reasonable
prices. **$$**
Terraces Café
185 Fairy Springs Road
Tel: 07-347 0027
At the top of the Skyline Gondola,
this is the perfect place for coffee
on a sunny day. All-day breakfast,
sandwiches, cakes, pizza and sushi. **$**
Zanelli's
1243 Amohia Street
Tel: 07-348 4908
www.zanellis.net.nz
A popular Italian restaurant famous
for its mussels, home-made gelato
and tiramisu. Everything is made

PRICE CATEGORIES

Price categories are per person for
dinner, including service and tax:
$ = NZ$15–25
$$ = NZ$25–40
$$$ = NZ$40 and over

TRANSPORT

ACCOMMODATION

EATING OUT

ACTIVITIES

A – Z

Seafood platter.

from scratch and you can taste the difference. **$$**

Taupo
Café Pinot
56 Huka Falls Road
Tel: 07-376 0260
This is Taupo's only winery restaurant, and serves up mouth-watering cuisine in an exquisite setting of landscaped gardens and Pinot Noir vines. Enjoy one of the chef's signature platters while seated on the expansive patio with panoramic views of Mount Tauhara and surrounds. Sample Huka Vineyard's fine wines at the cellar door adjacent to the restaurant. **$$$**
The French Café
101 Heu Heu Street
Tel: 07-378 9664
Authentic French breads and pastries and a menu that even includes snails and crêpes. Not to be missed. **$**
Huka Prawn Park Restaurant
Wairakei Tourist Park
Tel: 07-374 8474
www.hukaprawnpark.co.nz/restaurant
The Wairakei Geothermal Field harnesses the power of about 30,000 tonnes of hot water, and Huka Prawn Farm makes the most of the warmth to raise succulent tropical prawns. Tour the farm, fish for your own lunch using bamboo rods, or enjoy a delicious prawn feast while surveying the Waikato River as it begins its 425km (265-mile) journey to the sea. **$$**
Salute Deli Café
47 Horomatangi Street
Tel: 07-377 4478
The best place in Taupo to dine on freshly prepared salads, bagels and pitta bread. **$**
Zest Café
65 Rifle Range Road
Tel: 07-378 5397
A small café serving outstanding salads and fresh food. Takeout is also available. Open Mon–Sat. **$**

Poverty Bay and Hawke's Bay

Gisborne
The Colosseum
4 River Point Road, Matawhero
Tel: 06-867 4733
www.colosseum.net.nz
Contemporary country bistro-style café in a vineyard setting. Good use of seasonal and locally produced ingredients. À la carte Wed–Sat. **$$**
The Lone Star
1 Wharf Shed, 60 The Esplanade
Tel: 06-868 3257
www.lonestar.co.nz
With redneck ribs, buffalo wings, gourmet pizza and mains like the Kiwi Joker (350g premium aged sirloin or rib-eye), nobody goes home hungry. Budget-friendly, depending on what you order. **$$**
Ussco Bar and Bistro
16 Childers Road
Tel: 06-868 3246
www.ussco.co.nz
Located in the old Union Steam Ship Company Building, Ussco is one of New Zealand's top restaurants and its menu caters to all. Dinner from 4.30pm daily. **$$$**
Wharf Café, Bar and Restaurant
Waterfront
Tel: 06-868 4876
www.wharfbar.co.nz
Bookings are recommended because this restaurant has one of the best wine lists in the country and uses seafood and local produce to perfection. The NZ$15 express lunch menu is great value. **$$**

Hastings/Havelock North
The Old Church
199 Meeanee Road, Meeanee
Tel: 06-844 8866
www.theoldchurch.co.nz
Simply superb contemporary New Zealand cuisine in a renovated and atmospheric church building. **$$$**
Terroir
253 Waimarama Road, Havelock North
Tel: 06-873 0143

www.craggyrange.com
The restaurant attached to Craggy Bay winery has an impeccable pedigree and sophisticated, original fare, including notable desserts. A healthy children's menu is available. Open for lunch and dinner. **$$$**

Napier
Pacifica Restaurant
209 Marine Parade
Tel: 06-833 6335
www.pacificarestaurant.co.nz
A contemporary and award-winning seafood/game restaurant with a strong Pacific ambience. The menu changes often. Dinner from 6pm. **$$$**
Ujazi
28 Tennyson Street
Tel: 06-835 1490
Cosy café that is particularly interesting for its exhibitions by local artists, not to mention its freshly prepared and well-presented food. **$**
Westshore Fish Café
112A Charles Street, Westshore
Tel: 06-834 0227
www.westshorefishcafe.co.nz
Slightly outside the centre of town, but worth the journey for the excellent and inexpensive fish dishes. Takeaways available. **$**

Taradale
Church Road Cellar Door
150 Church Road
Tel: 06-833 8225
www.churchroad.co.nz
Fresh local produce is used to create elegant antipasto platters at lunchtime that complement the vineyard's range of wines. These can be enjoyed indoors or alfresco. **$**

Taranaki, Wanganui and Manawatu

New Plymouth
André L'Escargot Restaurant and Bar
37–41 Brougham Street
Tel: 06-758 4812
www.andres.co.nz
Run by Frenchman André Teissonnière, L'Escargot has a definite French feel. Signature dishes include roasted quail and eye fillet stroganoff. **$$$**
Arborio
Puke Ariki Museum, St Aubyn Street
Tel: 07-759 6060
Lively café in the museum overlooking the foreshore walkway. Enjoy locally roasted Ozone coffee, authentic Italian risottos, home-made pizzas and pasta dishes indoors or alfresco. Daily 9am until late. **$–$$**
Salt
1 Egmont Street

Tel: 06-769 5304
www.waterfront.co.nz
Right on the waterfront with superb
views from every table, Salt offers
contemporary New Zealand cuisine
daily from 7am until late. **$$$**
Table Restaurant
Nice Hotel, 71 Brougham Street
Tel: 06-758 6423
www.nicehotel.co.nz
This award-winning restaurant in the
gorgeous Nice Hotel serves designer
food using the best of locally sourced
ingredients available in season.
The owner's passion for wine is
showcased in the superb wine list,
and this is best enjoyed from the
outdoor deck surrounded by a lush
tropical garden. **$$$**

Palmerston North
Aberdeen Steakhouse and Bar
161 Broadway Avenue
Tel: 06-952 5570
www.aberdeenonbroadway.co.nz
Marbled walls, an earthen
fireplace and the menu provide a
Mediterranean atmosphere, and
there's a courtyard for year-round
alfresco dining. Wide range of dishes;
Angus steak is the speciality. **$$$**
Halikarnas
15 Fitzherbert Avenue
Tel: 06-357 5777
www.halikarnas.co.nz
Great Turkish cuisine in the heart of
town. Popular local haunt. Halikarnas
Chicken – stuffed chicken breast – is
their speciality. Open for lunch and
dinner. **$**
The Herb Farm Café
Grove Road, Ashhurst
Tel: 06-326 7479
www.herbfarm.co.nz
A short drive from Palmerston North,
this is Manawatu's most popular
destination café, in a tranquil
rural setting. It serves beautifully
presented, garden-fresh meals. Also
offers a range of herbal tours and
workshops, and a well-stocked studio
with herbal products, many of which
are manufactured on site. **$**

Wanganui
Redeye Café
96 Guyton Street
Tel: 06-345 5646
Freshly prepared food is available
from the chilled cabinet or can be
ordered from the blackboard menu, at
this popular café. **$**

Wellington and Surroundings

Wellington
Arbitrageur
125 Featherstone Street

Tel: 04-499 5530
www.arbitrageur.co.nz
Once described as a serious temple
of gustatory pleasure, Arbitrageur
continues to serve exquisite food
in an elegant 1930s European
ambience. The menu changes with
the seasons and it has a wine list of
400 bottles, 60 of which are available
by the glass. **$$$**
Atlanta
105 The Terrace
Tel: 04-499 5209
www.atlanta.co.nz
Open for breakfast, lunch and dinner
Mon–Fri, 7am until late. A popular
place to visit for a refreshing cold
drink, pizza and the most delicious
squid rings. **$$**
Boulcott Street Bistro
99 Boulcott Street
Tel: 04-499 4199
www.boulcottstreetbistro.co.nz
A pretty cottage just off Willis Street
houses this fine restaurant, which
has an air of relaxed formality. The
kitchen sources the freshest seasonal
produce to create some of New
Zealand's finest game and seafood
dishes, imaginatively prepared, full
of flavour, and served with grace and
style. Lunch Mon–Fri, dinner daily.
$$$
Capitol
Corner Majoribanks and Kent Terrace
Tel: 04-384 2855
www.capitolrestaurant.co.nz
Award-winning, classic Italian
restaurant, popular with locals and
renowned for its service. Open daily
for brunch, lunch and dinner. **$$**
The Flying Burrito Brothers
Corner Cuba and Vivian streets
Tel: 04-385 8811
www.flyingburritobrothers.co.nz
Upbeat Mexican-styled cantina and
tequileria in the Bohemian Cuba
quarter, with a good children's menu.
$$
Logan Brown Restaurant
192 Cuba Street
Tel: 04-801 5114
www.loganbrown.co.nz
Bistro-style food except for Saturday
night, when the chef offers a
degustation menu. Book in advance
to make sure you don't miss out
as this is one of the city's top
restaurants. **$$$**
**Martin Bosley's Yacht Club
Restaurant**
Royal Port Nicholson Yacht Club, 103
Oriental Parade
Tel: 04-920 8302
www.martin-bosley.com
Location doesn't come any better,
and with Bosley's flamboyant dishes
to match, the combination is perfect.

Bookings are essential. **$$$**
Matterhorn
106 Cuba Street
Tel: 04-384 3359
www.matterhorn.co.nz
Lively venue with an imaginative
28-dish range of tapas. Mon–Sat
3pm–late. **$–$$**
Monsoon Poon
12 Blair Street, Courtney Place
Tel: 04-803 3555
www.monsoonpoon.co.nz
A melting pot of the cuisines of the
Far East, this richly decorated eatery
resembles an Eastern trading house.
Diners can feast their eyes directly
on the large open kitchen where it all
happens. Takeaway is also available.
$$
One Red Dog
Steamship Building, North Queens Wharf
Tel: 04-918 4723
www.onereddog.co.nz
Wellington's leading gourmet pizza
restaurant, with more than 50 wines
by the glass and award-winning beers
on tap. **$$**
Osteria del Toro
60 Tory Street
Tel: 04-381 2299
www.osteriadeltoro.co.nz
Pasta, pizza and great Spanish
paellas are served in this wonderful
Mediterranean café. **$$**
Public Bar & Eatery
Corner Tory Street and Courtenay Place
Tel: 04-801 5115
www.public.net.nz.
Contemporary New Zealand cuisine.
$$$
Scopa
Corner Ghuznee and Cuba streets
Tel: 04-384 6020
www.scopa.co.nz
Italian kitchen in the heart of Cuba
Street renowned for its authentic thin-
crust pizza and home-made pasta. **$$**
Shed 5 Restaurant and Bar
Queens Wharf
Tel: 04-499 9069
www.shed5.co.nz
This restaurant occupies a well-
converted 1800s wool shed opposite
the Maritime Museum and is one of
Wellington's most iconic eateries,
serving smartly prepared seafood.
The menu includes a range of meats
as well. **$$$**
Sweet Mother's Kitchen
5 Courtenay Place

PRICE CATEGORIES

Price categories are per person for
dinner, including service and tax:
$ = NZ$15–25
$$ = NZ$25–40
$$$ = NZ$40 and over

Tel: 04-385 4444
www.sweetmotherskitchen.co.nz
New Orleans-style café and bar
featuring a Cajun and creole menu,
plus Mexican snack food. Gumbo
and blackboard specials are real a
highlight here. **$$**
Taste
2 Ganges Road, Khandallah
Tel: 04-479 8449
Taste is a good example of the type
of relaxed restaurant that features
dishes reflecting New Zealand's
diverse cultural influences. Dinner
bookings are essential. **$$$**
The Tasting Room
2 Courtenay Place
Tel: 04-384 1159
www.thetastingroom.co.nz
In the heart of the entertainment
district, this gastro-pub specialises in
traditional pub fare with a tasty twist,
matched to a wide range of beers. **$$**
Wholly Bagels & Pizza
Corner Willis and Bond streets
Tel: 04-472 2336

www.whollybagels.co.nz
Bagels made fresh daily using locally
sourced ingredients. Boiled and
baked in traditional New York style
using no preservatives or additives.
Coffee and pizzas are also sold here,
but the bagels are the drawcard. **$**
Zibibbo
25–29 Taranaki Street
Tel: 04-385 6650
www.zibibbo.co.nz
A family-run restaurant serving food
inspired by Italy and Spain. **$$$**

Outside Wellington
Café Bloom
284 Dry River Road, Martinborough
Tel: 06-306 9165
www.bloomrestaurant.co.nz
Located at the Murdoch James
Vineyard Café, Bloom serves a
range of contemporary New Zealand
cuisines, including tasty platters to
share. **$$**
The French Baker
81 Main Street, Greytown

Tel: 06-304 8873
French breads and delicious pastries,
including pain au raison (or chocolat),
plum brioche, almond croissant, and
tarte au citron. **$**
Main Street Deli
88 Main Street, Greytown
Tel: 06-304 9022
Freshly prepared deli fare served
indoors or out. Daily 8am–5pm. **$**
Salute
83 Main Street, Greytown
Tel: 06-304 9825
www.salute.net.nz
Tapas and pizzas are served with fine
wines that can be enjoyed next to a
blazing log fire on chilly Wairarapa
winter nights, or, come balmy summer
afternoons, alfresco under shady
oaks. **$$**
Wild Oats Café
127 High Street, Carterton
Tel: 06-379 5580
www.wildoatscafe.co.nz
A great range of fresh-from-the-oven
bakery items and sweet treats. **$**

SOUTH ISLAND

Nelson and Marlborough

Blenheim
Highfield Estate
Brookby Road, Omaka Valley
Tel: 03-572 9244
www.highfield.co.nz
Vineyard restaurant specialising in
matching fresh local produce with its
own wines. **$$**
Hotel d'Urville Restaurant
52 Queen Street
Tel: 03-577 9945
www.durville.com
Intimate restaurant set within
a boutique hotel with delicious
contemporary New Zealand cuisine.
It's very popular, so bookings are
recommended. **$$$**
Raupo Café
6 Symons Street
Tel: 03-577 8822
www.raupocafe.co.nz
Open from 7.30am until late, Raupo
Café is well known for its delicious
high teas and fresh muffins. An à la
carte and degustation menu is also
available. **$**
Rocco's Italian Restaurant
5 Dobson Street
Tel: 03-578 6940
Run by Italians, this place specialises
in home-made fresh pasta and
prosciutto, as well as New Zealand
seafood, lamb and chicken cooked in
the traditional Italian way. Extensive
menu and wine list. **$$$**

Twelve Trees Vineyard Restaurant
Allan Scott Wines and Estate, Jacksons
Road
Tel: 03-572 7123
www.allanscott.com
A winery restaurant with a menu that
perfectly showcases Allan Scott's
full-bodied wines. Gorgeous indoor/
outdoor setting, seven minutes out
of town towards the airport. Daily
9am–5pm. **$$**

Kaikoura
The Craypot Café and Bar
70 West End Road
Tel: 03-319 6027
Centrally located, this restaurant has
an open fire, and the varied menu
includes mulled wine, fresh crayfish
and vegetarian options. All-day dining
until late. **$$$**
Donegal House
School House Road
Tel: 03-319 5083
www.donegalhouse.co.nz
Located 3km (2 miles) north of
Kaikoura, this acclaimed Irish pub has
an excellent restaurant serving fresh
local seafood; seafood chowder and
the local rib-eye steak are specialities.
Good local wine selection, and, of
course, Guinness on tap. **$$**
Hislops Café
33 Beach Road, Kaikoura
Tel: 03-319 6971
www.hislops-wholefoods.co.nz
A very popular organic and whole food

café where much of the produce used is
grown on the family farm. Stoneground
bread is baked here daily. **$**

Nelson
Boat Shed Café
350 Wakefield Quay
Tel: 03-546 9783
www.boatshedcafe.co.nz
A very pleasant and popular
restaurant, with views across the
water and imaginative seafood
dishes. Open 10am until late.
Booking is essential. **$$$**
**Café in the Vineyard at Waimea
Estate**
59 Appleby Highway, Hope
Tel: 03-544 4963
www.cafeinthevineyard.co.nz
Pacific cuisine served in an ambient
vineyard setting. Open 10am–5pm
daily. **$$**
The Smokehouse
Shed Three, Mapua Wharf, Mapua
Tel: 03-540 2280
www.smokehouse.co.nz
A unique smokehouse and café that
uses the freshest local seafood.
Here you can pick up fish, poultry,
meat and vegetables, delicately hot-
smoked on site using a traditional
brick kiln and manuka shavings. **$$**

Picton and the Sounds
Le Café
14–26 London Quay, Picton
Tel: 03-573 5588

www.lecafepicton.co.nz
Great location on the waterfront, with an excellent menu featuring seasonal local produce and, wherever possible, organic fare. Over 50 wines, beers and a selection of cigars. **$$–$$$**

Café Cortado
30 London Quay
Tel: 03-573 5630
www.cortado.co.nz
Contemporary New Zealand food with an emphasis on seafood. Open from 8am until late. Great location. **$$**

Takaka
Dangerous Kitchen
46 Commercial Street
Tel: 03-525 8686
Bakes it own range of breads, including organic, and serves brick-oven gourmet pizzas. Always packed with locals. **$**

Christchurch and Surroundings

Akaroa
Ma Maison Restaurant and Bar
2 Rue Jolie
Tel: 03-304 7668
www.mamaison.co.nz
Waterfront location, with quality food and a good wine list. Open 10.30am until late. **$$**

The Trading Rooms Restaurant and Pantry
71 Beach Road
Tel: 03-304 7656
www.thetradingrooms.co.nz
In a stunning waterfront location. The lunch menu is great value. Try the Akaroa blue cod battered in Stella Artois and served with chips, home-made mushy peas and tartare sauce. Delicious! **$$**

Vangionis Trattoria
40F Rue Lavaud
Tel: 03-304 7714
www.vangionis.co.nz
The wide-ranging menu here includes fresh seafood and real Italian-style pizza, plus a blackboard menu that changes daily. Open from 5pm. **$$$**

Christchurch
After the Red Verandah
Corner Tancred and Worcester streets
Tel: 03-381 1109
www.utrv.co.nz
The owners of 'Under the Red Verandah' smartly rebranded and opened as 'After the Red Verandah' following the February 2011 earthquake. They serve popular all-day breakfasts, and excellent espresso, salads, risottos, organic house breads, sandwiches, muffins and cakes. **$**

Bealey's Speights Alehouse
Bealey Avenue
Tel: 03-366 9958
www.bealeysalehouse.co.nz
Stylish alehouse serving delicious Southern fare with dishes ranging from blue cod and chips through to slow-cooked lamb shanks, freshly smoked salmon, and beef steaks just how you like them. **$$**

Boatshed Café
Antigua Boat Sheds, Avon River
Tel: 03-366 6768
www.boatsheds.co.nz
Quick toasties, steak sandwiches, lasagne, chips, nachos and burgers are served at this casual café overlooking the Avon River. They also make up picnic baskets to enjoy in the park. **$**

Chopsticks Restaurant
376 Ilam Road, Fendalton
Tel: 03-351 2618
This restaurant is busy most nights of the week with locals who come for its delicious and inexpensive Chinese menu rather than its surrounds. **$**

Cook'n With Gas
23 Worcester Boulevard
Tel: 03-377 9166
www.cooknwithgas.co.nz
The atmosphere is casual but the food is seriously good in this converted villa opposite the site of the Arts Centre. Canterbury ingredients and New Zealand heritage foods feature on the menu. There's also a good selection of boutique beers. The Astro Lounge offers outdoor dining. **$$$**

Cup Café
Corner Hackthorne and Dyers Pass roads
Tel: 03-332 1270
The food is good and the view is probably the best in Christchurch, taking in the whole city. Well worth the drive. **$**

Five Star Vietnamese
Fendaltown Village Mall
Tel: 03-351 7178
If you have a huge appetite, this is the place to go but be sure to make a booking first as this place is always humming. If you enjoy seafood try the house speciality – salt and pepper squid. **$$**

Honeypot Café
458 Colombo Street
Tel: 03-366 5853
www.honeypotcafe.co.nz
Casual eatery serving full meals, as well as sandwiches and pizza. Great desserts and coffee too. **$$**

The Lakes Restaurant
1 Clearwater Avenue, Harewood
Tel: 03-360 1002
www.peppers.co.nz/clearwater
Located near the airport at the renowned

Peppers Clearwater Golf Resort, this contemporary restaurant overlooks a small private lake and is open for breakfast, lunch and dinner. **$$$**

Lone Star
116 Northlands Mall, Papanui
Tel: 03-352 6653
www.lonestar.co.nz
Hearty pub fare served in a relaxed family atmosphere. **$$**

Misceo Café and Bar
Corner Ilam and Clyde roads
Tel: 03-351 8011
A family-friendly eatery serving pizza, pasta and flatbreads. Booking ahead is recommended. **$–$$**

Native Garden Café at Untouched World
155 Roydvale Avenue, Burnside
Tel: 03-357 9499
www.untouchedworld.com
Located near the airport, this popular café serves fresh organic fare ordered from a blackboard which changes with the seasons. **$**

Tiffany's Restaurant
95 Oxford Terrace
Tel: 03-379 1350
www.tiffanys.co.nz
Fine wines, first-rate regional cuisine and top-class service are on offer here. Tiffany's has a picturesque riverside location, but is still close to the centre of town. Their alfresco lunches are recommended. **$$$**

Tutto Bene
192 Papanui Road, Merivale
Tel: 03-355 4744
www.tuttobene.co.nz
An authentic Italian restaurant and pizzeria, favoured by locals, and owned and operated by a well-established Italian family. Also has a take-out menu. **$$**

Canterbury

Aoraki Mount Cook National Park
The Old Mountaineers Café, Bar and Restaurant
Aoraki Mount Cook Village, next to the DOC Visitor Centre
Tel: 03-435 1890
www.mtcook.com/restaurant/
Sir Edmund Hillary is one of the mountaineers this café is named after. The extensive menu covers just about everything, from towering mountain burgers and steaks to

PRICE CATEGORIES

Price categories are per person for dinner, including service and tax:
$ = NZ$15–25
$$ = NZ$25–40
$$$ = NZ$40 and over

chicken and apple crumble, and focuses on fresh, organic food. Of note are the house speciality pork sausages named after the late Sir Ed. **$$**

The Panorama Room
Inside the Hermitage Hotel
Tel: 0800-686 800
www.hermitage.co.nz
Outstanding views, particularly at sunset. The Panorama Room is where Executive Chef Kane Bambery creates world-class cuisine. It is well worth splashing out to dine here, but bookings are absolutely essential; remember to ask for a window seat. **$$$**

Darfield
Terrace Café and Bar
20 Main South Terrace
Tel: 03-318 7303
www.terracecafe.co.nz
Seasonal menu featuring locally reared meat such as Canterbury lamb and local salmon. **$$**

Hanmer Springs
Hot Springs Hotel
2 Fraser Close
Tel: 03-315 7799
This is a friendly pub with a bistro menu. **$$**
Malabar Restaurant and Cocktail Bar
5 Conical Hill Road
Tel: 03-315 7745
www.malabar.co.nz
The finest Asian and Indian cuisine with an excellent selection of local wines. Reservations are essential. **$$**

Lake Tekapo
Pepe's Pizza
Shopping Mall 3, SH8
Tel: 03-680 6677
In a niche of its own among the many fine-dining establishments along Tekapo's ridge, Pepe's Pizza has a great atmosphere with fireside dining and a cosy bar, and incredibly good pizza. The Smoked Salmon Siesta – thin-crust pizza topped with smoked salmon, onion, baby spinach and mild wasabi sauce – as well as Vinnie's Venison, Grandma's smoked chicken and the vegetarian Vintage Cheese pizza, are especially recommended. **$$**
Reflections Restaurant
At the Lake Tekapo Scenic Resort, Main Highway
Tel: 03-680 6234
www.reflectionsrestaurant.co.nz
Fresh local produce including salmon and venison are on the menu here, accompanied by spectacular mountain and lake views. **$$$**

Methven
The Last Post
116 Main Street
Tel: 03-302 8259
www.thelastpostrestaurant.co.nz
Modern Kiwi-style menu with some European and Asian influence. Hearty lunches, dinners and snacks. Dinner booking recommended. **$$**

The West Coast

Fox Glacier
Café Neve
Main Road
Tel: 03-751 0110
A consistently good and long-running café/restaurant serving a variety of cuisine, including award-winning beef and lamb, seafood, venison and gourmet pizza. Also a good selection of pasta dishes and salads. Indoor and alfresco (summer only) dining. **$–$$**
High Peaks Bar and Restaurant
163 Cook Flat Road
Tel: 03-751 0131
www.highpeakshotel.co.nz
The place to sample authentic west-coast cuisine: the venison hotpot is one of its most popular dishes. The restaurant has an extensive wine list; the café has a good selection of bistro meals. Great views from every table. **$$**
Matheson Café
Lake Matheson Road
Tel: 03-751 0878
www.lakematheson.co.nz
Super coffee and deli-style sandwiches, cakes, savouries and salads. À la carte evening menu. Great location to view sunset over the glaciers and Mount Cook. Easy access to Lake Matheson walkway. **$**
The Salmon Farm Café (at South Westland Salmon)
SH6 Paringa (south of Fox)
Tel: 03-751 0837
www.salmonfarm.co.nz
Sample freshly hooked farmed salmon (you can catch your own if you wish) and hot-smoked salmon, plus a great selection of home-made cakes and slices. **$$**

Franz Josef Glacier
Alice May Bar & Restaurant
Corner Cowan and Cron streets
Tel: 03-752 0740
One of Franz's top locations, you can expect excellent service and a hearty menu. The venison here is very good. **$**
Blue Ice Café
SH6
Tel: 03-752 0707
The eclectic menu at this long-running West Coast café ranges from Italian and Indian dishes to

New Zealand cuisine, but pizzas are the speciality. Extensive wine list. Upstairs bar with pool table. **$$**
Picnics Bakery
SH6
Tel: 03-752 0667
A great place to stock up your picnic basket with ready-made pies, pastries and pasties. **$**
Priya Indian Restaurant
70 Cron Street
Tel: 03-752 0060
A busy restaurant opposite the Glacier Hot Pools. Authentic Indian and Tandoori cuisine. **$**
The Landing
SH6
Tel: 03-752 0229
www.thelandingbar.co.nz
Good hearty roast pork dinners and steak meals are popular here, along with well-priced burgers, salads and pizza. **$$**

Greymouth
The Smelting House Café
102 MacKay Street
Tel: 03-768 0012
Set in a converted historic west-coast bank building and specialising in home-style food. Mon–Sat 8am–5pm. **$**
Speights Ale House
130 Mawhera Quay
Tel: 03-768 0667
Dishes focus on West Coast fish and game such as wild pork, venison and whitebait. It's also popular for its well-priced steak meals, such as the 300g prime rump. **$$**

Haast
Fantail Café
Corner Mark Road and SH6
Tel: 03-750 0055
Dine in or get a takeaway at this conveniently located café, which serves standard café fare such as fish and chips, pies, vegetarian food and sandwiches. Menu features blue cod when available. Whitebait is a favourite here. Daily 7.30am–5pm. **$**

Hokitika
Bushman's Centre Café
SH6, Pukekura (south of Hokitika)
Tel: 03-755 4144
A popular lunch stop with an amusing menu including 'Roadkill Pies' filled with possum, venison, goat and rabbit meat. Everything is made from scratch daily, including quiche for vegetarians. **$**
Café de Paris
19 Tancred Street
Tel: 03-755 8933
www.cafedeparis.net.nz
Featuring genuine French cooking,

with a fabulous range of mouth-watering desserts in a place that's about as far from Paris as you can possibly get. Open daily for breakfast, lunch and dinner. **$$–$$$**

Stumpers Bar and Café
2 Weld Street
Tel: 03-755 6154
www.stumpers.co.nz
This warm and cosy café offers a wide-ranging menu featuring lamb shanks, fresh pasta, locally caught whitebait (in season) and venison, to name a few. Check out the copper artwork by local artists that adorns the walls. **$$**

Westport
Priya Indian Restaurant
110 Palmerston Street
Tel: 03-789 6255
www.priyaindianrestaurant.co.nz
This is where you can dine upon traditional ethnic Indian and Tandoori dishes with a New Zealand twist, such as the popular whitebait bhajis. **$**

The Townhouse
Corner Cobden and Palmerston streets
Tel: 03-789 7133
A popular local haunt with an upbeat chef and an ever-changing and exciting menu. An unusual but magical combination is the wild venison dish which comes served with parsnip purée, roast grapes, walnuts and feta. **$$**

Queenstown and Otago

Arrowtown
The Millhouse
Millbrook Resort
Tel: 03-441 7000, 8088-800 604
www.millbrook.co.nz
A fine-dining restaurant in a pretty setting at Millbrook Resort. Executive chef Russell Heron has won many recent awards, including the New Zealand Beef and Lamb Awards for Excellence for the past two years running. Open daily from 6pm. Bookings recommended due to popularity. **$$$**

Postmasters Residence
54 Buckingham Street
Tel: 03-442 0991
www.postmasters.co.nz
Award-winning restaurant in a meticulously restored historic house. Superb food, fine wine list and excellent service. Open for lunch and dinner. **$$$**

Gibbston Valley
Gibbston Valley Winery Restaurant
SH6
Tel: 03-442 6910
www.gibbstonvalleynz.com
Superb dining experience – dishes

team perfectly with the wines produced on site. **$$$**

Glenorchy
Glenorchy Hotel & Bar
Mull Street, Glenorchy
Tel: 03-442 9902
www.glenorchynz.com
Rustic fully licensed restaurant open for country-style breakfasts, and lunch and dinner. Sit beside the large stone fireplace during the winter or on the sun-drenched decks during the summer. **$**

Queenstown
The Bathhouse
28 Marine Parade
Tel: 03-442 5625
www.bathhouse.co.nz
An old bathhouse, built in 1911, right on the beach with amazing lake and mountain views. It offers nostalgic indoor and awe-inspiring outdoor dining from an award-winning menu. **$$$**

Botswana Butchery
Archers Cottage, 17 Marine Parade
Tel: 03-442 6994
www.botswanabutchery.co.nz
Cosy, contemporary restaurant with log fires and an extensive lunch and dinner menu. **$$$**

Brazz on the Green
1 Athol Street
Tel: 03-442 4444
www.brazz.co.nz
A steakhouse, bar and grill with a relaxed atmosphere and a wide-ranging menu, which also includes pizzas, salads and tapas. **$$$**

The Bunker
Cow Lane
Tel: 03-441 8030
www.thebunker.co.nz
Small, stylish restaurant serving simple, fresh, modern cuisine. Reservations advised. Daily for dinner. **$$$**

Fergburger
42 Shotover Street
Tel: 03-441 1232
www.fergburger.co.nz
Flavoursome gourmet burgers and fries. **$**

Habebes
Wakatipu Arcade, Rees Street
Tel: 03-442 9861
A favourite with locals for its fresh wraps and yummy vegetarian dishes, including fresh salads. **$**

Joe's Garage
Searle Lane
Tel: 03-442 5282
www.joes.co.nz
All-day breakfast/brunch; this is where the locals hang out with their dogs and kids, and eat real local Kiwi food like mince on toast with free-range eggs. **$**

Lone Star Café and Bar
14 Brecon Street
Tel: 03-442 9995
www.lonestar.co.nz
As the name implies, a Western-style restaurant where the portions are huge and the food is good. **$$**

Minami Jujisei
45 Beach Street
Tel: 03-442 9854
www.minamijujisei.co.nz/
Award-winning traditional Japanese cuisine, mixed with modern influences. Minami Jujisei is a particularly good choice for those who have never tried Japanese food before. **$$$**

Prime Waterfront Restaurant and Bar
2 Rees Street
Tel: 03-442 5288
www.primerestaurant.co.nz
Lakefront restaurant with panoramic views specialising in char-grilled steak and seafood – you can even bring in your own freshly caught trout for the chefs to cook. The wine list features many local Pinot Noirs, and there's an open fire on cold nights. Open daily from 5pm. **$$$**

Roaring Megs Restaurant
53 Shotover Street
Tel: 03-442 9676
www.roaringmegs.co.nz
Set in a gold miner's cottage dating back to the late 1800s, this restaurant specialises in unique South Island fare such as Marlborough hare, wild Fiordland venison, Canterbury duck, and Akaroa salmon. It has won awards for its European/Pacific Rim style of cuisine. Candlelit dining in a relaxed, cosy atmosphere. **$$$**

Solera Vino
25 Beach Street
Tel: 03-442 6082
An attractive place serving French Mediterranean cuisine and a good range of wines. **$$$**

Tatler Restaurant and Bar
5 The Mall
Tel: 03-442 8372
www.tatler.co.nz
Stylish restaurant with a cosy wood interior and lake views from outdoor tables. The extensive drinks list focuses on Central Otago wines and the menu features seasonal, regional specialities. Open daily for brunch and dinner from 10am. **$$$**

PRICE CATEGORIES

Price categories are per person for dinner, including service and tax:
$ = NZ$15–25
$$ = NZ$25–40
$$$ = NZ$40 and over

TRANSPORT
ACCOMMODATION
EATING OUT
ACTIVITIES
A – Z

Wanaka
Café Gusto
1 Lakeside Drive
Tel: 03-443 6639
Daily blackboard specials and lots of vegetarian and gluten-free options. Fresh baking daily. **$**
Creek Café and Bar
2 Dunmore Street
Tel: 03-443 6262
Built on the site of the old 1880 Wanaka jail, this spacious, newly renovated restaurant has an inviting ambience. The open stone fireplace is a draw, as is the tapas menu and wine list. **$–$$**
Kai Whakapai Café and Bar
Lakefront
Tel: 03-443 7795
Easy to find on the edge of Lake Wanaka, this café has panoramic views and prides itself on its freshly baked breads, pies, and a good selection of vegetarian dishes. Daily 8am–9pm. **$**

Dunedin

Dunedin
Bennu Café and Bar
12 Moray Place
Tel: 03-474 5055
www.bennu.co.nz
Brasserie with imaginative Pacific Rim flavours, delicious Mediterranean gourmet pizzas and a selection of great desserts, served amid the stylish decor of the old Savoy building. It is also renowned for its excellent coffee. Late-night lounge bar upstairs. **$$**
Etrusco at the Savoy
8A Moray Place
Tel: 03-477 3737
www.etrusco.co.nz
Located on the first floor of the historic Savoy Building, offering an extensive menu of Tuscan favourites – pasta dishes, thin-crust pizzas, Italian breads and antipasti. Strong Italian coffee, desserts and extensive wine list. **$$**
Ombrellos Kitchen and Bar
10 Clarendon Street
Tel: 03-477 8773
www.ombrellos.com
This restaurant features highly imaginative cuisine in an attractive, wood-panelled interior. Excellent wine list. Open Tue–Sat 10am until late, Sun–Mon10am–3pm. **$$$**
The Palms Restaurant
18 Queens Gardens
Tel: 03-477 6534
www.palmsrestaurant.co.nz
Popular with the locals, this elegant, relaxed restaurant serves up generous portions from a varied

menu. Enjoy lovely views over the Queens Gardens (on summer evenings) from the huge windows of this spacious turn-of-the-century building. Lunch and dinner Mon–Sat. **$$$**
Starfish Café
7/240 Forbury Road, St Clair
Tel: 03-455 5940
www.starfishcafe.co.nz
Within a stone's throw of beautiful St Clair beach, this is a popular café for brunch, lunch or a light meal. **$$**

Oamaru
Whitestone Cheese
3 Torridge Street
Tel: 03-434 8098
www.whitestonecheese.co.nz
Delicious platters featuring Whitestone Cheese, made on site. **$**

Southland

Colac Bay
The Pavilion
188 Colac Foreshore Road
Tel: 03-234 8445
Sample fresh local fare including that good old Southland stable, blue cod and chips. It comes cooked to your liking, battered or egg-washed, with potatoes or chips, salad and home-made tartare. Open Wed–Sun 10am until late. **$–$$**

Invercargill
The Cabbage Tree & Outpost Tavern
379 Dunns Road, Otatara, RD9
Tel: 03-213 1443
www.thecabbagetree.com
A European-inspired restaurant and wine bar with a warm atmosphere (four fireplaces) and mammoth à la carte menu featuring local seafood and produce. **$$**
First in Windsor
72 King Street, Windsor
Tel: 03-217 3905
Located in Invercargill's swish inner-city suburb of Windsor, First is a renowned lunch stop. **$$**
Paddington Arms
220 Bainfield Road
Tel: 03-215 8156
www.paddingtonarms.co.nz
Housed in a rambling old villa, this restaurant specialises in seafood (it's the only restaurant that fillets its own blue cod on site), but also caters amply to meat eaters. Open Tue–Fri from 5pm and Sat–Sun from 11am. **$$**

Milford Sound
Blue Duck Café
SH94
Tel: 03-249 7931

Great water views. Sandwiches and bakery fare by day, pub-style meals by night. **$–$$**

Te Anau
Olive Tree Café
52 Town Centre
Tel: 03-249 8406
www.olivetreecafe.co.nz
An à la carte menu is offered in this pleasant café, open 7am–10pm for breakfast, lunch and dinner. Great coffee. **$–$$**
Redcliff Café and Bar
12 Mokonui Street
Tel: 03-249 7431
Not to be missed, big-city-style cuisine is served in a delightful old cottage, sometimes with live entertainment. Evenings only, from 5pm. Friendly true-blue Kiwi service; highly recommended. **$$$**
Sandfly Café
9 The Lane
Tel: 03-249 9529
Tucked out of sight, this small but popular café does delicious wraps daily, and its cabinet is always bursting with freshly baked sweet treats. This is where the locals come to relax. **$**
La Toscana
108 Town Centre
Tel: 03-249 7756
www.latoscana.co.nz
A true taste of Tuscany in Te Anau, with excellent service. Word from the locals is that the al nonno pasta and cheesecake are divine. **$$**

Stewart Island
Church Hill Restaurant & Oyster Bar
36 Kamahi Road, Oban
Tel: 03-219 1123
www.churchhill.co.nz
Offers à la carte dining with panoramic sea views. Local produce such as blue cod, oysters, mussels, and squid are specialities here. Pasta is home-made daily and if you have a great appetite, consider the rib-eye steak. **$$–$$$**
South Sea Hotel
Foreshore, Oban
Tel: 03-219 1059
www.stewart-island.co.nz
No visit to Stewart Island is complete without dining at the South Seas Hotel, a local watering hole and the best place to sample freshly caught blue cod in crispy beer batter served with chunky fries, thick wedges of lemon and home-made tartare sauce. Crayfish is also on the menu here and mutton-bird tastings are sometimes available in season. **$$–$$$**

ACTIVITIES

THE ARTS, NIGHTLIFE, FESTIVALS, SHOPPING, OUTDOOR AND CHILDREN'S ACTIVITIES

THE ARTS

General

New Zealand's culture comprises a blend of influences, including Maori and Pacific Island, European, Asian, US and Australian. New Zealand performers, film-makers, writers, designers and musicians have made their mark with their own unique style and talent.

Art Galleries: New Zealand has a vibrant contemporary art scene, and most towns have art galleries. Keep an eye out for works by some of the country's leading artists, including Ralph Hotere, Michael Parekowhai, Robyn Kahukiwa, and the late Colin McCahon. The Dunedin Public Art Gallery (www.dunedin.art.museum) is the country's oldest viewing room.

Classical Music and Ballet: The country has three professional symphony orchestras, including the New Zealand Symphony Orchestra (www.nzso.co.nz), and its own professional ballet company, the Royal New Zealand Ballet (www.nzballet.org.nz). A number of contemporary dance companies are operating throughout the country, including Black Grace Dance Company (www.blackgrace.co.nz), The New Zealand Dance Company (www.nzdc.org.nz), Atamira Dance Company (www.atamiradance.co.nz) in Auckland, and Footnote Dance Company (www.footnote.org.nz) in Wellington.

Contemporary Music: The music scene varies from rappers and DJs to jazz musicians and opera singers. It has produced some world-class performers, from Kiri Te Kanawa and Neil Finn (Crowded House), to Pauly Fuemana (OMC) and Jemaine Clement, Bret McKenzie and Rhys Darby of Flight of the Conchords fame. Other Kiwi performers making a name for themselves include Kimbra, Tiki Tane, Gin Wigmore, King Kapisi and Hayley Westenra.

Theatre: Theatre is a thriving industry and New Zealand boasts a number of theatre companies, including Taki Rua in Wellington (www.takirua.co.nz) and the Auckland Theatre Company (www. atc.co.nz), Massive Company (www. massivecompany.co.nz) and Red Leap Theatre (www.redleaptheatre.co.nz) in Auckland. There are venues for live theatre in most towns and cities, and many fine repertory theatre companies throughout the country.

Festivals: Festivals are plentiful, and there are arts festivals in most major New Zealand towns – from Bluff in the South to the Bay of Islands in the North. (See page 355 for listings.)

Film: Movies such as Peter Jackson's *The Hobbit and The Lord of the Rings*, Niki Caro's *Whale Rider*, and the hit cult television series *Xena, Warrior Princess* have established the country's film-makers as some of the best in the world.

Listings: To find local cultural events, check the entertainment pages of provincial and local newspapers. Other useful sources of information found at major newsagents, libraries or online are: *NZ Musician* magazine for modern music (www.nzmusician.co.nz); *Music in New Zealand* for classical (www. musicinnz.com); *Rip it Up* magazine (www.ripitup.co.nz); and the online Groove Guide for pop/rock (www. grooveguide.co.nz).

North Island

Auckland

New Zealand's biggest city is home to several dance and theatre companies, its own arts festival and three theatres: the **Civic, Aotea Centre** and **Sky City Theatre**. The entertainment section of the *New Zealand Herald* is the best source of performance listings. Book for major events through **Ticketek** (Aotea Centre, Aotea Square, Queen Street, tel: 09-307 5000; www.ticketek.co.nz).

Theatre/Dance

The 700-seat **Sky City Theatre**, which opened in 1997 in the Casino Complex (entrance at the corner of Hobson and Wellesley streets, tel: 09-912 6000; www.skycity.co.nz); **Maidment Theatre** (in the university, corner of Princes and Alfred streets, tel: 09-308 2383; www.maidment. auckland.ac.nz), the **Herald Theatre** and **ASB Auditorium** (Aotea Centre complex, tel: 09-357 3355; www. the-edge.co.nz) are three of the most popular venues for drama. The opulent **Civic** (tel: 09-357 3355; www. civictheatre.co.nz) is usually used for touring musicals and shows.

Details of performances at various venues by Auckland's main theatre group, **Auckland Theatre Company**, are available at tel: 09-309 0390; www.atc.co.nz. For the **Auckland Music Theatre Company**, contact tel: 09-361 1000 (www. aucklandmusictheatre.org.nz).

Smaller venues producing more innovative work include **Silo** (Lower Greys Avenue in central Auckland, tel: 09-361 1551; www.silotheatre. co.nz) and **Depot Arts Space** (28 Clarence Street, Devonport, over the Harbour Bridge on the North Shore, tel: 09-963 2331; www.depotartspace.co.nz).

Auckland is also home to the all-male dance company **Black Grace**, featuring some of New Zealand's finest and most respected contemporary dancers (tel: 09-630 0835; www.blackgrace.co.nz).

Hamilton

Hamilton has a variety of entertainment on offer – from arts and film festivals to live theatre, music and dance. National and international touring groups visit Hamilton and play at one of three venues – **Founders Theatre**, the **Clarence Street Theatre** and **The Meteor**; all can be contacted on tel: 07-838 6600, www.hamiltontheatres.co.nz. The Academy of Performing Arts (tel: 07-858 5105; www.waikato.ac.nz/academy), located on the University of Waikato campus, hosts local dance and theatre, including Maori performing arts.

Check out **The Fuel Festival** (www.fuelfest.co.nz), held in Hamilton in June every other year (next held in 2014). The city has an abundance of nightclubs and bars, and some of the top DJs from Auckland often perform here.

Rotorua

The **Civic Theatre** is a popular venue for kapa haka and Maori performing arts, and there are Maori concerts and shows throughout Rotorua. The famous **Opera In The Pa** concerts are held in January at Rotowhio Marae. For more information, contact the **Rotorua i-site Visitor Centre** (tel: 07-348 5179; www.rotoruanz.com).

Tauranga/Mount Maunganui

Tauranga hosts a vast range of events, including jazz festivals, arts festivals and sports marathons. It also has a vibrant nightlife scene, and most bars around the Tauranga and Mount Maunganui region are packed during the weekends. The **Baycourt Theatre** stages a number of exhibitions,

Films

Wellington has more screens per capita than anywhere else in the country, which show mainstream and arthouse, international and local films. There is a highly regarded film festival every year. The **Embassy Theatre** (tel: 04-384 7657; www.deluxe.co.nz), at the end of Courtenay Place, is Wellington's grandest cinema.

festivals and events (tel: 07-577 7189; www.tauranga.govt.nz/baycourt).

Wellington

Wellington has three repertory theatres, a wide range of musical events and numerous music, art and theatre festivals. It's also home to the Royal New Zealand Ballet, New Zealand Symphony Orchestra, New Zealand String Quartet, Chamber Music New Zealand, Wellington Sinfonia and New Zealand Opera. At the end of the year, there are performances by the New Zealand School of Dance and the New Zealand Drama School, Toi Whakaari.

For ticketing details, contact Wellington's Ticketek office at tel: 04-384 3840; www.ticketek.co.nz.

Theatre/Ballet

Bats Theatre, 1 Kent Terrace, tel: 04-802 4175; www.bats.co.nz. This small and cosy venue has the courage to experiment with lesser-known works, which means you can often book tickets at short notice.

Circa Theatre, 1 Taranaki Street, tel: 04-801 7992; www.circa.co.nz. This theatre, managed by the actors themselves, offers stimulating drama in a waterside location, by Te Papa Museum. You can get cheap stand-by tickets an hour before the show.

Downstage Theatre, 2 Courtenay Place, tel: 04-801 6946; www.downstage.co.nz. Located in the restaurant and café district, this professional theatre stages a variety of plays – from modern authors to Shakespeare – plus performances by the leading Maori theatre company, Taki Rua (www.takirua.co.nz).

Royal New Zealand Ballet, 77–87 Courtenay Place, tel: 04-381 9000; www.nzballet.org.nz. The country's principal ballet company was formed in 1953, and is based at the St James Theatre. Tickets from Ticketek, tel: 04-384 3840.

St James Theatre, 77–87 Courtenay Place, tel: 04-802 4060; www.stjames.co.nz. The finest lyric theatre in New Zealand. This restored heritage building is the Wellington venue for opera, ballet and major musical shows. Also the site of the Ticketek box-office agency.

South Island

Christchurch

Christchurch is a fairly laid-back city with many artists and craftspeople. The theatre and concert scene is varied, and events are listed in the

Concert Venues

The main concert and opera venues in Auckland are the modern **Aotea Centre** and the **Town Hall** (Aotea Square, Queen Street, tel: 09-309 2677; www.the-edge.co.nz). There's also the **Bruce Mason Theatre** on the North Shore, which is mostly used for larger productions. For bookings, tel: 09-488 2940; www.bmcentre.co.nz. Smaller, part-time venues include the old theatre complexes in the city centre, which host concerts and shows by international DJs and musicians.

Authentic Maori ceremonies and dances are performed daily at 11am, noon, 1.30pm and 2.30pm in the **Auckland War Memorial Museum** (Auckland Domain, tel: 09-309 0443). Performances last approximately 45 minutes.

Christchurch and Canterbury Visitors' Guide. The Press newspaper also has details of current arts events. Christchurch is also home to the yearly Arts Festival, and the World Buskers Festival.

Theatre

Court Theatre, Bernard Street, Addington, tel: 03-963 0870; www.courttheatre.org.nz. Following the Christchurch earthquake, the Court Theatre has moved into a long-term temporary facility in Addington. Affectionately dubbed 'The Shed' due to its original purpose as a grain storage silo, performances will continue here until a new purpose-built venue is ready.

Isaac Theatre Royal, 145 Gloucester Street, tel: 03-366 6326; www.isaactheatreroyal.co.nz. Built in 1908, this Edwardian-style lyric theatre seats about 1,300 people and hosts concerts, comedy and a range of other events and arts performances. The theatre suffered earthquake damage and is due to reopen in mid-2014.

Concerts

The CBS Arena (55 Jack Hinton Drive, Addington, tel: 03-366 8899; www.convention.co.nz) currently plays host to Christchurch's major musical events. Meanwhile, the city's brand new Convention Centre is under construction and is scheduled to be open in March 2017.

Dunedin

Behind the facades of its once-elegant buildings, Dunedin is still a very youthful town. It is the home of

New Zealand's oldest university, and the large number of students give it a relaxed atmosphere, with plenty of pub music and theatre on offer. Dunedin has a vibrant live-music scene, and a number of excellent New Zealand bands have originated here. The **Fortune Theatre** (231 Stewart Street, tel: 03-477 8323; www.fortune theatre.co.nz), has a particularly good reputation and hosts both local and touring performances. Also the **Globe Theatre** (104 London Street, tel: 03-477 3274; www.globetheatre.org. nz), a Dunedin institution dedicated to bringing the best in classical and modern plays, has regular productions.

NIGHTLIFE

New Zealand's nightlife options can vary considerably, depending on the size of the place you are visiting. In small towns, you will find little more than a humble pub. Pubs are a great New Zealand social institution, and you will seldom find yourself short of conversation or an opinion. In recent years, many city pubs have become more sophisticated, with 'boutique' beer brewed on the premises and brasserie-style food.

The main cities have a variety of cosmopolitan dance clubs with a predominantly young clientele, as well as late-night bars. In Auckland and Wellington, and to a growing extent Christchurch, activity in the bars doesn't peak until after midnight. Auckland, Wellington and Queenstown are busy most nights of the week, while it is a little quieter in Christchurch until Friday and Saturday nights. Queenstown reaches a critical mass at times, such as during the winter festival, when the parties don't seem to stop.

North Island

Auckland

It's hard to escape the buzz of Auckland's nightlife. Walk along

Ticketek Tickets

Most major events can be booked through the national ticketing agency, **Ticketek**. There are more than 200 Ticketek outlets in New Zealand. Contact: **Auckland**, tel: 09-307 5000; **Wellington**, tel: 04-384 3840; **Christchurch**, tel: 03-377 8899; www.ticketek.co.nz.

Ponsonby Road, turn left into K Road, then down Queen Street and through to the viaduct and you'll hear music pulsating from every doorway.

Most clubs have dress codes and you won't get in wearing shorts or gym shoes. Some clubs are discreetly hidden away up staircases or down alleyways, and only the locals know they exist, but follow the music and you're bound to find them. Some of the popular bars include:

Caluzzi Bar and Cabaret, 461–463 Karangahape Road, CBD, tel: 09-357 0778; www.caluzzi.co.nz. For a unique, unforgettable night out with great food, this is the place. Plus a disco, DJs and an interactive show by award-winning drag artistes. NZ$65 for dinner and show.

Cartel, 224 Symonds Street, tel: 09 368 4574; www.cartelbar.co.nz. Housed in the basement of the old Post Office, Cartel is one of Auckland's best-kept secrets. Fine wines, cocktails and single malts.

Clooney, 33 Sales Street, CBD, tel: 09-358 1702; www.clooney. co.nz. Tucked in behind Victoria Park Market, this bar is inside a converted warehouse and has an extensive cocktail list.

Danny Doolans, Viaduct Harbour, 204 Quay Street, CBD, tel: 09-358 2554; www.dannydoolans.co.nz. Popular Irish bar in a good location with lots of old-world charm. Decor even includes a confessional box. Live music every night.

Honey, 5 O'Connell Street, tel: 09 369 5639. DJs play until late every night at this fashion and media haunt. More than 30 types of champagne are on offer, along with champagne cocktails and a range of international beer.

Khuja Lounge, 3rd Floor, 536 Queen Street, tel: 022-018 7844; www.khuja. co.nz. An intimate Havana/Cuban-themed bar hidden away up three flights of stairs. Live bands, vocalists, instrumentalists and local artists performing original compositions, plus the best jazz, soul, funk, Afro-Latino and dance music from around the world. Open Wed–Sat 8pm until late.

Rakinos, Level 1, 35 High Street, CBD, tel: 09-358 3535; www.rakinos.com. Trendy lounge bar with a DJ playing a blend of hip-hop, soul and funk.

The Whiskey, 210 Ponsonby Road, Ponsbony, tel: 09-361 2666. A hip Auckland joint with an extensive cocktail list that leans towards whiskey. Small and dark with candles at every table and low music so you can still hear yourself speak.

The Wine Cellar, St Kevin's Arcade, K Road, tel: 09-377 8293. Cosy bunker-

like space beneath the arcade and the hang-out for creative types who come here to enjoy the unpretentious environment. Live acoustic entertainment Sat–Sun.

Northland

Nightlife is pretty relaxed in Northland, but in most large towns there are plenty of bars and restaurants to choose from. The town of Paihia or the trendy area of the Town Basin in Whangarei are the best places to head for live music and bars.

Rotorua

Pubs/Bars
Henneseys Irish Bar, 1210 Tutanekai Street, tel: 07-343 7901; Mon–Sat 11am until late, Sun noon–1am. Live entertainment on Thursday. Outside seating available. Full bar menu and snacks.

Lava Bar, 1286 Arawa Street, tel: 07-348 8618. Loud and raucous, Lava Bar caters to the young backpacker market. Live music on Friday.

The Pheasant Plucker, Arawa Street, tel: 07-343 7071. Live music every night, ranging from classical jam to jazz, blues and soul, plus rock bands and cover bands. Gourmet pizza every night until midnight.

Pig and Whistle, corner Haupapa and Tutanekai streets, tel: 07-347 3025; www.pigandwhistle.co.nz. Naturally brewed beers, a garden bar with two big screens to watch live sport including rugby, hearty pub meals and live entertainment Thu–Sat.

Taupo

For a town of its size, Taupo has quite a number of bars to while away the evening hours. **Bond Lounge Bar** (tel: 07-377 2434) at 40 Tuwharetoa Street is one of the most popular nightspots. **Finn MacCuhal's** (tel: 07-378 6165; www.finns.co.nz), an Irish bar at the corner of Tuwharetoa and Tongariro streets, is another lively place to down a pint of Guinness. It has live entertainment Thu–Sat and big screens to watch sports matches.

Wellington

Alice, End of Forresters Lane, tel: 04-385 2242; www.whiterabbit.co.nz. Stylish cocktails, a Mad Hatters Tea Party, and lots of crazy creative types can be found here most nights of the week.

Bodega, 101 Ghuznee Street, tel: 04-384 8212; www.bodega.co.nz. Bodega specialises in New Zealand ale, including the local Tuatara beer, and serves the city's only hand-drawn

TRANSPORT

ACCOMMODATION

EATING OUT

ACTIVITIES

A – Z

ales plus 17 different tap beers. Also famous as a venue for live, original New Zealand music.

Boogie Wonderland, 25–29 Courtenay Place, tel: 04-385 2242; www.boogiewonderland.co.nz. Those who love to dance are guaranteed a good night at this authentic disco-pop nightclub. Featuring a Saturday Night Fever dance floor.

Concrete Bar, Level 1, Cable Car Lane, tel: 04-473 7427; www.concretebar.co.nz. Light evening meals and a superb range of cocktails are served in a distinct New York-style atmosphere.

Duke Carvell's Swan Lane Emporium, 6 Swan Lane, tel: 04-385 2240; www.dukecarvells.co.nz. Cool cocktail list, tapas and live music on Saturday nights.

Havana, 32 Wigan Street; tel: 04-384 7039; www.havanabar.co.nz. Open Mon–Sat 3pm until late, with live music most nights and lots of cool cocktails to choose from.

Hummingbird, 22 Courtenay Place, tel: 04-801 6336; www.hummingbird. co.nz. This is a stylish café and bar in a great location, and it attracts a more mature crowd than some of the other establishments along Courtenay Place.

Motel Bar, Forresters Lane, tel: 04-384 9084; www.motelbar.co.nz. Stuck in the 1970s – at least tunes-wise – more vinyl is played at this discreet cocktail lounge than anywhere else in New Zealand. Rather than just one cocktail list, Motel has several according to different themes and eras, which are constantly rotated.

Welsh Dragon Bar, Middle of the Road, Cambridge Terrace, tel: 04-385 6566; www.welshdragonbar.co.nz. This has been compared to the best pubs in Ireland for atmosphere, yet it is Welsh – the only one in NZ – complete with Welsh beer and owners. Live music three nights a week; there's a piano for impromptu performances.

South Island

Christchurch

On Fridays and Saturdays, nearly all pubs have live bands performing.

Cargo Bar, 359 Lincoln Road, tel: 03-338 9016; www.cargobar. co.nz. Cargo Bar was the first of the new 'Shipping Container' bars that popped up around Christchurch post-earthquake. A cool place to catch up for a quiet drink.

Dark Room Bar, 336 St Asaph Street, tel: 03-974 2425; www.darkroombar. co.nz. A pumping new post-quake venue with live music playing most

nights of the week.

The Dux Live, 363 Lincoln Road, Addington, tel: 03-366 6919; www. duxlive.co.nz. The Dux lives on post-quake at its new location in Addington, with a variety of live music booked weekly. Check the website for an up-to-date listing.

The Johnny Cash Bar within the **Lone Star** restaurant, on the corner Waimairie and Riccarton Roads (tel: 03-943 9434) is a comfortable place to meet for a casual beer.

Speights Ale House at Bealeys Hotel, 263 Bealey Avenue, tel: 03-379 8660; www.bealeyshotel.co.nz. Owned by an ex-All Black, Tane Norton, this is a good place to rub shoulders with locals.

Queenstown

Queenstown has plenty of superb bars and nightclubs that are often packed with international travellers and backpackers as well as local skiers and adventurers.

Bardeaux, Eureka Arcade, off The Mall, tel: 03-442 8284; www. goodgroup.co.nz. Sumptuous surroundings with comfy leather armchairs, extensive wine and cocktails list, plus a huge open fireplace make this a very popular spot for locals and tourists alike. Best to dress smart.

The Boiler Room, Steamer Wharf, tel: 03-441 8066; www.theboilerroomnz. com. A groovy cocktail bar with friendly bar staff. Leather loungers and music from the 1970s, '80s and '90s. Frequented by locals and visiting New Zealanders, this is the place to see and be seen, particularly if you have a penchant for dancing on tables.

Minus 5 Ice Bar, Beach Street; tel: 03-442 6050; www.minus5icebar. com. Chill out in a bar totally crafted from ice. The walls, furniture and even the glasses which hold some of the cocktails are totally crafted from the substance. Jackets, gloves and warm footwear are provided.

Pog Mahone's, 14 Rees Street, tel: 03-442 5382; www.pogmahones. co.nz. As Irish as they come in Queenstown. The Guinness flows smoothly, and it packs out when live bands are playing (usually Wed and Sun). Food available.

Searle Lane and Social, 15 Church Street, tel: 03-441 3934. New and groovy bar with good food and wine, and parties which last late into the night.

Surreal, 7 Rees Street, tel: 03-441 8492; www.surrealbar.co.nz. It's a restaurant in the early evening, but as the night comes on, lots of live sounds play here, from house, electro

and hip-hop to live jazz, rock and dub. Great food and service.

Tardis, Cow Lane, tel: 03-441 8397; www.tardisbar.com. Hip-hop every night of the week played by leading DJs. A small venue that fills quickly, so it pays to go early.

The World Bar, Restaurants and Nightclub, 27 Shotover Street, tel: 03-442 6757; www.theworldbar.com. Often filled with backpackers and young adventurers, this is a lively and often very noisy venue renowned for happy hours that go on until late. Live bands often play here.

Wanaka

Like Queenstown, the nightlife and entertainment in Wanaka tend to centre around the après-ski crowd in winter and adventure bunnies in summer. There are plenty of bars and a few nightclubs. Check out the **Slainte Irish Bar**, tel: 03-443 6755, in Lower Helwick Street, open daily from noon. It serves Irish and Kiwi fare, plus a huge variety of New Zealand and Irish beers.

Dunedin

A true university town, Dunedin's nightlife is lively and incorporates a mix of live music and poetry evenings, and is a hothouse for contemporary up-and-coming bands.

The Bog Irish Bar, Corner George and London streets, tel: 03 477 8035; www.thebog.co.nz. Irish tavern with live entertainment seven nights a week.

Craft Bar, 10 The Octagon, tel: 03-470 1426; www.craftbar.co.nz. A vibrant mix of live music and poetry readings; contemporary bands play here. Open until late, with Monteith's beer on tap.

Di Lusso, 117 Stuart Street, tel: 03-477 3885. A live – and loud – acoustic music venue, that stays open until late.

Mornington Tavern, 36 Mailer Street, tel: 03-453 6099; www. morningtontavern.co.nz. A popular sports bar perfect for catching live sports coverage, including rugby, on its huge screens.

Ra Bar, 21 The Octagon, tel: 03-477 6080; www.rabar.co.nz. Regular DJ and live local bands play here Thu–Fri nights. Happy hours are popular here, the times change often so check the website for current times.

Scotia Whisky Bar, 199 Upper Stuart Street, tel: 03-477 7704. A popular bar with over 300 whiskies, plus Emerson's award-winning beer and Bellhaven Scottish ale. Good wine list too.

Stadium Sports Bar, 91 St Andrew Street, tel: 03-477 2029; www.

Sailing in the Hauraki Gulf.

stadiumsportsbar.co.nz. With five huge screens and a good range of New Zealand beer, this is a great place to catch live sports coverage. Live music, karaoke, and poker and quiz nights are regularly held here.

FESTIVALS

January

Auckland

Anniversary Regatta – Annual sailing regatta that celebrates Auckland's birthday (one-day event). www.regatta.org.nz.

ASB Bank Classic – Leading international and national women tennis players battle it out in this annual one-week tournament. www.asbclassic.co.nz.

Auckland Festival – The region's biennial arts festival, presenting performance and arts events from New Zealand and the Pacific. www.aucklandfestival.co.nz.

Heineken Tennis Open – International men's ATP tennis tour that precedes the Australian Open (week-long event). www.heinekenopen.co.nz.

New Zealand Golf Open – New Zealand's official golf championship. An open event that features players from throughout Australasia (three-day event). www.nzopengolf.co.nz.

Christchurch

World Buskers Festival – The world's best street acts converge on Christchurch (10-day event). www.worldbuskersfestival.com.

Wellington

Summercity – A series of small festivals around the city supported by

the local council (two-month event). www.summercity.net.

February

Auckland

Devonport Wine and Food Festival – A two-day food and wine festival that is one of the highlights of the Auckland summer calendar. www.devonportwinefestival.co.nz.

Waiheke Island Wine Festival – An event for wine-lovers showcasing the island's vineyards. Located on Waiheke Island in the Hauraki Gulf (two-day event). www.tourismwaiheke.co.nz.

Blenheim

Marlborough Wine Festival – Gourmet cuisine, local wine, workshops and music make up this extremely popular festival (one-day event). www.wine-marlborough-festival.co.nz.

Canterbury

Coast to Coast – Longest-running multi-sport event in the world. National and international participants run, kayak and cycle 238km (148 miles) from the west coast to Sumner Bay (two-day event). www.coasttocoast.co.nz.

Christchurch

Garden City Festival of Flowers – Helps Christchurch live up to its billing as New Zealand's garden city with abundant floral displays. www.festivalofflowers.co.nz.

Hamilton

Hamilton Gardens Summer Festival A celebration of opera, theatre, concerts and performing arts in a garden setting. www.hamiltongardens.co.nz.

Napier

Art Deco Weekend – This Deco jewel of a town steps back in time en masse. Many Deco landmarks are open to the public on this weekend. www.artdeconapier.com.

Waitangi

Waitangi Day – The signing of the nation's founding document is celebrated in the Treaty House grounds with much pageantry, including a spectacular display of waka (canoes). www.waitangi.net.nz.

Wanganui

Masters Games – The largest multi-sport event in New Zealand (one-week event). Held in Wanganui odd-numbered years and Dunedin even-numbered years. www.nzmg.com.

March

Auckland

Auckland Cup – One of the biggest days in New Zealand for thoroughbred horse racing. www.aucklandcupweek.co.nz.

Hokitika Wild Foods Festival – This festival celebrates such gourmet delights as possum pie, huhu grub sushi, scorpions and the ever-popular euphemism – mountain (or prairie, depending where you come from) oysters. www.wildfoods.co.nz.

Pasifika Festival – The biggest one-day Pacific Island Festival, celebrating Pacific Island cultures with food, crafts, music, theatre, comedy and art. www.aucklandnz.com/pasifika.

Round the Bays – Its moderate distance of 8.6km (5 miles) makes for a high level of participation in this fun-run. www.roundthebays.co.nz.

Ngaruawahia

Ngaruawahia Regatta – The town's location at the meeting point of two rivers makes it the natural site for highly competitive Maori waka (canoe) races. This is an exciting event held annually for more than 100 years. It is also the only time the Turangawaewae Marae is open to the public. www.wakaama.co.nz.

Taupo

Ironman New Zealand – This is the longest endurance triathlon in New Zealand. It is one of the six qualifying races for the Ironman Triathlon World Championships (one-day event). www.ironman.co.nz.

Tauranga

National Jazz Festival – Tauranga's bars and nightclubs come alive with the sounds of jazz during this weekend festival. www.jazz.org.nz.

Waipara

Waipara Wine and Food Festival – Described as the 'biggest little best wine-and-food celebration', this festival features leading wine makers and purveyors of fine food. www.waiparavalleywineandfood.co.nz.

Wairarapa

Golden Shears – The world's premier shearing and wool-handling championships (four-day event) celebrate one of New Zealand's foremost rural industries. www.goldenshears.co.nz.

Wellington

New Zealand Arts Festival – This is unquestionably New Zealand's premier arts festival, featuring national and international acts (four-week event; even-numbered years only). www.festival.co.nz.

April

Arrowtown

Arrowtown Autumn Festival – There's no prettier town in autumn, and local heritage is celebrated with numerous performances, parades and markets. www.arrowtownautumnfestival.org.nz.

Auckland

Auckland Wine and Food Festival – Food event of the year. A unique opportunity for Aucklanders to treat their taste buds to a feast laid on by New Zealand's premier suppliers of cheeses, antipasto, continental meats, wine and premium beer. www.tasteofauckland.co.nz.

Royal Easter Show – Livestock competitions, arts and crafts awards, wine awards and one of the largest equestrian shows in the Southern Hemisphere (one-week event). www.royaleastershow.co.nz.

Waiheke Jazz Festival – First-rate acts in a magnificent setting, and an opportunity to hear quality New Zealand (and overseas) musicians. www.waihekejazz.co.nz.

Bluff

Bluff Oyster and Southland Seafood Festival – The annual celebration of Southland's most precious gourmet delight, with numerous oyster-themed events. www.bluffoysterfest.co.nz.

Christchurch

Montana Christchurch International Jazz Festival – New Zealand's biggest jazz festival, an annual event featuring local and international jazz luminaries. www.jazzfestivalnz.com.

Hamilton

Balloons Over Waikato – A five-day event during which up to 40 hot-air balloons grace the skies over the Waikato landscape. Includes a mass ascension of balloons at sunrise and sunset. The Night Glow event is unforgettable. www.balloonsoverwaikato.co.nz.

Taihape

Gumboot Day – Find out why Taihape is the gumboot capital of the world, as rural New Zealand puts on a light-hearted celebration of itself. www.taihape.co.nz.

Wanaka

Southern Lakes Festival of Colour – Wanaka hosts some of the country's most respected names in art, music, theatre and dance during this biennial celebration. www.festivalofcolour.co.nz.

May

Auckland

New Zealand International Comedy Festival – Comedy festival showcasing the best local, national and international comedians (two-week event). www.laugh.co.nz.

Manawatu

Manawatu International Jazz Festival – Live jazz at various venues throughout Palmerston North (one-week event). www.jazzandblues.co.nz.

June

Queenstown

Queenstown Winter Festival – One of the Southern Hemisphere's biggest and brightest winter parties, in downtown Queenstown. The events range from the zany and hilarious to serious winter sports competitions (two-week event). www.winterfestival.co.nz.

The Waikato

Fuel Festival of New Zealand Theatre – A biennial, three-week national festival of theatre held in Hamilton. www.fuelfest.co.nz.

National Agricultural Field Days – One of the largest agricultural shows in the world, held at Mystery Creek (three-day event). www.fieldays.co.nz.

July

Auckland and Wellington

International Film Festival – Three weeks of movie madness and the year's best films. www.nzff.co.nz.

Volcanic Plateau

The Ruapehu Mountain Mardi Gras – The Ruapehu and Turangi skiing areas of the North Island host a more sedate version of the Queenstown event (see June above). www.ohakune-mardigras.co.nz.

Wanaka

World Heli-Challenge – The annual gathering of the world's leading snowboarders and skiers in the premier helicopter-accessed free-ski and free-ride competition. The two-week event ends with the Wanaka Big Air (free-style ski and snowboard championships). www.worldhelichallenge.com.

August

Northland

Bay of Islands Jazz and Blues Festival – Jazz and blues on the streets and in selected venues in Paihia and Russell during this three-day event that draws both international and national talent. www.jazz-blues.co.nz.

September

Alexandra

Alexandra Blossom Festival – Central Otago celebrates the coming of spring with a parade, sheep-shearing competitions, entertainment and garden tours. www.blossom.co.nz.

Auckland

New Zealand Fashion Week – A showcase of some of New Zealand's best fashion designers, with catwalk shows and a trade exhibition (one-week event). www.nzfashionweek.com.

Hastings

Hastings Blossom Festival – Hawke's Bay is one of the country's leading apple exporters and Hastings is known as the fruit bowl of New Zealand, so the blossoms are outstanding this time of the year. Highlights of this celebration of spring include a huge parade, performances by celebrity artists, concerts and a big fireworks finale. www.visithastings.co.nz.

Wellington

Montana World of Wearable Art Awards – A fashion extravaganza of weird and wonderful designs by national and international designers and artists (three-day event). www.worldofwearableart.com.

Wellington Fashion Festival – The capital kicks off spring in style with fashion shows and in-store promotions (one-week event). www.wfweek.co.nz.

October

Gisborne

Gisborne Wine and Food Festival and International Chardonnay Challenge – The festival brings together a range of Gisborne wines and the culinary expertise of top New Zealand chefs using quality Gisborne produce (one-day event). www.gisbornewine.co.nz.

Hawke's Bay

Hawke's Bay Show – One of Hawke's Bay's biggest events, attracting 60,000 spectators each year. Plenty of attractions, competitions and entertainment, with and without an agricultural bias (two-day event). www.hawkesbayshow.co.nz.

Kaikoura

Kaikoura Seafest – A celebration of the abundance of the ocean and fine wines and foods predominantly from the Kaikoura, Marlborough and North Canterbury regions, with continuous live entertainment. Bookings essential. www.kaikoura.co.nz/seafest.

Nelson

Nelson Arts Festival – An annual two-week showcase of artists from all over New Zealand, with cabaret, music, theatre, comedy and visual art. www.nelsonfestivals.co.nz.

Taranaki

Taranaki Rhododendron Festival – This regional garden festival encompasses over 60 private gardens that are open to the public during the 10-day blooming period for rhododendrons (one-week event). www.rhodo.co.nz.

Tauranga

Tauranga Arts Festival – Street theatre, dance, literature and other performing arts are brought to the fore in this biennial event, which is staged throughout the region (10-day event). www.taurangafestival.co.nz.

Wellington

Wellington International Jazz Festival – One of the country's largest jazz festivals, representing many different kinds of music from New Orleans, swing and fusion to experimental jazz (three-week event). Features legendary musicians. www.jazzfestival.co.nz.

Various Locations

Fiji Day celebrates the anniversary of Fiji's independence, and involves communities throughout the country. A different theme is chosen every year. Call the Fiji High Commission, tel: 04-473 5401, for details.

November

Auckland

Waitakere Pacifica Living Arts Festival – Enjoy fashion shows and participate in creative activities in traditional craft workshops during this cultural celebration of Pacific art, music, crafts and fashion. www.pacificarts.org.

Christchurch

Cup Carnival – The strongly contested New Zealand Trotting and Galloping Cups are just a part of the celebrations that form the Christchurch A&P Show (see below). www.theshow.co.nz.

Royal New Zealand Show – The country's biggest A&P (agriculture and pastoral) show, with a programme of events for all ages (two-day event). www.theshow.co.nz.

Martinborough

Toast Martinborough – A wine, food and music festival that promotes the top-quality wine region of Martinborough. This is a hugely popular festival, so get tickets early (one-day event). www.toastmartinborough.co.nz.

December

Nelson

Nelson Jazz Festival – A variety of local and national jazz bands saturate Nelson with music in a week-long festival. www.nelsonjazzfest.co.nz.

Taranaki

Festival of Lights – New Plymouth's Pukekura Park is beautifully illuminated by lights each December; fluorescent pebble-paths and waterfalls come alight. The festival that is held when the lights are switched on is a one-day event, but the lights stay on for several weeks. www.festivaloflights.co.nz.

Wellington

Summercity – Not a big bash, but a series of small festivals that take place all around the city over two months. www.summercity.net.

SHOPPING

New Zealand offers a wide range of shopping opportunities, from exclusive high-street designer stores in its larger cities to boutique shops, and arts and crafts stores in its smaller towns and villages. If you are seeking quality and/or goods with a creative twist, look out for New Zealand-made products. Products that are manufactured in New Zealand will usually state this clearly on the packaging. These goods are guaranteed to be designed and manufactured in New Zealand; quality workmanship is a given.

What to Buy

Sheepskin

With more than 45 million sheep, it comes as no surprise that sheepskin and woollen products are on sale everywhere in New Zealand. You are unlikely to find cheaper sheepskin clothing anywhere in the world, and the colour and variety of items make them ideal gifts or souvenirs. Many shops stock a huge range of coats and jackets made from sheepskin, possum, deerskin, leather and suede.

Woollens

New Zealand is one of the world's major wool producers, and experienced manufacturers take the raw material right through to quality finished products such as the beautiful possum-merino garments, light, soft and so warm. Hand-knitted, chunky sweaters from naturally dyed wool or mohair are ideal if you are heading back to a northern winter. Innovative wall hangings created from home-spun yarns make another worthwhile purchase.

Woodcarvings

The time-honoured skills involved in Maori carvings have been passed down from one generation to the next. Carvings usually tell stories from mythology and often represent a special relationship with the spirits of

TRANSPORT

ACCOMMODATION

EATING OUT

ACTIVITIES

A – Z

the land. Maori carvings of wood and bone can command high prices.

Greenstone

New Zealand jade, more commonly referred to as greenstone, is a distinctive Kiwi product. The jade, found only on the west coast of the South Island, is worked into jewellery, figurines, ornaments and Maori *tiki*. Factories in the west-coast towns of Greymouth and Hokitika allow visitors to see the jade being worked.

Jewellery

Jewellery made from greenstone and the iridescent *paua* (abalone) shell and bone have been treasured by Maori for centuries. You can buy such ornaments and unique contemporary jewellery from specialised stores.

Jewellery Workshop

Bonz and Stonz, 16 Hamilton Street, Hokitika, tel: 03-755 6504, 0800-214 949; www.bonz-n-stonz.co.nz. Offers a full-day workshop where you can design and carve your own pendants in jade, bone, *paua* and mother-of-pearl shells. Advance bookings essential, especially in the summer months. No previous carving experience is necessary.

Handicrafts

There has been an explosion of handicrafts in recent years – sold by local craftspeople and by shops catering specifically to tourists. Pottery is perhaps the most widely available craft product, though patchwork, quilting, canework, kauri woodware, wooden toys, glassware and leather goods are among the enormous range of crafts available at the major tourist centres.

Sportswear and Outdoor Equipment

New Zealanders love the great outdoors, so it should come as little surprise that they have developed a wide range of hard-wearing clothing and equipment to match tough environmental demands. Warm and rugged farm-wear like Swanndri bush shirts and jackets are popular purchases, while mountaineering equipment, camping gear and backpacks set world standards. Some items have even become fashion success stories, such as the Kathmandu outdoor wear and the Canterbury range of rugby and yachting jerseys.

Contemporary Art

Quality contemporary art, from the conservative to the ground-breaking,

is surprisingly affordable in New Zealand. Artist's prints in particular are well priced and easy to transport. The larger cities have private galleries that usually keep a wide range of artwork in stock.

Designer Clothing

Labels from New Zealand designers, such as World, Karen Walker, Trelise Cooper, Sharon Ng, Sabatini, Nom*D and Zambesi, can be found at boutiques in the principal cities, along with a range of clothing from international designers.

Food and Wine

Processed items like local jams, chutney and honey do not need documentation, and make excellent gifts as they are often attractively packaged. Wine also makes a good purchase, in particular Sauvignon Blanc, Chardonnay and Pinot Noir.

Bookstores

Bearing in mind that New Zealand boasts the highest per capita readership of books and periodicals anywhere in the world, it is well worth paying a visit to some of New Zealand's fine bookshops. Whitcoull's (www.whitcoulls.co.nz) and Paper Plus (www.paperplus.co.nz) are the country's major bookstores (and stationers) and offer a good selection of quality titles. There is a wealth of reading related to New Zealand. Online stores include www.mightyape. co.nz, www.fishpond.co.nz and www. trademe.co.nz, where a search for 'New Zealand author', will bring up a number of books from which to choose. See page 385.

Greenstone necklace.

See page 385.

Where to Shop

North Island

Auckland

Auckland's **Queen Street** is a good place to start, as it has a range of souvenir shops, and from here other interesting shopping streets can be easily reached on foot. Modish **Vulcan Lane**, fashionable **High Street** and the **Chancery** shopping area are home to many chic boutiques and stores of New Zealand designers such as Karen Walker, World, Zambesi and Ricochet. Pauanesia in High Street (www.pauanesia.co.nz) stocks designer jewellery and ornaments from throughout the Pacific, while The Old Customhouse, corner of **Customs and Albert streets** (near the downtown Ferry Building) is the place to go for luxury labels and duty-free shopping.

Make sure you pay a visit to Victoria Park Market (www.victoria-park-market. co.nz), with its distinctive chimney stack on Victoria Street. It's filled with stalls, shops and cafés. On Friday and Saturday the stallholders gather at the Aotea Square Markets outside the Aotea Centre, Queen Street, and offer a variety of Pacific Rim arts and crafts, souvenirs and clothing – some collectable, some forgettable.

At the top of Queen Street is Karangahape Road. 'Karangahape' translates as 'winding ridge of human activity', an apt description of one of Auckland's busiest and oldest commercial streets (not to mention red-light district), where small second-hand clothing, ethnic shops and furniture stores compete for business.

Further afield, the inner-city suburbs of Parnell, Ponsonby and Newmarket also offer a wide choice. Check out the backstreets in Newmarket, where there are many interesting shops, and The Garden Party at 71 Ponsonby Road, Ponsonby (www.thegardenparty.co.nz), which specialises in unique and beautiful gifts made in New Zealand.

Across the harbour, Devonport has a range of boutique stores, including: Art of this World, Shop 1, 1 Queens Parade, tel: 09-446 0926; www.artofthisworld.co.nz, with art and sculpture by New Zealand-based artists; Flagstaff Gallery, 30 Victoria Road, tel: 09-445 1142; www.flagstaff.co.nz, offering contemporary New Zealand art; and Green Planet Enterprises Ltd, 87 Victoria Road, tel: 09-445 7404; www. greenplanet.co.nz, with its high-quality, New Zealand-made eco-friendly merchandise. Also on the North Shore in Birkenhead is the Next Door Gallery at 132 Hinemoa Street, tel: 09-480 9289; www.nextdoorgallery. co.nz, which showcases a collection of contemporary New Zealand creations and is well worth the trip.

For mainstream international brands, head to St Lukes in Mount Albert, Sylvia Park in Mount Wellington, Westfield in Albany, or 277 on Broadway in Newmarket.

Not to be missed is New Zealand's largest street market, the Otara Market (Sat 6am–noon; tel: 09-274 0830), located behind Otara Shopping Centre in the car park between Watford and Newbury streets in South Auckland.

Waikato/Bay of Plenty

There are several major shopping centres in the Bay, from Tauranga to Mount Maunganui's Phoenix Centre, Bayfair and Palm Beach Plaza. A wide range of arts and crafts are on offer in artisans' studios in the colonial-style Village on 17th (www. villageon17.co.nz), on 17th Avenue West in Tauranga. Cambridge is well known for its boutique shopping and authentic New Zealand souvenirs can be purchased from Cambridge Country Store (www.cambridgecountrystore. co.nz) at 92 Victoria Street. The House of Creations in Whitianga (www. houseofcreations.co.nz) also offers a good range of New Zealand-made gifts and souvenirs.

Paihia

Bring home New Zealand-made gifts from The Cabbage Tree shops (tel: 09-402 7318; www.thecabbagetree. co.nz) in Paihia. Choose from merino wool garments, hand-blown glassware, greenstone jewellery and more from its two shops, one in Williams Road, and one in the Maritime Building on the wharf.

Rotorua

With attractive wide streets, Rotorua provides an abundance of shops from clothing and fashion to souvenirs, food and pharmacies. Tutanekai and Hinemoa are the streets to visit, while City Focus Square is within walking distance. There are souvenir shops galore in the city, including **The Jade Factory** in Fenton Street, tel: 07-349 3968; www.mountainjade.co.nz, which showcases quality jade from throughout New Zealand and elsewhere. **The Souvenir Centre**, tel: 07-348 9515; www.thesouvenircentre.co.nz, also in Fenton Street, stocks a wide range of New Zealand arts and crafts.

Russell

The Strand is Russell's premier all-weather retail therapy centre, with everything from fine food to high fashion and gifts.

Warkworth/Matakana

Craft Co-Op @ Sheepworld, 324 SH1, Warkworth, tel: 09-425 7449; www.sheepworld.co.nz, has a dazzling variety of locally produced sheepskin goods and other souvenirs. It also has a good café, open daily 9am–5pm. **Honey Centre**, corner SH1 and Perry Road, Warkworth, tel: 09-425 8003; www.honeycentre.co.nz. Sells all varieties of New Zealand's excellent honey. **Morris and James Pottery and Café**, 48 Tongue Farm Road, Matakana, tel: 09-422 7116; www.morrisandjames. co.nz. This establishment has a devoted following among locals and tourists alike for its brightly coloured pottery.

Wellington

Wellington City is divided into several distinct shopping precincts – **Cuba Quarter** is where you'll find the more alternative, funky stores and second-hand shops. **Lambton Quarter** is home to five shopping centres, including the famous Kirkcaldie & Stains (www.kirkcaldies.co.nz) – the oldest classic department store in New Zealand – while **Willis Quarter** has local designer stores, sports shops and cafés. Wellington has a number of weekend markets. A variety of goods and produce is on offer at the Hill Street Farmers' Market and the Frank Kitts Underground Market on Saturdays, while the Victoria Street Market, Harbourside Market and City Market offer fresh produce on Sundays. For antiques shops, head to the character-filled streets of Wellington's historical district, **Thorndon**. Otherwise, nip over to the **Wairarapa**, where you'll discover amazing wineries and antiques and craft shops located inside beautiful historic houses.

South Island

Arrowtown

The Gold Shop on Buckingham Street makes reasonably priced contemporary jewellery, including lockets, from local natural gold nuggets; www.thegoldshop.co.nz.

Christchurch

Christchurch offers excellent prospects for shopping, and you will find a selection of designer stores, nationwide chain stores, souvenir shops and shopping malls.

Visitors to Christchurch can enjoy one of the most unique shopping experiences in New Zealand, Re:START, an upmarket and brightly coloured shipping container shopping mall and a temporary home for retailers displaced by Christchurch's earthquakes. It sits alongside Ballantyne's, Christchurch's iconic department store, which has re-opened its doors after an extensive refurbishment.

Good shopping centres include Westfield Mall at Riccarton, on Riccarton Road, and Northlands Mall at Papanui, on Main North Road. The Antarctic shop at the International Antarctic Centre opposite Christchurch Airport sells New Zealand-made products with a wintry theme, while Untouched World (www.untouchedworld.com), at 155 Roydvale Road, creates organic easy-care designer outdoor garments for men and women from sustainable and environmentally friendly materials including fine New Zealand machine-washable merino.

The Christchurch Farmers' Market takes place every Saturday 9am–noon on the grounds of Riccarton House (www.riccartonhouse.co.nz), while the former Arts Centre Markets are now held at Ferrymead Heritage Centre (www.ferrymead.org.nz) every weekend.

Dunedin

Shopping in Dunedin is relaxed and unhurried. The main shopping centre is located around the Octagon, and radiates out onto Lower Stuart Street, Princes Street, George Street and St Andrews. There are also a number of suburban centres with good shops at Mornington, The Gardens, Andersons Bay Road and Mosgiel.

Nelson/Marlborough

There are more than 350 full-time artists and craftspeople in the Nelson region, so expect to see plenty of craft shops in the centre of town. The Saturday morning market in Montgomery Square is popular, and there are stalls with everything from arts and crafts to regional produce and gourmet foods. There are also weekend markets in Motueka and Golden Bay. At the Nelson or Motueka information centres you can pick up a map which shows the location of the studios of more than 30 local artists and craftspeople.

Queenstown

Visitors to Queenstown will find

Sailing in the Bay of Plenty.

streets bristling with souvenir shops. To meet demand, Queenstown does not follow normal retail hours – most shops are open seven days a week for extended hours.

Wanaka

Everything you need is within walking distance in Wanaka. You'll find shops selling local arts and crafts, plenty of souvenir shops and such basic amenities as pharmacies, hardware and stationery shops.

West Coast Crafts

For genuine handcrafted South Island *pounamu* (greenstone), check out **Te Waipounamu Maori Heritage Centre**, 27 Sewell Street, Hokitika, tel: 03-755 8304; www.maoriheritage. co.nz, or Kotuku Gallery in Whataroa (6 Main Road; tel: 03-753 4249), where local carver Lou Armstrong has an incredible range of bone, wood and greenstone carvings on display. **Possum People**, at 20 Sewell Street, specialise in making items from possum fur and sheepskins, tel: 03-756 8090; www.possum-nz.com.

OUTDOOR ACTIVITIES

General

New Zealanders love the outdoors, and there are plenty of places to cycle, walk, swim, ski, climb, bungee jump, fish, play golf or go rafting. Because the country has a low population density and spectacular scenery, you are never very far from an outdoor activity, whether it's an organised adventure or a peaceful walk in the bush. The opportunity to participate in so many activities at low cost in some of the world's most beautiful locations is a major tourist draw, and local tourism operators have risen to

the challenge by meeting this demand with a high level of professionalism and, equally important, safety.

Spectator Sports

Watching sport of all descriptions is also easily accessible. Attending an **All Blacks** match is often high on visitors' agendas, although it is worth noting that during the summer season the team is frequently touring overseas, during the Northern Hemisphere's winter. Chances of catching a game are a lot higher during New Zealand's winter. Stadiums are located in all major cities including Eden Park in Auckland, Waikato Stadium in Hamilton, Wellington Regional Stadium, Otago Stadium in Dunedin and Rugby Park in Invercargill. To secure tickets and find out about matches that are being played, visit www.allblacks.co.nz. Information on games and ticketing is posted here, as it becomes available.

Watching regional rugby matches is also popular, and many games and practice matches can be attended free of charge. Join the spectators: New Zealanders will love any interest you show in local sports. Soccer is also undergoing something of a revival, and summer spectator sports that can be attended include cricket (played at the aforementioned regional stadiums), sailing, windsurfing, surfing, motor racing, horse racing, tennis, volleyball and softball. Check local newspapers or visit the local i-site for information on where games are being held.

Land Sports

Abseiling

New Zealand provides numerous opportunities to abseil down cliffs, waterfalls, canyons and some

spectacularly deep holes in the ground. In some cities, it is possible to perform the urban equivalent and rappel down the outside of skyscrapers.

Auckland

AWOL Adventures, Dominion Road, tel: 0800-462 965; www. awoladventures.co.nz. A range of options including a good beginners' abseil, 26 metres (85ft) down a dam.

Waikato

Waitomo Adventures, Waitomo Caves Village, tel: 07-878 7788, www. waitomo.co.nz. Abseiling tours into the Lost World (100-metre/328ft abseil plus dry caving); two trips daily, 4 or 7 hours in duration.

Queenstown

Climbing Queenstown, tel: 03-450 2119; www.climbingqueenstown. co.nz. Climb up the rung-way on Queenstown Hill and abseil back down. Trips depart at 9am and 1.30pm daily.

Ballooning

Ballooning is a wonderful way to see New Zealand's unique landscape. Balloons depart in the early morning, so be prepared to be up at the crack of dawn. On some tours you will get to assist in preparing the balloon for take-off; all will offer a safety briefing before your departure.

Christchurch

Up, Up and Away, tel: 03-381 4600, www.ballooning.co.nz. Traditional ballooning over Christchurch city and the Canterbury Plains. Flight lasts approximately 1 hour and concludes with a celebratory glass of champagne.

Hastings

Early Morning Balloons, 71 Rosser Road, tel: 06-879 4229; www.hotair. co.nz. You'll spend an hour drifting peacefully above Hawke's Bay, with a traditional balloon picnic at the end of the flight.

Methven

Aoraki Balloon Safaris, 121 Main Street, tel: 03-302 8172, 0800-256 837; www.nzballooning.com. Soar aloft for views of Mount Cook and the National Park Mountains, plus a full panorama of the entire Canterbury Plains.

Bungee Jumping/Sky Jumping

Developed in the 1980s by New Zealand adventurers A.J. Hackett and Henry Van Asch, this exhilarating experience of throwing oneself off a high platform with a large rubber-band attached to the ankles has become world-famous. Today, there are several official **A.J. Hackett** bungee-jump sites, and jumps are also offered by other operators.

Auckland

A.J. Hackett Bungy, Curran Street, Westhaven Reserve, tel: 0800-286 4958; www.ajhackett.com. This was the world's first harbour-bridge bungee jump, run by the outfit that originally developed the sport. The latest in adventure technology is used – with a purpose-built jump pod and retrieval system for maximum safety and comfort for the jumpers.

Skyjump, Sky Tower, corner Victoria and Federal streets, tel: 09-368 1835, 0800-759 586; www.skyjump.co.nz. Touting itself as a world-first adventure experience, the 192-metre (630ft) Skyjump is a cable-controlled base jump with great views. Jumpers drop at up to 80kmh (51mph).

Hanmer Springs

Thrillseekers Canyon Adventure Centre, Hanmer Springs, tel: 03-315 7046; www.thrillseekers.co.nz. Located 8 minutes from Hanmer, this one-stop action adventure land has it all – bungee, jet boating, quad biking and river rafting.

Queenstown

Queenstown is the home of bungee jumping, the place where it all began in 1988. The world's first bungee site, the Kawarau Bridge, has evolved into the **Kawarau Bungy Centre**, a busy hub from where A.J. Hackett (tel: 0800-286 495; www.ajhackett.com) operates the Bungy Shop, a café, the **Freefall Wine Bar** and the **Secrets of Bungy Tour**, a behind-the-scenes insight into the bungee phenomenon for those who don't fancy the real deal. This tour leaves hourly and includes the Bungy Theatre and Interactive Zone where you can get a first-hand look at bungee-cord making as well as exclusive access to viewing

Tekapo Tours Star Watching, Main Road, tel: 03-680 6960; www.earthandsky.co.nz. Take advantage of the unusually clear skies in this region to go on one of these spectacular, if sometimes chilly, night-time adventures. Tours depart at 10pm during the summer and 7–8pm during the winter months.

decks where you observe alongside the jump crews.

In addition to the Kawarau Bridge Bungy (adults NZ$180, children 10–15 years NZ$130), A.J. Hackett operates two other bungee sites around Queenstown, The Ledge Bungy (adults NZ$180, children 10–15 years NZ$130) and the Nevis Highwire Bungy (NZ$260 for adults and children), billed as the wildest. A package deal gives the option of all three for NZ$465, or try the Nevis Arc, a 120-metre (787ft) rope swing. This can also be done in tandem (adults NZ$180, tandem NZ$302, children 10–15 years NZ$130).

Taupo

Taupo Bungy, Spa Road, tel: 0800-888 408; www.taupobungy.co.nz. Solo and tandem jumps from above the Waikato River.

Canyoning

A super adrenaline rush, canyoning combines a range of skills, from abseiling and rock climbing to using zip lines to cross canyons.

Waitomo/Waikato

Canyonz, tel: 0800-422 696; www.canyonz.co.nz. Abseil down waterfalls and slide down the natural polished rock chutes of the Blue Canyons or the Sleeping God Canyon. Pick-up available in Auckland and Thames.

Waitomo Adventures, Waitomo Caves Road, tel: 07-878 7788, 0800-924 866; www.waitomo.co.nz. Offers various permutations of abseiling and canyoning into underground holes and down waterfalls.

Wanaka

The Deep Canyoning Company, 99 Ardmore Street, Wanaka, tel: 03-443 7922; www.deepcanyon.co.nz. Experience is not essential although water confidence and reasonable fitness are an advantage when you go

View from Bob's Peak.

canyoning with the Deep Canyoning Company. The season runs from early November until April. Wetsuits and harness are provided, along with comprehensive instruction.

Caving

New Zealand offers some of the most challenging and spectacular caving in the world, although you do not need to be a professional caver to make the most of the underworld. Guided tours range from an easy walk through the caves to as daring a climb as you like, but for the best range of activities head to the Waitomo region.

Te Anau

Real Journeys, Real Journeys Visitor Centre, Lakefront Drive, Te Anau, tel: 03-249 7416, 0800-656 501; www.realjourneys.co.nz. Enjoy a scenic cruise across Lake Te Anau, then venture underground on foot and on a small boat into the glow-worm grotto for a magical sight.

Waitomo

Waitomo Adventures, Waitomo Caves Road, tel: 07-878 7788, 0800-924 866; www.waitomo.co.nz. This adventure company offers a wide variety of cave experiences, from a two-hour black-water journey (floating through caves in the dark), to complex abseiling into underground holes and down waterfalls.

Climbing

Rock climbing has experienced a phenomenal growth in New Zealand. There are now lots of indoor climbing walls in towns and cities, rock-climbing clubs and excellent terrain to discover throughout the country. New Zealand has adopted the Australian 'Ewbank' numerical grading system, which uses a single numerical value to indicate route difficulty. Some of the best rock-climbing areas include

Wharepapa, south of the Waikato, which has more than 700 climbs, and the **Canterbury** area, which has more than 800 climbs.

For more information, contact: Climb New Zealand; www.climb.co.nz.

Aoraki Mount Cook National Park

Alpine Guides, tel: 03-435 1834; www.alpineguides.co.nz. Guided climbs of Aoraki Mount Cook and other peaks during the summer, as well as an intensive mountaineering course.

Queenstown

Climbing Queenstown, Via Ferrata, tel: 03-409 2508; www.climbingqueenstown.com. The Southern Hemisphere's first 'Iron Way' is simply a series of iron rungs, ladders and wires, attached to a mountainside, which enables the inexperienced to duplicate the experience of rock climbing. Rock-climbing and abseiling tours also depart daily at 9am and 1.30pm.

Wharepapa

Bryce's Rockclimbing, 1424 Owairaka Valley Road, Wharepapa, tel: 07-872 2533; www.rockclimb.co.nz. Located between Te Awamutu and Mangakino, **Wharepapa** is one of the best rock-climbing areas in New Zealand, with over 2,500 routes, more than 800 of these within a short, easy walk. There is an equipment store and café on site. Accommodation is also available.

Cycling

New Zealand's windy, rainy weather can sometimes take the pleasure out of cycling, as can the hilly terrain and narrow winding roads crowded with badly driven recreational vehicles. Cycle touring nevertheless offers huge rewards, and some organised tours include a bus to carry your luggage. Mountain bikes are widely available for hire throughout the country. Some of the best places for cycling are in the South Island, in areas such as Central Otago and **Queenstown**. Highlights include the Otago Central Rail Trail (www.otagocentralrailtrail. co.nz), cycling to explore abandoned gold-diggers' villages such as Macetown near Arrowtown, and the roads leading up to the ski resorts, which offer superb lakeland views. Queenstown's latest attraction is the new 110km (68-mile) Queenstown Trail, which connects the Wakatipu Basin, Gibbston Valley, Arrowtown, Lake Hayes and Queenstown Bay. Cyclists can choose to complete the full multi-day ride or spend a day or even an hour exploring the trail.

Auckland

Cycle Auckland, Shop 6, Devonport Wharf, Devonport, tel: 09-445 1189; www.cycleauckland.co.nz. Just a short ferry ride from the CBD, Devonport offers more than 20km (12 miles) of dedicated cycle tracks to explore.

Central Otago

Off the Rails, 32 Charlemont Street, Ranfurly, tel: 0800-633 7245; www.offtherails.co.nz. Guided cycling tours in Central Otago, including the popular Otago Central Rail Trail.

Christchurch

Mountain Bike Adventure Company, 68 Waltham Road, tel: 03-377 5952; www.cyclehire-tours. co.nz. Bike rentals with the choice of a challenging off-road mountain bike track, a gentle scenic cycle, or a ride to Sumner Beach.

New Plymouth

Cycle Inn, 133 Devon Street East, tel: 06-758 7418; www.cycleinn.co.nz. Bicycle hire.

Rotorua

Planet Bike, tel: 07-346 1717; www.planetbike.co.nz. Rotorua has world-class mountain biking in **Whakarewarewa Forest** close to the city centre. Choose from flat, easy rides for first-timers or fast, technical single-track action for the more experienced. Bikes can be hired independently, or you can join a tour. These include a half-day single-track exploration and full-day biking. Equipment, bikes, guides and refreshments are included.

Wellington

Burdans Gate Bike Shed, Muritai Road, Eastbourne; tel: 027-570 0180; www.daysbayboatshed.co.nz. Mountain bikes, pedal boats, rollerblades and scooters are hired from here to explore Eastbourne and the waterfront.

Gliding

One of the best ways to experience flying is in a glider, pulled aloft by a tow plane then set free to glide on air currents before landing back at base. Taupo and Omarama are the most popular places to glide in New Zealand.

Omarama

Glide Omarama, Omarama Airfield, tel: 03-438 9555; www.glideomarama. com. Short valley flights to longer flights exploring the Southern Alps. Two-day introduction training for contests.

Pan for Gold

Goldmine Experience, Main Road, SH25, Thames, tel: 07-868 8514; www.goldmine-experience. co.nz; daily 10am–4pm. In the heart of the gold-mining district, this unique attraction offers gold panning, guided tours underground and through the stamper battery, and a photographic museum.

Taupo

Taupo Gliding Club, Centennial Park, Taupo, tel: 07-378 56276; www.taupoglidingclub.co.nz. High-altitude, long-distance and long-duration flights are available, and there are six gliders to choose from. Instructors teach the basics – from how to stay up, to the intricacies of aerobatics.

Golf

There are around 400 golf courses in New Zealand, with an average green charge of around NZ$15 at smaller clubs, and equipment for hire at low cost; just turn up: you will be sure of a warm welcome.

Some of the finest and priciest courses in New Zealand include Kauri Cliffs (www.kauricliffs.com) and Peppers Carrington Resort (www.carrington.co.nz) in Northland, Millbrook Golf and Country Club (www. millbrook.co.nz) near Arrowtown, and Terrace Downs (www.terracedowns. co.nz) and Clearwater Resort (www. clearwaternz.com) in Christchurch. Other excellent courses, popular with locals, include the following:

Auckland

Akarana Golf Club, 1388 Dominion Road, Mount Roskill, tel: 09-621 0024; www.akaranagolf.co.nz. This course has tree-lined fairways, with bunkers protecting most greens and panoramic views from the clubhouse. **Aviation Country Club of NZ**, Tom Pearce Drive, Auckland International Airport, tel: 09-275 6265; www. aviationgolf.co.nz. Part of this 18-hole course at the airport runs beside the Manukau Harbour. **Muriwai Golf Club**, Muriwai Beach, tel: 09-411 8454; www. muriwaigolfclub.co.nz, is a links course with fantastic views over the west coast and undulating fairways over the natural landscape. **Titirangi Golf Club**, Links Road, New Lynn, tel: 09-827 5749; www.titirangi golf.co.nz. One of New Zealand's top courses, with tight fairways, deep gullies and subtle bunkers set amid exotic trees, native bush and streams.

Hanmer Springs
Hanmer Springs Golf Club, 133 Argelins Road, tel: 03-315 7110; www.hanmersprings.nzgolf.net. A challenging 18-hole course, amid breath-taking mountain scenery.

Paihia
Waitangi Golf Club, Paihia, tel: 09-402 7713; www.waitangigolf. co.nz. One of New Zealand's finest golf courses, with impressive scenery. Ideal as a golfing holiday destination as it's within an hour's drive of Kauri Cliffs and Peppers Carrington Resort.

Queenstown
Millbrook Resort, Malaghans Road, Arrowtown, tel: 03-441 7010; www. millbrook.co.nz. Play a round of golf at the Millbrook Resort's spectacular par-72 championship golf course, which was designed by New Zealand's renowned master golfer, Sir Bob Charles.

Taupo
Wairakei International Golf Course, SH1, Taupo, tel: 07-374 8152; www. wairakeigolfcourse.co.nz. Wairakei International Golf Course has magnificent fairways and large greens with 101 bunkers.

Whitianga
Mercury Bay Golf and Country Club, Golf Road, tel: 07-866 5479; www. mercurybaygolf.co.nz. An 18-hole course north of Thames. Idyllic surroundings, with level walking.

Golf Cross
This intriguing game of golf, played using a small oval ball, was developed by New Zealander Burton Silver. You can try this sport at several locations throughout New Zealand, including Ngawaro near Rotorua, Station Bush in Martinborough, Braemar Station near Lake Pukaki, and Rippon Vineyard in Wanaka. For further information, visit www.golfcross.com.

Hiking
With more than 5 million hectares (12½ million acres) of parks and reserves, New Zealand offers a wealth of walking opportunities, from short day hikes to multi-day tramps. Among these are nine longer routes, known as the **Great Walks**, for which you need a hut pass to use en route. These are obtainable from offices of the Department of Conservation (www.doc. govt.nz), and cost NZ$22–54 for a pass which lasts for the duration of the hike, or NZ$6–18 for a serviced campsite (which has flush toilets, tap water,

kitchen, laundry, hot showers, rubbish collection, picnic tables and some powered pitches). Alternatively, there's the option to purchase a six-month Backcountry Hut Pass ($92 adults, $46 youth) or one-year Backcountry Hut Pass ($122 adults, $61 youth). Youths are those who are under 18 years.

If you don't want to carry your pack, it is best to book a guided walk with a reputable trekking company:
Aoraki Mount Cook National Park, Alpine Guides, tel: 03-435 1834; www.alpineguides.co.nz. Hiking and guided climbs of Aoraki Mount Cook and other peaks.
Discovery Tours, tel: 03-435 0114; www.discoverytours.co.nz. Guided walking tours and heli-hiking tours.

Auckland
The Arataki Park Visitor Centre, Scenic Drive, Titirangi, tel: 09-817 0077. Provides guided walks of varying degrees of difficulty through some of West Auckland's most impressive stands of forest.

Blenheim
Southern Wilderness and Wilderness Guides, tel: 03-545 7544; www.southernwilderness.com. Guided walks (including Heaphy Track) with gourmet food and wine served along the way.

Catlins Coast
Catlins Wildlife Trackers, 5 Mirren Street, Papatowai, RD2 Owaka, tel: 03-415 8613; www.catlins-ecotours.

co.nz. Award-winning multi-day tours filled with wildlife encounters and fascinating historical and ecological commentary.

Central Plateau
Mount Ruapehu Alpine Guides, tel: 07-892 4000; www.mtruapehu.com. Leads hikes to the summit of Mount Ruapehu to see its crater lake during summer months. During the winter leads ski/hiking trips around the mountain.

Fiordland National Park
Kiwi Wilderness Walks, 31 Orawia Road, Tuatapere, tel: 021-359 592; www.nzwalk.com. Multi-day guided walks, including Waitutu Track and Dusky Track.
Mount Aspiring National Park
Adventure South, tel: 03-942 1222; www.advsouth.co.nz. Guided hikes in the Aspiring National Park and further afield, throughout the South Island.
Real Journeys, tel: 03-249 7416; www.realjourneys.co.nz. This company offers a taste of the Milford Track experience on a guided day walk of the track departing from Te Anau.
Ultimate Hikes, tel: 03-450 1940; www.ultimatehikes.co.nz. Multi-day hiking trips including the Milford Track, Routeburn track, Grand Traverse and a wide range of day walks.
Hollyford Track Guided Walks, tel: 03-442 3000; www.hollyfordtrack. co.nz. Guided tours of the Hollyford Track.

Northland
Native Nature Tours, Tipene Road, Towai, tel: 0800-668 873; www.native naturetours.co.nz. Guided day or multi-day eco-cultural walks through private tribal lands. Small groups. An intimate insight into the Maori way of life.

Stewart Island
Kiwi Wilderness Walks, 31 Orawia Road, Tuatapere, tel: 021-359 592; www.nzwalk.com. Multi-day guided walks, including Rakiura Track.
Ulva's Guided Walks, tel: 03-219 1216; www.ulva.co.nz. Guided half-day walks led by Ulva Amos, a descendant of the indigenous people of Stewart Island, and an authority on the area's flora and fauna.

Whangamata
Kiwi Dundee Adventures, Pauanui, Tairua and Whangamata, tel: 07-865 8809; www.kiwidundee.co.nz. Two of New Zealand's foremost guides offer personalised walks, hikes and tours, throughout the North Island.

TRANSPORT

ACCOMMODATION

EATING OUT

ACTIVITIES

A – Z

Horse Riding

Seeing New Zealand on horseback is one of the best ways of experiencing backcountry scenery and gaining an insight into the lives of rural people in New Zealand. Operators throughout the country organise treks, which range from half-day to full-day and overnight trips.

Hurunui
Hurunui Horse Treks, Ribbonwood, Hawarden, tel: 03-314 4500; www. hurunui.co.nz. This company conducts horseback tours through the farmland of North Canterbury.

Lake Tekapo
MacKenzie Alpine Trekking Company, Godley Peaks Road, tel: 0800-628 269; www.maht.co.nz. Horseback treks through the tussock grasslands, glacial lakes and forests of the Mackenzie High Country at Lake Tekapo, with the option for the 'Lake Stroll', a 6–7-day adventure hike over three famous sheep stations to enjoy stunning views of Aoraki Mount Cook. All levels catered for with treks from 1 hour to overnight.

Martinborough
Heavenly Horse Treks, RD2, Martinborough, tel: 06 307 8885; www.heavenlyhorsetreks.co.nz. Rides and overnight treks to suit all abilities depart from Riversdale Station, a working cattle station of some 10,500 acres.
Patuna Farm Adventures, RD1, Martinborough, tel: 06-306 9966; www.patunafarm.co.nz. Horse

rides through rural Martinborough countryside.

New Plymouth
Gumboot Gully, Piko Road, Okoki, tel: 06-752 3467. Rides and overnight excursions with this company range from half-day to week-long treks, including river crossings, old stock routes, native bush tracks, pine forests and high ridge tops with spectacular views and quiet, misty gullies. Overnight treks between November and May, and year-round for day rides.

Palmerston North
Timeless Horse Treks, Gorge Road, Ballance, Pahiatua, tel: 06-376 6157; www.timelesshorsetreks.co.nz. Rides include gentle river trails and challenging hill country and range from 1 hour to 14 days. Campfire cooked meals.

Rotorua
The Farm House, Sunnex Road, tel: 07-332 3771; www.thefarmhouse. co.nz. Hire ponies and horses and ride over 245 hectares (600 acres) of bush-edged farmland.

Taihape
Lazy H Horse Treks, 159 Maukuku Road, RD5, Taihape, tel: 06-388 1144; www.lazyh.co.nz. Short rides and overnight adventures.
River Valley Stables, RD2, Taihape, tel: 06-388 1444; www.rivervalley.co.nz. Amazing personalised horse-riding adventures through breathtakingly beautiful North Island high country.

Te Anau
High Ride Horse Treks and Quad Bike Adventures, Wilderness Road, RD2, tel: 03-280 0552; www.highride. co.nz. Scenic treks through a variety of backcountry terrain. A variety of horses is available to suit all levels of experience, and trained guides provide tuition.

Te Awamutu
Pirongia Clydesdales, RD6, Te Awamutu, tel: 07-871 9711; www. clydesdales.co.nz. Home to several equine stars from *The Lord of the Rings* trilogy. Horse rides and wagon rides are also available.

Warkworth/Matakana
Pakiri Beach Horse Rides, Rahuikiri Road, Pakiri Beach, tel: 09-422 6275; www.horseride-nz.co.nz. Ninety minutes' drive north of Auckland, with rides for all abilities. Daily 1- and 2-hour rides, half- and full-day rides and also multi-day safaris, including a 7-day Great Northern coast-to-coast ride.

Wanaka
Backcountry Saddle Expeditions, Cardrona Valley, tel: 03-443 8151, www.backcountrysaddles.co.nz. Organised horseback day tours of the Cardrona Valley. Appaloosa horses with Western saddles.

Hunting

In New Zealand's earlier colonial days, Europeans introduced many unwanted species, some of which have become pests and are controlled through hunting, a popular rural pastime. Game includes possum, deer, chamois, Himalayan tahr, rabbits, pigs, goats, and, near Waimate in the South Island, wallabies.

Wanganui
Wades Landing Outdoors, 11 Kaiteke Road, Raurium, tel: 07-895 5995; www. whanganui.co.nz. Hunting excursions plus trout fishing and kayaking.

Waimate
Ngahere Game Ranch, 617 Mill Road, RD8, Waimate, tel: 03-689 7809; www.tournz.com. Hunting wallabies in Waimate is something of a local sport, and visitors can take part by teaming up with locals, like Bruce and Mieke Fiett at the Ngahere Game Ranch. Trophy hunts for red stags, elk, fallow buck, goats and boars are also available.

Mountaineering

Before New Zealander Sir Edmund Hillary conquered Everest, he

---

Safety in the National Parks

A few simple precautions will help you enjoy some of the most beautiful scenery in the world. Always check with the local DOC Visitor Centre before you go tramping, as weather conditions can change very rapidly in New Zealand; even in the height of summer it is essential to be well prepared for adverse weather conditions. DOC staff can also provide advice on any natural threats, such as volcanic activity, as well as the availability of accommodation, time considerations, and food supplies required for each hike.

You may get more out of some walks and climbs with the assistance of a guide who knows the area well – guided group walks are available in most areas. The local

i-site information centre will be able to provide further details.

Do not set out on a tramp – long or short – without suitable thermal clothing and footwear. Bring a map, compass, torch, matches and a first-aid kit. Sunblock, sunglasses and a good raincoat are also essential. If required, there are plenty of shops where you can purchase or hire decent gear, including coats, gloves and hats.

For your own safety in case you get lost you should always inform someone else where you're going. On multi-day hikes log your movements at huts en route. Once you're off the beaten track, if you set out in the wrong direction it's extremely easy to get lost, and your hike could become a much longer walk than you'd planned.

practised in the Southern Alps, an area stretching more than 700km (435 miles) and larger than the French, Austrian and Swiss Alps combined. But even if your ambitions are less lofty, you'll find plenty of climbing opportunities in New Zealand. There are numerous mountaineering and climbing clubs, including the New Zealand Alpine Club, which has a strong nationwide membership. Contact: **New Zealand Alpine Club**, Unit 6, 6 Raycroft Street, Opawa, Christchurch, tel: 03-377 7595; www.alpineclub.org.nz.

Aoraki Mount Cook
Alpine Guides, tel: 03-435 1834; www.alpineguides.co.nz. Guided climbs of Aoraki Mount Cook and other peaks during the summer, as well as an intensive mountaineering course and private instruction.

Lake Tekapo
Alpine Recreation Canterbury, 30 Murray Place, tel: 03-680 6736; www.alpinerecreation.com. Climbing courses and guided ascents of major peaks and glaciers.

Wanaka
New Zealand Wild Walks, 99 Ardmore Street, tel: 03-443 9422; www.wildwalks.co.nz. Specialists in climbing in Mount Aspiring National Park. They guide small groups on single-day as well as overnight climbing trips and multi-day glacier treks.

Orienteering
This is a specialist activity, but for those who enjoy negotiating unknown terrain with just a map and a compass, New Zealand is the perfect spot. Its varied, often rugged landscape provides plenty of challenges, and courses cater to a variety of competence levels. There are a lot of clubs located throughout the country; to join a group, check with local information centres for details.

Geocaching has also caught on in New Zealand in a big way. Basically it is a high-tech game of hide and seek and can be combined with hiking, mountain biking and orienteering. For further information, visit www.geocaching.com, which has the largest directory of New Zealand geocache sites.

Paragliding/Parapenting/Hang-Gliding
Parapenting involves unfurling a canopy that lifts you from the ground as you take off down a hill. Once airborne you gain height and drift lazily around the sky. It can be done in tandem with an experienced operator. In hang-gliding, you are strapped to a giant kite (together with the pilot of course!) and literally run off a mountain.

Queenstown
Coronet Peak Tandems, 28 Lake Avenue, Frankton, tel: 0800-467 325; www.tandemparagliding.com. Experienced company offering paragliding and hang-gliding.
Queenstown Paraflights, Queenstown Main Pier, tel: 03-441 2242, 0800-225 520; www.paraflights.co.nz. Take off from a boat on Lake Wakatipu and feel yourself lift gently into the air, to rise up to 200 metres (656ft). Land back on the boat. Minimum age is 3.

Wanaka
Wanaka Paragliding, Wanaka, tel: 0800-359 754; www.wanakaparagliding.co.nz. Wanaka offers New Zealand's highest tandem paragliding (NZ$180). Also has door-to-door Flying Bus Transport service to Treble Cone (NZ$28).

Skydiving/Parachuting
If launching yourself into the air from a mountainside is too passé for you, try jumping from a plane. Tandem skydiving has made this thrill accessible to all. Attached to an experienced skydiver by a special harness, there is little you need to do except follow the instructions and keep control of your fear. The bonus with this thrill is the stunning views offered by the plane ride as you circle above the drop zone. Operators are found throughout the country, but the most popular jumps include Queenstown, Franz Josef and Taupo.

Franz Josef
Skydive Franz, Franz Josef, tel: 03-752 0714, 0800-458 677; www.skydivefranz.co.nz. World-class instructors (including members of the New Zealand freestyle ski-diving team). The company arranges jumps over glaciers, with stunning views of Mount Cook, the Southern Alps and the West Coast.

Queenstown
NZONE The Ultimate Jump, tel: 03-442 5867, 0800-376 796; www.nzone.biz. The tandem jumps are priced variably, depending on whether you jump at 2,743 metres (9,000ft), 3,658 metres (12,000ft) or the ultimate 4,572 metres (15,000ft).

Taupo
Skydive Taupo, tel: 07-378 4662, 0800-586 766; www.skydivetaupo.co.nz. Choose your jump height for stunning scenery of the Central Plateau. The higher you go, the longer it lasts!

Skywire/Sky-swing
A bit tamer than a skydive, Skywire or Sky-swings are basically seats attached to giant swings which are raised extremely high, then let go.

Nelson
Happy Valley Adventures, 194 Cable Bay Road, Nelson, tel: 03-545 0304; www.happyvalleyadventures.co.nz. The Skywire chair at Happy Valley is formed from four racing-car seats, and the ride takes you on an 800-metre (2,625ft) drop with speeds reaching 100kmh (62mph).

Queenstown
Nevis Swing, tel: 0800-286 4958, www.bungy.co.nz. An A.J. Hackett site with a 120-metre (394ft) solo or tandem rope swing.
Shotover Canyon Swing, tel: 03-442 6990; www.canyonswing.co.nz. A 109-metre (358ft) rope swing. You'll free-fall 60 metres (197ft) into the canyon until the ropes pendulum you in a giant arc (200 metres/656ft) at 150kmh (93mph). Minimum age is 10.

Taupo
Taupo Bungy, tel: 07-377 1135; www.taupobungy.co.nz. Home to the Cliff Hanger, an extreme swing ride reaching speeds of up to 70 kmh (43mph).

Zorbing
The only place to zorb in New Zealand is with **Zorb Rotorua**, Western Road, tel: 07-357 5100; www.zorb.co.nz. This unique sport was invented in New Zealand and involves tumbling, flipping and sliding inside a giant globe as it hurtles downhill at speeds of up to 30kmh (19mph).

Water sports

Diving
Diving in New Zealand's clear waters is an absolute delight, and not surprisingly the country has more divers per head of population than anywhere else in the world. The Poor Knights off the **Northland** coast is rated among the top-ten dives in the world. There are many shipwrecks to explore in the **Marlborough Sounds**, and at Matauri Bay in Northland you'll

TRANSPORT

ACCOMMODATION

EATING OUT

ACTIVITIES

A – Z

find the remains of the anti-nuclear Greenpeace ship, the *Rainbow Warrior*, which was bombed by French agents in 1985.

Marlborough Sounds
Go Dive, Picton, tel: 0800-463 483; www.godive.co.nz. A range of dives, including shipwreck tours.

Paihia/Northland
A to Z Diving, 13-15 Whatuwhiwhi Road, Karikari Peninsula; tel: 09 408 3336; www.atozdiving.co.nz. This is New Zealand's most northern dive school, which offers diving charters and hire equipment at Whatuwhiwhi, in the crystal-clear waters of the Karikari Peninsula.
Dive North, Main Wharf, tel: 09-402 5369; www.divenorth.co.nz. Takes divers to many dive locations in the Bay of Islands, including the wreck of the *Rainbow Warrior*, the Cavalli Islands and Cape Brett.
Paihia Dive, 12 Mako Lane, Paihia, tel: 09-402 7551, 0800-107 551; www.divenz.com. Trips to the *Rainbow Warrior*. Also runs diving courses.
Keri Dive, SH10, RD3, Kerikeri, tel: 09-401 6206; www.keridive.co.nz. Runs daily dive charters to various locations in the Far North including the Cavalli Islands. Wreck dives include the Rainbow Warrior and the HMNZS Canterbury.

Stewart Island
Shark Dive NZ, Oban Wharf, Stewart Island, tel: 0800-742 7569; www. sharkdivenz.com. Full-day tours to view Great White Sharks, the largest predatory fish in the sea, with the option to dive inside a shark cage for an even closer look.

Warkworth/Matakana
Goat Island Dive, 142A Pakiri Road, Leigh, tel: 09-422 6925, 0800-348 369; www.goatislanddive.co.nz. Diving operation and boat charter based at the magnificent Goat Island Marine Reserve.

Whangarei
Dive HQ Whangarei, 41 Clyde Street, Whangarei, tel: 0800-102 102; www. divenow.co.nz. A premier dive-training facility offering a full range of dive training and dives at the Poor Knights Islands.
Dive Tutukaka, Marina Road, Tutukaka RD3, tel: 09-434 3867, 0800-288 882; www.diving.co.nz. Centred on the Poor Knights Islands some 22km (14 miles) off the east coast at Tutukaka near Whangarei, this is rated among the 10 best dive spots in the world. If

you only have time for one dive in New Zealand, this is the place to do it.
Oceanblue Adventures, Tutukaka Marina, Berth A27; tel: 027-480 0459; www.oceanblue.co.nz. Dive trips and extended live-on-board diving trips to a range of dive spots at the Poor Knights Islands Marine Reserve.

Fishing Charters and Guides
From October to April, New Zealand's tranquil waters attract anglers from all over the world. One in four New Zealanders enjoys fishing, but there are plenty of fish to go around. One of the best places for charter fishing is Northland. For trout fishing head to Lake Rotorua in the Nelson Lake District, where guides will help you find brown trout up to 50cm (20ins) in length. **Lake Tarawera**, in the Rotorua region, and **Gore** in Southland are other renowned spots to angle for trout.

Hastings
Jack Trout Fishing Guides, 27 Tainui Drive, Havelock North, tel: 06-877 7642; www.jacktrout.co.nz. Professional guides provide one-on-one fishing at Hawke's Bay, opportunities for all levels, reaching the best spots by helicopter and raft.

Nelson Lakes
John Gendall Fly Fishing, tel: 03-548 7892; www.johngendallflyfishing.com. Experienced guides who will share all their favourite trout-fishing spots.

Northland
Hokianga Express, Opononi Wharf, Opononi, tel: 09-405 8872; www. hokiangaexpress.webs.com. Provides fishing trips on the Hokianga Harbour with all equipment provided.
Major Tom Charters, Russell Wharf, Russell, tel: 09-403 8553; www. majortom.co.nz. A serious fishing boat holding lots of world records for game fish including marlin and tuna. For game fishing, plan for mid-December to mid-May; fishing for grouper, kingfish, sea bass, snapper and saltfly is available year-round.
Oakura, Fish, Dive & Cruise, 207 Oakura Beach Road, Oakura, tel: 0800-625 872, www.fishingtrips. co.nz. Specialises in providing trips to learn how to use bait effectively to catch snapper, kingfish, tuna, shark and marlin.
Wild Bill Sport Fishing Charters, Opua Marina, Opua, tel: 09-402 7085; www.wildbill.co.nz. Operating from the Bay of Islands through to the Three King Islands, Wild Bill offers

big-game fishing, with everything you need provided.

Rotorua
Clearwater Cruises, 537 Spencer Road, Tarawera, tel: 07-345 6688; www.clearwater.co.nz. Trout fishing and other excursions on Lake Tarawera.

Taupo
Central Plateau Fishing Guides, tel: 07-378 8192; www.cpf.net.nz. Trout fishing is famous here in Taupo and guides from Central Plateau Fishing Guides will happily lead you to all their favourite spots. The rainbow trout in Lake Taupo average 2kg (4lb), while the brown trout average 3kg (6lb).
Bryce Curle Fly Fishing Guide, 59 Kahotea Drive, Motuoapa, tel: 07-386 6813; www.brycecurleflyfishing.com. Fly-fishing tuition and professional angling in all of Taupo's lakes, rivers and Central North Island backcountry streams and rivers. Quality tackle, waders, food and refreshments provided.

Tauranga/Mount Maunganui
Mission Charters, Tauranga Bridge Marina, Tauranga, tel: 0274-842 700; www.missioncharters.co.nz. This company organises a range of fishing trips, from single-day excursions to an extended cruise, anchoring in some idyllic bay for the evening. The crew are experienced and these trips are ideal for everyone, from novices to experts.

Whitianga
Waters Edge Charters, Whitianga, tel: 07-866 5760; www. watersedgecharters.co.nz. Experienced skipper Craig Donovan will take you out for a spot of bottom fishing, game fishing, diving or scenic tours, tailored to suit your needs.

Kayaking/Canoeing – Sea and Coastal
With so much water around, both along the coast and on the lakes, this sport is enjoying a veritable boom in New Zealand, particularly in **Marlborough Sounds**, **Abel Tasman National Park**, Northland and Paihia in the **Bay of Islands**. You can hire kayaks for guided or independent tours lasting one or more days.

Abel Tasman National Park
Abel Tasman Kayaks, RD2 Marahau, Motueka, tel: 03-527 8022; www.abel tasmankayaks.co.nz. Half-day, single-day or multi-day guided sea-kayaking trips with camping and boat-stay options.

Wilson's Abel Tasman, 265 High Street, Motueka, tel: 03-528 2022; www.abeltasman.co.nz. Choose from a wide range of one- or multi-day trips, including boat-cruise, walking and sea-kayaking options.

Akaroa

Captain Hectors, Foreshore, Beach Road, Akaroa, tel: 03-304 7866; www.akaroadolphins.co.nz/captain_hector.html. Paddle boats, kayaks, sea kayaks, motorboats, double canoes and rowing boats available.

Dunedin

Wild Earth Adventures, daily by arrangement; tel: 03-489 1951; www.wildearth.co.nz. This company offers sea-kayak tours ranging in duration from a few hours to several days, visiting the royal albatross and fur seal colonies by sea, and taking in a great variety of other wildlife on the way.

Fiordland National Park

Adventure Kayak and Cruise, tel: 03-249 6626; www.fiordland adventure.co.nz. Choose from a range of lake and sea-kayaking experiences.

Hahei

Cathedral Cove Sea Kayaking, 88 Hahei Beach Road, tel: 07-866 3877; www.seakayaktours.co.nz. Organises both half- and full-day tours to Hot Water Beach and Cathedral Cove.

Paihia

Coastal Kayakers, Te Karuwha Parade, Ti Bay, Waitangi, tel: 09-402 8105; www.coastalkayakers.co.nz. There are more than 150 scenic islands to explore by sea kayak. Coastal Kayakers conduct guided tours, from a half-day to three days.

Paparoa National Park

River Kayaking, State Highway 6, Punakaiki, tel: 03-731 1870; www.riverkayaking.co.nz. Rents out kayaks and canoes to explore the limestone gorges of the Pororari River.

Picton and the Sounds

Marlborough Sounds Adventure Company, The Waterfront, Picton, tel: 03-573 8827 or 0800-283 283; www.marlboroughsounds.co.nz. This company organises kayaking, and also conducts walks and bike trials around the 1,500km (930 miles) of bays in the area.

Te Urewera National Park

Lake Waikaremoana Motor Camp, tel: 06-837 3826; www.lake.co.nz. Kayak and fishing equipment rental.

Whanganui River
Blazing Paddles, Piriaka (10km/6 miles south of Taumarunui on SH4), tel: 07-895 5261; www.blazingpaddles.co.nz. Self-guided canoe trips on the river from 1 hour to 5 days, with various canoe options to choose from.
Wades Landing Outdoors, tel: 0800-226 631; www.whanganui.co.nz. Multi-day kayak and canoe trips on the Whanganui River, as well as trout fishing and hunting excursions.
Yeti Tours, tel: 06-385 8197; www.yetitours.co.nz. Experienced operators providing multi-day kayak adventures through the Whanganui National Park.

Kite Surfing

Kite surfing is very popular in New Zealand. Kite surfers ride boards and hold their kite/sail aloft in the breeze. Advanced riders are great to watch on windy days as they perform a series of jumps and flips. For the beginner, inland waterways and harbours provide the best learning conditions. Boards can be hired from trailers parked up at popular beaches throughout the summer.

Auckland

New Zealand Board Store, 5 Raymond Street, Pt Chevalier, tel: 09-815 0683; www.nzboardstore.co.nz. Provides kite-surfing lessons and rents out boards and gear.

Nelson

Kitesurf Nelson, 623 Rocks Road, Tahunanui, tel: 03-548 5958; www.kitesurfnelson.co.nz. Kite-surfing school and hire centre.

Ruakaka/Northland

Ruakaka Kite Sports, 3 Kepa Road, Ruakaka, tel: 021-654 149. Lessons for beginners to advanced.

Rafting/Jet Boating

Wild, untamed rivers and spectacular scenery provide the perfect backdrop for New Zealand's numerous wild-water rafting expeditions.

Jet boats, which are fast, manoeuvrable and skim the surface of the water, were invented by a New Zealand farmer. One of the best places for this activity is Queenstown's **Shotover River** and the **Wairaurahiri River in Fiordland**.

Alternatively, many of New Zealand's rivers are ideally suited to whitewater rafting, and you can enjoy the thrills and spills in an inflatable with up to seven other people.

Other intrepid souls can go black-water rafting through the caves

of Waitomo in the Waikato. You'll discover a labyrinth of dark caves with waterfalls, lit by glow-worms and providing endless fun.

Fiordland National Park

Hump Ridge Jet, Lake Hauroko, tel: 03-225 8174, 0800-270 556; www.wildernessjet.co.nz. An incredible jet-boat ride through the forest from Lake Hauroko in Fiordland National Park to the South Coast.

Haast

Waiatoto River Jet Boat Safaris, The Red Barn, SH6, Haast Junction, tel: 03-750 0780. An eco-jet-boat river safari exploring a remote part of the Southwest World Heritage Area.

Palmerston North

River Valley, Mangahoata Road, Pukeokahu, tel: 06-388 1444; www.rivervalley.co.nz. This location in the Rangitikei River canyon offers New Zealand's premier Grade 5 rafting trip through great rapids such as Fulcrum and Max's Drop. Trips run daily year-round. River Valley offers a variety of other activities, including horse trekking. Accommodation is available.

Queenstown

Shotover Jet, Shotover Jet Beach, Arthurs Point, Queenstown, tel: 03-442 8570; www.shotoverjet.co.nz. One of the best places for jet boating in Queenstown – and all of New Zealand – is the Shotover River. Courtesy shuttle from Queenstown Visitor Centre departs every half-hour.
Dart River Safaris, 27 Shotover Street, tel: 03-442 9992; www.dartriver.co.nz. This company takes you on an 80km (50-mile) safari by jet boat between mountains and glaciers into Mount Aspiring National Park, a World Heritage Area.
Challenge Rafting, The Station, corner of Shotover and Camp streets, tel: 03-442 7318; www.raft.co.nz. Enjoy the thrills and spills of whitewater rafting in an inflatable; some of the most exciting rivers are the Shotover and Kawarau.

Rotorua

Agrojet, Western Road, tel: 07-357 4747; www.agroventures.co.nz. A 450hp 4-metre (13ft) raceboat offers a thrilling ride, accelerating up to 100kmh (62mph) in just four seconds, with no slowing down for corners on a man-made watercourse.
Kaituna Cascades Raft and Kayak Expeditions, Trout Pool Road, Okere Falls, tel: 07-345 4199, 0800-524 886; www.kaitunacascades.co.nz. Offers

single-day and multi-day adventures down the Kaituna, Wairoa, Rangitaiki and Motu rivers. The company has award-winning guides, custom-built rafts and first-class equipment.

Waitomo
Waitomo Adventures, Waitomo Caves Road, tel: 07-878 7788, 0800-924 866; www.waitomo.co.nz. Well-known operator of cave-tubing trips; organises underground adventures of varying difficulty. Some trips involve abseiling (rappelling) and flying fox (zip line) rides.

Wanganui
Bridge to Nowhere Jet Boat Tours, tel: 06-385 4622; www.bridgeto nowheretours.co.nz. Escorted jet-boat tours of the magnificent Whanganui River, with an option to stay overnight at the Bridge to Nowhere Lodge.

Sailing/Cruises
The best conditions for sea sailing occur between October and April. You will find the widest range of sailing boats for one-day and longer trips, with or without a skipper, in the **Bay of Islands**, **Auckland** and the **Marlborough Sounds**.
 Chartering a fully equipped 12-metre (40ft) yacht costs between NZ$2,000 and NZ$3,000 a week, with smaller boats ranging from NZ$120 per day depending on the season. One of the most scenic trips you can make is the 'coastal cruise' along the coast of Auckland into the Bay of Islands. A day's sailing in a group costs around NZ$80–195 per person.

Abel Tasman
Abel Tasman Sailing Adventures, tel: 03-527 8375; www.sailing adventures.co.nz. Charter a yacht or hire a crew and explore the Marlborough Sounds. Alternatively, join a scenic sailing tour.

Aoraki Mount Cook National Park
Glacier Explorers, The Hermitage, Mount Cook, tel: 03-435 1641; www. glacierexplorers.com. Cruise the glacial lake formed by the melting face of New Zealand's largest glacier; touch and taste 500-year-old ice. Guides give an informative commentary.

Auckland
Sail NZ, tel: 03-359 5987, 0800-724 569; www.explorenz.co.nz. Auckland isn't called the City of Sails for nothing and you can take a daily cruise on the former America's Cup New Zealand yachts *NZL 40* and *NZL 41* or join in match racing

from October to April. Sail NZ also offers Dolphin and Whale Safari trips aboard the *Pride of Auckland*, and a 2½-hour dinner cruise on a 15-metre (49ft) yacht around Waitemata Harbour.

Hahei
Glass Bottom Boat, Hahei Beach Road, tel: 07-867 1962; www.glass bottomboatwhitianga.co.nz. Daily adventure boat trips in a glass-bottomed boat to see Hahei Marine Reserve's Cathedral Cove, islands, reefs and sea caves. Snorkel gear is also available for hire.

Nelson Lakes
Rotoiti Water Taxis, tel: 021-702 278; www.rotoitiwatertaxis.co.nz. Takes lake cruises and hires out rowboats.

Paihia
Fullers Bay of Islands, Maritime Building, Paihia Waterfront, tel: 09-402 7421; www.fboi.co.nz. The Bay of Islands is renowned for sailing, and Fullers has luxury cruises, the 90-minute high-speed Excitor Tour to Cape Brett and through the famous Hole in the Rock, plus 'swimming with dolphins' adventures.

Picton and the Sounds
Compass Charters, Unit 1, Commercial Building, Waikawa Marina, tel: 03-573 8332; www. compass-charters.co.nz. Explore the magical Marlborough Sounds on a yacht, runabout or launch.

Queenstown
TSS *Earnslaw*, Lake Wakatipu, tel: 03-442 7500, 0800-656 503; www. realjourneys.co.nz. Departs daily every 2 hours (summer 10am–8pm, winter noon–4pm). This grand, coal-fuelled old lady has graced the waters of Lake Wakatipu since 1912 when she was first used to carry goods to remote settlements. You may opt to visit Walter Peak High Country farm, a working farm, for lunch and a guided horse trek.

Russell
Fullers Russell, The Strand, tel: 09-403 7866; www.fboi.co.nz. The Cape Brett Hole in the Rock cruise includes the eponymous gap, Cape Brett Lighthouse and Grand Cathedral Cave, and includes a stop ashore on Urupukapuka Island.

Te Anau
Adventure Manapouri, 50 View Street, Manapouri, tel: 03-249 8070; www.adventuremanapouri.co.nz. This

company will take you by water taxi to the beginning of the Manapouri Track, only accessible by boat.
Milford Sound Red Boat Cruises, Milford Wharf, Milford Sound, tel: 03-441 1137; www. southerndiscoveries.co.nz. The highlight of a New Zealand holiday for many is a visit to the majestic scenery of Milford Sound, including Mitre Peak, waterfalls and abundant flora and fauna.

Whitianga
Cave Cruzer Adventures, Whitianga Wharf, tel: 07-866 0611; www.cave cruzer.co.nz. You can explore the Coromandel's scenic coastline in an ex-Navy inflatable rescue boat, and head into a sea cave to hear the amazing sound of dolphins and whales calling, plus Maori instrument demonstrations.

Surfing
New Zealand's surrounding coastline ranges from gentle sloping beaches to rocky cliffs. There are excellent surfing conditions throughout the country, from **Raglan** in the North Island to **Dunedin** in the South. Water temperatures vary, and the best waves are usually found in the winter months. A wetsuit is required most of the year, except in Northland – one of the best regions in New Zealand to surf – where surfers can get by with a rash guard shirt from November to May. You'll find clean, barrelling waves on the **east coast** and heavier sets, sometimes as big as 3 metres (10ft), on the **west coast**.
 For daily weather and surf conditions, up-to-date access to satellite images, surf cams and photographs of some of New Zealand's top surfing spots, plus information about contests, surf travel and surf stores around the country, check out: www.surf.co.nz, which gives a daily surf report/forecast.

Auckland
The best surf beaches in Auckland are on the west coast, and include Piha, Maori Bay, Muriwai and Bethells. Keep an eye on serious rips and tidal changes, as this coast is renowned for its danger spots. If unsure, check at the Surf Lifesaving Clubs before entering the water.

Dunedin
For anyone who is brave enough to venture into the freezing cold ocean, Dunedin offers some of the best waves in the country – and there

are 47km (29 miles) of beach within the city boundaries. The popular surf spots include **St Clair**, **St Kilda** and **Brighton**. If you plan to surf in winter, make sure you have a thick wetsuit, hat and booties.

Northland

At the top of the North Island above Auckland, sitting 12 degrees below the Tropic of Capricorn, this region's waters are mild throughout the year, and wetsuits are not required out in the summer. Surf is available at most beaches, however the most popular east-coast surf beaches include Mangawhai Heads, Waipu Cove and Ruakaka, while the west is famous for Shipwreck Bay, near Ahipara, and Baylys Beach.

Waikato

Raglan Beach is a popular resort on Waikato's rugged west coast. The point breaks of Indicators and Manu are the fastest and best surfing spots in Raglan; Whale Bay tends to provide a slower ride.

Swimming/Heated Pools

Franz Josef

Glacier Hot Pools, Cron Street, Franz Josef, tel: 0800-044 044; www. glacierhotpools.co.nz. Daily noon–10pm. Located within easy walking distance of town, these invitingly warm pools are set amid dripping rainforest.

Hanmer Springs

Hanmer Springs Thermal Pools and Spa, Amuri Avenue, tel: 03-315 0000, 0800-442 663; www.hanmersprings. co.nz. These hot mineral pools are set in a garden of giant conifers. Few experiences are more pleasurable than relaxing in the warmth of these open-air pools on a winter's night, watching the snowflakes dissolve silently in the steam.

Swimming Baths

Most towns in New Zealand have community pools, and entrance to these is generally very reasonably priced. There is also bathing in many local lakes, many of which are crystal-clear (if surrounded by native bush), and swimming in the sea. Generally the east coast provides the safest sea swimming, but be sure to look for signs which may indicate rips, and if the beach has a Surf Lifesaving Club, be sure to swim between the flags.

Hastings

Splash Planet, Grove Road, Hastings, tel: 06-873 8033; www.splashplanet. co.nz. This is a fun, family-oriented park, with such amusements as a full-size pirate ship, a castle, thrilling water slides and many more escapes from reality.

Helensville

Aquatic Park Parakai Springs, Parkhurst Road, Parakai, tel: 09-420 8998; www.parakaisprings.com. Enjoy a relaxing soak in the mineral pools, hire a private pool or have fun on the giant water slide. Daily 10am–9pm, until 10pm Fri–Sat.

Rotorua

Polynesian Spa, Lake end of Hinemoa Street, daily 8am–11pm; charge; tel: 07-348 1328; www. polynesianspa.co.nz. There are 31 thermal pools of varying temperatures, each with its own special mineral content.

Tekapo

Alpine Springs and Spa, Tekapo Winter Park, tel: 03-680 6550, 0800-353 3283; www.alpinesprings. co.nz. Fed by underground spring water, there are three pools to choose from, each differently shaped to reflect the local glacier lakes of the region. Heated pathways lead between the pools and the sauna, steam room and plunge pool.

Te Aroha

Te Aroha Mineral Pools, tel: 07-884 8717; www.tearohamineralspas.co.nz. Public and private pools, some in original 19th-century bathhouses. Lovely small-town atmosphere.

Whale/Dolphin/Penguin/Seal Watch

You can get close to whales at **Kaikoura**, on the east coast of the South Island. Here, huge Sperm whales swim barely 1km (½ mile) off the coast between April and June; orcas can also be seen during the summer, and humpbacks put in an appearance during June and July.

In the Bay of Islands, you'll encounter Bottlenose dolphins, orcas and Sperm whales. Some trips also allow you to get into the water to cavort with the dolphins.

Akaroa

Black Cat, 61 Beach Road, tel: 03-304 7641; www.blackcat.co.nz. Two-hour cruises observing fur seals, Blue penguins and the rare Hector's

dolphin. On the swimming tour, you can dive in and swim with the dolphins.

Dunedin

Penguin Place, Harrington Point, tel: 03-478 0286; www.penguinplace. co.nz. Daily tours at 10.15am, 11.45am, 1.15pm, 2.15pm, then every hour at quarter past until 7.15pm. Here, rare Chaplinesque Yellow-eyed penguins strut in the surf and can be observed at close proximity utilising a unique system of hides and tunnels.
Monarch Wildlife Cruises Ltd, tel: 03-477 4276; www.wildlife.co.nz. Unrivalled viewing of albatross, seals and penguins in their natural environment. Explore Taiaroa Head, Otago Harbour and the Peninsula on a one-hour cruise, or a half- or full-day tour.

Kaikoura

Kaikoura is world famous for its whale, dolphin and seal population. Huge sperm whales swim barely a kilometre (½ mile) off the coast between April and June; orcas can also be seen during the summer, and humpbacks put in an appearance during June and July.

The following companies organise trips to see both whales and dolphins; you should book a few days in advance:
Dolphin Encounter, 96 The Esplanade, tel: 03-319 6777, 0800-733 365; www.dolphin.co.nz.
Seal Swim Kaikoura, 58 West End, tel: 03-319 6182, www. sealswimkaikoura.co.nz. Boat and land based seal-snorkelling tours led by experienced guides.
Topspot Sealswims, 22 Deal Street, Kaikoura, tel: 03-319 5540. Slip into a wetsuit and get up close to New Zealand fur seals.
Whale Watch Kaikoura, Railway Station Road, tel: 03-319 6767, 0800-655 121; www.whalewatch.co.nz.
Wings Over Whales, Kaikoura Airfield, tel: 03-319 6580; www. whales.co.nz. Spectacular 30-minute whale-watching flights.

Paihia

Explore NZ, New Zealand Post Building, corner Marsden and Williams roads, tel: 0800-397 587; www.explorenz.co.nz. Runs regular dolphin discovery trips from Paihia and Russell to see Bottlenose dolphins, orcas and sperm whales.

Wellington

Seal Coast Safari, tel: 04-801 6040, 0800-732 527; www.sealcoast.com.

Departs daily at 10am and 1.30pm from the i-site Visitor Centre at the corner of Victoria and Wakefield streets; these boat trips get you up close to Wellington's resident seal colony.

Windsurfing

New Zealand is an ideal place for windsurfing because windless days are few and far between and there are miles of coastline, harbours and lakes in which to enjoy the sport. Windsurfing conditions similar to those of Hawaii can be found in the North Island province of Taranaki. Other good windsurfing destinations include Auckland's Orewa Beach, Mission Bay and Piha Beach (professionals only), **New Plymouth and Makatana Island** near Tauranga, and **Gisborne**. In the South Island, the wind and waves are particularly good at **Kaikoura**, **Whites Bay** (Blenheim), **Pegasus** and **Sumner** bays near Christchurch, and the bays around **Dunedin** and **Cape Foulwind** (Westport).

Those who prefer lakes will find plenty of room at Lake Taupo, the largest in the country, Lake Rotorua or on the Alpine lakes of the South Island. For more information, check out www.winzurf.co.nz, or call into local surf shops.

Auckland

There are plenty of great windsurfing spots in Auckland, including the popular **Point Chevalier** near the city centre, Orewa Beach and Piha Beach. Winds are consistent, but seldom very strong. You can hire from **New Zealand Board Store**, 5 Raymond Street, Point Chevalier, tel: 09-815 0683; www.nzboardstore.co.nz. This company offers windsurfing and kite surfing lessons.

Christchurch

Pegasus and Sumner bays near Christchurch offer good windsurfing and surfing conditions, but the water is freezing, so it is advisable to wear a wetsuit.

Winter Sports

Skiing, Snowboarding and Heli-Skiing

With the spectacular triple peaks of the North Island and the magnificent Alps, which run most of the length of the South Island, New Zealand is one of the world's great skiing destinations.

In winter, Kiwis are magically transformed into 'Skiwis'. Between July and October, as soon as sufficient new snow has accumulated, snow-loving New Zealanders migrate from the water to the mountains. There are 27 peaks higher than 3,000 metres (9,843ft), and another 140 exceeding 2,000 metres (6,562ft), and many of the ski resorts have spectacular views of green valleys and deep blue lakes far below. The snowline is usually at around 1,000 metres (3,300ft), and all the skiing areas are above the tree line. This means there is plenty of space for everyone, and conditions are particularly ideal for the popular sport of snowboarding. Most ski fields have impressive, long runs and a range of slopes from beginner to professional-only. Fields pride themselves on having long vertical drops.

The main ski season runs from July to September, though this is extended at the larger fields by using artificial snow. Typically a day pass costs around NZ$80 for adults. Multi-day passes and season passes are also available and these provide excellent value. Ski gear including boots, skis and poles can be hired for around NZ$60 a day and snowboards and boots for around NZ$50.

Heli-skiing is an affordable luxury in New Zealand: three to five runs a day cost between NZ$645 and NZ$945. There are also week-long private heli-skiing charters, as well as daily heli-skiing packages tailored to your ability.

Ski Centres

The major **ski centres** in the **South Island** are at:
Cardrona: www.cardrona.com
Coronet Peak: www.nzski.com/coronet
Craigieburn: www.craigieburn.co.nz

Skiing on Mount Ruapehu.

Mount Hutt: www.nzski.com/mthutt
Ohau: www.ohau.co.nz
Porter Heights: www.skiporters.co.nz
The Remarkables: www.nzski.com/remarkables
Temple Basin: www.templebasin.co.nz
Treble Cone: www.treblecone.co.nz

The major North Island ski centres are located at Tongariro National Park and around Mount Ruapehu, specifically Whakapapa (National Park or Whakapapa Village) and Turoa (Ohakune): www.MtRuapehu.com.

For more information, look up www.nzski.com and www.snow.co.nz.

Aoraki Mount Cook National Park

Alpine Guides Aoraki, Bowen Drive, Mount Cook, tel: 03-435 1834; www.skithetasman.co.nz or www.alpineguides.co.nz. Tasman Glacier is open for skiing from July to September, but access to its magnificent slopes is only via fixed-winged skiplanes. Be warned that skiing the Tasman can be an expensive affair, although heli-skiing in New Zealand is cheap compared to the US and Europe.

Christchurch

Mount Hutt, **Methven** and **Porter Heights** are a 90-minute drive away from Christchurch. Contact: **Mount Hutt Ski Area**, tel: 03-308 5074; www.nzski.com/mthutt or **Porters Ski Area**, tel: 03-318 4002; www.skiporters.co.nz.

Methven

Methven Heliskiing, Main Street, tel: 03-302 8108; www.methvenheli.co.nz. This company flies skiers by helicopter, deep into the heartland where there are long ski runs through unbeatable scenery.

New Plymouth

Manganui Club Ski Field, tel: 06-759 1119; www.skitaranaki.co.nz.

The Manganui Ski Club on Mount Taranaki welcomes visitors to its ski field and clubrooms.

Queenstown/Wanaka

The best-organised ski centres in the South Island are Cardrona (www.cardrona.co.nz), Treble Cone (www.treblecone.co.nz), Coronet Peak (www.nzski.com/coronet) and The Remarkables (www.nzski.com/remarkables), all close to Queenstown and Wanaka. Visit their websites for more info or contact the visitor centres at Queenstown and Wanaka.

Harris Mountains Heli-Ski offers a range of packages, including private heli-ski charters as well as week-long and daily heli-skiing packages tailored to your skiing ability. Skiers get to explore the vast terrains of the Southern Alps, with its untracked powder, massive peaks, stunning valleys and challenging chutes. The best time for heli-skiing is July to September. Contact: Harris Mountains Heli-Ski, The Station, corner Shotover and Camp streets, Queenstown, tel: 03-442 6722 or 99 Ardmore Street, Wanaka, tel: 03-443 7930 (winter only); www.heliski.co.nz.

Whakapapa Village/National Park

Whakapapa ski area is on the northwestern slopes of Mount Ruapehu and, on a clear day, has spectacular views across central North Island. Skiers either base themselves at Whakapapa Village, a 6km (4-mile) drive via Bruce Road to the foot of the slopes, or at National Park, a strangely named town, 15km (9 miles) to the west.

Turoa ski area is on the southwestern slopes of Ruapehu and has spectacular views out towards Mount Taranaki. A 17km (11-mile) drive up the Mountain Road above Ohakune Village (which has a wide range of accommodation, cafés and restaurants) will take you to the base of the slopes.

Check www.MtRuapehu.com for more information on skiing in these areas.

Ice Hiking/Glacier Walking

Ice hiking (also known as glacier walking) is the art of trying to stay upright while negotiating your way along an icy expanse full of stunning blue crevasses. This activity should certainly not be attempted alone: team up with a professional company which, as well as providing a knowledgeable and safety-conscious guide, will provide all the gear you will require, including crampons to attach

to your hiking boots. Trips are either half- or full-day, with the full day being better to suited to those who are in good shape physically. Heli-hikes transport you quickly to the heart of the action and are suitable for people of all levels of fitness.

Fox Glacier

Fox Glacier Guiding, Main Road, SH6, Franz Josef Glacier, tel: 03-751 0825, 0800-111 6000; www.foxguides.co.nz. This company operates glacier walks, ice climbing and heli-hikes on Fox Glacier. Short hike to reach start point at the glacier's base.

Franz Josef Glacier

Franz Josef Glacier Guides, Main Road, SH6, tel: 03-752 0763, 0800-484 337; www.franzjosefglacier.com. Glacier walks, ice climbing and heli-hikes on Franz Josef Glacier. All trips currently require a helicopter flight to reach the ice as the former track is unstable.

Wanaka

New Zealand Wild Walks, 99 Ardmore Street, tel: 03-443 9422; www.wildwalks.co.nz. This company specialises in climbing in Mount Aspiring National Park and also guides small groups on multi-day glacier treks.

Snow Safety

Be aware that even the most glorious mountain weather can deteriorate very rapidly, so be prepared for the worst conditions.

The NZ MetService provides weather forecasts for mountain areas, daily reports on ski conditions and the latest AA highway reports. Visit www.metservice.co.nz. For up-to-date information from ski areas on snow conditions, snow-cams and operating facilities, check out www.snow.co.nz.

When you're up on a mountain, you need to protect yourself from the elements. If you become cold, don't wait until you are shivering, move to shelter and warm up; if possible, have a hot drink. Remember that children tire more easily than adults. Carry snacks and eat regularly, as skiing and snowboarding are high-energy sports, and drink plenty of fluids. Don't forget lip balm, sunblock and sunglasses or goggles to prevent snow blindness.

Other Outdoor Activities

Four-Wheel-Drive Tours

Four-wheel-drive tours allow visitors to reach the seldom-seen scenery of New Zealand's backcountry with experienced and informative local guides.

Rotorua

Off Road NZ, SH5, tel: 07-332 5748; www.offroadnz.co.nz. This is for those thrill-seekers who like to go very fast and make a lot of noise, especially in self-drive four-wheel-drive vehicles. Open daily 9am–5pm.

Queenstown

Nomad Safaris, 37 Shotover Street, tel: 03-442 6699, 0800-688 222; www.nomadsafaris.co.nz. Tours depart at 8am, 8.15am, 8.30am and 1.30pm and last 4 hours. Various tour options include the spectacular off-road scenery of Middle-earth, Skippers Canyon and Macetown.

Scenic Flights

Scenic flights provide a great way to see New Zealand's landscapes and to get an overview of the area you're exploring. Flights range from relatively cheap to expensive, mostly depending on the size of the aircraft. You can charter your own scenic flight or join others, with prices starting at around NZ$70 and increasing depending on the length of flight.

Aoraki Mount Cook National Park

Aoraki Mount Cook Skiplanes, Mount Cook Airport, SH80, near Aoraki Mount Cook Village, tel: 03-430 8034, 0800-800 702; www.skiplanes.co.nz. Offers scenic flights to view the glaciers up close and the only fixed-wing snow landing in the Southern Alps.

Helicopter Line, tel: 03-435 1801, 0800-650 651; www.helicopter.co.nz. Flights depart from Glentanner and fly directly up to Mount Dark or to any point you choose. Heli-flights can be tailor-made to suit any time frame.

Central Plateau

Mountain Air, SH4, tel: 07-892 2812; www.mountainair.co.nz. Breath-taking scenic views of the mountains of the Tongariro National Park, its many iridescent lakes and the broad sweep of Lake Taupo.

Franz Josef/Fox Glacier

Fox Glacier & Franz Josef Heli Services, SH6, Franz Josef; tel:

TRANSPORT
ACCOMMODATION
EATING OUT
ACTIVITIES
A – Z

03-752 0793; www.scenic-flights.
co.nz. There's no better way to gain
a bird's-eye view of glacier country
than aboard a helicopter with a
glacier landing. A range of flights is
on offer, including the Grand Tour,
which explores both Fox and Franz
Josef Glaciers, then flies around
Mount Cook and Mount Tasman to
the Tasman Glacier before returning
to base.

Paihia

Salt Air, Paihia Waterfront, tel:
09-402 8338, 0800-472 582; www.
saltair.co.nz. Operates light plane
and helicopter flights to scenic spots
in the Bay of Islands and to Cape
Reinga. The latter combines with
a four-wheel drive tour of the sand
dunes at Ninety Mile Beach.

Rotorua

Volcanic Air Safaris, Rotorua City
lakefront, tel: 07-348 9984; www.
volcanicair.co.nz. Floatplane and
helicopter tours of the Rotorua
region and central volcanic plateau,
including Mount Tarawera and White
Island. Costs range from NZ$85 for an
8-minute flight (minimum 4 persons)
over the town area to NZ$800 for
a 3-hour helicopter flight to White
Island.

Marine Volcano Tours

Scrambling inside a volcano is not
everybody's cup of tea, but there
is nowhere else in the world where
a live marine volcano is as easily
accessible as at Whakatane, where
regular tours depart to explore the
fiery – and still active – crater of
White Island.

Whakatane

White Island Tours aboard PeeJay,
15 The Strand East, Whakatane, tel:
07-308 9588, 0800-733 529; www.
whiteisland.co.nz. Experience the
awesome might of a live volcanic
island. To get there, a boat ferries
you across to the island, where you
disembark to see the rusty ruins of
a former sulphur mine, before hiking
across a steaming, hissing crater
floor, to the island's crater lake.

Wildlife and Garden Tours

Wildlife tours provide the opportunity
to view some of New Zealand's
most important wildlife sites with
an experienced guide who provides
informative and in-depth information
on native flora and fauna. Garden tours
provide an insight into this art form,
and here you will see native plants
growing happily beside exotic species.

Franz Josef Glacier

Okarito Nature Tours, Franz Josef,
Whataroa, tel: 03-753 4014; www.
okarito.co.nz. Kayak deep into the
heart of the forest for awesome
Alpine views or to spot some of the 70
bird species in the area, notably the
kotuku (White heron).

White Heron Sanctuary Tours, SH6,
Whataroa, tel: 03-753 4120; www.
whiteherontours.co.nz. Visit New
Zealand's only White heron nesting
colony from late September to March
from hides located at an isolated
nesting site. A jet-boat ride provides
transport there and back.

Hastings

Gannet Safaris Overland,
Summerlee Station, 396 Clifton
Road, Te Awanga, Hastings, tel:
06-875 0888, 0800-427 232;
www.gannetsafaris.co.nz. On these
excursions, you ride in style and
comfort in four-wheel-drive vehicles,
for the unique experience of visiting
the largest mainland colony of
gannets in the world on the rugged
Cape Kidnappers Coast. Tours depart
daily at 9.30am and 1.30pm from
Sept–Apr.

Queenstown

Queenstown Garden Tours, tel:
03-441 3990; www.queenstown
gardentours.co.nz. Tours include at
least three splendid local residential
gardens, chosen according to season,
providing a delightful opportunity to
see New Zealand domestic gardening
at its best. Devonshire tea included.
The Garden Tour can be combined
with a Wine Tour – check details on
their website.

Kiwi and Birdlife Park, Brecon
Street, tel: 03-442 8059; www.
kiwibird.co.nz. Easy walking through
native bush leads to aviaries where
you will see not just *tui*, bellbirds,
fantails and kiwis, but also rare
and endangered birds and the rare
tuatara. Conservation shows daily
at 11am and 3pm, and kiwi-feeding
is held at 10am, noon, 1.30pm
and 4.30pm. Open daily from
9am–6pm.

Stewart Island

Ulva's Guided Walks, tel: 03-219
1216; www.ulva.co.nz. Guided half-day
walks led by Ulva Amos (see listing
page 363).

Te Anau

The Te Anau Wildlife Centre,
Lakefront Drive, Te Anau, tel: 03-249
7924. Focuses on native birds,
including the rare takahe.

Wellington

**Zealandia: The Karori Sanctuary
Experience**, Waiapu Road, tel:
04-920 9200; www.visitzealandia.
com. This wildlife oasis has 35km
(21 miles) of tracks within the 252
hectares (622 acres) of regenerating
forest. There's also a 19th-century
gold mine on the site. Night tours are
also possible.

Skywire/Cable Car/Luge

Skywire is somewhat similar to a
flying fox except you are seated inside
a carriage – it is best not attempted
immediately after lunch! A more
sedate way to enjoy scenery in a
moving carriage is aboard a cable car
or gondola. Attached to a cable, these
travel sedately uphill to a landing
platform, most often with a café/
restaurant or other optional activities
available at the summit, including the
luge, a three-wheeled cart that travels
on a purpose-built track.

Nelson

Happy Valley Adventures, 194 Cable
Bay Road, tel: 03-545 0304; www.
happyvalleyadventures.co.nz. Fifteen
minutes north of Nelson, this Skywire
ride is claimed to be New Zealand's
longest flying fox. Strapped in a four-
seat carriage suspended by a cable
high over native forest, you are flown
over 3km (2 miles) at speeds of up to
100kmh (62mph). Also popular are
the four-wheel bike rides and horse
treks departing from here through
farmland and native forest.

Queenstown

Skyline Gondolas, Brecon Street, tel:
03-441 0101; www.skyline.co.nz; daily
9am until late; charge. After the 790-
metre (2,600ft) climb by cable car,
take a chair-lift ride to reach the start
of the thrilling downhill luge. Minimum
age is 3 for luge rides.

Rotorua

Skyline Gondolas, Fairy Springs Road,
tel: 07-347 0027; www.skyline.co.nz.
Open daily from 8am until late, the
gondola travels 487 metres (1,598ft)
above sea level for panoramic views
of Rotorua City and the surrounding
lakes. At the top is a restaurant, café
and thrilling downhill luge rides.

Island Excursions

The main islands of the Hauraki
Gulf – Rangitoto, Waiheke, Motutapu
and Great Barrier – are accessible by
the fast ferries operated by **Fullers
Cruise Centre** (Ferry Building, 99
Quay Street, Auckland, tel: 09-367
9111; www.fullers.co.nz). Don't

miss the return ferry, as there is no accommodation on some islands, and alternative transport to the mainland is expensive. Tiritiri Matangi Island, an island bird sanctuary, can be reached with 360 Discovery Cruises (tel: 0800-360 3472; www.360discovery.co.nz).

If you wish to bring your car to Great Barrier Island, book with Sea Link, 45 Jellicoe Street, Auckland Viaduct, tel: 09-300 5900, 0800-732 546; www.sealink.co.nz.

Great Barrier Island is also serviced by flights. Contact Great Barrier Airlines, Auckland Domestic Airport Terminal, tel: 09-275 9120, 0800-900 600; www.greatbarrierairlines.co.nz.

Kawau Island and all the islands in the Hauraki Gulf are served by Kawau Water Taxis, Sandspit Wharf, Warkworth, tel: 09-425 8006, 0800-111 616; www.kawauwatertaxis.co.nz.

Stewart Island

Aside from the regular ferry service departing from Bluff, there are numerous local charter outfits, including adventure cruises, diving and fishing excursions, who can provide transport to Stewart Island.

Exploring Antarctica

Not an expedition to be undertaken lightly, an unforgettable journey to one of the world's most remarkable places can be booked and depart from Christchurch.

Heritage Expeditions, 53B Montreal Street, Christchurch, tel: 03-365 3500, 0800-262 8873; www.heritage-expeditions.com. Cruises to Antarctica and the sub-Antarctic Islands – the 'Galapagos of Antarctica' and among the last remaining unspoilt environments in the world. Groups number less than 50, and the emphasis is on getting you on shore as often and for as long as possible.

WINERIES AND TOURS

Scattered throughout the country are New Zealand's vineyards. Call in to sample local wines or join a vineyard tour.

North Island

Auckland Region

Ascension Vineyards and Café, 480 Matakana Road, Matakana, tel: 09-422 9601; www.ascensionvineyard. co.nz. Open for tastings and sales daily 11am–4pm, and excellent food is available in the café.

Auckland Wine Trail Tours, 11 Pentland Avenue, Mount Eden, tel: 09-630 1540; www.winetrailtours.co.nz. Half- and one-day tours of Auckland's premier wine-growing regions.
Babich Wines, Babich Road, Henderson, tel: 09-833 7859; www.babichwines.co.nz. Well-established winery within easy reach of the CBD offering cellar-door sales.
Heron's Flight Vineyards and Café, 49 Sharp Road, Matakana, tel: 09-950 6643; www.heronsflight.co.nz. Daily 11am–5pm, its courtyard café has a great view – and herons to spot if you're lucky.
Hyperion Wines, 188 Tongue Farm Road, Matakana, tel: 09-422 9375; www.hyperion-wines.co.nz. This winery produces mostly Cabernet Sauvignon and Merlot, also Pinot Gris and Chardonnay. Cellar door is open 10am–5pm weekends only.
Kumeu River Vineyard, 550 State Highway 16, Kumeu, tel: 09-412 8415; www.kumeuriver.co.nz. Cellar-door wine tasting Mon–Sat, but note no food is served on site.
Matua Valley Wines, Waikoukou Road, Waimauku, tel: 09-411 8301; www.matua.co.nz. Daily 10am–5pm. In a delightful garden setting, this winery offers cellar-door sales. Cheese platters can be ordered to accompany wine tastings.
Mudbrick Vineyard and Restaurant, Church Bay Road, tel: 09-372 9050; www.mudbrick.co.nz. A popular wine-and-dine location, featuring international cuisine.
Soljans Estate Winery, 366 SH16, Kumeu, tel: 09-412 5858; www.soljans.co.nz. Offers complimentary tastings and a café. Daily 9am–5.30pm.
Te Whau Vineyard, 218 Te Whau Road, Rocky Bay Waiheke Island, tel: 09-372 7191; www.tewhau.com. Breath-taking sea views, superb wine, cellar-door tastings and an award-winning restaurant make Te Whau a must-do for wine-lovers.
Villa Maria Estate, 118 Montgomerie Road, Mangere, tel: 09-255 1777; www.villamaria.co.nz. One of New Zealand's leading and longest-established wineries, near Auckland Airport. Cellar-shop tastings Mon–Fri 9am–6pm, Sat–Sun 9am–4pm, and winery tours depart daily at 11am and 3pm.
Westbrook, 215 Ararimu Valley Road, Waimauku, tel: 09-411 9924; www.westbrook.co.nz. Free tastings in an idyllic country setting. Wide open spaces and complimentary barbecues are provided for picnickers; alternatively cheese and/

or tasting platters can be purchased. There's also a giant chess set and a pétanque court available for visitors' enjoyment.

Gisborne Region

Matawhero Wines, 189 Riverpoint Road, Gisborne, tel: 06-867 6140; www.matawhero.co.nz. Family-owned vineyard with a range of white wines including Chardonnay, Pinot Gris, Viognier, Arneis and Gewürztraminer.
Millton Vineyard, 119 Papatu Road, Manutuke, tel: 06-862 8680; www.millton.co.nz. A certified organic vineyard with an atmospheric tasting room serving outstanding Chardonnay and organic grape juice. Open Mon–Fri 2pm–4pm.

Hawke's Bay Region

Church Road Winery, 150 Church Road, Taradale, tel: 06-844 2053; www.churchroad.co.nz. Working winery offering winery tours, a cellar-door experience, and wine museum on site.
Clearview Estate Winery, 194 Clifton Road, Te Awanga, tel: 06-875 0150; www.clearviewestate.co.nz. Boutique vineyard famous for its Chardonnay and Bordeaux-style reds. Wine tastings and accommodation available.
Craggy Range Vineyard, 253 Waimarama Road, Havelock North, tel: 06-873 0141; www.craggyrange. com. Posh vineyard experience with cellar-door tastings and award-winning cuisine served at its on-site restaurant.
Mission Estate, 198 Church Road, Taradale, tel: 06-845 9350; www.missionestate.co.nz. New Zealand's oldest winery, offering cellar-door tastings and sales, and classy on-site dining.
On Yer Bike Wine Tours, 129 Rosser Road, Hastings, tel: 06-650 4627; www.onyerbikehb.co.nz. Unique one-day cycling tours on level roads calling into the best of Hawke's Bay's vineyards, orchards, boutique farms and olive groves.

Northland Region

Cottle Hill Winery, SH10, Kerikeri, tel: 09-407 5203; www.cottlehill.co.nz. This small family-owned winery offers tastings and platters in a casual and relaxed atmosphere.
Longview Estate Vineyard and Winery, SH1, Otaika, Whangarei, tel: 09-438 7227; www.longviewwines. co.nz. Uses traditional techniques with modern technology to produce individual handcrafted wines with intense fruit flavours.

Marsden Estate Winery and Restaurant, Wiroa Road, Kerikeri, tel: 09-407 9398; www.marsdenestate. co.nz. Original cuisine and wines can be enjoyed in a relaxed courtyard overlooking the lake and vines. Also wine sales, tastings and tours.

Wairarapa/Martinborough

Atarangi, 14 Puruatanga Road, Martinborough, tel: 06-306 9570; www.atarangi.co.nz. Large vineyard and winery producing some of New Zealand's finest Pinot Noir. Cellar door open daily.

Martinborough Wine Tours, tel: 06-306 8032; www. martinboroughwinetours.co.nz. Comprehensive day tours of the Wairarapa wine growing region.

Martinborough Vineyard, Princess Street, Martinborough, tel: 06-306 9955; www.martinborough-vineyard. co.nz. Cellar door opens daily, serving wines crafted from hand-picked grapes.

Te Kairanga, Martins Road, Martinborough, tel: 06-306 9122; www.tkwine.co.nz. A warm welcome is assured at Te Kairanga, where its six vineyards supply the atmospheric tasting room, housed in old settler's cottage, with a selection of award-winning wines including Pinot Noir. Bring a picnic to enjoy between the vines, or select from a range of cheese, crackers and other produce, sold on site.

South Island

Nelson/Marlborough Region

Cloudy Bay, Jacksons Road, Blenheim, tel: 03-520 9140; www.cloudybay.co.nz. One of the best-known wineries, Cloudy Bay produces some of New Zealand's best wines. Offers tastings and sales of the vineyard's current releases, including limited-release wines daily 10am–5pm.

Montana Brancott Winery, SH1, Riverlands, tel: 03-520 6975; www. montana.co.nz. One of New Zealand's largest wineries and an excellent place to begin an exploration of Marlborough vineyards. Wine tours held daily at 11am and 2pm, plus wine tastings at the cellar door, a children's playground and restaurant.

Neudorf Vineyard, 138 Neudorf Road, Upper Moutere, Nelson, tel: 03-543 2643; www.neudorf.co.nz. Incredible wines served in a rustic stable/courtyard setting. Cheese platters are available, or visitors are welcome to bring their own picnics. Open daily 11am–5pm.

Ruby Bay Vineyard, 271 Pomona Road, Ruby Bay, tel: 03-540 3928; www.rubybayvineyard.co.nz. Boutique winery with vineyard accommodation.

Villa Maria Estate, corner Paynters and New Renwick roads, Fairhall, tel: 03-520 8470; www.villamaria. co.nz. Award-winning modern winery in an impressive location, specialising in Pinot Noir and Sauvignon Blanc.

Wairau River Winery, 264 Rapaura Road, Renwick, tel: 03-572 7950; www.wairauriverwines.co.nz. Good food crafted from Marlborough's local produce at the Wairau River Restaurant, and award-winning wines at cellar-door prices.

Waipara Region

Mud House Winery and Café, 780 Glasnevin Road, Waipara, tel: 03-314 6900; www.mudhousewineryandcafe. co.nz. Showcasing the best of Waipara wine, the cellar door and café at Mud House Winery is open daily 10am–5pm.

Pegasus Bay, Stockgrove Road, Waipara, tel: 03-314 6869; www. pegasusbay.com. A completely family-owned and operated vineyard with an ambient tasting room and award-winning restaurant serving delicious platters and lunches.

Central Otago Region

Amisfield Wine Company, 10 Lake Hayes Road, Lake Hayes, tel: 03-442 0556; www.amisfield.co.nz. A wine-tasting experience in a stunning lakeside location 10 minutes from Queenstown.

Black Ridge Vineyard, Conroy's Road, Alexandra, tel: 03-449 2059; www.blackridge.co.nz. Vibrant, full-bodied pinots are a speciality at this unassuming vineyard just a short drive from Alexandra. Cellar door open daily 10am–5pm.

Chard Farm, RD1, Queenstown, tel: 03-442 6110; www.chardfarm.co.nz. Situated on a backcountry byway which used to be part of the main coach link between Queenstown and Cromwell. Cellar door open daily 10am–5pm.

Gibbston Valley Wines, SH6, Gibbston, tel: 03-442 6910; www. gvwines.co.nz. Award-winning winery in stunning location. The wine tour is not to be missed. Very impressive wine cave.

Peregrine Wines, 2127 Kawarau Gorge Road, Queenstown, tel: 03-442 4000; www.peregrinewines. co.nz. Pinot Noir specialists with a vineyard in rugged mountain country in Gibbston Valley.

CHILDREN'S ACTIVITIES

Not all tourist attractions are suitable for children, and if you are travelling with children you will need to factor this into your travel plans. Fortunately, from restaurants to parklands, New Zealand is well equipped to cope with the wide-ranging needs of kids and provides a magnitude of entertainment – particularly outdoors – for all ages, just about everywhere you travel.

While all restaurants will be able to provide a high chair, many others also come with toy boxes, outdoor areas, and even separate play areas.

Children's parks are found in every small town and at a minimum offer swings and slides. Outdoor playgrounds of note include Masterton's Kids Own Playground, Whangarei's Town Basin Playground, and Rotorua's Lakefront Playground. In the larger cities there are large indoor playgrounds (look out for the franchised branches of Chipmunks, www.chipmunks.co.nz, and Lollipops, www.lollipopsplayland.co.nz), where, for a small charge, children have access to bouncy castles, huge slides and adventure play.

Rainbows End in Auckland is the country's largest theme park, and Auckland, Hamilton, Wellington and Christchurch all have their own zoos and Christchurch has a wildlife park.

Other family activities available in most of New Zealand's larger townships include mini golf, mazes and nature parks. Throughout the country there is a variety of bush and beach walks on offer which range from 10–30 minutes – perfect for younger legs, as well as longer hikes for the teens.

New Zealand's wealth of educational activities – thermal-pool walks, dolphin watching, glow-worm caves, farm tours and birdlife tours – are ideal for keeping young minds stimulated. Other novel activities such as Taupiri's Candyland (tel: 07-824 6818; www.candyland.co.nz; Mon–Fri 10am–5pm,), where you can make your own lollipops, and Wanaka's famous Puzzling World mazes (tel: 03-443 7489; www.puzzlingworld. co.nz; daily 8.30am–5pm) can be found along the way.

What's more, in New Zealand age seems to be no barrier to many activities: you can go rafting at age 3, bungee jumping at 10, tackle rapids at 13, and any age is considered suitable to swim with dolphins! Older kids can enjoy horse riding, hot-air ballooning and even paragliding.

A – Z

A HANDY SUMMARY OF PRACTICAL INFORMATION

A

Admission Charges

Unless visiting a beach, national park, scenic reserve or botanic gardens, the vast majority of attractions in New Zealand have an admission charge. Generally these average around NZ$20 for an adult and NZ$5–10 for children, although there are many attractions such as museums located in small towns or small community-run enterprises that request only a NZ$1 or NZ$2 donation (you may come across the term *koha* – Maori for donation). Honesty boxes abound in New Zealand; respect the locals' trusting nature by paying your dues.

Adventure activities tend to attract higher costs. These range roughly between NZ$75–200 depending on the activity, its duration and what is included in the price (ie the cost of lunch or dinner, or entry into several attractions). Special multi-attraction deals are on offer in larger cities and key tourist destinations including Rotorua and Queenstown. For information, check at the local i-site information office. Major discounts (sometimes up to half price) are often available for children, students and senior citizens. Children under 5 often go free, while children under 3 years almost always do.

Age Restrictions

The minimum driving age in New Zealand is 16, so don't be surprised when you encounter very young-looking drivers on the road. The age of consent in New Zealand is also 16, for both hetero- and homosexual persons. The legal drinking age is 18.

B

Budgeting for Your Trip

Ordering a standard beer and a glass of house wine at an average bar or pub will cost you around NZ$14–18. The main course meal for one person at a budget restaurant will set you back NZ$15–18, at a moderately priced establishment NZ$22–25, and anywhere between NZ$40–50 at a restaurant of high renown. The average price of accommodation varies from around NZ$100 to NZ$250 per night for two people. Motel rooms (self-contained units) tend to cost NZ$100–150, bed & breakfast NZ$100–200, hotel rooms NZ$140–250 and boutique-style rooms NZ$300 and up.

Car hire ranges from around NZ$45 per day for a small vehicle hired for a hire period of seven days or more, and increases up to around NZ$120 for a large vehicle. Short hire periods cost more, starting at around NZ$80 per day for a small vehicle, or NZ$150+ for a larger vehicle.

Taxi fares are relatively expensive. Typical city-centre-to-airport fees are anywhere from NZ$45–65 (in Christchurch) to NZ$60–80 (in Auckland) one-way. Airport shuttle buses cost around NZ$25–40. Other bus tickets start at around NZ$1.20 (depending on the city), and a one-day travel pass costs between NZ$12–16 (depending on the city).

C

Children

New Zealand is a great place to visit with children, with a range of activities for the whole family to enjoy. Most hotels offer a reliable babysitting service, and some have kids' clubs and activities. Motels and other accommodation usually have a contract with a local babysitting service and can organise fully police-vetted sitters on your behalf. Expect to pay from NZ$18 to NZ$30 per hour (depending on the city); most of the babysitters employed will be qualified nannies, so your children will be in good hands.

As a general rule, children under 3 years of age gain free entry to attractions, and this sometimes applies to under 5s. Most attractions offer cut-rate prices for older children, sometimes half-price or less. There are special offers during off-peak holiday periods (mid-April, the first half of July and early October).

For more information about family holidays in New Zealand visit www.newzealand.com. See also Children's Activities section, page 374.

Climate

New Zealand's climate is the reverse of that of the Northern Hemisphere. This means New Zealanders enjoy a warm Christmas in the sun, while June and July are the coldest months. The north of New Zealand, particularly Northland, has a subtropical climate, with very mild winters. The climate in

Southland, at the bottom of the South Island, is generally temperate, with rainfall spread fairly evenly throughout the year, although the weather is very changeable – not too dissimilar from that of the UK, albeit sunnier. During the winter, temperatures at night plummet dramatically.

Winds can be strong at any time on the Cook Strait, which separates the two main islands, but summer days are generally warm and pleasant in most of the regions. Winters can be cold in the central and southern North Island and coastal districts of the South Island, and can be severe in the central regions of the South Island.

The New Zealand weather service's website, www.metservice.co.nz, has details on weather conditions, and the National Institute of Water and Atmospheric Research (NIWA) at www. niwa.co.nz has further information on temperatures.

When to Visit

The summer and shoulder seasons from November to April are the most settled and sunniest, and the best time for a visit. New Zealanders traditionally take their main family holiday break at Christmas and into January, so visitors are advised to make advance bookings for accommodation and domestic transport over this period.

Remember to stock up on plenty of sunscreen and insect repellent during summer; this is readily available throughout the country.

What to Wear

(See also Etiquette, page 377)
For summer visits, you are advised to bring sweaters or wind-breakers for the cooler evenings or brisk days, especially if you are planning to travel to regions in the South Island. By day, a T-shirt or thin cotton shirt will suffice.

Medium-thick clothing (a T-shirt and sweater), plus a raincoat or umbrella, is adequate for most regions most of the year, but in midwinter in Rotorua, Taupo and most of the South Island including Queenstown, sturdy winter clothing and footwear are essential. The South Island is considerably colder during the winter than the North.

Note: New Zealand is noted for its high level of ultraviolet radiation and the brilliance of its light. This means you may get sunburnt even on cloudy days or when the air temperature is quite low. It is important to wear sunscreen lotions, a hat, sunglasses and protective clothing. Stay out of the summer sun around the middle of the day (especially in the North) and follow the Kiwi catch-cry to 'Slip, slop, slap, wrap and re-apply sunscreen regularly'.

Crime and Safety

New Zealand is considered to be one of the safer countries in the world for travellers and suffers only isolated incidences of serious crime. However, petty crime is a problem. Take precautions to secure and conceal your valuables at all times, and never leave them unattended in a car.

To report a crime, contact the nearest police station, where you will find police who are approachable and helpful. New Zealand police carry Taser stun guns, and the special force within the police known as the armed offenders squad, only called upon in emergencies, is heavily armed.

In an emergency dial 111 for ambulance, police or fire service. Emergency calls are free from public call boxes. For further information regarding safety and other general information regarding travelling in New Zealand, visit www.newzealand.com.

Drink-Driving

Drink-driving penalties are tough, regardless of where you are from. Random breath tests by police are often conducted and care should be taken not to exceed the limit of 0.8g of alcohol for each litre of blood.

Customs Regulations

New Zealand has three levels of control at all points of entry into the country: immigration, customs and The Ministry of Agriculture and Fisheries, otherwise known as MAF. On arrival, you must complete an arrival card. Present this to an immigration official with your passport, and, if required, a valid visa. For more on visas and entry requirements, see page 384.

A visitor over the age of 17 may import 200 cigarettes or 250g of tobacco; 50 cigars or a mixture of all three not exceeding 250g; 4.5 litres of wine or beer and three bottles, each not containing more than 1,125ml of spirits. Excess quantities are subject to customs charges.

Strict laws prevent the entry of drugs, weapons, illicit material, wildlife products, firearms and

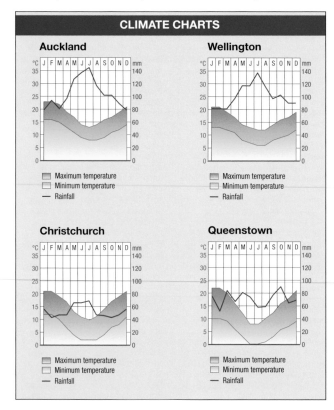

CLIMATE CHARTS

Auckland

°C J F M A M J J A S O N D mm

- ☐ Maximum temperature
- ☐ Minimum temperature
- — Rainfall

Wellington

°C J F M A M J J A S O N D mm

- ☐ Maximum temperature
- ☐ Minimum temperature
- — Rainfall

Christchurch

°C J F M A M J J A S O N D mm

- ☐ Maximum temperature
- ☐ Minimum temperature
- — Rainfall

Queenstown

°C J F M A M J J A S O N D mm

- ☐ Maximum temperature
- ☐ Minimum temperature
- — Rainfall

quarantine items. For a full list of banned items and further information on customs regulations, visit www.customs.govt.nz.

Farm Regulations

Because New Zealand relies heavily on agricultural and horticultural trade with the rest of the world, it has stringent regulations governing the import of animals, as well as vegetable and animal matter. Visitors planning to bring in any material of this sort should make enquiries at the New Zealand Government offices overseas before proceeding. Live animals legally brought into the country must undergo strict quarantine periods. For further information, visit www.biosecurity.govt.nz.

It is worth noting that if you complete your arrival card stating you are not carrying food of any kind, and food is in fact discovered, this attracts hefty fines of up to NZ$100,000 or a prison term of up to five years. Rubbish bins are provided in the customs area for the disposal of food items and all baggage entering the country is subsequently X-rayed prior to entry, so if you are carrying food of any description, either dispose of it, or declare it.

D

Disabled Travellers

New Zealand law requires every new building or major reconstruction to provide 'reasonable and adequate' access for people with disabilities. Most facilities have wheelchair access, but it pays to check when booking.

Parking concessions are available for people with disabilities, and temporary display cards can be issued for the length of the visitor's stay. For more information, check the Weka website, www.weka.net.nz, New Zealand's disability information website, which also provides brochures, or call tel: 0800-171 981. Weka can direct you to any of the 23

Emergency Numbers

If you are involved in an emergency in New Zealand you need to dial **111** (for ambulance, fire or police). This number is free regardless of whether you are using a mobile phone, landline or public telephone.

Local Disability Resource Centres around the country.

Most transport operators can cater for people with special needs, although most urban transport buses are not equipped to accommodate the disabled. A few tour operators provide custom holiday packages for individual and group travellers with disabilities. Contact:
Accessible Kiwi Tours, 34 Waipu Caves Estate Drive, Waipu, Northland, tel: 09-432 2575; www.toursnz.com.
Ucan Tours New Zealand Ltd, 8 Campbell Street, Sumner, Christchurch, tel: 03-326 7881.

E

Electricity

New Zealand's AC electricity supply operates at 230/240 volts, 50 hertz, which is the same as Australia's. Most hotels and motels provide 110-volt, 20-watt AC sockets for electric razors only. For all other equipment an adaptor/converter is required, unless the item has a multi-voltage option. Power outlets only accept flat three- or two-pin plugs, depending on whether an earth connection is fitted.

Embassies and Consulates

Overseas

There is a New Zealand Diplomatic Post finder at www.nzembassy.com, which details all New Zealand embassies and consulates around the world. Here are a few of them:
Australia: New Zealand High Commission, Commonwealth Avenue, Canberra, ACT 2600, Australia, tel: 02-6270 4211; email: nzhccba@bigpond.net.au.
Canada: New High Commission, 99 Bank Street, Suite 727, Ottawa, Ontario K1P 6GE, Canada, tel: 613-238 5991; email: info@nzhccottawa.org.
France: New Zealand Embassy, 7ter, rue Léonard de Vinci, 75116 Paris, France, tel: 01-4501 4343; email: embassy.nz.fr@gmail.com.
Germany: New Zealand Embassy, Friedrichstrasse 60, 10117 Berlin, Germany, tel: 030-206 210; email: nzembber@infoem.org.
Singapore: New Zealand High Commission, Ngee Ann City, Tower A #15-06/10, 391A Orchard Road, Singapore 238873, tel: 65-6235 9966; email: enquiries@nz-high-com.org.sg.

South Africa: New Zealand High Commission Pretoria, 125 Middel Street, New Muckleneuk 0181, South Africa, tel: 012-435 9000; email: enquiries@nzhc.co.za.
United Kingdom: New Zealand High Commission, New Zealand House, 80 Haymarket, London SW1Y 4TQ, United Kingdom, tel: 020-7930 8422; email: aboutnz@newzealandhc.co.uk.
United States of America: New Zealand Embassy, 37 Observatory Circle, Washington DC 20008, USA, tel: 202-328 4800; email: wshinfo@mfat.govt.nz.

In New Zealand

For information on foreign embassies in New Zealand, check the Ministry of Foreign Affairs and Trade website: www.mfat.govt.nz. Most foreign embassies are located in Wellington.
Australia: 72–76 Hobson Street, Thorndon, Wellington 6011, tel: 04-473 6411, email: nzinbox@dfat.gov.au.
Canada: Level 11, 125 The Terrace, Wellington 6011, tel: 04-473 9577, email: wlgtn@international.gc.ca.
France: 34–42 Manners Street, Wellington 6011, tel: 04-384 2555, email: ambassade@ambafrance-nz.org.
Ireland: Level 3, National Bank Tower, 205 Queen Street, Auckland, tel: 09-977 2252, email: consul@ireland.co.nz.
South Africa: Level 7, 1 Willis Street, Wellington, tel: 04-815 8484, email: wellington@dirco.gov.za.
United Kingdom: 44 Hill Street, Thorndon, Wellington 6011, tel: 04-924 2888.
United States: 29 Fitzherbert Terrace, Thorndon, Wellington 6011, tel: 04-462 6000.

Etiquette

New Zealanders are regarded as fairly casual dressers, although you will need to bring something dressy if you plan to go to any arts events and fancy restaurants. For clubbing, you should wear something smart. Some nightclubs and bars do not allow shorts, singlets, trainers or flip-flops (called jandells in New Zealand).

If you are invited to someone's home, casual dress is fine. If you are invited to attend church or a Maori marae, dress neatly but don't go over the top, as New Zealanders in general have a very laid-back approach to dressing up.

If you are invited to attend a barbeque, or meal at someone's home it is appropriate to bring something for your host; a bottle of wine, small box

Polynesian culture is celebrated in colour and style at the annual Pasifika Festival.

of chocolates or other small token will be graciously accepted.

If you happen to attend a community event that states everyone should 'bring a plate' – this means a plate filled with something to share with others, most usually finger-food. For visitors it is perfectly acceptable, should this arise, simply to bring a packet of shop-bought biscuits. On arrival, place them on the table.

G

Gay and Lesbian Travellers

New Zealand is a gay-tolerant country, although some prejudice persists in small towns. Homosexuality ceased being categorised as a criminal offence in 1986, and the age of consent was set at 16 (same as heterosexuals).

There are plenty of facilities in New Zealand catering for the gay, lesbian and bisexual traveller, and festivals include the Hero Festival in Auckland, Gay Ski Week in Queenstown and the Great Party weekend in Wellington.

The best organisation to contact for further information is Gay Tourism New Zealand: PO Box 19-299, Hamilton 3244, tel: 07-834 0137; www.gaytourismnewzealand.com. Other useful websites are www.gaytravel. co.nz, www.gaystaynewzealand.com and www.skigaynewzealand.com.

H

Health and Medical Care

Visitors are charged for taxpayer-funded health care in New Zealand,

so health insurance is highly recommended. To be eligible for the same health-care benefits as New Zealand residents, you must be able to prove your eligibility with a work permit for two years or more, refugee status, or proof that you are a Cook Islands, Niue or Tokelau New Zealand citizen. In the case of visiting children under 18 years, the child's legal guardian must prove their resident status. New Zealand does have reciprocal health agreements with a few countries including Australia and the UK, providing a limited range of health care. For more information visit www.health.govt.nz. Any ineligible patient who seeks general specialist treatment at a hospital – whether it is a public or a private hospital – or any medical centre will be prioritised alongside eligible patients if there is spare capacity. The estimated cost must be paid in advance and any additional costs paid at the end of the treatment.

All visitors, however, are entitled to initial, free acute (emergency) care following an accident, regardless of who is to blame, and this is covered by the government-run Accident Compensation Scheme (ACC). However, for any ongoing or subsequent treatment, you must apply to the ACC for approval, so it is best to have your own health insurance.

Free care is also provided by the New Zealand government for any visitor who has been admitted to hospital under a compulsory treatment order issued under the Tuberculosis Act, the Mental Health Act, or the Alcoholism and Drug Addiction Act.

Other Considerations

Tap water in New Zealand is safe to drink and is of a high quality thanks to its pristine environment. However, it is not wise to drink untreated water from lakes and streams, or to fill up a drink bottle in a public toilet, as it may be plumbed from a stream. In national parks, Department of Conversation (DOC) signs will state whether water sources are safe to drink.

Law prohibits smoking in all public buildings, restaurants and pubs.

There are no snakes or dangerous wild animals in New Zealand, although a bite from the native katipo spider and introduced Red-back spider and White-tail spider may require medical attention. Sandflies and mosquitoes are prevalent in some areas, although insect repellents are widely available.

Medical Services

For non-emergencies, full instructions for obtaining assistance are printed in the front of telephone directories. Hotels and motels normally have individual arrangements with duty doctors for guests' attention, and they can also assist you in finding a dentist.

New Zealand's medical and hospital facilities, both public and private, provide a high standard of treatment and care. It is important to note that medical services are not free to visitors, except as outlined above, for the treatment of injuries sustained in an accident.

Pharmacies

Pharmacies, or chemists, are generally open 8.30am–5.30pm weekdays and until noon on Saturdays. Some are also open for one late night a week.

In New Zealand there is no single pharmacy that remains open 24/7: this task is a shared responsibility, although public hospitals, listed below, will be able to advise the address and phone number of pharmacies which are on duty on any given night.

As well as dispensing pharmaceuticals and medicines, chemists also sell cosmetics and insect and sun protections. Some drugs sold over the counter in other countries may not be available without a prescription – this will involve a visit to a medical centre to obtain one.

Major North Island Hospitals

Auckland Hospital, tel: 09-367 0000
Hawke's Bay Hospital, tel: 06-878 8109
Rotorua Hospital, tel: 07-348 1199
Taranaki Hospital, tel: 06-753 6139
Taupo Hospital, tel: 07-376 1000
Waikato Hospital, tel: 07-839 8899
Wellington Hospital, tel: 04-385 5999
Whangarei Hospital, tel: 09-430 4100

Major South Island Hospitals

Christchurch Hospital, tel: 03-364 0640
Queenstown Hospital, tel: 03-441 0015
Dunedin Hospital, tel: 03-474 0999
Greymouth Hospital, tel: 03-768 0499
Nelson Hospital, tel: 03-546 1800
Southland Hospital, tel: 03-218 1949
Timaru Hospital, tel: 03-684 4000

Health and Beauty

Health Spas

The following are among the finest of the many natural and non-commercial spas to be found in New Zealand:

Te Wairua at Lake Tarawera is a well-kept secret reached by hiring a Clearwater Charters water taxi from Tarawera's Landing Café (tel: 07-362 8502; www.thelandinglaketarawera. co.nz). Once there, a short 2-minute walk along a bush track leads to a natural hot pool set in a tranquil glade amid the trees. It is a heavenly place to visit for a private hot spa – and an unforgettable experience. The steaming waters of nearby **Lake Tarawera's Hot Water Beach** provide the chance for a hot soak, but you will have to dig your own pool in the sand. Also accessible only by boat – and well worth the journey – are the **Parengarenga Pools** on Lake Rotoiti.

Kerosene Creek is a hot flowing stream with a variety of pools located just south of Rotorua near Wai-O-Tapu on SH5.

Over on the North Island's East Coast, the Coromandel's most famous spa experience is found at **Hot Water Beach**, where, for a couple of hours either side of low tide, you can dig your very own hot spring pool. Try some refreshing hydrotherapy: a hot soak followed by a quick splash about in the sea – it all comes free of charge.

Some of the best commercial sites include:

Hanmer Springs Thermal Pools and Spa, Amuri Avenue, Hanmer Springs, tel: 03-315 0000; www. hanmersprings.co.nz.

Maruia Springs Thermal Resort, SH7, Lewis Pass, tel: 03-523 8840; www.maruiasprings.co.nz.

Miranda Hot Springs, SH25, Miranda, tel: 07-867 3055; www. mirandahotsprings.co.nz.

Opal Hot Springs and Holiday Park, Okauia Springs Road, Matamata, tel: 07-888 8198; www.opalhotsprings. co.nz.

Parakai Hot Springs, 150 Parkhurst Road, Parakai, Auckland, tel: 09-420 8998; www.parakaisprings.co.nz.

Polynesian Spa, Lake End, 1000 Hinemoa Street, Rotorua, tel: 07-348 1328; www.polynesianspa.co.nz.

Te Aroha Mineral Spas, Boundary Street, Te Aroha, tel: 07-884 8717; www.tearohamineralspas.co.nz.

Wai Ora Spa at Hells Gate, SH30, Tikitere, Rotorua, tel: 07-345 3151; www.hellsgate.co.nz.

Waikite Valley Thermal Pools, Waikite Valley Road, Rotorua, tel: 07-333 1861; www.hotpools.co.nz.

Waiwera Thermal Resort and Spa, 21 Main Road, Waiwera, Auckland, tel: 09-427 8800; www.waiwera. co.nz.

See also Spas feature, page 193.

Beauty Therapy and Day Spas

Beauty-therapy clinics offering services such as sunbeds, day spas, manicures, pedicures, massages, body wraps, waxing, skin care and make-up can be found throughout New Zealand. Prices range from NZ$40 for a 40-minute massage to around NZ$500 for a full-day, complete beauty spa experience. Check the Yellow Pages (www.yellow. co.nz) for the nearest beauty salon or day spa.

Internet

There are numerous internet cafés in every city and small town in New Zealand that provide access to internet and email. All hotels provide internet access, as do the majority of motels and other accommodations. Most often this is for an additional charge, although in an increasing number of motels, lodges and boutique accommodations it is a complimentary service. You will need an RJ45-type plug to be able to connect your laptop into a computer socket in New Zealand, and an adaptor with a flat two- or three-point power plug to connect to the power supply.

Wireless is widely available nationwide, but to access you will need to obtain correct passwords, etc. Your accommodation will be able to provide you with information on local hotspots, and how to access and pay for these.

Websites

www.newzealand.com Tourism New Zealand's award-winning website is loaded with useful information. www.yellow.co.nz Provides listings of businesses nationwide, from hairdressers and hamburger joints through to medical centres and transport services. www.nzedge.com A comprehensive and eclectic site that explores the lives and achievements of New Zealanders living overseas and connects them on a global scale. The site contains a unique online shopping guide, news stories, a section dedicated to New Zealand 'heroes', image galleries, speeches, web links and a global register. www.nzmusic.com The diversity of the Pacific sound is at your fingertips here. It has a catalogue of Kiwi artists, biographies, music, news, an extensive gig guide and a section dedicated to forums.

www.allblacks.com Official site of the New Zealand Rugby Football Union and the All Blacks. www.caravan-parkfinder. co.nz Comprehensive guide to accommodation in New Zealand holiday parks and campgrounds for campervan hirers. www.doc.govt.nz/camping A guide to Department of Conservation campsites in New Zealand. www.aa.co.nz New Zealand's leading motoring organisation. Driver, accommodation and travel info. www.nzmuseums.co.nz An exhaustive listing of museums great and small, throughout the country.

Left Luggage

Key-operated luggage-storage facilities are available at all major train stations and bus stations. Most are coin or credit-card operated; others you will need to pay for at a desk. Many hotels will also happily store extra luggage if you plan to return to the hotel after taking a tour.

Lost Property

There is no central lost-property service in New Zealand, so if you lose something of value, advise your accommodation and contact the nearest police station. Chances are someone will hand the item in.

If you lose your passport you will need to advise your embassy as soon as possible, and should your credit card go astray, phone your credit card provider immediately.

Auckland Sky Tower.

M

Maps

Tourist information offices (i-sites) and car-hire companies distribute free maps. The New Zealand Automobile Association also produces regional maps and excellent district maps; a nominal sum is charged for North and South Island maps. *Hema Maps* produces a range of up-to-date road atlases which are widely available. The laminated *Insight Fleximap New Zealand*, found at most bookstores throughout New Zealand, is durable and detailed.

Media

Print

English is the most widely used language, followed by Maori, the indigenous language. There is a high level of literacy in New Zealand: most communities have a decent library, and sales of books, magazines and newspapers on a per capita basis are among the highest in the world. One in four people in Auckland reads *The New Zealand Herald*, the morning daily. Most large towns have their own newspaper, and small community newspapers have recently undergone a revival.

International newspapers can be found in the larger bookshops and outlets at New Zealand's international airports as well as in public libraries.

Cuisine magazine is an excellent guide to New Zealand food and wine, with regular new restaurant reviews from around the country; NZ Life and Leisure magazine has in-depth features about New Zealanders, travel destinations, food and wine; and North and South and The Listener comment on contemporary New Zealand issues.

TV and Radio

New Zealand has several public broadcasting channels. Two television channels are administered by a nominally independent government corporation: Television One and TV2. Two more channels, TV3 and Prime, are run by a Canadian-owned company. National and international news and current affairs programmes are usually carried on Television One, TV3 and Prime. Also of interest is Maori Television. Most programmes are in Te Reo, but subtitles make the storylines easy to follow. *Kapa*

haka competitions (dance shows) are often shown, along with excellent documentaries on modern-day living, which include fishing and hunting methods, gardening and cooking, geography and history, all of which are produced for local interest.

Free-view (digital) has seen the start-up of several new regional television stations – some of which broadcast nationwide. In addition, many New Zealanders, and most hotels and motels, have long subscribed to the Sky satellite TV service for international news and sports, movie and music channels, British drama, and a variety of other programming.

New Zealand has a selection of AM- and FM-band radio stations, satisfying a wide variety of tastes.

Money

The New Zealand dollar (NZ$), divided into 100 cents, is the unit of currency. Currency exchange facilities are available at Auckland, Wellington and Christchurch international airports, as well as most banks and bureaux de change in the larger cities and resorts.

There is no restriction on the amount of domestic or foreign currency (or traveller's cheques in New Zealand dollars) a visitor may bring into or take out of New Zealand. The New Zealand dollar is frequently called 'the kiwi' because the dollar coin features a kiwi, the national bird, on one side.

Credit Cards

Credit cards, including Visa, American Express, Diners Club and MasterCard, are widely accepted throughout New Zealand, and you will be able to use them to withdraw cash from automatic teller machines (ATMs), situated at banks and shopping centres throughout the country.
Amex, tel: 0800-656 660
Diners Club, tel: 0800-346 377
Mastercard, tel: 0800-449 140
Visa, tel: 0508-600 300

Goods and Services Tax

A goods and services tax (GST) of 15 percent is applied to the cost of all goods and services and by law is included in displayed prices. GST is not charged on duty-free goods, or where the items are posted by a retailer to an international visitor's home address. Neither is GST included in international air fares purchased in New Zealand. GST is added to accommodation, however, by law, and this is now included in the quoted price. There are no further hotel taxes.

Language

English is the common language of New Zealand. However, as this is a multicultural society, you may hear other languages spoken, including Te Reo Maori, the other official language. The vast majority of New Zealand place names are of Maori origin. There are also television and radio programmes which are broadcast entirely in the Maori language.

Useful Maori Phrases

Kia ora – hello
Kia ora tatou – hello everyone
Tena koe – greetings to you (said to one person)
Tena koutou – greetings to you all
Haere mai – welcome
Haere ra – farewell
Ka kite ano – until I see you again (goodbye)
moana – sea
puke – hill
roto – lake
whanga – bay
wai – water
tomo – cave
waitomo – water cave

Tipping

Tipping is becoming more widespread in New Zealand, although it is still regarded as a foreign custom. In the major centres, tipping is encouraged but not expected. You should tip 5–10 percent of your restaurant bill if you feel the service was worthy. Service charges are not added to hotel or restaurant bills.

O

Opening Hours

As a general rule, shops are open for business 8.30am–5.30pm (Mon–Fri), and usually stay open until 9pm one night of the week. Hours on Saturday and Sunday are usually from 9am until the late afternoon. Main cities and the larger tourist areas have extended opening hours, with many shops open seven days a week.

Banks are open 9.30am–4.30pm (Mon–Fri), and ATMs are plentiful.

Bars, pubs and taverns usually open 11am–late (Mon–Sun). Nightclubs usually open their doors 7.30–8pm and close around 3am.

Banks, post offices, government offices and some shops close on public holidays. Most nightclubs and bars also close at midnight the night before each public holiday.

P

Photography

Most New Zealanders don't mind being photographed, but it's best to ask before you click. There are professional photographic labs and camera centres throughout the country. They have the most up-to-date digital and film-processing technology, and the latest camera and video gear. At some stores you can even hire equipment. You can also drop your film off at local pharmacies to be processed and download your digital camera's memory card onto disk. There are also plenty of camera-repair services throughout New Zealand. Check the widely available Yellow Pages directory (www.yellow.co.nz) or the internet for camera store locations.

Postal Services

Post offices are generally open 9am–5pm (Mon–Fri). Some are also open Saturday mornings until midday. In smaller rural areas, postal services and stamps are also available in stationery shops and corner stores. In larger towns, in addition to stamps, post offices also sell magazines and a range of stationery. NZ Post also offers a courier service within New Zealand.

Post boxes are widely available and easily identified by their distinctive red-and-white design. If you are posting within New Zealand there is the choice of standard post or fast post. An average letter costs NZ70c to send by standard post, or NZ$1.40 by fast post.

Airmail is fairly swift, but because it is based on weight, it becomes expensive if you are sending a letter of more than one page. A one-page letter in a standard airmail-sized envelope to Australia costs NZ$1.90, as does a postcard or aerogramme; to anywhere else in the world a standard letter costs NZ$2.40 and a postcard or aerogramme costs NZ$1.90.

Mail to Australia takes 3–6 days to reach its destination; the rest of the world takes 6–10 days.

Public Toilets

Public toilets can be found at most beaches, parks and town centres. In wilderness areas and national parks, environmentally friendly composting and long-drop toilets are found in or near most car parks and at huts. During the summer it is wise to travel with your own supply of toilet paper, as smaller places sometimes struggle to cope with the demands placed upon their facilities, which are free of charge.

R

Religious Services

More than half of New Zealanders affiliate themselves with a Christian religion, with Anglican, Catholic and Presbyterian being the largest denominations. The largest non-Christian religions include Hindu, Buddhist, Muslim, Spiritualism/New Age, Sikh and Jewish religions.

Churches and other places of worship are located throughout New Zealand. To find out about local services, ask at your accommodation or at the nearest i-site.

S

Smoking

Although statistics report that one in five New Zealanders smokes, these days smoking has a social stigma attached to it and is banned in all public places, including bars. Endeavour not to light up within close proximity of other people and never inside a public space. A few hotels/motels still provide smoking rooms, but there is a trend towards providing smokers with comfortable outdoor places to indulge their habit.

Student Travellers

Discounts are offered to travelling students, although in many cases you will need to ask. Identification will be required in the form of an International Student Identity Card, although International Youth Travel Cards (www.isiccard.com) will sometimes be accepted. The Youth Hostel Association (www.yha.co.nz) is widely recognised in New Zealand. Its members are eligible for discounts of 10 to 25 percent on coach travel, adventure activities, and shopping. Visit the website www.yha.co.nz, click on membership, then on member discounts to see a sample list of savings.

T

Tax

A goods and services tax (GST) of 15 percent is applied to the cost of all goods and services as outlined on page 380. There are no further hotel taxes or sales taxes.

Telephones

To call New Zealand from overseas, dial its country code (64), but omit the 0 prefix on all area codes. Dial the 0 prefix of the area code only when calling within New Zealand. To phone overseas from New Zealand, dial 00 followed by the national code of the country you are calling.

Note: Some businesses have free 0800 or 0508 numbers which can only be dialled within New Zealand – there is no charge for these calls, even if you dial from a mobile phone.

Public Holidays

January New Year's Day (1st and 2nd, or observed on the next working days); provincial anniversaries: Southland (18th), Wellington (25th), Northland and Auckland (31st).
February Waitangi Day (6th); provincial anniversaries: Nelson/Buller Day (1st).
March Provincial anniversaries: Otago (22nd), Taranaki (8th). Good Friday and Easter Monday.
April Anzac Day (25th).
June Queen's Birthday (usually the first Monday).
September Provincial anniversaries:

South Canterbury (27th).
October Labour Day (usually the last Monday); provincial anniversaries: Hawke's Bay (22nd).
November Provincial anniversaries: Marlborough (1st), Canterbury (12th).
December Christmas (25th and 26th, or observed on the next working days).

    Note: Provincial anniversaries are usually observed on the Monday closest to the actual date. All banks, post offices, government and private offices and some shops close on public holidays.

0900 numbers are charged to the caller by the minute, and are charged at premium rates.

Phone numbers appear in the White Pages (alphabetical listings) and the Yellow Pages (business category listings).

Public phones: Most public phones accept cards that can be purchased from bookstalls and newsagents with a minimum value of NZ$5. Some public telephones also accept credit cards, and a few accept coins. Calls made from public telephones within the local area cost NZ$1 for the first 15 minutes, then 20 cents per minute thereafter.

Mobile phones: Check with your phone company before leaving home about international mobile roam facilities in New Zealand. Mobile phones can also be hired on arrival in New Zealand (outlets are available at international airports). To save on mobile phone bills, consider buying a prepaid phone card. Check with **NZ Telecom** (www.telecom.co.nz) and **Vodafone** (www.vodafone.com) shops in major towns and cities.

New Zealand Area Codes

Northland: 09
Auckland: 09
Waikato: 07
Bay of Plenty: 07
Gisborne: 06
Hawke's Bay: 06
Taranaki: 06
Wairarapa: 06
Wellington: 04
Nelson: 03
West coast and Buller: 03
Christchurch: 03
Timaru/Oamaru: 03
Otago: 03
Southland: 03

International Codes from New Zealand

Australia: 0061
Canada: 001

Ireland: 00353
South Africa: 0027
United Kingdom: 0044
United States: 001

Time Zone

There is only one time zone throughout most of the country: 12 hours ahead of Greenwich Mean Time (GMT), and 17 hours ahead of Eastern Standard Time in the USA. However, from early October until late March, time is advanced by one hour to give extended daylight throughout summer. Therefore, and taking British Summer Time and the US Daylight Saving Time into account, New Zealand time is in fact GMT +13/EST + 18 for much of the October–March period, and GMT + 11/EST + 16 from late March to October.

Time in the remote Chatham Islands, 800km (500 miles) east of Christchurch, is 45 minutes ahead of that in the rest of the country.

Early Start to the Day

Travellers from the Northern Hemisphere moving west into New Zealand lose a full day crossing the International Dateline, and regain a full day returning eastwards. Because the country is so advanced in time, given its proximity to the International Date Line, it is one of the very first nations to welcome each day, preceded only by the small Pacific Island nations of Fiji, Samoa, Tonga and Kiribati.

Tour Operators

New Zealand tour operators employ highly trained, professional and friendly staff who will often go out of their way to make sure your experience is the very best they can provide. A huge range of activities is on offer.

Sheep outnumber people by around twenty to one.

Tourist Information

New Zealand is well served in terms of visitor information. Desks offering information and booking services are provided at most airports, and information can also be found at over 100 prime locations including i-sites (visitor information centres) around the country. A good starting point is the **Tourism New Zealand** website, www.newzealand.com. It has comprehensive information in several languages. Alternatively, contact one of the following Tourism New Zealand offices:
London: New Zealand House, Level 7, 80 Haymarket, London SW1Y 4TE, tel: 0207-930 1662.
Los Angeles: 501 Santa Monica Boulevard, Suite 300, Santa Monica, CA 90401, tel: 310-395 7480.
Singapore: 391A Orchard Road, #15-06/10, Ngee Ann City Tower A#15-06/10, Ngee Ann City Tower A Singapore 238873, Singapore 238873, tel: 65-6738 5844.
Sydney: Level 12, 21 York Street, Sydney, NSW 1225, tel: 02-8299 4800.

Tourist Information Offices

Tourism offices, known as i-site Visitor Centres, are open daily 8.30am–5pm; opening hours are extended in some major cities, as listed below.

North Island

Auckland
Auckland i-site Visitor Centre, Atrium, Sky City, corner of Victoria and Federal streets; daily 8.30am–7pm; tel: 09-363 7182; www.aucklandnz.com.
Auckland i-site Visitor Centre, 137 Quay Street, Princes Wharf; daily 8.30am–6.30pm; tel: 09-307 0615; www.aucklandnz.com.

Cambridge
Cambridge Information Centre, corner of Victoria and Queen streets, tel: 07-823 3456; www.cambridge.co.nz.

Devonport
Devonport i-site Visitor Centre, 3 Victoria Road, tel: 09-446 0677; www.northshorenz.co.nz.

Doubtless Bay
Doubtless Bay Information Centre, Waterfront Drive, tel: 09-406 2046; www.doubtlessbay.co.nz.

Great Barrier Island
Great Barrier Island Visitor Information Centre, Claris Postal

Centre, tel: 09-363 7182; www.great barriernz.co.nz. Note: there are no banks on the island so do bring cash; credit card facilities are available at most commercial outlets.

Gisborne
Gisborne i-site Visitor Centre, 209 Grey Street, tel: 06-868 6139; www.gisbornenz.com.

Hamilton
Hamilton i-site Visitor Centre, 5 Garden Place, tel: 07-839 3580; www.visithamilton.co.nz.

Hastings
Hastings i-site Visitor Centre, corner Russell and Heretaunga streets, tel: 06-873 5526; www.visithastings.co.nz.

Kaitaia/Northland
Far North i-site Visitor Centre, corner Matthews and South roads, Kaitaia, tel: 09-408 0879; www.northlandnz.co.nz.

Napier
Napier i-site Visitor Centre, 100 Marine Parade, tel: 06-834 1911; www.isitehawkesbay.co.nz.

New Plymouth
New Plymouth i-site Visitor Centre Puke Ariki, 1 Ariki Street, tel: 06-759 6060, 0800-639 759; www.pukeariki.com. Town-centre museum, public library and visitor centre in one.

Ohakune
Ruapehu Visitor Centre, 54 Clyde Street, tel: 06-385 8427; www.visitruapehu.com.

Orewa
Orewa i-site Visitor Centre, 214A Hibiscus Coast Highway, Orewa, tel: 09-426 0076, www.orewabeach.co.nz.

Paihia
Bay of Islands i-site Visitor Centre, The Wharf, Marsden Road, tel: 09-402 7345; www.northlandnz.co.nz, www.paihia.co.nz.

Palmerston North
Palmerston North i-site Visitor Centre, 52 The Square, tel: 06-350 1922; www.manawatunz.co.nz.

Rotorua
Rotorua i-site Visitor Centre, 1167 Fenton Street, tel: 07-348 5179; www.rotoruanz.com.

Russell
Russell Information Centre, end of the Wharf, tel: 09-403 8020; www.

northlandnz.co.nz.

South Auckland
Franklin i-site Visitor Centre, SH1, Mill Road, Bombay, tel: 09-236 0670; www.franklincountry.com.
Auckland Airport i-site Visitor Centre, International Terminal, Mangere, tel: 09-275 6467; www.aucklandnz.com.

Taupo
Taupo i-site Visitor Centre, 30 Tongariro Street, tel: 07-376 0027; www.laketauponz.com.

Tauranga/Mount Maunganui
Tauranga i-site Visitor Centre, 95 Willow Street, tel: 07-578 8103; www.bayofplentynz.com.

Te Aroha
Te Aroha i-site Visitor Centre, 102 Whitaker Street, tel: 07-884 8052; www.tearoha-info.co.nz.

Te Urewera National Park
Aniwaniwa Visitor Centre, SH38, Aniwaniwa, Wairoa, tel: 06-837 3900; www.doc.govt.nz.

Thames
Tourism Coromandel, 1st Floor, Goldfields Shopping Centre, 100 Mary Street, tel: 07-868 0017; www.thecoromandel.com.

Waiheke Island
Waiheke Island i-site Visitor Centre, 2 Korora Road, Artworks, Oneroa, tel: 09-372 1234; www.aucklandnz.com.

Waitakere City and West Coast Beaches
Arataki Visitor Centre, 300 Scenic Drive, Titirangi, Auckland, tel: 09-366 2000; www.arc.govt.nz.

Waitomo
Waitomo i-site Visitor Centre, 21 Caves Road, Waitomo Caves, tel: 07-878 7640, 0800-474 839; www.waitomodiscovery.co.nz.

Wanganui
Wanganui i-site Visitor Centre, 31 Taupo Quay, tel: 06-349 0508; www.wanganui.com.

Warkworth Area
Warkworth i-site Visitor Centre, 1 Baxter Street, Warkworth, tel: 09-425 9081; www.warkworthnz.com. For Matakana see www.matakanacoast.com.

Wellington
Wellington i-site Visitor Centre, corner Wakefield and Victoria streets,

tel: 04-802 4860; www.wellingtonnz.com.

Whakapapa Village/National Park
Whakapapa Visitor Centre at DOC, Whakapapa Village, tel: 07-892 3729; www.doc.govt.nz.

Whangamata
Whangamata i-site Visitor Centre, 616 Port Road, tel: 07-865 8340; www.whangamatainfo.co.nz.

Whangarei
Whangarei i-site Visitor Centre, 92 Otaika Road, SH1, tel: 09-438 1079; also located at the Whangarei Town Basin; www.whangareinz.com.

Whitianga
Whitianga i-site Visitor Centre, Albert Street and Blacksmith Lane, tel: 07-866 5555; www.whitianga.co.nz.

South Island

Akaroa
Akaroa Information Centre, 120 Rue Jolie, tel: 03-304 8600; www.akaroa.com.

Aoraki Mount Cook National Park
Aoraki Mount Cook Visitor Centre, Larch Road, Mount Cook, tel: 03-435 1186; www.doc.govt.nz.

Arrowtown
Lakes District Museum information centre, 49 Buckingham Street, tel: 03-442 1824; www.arrowtown.org.nz.

Arthur's Pass
Arthur's Pass Visitor Information Centre, SH73, tel: 03-318 9211; www.doc.govt.nz.

Blenheim
Blenheim i-site Visitor Centre, Railway Station, SH1, tel: 03-577 8080; www.destinationmarlborough.com.

Christchurch
Christchurch and Canterbury i-site Visitor Centre, 9 Rolleston Avenue, tel: 03-379 9629; www.christchurchnz.com.

Dunedin
Dunedin i-site Visitor Centre, 48 The Octagon, tel: 03-474 3300; www.dunedin.govt.nz.

Fox Glacier
Fox Glacier Visitors Centre, Department of Conservation, SH6,

tel: 03-751 0807; www.west-coast.co.nz, www.glaciercountry.co.nz.

Franz Josef Glacier
Franz Josef Glacier Visitor Centre, Department of Conservation, SH6, tel: 03-752 0796; www.west-coast.co.nz, www.glaciercountry.co.nz.

Greymouth
Greymouth i-site Visitor Centre, 168 Mackay Street, tel: 03-768 5101; www.west-coast.co.nz.

Haast
Haast Visitor Centre, Department of Conservation, Haast Junction, tel: 03-750 0809; www.doc.govt.nz.

Hanmer Springs
Hurunui i-site Visitor Centre, 42 Amuri Avenue, tel: 03-314 8816; www.visithurunui.com.

Hokitika
Hokitika i-site Visitor Centre, Carnegie Building, Hamilton Street, tel: 03-755 6166; www.west-coast.co.nz.

Invercargill
Invercargill i-site Visitor Centre, 108 Gala Street, tel: 03-214 6243; www.invercargill.org.nz.

Kaikoura
Kaikoura i-site Visitor Centre, West End, tel: 03-319 5641; www.kaikoura.co.nz.

Lake Tekapo
Lake Tekapo Information Centre, Main Highway next to the (only) petrol station, tel: 03-680 6686; www.laketekapountouched.co.nz.

Methven
Methven i-site Visitor Centre, 160 Main Street, tel: 03-302 8955; www.methveninfo.co.nz.

Nelson
Nelson i-site Visitor Centre, Millers Acres Centre, 77 Trafalgar Street, tel: 03-548 2304; www.nelsonnz.com.

Picton and the Sounds
Picton i-site Visitor Centre, Auckland Street on the Foreshore, Picton, tel: 03-520 3113; www.destinationmarlborough.com.

Queenstown
Queenstown i-site Visitor Centre, Clock Tower Building, corner Shotover and Camp streets, tel: 03-442 4100, 0800-668 888; www.queenstownnz.co.nz.

Stewart Island
Rakiura National Park Visitor Centre, 15 Main Road, tel: 03-219 0002; www.doc.govt.nz is an indispensable source of information on how to make the most of this conservationists' paradise. Additional information is available at www.stewartisland.co.nz.

Te Anau
Fiordland i-site Visitor Centre, Lakefront Drive (next to Real Journeys Office), tel: 03-249 8900; www.fiordland.org.nz.

Wanaka
Lake Wanaka i-site Visitor Centre, Waterfront Log Cabin, 100 Ardmore Street, tel: 03-443 1233; www.lakewanaka.co.nz.

Visas and Passports

Visa requirements differ, depending on nationality, purpose of visit and length of stay. Many countries offer a reciprocal visa waiver agreement with New Zealand, and nationals of these countries can stay in New Zealand on the visa waiver programme for three months to six months. All visitors must be able to produce an onward or return ticket and sufficient funds to support themselves during their stay. Check with the New Zealand diplomatic or consular office in your country of residence (see Embassies and Consulates, page 377) or on www.immigration.govt.nz. All visitors to New Zealand require passports, which must be valid for at least three months beyond the date you intend leaving the country. See also Customs Regulations, page 376.

The following classes of people are prohibited by law from entering, either as tourists or immigrants, regardless of country of origin:

1) Those suffering from tuberculosis, or those with a relatively high probability of needing publicly funded health services during their stay in New Zealand.

2) Those convicted of an offence which drew a sentence of imprisonment of over one year.

3) Those who have previously been deported from New Zealand.

4) For further details, visit www.immigration.govt.nz and click on Find a Visa, then Visiting New Zealand.

The Shotover Jet.

Weights and Measures

New Zealand uses the metric system to record weights and measurements, and has done so for more than 35 years. This decision was based on the requirements of the country's trading and export partners, and although the movement towards metric began in 1969, it wasn't until 14th December 1976 that it was fully integrated.

Women Travellers

New Zealand is a relatively safe country to travel around as a female, but, as always when travelling, it pays to heed a few basic precautions.

Projecting confidence and looking busy – or as if you know where you are going – is one of the best ways to stay safe and avoid being hassled. Consider carrying a mobile phone as it provides a little extra security and travelling with as little luggage as possible. When you are overburdened, you become an easy target for thieves.

Avoid doing things at night that can be done in the light of day, like withdrawing money from an ATM. As elsewhere in the world, it is best not to walk alone at night in areas that are dimly lit. Catch a taxi back to your accommodation instead. Your accommodation can provide the name and phone number for a local taxi company they trust. Hitch-hiking alone at any time of day or night, or in isolated places, is also not advisable.

Accommodation-wise, staying in a busy hotel in the heart of town is a lot less inconspicuous than a cottage on the outskirts. Always put your safety first and remember that it's not all bad news: travelling alone as a woman makes you approachable.

FURTHER READING

History

The Penguin History of New Zealand by Michael King. This is the definitive New Zealand history.

Being Pakeha Now: Reflections and Recollections of a White Native by Michael King. The first serious analysis of what it means to be a non-Maori New Zealander.

Moko by Michael King and Marti Friedlander. An iconic Kiwi book, with photos by one of the country's most eminent photographers – Moko features portraits of Maori tattooing in the 20th century and the women who wore it.

Healing Our History – the Challenge of the Treaty of Waitangi by Robert Consedine and Joanna Consedine. Expands upon critical treaty issues: the foreshore and seabed debate, Maori access to political power, the Maori economy, Maori education and the Treaty settlement process.

Encircled Lands: Te Urewera, 1820–1921 by Judith Binney. A richly illustrated history and topical account of Te Urewera and the Tuhoe people's quest for authority in their lands.

Captain Cook's Apprentice by Anthony Hill. The enthralling and true story of Captain Cook's voyage on the Endeavour, as seen through the eyes of his cabin boy.

Forgotten Anzacs: The Campaign in Greece, 1941 by Peter Ewer. The history of the campaign in Greece and Crete, written from a truly Anzac perspective. Based on rarely accessed archives and more than 30 interviews with Australian, Greek and New Zealand veterans, this book gives overdue recognition to the brave, forgotten Anzacs of 1941.

Ask That Mountain by Dick Scott. This book draws on official papers, settler manuscripts and oral history to give the first complete account of what took place at Parihaka in Taranaki. Now in its ninth edition, this seminal work was named as one of the ten most important books published in New Zealand.

Literature/Fiction

The Bone People by Keri Hulme. Winner of the British McConnell Prize for fiction.

Dogside Story by Patricia Grace. Internationally acclaimed novel explores the strength and conflicts of the whanau (family), the power of the land, and the aroha (love) and humour of the community.

Landings by Jenny Patrick. Set on the Whanganui River at the turn of the 20th century, this historical novel weaves together the lives of the people who have made it their home.

The Denniston Rose by Jenny Pattrick. A bestseller, set in the 1880s, this is a story of isolation and survival, as spirited child Rose fends for herself in the bleak coal-mining settlement of Denniston, located high above New Zealand's west coast.

Katherine Mansfield New Zealand

Send Us Your Thoughts

We do our best to ensure the information in our books is as accurate and up-to-date as possible. The books are updated on a regular basis using local contacts, who painstakingly add, amend and correct as required. However, some details (such as telephone numbers and opening times) are liable to change, and we are ultimately reliant on our readers to put us in the picture.

We welcome your feedback, especially your experience of using the book "on the road". Maybe we recommended a hotel that you liked (or another that you didn't), or you came across a great bar or new attraction we missed.

We will acknowledge all contributions, and we'll offer an Insight Guide to the best letters received.

Please write to us at:
**Insight Guides
PO Box 7910
London SE1 1WE**
Or email us at:
insight@apaguide.co.uk

Stories edited by V. O'Sullivan. A collection of the New Zealand stories of New Zealand's most celebrated writer, and one of the key figures in the history of the short story in English.

Kitty by Deborah Challinor. In the untamed Bay of Islands, missionaries struggle to establish Victorian England across the harbour from the infamous whaling port of Kororareka, hell-hole of the Pacific.

Once Were Warriors by Alan Duff. With more than 85,000 copies in circulation in New Zealand, this is one of the most talked-about books ever published in this country, and is the basis of a powerful film.

Pounamu Pounamu by Witi Ihimaera. First published in 1972, Pounamu Pounamu introduced an exciting new voice into New Zealand literature, which continues to excite readers today. Most of Witi Ihimaera's stories, based on the East Coast, describe a traditional rural, communal way of life facing huge pressures from the drift by many Maori to the cities.

The Whale Rider by Witi Ihimaera. The story follows eight-year-old Kahu and her struggle to gain recognition as heir to chiefdom of Ngati Konohi – and her inherited ability to communicate with the whales. Made into a popular film.

As the Earth Turns Silver by Alison Wong. A story of two families set in the late 19th century – a young mother struggling to raise her family alone and a Chinese immigrant. Winner of the NZ Post Book Awards 2010 Fiction Award.

Poetry

Just This by Brian Turner. A collection of poems reflecting Turner's love affair with his homeland of Central Otago.

Fast Talking PI by Dr Selina Tusitala Marsh. Strong, sensuous poetry with clear rhythms and repetitions about Pacific life, family, community, ancestry and history.

The Yellow Buoy by C.K. Stead. Completed in his 80th year, this is an outstanding book of poems by one of New Zealand's most acclaimed novelists, literary critics and poets. He has won the Prime Minister's Award for Fiction and been made a CBE and ONZ for his services to literature.

Plants/Animals/ Environment

Field Guide to Native Edible Plants by Andrew Crowe. Over 190 trees, shrubs, herbs, ferns, mushrooms, lichens and seaweeds are described in this book, including information on which part is edible and when, and how plants have been utilised, particularly by Maori.
Introducing New Zealand Birds by Alina Arkins and Len Doel. A good guide to New Zealand's array of unique birdlife, including the history of birds in New Zealand, and their habitat.
New Zealand Frogs and Reptiles by Gill and Whitaker. Identify 59 species of frogs, tuataras, geckos, skinks, turtles and sea snakes.
New Zealand Fishes by L. Paul. Identification of fish in New Zealand waters. Species are described, with notes on distribution, life history and population.
From Weta to Kauri Janet Hunt and Rob Lucas. All-in-one guide to the New Zealand forest, covering over 300 species of insects, birds and plants, with pictures and photographs to help with identification. A great book to take tramping.
A Field Guide to the Alpine Plants of New Zealand by John Salmon. Ideal field companion for walkers. Detailed descriptions and photographs.
The Living Reef – The Ecology of New Zealand's Rocky Reefs by N. Andrew, M. Francis. Focuses on key species of fish, animal and plant life, while also profiling New Zealand's most important marine ecosystems, from the Kermadec Islands to Fiordland and Antarctica.
The Penguin Natural World of New Zealand by Gerard Hutching. Covers all aspects of New Zealand's natural history.

Geology

New Zealand Minerals and Rocks for Beginners by P.J. Forsyth and J.J. Aitken. Details of the minerals and rocks found in New Zealand, how they were formed and where you find them.
The Field Guide to New Zealand Geology by Jocelyn Thornton. A good introductory book to New Zealand geology. Written in simplified terms,

it includes an introductory chapter on general geology, a geological time chart and quick-reference maps of the North Island and the South Island for travellers.

Sport

All Black Magic – 100 Years of New Zealand Test Rugby by Bob Howitt and Dianne Haworth. A celebration of New Zealand's national game.
Te Araroa – The New Zealand Trail; The Long Pathway through New Zealand by Geoff Chapple. This is the story of an individual who pursued a dream, a walking trail from the far north of New Zealand to the far south, some 2,600km (1,600 miles).
The Complete NZ Fisherman – Saltwater and Freshwater Fishing by G. Thomas. Everything you need to know about fishing. Geoff Thomas, one of New Zealand's best-known fishermen, has written this comprehensive fishing guide specifically for New Zealand conditions.

Food and Wine

Kiwi Favourites by Simon and Alison Holst. Two of New Zealand's favourite cookbook writers provide over 100 popular Kiwi tried-and-true family recipes.
Go Fish: Recipes and Stories from the New Zealand Coast by Al Brown. A book which takes you back to the simple days when a great meal could be had by simply casting a line from a dinghy.
Free Range in the City by Annabel Langbein. New Zealand culinary superstar Annabel Langbein invites you into her home to share how her free-range cooking style can help you create a sustainable lifestyle no matter where you live. More than 220 recipes for living well in today's busy world.

Children

Hairy Maclary from Donaldson's Dairy by Lynley Dodd. The first book in a series of 12 following the adventures of Hairy Maclary, by one of New Zealand's most prominent children's authors, who has sold more than 5 million copies worldwide.
Bruce Goes Home by Donna Blaber and Rupert Shaw. The third book in the popular Kiwi Critters series in which Keri the Kiwi discovers New Zealand's native plants are disappearing and devises a plan to

save them by using a bungee rope to catapult the culprit, Bruce the Possum, home to Australia.
Book of Maori Mythology by A.W. Reed and Ross Calman. A revised edition of the classic Treasury of Maori Folklore, this book tells the stories of the creation of the universe, of Rangi and Papa and the children of earth and sky, of the demigods Maui and Tawhaki, and supernatural monsters and fairies.
Hunter by Joy Cowley (an award-winning children's author of more than 600 books). This is the story of 14-year-old Jordan who is in a plane crash on an isolated New Zealand coastline with her younger brother. A good read for older children.

Art and Culture

Rita Angus: An Artist's Life by Jill Trevelyan. In this revelatory and subtle book, Jill Trevelyan traces Angus's entire life, from her childhood in Napier and Palmerston North to her death in Wellington in 1970. Drawing on a wealth of newly available archives and letters, she brings Rita Angus to life, her attitudes and emotions, pacifist and feminist beliefs and her dedication, above all, to life as an artist.
Mana Pounamu – New Zealand Jade by Russell Beck. New Zealand jade has always played an important role in New Zealand, being pivotal to the development of Maori culture, traditionally serving as tool, weapon, adornment and currency.
Classic Kiwiana: an Essential Guide to New Zealand Popular Culture by Stephen Barnett and Richard Wolfe. A unique collection of images, which draws together Kiwis' national character.

Other Insight Guides

Insight Guides publish several other titles on the Australasian region:
Insight Guide: Australia, a superbly illustrated guide covering the island continent in detail.
Insight Guide: Tasmania is the complete guide to this magnificently scenic island.
Insight Step By Step Guide: New Zealand offers eighteen tailor-made itineraries to guide you around the country.
Insight Smart Guide: Sydney, a detailed look at the city in a handy A–Z format.
Insight Fleximap: New Zealand, a durable and practical laminated map, with a list of recommended sights.

CREDITS

Insight Guide Credits

Distribution

UK
Dorling Kindersley Ltd
A Penguin Group company
80 Strand, London, WC2R 0RL
customerservice@dk.com

United States
Ingram Publisher Services
1 Ingram Boulevard, PO Box 3006,
La Vergne, TN 37086-1986
ips@ingramcontent.com

Australia
Universal Publishers
PO Box 307
St Leonards NSW 1590
sales@universal
publishers.com.au

New Zealand
Brown Knows Publications
11 Artesia Close, Shamrock Park
Auckland, New Zealand 2016
sales@brownknows.co.nz

Worldwide
Apa Publications GmbH & Co. Verlag
KG (Singapore branch)
7030 Ang Mo Kio Avenue 5
08-65 Northstar @ AMK
Singapore 569880
apasin@singnet.com.sg

Printing
CTPS-China

© 2013 Apa Publications (UK) Ltd
All Rights Reserved

First Edition 1984
Tenth Edition 2013

www.insightguides.com

Project Editor
Tom Stainer

Series Manager
Carine Tracanelli

Art Editor
Ian Spick

Map Production
Original cartography Polyglott
Kartographie, updated by
Apa Cartography Department

Production
Tynan Dean and Rebeka Ellam

INDEX

Main references are in bold type